Lifegate
English
New
Testament

FIRST HARDCOVER PRINTING

Translation by: J. James Mancuso

Niskayuna, New York

April 2023

https://warner.house

For more information, contact:
Warner House Press
1325 Lane Switch Road
Albertville, AL 35951

Printed in the United States of America

ISBN: 978-1-951890-49-0

TO THE READER

The *Lifegate English New Testament* (LENT) is an essentially literal translation of the Greek New Testament, based primarily on the Majority Text, with regard to modern biblical scholarship. As a guiding principle for this work, the words in each verse of the LENT text must have their basis in the original Greek text, although in many verses, some extra words have been inserted to make a sentence sound more natural or to complete a thought.

Other English translations include some inserted words as well. For instance, in the King James Version, such words were *italicized*. But in the LENT these words have been placed in square brackets [ ]. This signals to the reader that the words are not actually found in the original Greek, but that given the nature and flow of English, they would be necessary for the reader to grasp the meaning. For the sake of clarity, in some places, a person's name has been inserted into a verse to clarify who is being referred to. Any words that are *italicized* indicate emphasis.

The LENT has been created to provide its readers with a version of the New Testament that uses common English wording to convey the meaning of the original Greek text, without adding to, subtracting from, or changing the text, so that the original meaning is conveyed in contemporary English clearly. This version can be easily read and understood by a speaker of 21st century American English. It was written to avoid using outdated words and phrases or confusing word order that might puzzle a contemporary reader. Although the verses are worded in a simple, straightforward style, every effort has been made to retain the literary beauty and rich meaning of the original.

The entire text has been reset for the style and usage of the 21st century. Some parts of the text have been reformatted so that the reader can see them as separate items, including:

➢ formatted lists
➢ some of the longer Old Testament quotations, indented and in a different typeface
➢ prayers, sayings, and hymns
➢ letters

LENT intentionally contains no footnotes, references, or explanatory notes. It has been designed to provide its readers with a contemporary style of writing more conducive for undistracted, devotional reading of scripture. This edition also contains all 150 psalms, which have been worded and formatted using the same principles and methods, as well a basic index to the New Testament.

The name "Lifegate" comes from a verse in a well-known hymn by Fanny Crosby, which refers to God giving His Son to open a life-gate that all may go in. The entire New Testament text points to this finished work of Christ—his sinless life, death on the cross, and resurrection— and how salvation is found only through repentance and belief in Him. Thus, this scripture forms a 'lifegate' that can lead a reader out of the bondage of sin and into eternal life.

–J. James Mancuso
14 January 2023

CONTENTS

MATTHEW

Chapter 1

¹The Record of the Genealogy of Jesus Christ, the Offspring of David, the Offspring of Abraham:

²Abraham was the father of Isaac, and Isaac the father of Jacob, and Jacob the father of Judah and his brothers, ³and Judah the father of Perez and Zerah by Tamar, and Perez the father of Hezron, and Hezron the father of Ram, ⁴and Ram the father of Amminadab, and Amminadab the father of Nahshon, and Nahshon the father of Salmon, ⁵and Salmon the father of Boaz by Rahab, and Boaz the father of Obed by Ruth, and Obed the father of Jesse, ⁶and Jesse the father of David the king. And David was the father of Solomon by [Bathsheba, formerly] the wife of Uriah, ⁷and Solomon the father of Rehoboam, and Rehoboam the father of Abijah, and Abijah the father of Asa, ⁸and Asa the father of Jehoshaphat, and Jehoshaphat the father of Joram, and Joram the father of Uzziah, ⁹and Uzziah the father of Jotham, and Jotham the father of Ahaz, and Ahaz the father of Hezekiah, ¹⁰and Hezekiah the father of Manasseh, and Manasseh the father of Amos, and Amos the father of Josiah, ¹¹and Josiah the father of Jechoniah and his brothers, at the time of the deportation to Babylon.

¹²And after the deportation to Babylon:

Jechoniah was the father of Shealtiel, and Shealtiel the father of Zerubbabel, ¹³and Zerubbabel the father of Abiud, and Abiud the father of Eliakim, and Eliakim the father of Azor, ¹⁴and Azor the father of Zadok, and Zadok the father of Achim, and Achim the father of Eliud, ¹⁵and Eliud the father of Eleazar, and Eleazar the father of Matthan, and Matthan the father of Jacob, ¹⁶and Jacob the father of Joseph the husband of Mary, of whom Jesus was born, who is called Christ.

¹⁷So the number of generations from Abraham to David was fourteen, and from David to the deportation to Babylon was also fourteen generations, and from the deportation to Babylon to the Christ was fourteen generations.

The Birth of Jesus

¹⁸Now the birth of Jesus Christ took place in this way: his mother Mary had been betrothed to Joseph, but before they came together, she was found to be pregnant by means of the Holy Spirit. ¹⁹Her husband Joseph, being a just man and unwill-

1

ing to put her to shame, resolved to break the engagement to her quietly. ²⁰But as he considered this–listen—an angel of the Lord appeared to him in a dream saying, "Joseph, son of David, do not be afraid to take Mary to be your wife, because what is conceived in her is of the Holy Spirit. ²¹She will bear a son, and you shall declare his name to be Jesus, for he will save his people from their sins." ²²All this happened to fulfill what the Lord had spoken by the prophet: ²³"Listen to this—a virgin shall conceive and bear a son, and he shall be known as Emmanuel" (which means "God with us"). ²⁴When Joseph awoke from sleep, he did as the angel of the Lord had commanded him: he took his wife, ²⁵but he did not have marital relations with her until after she had given birth to a son, and he declared his name Jesus.

Chapter 2

The Visit of the Wise Men

¹Sometime after Jesus was born in Bethlehem of Judea in the days of Herod the king—listen—Wise Men from the East came to Jerusalem, saying, ²"Where is the one who has been born king of the Jews? For we saw the rising of his star and have come to worship him." ³When King Herod heard this, he was troubled, and all of Jerusalem was along with him. ⁴Having assembled all the chief priests and scribes of the people, he asked them where the Christ was to be born. ⁵"In Bethlehem of Judea," they told him, "because it is written this way by the prophets: ⁶'And you, O Bethlehem, in the land of Judah, are by no means least among the rulers of Judah, for out of you shall come a ruler who will shepherd my people Israel.'"

⁷Then Herod summoned the Wise Men secretly and ascertained from them the point in time when the star had appeared. ⁸Then he sent them to Bethlehem, saying, "Go and search diligently for the child, and when you have found him report to me, so that I may come and worship him, too." ⁹Having listened to the king, they went on their way. You see, the star that they had seen at its rising went before them until it came to rest over the place where the child was. ¹⁰When they saw the star, they rejoiced greatly with extreme joy. ¹¹Upon entering the house, they saw the child with his mother Mary, and they fell down and worshiped him. Then, opening their treasures, they offered him gifts: gold, frankincense, and myrrh. ¹²And being warned in a dream not to return to Herod, they returned to their own country by a different route.

Fleeing to Egypt and Returning to Israel

¹³Now once they had departed—listen—an angel of the Lord appeared to Joseph in a dream and said, "Get up, take the child and his mother and escape to Egypt. Remain there until I tell you because Herod is about to search for the child to

2

destroy him." ¹⁴And he got up and took the child and his mother by night and departed to Egypt. ¹⁵Then he remained there until the death of Herod, in order to fulfill what the Lord had spoken by the prophet, "Out of Egypt I called my son."

¹⁶When Herod realized that he had been tricked by the Wise Men, he was furious, and he sent orders to kill all the male children in Bethlehem and the surrounding area who were two years old or under, according to the timing he had ascertained from the Wise Men. ¹⁷Then what was spoken by the prophet Jeremiah was fulfilled:

> ¹⁸"A voice was heard in Ramah:
> Weeping and loud lamentation,
> Rachel weeping for her children.
> She refused to be comforted because they were no more."

¹⁹But when Herod died—listen—an angel of the Lord appeared in a dream to Joseph in Egypt, saying, ²⁰"Get up, take the child and his mother, and go to the land of Israel, for those who were seeking the child's life are dead." ²¹And he got up and took the child and his mother and went to the land of Israel. ²²But when he heard that Archelaus was reigning over Judea in place of his father Herod, he feared going there. So, he withdrew to the district of Galilee, having been warned in a dream. ²³He went and lived in a city called Nazareth, so that what was spoken by the prophets might be fulfilled: "He shall be called a Nazarene."

Chapter 3

John Baptizes the Repentant

¹There came a time when John the Baptist was continually preaching in the wilderness of Judea, ²"Repent, for the kingdom of heaven is at hand." ³This is the one that the prophet Isaiah spoke of when he said,

> "The voice of one crying in the wilderness:
> Prepare a way for the Lord.
> Lay out a straight avenue to [welcome] him."

⁴Now John wore clothing made of camel's hair, and a leather belt around his waist, and his food was locusts and wild honey. ⁵Then the people of Jerusalem, Judea, and all the region around the Jordan, went out to him, ⁶and, confessing their sins, they were baptized by him in the river Jordan.

⁷But when he saw many of the Pharisees and Sadducees coming to him for baptism, he said to them, "You brood of vipers! Who warned you to flee from the wrath to come? ⁸Produce fruit in keeping with repentance. ⁹Do not presume to

reassure yourselves with, 'We have Abraham as our father'. For I tell you, God is able to raise up children to Abraham from these stones. [10]Even now the ax is laid to the root of the trees. Therefore, every tree that does not produce good fruit is cut down and thrown into the fire.

[11]"I baptize you with water for repentance, but the One coming after me is mightier than I– I am not even worthy to carry his sandals. He will baptize you with the Holy Spirit and with fire. [12]His winnowing fork is in his hand, and he will clear his threshing floor and gather his wheat into the barn, but he will burn the chaff with unquenchable fire."

[13]Then Jesus came from Galilee to the Jordan to John to be baptized by him. [14]Meaning to deter him, John responded, "I have need of being baptized by *you*, and yet you are coming to *me*?" [15]But Jesus answered him, "It should be done this way now, because it is a fitting way for us to fulfill all righteousness." Then he consented. [16]And when Jesus was baptized, he came up quickly out of the water—and listen—the heavens were opened and he saw the Spirit of God descending like a dove, and coming to rest on him, [17]and—listen—a voice from heaven, saying, "This is my beloved Son, with whom I am well pleased."

Chapter 4

The Devil Tempts Jesus in the Wilderness

[1]Then Jesus was led by the Spirit up into the wilderness where he was tempted by the devil. [2]After having fasted forty days and forty nights, he was hungry. [3]And the tempter came and said to him, "If you are the Son of God, command these stones to become loaves of bread." [4]But he replied, "It is written, 'Man shall not live by bread alone, but by every word that comes forth from the mouth of God.'"

[5]Then the devil took him to the holy city and set him on the pinnacle of the temple. [6]And he said to him, "If you are the Son of God, throw yourself down, for the scripture says, 'He will command his angels to care for you,' and 'They will hold you up with their hands so that you do not strike your foot against a stone.'" [7]Jesus replied to him, "Again the scripture says, 'You shall not put the Lord your God to the test.'" [8]Again, the devil took him to a very high mountain and showed him all the kingdoms of the world and their splendor. [9]And he told him, "I will give you all of these if you will fall down and worship me." [10]Then Jesus replied to him, "Be gone, Satan! For the scripture says, 'You shall worship the Lord your God, and you shall serve only him.'" [11]Then the devil departed from him—and listen—angels came and began attending to his needs.

[12]Now, when he heard that John had been arrested, he withdrew into Galilee.

¹³Leaving Nazareth, he went and lived in Capernaum by the sea, in the territory of Zebulun and Naphtali, ¹⁴so that what the prophet Isaiah had spoken might be fulfilled:

> ¹⁵"The land of Zebulun and the land of Naphtali,
> the way to the sea, across the Jordan, Galilee of the Gentiles,
> ¹⁶the people dwelling in darkness, have seen a great light,
> and on those dwelling in the land of the shadow of death
> a light has dawned."

¹⁷From that time Jesus began to preach, saying, "Repent, for the kingdom of heaven is at hand."

Jesus Calls the First Four Apostles

¹⁸As he walked by the Sea of Galilee, he saw two brothers, Simon (who is called Peter), and Andrew his brother who, as fishermen, were casting a net into the sea. ¹⁹And he said to them, "Follow me, and I will make you fishers of men." ²⁰They immediately left their nets and followed him. ²¹And going on from there he saw another pair of brothers, James the son of Zebedee and John his brother, in the boat with Zebedee their father, mending their nets, and he called them. ²²They immediately left the boat and their father and followed him.

²³And he went throughout all Galilee, teaching in their synagogues and proclaiming the gospel of the kingdom and healing every disease and every infirmity among the people. ²⁴So his fame spread throughout all Syria, and they brought him all the sick, those afflicted with various diseases and pains—demoniacs, epileptics, and paralytics—and he healed them. ²⁵And great crowds from Galilee, the Decapolis, Jerusalem, Judea, and from beyond the Jordan, followed him.

Chapter 5

The Sermon on the Mount

Beatitudes

¹Seeing the crowds, he went up on the mountain, and when he sat down his disciples came to him. ²And he began to teach them, saying:

> ³"Blessed are the poor in spirit, for theirs is the kingdom of heaven.
> ⁴"Blessed are those who mourn, for they shall be comforted.
> ⁵"Blessed are the meek, for they shall inherit the earth.
> ⁶"Blessed are those who hunger and thirst for righteousness,
> for they shall be satisfied.

5

[7]"Blessed are the merciful, for they shall be treated mercifully.

[8]"Blessed are the pure in heart, for they shall see God.

[9]"Blessed are the peacemakers, for they shall be called sons of God.

[10]"Blessed are those who are persecuted for the sake of righteousness,
for theirs is the kingdom of heaven.

[11]"Blessed are you when men denounce you and persecute you
and speak all kinds of evil things against you falsely on account of me.

[12]Rejoice and be extremely glad, for your reward in heaven is great,
for they persecuted the prophets who were before you in the same way.

Being Salt and Light

[13]"You are the salt of the earth, but if salt has lost its taste, how can its saltiness be restored? It is no longer good for anything except to be thrown out and be trampled underfoot.

[14]"You are the light of the world. A city situated on a hill cannot be hidden. [15]Nor would anyone light a lamp and put it under a basket, but rather on a stand, where it gives light to all in the house. [16]Let your light shine before men in such a way that they may see your good deeds and give glory to your Father who is in heaven.

Come to Fulfill the Law

[17]"Do not think that I have come to abolish the law and the prophets. I have come not to abolish them but to fulfill them. [18]For truly, I say to you, until heaven and earth pass away, not a single letter or period will vanish from the law until all has been accomplished. [19]So then, whoever lets up on one of the least of these commandments, and teaches others to do so, will be called least in the kingdom of heaven. But whoever practices and teaches them will be called great in the kingdom of heaven. [20]For I tell you, unless your righteousness surpasses that of the scribes and Pharisees, you will never enter the kingdom of heaven.

Commandments of the Old Testament:

Reconciling

[21]"You have heard that long ago our ancestors were told, 'You must not commit murder, and whoever does so will be subject to judgment.' [22]But I am telling you that everyone who is angry with his brother is already subject to judgment. Whoever insults his brother will be subject to the Sanhedrin, and whoever says, 'You fool!' is in danger of the fire of hell. [23]So if you are offering your gift at the altar, and there you remember that your brother has something against you, [24]leave your gift there before the altar. First go and be reconciled to your brother, and then come and offer your gift.

6

²⁵Resolve things quickly with your accuser while you are going with him to court. Do this so that your accuser does not hand you over to the judge, and the judge hand you over to the officer, and you get put in prison. ²⁶Truly, I say to you, you will never get out until you have paid the last penny.

Committing Adultery

²⁷"You have heard that it was said, 'You must not commit adultery.' ²⁸But I say to you that everyone who looks at a woman lustfully has already committed adultery with her in his heart. ²⁹If your right eye causes you to sin, gouge it out and throw it away. It is better to lose one of your members than to have your whole body be thrown into hell. ³⁰And if your right hand causes you to sin, cut it off and throw it away. It is better to lose one of your members than to have your whole body go into hell.

Divorce

³¹"It was also said, 'whoever divorces his wife, let him give her a certificate of divorce.' ³²But I say to you that everyone who divorces his wife, except on the grounds of unfaithfulness, makes her an adulteress, and whoever marries a divorced woman commits adultery.

Swearing Oaths

³³"Again you have heard that long ago our ancestors were told, 'You must not make an empty oath, but must actually carry out the oaths you have sworn to the Lord.' ³⁴But I tell you to not swear any oaths at all, either by heaven, for it is the throne of God, ³⁵or by the earth, for it is his footstool, or by Jerusalem, for it is the city of the great King. ³⁶And do not swear an oath by your head, for you do not even determine whether one hair is white or black. ³⁷Let your 'Yes' be simply 'Yes' and your 'No' be simply 'No.' Anything beyond this comes from the evil one.

Repaying Evil

³⁸"You have heard that it was said, 'An eye for an eye and a tooth for a tooth.' ³⁹But I am telling you to not resist an evil person. Rather, if anyone strikes you on the right cheek, turn the other one to him, too. ⁴⁰If anyone wants to sue you and take your tunic, let him have your cloak as well. ⁴¹If anyone forces you to go one mile, go two with him. ⁴²Give to anyone who begs from you, and do not refuse anyone who wants to borrow from you.

[43]"You have heard that it was said, 'You must love your neighbor and hate your enemy.' [44]But I am telling you to love your enemies and pray for those who persecute you, [45]so that you may be sons of your Father who is in heaven. For he makes his sun rise on the evil and on the good and sends rain on the righteous and on the unrighteous. [46]After all, if you love those who love you, what reward is there in that? Do not even the tax collectors do that? [47]And if you greet only your brothers, what are you doing that is more than others do? Do not even pagans do that? [48]You are to be perfect, as your heavenly Father is perfect.

Chapter 6

Deeds Done in Secret

[1]"Be careful not to do your good deeds in the presence of others in order to be seen by them; for then you will receive no reward from your Father who is in heaven. [2]"So, when you give to the needy, do not do so with the blast of a trumpet, as the hypocrites do in the synagogues and in the streets so that they will be praised by others. Truly, I say to you, they have already received all their reward. [3]But when you give to the needy, do not let your left hand know what your right hand is doing, [4]so that your act of giving remains in secret. And your Father who sees what is done in secret will reward you.

[5]"And when you pray, you must not be like the hypocrites, for they love to stand and pray in the synagogues and on the street corners, so that they may be seen by others. Truly, I tell you, they have already received all their reward. [6]But when you pray, go into your room and shut the door and pray to your Father who is in secret, and your Father who sees what is done in secret will reward you.

Father in Heaven

[7]"And when you are praying, do not keep chanting empty phrases as the pagans do. For they think that they will be heard by virtue of their wordiness. [8]Do not be like them, for your Father knows what you need before you ask him. [9]So then, pray like this:

The Lord's Prayer

Our Father in heaven, may your name be held as holy.
[10]*May your kingdom come; may your will be done on earth as it is in heaven.*
[11]*Give us today our daily bread,*
[12]*and forgive us our debts, as we also have forgiven our debtors.*
[13]*And do not let us yield to temptation, but deliver us from the evil one,*
For yours is the kingdom, and the power, and the glory, forever. Amen.

Forgiveness

[14]"For if you forgive other people for their sins against you, your heavenly Father will also forgive you. [15]But if you do not forgive other people for their sins, neither will your Father forgive your sins.

Fasting

[16]"And when you fast, do not look morose like the hypocrites who distort their faces so that others will realize that they are fasting. Truly, I tell you, they have already received all their reward. [17]But when you fast, put oil on your head and wash your face, [18]that your fasting may not be seen by other people, but by your Father who is in secret. And your Father who sees what is done in secret will reward you.

Heavenly Treasure

[19]"Do not store up treasures for yourselves on earth where moths and rust destroy and where thieves break in and steal, [20]but store up treasures for yourselves in heaven, where neither moth nor rust destroys and where thieves do not break in and steal. [21]For where your treasure is, there will your heart be also.

Lamp

[22]"The eye is the lamp of the body. So, if your eye is healthy, your whole body will be full of light. [23]But if your eye is bad, your whole body will be full of darkness. Then if the light in you is darkness, how great is the darkness!

Masters

[24]"No one can serve two masters. For either he will hate one of them and love the other, or he will be devoted to the one and despise the other. You cannot serve both God and money.

Not Being Anxious

[25]"Therefore I tell you, do not be anxious about your life, what you will eat or what you will drink, nor about your body and what you will wear. Is not life more than food, and the body more than clothing? [26]Look at the birds of the air: they do not sow or reap or gather food into barns, and yet your heavenly Father feeds them. Are you not of more value than they are? [27]Can anyone can add the least bit to his length of days, just by being anxious?

[28]And why are you anxious about clothing? Think about the lilies of the field and how they grow. They neither toil nor spin. [29]Yet I tell you, even Solomon in all

his splendor was not dressed like one of these. ³⁰But if this is how God clothes the grass of the field, which today is alive and tomorrow is tossed onto the fire, will he not clothe you much more, O you of little faith?

³¹Therefore do not be anxious, saying, 'What are we going to eat?' or 'What are we going to drink?' or 'What are we going to wear?' ³²For the pagans chase after all these things, and your heavenly Father is aware that you need them all. ³³Instead, seek his kingdom and his righteousness first, and all these things will be added to you.

³⁴"Therefore do not be anxious about tomorrow, for tomorrow will be anxious for itself. Each day has enough trouble of its own.

Chapter 7

Not Judging Others

¹"Do not pass judgment, so that you will not be judged. ²For in the same way you judge you will be judged, and however much you give will be what you receive back. ³Why do you focus on the speck that is in your brother's eye, but fail to notice the plank that is in your own eye? ⁴Or how can you say to your brother, 'Let me take that speck out of your eye,' when there is the plank in your own eye? ⁵You hypocrite! First take the plank out of your own eye, and then you will see clearly to take the speck out of your brother's eye.

Pearls Laid out for Hogs

⁶"Do not give dogs what is holy, and do not lay out your pearls in front of hogs, or else they will trample them underfoot and then turn to attack you.

Receiving When You Ask

⁷"Keep on asking, and it will be given to you; keep on seeking, and you will find; keep on knocking, and it will be opened to you. ⁸For everyone who asks receives, and everyone who seeks finds, and to the one who knocks it will be opened. ⁹Or which one of you, if his son should ask him for bread, would give him a stone? ¹⁰Or if he should ask for a fish, would give him a snake? ¹¹So then, if you, who are evil, know how to give good gifts to your children, how much more will your Father who is in heaven give good things to those who ask him! ¹²So in all things, do to others whatever you would want them to do to you, for this sums up the Law and the Prophets.

Search for the Narrow Gate

¹³"Enter by the narrow gate for the gate that leads to destruction is wide, and the way is easy, and those who enter by it are many. ¹⁴But the gate that leads to life is narrow, and the way is hard, and those who find it are few.

Trees and Their Fruit

¹⁵"Beware of false prophets, who come to you in sheep's clothing but inside are ravenous wolves. ¹⁶You will know them by their fruits. Are grapes gathered from thorns, or figs from thistles? ¹⁷So, every healthy tree bears good fruit, but the bad tree bears evil fruit. ¹⁸A healthy tree cannot bear evil fruit, nor can a bad tree bear good fruit. ¹⁹Every tree that does not bear good fruit is cut down and thrown into the fire. ²⁰So it is by their fruits that you will recognize them.

Who Will Enter the Kingdom of Heaven?

²¹"Not everyone who says to me, 'Lord, Lord,' will enter the kingdom of heaven, but the one who does the will of my Father who is in heaven will. ²²On that day many will say to me, 'Lord, Lord, did we not prophesy in your name, and cast out demons in your name, and do many powerful things in your name?' ²³And then will I declare to them, 'I never knew you. Depart from me, you who practice wickedness.'

Wise Men versus Foolish Men

²⁴"Everyone then who hears these words of mine and puts them into practice will be like a wise man who built his house on the rock. ²⁵The rain fell, and the floods came, and the winds blew and beat against that house, but it did not fall, because its foundation was on the rock. ²⁶Everyone who hears these words of mine and does not put them into practice will be like a foolish man who built his house on the sand. ²⁷The rain fell, and the floods came, and the winds blew and beat against that house, and it fell—and great was its collapse."

²⁸When Jesus had finished saying these things, the crowds stood astonished at his teaching ²⁹because he taught them like someone who had authority, unlike their religious leaders.

Chapter 8

Jesus Heals a Leper

¹When he came down from the mountain, huge crowds followed him. ²And listen—a leper came to him and knelt before him, saying, "Lord, if you are willing

to, you can make me clean." [3]And [Jesus] stretched out his hand and touched him, saying, "I am willing; be clean." And immediately his leprosy was cleansed. [4]Then Jesus said to him, "Make sure that you do not say anything to anyone. But instead, go and show yourself to the priest and offer the gift instituted by Moses as a proof to the people."

The Faithful Centurion

[5]As he entered Capernaum, a centurion came forward to him, begging him earnestly [6]and saying, "Lord, my servant is at home, lying paralyzed, in terrible distress." [7]And he said to him, "I will come and heal him." [8]But the centurion answered him, "Lord, I am not worthy to have you come under my roof, but just say the word, and my servant will be healed. [9]For I am a man under authority, with soldiers under me. And I say to one, 'Go,' and he goes, and to another, 'Come,' and he comes, and to my servant, 'Do this,' and he does it."

[10]When Jesus heard him, he marveled and said to those who followed him, "Truly, I say to you, I have not found such faith elsewhere—even within Israel. [11]I tell you, many will come from east and west and sit at table with Abraham, Isaac, and Jacob in the kingdom of heaven, [12]while the sons of the kingdom will be thrown into the outer darkness, where there will be weeping and gnashing of teeth." [13]Then Jesus said to the centurion, "Go—may it be done for you as you have believed." And the servant was healed at that very moment.

Peter's Sick Mother-in-Law

[14]On entering Peter's house, Jesus saw [Peter's] mother-in-law lying sick with a fever. [15]He touched her hand, and the fever left her, and she got up and began to wait on him. [16]That evening they brought many who were possessed with demons to him. He cast out the spirits with a word and healed all who were sick. [17]This was to fulfill what was spoken by the prophet Isaiah, "He took away our sicknesses and bore our diseases."

The Cost of Discipleship

[18]Now when Jesus saw great crowds around himself, he gave orders to go over to the other side. [19]A scribe came up and said to him, "Teacher, I will follow you wherever you go." [20]And Jesus said to him, "Foxes have holes, and birds of the air have nests, but the Son of Man has nowhere to lay his head." [21]Another of the disciples said to him, "Lord, let me first go and bury my father." [22]But Jesus said to him, "Follow me and leave the dead to bury their own dead."

Jesus Calms a Storm at Sea

²³Once he had gotten into the boat, his disciples followed him. ²⁴Listen—a great storm arose on the sea, so that the boat was being swamped by the waves. But Jesus was asleep. ²⁵So, they went over and woke him up, exclaiming, "Save us, Lord. We are going to die!" ²⁶And he said to them, "Why are you afraid, O men of little faith?" Then he rose and rebuked the winds and the sea, and there was a great calm. ²⁷The men were then awestruck, saying, "What kind of man is this, that even the winds and the sea obey him?"

Demons Cast into a Herd of Hogs

²⁸And when he came to the other side, to the country of the Gadarenes, two demoniacs met him, coming out of the tombs. They were so fierce that no one could get through that way. ²⁹And listen—they cried out, "What do you have to do with us, O Son of God? Have you come here to torment us before the appointed time?" ³⁰Now a herd of many hogs was feeding a short distance from them. ³¹And the demons begged him, "If you cast us out, send us away into the herd of hogs." ³²He replied, "Be gone." So, they came out of him and went into the hogs. Listen—the whole herd rushed down the steep bank into the sea and died in the waters. ³³The herdsmen ran away, and as they came into the city, they reported everything, and what had happened to the demoniacs. ³⁴And listen—the whole city came out to meet Jesus. And when they saw him, they begged him to leave their area.

Chapter 9

Jesus Heals a Paralyzed Man

¹Getting into a boat, he crossed over and came to his own town. ²Listen, some people brought a paralyzed man lying on his mat to him. When Jesus saw their faith, he said to the paralyzed man, "Take heart, my son; your sins are forgiven." ³Listen—some of the scribes said to themselves, "This man is blaspheming." ⁴But Jesus, knowing their thoughts, asked [them], "Why are you pondering evil in your hearts? ⁵Which one is easier: saying 'Your sins are forgiven,' or saying 'Get up and walk'? ⁶Actually, it is so that you may know that the Son of Man has authority on earth to forgive sins." He then said to the paralyzed man, "Get up. Pick up your mat and go home." ⁷And he got up and went home. ⁸When the crowds saw this, they were awestruck, and they gave the glory to God, who had given such authority to men.

Jesus Calls Matthew, a Sinner

[9]As Jesus passed on from there, he saw a man called Matthew sitting at the tax booth, and he said to him, "Follow me." So, he got up and followed him. [10]Later, as he was sitting at the table in the house, many tax collectors and sinners came and sat down with Jesus and his disciples. [11]Now, when the Pharisees saw this, they asked his disciples, "Why does your teacher eat with tax collectors and sinners?" [12]But when he heard it, he said, "Those who are well have no need of a physician, but those who are sick do. [13]Go and learn what this means: 'I desire mercy and not sacrifice.' For I came not to call the righteous but sinners."

New Wineskins

[14]Then John's disciples came to him and asked, "Why do we and the Pharisees practice fasting, but your disciples do not?" [15]Jesus replied, "Can the wedding guests mourn while the bridegroom is still with them? The days will come when the bridegroom is taken away from them, and then they will fast. [16]And no one puts a piece of unshrunk cloth on an old garment because the patch tears away from the garment, and a worse tear is made. [17]Neither is new wine put into old wineskins. If it is, the skins burst, and the wine is spilled, and the skins are destroyed—whereas new wine is put into fresh wineskins, and so both are preserved."

Jesus Heals People

A Woman Touches his Garment

[18]While he was telling them these things, a ruler came in and knelt before him, saying, "My daughter has just died. But, come and lay your hand on her, and she will live." [19]And Jesus rose and followed him, along with his disciples. [20]Well, a woman who had suffered from a hemorrhage for twelve years came up behind him and touched the fringe of his garment, [21]for she said to herself, "If I only touch his garment, I will be made well." [22]Jesus turned, and seeing her he said, "Take heart, daughter; your faith has made you well." And instantly the woman was made well.

A Dead Girl Comes to Life

[23]And when Jesus came to the ruler's house, and saw the flute players, and the crowd making a tumult, [24]He said, "Go away—the girl is not dead but sleeping." And they laughed at him. [25]But once the crowd had been put outside, he went in and took her by the hand, and the girl got up. [26]And the news about this spread throughout the whole region.

Two Blind Men See

²⁷Then as Jesus passed on from there, two blind men followed him, exclaiming, "Have mercy on us, Son of David." ²⁸When he entered the house, the blind men came to him, and Jesus said to them, "Do you believe that I am able to do this?" They answered, "Yes, Lord." ²⁹Then he touched their eyes, saying, "Let it be done to you according to your faith." ³⁰And their eyes were opened. Then Jesus sternly charged them, "See to it that no one knows about this." ³¹But on the contrary, they went away and spread his fame throughout all of that region.

A Mute Man Speaks

³²As they were going away, a mute, demon-possessed man was brought to him. ³³And when the demon had been cast out, the mute man spoke. The crowds marveled, saying, "Never has anything like this been seen in Israel." ³⁴However, the Pharisees said, "He casts out demons by the prince of demons." ³⁵And Jesus went about all the cities and villages, teaching in their synagogues and preaching the gospel of the kingdom and healing every disease and every sickness.

Laborers into the Harvest

³⁶When he saw the crowds, he had compassion for them because they were harassed and helpless, like sheep lacking a shepherd. ³⁷Then he said to his disciples, "The harvest is plentiful, but the laborers are few. ³⁸So, prayerfully ask the Lord of the harvest to send out laborers into his harvest."

Chapter 10

The Twelve Apostles Sent Out

¹He called his twelve disciples to himself and gave them authority for casting out evil spirits and for healing every disease and every sickness. ²The names of the twelve apostles are these: first, Simon, who is called Peter, and Andrew his brother; James the son of Zebedee, and John his brother; ³Philip and Bartholomew; Thomas and Matthew the tax collector; James the son of Alphaeus, and Thaddaeus; ⁴Simon the Canaanean, and Judas Iscariot, who [later] betrayed him.

⁵Jesus sent these twelve out, instructing them, "Do not go anywhere among the Gentiles, or enter any town of the Samaritans, ⁶but instead, go to the lost sheep of the house of Israel. ⁷And as you go, proclaim this message: 'The kingdom of heaven is at hand.' ⁸Heal the sick, raise the dead, cleanse lepers, cast out demons. You received without paying, give without pay. ⁹Do not take along any gold, or silver, or copper in your belts, ¹⁰or a bag for your journey, or two tunics, or sandals, or a staff—for the laborer deserves his food.

[11]In whatever town or village you enter, find out who is worthy in it and stay with him until you depart. [12]As you enter the house, give it your greeting. [13]And if the house is worthy, let your peace come to it. But if it is not worthy, let your peace return to you. [14]If anyone will not receive you or listen to your words, shake off the dust from your feet as you leave that house or town. [15]Truly, I say to you, on Judgment Day it will be more tolerable for the land of Sodom and Gomorrah than for that town.

You Will Be Persecuted

[16]"Listen, I am sending you out as sheep in the midst of wolves, so be as shrewd as snakes and as harmless as doves. [17]Be on your guard against men, for they will hand you over to local councils, and flog you in their synagogues. [18]For my sake, you will be dragged before governors and kings, to bear witness before them and the Gentiles. [19]Now, when they hand you over, do not be anxious about how you are to speak or what you are to say. What you are to say will be given to you in that moment, [20]for it is not *you* speaking, but the Spirit of your Father speaking through you.

[21]Brother will deliver brother over to death, and the father his child, and children will rise against parents and have them put to death. [22]You will be hated by all for the sake of my name, but the one who endures to the end will be saved. [23]When they persecute you in one town, flee to the next. For truly, I tell you, you will not have gone through all the towns of Israel before the Son of Man comes.

[24]"A disciple is not above his teacher, nor is a servant above his master. [25]It is enough for the disciple to be like his teacher, and the servant like his master. If they have called the Master of the house 'Beelzebub', how much more will they do so to those of his household?

[26]"So have no fear of them, for nothing is covered that will not be revealed, or hidden that will not be known. [27]What I tell you in the dark, repeat in the light. What you hear whispered, proclaim upon the housetops. [28]And do not fear those who kill the body but cannot kill the soul. Instead, fear him who can destroy both soul and body in hell. [29]Are not two sparrows sold for a penny? And not one of them will fall to the ground outside of your Father's will. [30]Now, even the hairs of your head are all numbered. [31]So, do not be afraid; you are far more valuable than a large number of sparrows. [32]Now, as for anyone who confesses me before men—I will also confess him before my Father who is in heaven. [33]But as for anyone who disowns me before men—I will also disown him before my Father who is in heaven.

Not Peace, but a Sword

³⁴"Do not think that I have come to bring peace on earth. I have not come to bring peace, but a sword. ³⁵For I have come to set a man against his father, and a daughter against her mother, and a daughter-in-law against her mother-in-law; ³⁶and a man's foes will be those of his own household. ³⁷Whoever loves father or mother more than me is not worthy of me. Whoever loves son or daughter more than me is not worthy of me. ³⁸Whoever does not take his cross and follow me is not worthy of me. ³⁹Whoever finds his life will lose it, and whoever loses his life for my sake will find it.

⁴⁰"Whoever receives you receives me, and the one who receives me receives him who sent me. ⁴¹The one who receives a prophet because he is a prophet shall receive a prophet's reward, and the one who receives a righteous man because he is a righteous man shall receive a righteous man's reward. ⁴²And whoever, on account of being named a disciple, gives even a cup of cold water to one of these little ones—I tell you truly—will not lose his reward."

Chapter 11

The Work of John the Baptist

¹And when Jesus had finished instructing his twelve disciples, he went on from there to teach and preach in their cities. ²Now when John heard in prison about what Christ had done, he sent word by his disciples ³and asked him, "Are you the one who is to come, or should we look for another?" ⁴And Jesus answered them, "Go and tell John what you hear and see: ⁵the blind are able to see and the lame walk, lepers are cleansed and the deaf hear, and the dead are raised up, and the poor have good news preached to them. ⁶And blessed is the one who is not offended by me."

⁷As [John's disciples] were leaving, Jesus began to speak to the crowds about John: "What did you go out into the wilderness to see? A reed shaken by the wind? ⁸Then what *did* you go out to see? A man dressed in soft clothing? Look, those who wear soft clothing are in kings' palaces. ⁹Then why did you go out? To see a prophet? Yes, I tell you, and more than a prophet. ¹⁰This is the one of whom it is written, 'Look, I send my messenger before your face, who shall prepare your way before you.' ¹¹Truly, I tell you, among those born of women there has arisen no one greater than John the Baptist. Yet the one who is least in the kingdom of heaven is greater than he [is]. ¹²From the days of John the Baptist until now the kingdom of heaven has been enduring violence, and men of violence take it by force. ¹³For all the Prophets and the law prophesied up until John [came]. ¹⁴And,

if you are willing to accept this, he is the expected Elijah. ¹⁵If anyone has ears to hear with, let him hear this.

¹⁶"But what should I compare this generation to? It is like children sitting in the marketplaces calling to their playmates, ¹⁷'When we played the flute for you, you did not dance. When we wailed, you did not mourn.' ¹⁸For John came neither eating nor drinking, and they say, 'He has a demon,' ¹⁹whereas the Son of Man came eating and drinking, and they say, 'Look at this: a glutton and a drunkard, a friend of tax collectors and sinners!' Still and all, wisdom is vindicated by her outcome."

Woe to Unbelieving Cities

²⁰Then he began to denounce the cities where most of his miracles had been performed, because they did not repent. ²¹"Woe to you, Chorazin! Woe to you, Bethsaida! For if the miracles performed in you had been done in Tyre and Sidon, they would have repented in sackcloth and ashes long ago. ²²But I tell you that on the Judgment Day it will be more bearable for Tyre and Sidon than for you. ²³And you, Capernaum, will you be exalted to heaven? You will be brought down to Hades. For if the miracles performed in you had been done in Sodom, it would have remained until this day. ²⁴But I tell you that on the Judgment Day it will be more bearable for the land of Sodom than for you."

²⁵At that moment Jesus addressed them and said, "I thank you, Father, Lord of heaven and earth, that you have hidden these things from the wise and the learned and revealed them to young children. ²⁶Indeed, Father, it was your gracious will to do so. ²⁷My Father has turned over all things to me, and no one knows the Son, except the Father, and no one knows the Father except the Son and anyone to whom the Son chooses to reveal him.

His Yoke is Easy

²⁸Come to me, all who toil and are heavy burdened, and I will give you rest. ²⁹Take my yoke on yourselves, and learn from me, for I am gentle and lowly in heart, and you will find rest for your souls. ³⁰For my yoke is easy, and my burden is light."

Chapter 12

Lord of the Sabbath

¹One time as Jesus was walking through fields of the grain on the Sabbath, his disciples got hungry, and they began picking heads of grain and eating them. ²But

when the Pharisees saw this, they said to him, "Look, your disciples are doing what is not lawful to do on the Sabbath." ³He replied, "Have you not read what David did, when he was hungry, along with those who were with him: ⁴how he entered the house of God and ate the consecrated bread, which was unlawful for him or for those who were with him to eat, but only for the priests? ⁵Or have you not read in the law how on the Sabbath the priests in the temple profane the Sabbath, yet remain innocent? ⁶I tell you–the one who is something greater than the temple is here now. ⁷In addition, if you had perceived what this means, 'I desire mercy, and not sacrifice,' you would not have condemned the innocent. ⁸For the Son of Man is Lord, even of the Sabbath."

The Man with a Shriveled Hand

⁹Going on from that place, he entered their synagogue. ¹⁰Now, a man with a shriveled hand was there. So, looking for a way to accuse him, the [Pharisees] asked [Jesus], "Is it lawful to heal on the Sabbath?" ¹¹He replied, "Which one of you, if he had a sheep that fell into a pit on the Sabbath, would not grab it and lift it out? ¹²How much more valuable is a man than a sheep! So, it is lawful to do good on the Sabbath." ¹³Then he said to the man, "Stretch out your hand." So, the man stretched it out, and it was totally restored, as sound as the other. ¹⁴But as for the Pharisees, they went out and plotted how they might kill Jesus.

Isaiah's Prophecy Fulfilled

¹⁵Aware of this, Jesus withdrew from there. Many followed him, and he healed them all, ¹⁶and he instructed them to not make him known. ¹⁷This was to fulfill what the prophet Isaiah spoke:

> ¹⁸"Here is my servant whom I have chosen,
>   my beloved with whom my soul is well pleased.
>   I will place my Spirit on him,
>   and he shall proclaim justice to the nations.
> ¹⁹He will not struggle or cry out,
>   nor will anyone hear his voice in the streets.
> ²⁰He will not break a bruised reed,
>   nor snuff out a smoldering wick,
>   until he brings justice to victory.
> ²¹And the nations will place their hope in his name."

Blasphemy Against the Holy Spirit

²²Then a demon-possessed man, blind and mute, was brought to him, and he healed him so that the disabled man could both speak and see. ²³Then all the

people were amazed and pondered, "Can this be the Son of David?" ²⁴But when the Pharisees heard it, they said, "It is only by Beelzebub, the prince of demons, that this man casts out demons." ²⁵Knowing their thoughts, he said to them, "Every kingdom divided against itself comes to ruin, and no city or house divided against itself will stand. ²⁶And if Satan casts out Satan, he is divided against himself. How then will his kingdom stand? ²⁷And if I cast out demons by Beelzebub, by whom do your sons cast them out? Therefore, they shall be your judges. ²⁸But if it is by the Spirit of God that I cast out demons, then the Kingdom of God has come to you. ²⁹Or how can someone enter a strong man's house and carry off his possessions, unless he first ties up the strong man? Then indeed he may plunder his house. ³⁰Whoever is not with me is against me, and whoever does not gather with me scatters. ³¹Therefore I tell you, people will be forgiven of every sin and blasphemy, but the blasphemy against the Holy Spirit will not be forgiven. ³²And whoever speaks a word against the Son of Man will be forgiven. But whoever speaks against the Holy Spirit will not be forgiven, either in this age or in the age to come.

Trees Known by Their Fruit

³³"Either make the tree good, and its fruit good, or make the tree bad, and its fruit bad. The tree is known by its fruit. ³⁴You brood of vipers! How can you speak what is good when you are evil? For the mouth speaks what overflows from the heart. ³⁵The good man brings forth good out of his good treasure, whereas the evil man brings forth evil out of his evil treasure. ³⁶I tell you, on the Day of Judgment men will give an account for every careless word they have spoken. ³⁷For by your words you will be justified, and by your words you will be condemned."

The Sign of Jonah

³⁸Then some of the scribes and Pharisees responded to him saying, "Teacher, we wish to see a sign from you." ³⁹But he answered them, "A wicked and adulterous generation seeks for a sign, but no sign shall be given to it except the sign of the prophet Jonah. ⁴⁰For just as Jonah was in the belly of the great fish for three days and three nights, so will the Son of Man be in the heart of the earth for three days and three nights. ⁴¹The men of Nineveh will rise up at the judgment with this generation and condemn it, for they repented at the preaching of Jonah, and take notice: the one who is much greater than Jonah is here. ⁴²The queen of the South will arise at the judgment with this generation and condemn it, for she came from the ends of the earth to hear the wisdom of Solomon and take notice: the one who is much greater than Solomon is here.

An Evil Spirit Returns

⁴³"When the evil spirit has gone out of a man, it passes through waterless places seeking rest, but it finds none. ⁴⁴Then it says, 'I will return to my house where I came from.' And when it comes it finds it empty, swept, and put in order. ⁴⁵Then it goes and brings with it seven other spirits more evil than itself, and they enter and dwell there. Then the last state of that person ends up worse than the first. So shall it be also with this wicked generation."

Who Are Jesus' Mother and Brothers?

⁴⁶While he was still speaking to the people—listen—His mother and his brothers were standing outside, asking to speak to him. ⁴⁷Someone told him, "Your mother and your brothers are standing outside, asking to speak to you." ⁴⁸But he replied to the man who told him, "Who is my mother, and who are my brothers?" ⁴⁹And stretching out his hand toward his disciples, he said, "Here are my mother and my brothers! ⁵⁰For whoever does the will of my Father in heaven is my brother, and sister, and mother."

Chapter 13

The Parable of the Seed Sower

¹[Later] that same day Jesus left the house and went and sat on the shore of the lake. ²Such large crowds gathered around him that he got into a boat and sat there while all the crowds stood on the shore.

³Then he told them many things in parables. He said, "A seed sower went out to sow. ⁴Now as he sowed, some seeds fell along the path, and the birds came and devoured them. ⁵Other seeds fell on rocky ground where they had little soil, and they did spring up right away, though they had no depth of soil. ⁶But when the sun rose, they were scorched, and since they had no root they withered away. ⁷Other seeds fell among thorns, and the thorns grew up and choked the [plants]. ⁸Other seeds fell on good soil and produced a crop, some a hundred, some sixty, some thirty times as much. ⁹If anyone has ears to hear with, let him hear this."

Jesus Explains the Use of Parables

¹⁰Then the disciples came and asked him, "Why do you speak to them in parables?" ¹¹He answered them, "Knowing the secrets of the kingdom of heaven has been granted to you, but it has not been given to them. ¹²As for to the one who has, more will be given to him, and he will have abundance. But as for the one who is lacking, even what he does have will be taken away. ¹³This is why I speak

to them in parables: seeing they do not see, and hearing they do not hear, nor do they understand. [14]With them indeed is fulfilled the prophecy of Isaiah that says:

"Even hearing, you will hear but never understand,
and even seeing, you will see but never perceive.
[15]For this people's heart has grown dull,
and their ears are weary of hearing,
and they have closed their eyes.
Otherwise, they might perceive with their eyes,
and hear with their ears,
and understand with their heart,
and turn, and I would heal them."

[16]But blessed are your eyes because they *do* see, and your ears because they *do* hear. [17]Truly, I tell you, many prophets and righteous men longed to see what you see, and did *not* see it, and to hear what you hear, and did *not* hear it.

[18]"Then listen with understanding to the parable of the seed sower. [19]When anyone hears the word of the kingdom and does not understand it, the evil one comes and snatches away what was sown in his heart; this is what was sown along the path. [20]As for what was sown on rocky ground, this is the one who hears the word and immediately receives it with joy. [21]But since he has no root in himself, he endures for but a short time, and when tribulation or persecution comes about on account of the word, he immediately falls away. [22]As for what was sown among thorns, this is the one who hears the word, but the cares of the world and the deceitful [delight] in wealth choke the word, making it unfruitful. [23]As for what was sown on good soil, this is the one who hears the word and understands it. He indeed bears fruit and yields, in one case a hundred, in another sixty, and in another thirty times as much."

The Parable of Wheat and Weeds

[24][Jesus] offered them another parable. He said, "The kingdom of heaven may be compared to a man who sowed good seed in his field. [25]But while everyone was asleep, his enemy came and sowed weeds among the wheat, and went away. [26]So when the wheat plants sprouted and bore grain, then the weeds appeared also. [27]Then the servants of the estate owner came and said to him, 'Sir, did you not sow good seed in your field? How can it be that it has weeds?' [28]He replied, 'An enemy has done this.' The servants said to him, 'Then do you want us to go and tear them out?' [29]But he said, 'No—so that you do not uproot the wheat in the process of tearing out the weeds. [30]Let both of them grow together until the har-

vest. And at harvest time I will tell the reapers, 'Gather the weeds first and bind them in bundles to be burned but gather the wheat into my barn'."

The Mustard Seed and the Leaven

[31]Then he offered them another parable. He said, "The kingdom of heaven is like a grain of mustard seed that a man took and sowed in his field. [32]It is the smallest of all seeds, but when it has grown it is the largest of the garden plants and becomes a tree, so that the birds of the air come and make nests in its branches."

[33]He told them another parable. "The kingdom of heaven is like leaven that a woman took and worked into three measures of flour, till it was all leavened."

[34]Jesus said all this to the crowds in parables. Actually, he said nothing to them without [using] a parable. [35]This was to fulfill what was spoken by the prophet: "I will start speaking in parables. I will speak what has been hidden since the formation of the world."

Explanation of the Weed Parable

[36]Then he left the crowds and went [back] into the house. His disciples came to him, saying, "Explain the parable of the weeds of the field to us." [37]He answered, "The one who sows the good seed is the Son of Man. [38]The field is the world, and the good seed means the sons of the kingdom. The weeds are the sons of the evil one, [39]and the enemy who sowed them is the devil. The harvest is the close of the age, and the reapers are angels. [40]Just as the weeds are gathered and burned with fire, so will it be at the close of the age. [41]The Son of Man will send his angels, and they will gather all causes of sin and all evildoers out of his kingdom, [42]and throw them into the fiery furnace, where there will be weeping and gnashing of teeth. [43]Then the righteous will shine like the sun in the kingdom of their Father. If anyone has ears to hear with, let him hear this.

The Kingdom of Heaven Is Like...

Hidden Treasure

[44]"The kingdom of heaven is like treasure hidden in a field: when a man found it, he covered it back up and then in his joy he went and sold all his possessions and bought that field.

A Pearl of Great Worth

[45]"Again, the kingdom of heaven is like a merchant in search of fine pearls, [46]who, on finding one pearl of great worth, went and sold all that he had and bought it.

Good Fish Sorted from Bad

47"Again, the kingdom of heaven is like a net thrown into the sea that gathered fish of every kind: 48when it was full, men pulled it ashore and sat down and sorted the good into baskets but threw away the bad.

Judgment Day

49So it will be at the close of the age. The angels will come out and separate the evil from the righteous, 50and throw them into the furnace of fire where there will be weeping and gnashing of teeth. 51Have you understood all this?" They answered, "Yes." 52And he said to them, "Therefore, every scribe who has been trained for the kingdom of heaven is like a master of a household who brings out of his treasure what is new and what is old."

A Prophet Without Honor in his Hometown

53And when Jesus had finished these parables, he left that place, 54and coming to his own hometown area he began teaching them in their synagogue, so that they were astonished, and said, "Where did this man receive this wisdom from? And these miracles! 55Isn't this the carpenter's son? Isn't his mother called Mary? And aren't his brothers James and Joseph and Simon and Judas? 56And aren't all his sisters with us? Where then did this man get all this?" 57And they took offense at him. But Jesus said to them, "A prophet is honored everywhere but in his own hometown and in his own house." 58And so, he did not perform many miracles there because of their lack of faith.

Chapter 14

John the Baptist is Beheaded

1At that time Herod the tetrarch heard about the fame of Jesus, 2and he said to his servants, "This is John the Baptist; he has been raised from the dead. That is why these powers are at work in him."

3For Herod had seized John and had bound him and had put him in prison, on account of Herodias, his brother Philip's wife, 4because John had been telling him, "It is not lawful for you to have her." 5Although [Herod] had been wanting to put him to death, he was afraid of the people, because they considered him to be a prophet. 6But when Herod's birthday came, the daughter of Herodias danced in front of the party guests, and pleased Herod 7so much that he promised with an oath to give her whatever she would ask for. 8Prompted by her mother, she said, "Give me the head of John the Baptist here on a platter." 9Then the king was sorry, but because of his oaths and his guests he ordered that the request be granted. [10]So he sent the guards and had them behead John in the prison, [11]and his head was brought on a platter and given to the girl, who brought it to her mother. [12][John's] disciples came and took the body and buried it, and they went and told Jesus.

Jesus Feeds 5,000 Miraculously

[13]Now when Jesus heard this news, he withdrew from there by himself in a boat to a desolate place. Hearing about this, the crowds followed him on foot from the towns. [14]As he landed, he saw the great crowd, and had compassion on them, and healed their sick. [15]When evening was coming, the disciples came to him and said, "This is a remote place, and the day is now over. Send the crowds away to go into the villages and buy food for themselves." [16]Jesus replied, "They do not need to go away. You give them something to eat." [17]They said to him, "We only have five loaves and two fish here." [18]So he said, "Bring them here to me." [19]Then he ordered the crowds to sit down on the grass. Taking the five loaves and the two fish, he looked up to heaven and said a blessing. Then he broke the loaves and gave them to the disciples, and the disciples gave them to the crowds. [20]They all ate and were satisfied, and they picked up twelve baskets full of the broken leftover pieces. [21]Those who ate numbered about five thousand men, besides the women and children.

Jesus Walks on Water

[22]Right after that, Jesus made the disciples get into the boat and go on ahead of him to the other side while he dismissed the crowds. [23]Then, having dismissed them, he went up on the mountain by himself to pray. When evening came, he was there alone, [24]but by this time the boat was a considerable distance from land, being buffeted by the waves, because the wind was against them. [25]During the fourth watch of the night, Jesus came to them, walking on the sea. [26]But when the disciples saw him walking on the sea, they were terrified. "It is a ghost!" they said, crying out in fear. [27]But he immediately spoke to them, saying, "Take heart, it is I; do not be afraid." [28]Peter responded, "Lord, if it is you, tell me to come to you on the water." [29]"Come," he said. So, Peter got out of the boat and walked on the water and came toward Jesus. [30]But when he saw the wind, he was afraid, and beginning to sink he cried out, "Lord, save me." [31]Jesus immediately reached out his hand and caught him, saying to him, "O you of little faith, why did you doubt?" [32]And when they climbed into the boat, the wind ceased. [33]Then those who were in the boat worshiped him, saying, "Truly you are the Son of God."

³⁴And when they had crossed over, they landed at Gennesaret. ³⁵Now when the men of that place recognized him, they sent word all around that area, and they brought all the sick people to him, ³⁶and begged him to let them just touch the fringe of his garment. And all those who did touch it were healed.

Chapter 15

Traditions and Commandments

¹Then Pharisees and scribes came to Jesus from Jerusalem and asked, ²"Why do your disciples break the tradition of the elders? When they eat, they do not wash their hands." ³He answered them, "And why do you break the commandment of God for the sake of your tradition? ⁴For God commanded, 'Honor your father and your mother,' and, 'Anyone who speaks evil of his father or mother must indeed be put to death.' ⁵But you say, 'If anyone tells his father or his mother, "What you would have gained from me is given to God," he need not honor his father.' ⁶So, for the sake of your tradition, you have nullified the word of God. ⁷You hypocrites! Isaiah prophesied well about you when he said:

⁸**This people honors me with their lips, but their heart is far from me.**
⁹**They worship me in vain, teaching man's ideas as doctrines."**

What Defiles a Man

¹⁰Jesus called the people to himself and said to them, "Hear and understand: ¹¹it is not what goes into the mouth that makes him unclean, rather, it is what comes out of the mouth that makes a man unclean." ¹²Then the disciples came and asked, "Are you aware that the Pharisees were offended when they heard what you said?" ¹³He answered, "Every plant that my heavenly Father has not planted will be pulled up by the roots. ¹⁴Leave them alone; they are blind guides. If a blind man leads a blind man, both will fall into a pit." ¹⁵But Peter said to him, "Explain the parable to us."

¹⁶"Are you also still lacking understanding?" Jesus replied. ¹⁷Do you not see that whatever goes into the mouth passes into the stomach and is pushed out into the latrine? ¹⁸But what comes out of the mouth issues forth from the heart, and this is what makes a man unclean. ¹⁹For out of the heart come evil thoughts, murder, adultery, sexual immorality, theft, false testimony, and slander. ²⁰These are what make a man unclean, but eating with unwashed hands does not make him unclean."

Healing a Canaanite Girl

²¹Then Jesus left that place and withdrew to the region of Tyre and Sidon. ²²A Canaanite woman from that area came to him, crying out, "Have mercy on me, O Lord, Son of David. My daughter is severely possessed by a demon." ²³But, he did not answer her a word. So His disciples came and urged him, saying, "Send her away, for she keeps on crying after us." ²⁴He answered, "I was sent only to the lost sheep of the house of Israel." ²⁵But she came and knelt before him, saying, "Lord, help me." ²⁶And he answered, "It is not fitting to take the children's bread and throw it to the dogs." ²⁷"Yes, Lord, she replied, "but even the dogs eat the crumbs that fall from their masters' table." ²⁸Then Jesus answered her, "Woman, your faith is great! Let this be done for you as you desire." And her daughter was healed at that very moment.

Jesus Heals Many

²⁹Then Jesus went on from there and passed along the Sea of Galilee and made his way up on the mountainside and sat down there. ³⁰Then great crowds came to him, bringing with them the lame, the crippled, the blind, the dumb, and many others, and they laid them at his feet, and he healed them. ³¹When they saw the dumb speaking, the crippled made whole, the lame walking, and the blind seeing they were amazed, and they gave glory to the God of Israel.

Jesus Feeds 4,000 Miraculously

³²Then Jesus called his disciples to himself and said, "I have compassion on the crowd, because they have been with me for three days now and have nothing to eat. I am not willing to send them away hungry; they might collapse on the way." ³³The disciples responded, "Where could we acquire enough [food] in such a remote place to feed so great a crowd?" ³⁴So Jesus asked them, "How many loaves *do* you have?" They answered, "Seven, and a few small fish." ³⁵So, commanding the crowd to sit down on the ground, ³⁶He took the seven loaves and the fish, and having given thanks he broke them and gave them to the disciples, and the disciples gave them to the crowds. ³⁷They all ate and were satisfied, and afterward they picked up seven baskets full of the leftover broken pieces. ³⁸The ones who ate numbered four thousand men, not including women and children. ³⁹After Jesus had sent away the crowds, he got into the boat and went to the region of Magadan.

Chapter 16

Looking for a Sign

[1]Then came the Pharisees, along with the Sadducees, and to test him they asked him to show them a sign from heaven. [2]He responded, "When the evening comes, you say, 'It will be fair weather; for the sky is rosy.' [3]And in the morning, 'Today it will be stormy, for the sky is red and threatening.' You know how to interpret the appearance of the sky, but you cannot interpret the signs of the times. [4]An evil and adulterous generation seeks after some miraculous sign, but no sign shall be given to it except the sign of Jonah." Jesus then left them and departed.

The Leaven of the Pharisees

[5]When the disciples reached the other side, they had forgotten to bring any bread. [6]"Take care," Jesus said to them, "beware of the yeast of the Pharisees and Sadducees." [7]They discussed this among themselves, saying, "We brought no bread." [8]But as he was aware of this, Jesus asked, "O men of little faith, why are you discussing among yourselves the fact that you have no bread? [9]Do you still not understand? Do you not remember the five loaves for the five thousand, and how many basketfuls of leftovers you gathered? [10]Or the seven loaves for the four thousand, and how many basketfuls of leftovers you gathered? [11]How is it that you fail to understand that I was not talking about bread? Beware of the yeast of the Pharisees and Sadducees." [12]Then they realized that he was not telling them to beware of yeast used in bread, but of the teachings of the Pharisees and Sadducees.

Who do People Say I Am?

[13]Now when Jesus came into the district of Caesarea Philippi, he asked his disciples, "Who do people say that the Son of Man is?" [14]They replied, "Some say John the Baptist, others say Elijah, and others Jeremiah or one of the prophets." [15]"And you—" he asked, "who do *you* say that I am?" [16]Simon Peter answered, "You are the Christ, the Son of the living God." [17]Jesus answered him, "Blessed are you, Simon son of Jonah! For it was not flesh and blood that revealed this to you but my Father who is in heaven. [18]And I tell you, you are Peter, and on this rock I will build my church, and the gates of Hell shall not withstand its assault. [19]I will give you the keys of the kingdom of heaven, and whatever you bind on earth shall be bound in heaven, and whatever you loosen on earth shall be loosed in heaven." [20]Then he strictly charged the disciples to tell no one that he was the Christ.

Jesus Foretells his Own Death

²¹From that time Jesus began to show his disciples that he must go to Jerusalem and suffer many things from the elders and chief priests and scribes, and be killed, and be raised on the third day. ²²And Peter took him [aside] and began to rebuke him, saying, "God forbid, Lord! This shall never happen to you." ²³But he turned and said to Peter, "Get behind me, Satan! You are a hindrance to me, for you are not on the side of God, but of men."

²⁴Then Jesus told his disciples, "If anyone should want to follow me, he must deny himself and take up his cross and follow me. ²⁵For whoever wants to save his life will lose it, and whoever loses his life for my sake will find it. ²⁶For what good will it be for a man, if he gains the whole world and forfeits his soul? Or what shall a man give in return for his life? ²⁷For the Son of Man is going to come with his angels in the glory of his Father, and then he will repay every man for what he has done. ²⁸Truly, I say to you, some who are standing here will not taste death before they see the Son of Man coming in his kingdom."

Chapter 17

Transfiguration on the Mount

¹Six days later Jesus took Peter, and James and John his brother, with him, and led them up a high mountain by themselves. ²There he was transfigured before them, and his face shone like the sun, and his clothes became as white as light. ³Just then, Moses and Elijah appeared to them, talking with Jesus. ⁴Peter said to Jesus, "Lord, it is great that we are here. If you want, I will build three shrines here, one for you and one for Moses and one for Elijah." ⁵While he was still speaking, a bright cloud overshadowed them, and a voice from the cloud said, "This is my beloved Son, with whom I am well pleased; listen to him." ⁶When the disciples heard this, they fell on their faces, and were filled with awe. ⁷But Jesus came and touched them, saying, "Rise up, and do not be afraid." ⁸When they lifted up their eyes, they saw no one but Jesus only.

⁹Then as they were coming down the mountain, Jesus commanded them, "Do not tell anyone about this vision, until the Son of Man has been raised from the dead." ¹⁰And the disciples asked him, "Then why do the scribes say that Elijah must come first?" ¹¹He replied, "Indeed, Elijah comes and restores all things. ¹²But I tell you that Elijah has already come, and they did not recognize him, but rather did to him whatever they wished. So, the Son of Man will also suffer at their hands." ¹³Then the disciples understood that he was talking to them about John the Baptist.

Disciples Unable to Exorcise a Demon

[14]When they came to the crowd, a man came up to him and knelt in front of him. [15]"Lord, have mercy on my son," he cried out, "for he is an epileptic, and he suffers terribly. He often falls into the fire, and often into the water. [16]And I brought him to your disciples, but they could not heal him." [17]Jesus answered, "O faithless and perverse generation, how long am I to be with you? How long am I to put up with you? Bring him here to me." [18]Jesus rebuked the demon and it came out of him, and the boy was cured instantly. [19]Then the disciples came to Jesus privately and asked, "Why could we not drive it out?" [20]He replied, "On account of the smallness of your faith. For truly, I say to you, if you have faith as [small as] a grain of mustard seed, you can say to this mountain, 'Move from here to there,' and it will move. Nothing will be impossible to you." [21]But this kind [of demon] never comes out except by prayer and fasting.

Jesus Foretells his Death Again

[22]Once they had gathered together in Galilee, Jesus said to them, "The Son of Man is to be betrayed into the hands of men, [23]and they will kill him. But on the third day he will be raised again." At that they grieved mightily.

The Coin in the Fish's Mouth

[24]After they arrived in Capernaum, the collectors of the two-drachma tax went up to Peter and asked, "Does your teacher not pay the two-drachma tax?" [25]"Yes," he answered. And when he came home, Jesus spoke to him first, saying, "What do you think, Simon? From whom do kings of the earth collect duties and taxes? From their own sons or from others?" [26]"From others," Peter answered. And Jesus said to him, "Then the sons are free. [27]However, so as not to give offense to them, go to the sea and cast out a fishhook. Take the first fish that comes up, and when you open its mouth you will find a four-drachma coin. Take that and give it to them for me and for yourself."

Chapter 18

Greatest in the Kingdom

[1]At that time the disciples came to Jesus, asking, "Who is the greatest in the kingdom of heaven?" [2]And summoning a child to himself, he put him in the midst of them, [3]and said, "Truly, I say to you, unless you change and become like children, you will never enter the kingdom of heaven. [4]Whoever humbles himself like this child is the greatest in the kingdom of heaven. [5]"Whoever receives one such child

in my name receives me. ⁶But as for the one who causes one of these little ones who believe in me to sin, it would be better for him to have a great millstone fastened around his neck and to be drowned in the depths of the sea.

Temptations to Sin

⁷"Woe to the world for its temptations to sin! For it is necessary that temptations come, but woe to the person by whom the temptation comes! ⁸And if your hand or your foot causes you to sin, cut it off and throw it away. It is better for you to enter life maimed or lame than to be thrown into the eternal fire with two hands or two feet. ⁹And if your eye causes you to sin, pluck it out and throw it away. It is better for you to enter life with one eye than to be thrown into the hell of fire with two eyes.

Recovering the Lost Sheep

¹⁰"See that you do not despise one of these little ones. For I tell you that in heaven their angels always gaze on the face of my Father who is in heaven, ¹¹for the Son of Man came to save the lost. ¹²What do you think? If a man has a hundred sheep, and one of them has gone astray, does he not leave the ninety-nine on the mountains and go in search of the one that went astray? ¹³And if he finds it—truly I say to you—he rejoices over it more than over the ninety-nine that never went astray. ¹⁴So it is not the will of my Father who is in heaven that one of these little ones should perish.

Reconciling with Your Brother

¹⁵"If your brother sins against you, go and tell him his fault, between you and him alone. If he listens to you, you have gained your brother. ¹⁶But if he does not listen, take one or two others along with you, so that every charge may be established by the evidence of two or three witnesses. ¹⁷If he refuses to listen to them, tell it to the church. And if he refuses to listen even to the church, let him be like a Gentile or a tax collector to you. ¹⁸Truly, I say to you, whatever you bind on earth shall be bound in heaven, and whatever you loosen on earth shall be loosed in heaven. ¹⁹Again I say to you, if two of you agree on earth about anything they ask, it will be done for them by my Father in heaven. ²⁰For where two or three are gathered in my name, there am I in the midst of them."

Forgive 490 Times

²¹Then Peter came up and said to him, "Lord, how often should my brother sin against me, and I still forgive him? As many as seven times?" ²²Jesus replied to him, "I would not tell you seven times, but seventy times seven.

Parable of the Unforgiving Servant

²³"Therefore the kingdom of heaven may be compared to a king who once wanted to settle accounts with his servants. ²⁴When he began the reckoning, one was brought to him who owed him ten thousand talents. ²⁵Since he could not pay, his master ordered him to be sold, with his wife and children and all that he had, and payment to be made. ²⁶So the servant fell on his knees, imploring him, 'Sir, have patience with me, and I will pay you everything.' ²⁷And out of pity for him the master of that servant released him and forgave him the debt.

²⁸But as he went out, that same servant happened to meet one of his fellow servants who owed him a hundred denarii. And seizing him by the throat he said, 'Pay what you owe [me].' ²⁹So his fellow servant fell down and pleaded with him, 'Have patience with me, and I will pay you.' ³⁰He refused and went and put him in prison till he could pay the debt. ³¹When his fellow servants saw what had taken place, they were greatly distressed, and they went and reported to their master all that had taken place. ³²Then his master summoned him and said to him, 'You wicked servant! I forgave you all that debt because you begged me. ³³Now should you not have had mercy on your fellow servant, as I had mercy on you?' ³⁴And in anger his master delivered him to the jailers, till he could pay all his debt. ³⁵So my heavenly Father will do [the same] to every one of you, if you do not forgive your brother from your heart."

Chapter 19

Divorce and Remarriage

¹Now when Jesus had finished saying these things, he went away from Galilee and entered the region of Judea beyond the Jordan. ²And large crowds followed him, and he healed them there.

³And Pharisees came up to him and tested him by asking, "Is it lawful to divorce one's wife on the basis of any cause?" ⁴He answered, "Have you not read that he who made them from the beginning made them male and female, ⁵and said, 'For this reason a man shall leave his father and mother and be joined to his wife, and the two shall become one flesh'? ⁶So they are no longer two but one flesh. Therefore, do not allow man to tear apart what God has joined together." ⁷They asked him, "Then why did Moses permit a man to just give [his wife] a certificate of divorce, and send her away?" ⁸He replied, "Because of your hardness of heart, Moses allowed you to divorce your wives, but from the beginning it was not [supposed to be] that way. ⁹And I tell you: whoever divorces his wife, except for sexual immorality, and marries, commits adultery."

¹⁰The disciples said to him, "If this is the situation between a man and his wife, it is not expedient to marry." ¹¹But he said to them, "Not everyone can accept this statement, but only those to whom it is given can. ¹²For there are eunuchs who have been so from birth, and there are eunuchs who have been made eunuchs by men, and there are eunuchs who have made themselves eunuchs for the sake of the kingdom of heaven. The one who is able to accept this should accept it."

Bring the Children

¹³Then children were brought to him that he might lay his hands on them and pray. The disciples rebuked the people, ¹⁴but Jesus said, "Allow the children come to me, and do not hinder them, for the kingdom of heaven belongs to such [as them]." ¹⁵And he laid his hands on them and went away.

The Rich Young Ruler

¹⁶Note this—a fellow came up to him and asked, "Teacher, what good deed must I do to have eternal life?" ¹⁷And he said to him, "Why is it that you ask me about what is good? There is only one who is good. If you should want to enter into life, keep the commandments." ¹⁸He asked him, "Which ones?" And Jesus said, "You shall not kill, You shall not commit adultery, You shall not steal, You shall not give false testimony, ¹⁹Honor your father and mother, and, You shall love your neighbor as yourself." ²⁰The young man said to him, "I have observed all these. What am I still lacking?" ²¹Jesus said to him, "If you should want to be perfect, go, sell what you possess and give to the poor, and you will have treasure in heaven, and come, follow me." ²²When the young man heard this, he went away sorrowful, for he had great possessions.

Rich People and Who is First and Last

²³And Jesus said to his disciples, "Truly, I say to you, it will be hard for a rich man to enter the kingdom of heaven. ²⁴Again I tell you, it is easier for a camel to go through the eye of a needle than for a rich man to enter the kingdom of God." ²⁵When the disciples heard this they were greatly astonished, saying, "Who then can be saved?" ²⁶But Jesus looked at them and said to them, "With men this is impossible, but with God all things are possible."

²⁷Then Peter said in reply, "See, we have left everything and followed you. What are we going to have?" ²⁸Jesus said to them, "Truly, I say to you, in the new world, when the Son of Man will sit on his glorious throne, you who have followed me will also sit on twelve thrones, judging the twelve tribes of Israel. ²⁹And everyone who has left houses or brothers or sisters or father or mother or children or lands

for my name's sake will receive a hundred times as much and inherit eternal life. [30]But many [who are] first will be last, and the last [will be] first.

Chapter 20

Parable of the Vineyard Workers and their Wages

[1]"For the kingdom of heaven is like the owner of an estate who went out early in the morning to hire laborers for his vineyard. [2]After agreeing to pay the laborers a denarius a day, he sent them into his vineyard. [3]About three hours into the workday, he went out and saw others standing idle in the marketplace. [4]He said to them, 'You go into the vineyard too, and I will pay you a fair wage.' So they went. [5]Going out again around noon and around three in the afternoon, he did the same. [6]And about five o'clock he went out and found others standing around and he asked them, 'Why are you standing around here idle all day?' [7]They answered, 'Because no one has hired us.' he said to them, 'You go into the vineyard too.' [8]Now when evening came, the owner of the vineyard said to his foreman, 'Call the laborers and pay them their wages, beginning with the last, up to the first.' [9]And when the ones hired about the eleventh hour came, each of them received a denarius. [10]Now when the first [ones hired] came up, they thought they would receive more; but each of them also received one denarius. [11]And on receiving it they grumbled at the owner of the estate, [12]saying, 'These last ones worked only one hour, and you have made them equal to us who have borne the burden of the day and the scorching heat.' [13]But he replied to one of them, 'Friend, I am doing you no wrong. Did you not agree with me for [the wage of one] denarius? [14]Take what belongs to you and go. I choose to give to these last ones in the same way as I am giving it to you. [15]Do not I have the right to do what I choose with what belongs to me? Or do you begrudge my generosity?' [16]So the last will be first, and the first [will be] last."

Jesus Foretells his Death a Third Time

[17]And as Jesus was going up to Jerusalem, he took the twelve disciples aside, and on the way he said to them, [18]"Look, we are going up to Jerusalem, and the Son of Man will be delivered to the chief priests and scribes. They will condemn him to death [19]and deliver him to the Gentiles to be mocked and scourged and crucified. And then he will be raised on the third day."

Greatest in the Kingdom

[20]Then the mother of the sons of Zebedee came up to him, with her sons, and kneeling before him she made a request of him. [21]And he said to her, "What do

you want?" She said to him, "Command that these two sons of mine may sit, one at your right hand and one at your left, in your kingdom." ²²But Jesus answered, "You do not know what you are asking. Are you able to drink the cup that I am to drink?" They said to him, "We are able." ²³He said to them, "You will drink my cup, but to sit at my right hand and at my left is not mine to grant, but it is for those for whom it has been prepared by my Father." ²⁴And when the other ten heard that, they were indignant at the two brothers. ²⁵But Jesus called them to himself and said, "You know that the rulers of the Gentiles lord it over them, and their great men exercise authority over them. ²⁶It shall not be so among you—rather, whoever would want to be great among you must be your servant, ²⁷and whoever would want to be first among you must be your slave, ²⁸just as the Son of Man came not to be served but to serve, and to give his life as a ransom for many."

Jesus Heals Two Blind Men

²⁹And as they left Jericho, a great crowd followed him. ³⁰Now two blind men were sitting alongside the road, and when they heard that Jesus was passing by, they cried out, "Have mercy on us, Son of David!" ³¹The crowd rebuked them, telling them to be silent. But they cried out all the more, "Lord, have mercy on us, Son of David!" ³²And Jesus stopped and called them, saying, "What do you want me to do for you?" ³³They said to him, "Lord, let our eyes be opened." ³⁴And in pity Jesus touched their eyes, and immediately they received their sight and followed him.

Chapter 21

The Triumphal Entry

¹As they were approaching Jerusalem and had come to Bethphage on the Mount of Olives, Jesus sent two disciples, ²saying to them, "Go into the village ahead of you, and immediately you will find a donkey tied up, with her colt by her. Untie them and bring them to me. ³If anyone says anything to you, say, 'The Lord has need of them,' and he will send them right away." ⁴This took place to fulfill what was spoken by the prophet who said, ⁵"Tell the daughter of Zion, 'Look—your king is coming to you, humble, and mounted on a donkey, and on a colt, the foal of a donkey'."

⁶The disciples went and did as Jesus had instructed them. ⁷They brought the donkey and the colt, and put their cloaks on them, and he sat on them. ⁸Most of the crowd spread their cloaks on the road, while others cut branches from the trees and spread them on the road. ⁹Then the crowds that went before him and that followed him shouted, "Hosanna to the Son of David! Blessed is he who comes in the name of the Lord! Hosanna in the highest!" ¹⁰And when he entered Jeru-

salem, the whole city was excited, asking, "Who is this?" [11]And the crowds said, "This is the prophet Jesus from Nazareth of Galilee."

Jesus Clears the Temple

[12]Then Jesus entered the temple of God and drove out all who were buying and selling in the temple, and he overturned the tables of the moneychangers and the benches of those who sold doves. [13]He said to them, "The scripture says, 'My house shall be called a house of prayer'; but you are making it a den of thieves."

[14]The blind and the lame came to him in the temple, and he healed them. [15]But when the chief priests and the scribes saw the amazing things that he did, and the children crying out in the temple, "Hosanna to the Son of David!" they were indignant. [16]And they asked him, "Do you hear what these children are saying?" And Jesus said to them, "Indeed! Have you never read, 'You have determined praise to come forth out of the mouths of babies and infants'?" [17]And leaving them, he went out of the city to Bethany and lodged there.

Jesus Curses a Fig Tree

[18]In the morning, as he was returning to the city, he grew hungry. [19]Seeing a fig tree on the roadside he went over to it but found nothing on it except leaves. He said to it, "May no fruit ever come from you again!" Immediately the fig tree withered. [20]When the disciples saw it they were amazed and asked, "How did the fig tree wither so quickly?" [21]Jesus answered them, "Truly, I say to you, if you have faith and never doubt, you will not only do what has been done to the fig tree, but even if you say to this mountain, 'Be taken up and cast into the sea,' it will be done. [22]And whatever you ask in prayer, you will receive, if you have faith."

By Whose Authority?

[23]And when he entered the temple, the chief priests and the elders of the people came up to him as he was teaching, and asked, "By what authority are you doing these things, and who gave you this authority?" [24]Jesus answered them, "I will ask you a question too, and if you can tell me the answer, then I also will tell you by what authority I do these things. [25]The baptism of John: where did it come from? From heaven or from men?" So they debated with one another, "If we say, 'From heaven,' he will say to us, 'Then why did you not believe him?' [26]But if we say, 'From men,' we have the crowds to fear, for everyone considers John a prophet." [27]So they answered Jesus, "We do not know." And he said to them, "Neither will I tell you by what authority I do these things.

Which Son Obeyed?

²⁸"What do you think [of this]? A [certain] man had two sons. He went to the first one and said, 'Son, go and work in the vineyard today.' ²⁹And he answered, 'I will not'; but later on he changed his mind and did go. ³⁰He went to the other son and said the same. He answered, 'I will go, sir,' but he did not go. ³¹Which of the two did the will of his father?" "The first," they replied. Jesus said to them, "Truly, I say to you, the tax collectors and the harlots are entering the kingdom of God before you. ³²For John came to you in the way of righteousness, and you did not believe him, but the tax collectors and the harlots believed him. Even when you realized this, you did not repent later on and believe him.

The Parable of the Wicked Tenants

³³"Listen to another parable: There was a landowner who planted a vineyard, and built a hedge around it, and dug a winepress in it, and built a watchtower, and rented it out to tenants and journeyed into another country. ³⁴When the harvest time approached, he sent his servants to the tenants to collect his fruit. ³⁵The tenants took his servants and beat one, killed another, and stoned another. ³⁶Again he sent some other servants—more than the first time—and they did the same to them. ³⁷Finally he sent his son to them, saying, 'They will respect my son.' ³⁸But when the tenants saw the son, they said to themselves, 'This is the heir; come, let's kill him and take his inheritance.' ³⁹So they took him and threw him out of the vineyard and killed him. ⁴⁰Now then, when the owner of the vineyard comes, what will he do to those tenants?" ⁴¹They said to him, "He will put those wretches to a miserable death and rent out the vineyard to other tenants who will give him the share of the crop at harvest time."

The Chief Cornerstone

⁴²Jesus said to them, "Have you never read in the scriptures: 'The very stone that the builders rejected has become the capstone. This was the Lord's doing, and it is marvelous in our eyes'? ⁴³Therefore I tell you the kingdom of God will be taken away from you and given to a people who will produce kingdom fruit." ⁴⁴The one who falls on this stone will be broken to pieces, and when it falls on anyone, it will crush him.

⁴⁵When the chief priests and the Pharisees heard his parables, they perceived that he was talking about them. ⁴⁶They tried to arrest him, but they were afraid of the crowds because the [crowds] considered him a prophet.

Chapter 22

The Parable of the Wedding Feast

¹And again Jesus spoke to them in parables, saying, ²"The kingdom of heaven may be compared to a king who gave a wedding feast for his son ³and sent his servants to call those who were invited to the wedding feast, but they refused to come. ⁴Again he sent other servants, saying, 'Tell those who are invited, Look, I have made ready my dinner, my oxen and my fattened calves have been slaughtered, and everything is ready. Come to the wedding feast.' ⁵But they ignored it and went off, one to his farm, another to his business, ⁶while the rest seized his servants, treated them horribly, and killed them. ⁷The king was angry, so he sent his troops to slay those murderers and burn their city. ⁸Then he said to his servants, 'The wedding feast is ready, but those who were invited are not worthy. ⁹So, go out to the main roads, and invite whomever you find to the wedding feast.' ¹⁰So the servants went out into the streets and gathered everyone they found, both bad and good. So, the wedding hall was filled with guests.

¹¹"But when the king came in to look at the guests, he saw a man there not dressed in wedding attire. ¹²When he asked him, 'Friend, how did you get in here without any wedding clothes?' he fell speechless. ¹³Then the king said to the attendants, 'Bind him hand and foot, and cast him into the outer darkness where there will be weeping and gnashing of teeth.' ¹⁴For many are called, but few are chosen."

Paying Taxes to Caesar

¹⁵Then the Pharisees went and started plotting how to entangle him in his words. ¹⁶So they sent their disciples to him, along with the Herodians, and they said, "Teacher, we know that you are truthful, and teach the way of God truthfully, and you do not care about anyone's opinion, because you have no regard for outward appearances. ¹⁷Tell us, then, what you think: Is it lawful to pay taxes to Caesar, or not?" ¹⁸But Jesus, aware of their malice, replied, "You hypocrites, why are you putting me to the test? ¹⁹Show me the coin for the tax." They brought him a denarius, ²⁰and Jesus asked them, "Whose image and inscription is this?" ²¹"Caesar's," they answered. Then he replied to them, "Therefore render to Caesar the things that are Caesar's, and to God the things that are God's." ²²When they heard it, they marveled, and they left him and went away.

Sadducees and the Resurrection

²³On that same day Sadducees, who say that there is no resurrection, came to him and they posed a question to him, ²⁴saying, "Teacher, Moses said, 'If a man dies,

having no children, his brother must marry the widow, and raise up children for his brother.' [25]Now there were seven brothers among us. The first one married, and died, and having no children left his wife to his brother. [26]So too the second one and third one, down to the seventh one. [27]After all of them, the woman died. [28]So then, in the resurrection, of the seven of them, whose wife will she be? For they all had her."

[29]But Jesus answered them, "Your reasoning is faulty because you know neither the scriptures nor the power of God. [30]For in the resurrection they neither marry nor are given in marriage, but are like angels in heaven. [31]And as for the resurrection of the dead, have you not read what God said to you, [32]'I am the God of Abraham, and the God of Isaac, and the God of Jacob'? He is not God of the dead, but of the living." [33]And on hearing this, the crowd was astonished at his teaching.

The Greatest Commandment

[34]But when the Pharisees heard that he had silenced the Sadducees, they convened. [35]And one of them, a lawyer, asked him a question to test him. [36]"Teacher, which commandment in the law is the greatest?" [37]He answered him, "You shall love the Lord your God with all your heart, and with all your soul, and with all your mind. [38]This is the greatest and first commandment. [39]And a second is like it: You shall love your neighbor as yourself. [40]All the law and the prophets depend on these two commandments."

Whose Son is Christ?

[41]Now while the Pharisees were gathered together, Jesus asked them a question, [42]saying, "What do you think of the Christ? Whose son is He?" They replied, "David's." [43]He said to them, "How then is it that David, inspired by the Spirit, calls him Lord, saying, [44]'The Lord said to my Lord, "Sit at my right hand, until I put your enemies under your feet"? [45]Then if David calls him Lord, how can the Lord be his son?" [46]No one was able to answer him a word, nor from that day on did anyone dare to question him any further.

Chapter 23

Jesus Denounces the Scribes and Pharisees

[1]Then Jesus said to the crowds and to his disciples, [2]"The scribes and the Pharisees sit on Moses' seat. [3]So practice and observe whatever they tell you, but not what they do, for they preach, but do not practice. [4]They tie up heavy burdens

that are hard to bear, and lay them on men's shoulders, but they themselves are not willing to lift a finger to move them. [5]They do all their deeds to be seen by others. For they make their phylacteries broad and their fringes long, [6]and they love the place of honor at feasts and the best seats in the synagogues, [7]and greetings in the marketplace, and being called rabbi by others. [8]But you are not to be called rabbi, for you have one teacher, and you are all brothers. [9]And call no man on earth your father, for you have one Father, who is in heaven. [10]Neither be called master teachers, for you have one master teacher, the Christ. [11]Now then, the one who is greatest among you shall be your servant. [12]Whoever exalts himself will be humbled, and whoever humbles himself will be exalted.

Jesus Pronounces Seven Woes

[13]"But, woe to you, scribes and Pharisees, hypocrites! For you shut people out of the kingdom of heaven—you neither enter yourselves, nor allow those who would enter to go in.

[14]"Woe to you, scribes and Pharisees, hypocrites! For you devour widows' houses and for a pretense you make long prayers. On account of that you will receive the greater condemnation.

[15]"Woe to you, scribes and Pharisees, hypocrites! For you travel over sea and land to make a single proselyte, and when he becomes one, you make him twice as much a son of hell as yourselves.

[16]"Woe to you, blind guides, who say, 'If anyone swears by the temple, it is nothing. But if anyone swears by the gold of the temple, he is bound by his oath.' [17]You blind fools! For which is greater, the gold or the temple that has made the gold sacred? [18]And you say, 'If anyone swears by the altar, it is nothing. But if anyone swears by the gift that is on the altar, he is bound by his oath.' [19]You blind men! Which one is greater, the gift or the altar that makes the gift sacred? [20]So the one who swears by the altar swears by it and by everything on it. [21]And the one who swears by the temple swears by it and by him who dwells in it. [22]And the one who swears by heaven swears by the throne of God and by him who sits on it.

[23]"Woe to you, scribes and Pharisees, hypocrites! For you tithe mint and dill and cumin and have neglected the weightier matters of the law: justice and mercy and faith. You ought to have done these [things], without neglecting the others. [24]You blind guides, straining out an ant and swallowing a giant!

[25]"Woe to you, scribes and Pharisees, hypocrites! For you cleanse the outside of the cup and of the plate, but inside they are full of extortion and self-indulgence.

[26]You blind Pharisee! First cleanse the inside of the cup and of the plate, so that the outside may also be clean.

[27]"Woe to you, scribes and Pharisees, hypocrites! For you are like whitewashed tombs, which outwardly appear beautiful, but inside are full of dead men's bones and all uncleanness. [28]In the same way you also have an outward appearance of righteousness to men, but inside you are full of hypocrisy and iniquity.

[29]"Woe to you, scribes and Pharisees, hypocrites! For you erect tombs for the prophets and adorn the monuments of the righteous, [30]claiming, 'If we had lived in the days of our fathers, we would not have taken part with them in shedding the blood of the prophets.' [31]In this way you witness against yourselves, that you are sons of those who murdered the prophets. [32]Then fill up the measure of your fathers' [guilt]. [33]You serpents, you brood of vipers, how are you to escape being sentenced to hell? [34]Therefore I send you prophets and wise men and scribes, some of whom you will kill and crucify, and some you will flog in your synagogues and persecute from city to city, [35]so that upon you shall come all the righteous blood that has been shed on earth, from the blood of innocent Abel to the blood of Zechariah the son of Barachiah, whom you murdered between the sanctuary and the altar. [36]Truly, I say to you, all this will come upon this generation.

Jesus Laments Over Jerusalem

[37]"O Jerusalem, Jerusalem, killing the prophets and stoning those who are sent to it! How often would I have gathered your children together as a hen gathers her brood under her wings, and you were unwilling! [38]Look—your house is forsaken and desolate. [39]For I tell you, you will not see me again, until you say, 'Blessed is he who comes in the name of the Lord.' "

Chapter 24

The Destruction of the Temple and Signs of the End of the Age

[1]Jesus left the temple and was going away when his disciples came to point out the buildings of the temple to him. [2]But he answered them, "You see all these, do you not? Truly, I say to you, there will not be one stone left on top of another in this place that will not be thrown down."

[3]As he was sitting on the Mount of Olives, the disciples came to him privately, saying, "Tell us when this will be, and what will be the sign of your coming and of the close of the age?" [4]And Jesus answered them, "Be careful that no one leads you astray. [5]For many will come in my name, saying, 'I am the Christ,' and they will lead many astray. [6]And you will hear of wars and rumors of wars, but see that you

are not alarmed. For though this must take place, the end is not yet. [7]For nation will rise against nation, and kingdom against kingdom, and there will be famines and earthquakes in various places: [8]all this is but the beginning of the birth pangs.

[9]"Then they will deliver you up to tribulation and put you to death. And you will be hated by all nations for my name's sake. [10]And then many will fall away and betray one another and hate one another. [11]And many false prophets will arise and lead many astray. [12]And because lawlessness will be so much greater, many people's love will grow cold. [13]But whoever endures to the end will be saved. [14]And this gospel of the kingdom will be preached throughout the whole world as a testimony to all nations, and then the end will come.

The Abomination Causing Desolation

[15]"So when you see the abomination [causing] desolation, whom the prophet Daniel spoke about, standing in the holy place (let the reader understand), [16]then let those who are in Judea flee to the mountains. [17]Let anyone on the housetop not go down to take what is in his house. [18]Let him who is in the field not turn back to grab his overcoat. [19]And how awful for the women who are pregnant and for the nursing mothers in those days! [20]Pray that your flight may not be in winter or on a Sabbath. [21]For then there will be great tribulation, such as has not been from the beginning of the world until now, no, and never will be [again]. [22]And if those days had not been cut short, no human being would be saved. But for the sake of the chosen ones, those days will be cut short.

[23]At that time if anyone says to you, 'Look, here is the Christ!' or 'There he is!' do not believe it. [24]For false Christs and false prophets will arise and show great signs and wonders, so as to lead astray, if possible, even the chosen ones. [25]Listen—I have told you beforehand. [26]So if they say to you, 'Look, he is in the wilderness,' do not go out. If they say, 'Look, he is in the inner rooms,' do not believe it. [27]For as the lightning comes from the east and shines as far as the west, so will be the coming of the Son of Man. [28]Wherever the corpse is, there will the vultures gather together.

The Son of Man's Return

[29]"Immediately after the tribulation of those days, the sun will be darkened, and the moon will not give its light, and the stars will fall from heaven, and the powers of the heavens will be shaken. [30]Then the sign of the Son of Man will appear in heaven, and then all the tribes of the earth will mourn. They will see the Son of Man coming on the clouds of heaven with power and great glory, [31]and he will send out his angels with a loud trumpet call, and they will gather his chosen ones from the four winds, from one end of heaven to the other.

³²"Learn the lesson from the fig tree: as soon as its branch becomes tender and puts forth its leaves, you know that summer is near. ³³So also, when you see all these things, you will know that he is near, even at the gates. ³⁴Truly, I say to you, this generation will not pass away till all these things take place. ³⁵Heaven and earth will pass away, but my words will not pass away.

No One Knows the Day or Hour

³⁶"But of that day and hour no one knows, not even the angels of heaven, nor the Son, but the Father only. ³⁷As were the days of Noah, so will be the coming of the Son of Man. ³⁸For as in those days before the flood they were eating and drinking, marrying and giving in marriage, until the day when Noah entered the ark. ³⁹But they did not know until the flood came and swept them all away. So will be the coming of the Son of Man. ⁴⁰Then two men will be in the field; one is taken and one is left. ⁴¹Two women will be grinding at the mill; one is taken, and one is left. ⁴²Keep watch therefore, for you do not know on what day your Lord is coming. ⁴³But know this, that if the master of the house had known in what part of the night the thief was coming, he would have kept watch and would not have let someone break into his house. ⁴⁴Therefore you also must be ready, for the Son of Man is coming at an unexpected hour.

⁴⁵"Who then is the faithful and wise servant, whom his master has put in charge of his household, to give them their food at the proper time? ⁴⁶Blessed is that servant whom his master will find doing so when he comes. ⁴⁷Truly, I say to you, he will put him in charge of all his possessions. ⁴⁸But if that wicked servant says to himself, 'My master is delayed,' ⁴⁹and begins to beat his fellow servants, and eats and drinks with the drunken ones, ⁵⁰the master of that servant will return on a day when he does not expect him and at an hour he does not know. ⁵¹He will cut him off and assign him a place with hypocrites where there will be weeping and gnashing of teeth.

Chapter 25

Five Wise and Five Foolish Virgins

¹"So then the kingdom of heaven can be compared to ten maidens who took their lamps and went to meet the bridegroom. ²Five of them were foolish, and five were wise. ³When the foolish took their lamps, they took no oil with them. ⁴But the wise brought along flasks of oil with their lamps. ⁵As the bridegroom was delayed, they all slumbered and slept. ⁶But at midnight came a cry, 'Look, it's the bridegroom! Come out to meet him.' ⁷Then all those maidens got up and made their lamps ready. ⁸The foolish said to the wise, 'Give us some of your oil because our lamps are going

out.' ⁹But the wise responded, 'There would not be enough for us *and* for you, too. Instead, go to the dealers and buy some for yourselves.' ¹⁰While they were gone to buy oil, the bridegroom came, and those who were ready entered the wedding feast with him, and the door was shut. ¹¹Afterward the other maidens came back, saying, 'Lord, lord, open the door for us.' ¹²But he replied, 'Truly, I say to you, I do not know you.' ¹³Therefore, keep watch because you know neither the day nor the hour.

The Parable of the Talents

¹⁴"For it will be as when a man going on a journey called his servants and entrusted his property to them. ¹⁵To one he gave five talents, to another two, to another one, in accordance with each one's ability. Then he went away. ¹⁶The one who had received the five talents went at once and did trading with them, and he made five talents more. ¹⁷So also, the one who had the two talents made two talents more. ¹⁸But the one who had received the one talent went and dug a hole in the ground and hid his master's money.

¹⁹Now after a long time the master of those servants came [back] and settled accounts with them. ²⁰And the one who had received the five talents came forward, bringing five talents more, saying, 'Master, you entrusted me with five talents. Here—I have made five talents more.' ²¹His master said to him, 'Well done, good and faithful servant. You have been faithful over a little; I will put you in charge over much. Enter into the joy of your master.' ²²Then the one who had the two talents came forward, saying, 'Master, you entrusted me with two talents. Here—I have made two talents more.' ²³His master said to him, 'Well done, good and faithful servant. You have been faithful over a little; I will put you in charge over much. Enter into the joy of your master.'

²⁴Then, the one who had received the one talent also came forward, saying, 'Master, I knew you to be a hard man, reaping where you did not sow, and gathering where you did not scatter seed. ²⁵So I was afraid, and I went and hid your talent in the ground. Here you have what is yours.' ²⁶But his master answered him, 'You wicked and slothful servant! You knew that I reap where I have not sown, and gather where I have not scattered seed? ²⁷Then you should have invested my money with the bankers, and at my coming I should have received what was my own with interest. ²⁸So take the talent from him and give it to the one who has the ten talents. ²⁹For more will be given to everyone who has, and he will have abundance. But from the one who is lacking, even what he does have will be taken away. ³⁰And cast the worthless servant into outer darkness where there will be weeping and gnashing of teeth.'

Separating the Righteous from the Wicked

[31]"When the Son of Man comes in his glory, and all the angels with him, then he will sit on his glorious throne. [32]All the nations will be gathered before him, and he will separate them one from another as a shepherd separates the sheep from the goats, [33]and he will put the sheep on his right side, but the goats on his left.

[34]"Then the King will say to those on his right, 'Come, my Father's blessed ones, inherit the kingdom prepared for you from the foundation of the world. [35]For:

> I was hungry and you gave me food,
> I was thirsty and you gave me drink,
> I was a stranger and you welcomed me,
> [36]I was naked and you clothed me,
> I was sick and you visited me,
> I was in prison and you came to me.'

[37]Then the righteous will answer him, 'Lord, when did we see you hungry and feed you, or thirsty and give you drink? [38]And when did we see you a stranger and welcome you, or naked and clothe you? [39]And when did we see you sick or in prison and visit you.' [40]And the King will answer them, 'Truly, I say to you, as you did so to one of the least of these my brothers, you did so to me.'

[41]"Then he will say to those at his left hand, 'Depart from me, you cursed ones, into the eternal fire prepared for the devil and his angels. [42]For:

> I was hungry and you gave me no food,
> I was thirsty and you gave me no drink,
> [43]I was a stranger and you did not welcome me,
> naked and you did not clothe me,
> sick and in prison and you did not visit me.'

[44]Then they also will answer, 'Lord, when did we see you hungry or thirsty or a stranger or naked or sick or in prison, and did not minister to you?' [45]Then he will answer them, 'Truly, I say to you, as you did not do so to one of the least of these, you did not do so to me.' [46]And they will go away into eternal punishment, but the righteous into eternal life."

Chapter 26

Chief Priests Plot to Kill Jesus

[1]When Jesus had finished saying all these things, he said to his disciples, [2]"You know that after two days the Passover is coming, and the Son of Man will be delivered up to be crucified."

³Then the chief priests and the elders of the people gathered in the palace of the high priest, who was called Caiaphas, ⁴and took counsel together in order to arrest Jesus by stealth and kill him. ⁵But they said, "Not during the feast, so that there will not be an uprising among the people."

Jesus Anointed and then Betrayed

⁶Now when Jesus was in Bethany at the house of Simon the leper, ⁷a woman came up to him with an alabaster flask of very expensive ointment, and she poured it on his head, as he sat at table. ⁸But when the disciples saw it, they were indignant, saying, "Why this waste? ⁹For this ointment might have been sold for a large sum, and given to the poor." ¹⁰But Jesus, aware of this, said to them, "Why do you trouble the woman? For she has done a beautiful thing for me. ¹¹For you always have the poor with you, but you will not always have me. ¹²In pouring this ointment on my body she has done it to prepare me for burial. ¹³Truly, I say to you, wherever this gospel is preached in the whole world, what she has done will be told in memory of her."

¹⁴Then one of the Twelve, who was called Judas Iscariot, went to the chief priests ¹⁵and said, "What will you give me if I deliver him to you?" And they paid him thirty pieces of silver. ¹⁶And from that moment on he sought an opportunity to betray him.

The Passover with the Disciples

¹⁷Now on the first day of Unleavened Bread the disciples came to Jesus, saying, "Where will you have us prepare for you to eat the Passover?" ¹⁸He said, "Go into the city to a certain one, and say to him, 'The Teacher says, "My time is at hand. I will keep the Passover at your house with my disciples."'" ¹⁹And the disciples did as Jesus had directed them, and they prepared the Passover.

²⁰When it was evening, he sat at table with the twelve disciples. ²¹ And as they were eating, he declared, "Truly, I say to you, one of you will betray me." ²²So they were very sorrowful, and one after another they began to ask him, "Is it I, Lord?" ²³He answered, "The one who has dipped his hand in the dish with me will betray me. ²⁴The Son of Man goes as it is written of him, but woe to that man by whom the Son of Man is betrayed! It would have been better for that man if he had not been born." ²⁵Judas, who betrayed him, said, "Is it I, Master?" he said to him, "You have said so."

The Lord's Supper

[26]Now as they were eating, Jesus took bread, and blessed, and broke it, and gave it to the disciples and said, "Take, eat: this is my body." [27]And he took a cup, and when he had given thanks, he gave it to them, saying, "Drink of it, all of you, [28]for this is my blood of the covenant, which is poured out for many for the forgiveness of sins. [29]I tell you I will not drink again of this fruit of the vine until that day when I drink it new with you in the Kingdom of my Father."

Jesus Foretells Peter's Denial

[30]And once they had sung a hymn, they went out to the Mount of Olives. [31]Then Jesus said to them, "You will all fall away because of me this night. For the scripture says, 'I will strike the shepherd, and the sheep of the flock will be scattered.' [32]But after I am raised up, I will go before you to Galilee." [33]Peter declared to him, "Even if they all fall away because of you, I will never fall away." [34]Jesus said to him, "Truly, I say to you, this very night, before the cock crows, you will deny me three times." [35]Peter said to him, "Even if I must die with you, I will not deny you." And all the disciples pledged the same.

The Prayer in the Garden of Gethsemane

[36]Then Jesus went with them to a place called Gethsemane, and he said to his disciples, "Sit here, while I go over there to pray." [37]And taking along Peter and the two sons of Zebedee, he began to be sorrowful and troubled. [38]Then he said to them, "My soul is very sorrowful, even to death. Stay here and keep watch with me." [39]And going a little farther, he fell on his face and prayed, "My Father, if it be possible, let this cup pass from me. Nevertheless, not as I will, but as you will." [40]And he came to the disciples and found them sleeping, and he remarked to Peter, "So, could not you [even] watch with me [for] one hour? [41]Watch and pray that you may not enter into temptation; the spirit indeed is willing, but the flesh is weak." [42]Again, for the second time, he went away and prayed, "My Father, if this cannot pass unless I drink it, your will be done." [43]And again he came and found them sleeping, for their eyelids had grown heavy. [44]So, leaving them again, he went away and prayed for the third time, saying the same words. [45]Then he came to the disciples and said to them, "Are you still sleeping and taking your rest? Look—the hour is at hand, and the Son of Man is betrayed into the hands of sinners. [46]Get up, let's be going. Look—my betrayer is at hand."

Jesus Betrayed and Arrested

[47]As he was still speaking, there came Judas, one of the Twelve, and with him a great crowd with swords and clubs, from the chief priests and the elders of the people. [48]Now the betrayer had given them a sign, saying, "The one I shall kiss is the man; seize him." [49]And he immediately came up to Jesus and said, "Greetings, Rabbi!" And he kissed him. [50]Jesus said to him, "Friend, why are you here?" Then they came up and laid hands on Jesus and seized him. [51]And listen—one of those who were with Jesus stretched out his hand and drew his sword, and struck the slave of the high priest, and cut off his ear. [52]Then Jesus told him, "Put your sword back into its place, for all who use the sword will die by the sword. [53]Do you think that I could not appeal to my Father, and he would at once send more than twelve legions of angels to me? [54]But then how would the scriptures that say this must occur be fulfilled?" [55]At that moment Jesus addressed the crowds: "Have you come out to capture me as [you would] against a robber—with swords and clubs? Day after day I sat in the temple teaching, and you did not seize me. [56]But all this has taken place so that the scriptures of the prophets might be fulfilled." Then all the disciples abandoned him and fled.

Jesus Before Caiaphas

[57]Then those who had seized Jesus led him to Caiaphas the high priest, where the scribes and the elders had gathered. [58]But Peter followed him at a distance, as far as the courtyard of the high priest, and going inside he sat with the guards to see the result. [59]Now the chief priests and the whole council were seeking false testimony against Jesus so that they might put him to death, [60]but they found none, though many false witnesses came forward. At last two came forward [61]and said, "This fellow said, 'I am able to demolish the temple of God, and to rebuild it in three days.' " [62]And the high priest stood up and said, "Have you no answer to make? What is it that these men testify against you?" [63]But Jesus was silent. And the high priest said to him, "I demand by the living God that you tell us if you are the Christ, the Son of God." [64]Jesus replied to him, "You have said so. But I tell you, in the future you will see the Son of Man seated at the right hand of power and coming on the clouds of heaven." [65]Then the high priest tore his robes, and said, "He has uttered blasphemy. Why do we still need witnesses? You have now heard his blasphemy. [66]What is your judgment?" They answered, "He deserves death." [67]Then they spit in his face and struck him. Some of them slapped him, [68]saying, "Prophesy to us, you Christ! Who is it that struck you?"

Peter Denies Jesus Three Times

⁶⁹Now Peter was sitting outside in the courtyard, and a maid came up to him, and said, "You were with Jesus the Galilean, too." ⁷⁰But he denied it before them all, insisting, "I do not know what you mean." ⁷¹And when he went out to the porch, another maid saw him, and she said to the bystanders, "This man was with Jesus of Nazareth." ⁷²And again he denied it with an oath, "I do *not* know the man." ⁷³After a little while the bystanders came up and said to Peter, "Certainly you are also one of them, because your accent betrays you." ⁷⁴Then he began to invoke a curse on himself and to swear, "I do *not* know the man." And immediately the cock crowed. ⁷⁵Then Peter remembered the words of Jesus, "Before the cock crows, you will deny me three times." And he went out and wept bitterly.

Chapter 27

Jesus Taken to Pilate

¹When morning came, all the chief priests and the elders of the people conferred against Jesus, on a way to have him put to death. ²Accordingly, they bound him and led him away and handed him over to Pilate the governor.

Judas Kills Himself

³Then when Judas, his betrayer, saw that [Jesus] was condemned, he repented and brought back the thirty silver coins to the chief priests and the elders, ⁴saying, "I have sinned by betraying innocent blood." "What is that to us?" they replied. See to [that] yourself." ⁵Throwing down the silver coins in the temple, he departed, and he went and hanged himself. ⁶But, taking the silver coins, the chief priests said, "It is against the law to put them into the treasury, since this is blood money." ⁷So having conferred about it, they used them to buy the potter's field, to bury strangers in. ⁸Therefore to this day that field has been called the Field of Blood. ⁹Then what had been spoken by the prophet Jeremiah was fulfilled:

"And they took the thirty pieces of silver,
the price set on him by some of the sons of Israel,
¹⁰and they used them to buy the potter's field,
as the Lord directed me."

Jesus Before Pilate

¹¹Meanwhile Jesus was standing before the governor, and the governor asked him, "Are you the King of the Jews?" Jesus replied, "You have said so." ¹²But he gave no response when accused by the chief priests and elders. ¹³Then Pilate asked

49

him, "Do you not hear how many things they testify against you?" [14]But he made no reply, not even to a single charge, to the great amazement of the governor.

Barabbas is Chosen for Release

[15]Now [on the day of] the feast it was the custom of the governor to release any one prisoner that the crowd called for. [16]At that time they had a notorious prisoner called Barabbas. [17]So when the crowd had gathered, Pilate asked them, "Which one shall I release for you, Barabbas or Jesus, who is called Christ?" [18]For he knew that it was out of envy that they had handed Jesus over to him.

[19]Now while he was sitting on the judgment seat his wife sent word to him: "Have nothing to do with that righteous man, for today in a dream I have suffered a great deal on account of him." [20]But the chief priests and the elders persuaded the people to ask for Barabbas and to execute Jesus. [21]The governor asked them again, "Which of the two shall I release for you?" And they cried out, "Barabbas." [22]Pilate said to them, "Then what shall I do with Jesus who is called Christ?" They all shouted, "Have him crucified."

Pilate Hands Over Jesus for Crucifixion

[23]So he pleaded, "Why? What evil has he done?" But they shouted all the more, "Have him crucified." [24]So when Pilate saw that he was gaining nothing, but rather that a riot was beginning, he took water and washed his hands in front of the crowd, saying, "I am innocent of this man's blood; see to it yourselves." [25]And all the people answered, "May his blood be on us and on our children!" [26]Then he released Barabbas for them, and having scourged Jesus, he handed him over to be crucified.

The Soldiers Mock Jesus

[27]Then the soldiers of the governor took Jesus into the headquarters, and they gathered the whole battalion before him. [28]And they stripped him and put a scarlet robe on him, [29]and twisted together a crown of thorns that they put on his head. They put a staff in his right hand, and kneeling before him they mocked him, saying, "Hail, King of the Jews!" [30]And they spit on him, and took the staff and struck him on the head. [31]And when they had mocked him, they stripped him of the robe, and put his own clothes back on him, and led him away to crucify him.

[32]As they went out, they encountered a man of Cyrene, Simon by name, and they compelled this man to carry his cross. [33]And when they came to a place called Golgotha (which means "the place of a skull"), [34]they offered him wine mixed with gall to drink. But when he tasted it, he would not drink it. [35]And once they

had crucified him, they divided his garments among themselves by casting lots. [36]Then they sat down and kept watch over him there. [37]And over his head they put the charge against him, which read,

THIS IS JESUS, THE KING OF THE JEWS.

[38]Then two thieves were crucified with him, one on the right and one on the left. [39]And those who passed by derided him, wagging their heads [40]and saying, "You who would demolish the temple and rebuild it in three days, save yourself! If you are the Son of God, come down from the cross." [41]The chief priests, with the scribes and elders, mocked him similarly as well, saying, [42]"He saved others—He cannot save himself. He is the King of Israel—let him come down now from the cross, and we will believe in him. [43]He trusts in God—let God rescue him now, if he desires him, for he said, 'I am the Son of God'." [44]And the thieves who were crucified with him also taunted him in the same way.

The Death of Jesus

[45]Now darkness came over all the land from noon until three o'clock in the afternoon. [46]About three o'clock in the afternoon, Jesus cried with a loud voice, "Eloi, Eloi, lama sabachthani?" which means, "My God, my God, why have you forsaken me?" [47]When some of the bystanders heard this, they said, "He is calling Elijah." [48]Immediately one of them ran and got a sponge, filled it with vinegar, and put it on a stick, and offered it to him to drink. [49]But the others said, "Wait, let's see whether Elijah will come to save him." [50]And Jesus cried again with a loud voice and yielded up his spirit.

[51]Listen—the curtain of the temple was torn in two, from top to bottom, and the earth shook, and the rocks were split open. [52]Tombs broke open as well, and many bodies of the saints who had fallen asleep were raised. [53]After his resurrection they came out of the tombs and went into the holy city and appeared to many. [54]When the centurion and those who were with him, keeping watch over Jesus, saw the earthquake and what took place, they were filled with awe, and said, "Truly this was the Son of God!"

[55]In addition, many women were also there, watching from a distance. They had followed Jesus from Galilee, ministering to him, and [56]among them were Mary Magdalene, and Mary the mother of James and Joseph, and the mother of the sons of Zebedee.

The Burial of Jesus

[57]When it was evening, there came a rich man from Arimathea, named Joseph, who was also a disciple of Jesus. [58]He went to Pilate and asked for the body of Jesus, and Pilate ordered it to be given to him. [59]So, Joseph took the body and wrapped it in a clean linen shroud, [60]and laid it in his own new tomb, which he had hewn in the rock. He rolled a large stone in front of the entrance to the door of the tomb and went away. [61]Mary Magdalene and the other Mary were sitting there, across from the tomb.

[62]On the next day, after the Day of Preparation, the chief priests and the Pharisees gathered before Pilate [63]and said, "Sir, we remember how that impostor, while he was still alive, claimed 'After three days I will rise again.' [64]Therefore order the tomb to be secured until the third day. Otherwise, his disciples might come and steal his body, and tell the people, 'He has risen from the dead.' Then the last deception would be worse than the first." [65]Pilate said to them, "You have a guard of soldiers. Go make it as secure as you can." [66]So they went and made the tomb secure by sealing the stone and setting a guard.

Chapter 28

The Resurrection of Jesus

[1]Now at the end of the Sabbath day, just before dawn on the first day of the week, Mary Magdalene and the other Mary went to see the tomb. [2]Mark this well: suddenly there was a great earthquake, for an angel of the Lord descended from heaven and came and rolled back the stone and sat on it. [3]His appearance was like lightning, and his clothing as white as snow. [4]The guards were so terrified of him that they trembled and fainted dead away. [5]But the angel said to the women, "Do not be afraid, for I know that you seek Jesus, who was crucified. [6]He is not here, for he has risen, as he said. Come, see the place where the Lord was lying. [7]Then go quickly and tell his disciples that he has risen from the dead—and listen—He is going before you to Galilee. You will see him there. See, I have told you." [8]So they hurried away from the tomb with fear and great joy and ran to tell his disciples. [9]Suddenly, Jesus met them and said, "Greetings!" And they came up and took hold of his feet and worshiped him. [10]Then Jesus said to them, "Do not be afraid. Go and tell my brothers to go to Galilee, and they will see me there."

The Guard Reports

[11]Now, while they were going, some of the guard went into the city and told the chief priests all that had taken place. [12]So when [the chief priests] had assembled

with the elders and devised a plan, they gave a sum of money to the soldiers [13]and said, "Tell people, 'His disciples came by night and stole him away while we were asleep.' [14]And if this report is heard by the governor, we will satisfy him and keep you out of trouble." [15]So they took the money and did as they were directed. And to this day, this story has been spread among the Jews.

The Great Commission

[16]Now the eleven disciples went to Galilee, to the mountain that Jesus had directed them to. [17]And when they saw him they worshiped him, though some were doubtful. [18]And Jesus came and said to them, "All authority in heaven and on earth has been given to me. [19]Therefore, having set out, make disciples from all peoples, baptizing them in the name of the Father and of the Son and of the Holy Spirit, [20]teaching them to observe all that I have commanded you. Listen, surely I am with you always, even to the end of the age."

MARK

Chapter 1

John the Baptist Preparing the Way

[1]Here begins the gospel of Jesus Christ, the Son of God. [2]This is written in [the book of] Isaiah the prophet:

> "Listen, I will send my messenger ahead of you;
> he will prepare your way—
> [3]the voice of one crying in the wilderness:
> 'Prepare a way for the Lord.
> Lay out a straight avenue to [welcome] him.'"

[4]In the wilderness there appeared a man, John the Baptist, preaching a baptism of repentance for the forgiveness of sins. [5]All the country [folk] of Judea, and all the people of Jerusalem were going out to him and were being baptized by him in the river Jordan, confessing their sins. [6]Now John was clothed with camel's hair, and had a leather belt around his waist, and ate locusts and wild honey. [7]And he preached, saying, "After me will come the One who is mightier than I [am], and I am unworthy to even stoop down and untie the strap of his sandals. [8]I have baptized you with water, but he will baptize you with the Holy Spirit."

Jesus is Baptized and Tempted

[9]And it came to pass in those days that Jesus came from Nazareth of Galilee and was baptized by John in the Jordan [River]. [10]And when he came up out of the water, he immediately saw the heavens being torn open and the Spirit descending on top of him like a dove; [11]and a voice came from heaven, "You are my beloved Son; with you I am well pleased." [12]Right away the Spirit drove him out into the wilderness, [13]and he stayed in the wilderness for forty days, being tempted by Satan. He was with the wild animals, and the angels ministered to him.

Jesus Begins his Ministry and Calls Disciples

[14]Now after John was arrested, Jesus came into Galilee, preaching the gospel of God, [15]and saying, "The time is fulfilled, and the kingdom of God is at hand. Repent and believe in the gospel." [16]Now, as he was passing along by the Sea of Galilee, he saw Simon and Andrew (the brother of Simon) casting a net in the sea,

for they were fishermen. [17]And Jesus said to them, "Follow me and I will make you fishers of men." [18]They promptly left their nets and followed him. [19]And going on a little farther, he saw James the son of Zebedee and John his brother, who were in their boat mending the nets. [20]Right then he called them. They left their father Zebedee in the boat with the hired servants and followed him, and [21]they went into Capernaum.

Jesus Begins to Heal People

Soon after, he entered the synagogue on the Sabbath and started teaching. [22]Now, they were astonished at his teaching, for he taught them as one who had authority, unlike the scribes. [23]Right then a man with an evil spirit was in their synagogue, [24]and he cried out, "What do you have to do with us, Jesus of Nazareth? Have you come to destroy us? I know who you are—the Holy One of God!" [25]But Jesus rebuked him, saying, "Be silent, and come out of him!" [26]Convulsing him and crying with a loud voice, the evil spirit came out of him. [27]Everyone was so amazed that they questioned among themselves, saying, "What is this? A new teaching! He commands even the evil spirits with authority, and they obey him." [28]And at once his fame spread everywhere throughout all the surrounding region of Galilee.

[29]Soon afterward, he left the synagogue, and entered the house of Simon and Andrew, with James and John. [30]Now Simon's mother-in-law lay sick with a fever, and they told him about her right away. [31]He came and taking her by the hand he lifted her up, and the fever left her, and she began serving them. [32]That evening, at sundown, they brought all who were sick or possessed with demons to him, [33]and the whole community was gathered together around the door. [34]And he healed many who were sick with various diseases and cast out many demons. And because they recognized him, he would not allow the demons to speak.

Jesus Continues to Preach and Heal

[35]Rising well before the dawn the next morning, he went out to a deserted place, and there he prayed. [36]Then Simon and those who were with him went looking for him, [37]and they found him and said to him, "Everyone is searching for you." [38]He said to them, "Let's go on to the next towns, so that I may preach there too, for that is the reason I left." [39]And he went throughout all of Galilee, preaching in its synagogues and casting out demons.

[40]Now, a leper came to him imploring him. Kneeling down, he said to him, "If you want to, you can make me clean." [41][Jesus] was deeply grieved [over his plight], so he stretched out his hand and touched him and said to him, "I do want

to. Be clean." ⁴²Immediately the leprosy left him, and he was cleansed. ⁴³Jesus sternly commanded him and sent him away at once, ⁴⁴saying to him, "See that you say nothing to anyone. Instead, go show yourself to the priest, and for your cleansing offer what Moses commanded, as a proof to the people." ⁴⁵But he went out and began to spread the news and to talk about it so freely that Jesus could no longer openly enter a town, but had to remain in the deserted places, and people came to him from every quarter.

Chapter 2

¹When he returned to Capernaum after a few days, it was reported that he was at home. ²So many were gathered together that there was no longer room for them, not even outside the door, and he was preaching the Word to them. ³Some men came, bringing to him a paralytic that was carried by four of them. ⁴And when they could not get near him because of the crowd, they removed [part of] the roof above him. And having made an opening, they let down the pallet that the paralytic was lying on. ⁵Now when Jesus observed their faith, he said to the paralytic, "Son, your sins are forgiven." ⁶Now some of the scribes were sitting there, questioning in their hearts, ⁷"Why is this man speaking like this? It is blasphemy! Who can forgive sins but God alone?" ⁸So right then Jesus, perceiving in his spirit that they were questioning like that, asked them, "Why do you question that way in your hearts silently? ⁹Which is easier to say to the paralytic, 'Your sins are forgiven,' or to say, 'Rise, take up your straw bed and walk'? ¹⁰But so that you may know that the Son of Man has authority on earth to forgive sins" –he said to the paralytic—¹¹"I say to you, get up, pick up your straw bed and go home." ¹²And he rose, and immediately took up the straw bed and walked out in front of everyone, so that they were all amazed and glorified God, saying, "We have never seen anything like this!"

Levi is Called

¹³He went out again alongside the sea, and the whole crowd gathered around him, and he taught them. ¹⁴And as he was passing by, he saw Levi the son of Alphaeus sitting at the tax office, and he said to him, "Follow me," and he rose and followed him.

¹⁵As he reclined at table in his house, many tax collectors and sinners were reclining with Jesus and his disciples, for there were many who followed him. ¹⁶When the scribes and the Pharisees saw that he was eating with sinners and tax collectors, they said to his disciples, "Why does he eat and drink with tax collectors and sinners?" ¹⁷And when Jesus heard it, he said to them, "It's not those who are well who have need of a physician, but those who are sick. I came not to call the righteous, but sinners."

56

Question about Fasting and the Sabbath

¹⁸John's disciples and the Pharisees were fasting. So people came and asked him, "Why are John's disciples and the disciples of the Pharisees fasting, but your disciples are *not* fasting?" ¹⁹And Jesus replied to them, "Can the wedding guests fast while the bridegroom is with them? They cannot fast as long as they have the bridegroom with them. ²⁰The days will come, when the bridegroom is taken away from them, and on that day they *will* fast. ²¹No one sews a piece of unshrunk cloth on an old garment. If he does, the patch tears away from it—the new from the old—and a worse tear is made. ²²Also, no one puts new wine into old wineskins. If he does, the wine will burst those skins, and then the wine is lost, and so are the skins. Rather, new wine is for fresh skins."

²³One Sabbath he was passing through the grain fields, and his disciples began to pick heads of grain as they made their way through. ²⁴And the Pharisees said to him, "Look, why are they doing what is not lawful on the Sabbath?" ²⁵So he replied to them, "Have you never read what David did, when he was in need and was hungry—he and those who were with him—²⁶how he entered the house of God, when Abiathar was high priest, and ate the bread of the Presence, which is not lawful to be eaten by anyone but the priests, and how they also gave it to those who were with him?" ²⁷And he added, "The Sabbath was made for man, not man for the Sabbath. ²⁸So, the Son of Man is Lord of even the Sabbath."

Chapter 3

The Man with a Withered Hand

¹Another time he entered the synagogue, and a man who had a withered hand was there. ²And they watched Jesus, to see whether he would heal him on the Sabbath, so that they could accuse him. ³He beckoned the man who had the withered hand, "Come here," ⁴and he asked them, "Is it lawful on the Sabbath to do good or to do harm, to save life or to kill?" But they were silent, ⁵and he looked around at them angrily, grieved at their hardness of heart, and said to the man, "Stretch out your hand." he stretched it out, and his hand was restored. ⁶The Pharisees went out and immediately began plotting against him with the Herodians, as to how to destroy him.

A Huge Crowd of Followers

⁷Jesus withdrew to the seashore with his disciples, followed by a huge crowd from Galilee and from Judea ⁸and Jerusalem and Idumea and from beyond the Jordan and from around Tyre and Sidon. When this huge crowd heard all that he did,

they came to him. [9]Jesus told his disciples to have a boat ready for him in case the crowd should start to crush him. [10]Because he had healed many, all who had diseases pressed up close to him in order to touch him. [11]And whenever the evil spirits caught sight of him, they fell down in front of him and cried out, "You are the Son of God." [12]But he strictly ordered them not to make him known.

[13]Afterwards he went up on the mountainside and summoned those he wanted, and they came to him. [14]He appointed twelve as apostles to be with him, and to be sent out to preach, [15]and to have authority to cast out demons: [16]Simon, whom he surnamed Peter; [17]James the son of Zebedee, and John the brother of James, (whom he surnamed Boanerges, which means "Sons of Thunder") [18]Andrew, and Philip, and Bartholomew, and Matthew, and Thomas, and James the son of Alphaeus, and Thaddaeus, and Simon the Zealot, [19]and Judas Iscariot, who [later] betrayed him. [20]When he returned home, such a crowd gathered again that they could not manage to eat a meal. [21]When his family heard about it, they went out to get him, for people were saying, "He is worn out."

Blaspheming Against the Holy Spirit

[22]Now the scribes who came down from Jerusalem claimed, "He is possessed by Beelzebub, and he is casting out demons by the prince of demons." [23]So Jesus called them to himself, and spoke to them in parables, "How can Satan cast out Satan? [24]If a kingdom is divided against itself, that kingdom cannot stand. [25]And, if a house is divided against itself, that house cannot stand. [26]If Satan has risen up against himself and is divided, he cannot stand—rather, his end is coming. [27]In fact, no one can enter a strong man's house and rob his possessions unless he first ties up the strong man. Then indeed he may rob his house. [28]"Truly, I say to you, the children of men will be forgiven of their sins, and whatever blasphemies they utter. [29]But, whoever blasphemes against the Holy Spirit never has forgiveness, but is guilty of an eternal sin." [30](For they had been saying, "He has an evil spirit.")

Jesus' Family Comes

[31]Then his mother and his brothers came, and, standing outside, they sent [word] to him and called for him. [32]A crowd was sitting around him, and they told him, "Your mother and your brothers are outside asking for you." [33]He asked in response, "Who are my mother and my brothers?" [34]Looking around at those who sat near him, he said, "Here are my mother and my brothers! [35]Whoever does the will of God is my brother, and sister, and mother."

Chapter 4

The Parable of the Sower of the Seed

[1]Jesus began to teach alongside the shore again, and a huge crowd gathered around him. So, he got into a boat and sat in it out on the lake, while the whole crowd was beside the lake on the land. [2]He taught them many things in parables, and in [the course of] his teaching he said to them: [3]"Listen! A sower went out to sow. [4]And as he sowed, some seed fell along the path, and the birds came and devoured it. [5]Other seed fell on rocky ground, where it had little soil, and it sprang up immediately. But, since it had no depth of soil, [6]when the sun rose it was scorched. And since it had no root it withered away. [7]Other seed fell among thorns and the thorns grew up and choked it, and it yielded no grain. [8]Still other seeds fell into good soil and produced grain, growing up and increasing and yielding thirty and sixty and even a hundred times as much." [9]And he said, "If anyone has ears to hear with, let him hear this."

Parables Explained

[10]Later when he was off with just the Twelve and some others who were close to him, they asked him about the parables. [11]He replied, "To you has been given the secret of the kingdom of God, but for those on the outside everything happens in parables; [12]such that they are ever seeing but not perceiving, and ever hearing but not understanding. For if they did, they would repent and be forgiven." [13]And he said to them, "Do you not understand this parable? Then how will you understand all the parables? [14]The sower sows the word, [15]and these are the ones along the path, where the word is sown. When they hear, Satan immediately comes and snatches away the word that is sown in them. [16]Similarly, these are the ones sown on rocky ground, who, when they hear the word, immediately receive it with joy. [17]But, not being firmly rooted, they last only for a while. Then, when tribulation or persecution arises on account of the word, they fall away immediately. [18]Others are the ones sown among thorns: they are those who hear the word, [19]but the worries of this life, and the deceitfulness of riches, and the desire for other things, enter in and choke the word, making it unfruitful. [20]But those that were sown on the good soil are the ones who hear the word and accept it and bear fruit—thirty, and sixty, and even a hundred times as much."

The Lamp Under the Basket

[21]He said to them, "Is a lamp brought in to be put under a basket, or under a bed, and not on a stand? [22]For there is nothing hidden that shall not be realized

someday, nor is anything secret that shall not come to light. [23]If anyone has ears to hear with, let him hear this." [24]And he said to them, "Pay attention to what you are hearing: however much you give will be what you receive back, and still more will be given to you. [25]For more will be given to the one who has, but as for the one who is lacking, even what he has will be taken away."

The Parable of the Seed

[26]He also said, "The kingdom of God is like this: A man scatters seed on the ground. [27]He sleeps and rises day and night, and the seed sprouts and grows, but he does not know how. [28]The earth produces by itself: first the stalk, then the head, then the full grain in the head. [29]As soon as the grain is ripe, he puts the sickle to it, because the harvest has come."

The Parable of the Mustard Seed

[30]Again he asked, "What can we compare the kingdom of God with, or what parable should we use [to describe] it? [31]It is like a grain of mustard seed, which is the smallest of all the seeds in world that are sown into the ground. [32]Yet, when it is sown it grows up and becomes the largest of all garden plants and puts forth large branches so that the birds of the air can make nests in its shade."

[33]As they were able to grasp it, he spoke the word to them with many such parables. [34]He did not speak to them without [using] a parable, but in private he did explain everything to his own disciples.

Jesus Calms a Storm

[35]Later that day, when evening had come, Jesus said to them, "Let's cross over to the other side." [36]Leaving the crowd behind, they took him with them in the boat, just as he was, and some other boats were with him. [37]Then a great windstorm arose, and the waves began breaking into the boat, so that the boat was already getting swamped. [38]But Jesus was in the stern asleep on the cushion, and they woke him up and said to him, "Teacher, don't you care that we might die?" [39]He woke up and rebuked the wind, and said to the lake, "Peace! Be still!" And the wind ceased, and there was a great calm. [40]He said to them, "Why are you afraid? Do you have no faith?" [41]They were greatly awed and pondered among themselves, "Then who is this, that even the wind and the lake obey him?"

Chapter 5

Jesus Casts out a Legion of Demons

[1]They came to the other side of the lake, to the region of the Gerasenes. [2]Right when Jesus had come out of the boat, a man with an evil spirit came up to him there, out of the tombs. [3]He lived among the tombs, and no one could bind him anymore, even with a chain. [4]For, he had often been bound with shackles and chains, but he yanked apart the chains, and he broke the shackles in pieces. No one had the strength to subdue him. [5]Day and night he was among the tombs and on the hills, always crying out and cutting himself with stones. [6]Now when he saw Jesus from afar, he ran and worshiped him. [7]Crying out with a loud voice, he said, "What do you have to do with me, Jesus, Son of the Most High God? I earnestly beg you to swear by God that you will not torment me." [8]For Jesus had said to him, "Come out of the man, you evil spirit!" [9]Jesus asked him, "What is your name?" he replied, "My name is Legion, for we are many." [10]And he pleaded with him earnestly that he not send them out of the country.

[11]Now, a great herd of pigs was feeding there on the hillside, [12]and they begged him, "Send us into the pigs, let us enter them." [13]So he allowed them to do so, and the evil spirits came out, and entered the pigs. The herd, numbering about two thousand, rushed down the steep bank into the lake, and drowned in it. [14]The herdsmen fled and reported it in the city and in the country. So, people came to see what it was that had happened. [15]And they came to Jesus, and saw the demoniac sitting there, clothed and in his right mind—the man who had had the legion [of demons]—and they were afraid. [16]And those who had seen it told [them] what had happened to the demoniac and to the pigs. [17]And they began begging Jesus to depart from their region. [18]And as he was getting into the boat, the man who had been possessed with demons begged to accompany him. [19]But he refused and said to him, "Go home to your people, and tell them how much the Lord has done for you and how he has had mercy on you." [20]And he went away and began to proclaim in the Decapolis [region] how much Jesus had done for him, and everyone marveled.

Jesus Raises Jairus' Daughter from the Dead

[21]When Jesus had crossed back to the other side by boat, a great crowd gathered around him, and he was beside the lake. [22]Then one of the rulers of the synagogue, Jairus by name, came, and seeing him he fell at his feet [23]and implored him earnestly, saying, "My little daughter is at the point of death. Come and lay your hands on her, so that she may be healed and live." [24]So, he left with him.

Now, a great crowd followed him and pressed closely around him. ²⁵A woman who had had a bleeding problem for twelve years was there. ²⁶She had suffered much while under the care of many doctors and had spent all that she had. She was no better, but rather had grown worse. ²⁷Having heard the reports about Jesus, she came up from behind in the crowd and touched his garment. ²⁸For she thought, "If I even touch his garments, I shall be healed." ²⁹The hemorrhage stopped immediately, and she felt in her body that she was healed of her disease. ³⁰And Jesus, perceiving in himself that power had gone forth from him, immediately turned around in the crowd and asked, "Who touched my garments?" ³¹His disciples responded, "You see the crowd pressing in all around you, and yet you ask [us], 'Who touched me?'" ³²So he looked around to see who had done it. ³³But the woman, knowing what had happened to her, came and fell down in front of him, trembling with fear, and told him the whole truth. ³⁴And he said to her, "Daughter, your faith has made you well; go in peace and be healed of your disease."

³⁵While he was still speaking, some men came from [Jairus] the ruler's house who said, "Your daughter is dead. Why trouble the Teacher any further?" ³⁶But dismissing what they said, Jesus said to the ruler of the synagogue, "Do not be afraid, just believe." ³⁷He allowed no one to follow him except Peter and James and John the brother of James. ³⁸When they came to the house of the ruler of the synagogue, Jesus saw a commotion and people weeping and wailing loudly. ³⁹When he had entered, he asked them, "Why are you making such a commotion and weeping? The child is not dead but sleeping."

⁴⁰And they ridiculed him, but he made them all go outside. And taking the child's father and mother and those who were with him, he went in where the child was. ⁴¹He took her by the hand and said to her, "Talitha cumi." (which means, "Little girl, I say to you, get up.") ⁴²And the girl promptly got up and starting walking (she was twelve years of age), and they were immediately overcome with amazement. ⁴³But he strictly charged them that no one should know about this, and he told them to give her something to eat.

Chapter 6

¹He left that place and returned to his own home area with his disciples following him. ²And with the coming of the Sabbath, he began to teach in the synagogue, and many who heard him were astonished, exclaiming, "Where did this man get all this? What is this wisdom that has been given to him? What miracles are done by his hands! ³Isn't this the carpenter, the son of Mary and brother of James and Joses and Judas and Simon, and aren't his sisters here with us?" And they were taking offense at him. ⁴Jesus said to them, "A prophet is not without honor, except

in his own home area, and among his own people, and in his own house." [5]He was not able to do any miracles there except for laying his hands on a few sick people and healing them, [6]and he was amazed at their unbelief. And he went around from village to village teaching.

Jesus Sends Out the Twelve Apostles

[7]And he called the Twelve to himself and began to send them out two by two and gave them authority over evil spirits. [8]He instructed them to take nothing for their journey except a walking staff–no bread, no bag, no money in their belts–[9]and to wear sandals and to not put on two tunics. [10]He said to them, "Whenever you enter a house, stay there until you leave that town. [11]And if any place will not accept you and they refuse to hear you, shake its dust off your feet when you are leaving as a testimony against them." [12]So they went out and preached that people should repent. [13]And they cast out many demons and anointed many sick people with oil and healed them.

King Herod Has John Beheaded

[14]King Herod heard about this for Jesus' name had become [commonly] known. Some were saying, "John the Baptist has been raised from the dead; that is why these [miraculous] powers are at work in him." [15]But others were saying, "It is Elijah." And others said, "He is a prophet, like one of the prophets of old." [16]But when Herod heard of it he said, "John, whom I beheaded, has been raised." [17]For Herod was the one who had sent for John, and had seized him and bound him in prison because Herod had married Herodias, his brother Philip's wife. [18]John had said to Herod, "It is not legal for you to have your brother's wife." [19]So Herodias had a grudge against him and wanted to kill him. But she had not been able to do so [20]because Herod feared John and kept him safe, knowing that he was a righteous and holy man. When Herod heard him, he was very perplexed, and yet he was glad to listen to him. [21]But an opportunity came on Herod's birthday when he was giving a banquet for his courtiers and military officers and the leading men of Galilee. [22]When Herodias' daughter came in and danced, she was pleasing to Herod and his guests. So the king said to the girl, "Ask me for whatever you wish, and I will give it to you." [23]He even vowed to her, "I will give you whatever you ask me, even up to half of my kingdom." [24]So she went out and asked her mother, "What should I ask for?" And she replied, "The head of John the Baptist." [25]So she immediately rushed back to the king, and made her request, "I want you to give me the head of John the Baptist on a platter right away." [26]Now the king was extremely sorry, but on account of his oaths and his guests he did not want to

break his word to her. ²⁷So, the king promptly sent out an executioner and gave orders to bring [John's] head. He went and beheaded him in the prison ²⁸and brought his head on a platter, and gave it to the girl, and the girl gave it to her mother. ²⁹When his disciples heard about it, they came and took his body and laid it in a tomb.

Jesus Feeds the Multitudes Miraculously

³⁰Together the apostles returned to Jesus and told him all that they had done and taught. ³¹And he said to them, "Come away by yourselves to a deserted place and rest a while." For many were coming and going, and they had no leisure to even eat. ³²And they went away in the boat to a deserted place by themselves. ³³Now many saw them going, and recognizing them, they ran there on foot from all the towns, and got there ahead of them. ³⁴As he went ashore he saw a great crowd, and he had compassion on them, because they were like sheep without a shepherd. He started teaching them many things.

³⁵And when it got late, his disciples came to him and said, "This is a deserted place, and it's now late in the day. ³⁶Send them off to go into the surrounding countryside and villages and buy themselves something to eat." ³⁷But he answered them, "You give them something to eat." And they said to him, "Should we go and buy two hundred denarii worth of bread, and give it to them to eat?" ³⁸So he asked them, "How many loaves *do* you have? Go and check." And when they had found out, they said, "Five, and two fish." ³⁹Then he commanded them all to sit down in groups on the green grass. ⁴⁰So they sat down in groups, by hundreds and by fifties. ⁴¹And taking the five loaves and the two fish he looked up to heaven, and he blessed and broke the loaves, and gave them to the disciples to set before the people. Then he divided the two fish among them all, ⁴²and they all ate and were satisfied. ⁴³Then they gathered up twelve baskets full of the leftover fragments of bread and fish. ⁴⁴Those who ate the loaves numbered five thousand men. ⁴⁵Right after that, he made his disciples get into the boat and go to Bethsaida on the other side before him while he dismissed the crowd.

Jesus Walks on Water

⁴⁶After he had left them he ascended the hill to pray. ⁴⁷When evening came, the boat was out on the lake, and he was alone on the land. ⁴⁸He saw that they were making headway arduously, for the wind was against them. Around the fourth watch of the night, he came to them walking on the water. He meant to pass by them, ⁴⁹but when they saw him walking on the lake, they thought it was a ghost and cried out, ⁵⁰for they all saw him and were terrified. But immediately he

spoke to them and said, "Take heart—I AM. Do not be afraid." [51]Then he got into the boat with them, and the wind ceased. They were completely astonished [52]because they still did not grasp the [miracle] of the bread, but—their hearts were hardened.

[53]Having crossed over, they landed at Gennesaret, and moored to the shore. [54]And when they got out of the boat, the people immediately recognized him [55]and ran around the whole area and began to bring sick people on their straw beds wherever they heard he was. [56]And wherever he went—in villages, cities, or the countryside—they laid the sick in the marketplaces and begged him that they might touch even the fringe of his garment, and everyone who touched it was healed.

Chapter 7

Jesus Confronts the Pharisees

[1]Now when the Pharisees were gathering together around him, along with some of the scribes who had come from Jerusalem, [2]they noticed that some of his disciples were eating bread with hands that were defiled, that is, unwashed. [3](For, observing the tradition of the elders, the Pharisees and all the Jews do not eat unless they ceremoniously wash their clenched hands. [4]And when they come from the marketplace, they do not eat unless they purify themselves. And they observe many other traditions: the washing of cups and pots and copper vessels and dining couches.)

[5]So the Pharisees and the scribes asked him, "Why do your disciples not do things according to the tradition of the elders, but instead eat with defiled hands?" [6]He answered them, "Isaiah prophesied well concerning you hypocrites, when he wrote, 'This people honors me with their lips, but their heart is far from me; [7]in vain do they worship me, teaching man-made laws as doctrine.' [8]You cast aside the commandment of God, yet cling firmly to the tradition of men." [9]And he said to them, "You have a fine way of rejecting the commandment of God, in order to preserve your tradition! [10]For Moses said, 'Honor your father and your mother'; and, 'Whoever curses father or mother, must surely die'; [11]but you say, 'If a man tells his father or his mother, "What you would have gained from me is Corban" (which means "given to God")', [12]then you no longer have him do anything for his father or mother, [13]thereby nullifying the word of God through your tradition that you have handed down. You do many such things."

Jesus Explains True Defilement

[14]Calling the people to himself again, he said to them, "Hear me, all of you, and understand: [15]there is nothing outside a person that can defile him by going into him. On the contrary, the things that come out of a man are what defile him." [16]If anyone has ears to hear with, let him hear this.

[17]When he had entered the house, away from the people, his disciples asked him about the parable. [18]He responded, "Well, do you not understand either? Do you not see that whatever goes into someone from outside cannot defile him, [19]since it enters not his heart but his stomach, and comes out into the latrine?" (In that way he declared all foods clean.) [20]He went on, "What comes out of a person is what defiles that person. [21]For from within, out of a person's heart, come evil thoughts, sexual immorality, theft, murder, adultery, [22]coveting, wickedness, deceit, lewdness, envy, slander, pride, and foolishness. [23]All these evil things come from within, and they defile a person."

Jesus Exorcises a Syrophoenician Girl

[24]From there he rose up and went away to the region of Tyre and Sidon. There he entered a house and did not want anyone to know, yet he could not remain hidden. [25]Right away a woman, whose little daughter was possessed by an evil spirit, heard of him and came and fell down at his feet. [26]Now the woman was a Greek, a Syrophoenician by birth, and she begged him to cast the demon out of her daughter. [27]He said to her, "Let the children be fed first, for it is not right to take the children's bread and throw it to the dogs." [28]But she answered him, "Indeed, Lord. Yet even the dogs under the table eat the children's crumbs." [29]And he said to her, "On account of that statement you may go your way; the demon has left your daughter." [30]And she went home and found the child lying in bed, and the demon gone.

Jesus Heals a Deaf Man

[31]Then he returned from the region of Tyre, and went through Sidon to the Sea of Galilee, through the region of the Decapolis. [32]And they brought a man who was deaf and had a speech impediment to him, and they begged him to lay his hand on him. [33]So taking him aside from the crowd privately, he put his fingers into his ears, and he spat and touched his tongue. [34]Looking up to heaven, he sighed and said to him, "Ephphatha," (which means "Be opened.") [35]His ears were opened, his tongue was released, and he spoke plainly. [36]He commanded them to tell no one, but the more he commanded them, the more zealously they proclaimed it. [37]And they were astonished beyond measure, saying, "He has done all things well. He even makes the deaf hear and the dumb speak."

Chapter 8

Jesus Again Feeds the Multitude Miraculously

[1]In those days, when a large crowd had gathered again, and they had nothing to eat, he called his disciples to himself and said to them, [2]"I have compassion on the crowd, because they have been with me now three days, and have nothing to eat. [3]If I send them away hungry to their homes, they will faint on the way—and some of them have come a long way." [4]His disciples answered him, "How can one feed these people with bread here in this deserted place?" [5]So he asked them, "How many loaves of bread do you have?" They answered, "Seven." [6]So he directed the crowd to sit down on the ground. He took the seven loaves, and having given thanks, he broke them and gave them to his disciples to set before the people, and they set them before the crowd. [7]They had a few small fish, and having blessed them, he commanded that these should be set before them also. [8]Then they ate, and were satisfied, and they took up the leftover fragments, seven baskets full. [9](There were about four thousand people). [10]Then he sent them away, and next he got into the boat with his disciples and went to the district of Dalmanutha.

Pharisees Seeking a Sign

[11]The Pharisees arrived and began to argue with him, seeking a sign from heaven from him to test him. [12]He sighed deeply in his spirit, and said, "Why does this generation seek a sign? Truly, I say to you, no sign shall be given to this generation." [13]And he left them and got back into the boat and departed to the other side.

Apostles Still Lack Understanding

[14]Now, they had forgotten to pack [more] bread, so they had only one loaf with them in the boat. [15]And he cautioned them, saying, "Watch out, beware of the leaven of the Pharisees and the leaven of Herod." [16]They began discussing this with one another, saying, "We have no bread." [17]And being aware of it, Jesus said to them, "Why are you talking about not having any bread? Do you not perceive or understand yet? Are your hearts hardened? [18]Do you have eyes, but still not see, and do you have ears, but still not hear? And do you not remember? [19]When I broke the five loaves for the five thousand, how many baskets full of broken pieces did you gather up?" They replied, "Twelve." [20]"And the seven [loaves] for the four thousand, how many baskets full of broken pieces did you gather up?" "Seven," they replied. [21]He asked them, "Do you still not understand?"

Jesus Heals a Blind Man

²²They came to Bethsaida, and some people brought a blind man to him and begged him to touch him. ²³So he took the blind man by the hand and led him out of the village. When he had spit on his eyes and laid his hands on him, he asked him, "Do you see anything?" ²⁴He looked up and said, "I see men, but they look like trees walking." ²⁵Then Jesus laid his hands on his eyes again, and he looked hard and [his sight] was restored, and he saw everything clearly. ²⁶Jesus sent him away to his home, saying, "Do not even enter the village."

"Who Do Men Say I Am?"

²⁷And Jesus went on with his disciples to the villages of Caesarea Philippi. On the way he asked his disciples, "Who do people say that I am?" ²⁸They told him, "John the Baptist, and others say Elijah—and others say one of the prophets." ²⁹Then he asked them, "But who do *you* say that I am?" Peter answered him, "You are the Christ." ³⁰And he commanded them to tell no one about him.

³¹And he began to teach them that the Son of Man must suffer many things and be rejected by the elders and the chief priests and the scribes and be killed and rise again on the third day. ³²He said this plainly. Then Peter took him aside and began to rebuke him. ³³But turning and seeing his disciples, he rebuked Peter, and said, "Get behind me, Satan! For you are not on the side of God, but of men." ³⁴Then summoning the crowd with his disciples, he said to them, "If anyone would want to follow after me, let him deny himself and take up his cross and follow me. ³⁵For whoever would want to save his life will lose it, whereas whoever loses his life for the sake of me and the gospel will save it. ³⁶For what does it profit a man to gain the whole world and forfeit his soul? ³⁷For what can a man give in return for his soul? ³⁸For the Son of Man, when he comes in the glory of his Father with the holy angels, will be ashamed of whoever is ashamed of me and of my words in this adulterous and sinful generation."

Chapter 9

¹He also said to them, "Truly, I say to you, some of those standing here will not taste death until they see the kingdom of God having come in power."

The Transfiguration and Moses and Elijah

²And after six days Jesus took Peter and James and John along with him, and he led them up a high mountain apart by themselves. Then he was transfigured before them, ³and his clothes became radiant, intensely white, as no cloth dyer on earth could bleach them. ⁴And Elijah, along with Moses, appeared to them,

and they were talking to Jesus. [5]Peter said to Jesus, "Master, it is good that we are here. We should make three shrines: one for you, and one for Moses, and one for Elijah," [6]because they were terrified and did not know what to say. [7]A cloud overshadowed them, and a voice came out of the cloud, "This is my beloved Son: listen to him." [8]And suddenly, looking around they no longer saw anyone with them but Jesus only. [9]Then as they were coming down the mountain, he commanded them to tell no one what they had seen until the Son of Man had risen from the dead. [10]So they kept the matter to themselves, questioning what this 'rising from the dead' might mean, [11]and they asked him, "Why do the scribes say that first Elijah must come?" [12]He replied to them, "Elijah does come first to restore all things. How is it written of the Son of Man, that he should suffer many things and be treated with contempt? [13]But I tell you that Elijah has come, and they did whatever they pleased to him, as it is written of him."

Jesus Exorcises a Boy

[14]When they came to the disciples, they saw a great crowd around them and scribes arguing with them. [15]When the whole crowd saw [Jesus], right away they were greatly amazed and ran up to him and greeted him. [16]He asked them, "What are you arguing about with them?" [17]Someone in the crowd answered him, "Teacher, I brought my son to you, for he has a spirit that makes him mute, [18]and whenever it seizes him, it throws him down. And he foams at the mouth and grinds his teeth and becomes rigid. I asked your disciples to cast it out, but they were unable to." [19]He answered them, "O faithless generation, how long am I to be with you? How long am I to bear with you? Bring him to me."

[20]So they brought the boy to him, and when the spirit saw him, it immediately convulsed the boy, and he fell on the ground and rolled about, foaming at the mouth. [21]Jesus asked his father, "How long has this been happening to him?" He replied, "From childhood, [22]and it has often thrown him into the fire and into the water, to destroy him. But if you can do anything, have pity on us and help us." [23]Jesus said to him, " 'If you can!' All things are possible to him who believes." [24]Immediately the father of the child cried out and said, "I do believe; help my unbelief!" [25]When Jesus saw that a crowd came running together, he rebuked the evil spirit, saying to it, "You dumb and deaf spirit, I command you, come out of him and never enter him again." [26]And after crying out and convulsing him terribly, it came out, and the boy was like a corpse, so that most of them said, "He is dead." [27]But Jesus took him by the hand and lifted him up, and he got up. [28]When he had entered the house, his disciples asked him privately, "Why could we not cast it out?" [29]He responded to them, "This kind cannot be driven out by anything but prayer."

³⁰They went on from there and passed through Galilee, but Jesus did not want anyone to know ³¹because he was teaching his disciples, saying to them, "The Son of Man will be delivered into the hands of men, and they will kill him. Once he has been killed, he will rise again on the third day." ³²But they did not understand this statement, and they were afraid to question him [about it].

Who Will be the Greatest?

³³Next they came to Capernaum, and when he was in the house, he asked them, "What were you debating on the way?" ³⁴But they were silent, for on the way they had been arguing with one another about which one was the greatest. ³⁵So he sat down and called the Twelve, and told them, "If anyone should want to be first, he must be last of all and servant of all." ³⁶He took a child and put him in the their midst. And taking him in his arms, he said to them, ³⁷"Whoever receives one such child in my name receives me, and whoever receives me, receives not me but him who sent me."

³⁸John said to him, "Teacher, we saw a man casting out demons in your name, and we forbid him to because he was not following us." ³⁹But Jesus said, "Do not forbid him, for no one who does a mighty work in my name will be able to speak evil of me soon afterward. ⁴⁰For whoever is not against us is for us. ⁴¹For truly, I say to you, whoever gives you a cup of water to drink because you belong to Christ will by no means lose his reward.

Warnings About Hell

⁴²"Whoever causes one of these little ones who believe in me to sin would be better off if a great millstone were hung around his neck and he were thrown into the sea. ⁴³And if your hand causes you to sin, cut it off. It is better for you to enter life maimed than to go with two hands to hell, to the unquenchable fire, ⁴⁴where their worm does not die, and the fire is not quenched. ⁴⁵And if your foot causes you to sin, cut it off. It is better for you to enter life lame than to be thrown with two feet into hell, ⁴⁶where their worm does not die, and the fire is not quenched. ⁴⁷And if your eye causes you to sin, pluck it out. It is better for you to enter the kingdom of God with one eye than to be thrown with two eyes into hell, ⁴⁸where their worm does not die, and the fire is not quenched. ⁴⁹For everyone will be salted with fire, and every sacrifice will be salted with salt. ⁵⁰Salt is good, but if the salt has lost its saltiness, how will you make it salty again? Have salt in yourselves and be at peace with each other."

Chapter 10

Questions About Divorce

¹Then he left there and went to the region of Judea and beyond the Jordan, and again crowds gathered to him, and again, as was his custom, he taught them. ²Then Pharisees came up [to him], and in order to test him they asked, "Is it lawful for a man to divorce his wife?" ³He asked them, "What did Moses command you?" ⁴They replied, "Moses allowed a man to write a certificate of divorce and to send her away." ⁵But Jesus said to them, "He wrote you this commandment because of your hardness of heart. ⁶But from the beginning of creation, 'God made them male and female.' ⁷For this reason a man shall leave his father and mother and be joined to his wife, ⁸and the two shall become one flesh.' So they are no longer two but one flesh. ⁹Therefore let not man break apart what God has joined together."

¹⁰Once in the house, the disciples asked him again about this matter. ¹¹He responded, "Whoever divorces his wife and marries another commits adultery against her. ¹²And, if she divorces her husband and marries another, she commits adultery."

"Let the Children Come to Me"

¹³They were bringing children to him so that he might touch them, and the disciples rebuked them. ¹⁴But when Jesus saw it he was indignant, and said to them, "Let the children come to me. Do not hinder them, for the kingdom of God belongs to such as them. ¹⁵Truly, I say to you, whoever does not receive the kingdom of God like a child shall not enter it." ¹⁶And he took them in his arms and blessed them, laying his hands on them.

The Rich Young Ruler

¹⁷And as he was setting out on his journey, a man ran up and knelt before him, and asked him, "Good Teacher, what must I do to inherit eternal life?" ¹⁸Jesus questioned him, "If no one but God alone is good, then why are you calling *me* good? ¹⁹You know the commandments: 'Do not kill, Do not commit adultery, Do not steal, Do not testify falsely, Do not defraud, Honor your father and mother.'" ²⁰He answered him, "Teacher, I have observed all these since I was young." ²¹And looking at him, Jesus loved him and said to him, "You lack one thing: go, sell what you have, and give to the poor, and you will have treasure in heaven. And come, follow me." ²²Greatly disheartened by these words, he went away sorrowful, for he owned great possessions.

The First Shall Be Last

²³Jesus looked around and said to his disciples, "How difficult [it is] for those who have wealth to enter the kingdom of God!" ²⁴The disciples were amazed at his words. But Jesus said to them again, "Children, how difficult it is for those who trust in wealth to enter the kingdom of God! ²⁵It is easier for a camel to go through the eye of a needle than for a rich person to enter the kingdom of God." ²⁶And they were extremely astounded, and said to him, "Then who can be saved?" ²⁷Jesus looked at them and said, "With man it is impossible—but not with God, for all things are possible with God." ²⁸Peter began responding, saying to him, "See, we have left everything and followed you." ²⁹Jesus said, "Truly, I say to you, there is no one who has left house or brothers or sisters or mother or father or children or lands, for my sake and for the gospel, ³⁰who will not receive back in this present age a hundred times as much, [in the way of] houses and brothers and sisters and mothers and children and lands, along with persecutions, and eternal life in the age to come. ³¹But many who are first will be last, and the last first."

Jesus Foretells his Own Death

³²Later they were on the road, heading up to Jerusalem with Jesus walking ahead of them. They were amazed, while those who followed were afraid. Taking the Twelve aside again, he began to tell them what was going to happen to him, ³³saying, "Look, we are going up to Jerusalem. The Son of Man will be delivered to the chief priests and the scribes, and they will condemn him to death and deliver him to the Gentiles. ³⁴They will mock him and spit on him and flog him and kill him. And on the third day he will rise again."

Servant Leadership

³⁵Now James and John, the sons of Zebedee, approached him and said to him, "Teacher, we want you to do for us whatever we ask of you." ³⁶"What do you want me to do for you?" he asked. ³⁷And they replied, "Grant that in your glory we may sit one at your right hand and one at your left." ³⁸But Jesus told them, "You do not know what you are asking. Are you able to drink the cup that I drink, or to be baptized with the baptism that I am baptized with?" ³⁹They replied, "We are able to." But Jesus said to them, "You will drink the cup that I drink, and you will be baptized with the baptism that I am baptized with. ⁴⁰But, to sit at my right hand or at my left is not mine to grant, but it is for those that it has been prepared for." ⁴¹When the [other] ten heard this, they began to be indignant at James and John. ⁴²So Jesus called them to himself and said to them, "You know that those who are considered rulers over the Gentiles lord it over them, and their great men

exercise authority over them. ⁴³But it must not be that way among you. Instead, whoever might want to be great among you must be your servant, ⁴⁴and whoever might want to be first among you must be the slave of all. ⁴⁵For even the Son of Man came not to be served but to serve, and to give his life as a ransom for many."

Jesus Heals a Blind Man

⁴⁶They went to Jericho, and as he was leaving Jericho with his disciples and a large crowd, Bartimaeus, a blind beggar, (the son of Timaeus), was sitting alongside the road. ⁴⁷Now when he heard that it was Jesus of Nazareth, he began to cry out and say, "Jesus, Son of David, have mercy on me!" ⁴⁸Many people rebuked him, telling him to be silent. But he cried out all the more, "Son of David, have mercy on me!" ⁴⁹Jesus stopped and said, "Call him." And they called the blind man, saying to him, "Take heart. Get up—He is calling you." ⁵⁰Throwing off his cloak he sprang up and came to Jesus. ⁵¹And Jesus asked him, "What do you want me to do for you?" And the blind man said to him, "Master, let me recover my sight." ⁵²And Jesus replied, "Go your way. Your faith has made you well." And he did recover his sight immediately and followed him on the way.

Chapter 11

The Triumphal Entry

¹When they were approaching Jerusalem, by Bethphage and Bethany, at the Mount of Olives, he sent two of his disciples, ²saying to them, "Go into the village in front of you, and as soon as you enter it, there you will find tied up a colt that no one has ever ridden on. Untie it and bring it. ³If anyone questions you, 'Why are you doing this?' say, 'The Lord has need of it [now] and will send it back here right away.'" ⁴And they went away, and outside in the street they found a colt tied at the door, and they untied it. ⁵And some of the ones standing there questioned them, "What are you doing, untying the colt?" ⁶So, they told them what Jesus had said, and they permitted them. ⁷They brought the colt to Jesus and threw their garments on it, and he sat on it. ⁸Many people spread their garments on the road, and others spread leafy branches that they had cut from the fields. ⁹And those who walked in front and those who followed after [him] shouted, "Hosanna! Blessed is he who comes in the name of the Lord! ¹⁰Blessed is the coming kingdom of our father David! Hosanna in the highest!"

¹¹And so he made his way into Jerusalem and went into the temple, and once he had looked around at everything, he went out to Bethany with the Twelve, since it was already late in the day.

[12]The next day, as they were returning from Bethany, he was hungry. [13]Seeing a fig tree in leaf in the distance, he went to see if he could find anything on it. When he got to it, he found nothing but leaves, for it was not the season for figs. [14]And in response, he said, "May no one ever eat fruit from you again," which his disciples heard.

Jesus Overturns the Tables

[15]They arrived in Jerusalem, and he entered into the temple and began to drive out those who were selling as well as those who were buying in the temple, and he overturned the tables of the money-changers and the seats of those who were selling pigeons. [16]And he would not allow anyone to carry merchandise through the temple courts. [17]He lectured them, saying, "Is it not written, 'My house shall be called a house of prayer for all the nations'? But you have made it a den of thieves." [18]When the chief priests and the scribes heard it, they began looking for a way to destroy him, for they feared him because the whole crowd was spellbound at his teaching. [19]And as evening was coming on, [Jesus and the disciples] left the city.

The Withered Fig Tree

[20]In the morning, as they were passing by the fig tree, they saw it withered away to its roots. [21]Peter remembered and said to him, "Master, look! The fig tree that you cursed has withered." [22]And Jesus addressed them and said, "Have faith in God. [23]Truly, I say to you, whoever says to this mountain, 'May you be lifted up and hurled into the sea,' and does not doubt in his heart, but believes that what he says will happen, it will be done for him. [24]Therefore I tell you, whatever you ask in prayer, believe that you are receiving it, and it will be yours. [25]And whenever you stand praying, forgive, if you have anything against anyone, so that your Father who is in heaven may also forgive you your sins. [26]But if you do not forgive, neither will your Father who is in heaven forgive your sins."

By Whose Authority?

[27]They arrived back in Jerusalem, and as Jesus was walking in the temple, the chief priests and the scribes and the elders came to him, [28]and they questioned him, "By what authority are you doing these things, or who gave you this authority to do them?" [29]Jesus replied, "I shall pose a question to you. Answer me, and I will tell you by what authority I do these things. [30]John's baptism: was it from heaven or from man? Answer me." [31]And they debated it among themselves, saying, "If we say, 'From heaven,' he will say, 'Then why did you not believe him?' [32]On the other hand, should we say, 'From man'?" Now, they were fearful of the people, for all of them held [the opinion] that John was indeed a prophet. [33]So

they answered Jesus, "We don't know." So, Jesus said to them, "Then neither will I tell you by what authority I do these things."

Chapter 12

The Parable of the Owner of the Vineyard

[1]Then he began to speak to them in parables: "A man planted a vineyard and set a fence around it and dug out the winepress pit, and built a watchtower. He leased it to tenants and then left the country. [2]When the right time had come, he sent a servant to the tenants to obtain some of the fruit of the vineyard from them. [3]But they took him and beat him and sent him away empty-handed. [4]Again he sent another servant to them, and they struck him on the head and abused him. [5]Then he sent another whom they killed. And so on with many others: they beat some and they killed some. [6]He only had one more: a beloved son. He finally sent him to them, saying, 'They will respect my son.' [7]But those tenants said to one another, 'This is the heir. Come on, let's kill him, and then the inheritance will be ours.' [8]So, they took him and killed him and hurled his body out of the vineyard. [9]What then will the owner of the vineyard do? He will come and destroy the tenants and give the vineyard to others. [10]Have you never read this scripture: 'The very stone that the builders rejected—that one has become the cornerstone. [11]This was the Lord's doing, and it is marvelous in our eyes'?" [12]Since they perceived that he had told this parable against them, they wanted to arrest him, but they feared the crowds, so they left him and went away.

Jesus Debates with the Pharisees and Scribes

[13]Next, they sent some of the Pharisees and some of the Herodians to him to trap him by his words. [14]They came and said to him, "Teacher, we know that you are true, and do not care about what people think, for you are not impressed by people's outward appearances, but rather you truthfully teach the way of God. Is it lawful to pay taxes to Caesar or not? [15]Should we pay them, or shouldn't we?" But Jesus, knowing their hypocrisy, replied, "Why are you testing me? Bring me a denarius coin to look at." [16]They brought one, and he asked them, "Whose image and inscription is this?" They said to him, "Caesar's." [17]Jesus said to them, "Offer up to Caesar the things that are Caesar's, and to God the things that are God's." And they marveled at him.

[18]Then [some] Sadducees, who claim that there is no resurrection, came up to him and asked him a question, saying, [19]"Teacher, Moses wrote for us that if a man's brother dies and leaves a wife, but leaves no child, the man must take the widow, and raise up children for his brother. [20]There were seven brothers; the first

one took a wife, and when he died left no children. [21]Then the second took her, and died, leaving no children, and the same with the third one, [22]so that the seven of them left no children. Last of all the woman died, too. [23]In the resurrection, when they rise again, whose wife will she be? For [all] seven had her as wife."

[24]Jesus responded, "You know neither the scriptures nor the power of God. Is that not why you are mistaken? [25]For when they rise from the dead, they neither marry nor are given in marriage, but are like angels in heaven. [26]And as for the dead being raised, have you not read in the book of Moses, in the passage about the bush, how God said to him, 'I am the God of Abraham, and the God of Isaac, and the God of Jacob'? [27]He is not God of the dead, but of the living. You are greatly mistaken."

[28]Then one of the scribes came up and listened to them engaged in dispute, and seeing that he answered them well, asked him, "Which commandment is the most primary one of all?" [29]Jesus answered, "The primary one is: 'Hear, O Israel: The Lord our God, the Lord is one, and you shall love the Lord your God with all your heart, and with all your soul, and with all your mind, and with all your strength.' [31]The secondary one is this: 'You shall love your neighbor as yourself.' There is no other commandment greater than these." [32]And the scribe said to him, "You are right, Teacher; you have truthfully said that he is one, and there is no other but him. [33]And, to love him with all the heart, and with all the understanding, and with all the strength, and to love one's neighbor as oneself, is much more than all the burnt offerings and sacrifices." [34]Then, seeing that he answered wisely, Jesus said to him, "You are not far from the kingdom of God." Then no one dared to question him anymore.

[35]Once when Jesus was teaching in the temple, he answered [a question] by saying, "How can the scribes say that the Christ is the son of David? [36]David himself, inspired by the Holy Spirit, declared, 'The Lord said to my Lord, "Sit at my right hand, till I put your enemies under your feet."' [37]David himself calls him Lord. So then how is he his son?" The large crowd listened to him with great delight. [38]As he was teaching he warned, "Beware of the scribes, who like to walk around in long robes and be greeted in the marketplace [39]and who have the best seats in the synagogues and the places of honor at festivals: [40]they gobble up the property of widows and pretentiously say long prayers. They will receive the greater condemnation."

The Widow's Penny

[41]Then he sat down across from the treasury and watched as the people were

putting money into the offering box. Many rich people put in large donations. [42]Then a poor widow came and put in two copper coins, which add up to a penny. [43]And calling his disciples over to himself, he said to them, "Truly, I tell you, this poor widow has put in more than all the others who are contributing to the treasury. [44]For they all contributed out of their abundance, but out of her poverty she has put in everything she had—all she had to live on."

Chapter 13

Not One Stone Left on Another

[1]As he was coming out of the temple, one of his disciples said to him, "Look, Teacher, what great stones and what great buildings!" [2]And Jesus said to him, "Do you see these great buildings? There will not be one stone here left on another that will not be thrown down."

Final Instructions and the End of the World

[3]Later, as he sat on the Mount of Olives opposite the temple, Peter and James and John and Andrew asked him in private, [4]"Tell us, when will this be, and what will be the sign when these things are all to be fulfilled?" [5]Jesus started to tell them: "See to it that no one misleads you. [6]Many will come in my name, saying, 'I am he!' and they will mislead many. [7]And when you hear of wars and rumors of wars, do not be alarmed. This must happen, but it is not the end yet. [8]For nation will rise against nation, and kingdom against kingdom. There will be earthquakes in various places, there will be famines. These are but the beginning of the birth pangs.

[9]"Still, watch out for yourselves, for they will deliver you up to councils. You will be beaten in synagogues, and you will stand in front of governors and kings for my sake, to give testimony before them. [10]But first the gospel must be preached to all nations. [11]And when they bring you to trial and deliver you up, do not be anxious beforehand about what you are to say. Rather, say whatever is given to you at that moment, for it is not you who speak, but the Holy Spirit. [12]And brother will deliver up brother to death, and the father his child, and children will rise up against [their] parents and have them put to death. [13]And you will be hated by everyone for [the sake of] my name. Yet, the one who endures to the end—that one will be saved.

[14]"But when you see the abomination [causing] desolation standing where he should not be (let the reader understand), then let those who are in Judea flee to the mountains. [15]No one who is on his housetop should go down, nor enter his

house to take anything out. [16]And no one who is in the field should turn back to grab his cloak. [17]And how awful for pregnant women and for the nursing mothers in those days! [18]Pray that it may not happen in winter. [19]For in those days there will be such tribulation as has not been from the beginning of the universe that God created until now, and never will be [again]. [20]And if the Lord had not shortened the days, no human being would be saved. But for the sake of the chosen ones, whom he chose, he shortened the days. [21]And then if anyone says to you, 'Look, here is the Christ!' or 'Look, there he is!' do not believe it. [22]For false Christs and false prophets will rise up and perform signs and wonders to mislead even the chosen ones, if possible. [23]So watch out for yourselves. I have told you everything ahead of time.

[24]"Now in those days, after that tribulation, the sun will be darkened, and the moon will not give its light, [25]and the stars will be falling from heaven, and the powers in the heavens will be shaken. [26]And then the Son of Man will be seen coming in clouds with great power and glory. [27]And then he will send out the angels and gather his chosen ones from the four winds, from the ends of the earth to the ends of heaven.

[28]"Learn the lesson from the fig tree: as soon as its branch becomes tender and puts forth its leaves, you know that summer is near. [29]So also, when you see these things happening, you will know that he is near, even at the gates. [30]Indeed, I tell you this generation will not pass away before all these things take place. [31]Heaven and earth will pass away, but my words will not pass away. [32]"However, no one knows that day or that hour—not even the angels in heaven, nor the Son, but only the Father. [33]Keep watching and stay awake. For you do not know when the time will come. [34]It is like a man going on a journey: he leaves home and puts his servants in charge, each with his duties, and commands the doorkeeper to stay awake. [35]Therefore, stay awake because you do not know when the master of the house will return—in the evening, or at midnight, or at rooster crowing time, or in the morning—[36]so that he does not find you asleep if he should come suddenly. [37]And I tell you what I tell everyone: Keep watch."

Chapter 14

Jesus Anointed and then Betrayed

[1]Now it was two days before the Passover and the feast of Unleavened Bread. And the chief priests and the scribes were looking for some way to arrest him on the sly and the kill him [2]because they said, "Not during the festival, so there will not be an uproar among the people." [3]So, Jesus was in Bethany at the house of Simon

the leper, and as he sat at table, a woman came with an alabaster flask of very costly ointment made of pure nard, and she broke the flask and poured it over his head. ⁴But there were some who said to themselves indignantly, "Why was the ointment wasted like that? ⁵For this ointment might have been sold for more than three hundred denarii and [the money] given to the poor." So, they scolded her. ⁶But Jesus said, "Leave her alone. Why are you bothering her? She has done something beautiful for me. ⁷For you always have the poor with you, and you can do good things for them whenever you wish to, but you will not always have *me*. ⁸She has done what she was able to do: she has anointed my body for burial in advance. ⁹And indeed—I tell you that wherever the gospel is preached in the whole world, what she has just done will be told in memory of her."

¹⁰Then Judas Iscariot, who was one of the Twelve, went to the chief priests in order to betray him to them. ¹¹When they heard it, they were delighted and promised to give him money. So, he started looking for an opportunity to betray him.

The Last Supper

¹²Now on the first day of Unleavened Bread, when they sacrificed the Passover lamb, Jesus' disciples said to him, "Where do you want us go to prepare to eat the Passover?" ¹³So he sent off two of his disciples, saying to them, "Go into the city, and a man carrying a jar of water will meet you. Follow him, ¹⁴and wherever he enters, say to the master of the house, 'The Teacher says, "Where is a guest room for me, where I am to eat the Passover with my disciples?"' ¹⁵He will show you a large upper room furnished and ready. Prepare for us there." ¹⁶And the disciples set out and went to the city, and found things just as he had told them, and they prepared the Passover. ¹⁷And when it was evening he came with the Twelve. ¹⁸And as they were at table eating, Jesus said, "Truly, I say to you, one of you will betray me—one who is eating with me." ¹⁹They began to be sorrowful, and to ask him one by one, "Is it I?" ²⁰He said to them, "It is one of the Twelve, one who is dipping bread into the dish with me. ²¹For the Son of Man goes as it is written of him, but woe to that man by whom the Son of Man is betrayed! It would have been better for that man if he had not been born."

²²As they were eating, he took bread, and having blessed it he broke it and gave it to them and said, "Take, this is my body." ²³Then he took a cup, and when he had given thanks, he gave it to them, and they all drank from it. ²⁴And he said to them, "This is my blood of the covenant, which is poured out for many. ²⁵Truly, I say to you, I shall not drink of the fruit of the vine again until that day when I drink it new in the kingdom of God."

^{26}When they had sung a hymn, they went out to the Mount of Olives. ^{27}And Jesus said to them, "You are going to fall away; for it is written, 'I will strike the shepherd, and the sheep will be scattered.' ^{28}But after I am raised up, I will go to Galilee ahead of you." ^{29}Peter said to him, "Maybe they might all fall away, but I will not." ^{30}And Jesus replied to him, "Truly, I say to you, this very night, before the cock has crowed twice, you will deny me three times." ^{31}But Peter said emphatically, "Even if I have to die with you, I will not deny you." And they all said the same thing.

In the Garden of Gethsemane

^{32}Next they went to a place that was named Gethsemane, and he said to his disciples, "Sit here while I pray." ^{33}And he took Peter and James and John with him and began to be greatly distressed and troubled. ^{34}And he said to them, "My soul is in great sorrow, to the point of death. Stay here and watch." ^{35}Then he went little farther, and he fell to the ground and prayed that, if it were possible, the hour might pass from him. ^{36}And he said, "Abba, Father, all things are possible to you—remove this cup from me. Yet not what I will, but what you will." ^{37}On returning he found them asleep, and he said to Peter, "Simon, are you asleep? Could you not stay awake for one hour? ^{38}Watch and pray that you may not enter into temptation. The spirit indeed is willing, but the flesh is weak." ^{39}Again he went away and prayed, saying the same words. ^{40}And again he came and found them asleep, for their eyelids were very heavy, and they did not know how to answer him. ^{41}He came the third time and said to them, "Are you still sleeping and taking a rest? It is enough; the hour has come; the Son of Man is betrayed into the hands of sinners. ^{42}Get up. Let's be going. Look–my betrayer is here.

Jesus is Betrayed, Arrested, and Questioned

^{43}Right then, while he was still speaking, came Judas, one of the Twelve, and along with him a crowd with swords and clubs, from the chief priests and the scribes and the elders. ^{44}Now the betrayer had given them a sign, saying, "The one I kiss is the one. Seize him and lead him away under guard." ^{45}When Jesus came, Judas went up to him at once and said, "Master!" and he kissed him. ^{46}Then they laid hands on him and seized him. ^{47}But one of those standing nearby drew his sword and struck the slave of the high priest and cut off his ear. ^{48}Jesus said to them, "Have you come out with swords and clubs to capture me, as you would a robber? ^{49}Day after day I was with you in the temple teaching, and you did not seize me. But let the scriptures be fulfilled." ^{50}And they all abandoned him and fled. ^{51}A young man followed him, with nothing but a linen cloth around his body. They even grabbed him, ^{52}but he fled, leaving the linen cloth, and ran away naked.

[53]They led Jesus to the high priest, and all the chief priests and the elders and the scribes assembled. [54]Peter had followed him at a distance, right into the courtyard of the high priest, and he was sitting with the guards, warming himself by the fire. [55]Now the chief priests and the whole council were seeking testimony against Jesus to put him to death. But they found none, [56]for many gave false accounts against him, and their accounts did not agree. [57]Some stood up and gave a false testimony against him, saying, [58]"We heard him say, 'I will destroy this temple that has been built by hand, and in three days I will build another one, not by hand.'" [59]Yet even so, their testimonies did not agree. [60]Then the high priest stood up among them and asked Jesus, "Do you not have any answer to give? What then are these men testifying against you?" [61]But he was silent and gave no answer. Again, the high priest questioned him, saying to him, "Are you the Christ, the Son of the Blessed?" [62]And Jesus said, "I am, and you will see the Son of Man seated at the right hand of Power, and coming with the clouds of heaven." [63]And the high priest tore his garments and said, "What additional testimony do we need? [64]You heard his blasphemy! What is your decision?" And they all condemned him as deserving death. [65]Some began to spit on him. They covered up his face and struck him, saying to him, "Prophesy!" When the guards got him, they struck him.

Peter Denies Jesus

[66]As Peter was below in the courtyard, one of the servant girls of the high priest came along. [67]Seeing Peter warming himself, she looked at him and said, "You were with the Nazarene, Jesus, too." [68]But he denied it, saying, "I do not know, nor do I understand, what you mean," and he went out into the gateway and the cock crowed. [69]Then the servant girl saw him, and again began saying to the bystanders, "This man is one of them." [70]But he denied it again. And after a little while the bystanders said to Peter again, "You surely are one of them because you are a Galilean." [71]But he began to invoke a curse on himself and to swear, "I do not know this man that you are talking about." [72]And immediately the cock crowed a second time. And Peter remembered how Jesus had said to him, "Before the cock crows twice, you will deny me three times," and he broke down and wept.

Chapter 15

Pilate Delivers Jesus to be Crucified

[1]Now first thing in the morning, the chief priests, along with the elders and scribes, and the whole council held a consultation. They bound Jesus and led him away and delivered him to Pilate. [2]Pilate asked him, "Are you the King of the Jews?" he responded to him by saying, "You say so." [3]The chief priests accused him of many

things, ⁴so Pilate again questioned him, saying "Do you not have any response? Look how many charges they are bringing against you." ⁵But the fact that Jesus gave no further answer amazed Pilate.

⁶Now at the festival Pilate customarily released to them one prisoner that they requested. ⁷Among the rebels in prison who had committed murder in the insurrection was a man called Barabbas. ⁸And the crowd came up and began to ask Pilate to do what he usually did for them. ⁹He answered them, "Do you want me to release the King of the Jews for you?" ¹⁰because he realized that it was out of envy that the chief priests had handed over Jesus to him. ¹¹But the chief priests stirred up the crowd to have him release Barabbas for them instead. ¹²Pilate asked them again, "Then what should I do with the man you call the King of the Jews?" ¹³And they shouted out again, "Crucify him." ¹⁴Pilate said to them, "Why? What wrong has he done?" But they shouted all the more, "Crucify him." ¹⁵So Pilate, wanting to satisfy the crowd, released Barabbas for them. And having had Jesus flogged, he delivered him to be crucified.

¹⁶The soldiers led him away inside the palace (that is, the headquarters), and they called together the whole battalion. ¹⁷They dressed him in a purple cloak, and they wove a crown of thorns and put it on him. ¹⁸They began saluting him, "Hail, King of the Jews!" ¹⁹And they struck his head with a reed and spit on him, and they knelt down to pay homage to him. ²⁰When they had mocked him, they stripped off his purple cloak and put his own clothes back on him, and they led him out to crucify him. ²¹And they compelled a passer-by, Simon of Cyrene (the father of Alexander and Rufus), who was coming in from the country, to carry his cross. ²²And they brought him to the place called Golgotha (which means "the place of a skull"). ²³And they offered him wine mixed with myrrh, but he did not take it. ²⁴And they crucified him, and divided his garments among them, casting lots for them, to decide what each should take. ²⁵It was nine o'clock in the morning when they crucified him, ²⁶ and the inscription of the charge against him read:

THE KING OF THE JEWS.

²⁷They crucified two robbers along with him, one on his right and one on his left. ²⁸Thus the scripture was fulfilled: "He was numbered among criminals."

²⁹And those who passed by derided him, wagging their heads, and saying, "Ha! So, you would destroy the temple and rebuild it in three days? ³⁰Save yourself and come down from the cross!" ³¹In the same way the chief priests also mocked him among themselves with the scribes, saying, "He saved others; he cannot save himself. ³²Let the Christ, the King of Israel, come down from the cross now so that we may see and believe." Those who were crucified with him also reviled him.

³³When noon had come, there was darkness over the whole land until three o'clock in the afternoon. ³⁴At three o'clock Jesus cried out in a loud voice, "Eloi, Eloi, lema sabachthani?" which means, "My God, my God, why have you forsaken me?" ³⁵Hearing that, some of the bystanders said, "Listen, he is calling Elijah." ³⁶Some of them ran and, filling a sponge full of sour wine, put it on a reed and gave it to him to drink, saying, "Wait, let's see if Elijah comes to take him down." ³⁷Then Jesus uttered a loud cry, and breathed his last. ³⁸The veil of the temple was torn in two, from top to bottom. ³⁹When the centurion, who stood facing him, saw the way that he cried out and breathed his last, he said, "Truly this man was the Son of God!"

⁴⁰There were also women looking on from afar, among whom were: Mary Magdalene; Mary, the mother of James the younger and of Joses; Salome, ⁴¹who followed him and ministered to him when he was in Galilee; and many other women who came up to Jerusalem with him, also.

⁴²And when evening had come, since it was the day of Preparation (that is, the day before the Sabbath) ⁴³Joseph of Arimathea, a respected member of the council, who himself was also looking for the kingdom of God, took courage and went to Pilate and requested Jesus' body. ⁴⁴Pilate was surprised that he was already dead, and summoning the centurion, he asked him whether he was indeed already dead. ⁴⁵When he learned from the centurion that he was dead, he granted the corpse to Joseph, ⁴⁶who bought a linen shroud, and took him down and wrapped him in the linen shroud. He laid him in a tomb that had been hewn out of the rock, and he rolled a stone against the entrance of the tomb. ⁴⁷Mary Magdalene and Mary the mother of Joses saw where he was laid.

Chapter 16

Jesus Rises from the Dead

¹And when the Sabbath was past, Mary Magdalene, and Mary the mother of James, and Salome bought spices, so that they might go and anoint him. ²Very early on the first day of the week, once the sun had risen, they went to the tomb. ³They were wondering to one another, "Who will roll the stone away from the entrance of the tomb for us?" ⁴And looking up, they saw that the stone, which was very large, had already been rolled back. ⁵And entering the tomb, they saw a young man sitting on the right side, dressed in a white robe, which dumbfounded them. ⁶And he said to them, "Do not be alarmed. You seek Jesus of Nazareth, who was crucified. He has risen; he is not here. See the place where they laid him. ⁷But go, tell his disciples and Peter that he is going on ahead of you to Galilee. You will see him there, as he told you." ⁸They went back out, and because they were

gripped with trembling from their astonishment, they fled from the tomb, and because they were fearful, they said nothing to anyone.

[9]Now when [Jesus] rose early on the first day of the week, he appeared first to Mary Magdalene, from whom he had cast out seven demons. [10]She went and told those who had been with him, as they were mourning and weeping. [11]But when they heard that he was alive and that she had seen him, they would not believe it.

Jesus Appears to the Apostles

[12]After this, he appeared in another form to two of them, as they were walking on their way into the country, [13]and they went back and told the rest, but they did not believe them. [14]Afterward he appeared to the eleven themselves as they sat at table, and he reproved them for their unbelief and hardness of heart because they had not believed those who saw him after he had risen. [15]He also said to them, "Having set out into all the world, proclaim the gospel to the whole world. [16]Anyone who believes and is baptized will be saved, but anyone who does not believe will be condemned. [17]And these signs will accompany those who believe:

- ➢ In my name they will cast out demons.
- ➢ They will speak in new tongues.
- ➢ [18]They will not be harmed if they pick up snakes or drink anything lethal.
- ➢ They will lay their hands on the sick and they will recover."

Jesus Ascends into Heaven

[19]So then the Lord Jesus, after he had spoken to them, was taken up into heaven and sat down at the right hand of God. [20]And [the disciples] went forth and preached everywhere, while the Lord worked with them and confirmed the message by the accompanying signs. Amen.

Chapter 1

Dedication

¹Since many others have undertaken compiling a narrative of the things that have been done in our midst, ²and whereas it was those who were eyewitnesses from the beginning and ministers of the word who conveyed it all to us, ³it seemed good to me, having a solid understanding of all these things for some time now, to record an accurate account for you, most excellent Theophilus, ⁴so that you would be certain about the things you have been taught.

Birth of John the Baptist Foretold

⁵It came to pass that in the days of Herod, king of Judea, there was a priest named Zechariah, of the division of Abijah, and he had a wife, from the daughters of Aaron, whose name was Elizabeth. ⁶They were both righteous before God, behaving impeccably in terms of all the commandments and statutes of the Lord. ⁷They were quite old but still childless because Elizabeth was barren.

⁸Now it so happened that once when Zechariah's division was on duty, and he was serving as priest before God, ⁹according to the custom of the priesthood, he was chosen by lot to enter the temple of the Lord and burn incense. ¹⁰A whole multitude of people were praying outside at the hour of incense burning. ¹¹An angel of the Lord appeared to him, standing on the right side of the altar of incense. ¹²Seeing him, Zechariah was shocked, and fear fell upon him. ¹³But the angel said to him,

"Do not be afraid, Zechariah, for your prayer has been heard, and your wife Elizabeth will bear you a son, and you shall declare his name to be John. ¹⁴You shall have joy and gladness, and many will rejoice at his birth, ¹⁵because he will be great before the Lord. He must not drink wine or hard liquor. He shall be filled with the Holy Spirit, even while still in his mother's womb. ¹⁶He shall turn many of the children of Israel to the Lord their God, ¹⁷and he shall come before him in the spirit and power of Elijah, to turn the hearts of the fathers toward their children, and to turn the disobedient ones toward the wisdom of the just, and to prepare a people who are ready for the Lord."

¹⁸Then Zechariah said to the angel, "How can I be sure of this? For I am an old man, and my wife is quite old." ¹⁹The angel answered him,

> "I am Gabriel. I stand in the presence of God, and I was sent to speak to you and to bring you this good news. ²⁰Listen, because you did not believe my words, which will be fulfilled in their time, you will fall silent and be unable to speak until such time as these things take place."

²¹Now the people were waiting for Zechariah, and they were wondering about his delay in the temple. ²²When he did come out, he was unable to speak to them, and they realized that he had seen a vision in the temple. He kept making signs to them and he remained mute. ²³And when his time of service was ended, he went home.

²⁴After these days his wife Elizabeth conceived, and for five months she kept herself hidden, saying, ²⁵"This is what Lord has done for me in the days when he took notice of me, to take away my public disgrace."

The Annunciation

²⁶In the sixth month the angel Gabriel was sent from God to a city of Galilee named Nazareth, ²⁷to a virgin legally pledged to be married to a man by the name of Joseph, of the lineage of David; the virgin's name was Mary. ²⁸He came to her and said, "Greetings, O woman of the Lord's favor, the Lord is with you!" ²⁹But on seeing him, she was greatly troubled by his words, and tried to discern what sort of greeting this might be. ³⁰And the angel said to her, "Do not be afraid, Mary, for you have found favor with God. ³¹See, you shall conceive in your womb and bear a son, and you shall declare his name to be Jesus. ³²He shall be great and shall be called the Son of the Most High, and the Lord God shall give him the throne of his father David. ³³He shall reign over the house of Jacob forever, and his kingdom shall never end."

³⁴Mary said to the angel, "How can this come about, since I am still a virgin?" ³⁵The angel answered her, "The Holy Spirit will come on you, and the power of the Most High will overshadow you. Therefore, the child to be born will be called holy–the Son of God. ³⁶And indeed, your relative Elizabeth, even in her old age, has also conceived a son. Now she who was called barren is in her sixth month, ³⁷for with God nothing is impossible." ³⁸Then Mary responded, "So be it, I am the servant of the Lord; let it happen to me as you have said." Then the angel departed from her.

The Visitation

³⁹In those days Mary arose and hastened into the hill country, to a town in Judah, ⁴⁰and she entered the house of Zechariah and greeted Elizabeth. ⁴¹When Elizabeth heard Mary's greeting, her unborn baby leaped in her womb. Elizabeth was filled with the Holy Spirit, ⁴²and she exclaimed with a loud cry, "Blessed are you among women, and blessed is the fruit of your womb! ⁴³And why is this for me—that the mother of my Lord should come to me? ⁴⁴You see, when the sound of your greeting came to my ears, the baby in my womb leaped for joy. ⁴⁵And blessed is she who believed, for there will be a fulfillment of what was spoken to her from the Lord."

Mary's Hymn of Praise: The 'Magnificat'

⁴⁶And Mary said:

"My soul does magnify the Lord, ⁴⁷and my spirit has rejoiced in God my Savior,
⁴⁸for he has taken notice of the humble estate of his servant.
For, yes, from now on all generations shall call me blessed,
⁴⁹for he who is mighty has done great things for me and holy is his name.
⁵⁰And his mercy is for those who fear him from generation to generation.
⁵¹He has shown strength with his arm.
He has scattered the proud in the vain imaginations of their hearts.
⁵²He has brought down the mighty from their thrones and exalted the lowly.
⁵³He has filled the hungry with good things, but he has sent away the rich empty-handed.
⁵⁴He has come to the aid of his servant Israel, in remembrance of his mercy,
⁵⁵as he declared to our fathers, to Abraham, and to his offspring forever."

⁵⁶Mary remained with her about three months and then returned to her home.

The Birth of John the Baptist

⁵⁷Now the time came for Elizabeth to give birth, and she give birth to a son. ⁵⁸Her neighbors and relatives heard that the Lord had shown her great mercy, and they rejoiced with her. ⁵⁹On the eighth day they came to circumcise the child. Now they would have called him Zechariah, that being the name of his father, ⁶⁰but his mother answered, "No, he shall be called John." ⁶¹So they said to her, "Not one of your relatives is called by this name." ⁶²So they made signs to his father, inquiring what he wanted him to be called. ⁶³He asked for a writing tablet and wrote, "His name is John," which puzzled them all. ⁶⁴Immediately his mouth was opened, and his tongue loosened, and he spoke, blessing God. ⁶⁵Fear came upon all their neighbors. All these things were talked about throughout all the hill country of Ju-

dea, ⁶⁶and all who heard them treasured them in their hearts, pondering, "Who will this child turn out to be?" for the hand of the Lord was [obviously] with him.

The Prophecy of Zechariah

⁶⁷Then his father Zechariah was filled with the Holy Spirit and prophesied, saying:

⁶⁸*"Blessed be the Lord, the God of Israel,*
for he has visited and redeemed his people.
⁶⁹*And for us he has raised up a horn of salvation*
in the house of his servant David,
⁷⁰*as he said by the mouth of his holy prophets from ancient times,*
⁷¹*to save us from our enemies and from the hand of all who hate us,*
⁷²*to show the mercy promised to our fathers*
and to remember his holy covenant
⁷³*–the oath that he swore to our father Abraham–*
to grant ⁷⁴*that we, being delivered from the hand of our enemies,*
could serve him without fear,
⁷⁵*in holiness and righteousness before him all our days.*
⁷⁶*And you, child, will be called the prophet of the Most High,*
for you will go before the Lord to prepare the way for him,
⁷⁷*to give his people the knowledge of salvation in the forgiveness of their sins,*
⁷⁸*because of the tender mercy of our God,*
when the sunrise dawns on us from on high
⁷⁹*to shine a light for those who sit in darkness and in the shadow of death,*
to guide our feet into the way of peace."

⁸⁰And the child grew and became strong in spirit, and he was in the wilderness until the day of his public appearance to Israel.

Chapter 2

The Nativity

¹In those days an edict went out from Caesar Augustus that all the world should be registered. ²This was the first registration when Quirinius was governor of Syria. ³And all went to be registered, each to his own town. ⁴So, Joseph also went up from Galilee, from the town of Nazareth, to Judea, to the city of David, which is called Bethlehem, because he was of the family and lineage of David, ⁵to be registered with Mary, his wife, who was pregnant. ⁶While they were there, the time came for her to give birth. ⁷She gave birth to her firstborn son and wrapped him in swaddling clothes and laid him in a manger, because there was no room for them in the guesthouse.

Angels appear to Shepherds

[8]And in the same region there were shepherds out in the field, keeping watch over their flock by night. [9]And an angel of the Lord appeared to them, and the glory of the Lord shone around them, and they were quite afraid. [10]And the angel said to them, "Do not be afraid, for you see—I bring you good news of great joy that will be for all the people. [11]For a Savior, who is Christ the Lord, is born to you this day in the city of David. [12]And this shall be a sign for you: you will find a baby wrapped in swaddling clothes and lying in a manger." [13]And suddenly there with the angel was a multitude of the heavenly host praising God and saying, [14]"Glory to God in the highest place, and on earth peace among the people whom he is pleased with!"

[15]When the angels had gone away from them into heaven, the shepherds said to one another, "Let's go over to Bethlehem and see this thing that has happened, which the Lord has made known to us." [16]So they hurried and found Mary and Joseph, and the baby lying in a manger. [17]Now, seeing this, they told them what had been told to them concerning this child. [18]All of them who heard what the shepherds told them marveled about it. [19]But Mary treasured up all these things, pondering them in her heart. [20]Then the shepherds returned, glorifying and praising God for all that they had heard and seen, just as it had been told to them.

[21]When he was circumcised at the end of eight days, he was called Jesus, the name given by the angel before he was conceived in the womb.

The Presentation at the Temple

[22]When the time came for their purification according to the law of Moses, they brought him up to Jerusalem to present him to the Lord [23](as it is written in the law of the Lord, "Every male who first opens the womb shall be called holy to the Lord") [24]and to offer a sacrifice according to what is required in the law of the Lord, "a pair of turtledoves, or two young pigeons."

[25]Now there was a man in Jerusalem, whose name was Simeon, and this man was righteous and devout, waiting for the consolation of Israel, and the Holy Spirit was on him. [26]It had been revealed to him by the Holy Spirit that he would not see death before he had seen the Anointed One of the Lord. [27]And by the [leading of] the Spirit he came into the temple, and when the parents brought in the child Jesus, to perform the customary legal rite for him, [28]he took him up in his arms and blessed God and said:

[29]*"Lord, now you are granting*
that your servant may depart in peace,
according to your word,

30for my eyes have seen your salvation
31that you have prepared in the sight of all peoples:
32a light for revelation to the Gentiles,
and for glory to your people Israel."

33His father and mother marveled at what was said about him. 34Simeon blessed them and said to Mary his mother, "You see, this child is destined to cause the falling and rising of many in Israel, as a sign that will be rejected, 35so that the thoughts of many hearts will be revealed. A sword will pierce through your own soul as well."

36Anna, a prophetess, and the daughter of Phanuel, of the tribe of Asher was there also. She was quite old, having lived with her husband seven years from when she was a virgin, 37and then as a widow until she was the age of eighty-four. She never left the temple, worshiping with fasting and prayer night and day. 38And coming up at that very hour, she began to give thanks to God and to speak about him to everyone who was waiting expectantly for the redemption of Jerusalem.

39Once they had performed everything according to the law of the Lord, they returned into Galilee, to their own town of Nazareth. 40The child grew up and became strong, filled with wisdom, and the favor of God was on him.

The Boy Jesus in the Temple

41Now every year his parents went to Jerusalem for the Feast of the Passover, 42and when he was twelve years old, they went up according to their custom of [attending] the feast. 43As they were returning [home] after the feast had ended, the boy Jesus stayed behind in Jerusalem, though his parents were not aware of it. 44Assuming that he was in their group, they went one day's journey, but then they began to search for him among their relatives and acquaintances. 45Not finding him, they returned to Jerusalem, searching for him.

46After three days they found him in the temple, sitting among the teachers, listening to them and asking them questions. 47Now, all who were listening to him were amazed at his understanding and his answers. 48When [his parents] saw him, they were astonished, and his mother said to him, "Son, why have you treated us this way? Listen, your father and I have been searching for you in great distress." 49He said to them, "Why were you looking for me? Did you not realize that I must be in my Father's house?" 50They did not understand the saying that he spoke to them. 51Then he went down with them and came to Nazareth and was obedient to them. His mother treasured up all these things in her heart.

52Then Jesus increased in wisdom, and in stature, and in favor with God and man.

Chapter 3

John the Baptist begins his Ministry

[1]It was the fifteenth year of the reign of Tiberius Caesar; Pontius Pilate was governor of Judea; Herod was tetrarch of Galilee, and his brother Philip was tetrarch of the region of Ituraea and Trachonitis; Lysanias was tetrarch of Abilene, [2]and the high priests were Annas and Caiaphas. The word of God came to John, the son of Zechariah, in the wilderness. [3]He went into all the region around the Jordan, proclaiming a baptism of repentance for the forgiveness of sins. [4]As it is written in the book of the words of Isaiah the prophet,

"The voice of one crying in the wilderness:
'Prepare the way of the Lord.
Lay out a straight avenue to [welcome] him.
[5]Every valley shall be filled,
and every mountain and hill shall be made low,
and the crooked shall become straight,
and the rugged places shall become level,
[6]and all mankind shall see salvation from God.'"

[7]Therefore he said to the crowds that came out to be baptized by him, "You brood of vipers! Who warned you to run away from the wrath to come? [8]Bear fruits in keeping with repentance. And do not start saying to yourselves, 'We have Abraham as our father.' For I tell you, God is able to raise up children for Abraham from these stones. [9]Even now the axe is laid to the root of the trees. Therefore every tree that does not bear good fruit is cut down and thrown into the fire." [10]And the crowds asked him, "Then what should we do?" [11]And he answered them, "Whoever has two tunics is to share with someone who has none, and whoever has food is to do likewise." [12]Tax collectors also came to be baptized and asked him, "Teacher, what should we do?" [13]And he said to them, "Collect no more than you are authorized to do." [14]Soldiers also asked him, "And we, what should we do?" And he said to them, "Do not extort money from anyone by threats or by false accusation and be content with your wages."

[15]As the people were in expectation, all were questioning in their hearts concerning John, whether he might be the Christ. [16]But John answered them all, saying, "I baptize you with water, but he who is mightier than I am is coming, and I am not even worthy to untie the strap of his sandals. He will baptize you with the Holy Spirit and with fire. [17]His winnowing fork is in his hand, to clear his threshing floor and to gather the wheat into his barn, but he will burn the chaff with unquenchable fire." [18]He preached the good news to the people with many other such exhortations.

[19]But Herod the tetrarch, whom John had [openly] criticized for taking Herodias, his brother's wife, and for all the evil things that Herod had done, [20]added this to them all: that he [would eventually] lock up John in prison. [21]Now when all the people were baptized, and when Jesus also had been baptized and was praying, the heavens were opened, [22]and the Holy Spirit descended on him in bodily form, like a dove. A voice came from heaven [saying], "You are my beloved Son; with you I am well pleased."

The Genealogy of Jesus Christ

[23]When he began his ministry, Jesus was about thirty years of age, being the son (as was supposed) of Joseph, the son of Heli, [24]the son of Matthat, the son of Levi, the son of Melchi, the son of Jannai, the son of Joseph, [25]the son of Mattathias, the son of Amos, the son of Nahum, the son of Esli, the son of Naggai, [26]the son of Maath, the son of Mattathias, the son of Semein, the son of Josech, the son of Joda, [27]the son of Joanan, the son of Rhesa, the son of Zerubbabel, the son of Shealtiel, the son of Neri, [28]the son of Melchi, the son of Addi, the son of Cosam, the son of Elmadam, the son of Er, [29]the son of Joshua, the son of Eliezer, the son of Jorim, the son of Matthat, the son of Levi, [30]the son of Simeon, the son of Judah, the son of Joseph, the son of Jonam, the son of Eliakim, [31]the son of Melea, the son of Menna, the son of Mattatha, the son of Nathan, the son of David, [32]the son of Jesse, the son of Obed, the son of Boaz, the son of Sala, the son of Nahshon, [33]the son of Amminadab, the son of Admin, the son of Arni, the son of Hezron, the son of Perez, the son of Judah, [34]the son of Jacob, the son of Isaac, the son of Abraham, the son of Terah, the son of Nahor, [35]the son of Serug, the son of Reu, the son of Peleg, the son of Eber, the son of Shelah, [36]the son of Cainan, the son of Arphaxad, the son of Shem, the son of Noah, the son of Lamech, [37]the son of Methuselah, the son of Enoch, the son of Jared, the son of Mahalaleel, the son of Cainan, [38]the son of Enos, the son of Seth, the son of Adam, the son of God.

Chapter 4

Jesus Endures Temptations

[1]Then Jesus, full of the Holy Spirit, returned from the Jordan and was led by the Spirit into the wilderness [2]for forty days, where he was tempted by the devil. He ate nothing during those days. So, when they were ended, he was hungry. [3]The devil said to him, "If you are the Son of God, command this stone to become bread." [4]But Jesus answered him, "It is written, 'Man shall not live by bread alone.'" [5]Then the devil took him up and showed him all the kingdoms of the world in a moment of time, [6]and said to him, "I will give you all this authority and

glory, for all of it has been handed over to me, and I give it to whomever I will. [7]If you, then, will worship me, it will all be yours." [8]But Jesus answered him, "It is written, "'You shall worship the Lord your God, and you shall serve only him.'"

[9]Then he took him to Jerusalem and put him on the pinnacle of the temple and said to him, "If you are the Son of God, throw yourself down from here, [10]for it is written, "'For your sake he will command his angels to keep you safe,' [11]and "'They will hold you up on their hands, so that you will not knock your foot against a stone.'" [12]But Jesus answered him, "It is said, 'You shall not put the Lord your God to the test.'" [13]So when the devil had ended every temptation, he departed from him until an opportune time.

Jesus Begins his Ministry

[14]Then Jesus returned to Galilee in the power of the Spirit, and a report about him went out through all the surrounding country. [15]He taught in their synagogues, being glorified by all.

[16]He came to Nazareth, where he had been brought up. And as was his custom, he went to the synagogue on the Sabbath day and stood up to read. [17]When the scroll of the prophet Isaiah was given to him, he unrolled the scroll and found the place where it was written:

[18]"The Spirit of the Lord is on me
because he has anointed me
to proclaim good news to the poor.
He has sent me to proclaim liberty to the captives
and the recovering of sight to the blind,
to liberate those who are oppressed,
[19]and to proclaim the year of the Lord's favor."

[20]Then he rolled up the scroll and gave it back to the attendant and sat down. The eyes of all in the synagogue were fixed on him. [21]And he began by saying to them, "Today this scripture has been fulfilled as you heard it read." [22]All spoke well of him and marveled at the gracious words that were coming from his mouth. And they commented, "Isn't this Joseph's son?" [23]He said to them, "Doubtless you will quote to me this proverb, 'Physician, heal yourself.' What we have heard you did at Capernaum, do here in your hometown as well." [24] he said, "Truly, I say to you, no prophet is accepted with honor in his hometown. [25]But in truth, I tell you, there were many widows in Israel in the days of Elijah, when the heavens were shut up for three years and six months, and a great famine came over all the land, [26]and Elijah was sent to none of them except Zarephath, in the land of Sidon, to

a woman who was a widow. ²⁷And there were many lepers in Israel in the time of the prophet Elisha, and none of them was cleansed, but only Naaman the Syrian."

²⁸When they heard these things, all in the synagogue were filled with wrath. ²⁹They got up and drove him out of the town and brought him to the edge of the hill that their town was built on, so that they could throw him off the cliff. ³⁰But passing through their midst, he went on his way.

Jesus Heals a Man with a Demon and Others

³¹Then he went down to Capernaum, a city of Galilee, and he was teaching them on the Sabbath, ³²and they were astonished at his teaching because of the authority in his word. ³³And in the synagogue was a man who had the spirit of an evil demon, and he cried out with a loud voice, ³⁴"Ha! What do you have to do with us, Jesus of Nazareth? Have you come to destroy us? I know who you are—the Holy One of God." ³⁵But Jesus rebuked him, saying, "Be silent and come out of him!" And when the demon had thrown him down in their midst, he came out of him, having done him no harm. ³⁶They were all amazed and said to one another, "What word is this? For he commands the evil spirits with authority and power, and they come out!" ³⁷And reports about him went out into every place in the surrounding region.

³⁸Then he got up and left the synagogue and entered Simon's house. Now Simon's mother-in-law was sick with a high fever, and they appealed to him on her behalf. ³⁹So he stood over her and rebuked the fever, and it left her, and she immediately got up and began to wait on them.

⁴⁰At sunset that day, all those who had any who were sick with various diseases brought them to him, and he laid his hands on every one of them and healed them. ⁴¹Demons also came out of many, crying, "You are the Son of God!" But he rebuked them and would not allow them to speak because they knew that he was the Christ.

Preaching in the Synagogues

⁴²The next morning he departed and went into a desolate place. The people sought him and came to him and would have kept him from leaving them. ⁴³But he said to them, "I must preach the good news of the kingdom of God to the other towns as well, for I was sent for this purpose." ⁴⁴And he went preaching in the synagogues of Judea.

Chapter 5

Fishers of Men

¹It happened that once while he was standing by the lake of Gennesaret, the crowd was pressing in on him to hear the word of God. ²And he saw two boats by the lake, but the fishermen had gotten out of them and were washing their nets. ³Getting into one of the boats, which was Simon's, he asked him to put out a little from the shore. He sat down and taught the people from the boat. ⁴When he had finished speaking, he said to Simon, "Put out into the deep [water] and let down your nets for a catch." ⁵Simon answered, "Master, we labored all night and took nothing! But if you say so, I will let down the nets." ⁶When they had done this, they enclosed such a large number of fish that their nets were breaking. ⁷So, they signaled to their partners in the other boat to come and help them. They came and filled both the boats with so much that they began to sink. ⁸But when Simon Peter saw it, he fell down at Jesus' knees, saying, "Depart from me, for I am a sinful man, O Lord." ⁹For he and all who were with him were astonished at the catch of fish that they had taken, ¹⁰and James and John, sons of Zebedee, who were partners with Simon, were also. But Jesus said to Simon, "Do not be afraid. From now on you will be fishers of men." ¹¹When they had brought their boats to land, they left everything and followed him.

Cleansing a Leper

¹²While he was in one of the cities, there came a man full of leprosy, and when he saw Jesus, he fell on his face and begged him, "Lord, if you are willing, you can make me clean." ¹³Jesus stretched out his hand and touched him, saying, "I am willing; be clean." And immediately the leprosy left him. ¹⁴He charged him to tell no one, but told him "go and show yourself to the priest and make an offering for your cleansing, as Moses commanded, for a proof to them." ¹⁵But then the report about him went abroad even more, and great crowds gathered to hear him and to be healed of their infirmities. ¹⁶Still, he routinely withdrew to desolate places to pray.

Healing a Paralytic

¹⁷And it happened that one day, as he was teaching, Pharisees and teachers of the law, who had come from every village of Galilee and Judea and from Jerusalem, were sitting there. Now the power of the Lord to heal was with him, ¹⁸and right then, some men were bringing a paralyzed man on a bed. They were intending to bring him in and lay him before Jesus, ¹⁹but finding no way to bring him

in, because of the crowd, they went up on the roof and let him down with his bed through the tiles into the midst in front of Jesus. [20]When he saw their faith, he said, "Man, your sins are forgiven you." [21]The scribes and the Pharisees began to question [this], asking, "Who is this who speaks blasphemies? Who but God alone can forgive sins?" [22]When Jesus perceived their thoughts, he answered them, "Why do you question in your hearts? [23]Which is easier, to say, 'Your sins are forgiven you,' or to say, 'Get [up] and walk'? [24]But so that you may know that the Son of Man has authority on earth to forgive sins, he said to the man who was paralyzed, "I say to you, get up, pick up your bed and go home." [25]Immediately he got up in front of them and picked up what he had been lying on and went home, glorifying God. [26]Amazement seized them all, and they glorified God and were filled with awe, saying, "Today we have seen extraordinary things."

The Calling of Levi

[27]After this he went out and saw a tax collector named Levi, sitting at the tax booth, and he said to him, "Follow me." [28]So leaving everything, he got up and followed him. [29]Then Levi made a great feast for him at his house, and there was a large company of tax collectors and others reclining at table with them. [30]The Pharisees and their scribes grumbled at his disciples, saying, "Why do you eat and drink with tax collectors and sinners?" [31]Jesus answered them, "It is not the well who have need of a physician, but the sick. [32]I have not come to call the righteous to repentance, but sinners."

A Question About Fasting

[33]Then they said to him, "The disciples of John fast often and offer prayers, and so do the disciples of the Pharisees, but yours eat and drink." [34]Jesus responded, "Can you make wedding guests fast while the bridegroom is with them? [35]The time will come when the bridegroom is taken away from them, and then they will fast in those days." [36]He also told them a parable: "No one tears a piece from a new garment and puts it on an old garment. If he does, he will tear the new, and the piece from the new will not match the old. [37]In addition, no one puts new wine into old wineskins. If he does, the new wine will burst the skins and it will be spilled, and the skins will be destroyed. [38]But new wine must be put into fresh wineskins. [39]And no one after drinking old wine desires new, for he says, 'The old is good.'"

Chapter 6

Lord of the Sabbath

¹While he was going through the grain fields on a Sabbath, his disciples plucked and ate some heads of grain, rubbing them in their hands. ²Then some of the Pharisees asked, "Why are you doing something that's not lawful to do on the Sabbath?" ³Jesus answered them, "Have you not read what David did when he was hungry—he and those who were with him—⁴how he entered the house of God and took and ate the bread of the Presence, which is not lawful for anyone but the priests to eat, and also gave it to those with him?" ⁵He declared to them, "The Son of Man is lord of the Sabbath."

A Man with a Withered Hand

⁶Now it so happened that on another Sabbath, he entered the synagogue and was teaching, and a man with a withered right hand was there. ⁷The scribes and the Pharisees were watching him to see whether he would heal on the Sabbath, so that they might find a reason to accuse him. ⁸But he knew their thoughts, and he said to the man with the withered hand, "Come and stand here," and he rose and stood there. ⁹Jesus said to them, "I ask you, is it lawful on the Sabbath to do good or to do harm, to save life or to destroy it?" ¹⁰And after looking around at all of them, he said to him, "Stretch out your hand." he did so, and his hand was restored. ¹¹But they were filled with fury and plotted among themselves what they might do to Jesus.

The Twelve Apostles

¹²Now it so happened in those days that he went up to the mountain to pray and spent the whole night in prayer to God. ¹³When morning came, he summoned his disciples and chose twelve of them, whom he named apostles: ¹⁴Simon, whom he called Peter, and Andrew his brother, and James and John, and Philip, and Bartholomew, ¹⁵and Matthew, and Thomas, and James the son of Alphaeus, and Simon who was called the Zealot, ¹⁶and Judas the son of James, and Judas Iscariot, who one day became a traitor.

Jesus Ministers to a Great Crowd

[17]And he came down with them and stood on a level place, with a great crowd of his disciples and a great multitude of people from all Judea and Jerusalem and the seacoast of Tyre and Sidon, [18]who had come to hear him and to be healed of their diseases. Those who were troubled with evil spirits were cured, [19]and all the crowd sought to touch him, for power came out from him and healed them all.

The Beatitudes and the Woes

[20]And he lifted up his eyes on his disciples, and said:

"Blessed are you who are poor, for yours is the kingdom of God.
[21] *"Blessed are you who are hungry now, for you shall be satisfied.*
"Blessed are you who weep now, for you shall laugh.
[22]*"Blessed are you when people hate you and when they exclude you and revile you and reject your name as evil, on account of the Son of Man!*
[23] *Rejoice in that day, and leap for joy, for look–your reward is great in heaven, for their fathers did likewise to the prophets.*
[24]*"But woe to you who are rich, for you have received your consolation.*
[25]*"Woe to you who are full now, for you shall be hungry.*
"Woe to you who laugh now, for you shall mourn and weep.
[26]*"Woe to you, when all people speak well of you, for their fathers did likewise to the false prophets.*

Love Your Enemies

[27]"But I tell you who are hearing [this] to love your enemies:

> ➤ Do good to those who hate you.
> ➤ [28]Bless those who curse you;
> ➤ Pray for those who abuse you.
> ➤ [29]If someone strikes you on the cheek, offer the other one also,
> ➤ and do not withhold your tunic from the one who takes away your cloak.
> ➤ [30]Give to everyone who begs from you,
> ➤ and do not demand your goods back from the one who takes them away.
> ➤ [31]Treat others in the same way as you wish that they would treat you.

[32]"If you do love those who love you, what credit is that to you? For even sinners love those who love them. [33]And if you do good to those who do good to you, what credit is that to you? For even sinners do the same. [34]And if you lend to people you expect to receive [something] from, what credit is that to you? Even sinners lend to sinners, to receive the same amount back. [35]But love your enemies, and do good, and lend, expecting nothing in return, and your reward will be great, and

98

you will be sons of the Most High, for he is kind to the ungrateful and the wicked. [36]Be merciful, just as your Father is merciful.

Judging Others

[37]"Do not judge, and you will not be judged. Do not condemn, and you will not be condemned. Forgive, and you will be forgiven. [38]Give, and it will be given to you. A goodly measure, pressed down, shaken together, running over, will be poured into your lap. For you will receive back by the same measure you give out."

[39]He also told them a parable: "Can a blind man guide [another] blind man? Will they not both fall into a pit? [40]A disciple is not superior to his teacher, but everyone will be like his teacher once he is fully trained. [41]Why do you see the speck that is in your brother's eye, but fail to notice the log in your own eye? [42]How can you say to your brother, 'Brother, let me remove the speck in your eye,' when you yourself do not see the log in your own eye? You hypocrite, first remove the log from your own eye, and then you will see clearly to remove the speck from your brother's eye.

A Tree and Its Fruit

[43]"For no good tree produces bad fruit, neither does a bad tree produce good fruit, [44]for each tree is known by its own fruit. Figs are not gathered from thorn bushes, nor are grapes picked from a bramble bush. [45]The good person out of the treasure of good in his heart produces good, and the evil person out of his store of evil produces evil, for his mouth speaks what is flowing out of the heart.

Building Your House on the Rock

[46]"Why do you call me 'Lord, Lord,' and neglect doing what I tell you? [47]I will show you what everyone who comes to me and hears my words and acts on them is like: [48]He is like a man who, when building a house, dug deep and laid the foundation on rock. When a flood arose, the torrents crashed against that house and [yet] could not shake it because it had been built on rock. [49]But the one who hears my words and does not act on them is like a man who built a house on the ground without a foundation. When the torrents crashed against it, it fell immediately, and the destruction of that house was great."

Chapter 7

Healing a Centurion's Servant

[1]After [Jesus] had finished all his sayings for the people to hear, he entered Capernaum. [2]Now a centurion had a highly valued servant who was gravely ill—at the point of death. [3]When the centurion heard about Jesus, he sent Jewish elders to him, requesting that he come and heal his servant. [4]When they came to Jesus, they earnestly pleaded with him, saying, "He is worthy to have you do this for him, [5]for he loves our nation, and he is the one who built us our synagogue." [6]So Jesus went with them. When he was not far from the house, the centurion sent friends who said to him, "Lord, do not trouble yourself, for I am not worthy to have you come under my roof, [7]which is why I did not presume to come to you. Just speak the word, that my servant may be healed. [8]For I am a man placed under authority too, with soldiers under me. I say to one, 'Go,' and he goes; and to another, 'Come,' and he comes; and to my servant, 'Do this,' and he does it." [9]When Jesus heard these things, he marveled at him, and turning to the crowd that was following him, he said, "I tell you, not even in Israel have I found such faith." [10]Then when those who had been sent returned to the house, they found the servant well.

Raising a Widow's Son from the Dead

[11]Now it came to pass that soon afterward he went to a town called Nain, and his disciples and a large crowd accompanied him. [12]As he approached the gate of the town, a man who had died was being carried out. [He was] the only son of his mother, and she was a widow, and a sizable crowd of townspeople was with her. [13]Now when the Lord saw her, he took compassion on her, saying to her, "Do not weep." [14]Then he came up and touched the bier, and the bearers stood still. And he said, "Young man, I say to you, arise." [15]The dead man sat up and began to speak, and he gave him to his mother. [16]Fear seized all of them, and they gave glory to God, saying, "A great prophet has arisen among us!" and "God has come to the aid of his people!" [17]This report about him spread throughout all of Judea and all the neighboring countryside.

Messengers from John the Baptist

[18]The disciples of John reported all these things to him. So John,[19]summoning two of his disciples to himself, sent them to the Lord to ask, "Are you the one who is to come, or should we be looking for another?" [20]When the men had come to him, they said, "John the Baptist has sent us to you to ask, 'Are you the one who is to

come, or should we be looking for another?'" ²¹So right then he healed many people of diseases and plagues and evil spirits, and he gave sight to many who were blind. ²²Then he answered them, "Go and tell John what you have just seen and heard: the blind see again, the lame walk, the lepers are cleansed, the deaf hear, the dead are raised up, the poor have good news preached to them. ²³And blessed is the one who is not offended by me."

²⁴When John's messengers had gone, Jesus began to speak to the crowds about John: "What did you go out into the wilderness to see? A reed shaken by the wind? ²⁵What then did you go out to see? A man dressed in soft clothing? Look, those who are dressed in splendid clothing and live in luxury are in kings' courts. ²⁶So, what then *did* you go out to see? A prophet? Yes, I tell you, and more than a prophet. ²⁷This is the one about whom it is written, "'You see, in advance of you I am sending my messenger who will prepare your way before you.' ²⁸I tell you, among those born of women none is greater than John. Yet the one who is least in the kingdom of God is greater than he [is]." ²⁹(When all the people heard this, including the tax collectors too, having been baptized with John's baptism, they acknowledged God as just. ³⁰But, the Pharisees and the lawyers, not having been baptized by him, rejected the purpose of God for themselves.)

³¹"Then what should I compare the people of this generation to, and what do they resemble? ³²They are like children sitting in the marketplace and calling to one another, "We played the flute for you, and you did not dance; we sang a dirge, and you did not weep.' ³³For John the Baptist has come eating no bread and drinking no wine, and you say, 'He has a demon.' ³⁴The Son of Man has come eating and drinking, and you say, 'Look at him! A glutton and a drunkard, a friend of tax collectors and sinners!' ³⁵Nonetheless, wisdom is vindicated by her outcome."

A Sinful Woman Forgiven

³⁶One of the Pharisees asked Jesus to eat with him, so he went into the Pharisee's house and took his place at the table. ³⁷Now then, a woman of the city, who was a sinner, learned that he was reclining at table in the Pharisee's house, so she brought an alabaster flask of ointment. ³⁸Standing behind him at his feet, weeping, she began to wet down his feet with her tears and wiped them with the hair of her head, and she kissed his feet and anointed them with the ointment. ³⁹Now when the Pharisee who had invited him observed this, he said to himself, "If this man were a prophet, he would have known who and what sort of woman was touching him, for she is a sinner."

⁴⁰And responding, Jesus said to him, "Simon, I have something to say to you." "Teacher," he replied, "Go ahead and speak." ⁴¹"A certain moneylender had two debtors. One owed [him] five hundred denarii, and the other fifty. ⁴²With neither of them able to repay, he cancelled both of their debts. Now which of them will love him more?" ⁴³Simon answered, "I suppose the one who had the larger debt forgiven." And he said to him, "You have judged correctly." ⁴⁴Then turning toward the woman he said to Simon, "Do you see this woman? I entered your house. You gave me no water for my feet, but she has washed my feet with her tears and wiped them dry with her hair. ⁴⁵You gave me no kiss, but from the time I came in she has not stopped kissing my feet. ⁴⁶You did not anoint my head with oil, but she has anointed my feet with ointment. ⁴⁷Therefore I tell you, her sins, which are many, are forgiven for she has shown much love. But he who is forgiven little, loves little." ⁴⁸Then he said to her, "Your sins are forgiven." ⁴⁹Then those who were at table with him started saying among themselves, "Who is this, who even forgives sins?" ⁵⁰And he told the woman, "Your faith has saved you; go in peace."

Chapter 8

Women Accompanying Jesus

¹It came to pass that soon afterward he passed through cities and villages, preaching and bringing the good news of the kingdom of God. The Twelve were with him, ²along with some women who had been healed of evil spirits and illnesses: Mary, called Magdalene, (seven demons had come out of her); ³and Joanna, the wife of Chuza, Herod's household manager; and Susanna, and many others who provided for them out of their resources.

The Parable of the Sower

⁴As a large crowd was gathering, and the townspeople were coming to him, he spoke by means of a parable: ⁵"A sower went out to sow his seed. And as he sowed, some fell along the path and was trampled underfoot, and the birds of the air devoured it. ⁶Some fell on the rock, and as it grew up, it withered away for lack of moisture. ⁷Some fell among thorns, and the thorns grew up with it and choked it. ⁸Some fell into good soil and grew and yielded a hundredfold." As he said these things, he called out, "If anyone has ears to hear with, let him hear this."

The Purpose of the Parables

⁹Then his disciples asked him what this parable meant. ¹⁰He replied, "The knowledge of the secrets of the kingdom of God is given to you, but to others they are in parables, such that 'though seeing they do not perceive, and though hearing

they do not understand.' ¹¹Now the parable is this: The seed is the word of God. ¹²The ones along the path are those who have heard, but then the devil comes and snatches away the word from their hearts, so that they may not believe and be saved. ¹³The ones on the rock are those who, when they hear the word, receive it with joy. But these have no root; they do believe for a while but fall away in a time of testing. ¹⁴As for what fell among the thorns, they are those who hear, but as they are going on their way they get choked by the cares and riches and pleasures of life, and they do not reach maturity. ¹⁵But as for those in the good soil, they are those who, hear the word, and securely hold it in an honest and good heart, patiently bearing fruit.

A Lamp Under a Jar

¹⁶"No one, after lighting a lamp covers it with a jar or puts it under a bed. Instead, he puts it on a stand so that those who come in can see the light. ¹⁷For nothing is hidden that will not be revealed, nor is anything secret that will not be known and come to light. ¹⁸Listen carefully, for more will be given to the one who has, and from the one who does not have, even what he imagines he has will be taken away."

Jesus' Mother and Brothers

¹⁹Then his mother and his brothers came to him, but they could not manage to reach him on account of the crowd. ²⁰And he was told, "Your mother and your brothers are standing outside, wanting to see you." ²¹But he answered them, "My mother and my brothers are those who hear the word of God and act on it."

Calming a Storm

²²One day it happened that he got into a boat with his disciples, and he said to them, "Let's go across to the other side of the lake." So, they set out, ²³and while they were sailing he fell asleep. Then a windstorm descended onto the lake, and they were becoming swamped with water and were in danger. ²⁴They went and woke him, exclaiming, "Master, Master, we are perishing!" And he awoke and rebuked the wind and the raging waves, and they ceased, and all was calm. ²⁵He said to them, "Where is your faith?" But they were afraid, and they wondered out loud to each other, "Then who *is* this who commands the winds and the water, and even they obey him?"

Healing the Gerasene Demoniac

[26]Then they sailed to the region of the Gerasenes, which is across the lake from Galilee. [27]When Jesus had stepped out on land, a man from the city who had had demons for a long time met him. He wore no clothes, and he did not live in a house, but among the tombs. [28]When he saw Jesus, he cried out and fell down in front of him and exclaimed in a loud voice, "What am I to you, Jesus, Son of the Most High God? I beg you not to torment me." [29](For he had commanded the evil spirit to come out of the man. It had seized him many times. He was kept under guard and bound with chains and shackles, but he would break the bonds and be driven by the demon into the wilderness.) [30]Jesus then asked him, "What is your name?" And he said, "Legion," because many demons had come inside him. [31]And they begged him not to command them to depart into the abyss.

[32]Now a large herd of pigs was feeding there on the hillside, so the [demons] begged him to let them enter the [pigs]. So, he allowed it. [33]Then the demons came out of the man and entered the pigs, and the herd rushed down the embankment into the lake and drowned. [34]When the herdsmen saw what had happened, they fled and talked about it in the city and in the country. [35]Then people went out to see what had happened, and they came to Jesus and found the man from whom the demons had gone, sitting at the feet of Jesus, clothed and in his right mind, and they were afraid. [36]The eyewitnesses told them how the demon-possessed man had been healed. [37]Then all the people of the surrounding region of the Gerasenes asked him to depart from them, for they were seized with great fear. So, he got into the boat and returned. [38]The man from whom the demons had gone begged that he might stay with him, but Jesus sent him away, saying, [39]"Return to your home and declare what great things God has done for you." So he went away, proclaiming throughout the whole city what great things Jesus had done for him.

Healing a Woman and Jairus's Daughter

[40]Now on Jesus' return, the crowd welcomed him, for they were all awaiting him. [41]Just then there came a man named Jairus, who was a leader of the synagogue. Falling at Jesus' feet, he begged him to come to his home [42]because his only daughter, who was about twelve years old, was dying.

As Jesus went, the people pressed around him. [43]Now there was a woman who had had a discharge of blood for twelve years, and though she had used up all her assets on physicians, no one had been able to cure her. [44]She came up behind him and touched the fringe of his garment, and immediately her discharge of blood ceased. [45]Jesus asked, "Who just touched me?" When all denied it, Peter said, "Master, the crowds surround you and are pressing in on you! And yet you ask, 'Who touched me?'" [46]But Jesus said, "Someone touched me because I sense that power has gone out from me." [47]When the woman saw that she could not stay hidden, she came trembling, and fell down in front of him. In the presence of all the people, she declared why she had touched him, and how she had been healed immediately. [48]He said to her, "Daughter, your faith has made you well; go in peace."

[49]While he was still speaking, someone from the house of the leader of the synagogue came and reported, "Your daughter is dead; no need to trouble the Teacher anymore." [50]But on hearing this Jesus responded, "Do not be afraid. Just believe, and she will be delivered." [51]When he came to the house, he allowed no one to enter with him, except Peter, John, James, and the father and mother of the child. [52]They were all weeping and mourning for her, but he said, "Do not weep, for she is not dead but sleeping." [53]And they derided him, knowing that she was dead. [54]But taking her by the hand he called out, saying, "Child, get up!" [55]And her spirit returned, and she got up at once. He told them to give her something to eat. [56]Her parents were astounded, but he commanded them not to tell anyone what had happened.

Chapter 9

Sending Out the Twelve Apostles

[1]On calling the Twelve together, he gave them power and authority over [driving out] all demons and curing diseases, [2]and he sent them out to proclaim the kingdom of God and to heal the sick. [3]And he said to them, "Take nothing for your journey—no staff, no bag, no bread, no money—and do not carry a spare tunic. [4]In whatever home you take up lodging, stay there until you leave [town]. [5]Wherever people do not welcome you, shake the dust off your feet when leaving that town as a testimony against them." [6]Then they departed and went through the villages, preaching the gospel and performing acts of healing everywhere.

Herod Wonders Who Jesus Is

[7]Now Herod the tetrarch heard about all that was happening, and he was disconcerted because some people said that John had been raised from the dead, [8]some said that Elijah had appeared, and others said that one of the prophets of old had risen. [9]Herod said, "I beheaded John, but who is *this* that I am hearing such things about?" So, he looked for a chance to see him.

Feeding the Five Thousand

[10]On their return, the apostles told [Jesus] all that they had done. He took them and they went away by themselves to a town called Bethsaida. [11]When the crowds found out about it, they followed him, and he welcomed them and spoke to them about the kingdom of God and cured those who had need of healing. [12]As the daylight was fading, the Twelve came and said to him, "Send the crowd away to go into the surrounding villages and countryside to find lodging and obtain food because we are here in a remote place." [13]But he said to them, "You give them something to eat." They said, "We have nothing more than five loaves and two fish—unless we were to go and buy food for all these people." [14](For there were about five thousand men.) So, he told his disciples, "Have them sit down in groups of about fifty each." [15]They did so, having all of them all sit down. [16]And taking the five loaves and the two fish, he looked up to heaven and blessed them, and broke them and gave them to the disciples to set before the crowd. [17]They all ate their fill, and twelve baskets of left-over broken pieces were picked up.

Peter Confesses Jesus as the Christ

[18]Now it happened that once when Jesus was praying alone, with the disciples there near him, he asked them, "Who do the crowds say that I am?" [19]They answered, "John the Baptist, though others say, Elijah, and others, that one of the prophets of old has risen." [20]So, he asked them, "But who do *you* say that I am?" And Peter responded, "The Christ of God."

[21]He strictly charged and commanded them to tell this to no one, [22]saying, "The Son of Man must suffer many things and be rejected by the elders and chief priests and scribes, and be killed, and be raised [from the dead] on the third day."

[23]Then he said to them all, "If anyone wants to come follow me, let him deny himself and take up his cross daily and follow me. [24]For whoever should want to save his life will lose it, but whoever loses his life for my sake will save it. [25]For what does it profit a man if he gains the whole world and loses or forfeits himself? [26]For when the Son of Man comes in his glory and the glory of the Father and of the holy angels, he will be ashamed of whoever is ashamed of me and of my words. [27]But I tell you truly, some who are standing here will not taste death until they see the kingdom of God."

The Transfiguration

[28]Now about eight days after these statements he took Peter and John and James with him and went up on the mountain to pray. [29]And as he was praying, the

appearance of his face became different, and his clothing became dazzling white. [30]Suddenly, two men, who were Moses and Elijah, were talking with him. [31]They appeared in glory and spoke of his demise, which he was about to see completed in Jerusalem. [32]Now Peter and those who were with him were heavy with sleep, but once they woke up fully, they saw his glory and the two men who were standing [there] with him. [33]Just as the men were parting from him, Peter, not realizing what he was saying, said to Jesus, "Master, it is a great thing that we are here. Let's make three tabernacles: one for you and one for Moses and one for Elijah." [34]As he was saying these things, a cloud came and overshadowed them, and they were fearful as they entered the cloud. [35]Then a voice came from the cloud, saying, "This is my Son, my Chosen One; listen to him!" [36]Once the voice had spoken, Jesus was found to be alone. And they kept silent, and in those days they told no one any of the things they had seen.

Healing a Boy with an Evil Spirit

[37]On the next day, when they had come down from the mountain, a great crowd met him. [38]Right then, a man from the crowd cried out, "Teacher, I beg you to look at my son, for he is my only child. [39]A spirit seizes him suddenly, and all at once he cries out. It convulses him so that he foams at the mouth, and tears him up, and will hardly leave him. [40]I begged your disciples to cast it out, but they could not." [41]Jesus answered, "O faithless and twisted generation, how long am I to be with you and bear with you? Bring your son here." [42]While he was coming, the demon threw him to the ground and convulsed him. But Jesus rebuked the evil spirit and healed the boy and gave him back to his father. [43]And all were astonished at the majesty of God.

Jesus Again Foretells his Death

But while they were all marveling at everything he was doing, Jesus said to his disciples, [44]"Let these words sink into your ears: The Son of Man is about to be betrayed into the hands of men." [45]But they did not understand this saying, and it was concealed from them, so that they might not perceive it. And they were afraid to ask him about this saying.

Who Is the Greatest?

[46]An argument arose among them as to which of them was the greatest. [47]But Jesus, knowing the reasoning of their hearts, took a small child and put him by his side [48]and said to them, "Whoever welcomes this child in my name welcomes me, and whoever welcomes me welcomes him who sent me. For the one who is least among you all is the one who is great."

Anyone Not Against Us Is for Us

⁴⁹John answered, "Master, we saw someone casting out demons in your name, and we tried to stop him because he does not follow with us." ⁵⁰But Jesus said to him, "Do not stop him, for the one who is not against you is for you."

A Samaritan Village Rejects Jesus

⁵¹When the days for him to be taken up drew near, he set his mind on going to Jerusalem. ⁵²He sent messengers on ahead of him, who went and entered a village of the Samaritans, to prepare a place for him. ⁵³But because he was heading to Jerusalem, the people did not welcome him. ⁵⁴When his disciples James and John saw this, they said, "Lord, do you want us to tell fire to come down from heaven and consume them, as Elijah did?" ⁵⁵But he turned and rebuked them. ⁵⁶And they went on to another village.

The Cost of Following Jesus

⁵⁷As they were going along the road, someone said to him, "I will follow you wherever you go." ⁵⁸But Jesus said to him, "Foxes have holes, and birds of the air have nests, but the Son of Man has nowhere to lay his head." ⁵⁹To another he said, "Follow me." But he said, "Lord, first let me go and bury my father." ⁶⁰But Jesus said to him, "Leave the dead to bury their own dead. But as for you, go and proclaim the kingdom of God." ⁶¹Yet another said, "I will follow you, Lord, but let me first say farewell to those at my home." ⁶²Jesus said to him, "No one who puts his hand to the plow and looks back is fit for the kingdom of God."

Chapter 10

Jesus Sends Out the Seventy-Two

¹After this the Lord appointed seventy-two others and sent them on ahead of him, in pairs, into every town and place where he himself was about to go. ²He said to them, "The harvest is plentiful, but the laborers are few. Therefore, pray earnestly to the Lord of the harvest to send out laborers into his harvest. ³Go your way. Listen, I am sending you out as lambs in the midst of wolves. ⁴Carry no moneybag, no knapsack, no sandals, and on your way greet no one. ⁵In whatever house you enter, first say, 'Peace be to this house!' ⁶And if a person of peace is there, your peace will rest on him. But if not, it will return to you. ⁷Remain in the same house, eating and drinking what they provide, for the laborer deserves his wages. Do not move about from house to house. ⁸Whenever you enter a town and you are welcomed, eat what is set in front of you. ⁹Heal the sick in it and tell

them, 'The kingdom of God has come close to you.' ¹⁰But whenever you enter a town and you are not welcomed, go into its streets and say, ¹¹'Even the dust of your town that clings to our feet we wipe off against you. Nevertheless, know this, that the kingdom of God has come near.' ¹²I tell you, on that Day it will be more bearable for Sodom than for that town.

Woe to Unrepentant Cities

¹³"Woe to you, Chorazin! Woe to you, Bethsaida! For if the mighty deeds done in you had been done in Tyre and Sidon, they would have repented long ago, sitting in sackcloth and ashes. ¹⁴But in the judgment it will be more bearable for Tyre and Sidon than for you. ¹⁵And you, Capernaum, will you be exalted to heaven? You shall be brought down to Hades.

¹⁶"The one who hears you hears me, and the one who rejects you rejects me, and the one who rejects me rejects him who sent me."

The Return of the Seventy-Two

¹⁷The seventy-two returned joyfully, saying, "Lord, in your name even the demons submit to us!" ¹⁸He said to them, "I observed Satan falling like lightning from heaven. ¹⁹Indeed, I have given you authority to tread on serpents and scorpions, and authority over all the power of the enemy, and [yet] nothing shall hurt you. ²⁰Nevertheless, do not rejoice in this—that the spirits submit to you—but rejoice that your names are written in heaven."

Jesus Rejoices in the Father's Will

²¹In that same hour he rejoiced in the Holy Spirit and said, "I thank you, Father, Lord of heaven and earth, that you have hidden these things from the wise and the intelligent and have revealed them to little children. Yes, Father, for it pleased you that it be so. ²²My Father has handed all things over to me, and no one knows who the Son is except the Father, or who the Father is except the Son and anyone to whom the Son chooses to reveal him."

²³Then turning to the disciples he said privately, "Blessed are the eyes that see what you see! ²⁴For I tell you that many prophets and kings longed to see what you see, but did not see it, and to hear what you hear, but did not hear it."

The Parable of the Good Samaritan

²⁵Listen, an expert in the law stood up, and to test him asked, "Teacher, what should I do to inherit eternal life?" ²⁶[Jesus] said to him, "What is written in the law? How do you read it?" ²⁷He answered, "You shall love the Lord your God

with all your heart and with all your soul and with all your strength and with all your mind, and your neighbor as yourself." [28]Jesus replied to him, "You have answered correctly; do this, and you will live."

[29]But, wanting to justify himself, he asked Jesus, "And who is my neighbor?" [30]Jesus replied, "A man was going down from Jerusalem to Jericho, and he fell into the hands of robbers, who stripped him and beat him and departed, leaving him half dead. [31]Now by chance a priest was going down that road, and when he saw him, he passed by on the other side. [32]Similarly a Levite, when he came to the place and saw him, also passed by on the other side. [33]But a Samaritan, as he journeyed, came to where he was, and when he saw him, he had compassion on him. [34]He went to him and bound up his wounds, pouring on oil and wine. Then he set him on his own animal and brought him to an inn and took care of him. [35]The next day he took out two denarii and gave them to the innkeeper, saying, 'Take care of him, and, I will repay you whatever more you spend when I come back.' [3]Of these three, which one do you think acted like a neighbor to the man attacked by the robbers?" [37]He replied, "The one who showed him mercy." So, Jesus said to him, "Go and do likewise."

Martha and Mary

[38]Now as they were going on their way, Jesus entered a certain village where a woman named Martha welcomed him into her home. [39]She had a sister named Mary who sat herself down at the feet of the Lord to listen carefully to his every word. [40]But Martha was distracted, doing a lot of serving, and she went up to him and said, "Lord, do you not care that my sister has left me to do the work of serving alone? Please tell her to help me." [41]But the Lord answered her, "Martha, Martha, you are anxious and fretful about many things, [42]though only one thing is necessary. Mary has chosen the good part, which will not be taken away from her."

Chapter 11

The Lord's Prayer

[1]Now it so happened that Jesus was praying in a certain place, and on finishing, one of his disciples said to him, "Lord, teach us to pray, just as even John taught his disciples." [2]He said to them, "When you pray, say:

"Father, may your name be held as holy.
May your kingdom come,
³*Give us this day our daily bread,*
⁴*and forgive us our sins*
for we forgive everyone indebted to us.
And do not let us yield to temptation."

⁵And he said to them, "Now suppose that you have a friend, and you go to him at midnight and say to him, 'Friend, lend me three loaves, ⁶for a friend of mine has arrived at my [house] on a journey, and I have no [food] to set in front of him.' ⁷And he answers from within, 'Don't bother me. The door is already locked, and my children and I have all gone to bed. I can't get up and give you anything.' ⁸I tell you that he will not get up and give him something on account of being his friend, but because of his dogged persistence he will get up and give him whatever he needs. ⁹So I tell you: Ask, and it will be given to you; seek, and you will find; knock, and it will be opened to you. ¹⁰For everyone who asks receives, and the one who seeks finds, and to the one who knocks it will be opened.

¹¹What father among you, if his son should ask for bread would give him a stone, or if he should ask for a fish, would give him a snake? ¹²Or, if he should ask for an egg, would give him a scorpion? ¹³If you then, being evil, know how to give good gifts to your children, how much more will the heavenly Father give the Holy Spirit to those who ask him!"

Jesus and Beelzebub

¹⁴Now he was casting out a demon that was mute. When the demon had gone out, the mute man spoke, and the people marveled. ¹⁵But some of them said, "He casts out demons by Beelzebub, the leader of the demons." ¹⁶Meanwhile, to test him, others kept seeking a sign from heaven from him. ¹⁷But, knowing their thoughts, he said to them, "Every kingdom divided against itself is destroyed, and a house divided falls. ¹⁸If Satan also is divided against himself, how will his kingdom stand? For you say that I cast out demons by Beelzebub. ¹⁹Now if I cast out demons by Beelzebub, whom do your sons cast them out by? Therefore, they will be your judges. ²⁰But, if it is by the finger of God that I cast out demons, then the kingdom of God has come on you. ²¹When a strong man, fully armed, guards his own castle, his belongings are safe. ²²But when a man stronger than he is attacks him and wins the victory over him, he takes away his armor that he trusted in and divides his spoil. ²³Whoever is not with me is against me, and whoever does not gather with me scatters.

Return of an Evil Spirit

²⁴"When the evil spirit has gone out of a person, it passes through barren places seeking rest, and finding none it says, 'I will return to my house that I came from.' ²⁵And when it comes, it finds the house swept and put in order. ²⁶Then it goes and brings seven other spirits more evil than itself, and they go in and take up residence there. And the last state of that person is worse than the first."

True Blessedness

²⁷As he said these things, a woman in the crowd raised her voice and said to him, "Blessed is the womb that bore you, and the breasts that nursed you!" ²⁸But he replied, "Rather, blessed are those who hear the word of God and keep it!"

The Sign of Jonah

²⁹As the crowds were increasing, he began speaking: "This generation is an evil generation. It seeks for a sign, but no sign will be given to it except the sign of Jonah. ³⁰For as Jonah became a sign to the people of Nineveh, so the Son of Man will be to this generation. ³¹The queen of the South will rise up at the judgment with the men of this generation and condemn them, for she came from the ends of the earth to listen to the wisdom of Solomon, but indeed, something greater than Solomon is here. ³²The men of Nineveh will rise up at the judgment with this generation and condemn it, for they repented at the preaching of Jonah. But listen, something greater than Jonah is here.

The Light in You

³³"After lighting a lamp, no one puts it in a cellar or under a basket, but on a stand, so that those who enter may see the light. ³⁴Your eye is the lamp of your body. When your eye is healthy, your whole body is full of light, but when it goes bad, your body is full of darkness. ³⁵Therefore take care that the light in you not become darkness. ³⁶Then if your whole body is full of light, having no part dark, it will be completely lit, as when a shining lamp gives you light."

Woes to the Pharisees and Lawyers

³⁷While he was speaking, a Pharisee invited him to dine with him, so he went in and took his place at the table. ³⁸The Pharisee was astonished to see that he did not first wash before dinner. ³⁹Then the Lord said to him, "Now you Pharisees cleanse the outside of the cup and of the dish, but inside you are full of greed and wickedness. ⁴⁰You fools! Did not the one who made the outside make the inside also? ⁴¹So give those things that are within as alms, and see, everything will be clean for you.

⁴²"But woe to you Pharisees! For you do tithe mint and rue and all kinds of herbs but overlook the need for justice and the love of God. You should have done these things without neglecting the others. ⁴³Woe to you Pharisees! For you love the best seat in the synagogues and greetings in the marketplaces. ⁴⁴Woe to you! For you are like unmarked graves that people walk over unwittingly."

⁴⁵One of the law experts answered him, "Teacher, by saying these things you also insult us." ⁴⁶And he said, "Woe to you, too, law experts! For you load up people with burdens hard to bear, and you yourselves do not lift a finger to ease the burdens. ⁴⁷Woe to you! For you build the tombs of the prophets whom your ancestors killed. ⁴⁸So you are witnesses and you consent to the deeds of your fathers, for they killed them, and you build their tombs. ⁴⁹Therefore the Wisdom of God also stated, 'I will send them prophets and apostles, some of whom they will kill and persecute,' ⁵⁰so that this generation may be charged with the blood of all the prophets, shed since the foundation of the world, ⁵¹from the blood of Abel to the blood of Zechariah, who perished between the altar and the sanctuary. Yes, I tell you, the charge will be laid against this generation. ⁵²Woe to you, law experts! For you have taken away the key of knowledge. You did not enter yourselves, and you hindered those who were entering."

⁵³As he passed on from there, the scribes and the Pharisees started pressing him hard and provoking him to speak about many things, ⁵⁴lying in wait, [hoping] to trap him by what [came] from his mouth.

Chapter 12

Beware of the Pharisees

¹In the meantime, when so many thousands of people had gathered together that they were trampling one another, he began to speak first to his disciples, "Beware of the yeast of the Pharisees, which is hypocrisy. ²Nothing is covered up that will not be revealed nor hidden that will not be known. ³Therefore whatever you have said in the dark shall be heard in the light, and what you have whispered in private rooms shall be proclaimed on the housetops.

Have No Fear

⁴"I tell you, my friends, do not fear those who kill the body, and afterwards can do no more damage. ⁵But I will warn you whom to fear: fear him who, after he has killed, has authority to cast into hell. Yes, I tell you, fear him! ⁶Are not five sparrows sold for two pennies? Yet in God's eyes not one of them is forgotten. ⁷Why, even the hairs of your head are all numbered. Do not be afraid. You are worth much more than many sparrows.

Acknowledge Christ Before Men

[8]"And I tell you, the Son of Man also will acknowledge in the presence of the angels of God everyone who acknowledges me before men, [9]but the one who denies me before men will be denied in the presence of the angels of God. [10]And everyone who speaks a word against the Son of Man will be forgiven, but the one who blasphemes against the Holy Spirit will not be forgiven. [11]And when they drag you before the synagogues and the rulers and the authorities, do not be anxious about how you should defend yourself or what you should say, [12]for at that very moment the Holy Spirit will instruct you what you should say."

The Parable of the Rich Fool

[13]Someone in the crowd said to him, "Teacher, tell my brother to divide up our inheritance with me." [14]But he said to him, "Man, who made me a judge or arbitrator over you?" [15]And he said to them, "Take care, and be on your guard against all greed, for one's life does not consist in the abundance of his possessions." [16]Then he told them a parable, saying, "The land of a rich man produced plentifully, [17]and he thought to himself, 'What shall I do, for I have nowhere to store my crops?' [18]And he said, 'I will do this: I will tear down my barns and build larger ones, and there I will store all my grain and my goods. [19]And I will say to my soul, Soul, you have ample goods laid up for many years; relax, eat, drink, be merry.' [20]But God said to him, 'Fool! This very night your soul shall be required of you, and the things you have prepared, whose will they be?' [21]Such is the one who lays up treasure for himself and is not rich toward God."

Do Not Be Anxious

[22]And he said to his disciples, "Therefore I tell you, do not be anxious about your life, what you will eat, nor about your body, what you will wear. [23]For life is more than food, and the body more than clothing. [24]Consider the ravens: they neither sow nor reap, they have neither storehouse nor barn, and yet God feeds them. Of how much more value are you than the birds! [25]And which one of you by being anxious can add a single hour to his span of life? [26]If then you are not able to do as small a thing as that, why are you anxious about the rest? [27]Consider the lilies, how they grow: they neither toil nor spin, yet I tell you, even Solomon in all his glory was not arrayed like one of these. [28]But if God so clothes the grass, which is alive in the field today, and tomorrow is thrown into the oven, how much more will he clothe you, O you of little faith! [29]And do not focus on what you are to eat and what you are to drink, nor be worried. [30]For all the nations of the world chase after these things, and your Father knows that you need them. [31]Instead, seek his kingdom, and these things will be added to you.

³²"Fear not, little flock, for it is your Father's good pleasure to give you the kingdom. ³³Sell your possessions and give to the needy. Provide yourselves with moneybags that do not grow old, with a treasure in the heavens that does not fail, where no thief stands nearby, and no moth destroys. ³⁴For where your treasure is, there your heart will be also.

You Must Be Ready

³⁵"Stay dressed for action, with your lamps lit, ³⁶and be like men who are waiting for their master to come home from the wedding feast, so that they may open the door to him as soon as he comes and knocks. ³⁷Blessed are those servants whom the master finds awake when he comes. Truly, I say to you, he will dress himself for service and have them take their places at the table, and he will come and serve them. ³⁸If he comes in the second watch [of the night], or in the third, and finds them awake, blessed are those servants! ³⁹But know this, that if the master of the house had known at what hour the thief was coming, he would have stayed awake and not have left his house to be broken into. ⁴⁰You also must be ready, for the Son of Man is coming at an hour you do not expect."

⁴¹Peter asked, "Lord, are you telling this parable for us or for everyone?" ⁴²And the Lord said, "Who then is the faithful and wise manager, whom his master will put in charge of his servants, to give them their portion of food at the proper time? ⁴³Blessed is that servant that his master will find working when he arrives. ⁴⁴Truly, I say to you, he will put him in charge of all his possessions. ⁴⁵But if that servant says to himself, 'My master is delayed in getting back,' and begins to beat the male and female servants, and to eat and drink and get drunk, ⁴⁶the master of that servant will come on a day when he does not expect him and at an hour he does not know and will cut him in pieces and put him with the unfaithful. ⁴⁷That servant who knew his master's will, but did not get ready or act according to his will, will receive a severe beating. ⁴⁸But the one who did not know, and did what deserved a beating, will receive a light beating. Much will be required from everyone whom much was given to, and more will be demanded from the one whom much has been entrusted to.

Not Peace, but Division

⁴⁹"I have come to bring fire to the earth, and how I wish it were already kindled! ⁵⁰I have a baptism to be baptized with, and how great is my distress until it is accomplished!

⁵¹Do you think that I have come to give peace on earth? No, I tell you, but rather division. ⁵²For from now on a household of five will be five divided, three against

two and two against three. [53]They will be divided, father against son and son against father, mother against daughter and daughter against mother, mother-in-law against her daughter-in-law and daughter-in-law against mother-in-law."

Interpreting the Times

[54]He also said to the crowds, "When you see a cloud rising in the west, you say at once, 'A rain shower is coming;' and so it happens. [55]And when you see the south wind blowing, you say, 'There will be scorching heat,' and it happens. [56]You hypocrites! You know how to interpret the appearance of earth and sky, but why do you not know how to interpret the present time?

Settle with Your Accuser

[57]"And why do you not judge for yourselves what is right? [58]As you go with your accuser before the magistrate, make an effort to settle with him on the way, so that he does not drag you to the judge, and the judge hand you over to the officer, and the officer throw you in prison. [59]I tell you, you will never get out until you have paid the very last penny."

Chapter 13

Repent or Perish

[1]Some who were present at that very time told him about the Galileans whose blood Pilate had mingled with their sacrifices. [2]He asked them, "Do you think that these Galileans suffered in this way because they were worse sinners than all the other Galileans? [3]No, I tell you. But, unless you repent, you will all perish in the same way. [4]Or those eighteen who were killed when the tower in Siloam fell on them: do you think that they were worse offenders than all the others who lived in Jerusalem? [5]No, I tell you. But, unless you repent, you will all perish in the same way.

The Parable of the Barren Fig Tree

[6]Then he told this parable: "A man had a fig tree planted in his vineyard, and he came seeking fruit on it and found none. [7]He said to the caretaker of the vineyard, 'Look, for three years now I have come looking for fruit on this fig tree, but I have found none. Cut it down. Why should it use up the soil?' [8]He replied, 'Sir, leave it alone this year as well, until I dig around it and apply some fertilizer. [9]Then, that's great if it should bear fruit in the time to come, but if not, you can have it cut down.'"

A Woman with a Disabling Spirit

[10]Now once as he was teaching in one of the synagogues on the Sabbath, [11]there came a woman who had had a disabling spirit for eighteen years, and she was bent over and unable to stand up straight. [12]When Jesus saw her, he called her over and said to her, "Woman, you are set free from your disability." [13]He laid his hands on her, and immediately she straightened up, and she gave God the glory. [14]But the leader of the synagogue, indignant because Jesus had healed on the Sabbath, said to the crowd, "There are six days on which work should be done. Come on those days to be healed, and not on the Sabbath day." [15]But the Lord responded to him, "You hypocrites! Does not each one of you untie his ox or his donkey from the manger and lead it away to give it water on the Sabbath? [16]Likewise, should not this woman, a daughter of Abraham whom Satan bound for eighteen years, be set free from this bondage on the Sabbath day?" [17]As he said these things, all his adversaries were put to shame, and all the people rejoiced at all the glorious things done by him.

The Mustard Seed and the Leaven

[18]He said therefore, "What is the kingdom of God like? And what shall I compare it to? [19]It is like a mustard seed that a man took and sowed in his garden, which grew and became a tree, and the birds of the air made nests in its branches."

[20]And again he said, "What shall I compare the kingdom of God to? [21]It is like yeast that a woman took and worked into three measures of flour until it was all leavened."

The Narrow Door

[22]He went on his way through towns and villages, teaching as he journeyed toward Jerusalem. [23]Once someone asked him, "Lord, will those who get saved be few in number?" He replied, [24]"Strive to enter through the narrow door. For, I tell you, many will seek to enter and will not be able. [25]Once the master of the house has risen and shut the door, and you begin to stand outside and to knock at the door, saying, 'Lord, open to us,' then he will answer you, 'I do not know where you are from.' [26]Then you will begin to say, 'We ate and drank in your presence, and you taught in our streets.' [27]But he will say, 'I tell you, I do not know where you are from. Depart from me, all you evildoers!' [28]In that place will be weeping and gnashing of teeth, when you see Abraham and Isaac and Jacob and all the prophets in the kingdom of God but you yourselves cast out. [29]Then people will come from east and west, and from north and south, and take their places at the table in the kingdom of God. [30]Indeed, some who are last shall be first, and some who are first shall be last."

Lament over Jerusalem

³¹At that moment some Pharisees came and said to him, "Get away from here, for Herod wants to kill you." ³²He said to them, "Go and tell that fox, 'Look, I am casting out demons and doing healing today and tomorrow, and on the third day I will complete my task. ³³Still, I must go on my way today and tomorrow and the day following, for it cannot be that a prophet should be killed outside of Jerusalem.' ³⁴O Jerusalem, Jerusalem, the city that kills the prophets and stones those who are sent to it! How often have I wanted to gather your children together as a hen gathers her brood under her wings, and you were not willing! ³⁵Take heed—your house is forsaken. I tell you: you will not see me until you say, 'Blessed is he who comes in the name of the Lord!'"

Chapter 14

Healing of a Man on the Sabbath

¹One Sabbath, when he had gone to dine at the house of one of their rulers, the Pharisees were watching him carefully. ²And right then, a man who had dropsy was there in front of him. ³Addressing the law experts and Pharisees, Jesus asked, "Is it lawful to heal on the Sabbath, or not?" ⁴As they remained silent, he took him and healed him and sent him on his way. ⁵Then he asked them, "Which of you would not immediately pull out a son—or even an ox—that has fallen into a well on a Sabbath day?" ⁶And they could not come up with a reply to him about these things.

The Parable of the Wedding Feast

⁷When he noticed how those who were invited [to dinner] had chosen the places of honor, he told them a parable, saying to them, ⁸"When you are invited by someone to a wedding feast, do not take your seat in a place of honor, in case someone more distinguished than you has been invited by the host, ⁹and whoever invited you both should come and say to you, 'Give your place to this person,' and then in disgrace you start taking the lowest place. ¹⁰Instead, when you are invited, go and sit down in the lowliest place, so that when your host comes, he may say to you, 'Friend, move up higher.' Then you will be honored in the presence of all who are seated at the table with you. ¹¹For everyone who exalts himself will be humbled, and the one who humbles himself will be exalted."

The Parable of the Great Banquet

[12]In addition, he said to the man who had invited him, "When you give a dinner or a banquet, do not invite your friends or your brothers or your relatives or rich neighbors, in case they should also invite you in return and you be repaid. [13]But when you give a feast, invite the poor, the crippled, the lame, and the blind, [14]and you will be blessed, because they cannot repay you. For you will be repaid at the resurrection of the righteous."

[15]When one of those who were at the table with him heard this, he said to him, "Blessed is everyone who will eat bread in the kingdom of God!"

[16]Then [Jesus] said to him, "A man once gave a great banquet and invited many people. [17]At the time for the banquet he sent his servant to say to those who had been invited, 'Come, for everything is ready now.' [18]But each one of them began to make excuses. The first said to him, 'I have bought a field, and I must go out and see it. Please have me excused.' [19]Another said, 'I have just bought five yoke of oxen, and I am on my way to examine them. Please have me excused.' [20]Another said, 'I have just gotten married, and therefore I cannot come.' [21]So the servant came and reported these things to his master. Then the master of the house became angry and said to his servant, 'Quickly—go out to the streets and avenues of the city, and bring in the poor, the crippled, the blind, and the lame.' [22]The servant said, 'Sir, what you commanded has been done, and there is still room.' [23]Then the master commanded the servant, 'Go out to the highways and back roads and force people to come in, so that my house may be full. [24]For I tell you, none of those men who were invited shall taste my banquet.'"

The Cost of Discipleship

[25]Then great crowds were accompanying him, and he turned and said to them, [26]"If anyone comes to me and does not hate his own father and mother and wife and children and brothers and sisters, yes, and even his own life, he cannot be my disciple. [27]Whoever does not bear his own cross and follow me cannot be my disciple. [28]For which of you, setting out to build a tower, does not first sit down and figure out the cost, to see if he has enough to complete it? [29]Otherwise, when he has laid a foundation and cannot finish [it], all who see it will begin to ridicule him, [30]saying, 'This man began to build but could not finish.' [31]Or what king, going out to wage war with another king, does not first sit down to determine whether he is able with ten thousand [men] to oppose the one who comes against him with twenty thousand? [32]And, if not, while the other is yet a great way off, he

sends a delegation and asks for peace [terms]. ³³So therefore, any one of you who does not renounce all he owns cannot be my disciple.

Salt Without Taste Is Worthless

³⁴"Salt is good, but if salt has lost its taste, how shall it be made salty again? ³⁵It is of no use either for the soil or for the compost heap; it is thrown away. If anyone has ears to hear with, let him hear this."

Chapter 15

¹Now the tax collectors and sinners were all approaching to hear him. ²And the Pharisees and the scribes grumbled, saying, "This man welcomes sinners and eats with them."

The Parable of the Lost Sheep

³So he told them this parable: ⁴"Which one of you who owns a hundred sheep and loses one of them does not leave the ninety-nine in the open country to seek the one that is lost until he finds it? ⁵...And then once he has found it, lays it on his shoulders, rejoicing. ⁶...And when he comes home, calls together his friends and his neighbors, saying to them, 'Rejoice with me, for I have found my sheep that was lost.' ⁷I tell you that in the same way there will be more joy in heaven over one sinner who repents than over ninety-nine righteous persons who have no need of repentance.

The Parable of the Lost Coin

⁸"Or what woman who has ten silver coins and loses one of them, does not light a lamp and sweep the house and search diligently until she finds it? ⁹And when she has found it, she calls her friends and neighbors together, saying, 'Rejoice with me, for I have found the coin that I had lost.' ¹⁰I tell you that in the same way there is joy in the presence of the angels of God over one sinner who repents."

The Parable of the Prodigal Son

¹¹Then Jesus said, "A certain man had two sons. ¹²And the younger of them said to his father, 'Father, give me the share of property that will become mine,' so he divided his property between them. ¹³A few days later, the younger son packed up everything and traveled to a distant country, and there he squandered his property in reckless living. ¹⁴When he had spent everything, a severe famine came about in that country, and he began to be in need. ¹⁵So he went and hired himself out to one of the citizens of that country, who sent him into his fields to feed pigs. ¹⁶He

longed to fill his stomach, even with the pods that the pigs ate, but no one gave him anything.

[17]"But when he came to his senses, he thought, 'How many of my father's hired servants have more than enough bread, but here I am dying of hunger! [18]I will get up and go to my father, and I will say to him, "Father, I have sinned against heaven and in your presence. [19]I am no longer worthy to be called your son. Treat me as one of your hired servants."' [20]And he got up and returned to his father. But while he was still a long way off, his father saw him and had compassion, and ran and hugged him and kissed him. [21]The son said to him, 'Father, I have sinned against heaven and in your presence. I am no longer worthy to be called your son.' [22]But the father said to his servants, 'Quickly bring the best robe, and put it on him, and put a ring on his hand, and shoes on his feet. [23]Go get the fattened calf and kill it; let's eat and celebrate. [24]For this son of mine was dead but is alive again; he was lost but [now] is found.' And they started celebrating.

[25]"Now his older son was in the field, and as he came and drew near to the house, he heard music and dancing. [26]And he called one of the servants and asked what these things meant. [27]And he said to him, 'Your brother has come, and your father has killed the fattened calf, because he has received him back unharmed.' [28]But he was angry and refused to go in. His father came out and begged him, [29]but he answered his father, 'Look, I have served you these many years, and I never disobeyed your command, yet you never even gave me a young goat, so that I could celebrate with my friends. [30]But when this son of yours came [back], having squandered your life's earnings on prostitutes, you killed the fattened calf for him!' [31]And he said to him, 'Son, you are always with me, and all that is mine is yours. [32]It was fitting to celebrate and be glad, for this brother of yours was dead, but is alive again; he was lost, but now is found.'"

Chapter 16

The Parable of the Shrewd Manager

[1]He also said to the disciples, "A certain rich man had a manager, and charges were brought to him that this man was squandering his possessions. [2]So he summoned him and said to him, 'What is this that I hear about you? Turn in the account of your management, for you can no longer be manager.' [3]Then the manager said to himself, 'What am I going to do now that my master is taking the management away from me? I am not strong enough to dig, and I am ashamed to beg. [4]I have decided what to do, so that when I am dismissed as manager, people might welcome me into their homes.' [5]So, summoning his master's debtors one

by one, he asked the first one, 'How much do you owe my master?' [6]He said, 'A hundred measures of oil.' he said to him, 'Take your bill, and sit down quickly and make it fifty.' [7]Then he asked another, 'And how much do you owe?' he replied, 'A hundred measures of wheat.' he said to him, 'Take your bill, and make it eighty.' [8]The master commended the dishonest manager for his shrewd dealings. For the sons of this world are shrewder in dealing with their own generation than the sons of light. [9]And I tell you, make friends for yourselves by means of unrighteous wealth, so that when it fails you may be welcomed into the eternal homes.

"One who is faithful in a very little is also faithful in much, and one who is dishonest in a very little is also dishonest in much. [11]If then you have not been faithful in the dishonest wealth, who will entrust the true riches to you? [12]And if you have not been faithful in what belongs to another, who will give you what is your own? [13]No servant can serve two masters, for either he will hate the one and love the other, or he will be devoted to the one and despise the other. You cannot serve [both] God and wealth."

The Law and the Kingdom of God

[14]The Pharisees, who were lovers of money, heard all these things, and they ridiculed him. [15]So he said to them, "You are those who justify yourselves in the sight of other men, but God knows your hearts. For what is highly esteemed among men is an abomination in the sight of God.

[16]"The Law and the Prophets stood until John. Since then the good news of the kingdom of God is being proclaimed, and everyone [tries to] force his way into it. [17]But it is easier for heaven and earth to pass away than for one dot of the law to be nullified.

Divorce and Remarriage

[18]"Every man who divorces his wife and marries another commits adultery, and whoever marries a woman divorced from her husband commits adultery.

The Rich Man and Lazarus

[19]"Now, a certain rich man who was clothed in purple and fine linen feasted sumptuously every day. [20]A poor beggar named Lazarus, covered with sores, was laid at his gate.[21]He longed to be fed with what fell from the rich man's table. Even the dogs came and licked his sores. [22]The poor man died and was carried off by the angels to Abraham's side. The rich man also died and was buried. [23]In Hades, being in torment, he lifted up his eyes and saw Abraham far off and Lazarus at his side. [24] he called out, 'Father Abraham, have mercy on me, and send Lazarus to

dip the tip of his finger in water and cool my tongue; for I am in anguish in these flames.' ²⁵But Abraham said, 'Child, remember that during your lifetime you received your good things, and Lazarus in like manner bad things. But now he is comforted here, and you are in agony. ²⁶Besides all this, a huge chasm has been fixed between you and us, in order that those who might want to pass from here to you cannot, and none may cross from there to us.'

²⁷He replied, 'Then I beg you, father, to send him to my father's house, ²⁸for I have five brothers, so that he might warn them, so that they might not come into this place of torment also.' ²⁹Abraham replied, 'They have Moses and the Prophets: let them heed them.' ³⁰He said, 'No, father Abraham, but if someone goes to them from the dead, they will repent.' ³¹He said to him, 'If they do not heed Moses and the Prophets, neither will they be convinced even if someone should rise from the dead.'"

Chapter 17

¹Jesus said to his disciples, "Stumbling blocks will surely come, but woe to the one through whom they come! ²It would be better for him if a millstone were hung around his neck and he were cast into the sea than that he should cause one of these little ones to sin. ³Guard yourselves! If your brother sins, rebuke him, and if he repents, forgive him. ⁴And if he sins against you seven times in a day, and returns to you seven times, saying, 'I repent,' you must forgive him."

Increase Our Faith

⁵The apostles said to the Lord, "Increase our faith!" ⁶The Lord replied, "If you had faith like a grain of mustard seed, you could say to this mulberry tree, 'Uproot yourself and plant yourself in the sea,' and it would obey you.

Unworthy Servants

⁷"Who among you who has a servant plowing or keeping sheep would say to him when he has come in from the field, 'Come at once and take your place at the table'? ⁸Rather, will he not say to him, 'Prepare supper for me, and dress properly, and serve me while I eat and drink, and afterward you will eat and drink'? ⁹Does he thank the servant because he did what he was commanded to do? ¹⁰So, once you have done all that you were commanded, you also should say, 'We are unworthy servants; we have only done what we were assigned to do.'"

Cleansing Ten Lepers

¹¹Now it so happened that on the way to Jerusalem Jesus was passing along between Samaria and Galilee. ¹²As he entered a village, he was met by ten lepers,

who stood at a distance [13]and lifted up their voices, crying out, "Jesus, Master, have mercy on us." [14]When he saw them he said to them, "Go and show yourselves to the priests." As they went they were cleansed. [15]Then one of them, when he saw that he was healed, turned back, praising God with a loud voice, [16]and he fell on his face at Jesus' feet, giving him thanks. Now he was a Samaritan. [17]Then Jesus asked, "Were not ten cleansed? Where are the other nine? [18]Was no one found to return and give praise to God except this foreigner?" [19]And he said to him, "Stand up and go on your way. Your faith has made you well."

The Coming of the Kingdom

[20]Once when Jesus was asked by the Pharisees when the kingdom of God would come, he answered them, "The kingdom of God is not coming with signs that can be observed, [21]nor will anyone be able to say, 'Look, it's here—or, over there!' for indeed, the kingdom of God is in the midst of you." [22]Then he said to the disciples, "The days are coming when you will long to see one of the days of the Son of Man, and you will not see it. [23]They will say to you, 'Look there!' or 'Look here!' Do not go out or follow them. [24]For as the lightning flashes and lights up the sky from one part to another, so will the Son of Man be in his day. [25]But he must first suffer many things and be rejected by this generation.

[26]Just as it was in the days of Noah, so it will be in the days of the Son of Man. [27]They were eating and drinking and marrying and being given in marriage, until the day when Noah entered the ark, and the flood came and destroyed them all. [28]Likewise, just as it was in the days of Lot: they were eating and drinking, buying and selling, planting and building, [29]but on the day when Lot withdrew from Sodom, fire and sulfur rained down from heaven and destroyed them all. [30]So will it be on the day when the Son of Man is revealed. [31]On that day, let the one who is on the housetop, with his goods in the house, not go down to take them away, and likewise let the one who is in the field not turn back. [32]Remember Lot's wife. [33]Whoever seeks to preserve his life will lose it, but whoever loses his life will keep it. [34]I tell you, in that night there will be two in one bed; one will be taken and the other left. [35]There will be two women grinding meal together; one will be taken and the other left." [36]Two men will working in the field; one will be taken and the other left." [37]They asked of him, "Where, Lord?" he said to them, "Where the [dead] body lies, there will the vultures gather."

Chapter 18

The Parable of the Persistent Widow

¹Then Jesus told them a parable showing their need to pray at all times and to not lose heart. ²He said, "In a certain city was a judge who neither feared God nor respected man. ³Now a widow in that city kept coming to him and saying, 'Give me justice against my adversary.' ⁴For a while he refused, but eventually he said to himself, 'Though I neither fear God nor respect man, ⁵yet because this widow keeps bothering me, I will grant her justice, so that she will not wear me out by her continual coming.'" ⁶The Lord said, "Hear what the unrighteous judge says. ⁷And will not God grant justice to his chosen ones, who cry to him day and night? Will he delay long over them? ⁸I tell you, he will grant justice to them swiftly. Nonetheless, when the Son of Man comes, will he find faith on earth?"

The Pharisee and the Tax Collector

⁹He also told this parable to some who trusted that they were righteous in themselves, and yet treated others with disdain: ¹⁰"Two men, one a Pharisee and the other a tax collector, went up into the temple to pray. ¹¹The Pharisee, standing by himself, prayed thus: 'God, I thank you that I am not like other men—extortioners, rogues, adulterers—or even like this tax collector. ¹²I fast twice a week; I give tithes of all that I receive.' ¹³But the tax collector, standing far off, would not even lift up his eyes to heaven, but beat his breast, saying, 'God, be merciful to me, a sinner!' ¹⁴I tell you, this man, rather than other, went down to his house justified. For everyone who exalts himself will be humbled, but the one who humbles himself will be exalted."

Let the Children Come to Me

¹⁵Now some people were even bringing babies to him so that he might touch them. When the disciples saw it, they rebuked them. ¹⁶But Jesus summoned them and said, "Allow the children to come to me, and do not hinder them, for to such belongs the kingdom of God. ¹⁷Truly, I say to you, whoever does not accept the kingdom of God like a child shall not enter into it."

The Rich Ruler

¹⁸A certain ruler asked him, "Good Teacher, what must I do to inherit eternal life?" ¹⁹Jesus said to him, "If [it's true that] no one is good except God alone, why do you call *me* good? ²⁰You know the commandments: 'You shall not commit adultery, You shall not murder, You shall not steal, You shall not bear false wit-

ness, Honor your father and mother.'" ^{21}He replied, "from the time of my youth I have kept all of these." ^{22}When Jesus heard this, he said to him, "One thing yet remains to be done: Sell all that you own and distribute to the poor, and you will have treasure in heaven. And come, follow me." ^{23}But when he heard these things, he became quite sad, for he was extremely rich. ^{24}Jesus, seeing that he had become sad, said, "How difficult it is for those who have wealth to enter the kingdom of God! ^{25}For it is easier for a camel to go through the eye of a needle than for a rich person to enter the kingdom of God." ^{26}Those who heard it said, "Then who can be saved?" ^{27}But he said, "What is impossible with men is possible with God." ^{28}Then Peter said, "Look, we have left our homes and followed you." ^{29}And he said to them, "Truly, I tell you, there is no one who has left house or wife or brothers or parents or children, for the sake of the kingdom of God, ^{30}who will not receive much more in the present age, and eternal life in the age to come."

Jesus Foretells his Death a Third Time

^{31}Then taking the Twelve aside, he said to them, "You see, we are going up to Jerusalem, and then everything written by the prophets about the Son of Man will be accomplished. ^{32}For he will be handed over to the Gentiles and will be mocked and mistreated and spit on. ^{33}And having flogged him, they will kill him, and on the third day he will rise again." ^{34}But they understood none of these things; what he said was hidden from them, and they did not grasp what was said.

Jesus Heals a Blind Beggar

^{35}As he approached Jericho, a blind man was sitting by the roadside begging. ^{36}And hearing a crowd going by, he inquired what was happening. ^{37}They told him, "Jesus of Nazareth is passing by." ^{38}He cried out, "Jesus, Son of David, have mercy on me!" ^{39}Those who were in front rebuked him, telling him to be silent. But he cried out all the more, "Son of David, have mercy on me!" ^{40}Jesus stopped and ordered him to be brought to him. And when he came near, he asked him, ^{41}"What do you want me to do for you?" he said, "Lord, let me see again." ^{42}Jesus said to him, "Then see again; your faith has made you well." ^{43}Immediately he could see again, and he followed him, glorifying God. When they saw it, all the people gave praise to God.

Chapter 19

Zacchaeus Receives the Lord

^{1}And having entered it, he was passing through Jericho. ^{2}A man was there by the name of Zacchaeus. He was a chief tax-collector, and he was rich. ^{3}He wanted to see who Jesus was, but on account of the crowd he was not able to, because he was short. [4]So, having run ahead of the crowd, he climbed up into a sycamore tree so that he might be able to see him, for he was about to pass along that way. [5]And as he came to the place, Jesus, looking up, said to him, "Zacchaeus, hurry down, for today I must stay at your house." [6]And hurrying, he came down and welcomed him rejoicing. [7]Now seeing this, all the people murmured, "He has gone to be the guest of a man who is a sinner."

[8]Standing up, Zacchaeus said to the Lord, "Lord, look—I shall give half of my possessions to the poor. And if I have defrauded anyone of anything, I shall restore four times as much." [9]Jesus said to him, "Today salvation has come to this house, since he is a son of Abraham, [10]for the Son of Man came to seek and save the lost."

The Parable of the Ten Minas

[11]As they heard this, he went on to tell them a parable, because he was near Jerusalem, and because they thought that the kingdom of God was about to appear. [12]Then he said, "A certain nobleman set out for a distant land to receive a kingdom for himself and then return. [13]Calling ten of his servants, he gave them each a mina, and said to them, 'Conduct business until I return.' [14]But his citizens hated him and sent a delegation to follow after him saying, 'We do not want this man to rule over us.'

[15]And it came to pass that he received the kingdom, and when he returned he commanded that the servants to whom he had given money be brought to him, so that he could determine what they had gained through business. [16]The first one came before him, saying, 'Lord, your mina has yielded ten minas more.' [17]And he said to him, 'Well done, good servant. Because you have been faithful with a little, you shall be in charge of ten cities.'

[18]And the second one came, saying, 'Lord, your mina has yielded five minas.' [19]And he said to him, 'And you shall be over five cities.'

[20]Then another one came, saying, 'Lord, here is your mina, which I kept hidden in a handkerchief [21]for I feared you, because you are a demanding man. You draw out what you have not put in and reap what you have not sown.' [22]He said to him, 'I condemn you with your own words, you wicked servant. So...you knew that I am a demanding man who draws out what I did not put in, and reaps what I didn't sow? [23]Then why didn't you put my money in the bank, and then on my return I might have collected it with interest?' [24]And he said to those who stood nearby, 'Take the mina away from him and give it to the one who has the ten minas." [25]And they said to him, 'Lord, he already has ten minas.' [26]I tell you that

127

more will given to everyone who has, but from the one who does not have, even what he does have shall be taken away. [27]But now, as for my enemies who did not want me to rule over them, bring them here and slay them in my presence.'"

Jesus Enters Jerusalem in Triumph

[28]And when he had said these things, he went on ahead, going up to Jerusalem. [29]When he approached Bethphage and Bethany, at the mount called Olivet, he sent two of the disciples, saying, [30]"Go into the town in front of you. On entering it you will find a colt tied up, that no one has ridden on yet. Untie it and bring it here. [31]If anyone should ask you, 'Why are you untying it?' you are to tell them, "the Lord has need of it." [32]So then the ones who were sent went away and found it just as he had told them. [33]And as they untied the colt, its owners asked them, "Why are you untying it?" [34]And they replied, "The Lord has need of it." [35]And they brought it to Jesus, and casting their garments on the colt, they placed Jesus on it. [36]And as he rode along, they spread their garments on the road. [37]As he was approaching, already on the way down the Mount of Olives, the whole crowd of his disciples started to rejoice and praise God with a loud voice for all the powerful works that they had seen, [38]saying, "Blessed is he who comes in the name of the Lord! Peace in heaven and glory in the highest." [39]And some of the Pharisees in the crowd said to him, "Teacher, rebuke your disciples." [40]He responded, "I tell you, if they were to remain silent, the stones would cry out."

Jesus Weeps Over Jerusalem

[41]And when he approached and saw the city, he wept over it, [42]saying, "O would that you, even you, would have recognized today those things that make for peace. But now they are hidden from your eyes. [43]For the time shall come on you, when your enemies will raise up a barricade around you, and surround you, and press you in on all sides, [44]and tear you down to the ground, you and your children within you. And they shall not leave one stone on top of another in you—[all] because you did not recognize the time of your visitation.

Jesus Cleanses the Temple

[45]Then he entered the temple and started to drive out the sellers, [46]saying to them, "The scripture says, 'My house shall be a house of prayer', but you have made it a den of thieves." [47]And then he taught in the temple daily. The chief priests and the scribes and the leaders of the people looked for a way to kill him, but they could not find anything that they could do, because the people were listening attentively to his words.

Chapter 20

Authority of Jesus Challenged

[1]It came to pass that one day as Jesus was in the temple teaching the people and preaching the gospel, the chief priests and the scribes, along with the elders, came up [2]to him and said, "Tell us by what authority you do these things, or at least, who gave you this authority." [3]He answered them, "I will ask you a question as well. So, tell me, [4]was the baptism of John from heaven or from man?" [5]At this, they deliberated among themselves, saying, "If we say 'From heaven,' he will ask, 'Why did you not believe him?' [6]But, if we say, 'From man,' all the people will stone us, for they are convinced that John was a prophet." [7]So, they answered that they did not know its source. [8]So Jesus responded to them, "Then neither will I tell you by what authority I do these things."

Parable of the Wicked Tenants

[9]And then he started telling the people this parable: "A man planted a vineyard and leased it to tenants and left town for a long time. [10]When the right time came he sent a servant to the tenants so that they would give him some of the fruit of the vineyard. But the tenants beat him and sent him away empty-handed. [11]Next he sent another servant; they also beat and abused him and sent him away empty-handed. [12]Then he sent yet a third one whom they also injured and threw out. [13]Then the master of the vineyard said, 'What shall I do? I will send my beloved son; perhaps they will show respect for him.' [14]But on seeing him, the tenants said to themselves, 'This is the heir. Let's kill him so that the inheritance might be ours.' [15]And they threw him out of the vineyard and killed him. Now how will the master of the vineyard deal with them? [16]He will come and destroy those tenants and give the vineyard to others." Hearing this, they said, "May it never happen!" [17]But he looked right at them and asked, "Then, what does this scripture mean: 'The stone rejected by the builders has become the cornerstone'? [18]Everyone who falls on that stone will be shattered, and when it falls on top of someone, it will crush him."

Paying Taxes to Caesar

[19]At that time the scribes and chief priests searched for a way to lay hands on him, since they did perceive that he had told that parable about them, but they feared the people. [20]So, they watched him, and they sent spies who feigned sincerity in order to catch him in something that he said, so that they could hand him over to the authority and jurisdiction of the governor. [21]Then they asked him, "Teacher, we

129

know that you speak and teach correctly, and are not partial to any, but teach the way of God in a truthful way. [22]Is it lawful for us to pay taxes to Caesar, or not?"

[23]But he perceived their guile and said to them, [24]"Show me a denarius. Whose image and inscription does it bear?" They responded, "Caesar's." [25]He said to them, "Then render to Caesar the things that are Caesar's, and to God the things that are God's." [26]So they were not able to use his words to trap him in the presence of the people, but instead they fell silent, [stunned and] wondering about his reply.

A Debate About the Resurrection

[27]There came to him some Sadducees, the ones who deny that there is a resurrection from the dead, and they asked him, [28]"Teacher, Moses wrote for us that if a man's brother should die, having a wife but no children, that man must marry the widow and raise up offspring for the sake of his [dead] brother. [29]Now, there were seven brothers. The first one took a wife and died childless. [30]And the second brother and [31]the third one each took her as wife, and all seven of them did likewise, but left no children and died. [32]Finally the woman died, too. [33]That being the case, whose wife will the woman be in the resurrection? For she had been the wife of seven men."

[34]Jesus answered them, "The children of this present age marry and are given in marriage, [35]but those who are judged to be worthy of having a place in that age [to come] and to the resurrection from the dead neither marry nor are given in marriage, [36]for they cannot die anymore, because they are like angels and are children of God, being children of the resurrection. [37]In the passage about the bush, even Moses showed the fact that the dead are raised: in it he speaks of the Lord as the God of Abraham and the God of Isaac and the God of Jacob. [38]Now he is not the God of the dead, but of the living, for to him, all of them are alive." [39]Then some of the scribes answered, "Teacher, you have spoken well," [40]because they no longer dared to ask him any more questions.

[41]Then he said to them, "How can they say that the Christ is David's son? [42]For David himself says in the book of the Psalms: 'The Lord said unto my Lord, "Sit at my right hand [43]until I make your enemies your footstool".' [44]David thus calls him Lord, so how can he be his son?"

Beware of the Scribes

[45]Then, as all the people were listening, he said to the disciples, [46]"Beware of the scribes, who enjoy walking around in long robes, and love respectful greetings in the marketplaces, and the most prominent seats in the synagogues, and places of

honor at banquets. [47]They cheat widows out of their houses and say long prayers for the sake of appearance. They will receive the greater condemnation."

Chapter 21

The Widow's Offering

[1]Jesus looked up and saw the rich putting their gifts into the offering box, [2]and he watched a poor widow put in two small copper coins. [3]He said, "Truly, I tell you, this poor widow has put in more than all of them. [4]For they all contributed out of their abundance, but whereas out of her poverty she put in all she had to live on."

Jesus Foretells Times of Great Destruction

[5]While some were speaking about the temple–how it was adorned with noble stones and things dedicated to God–he said, [6]"As for these things that you see, the days will come when not a single stone here will be left on top of another; they will all be hurled down." [7]They asked him, "Teacher, when will these things be, and what sign will indicate when these things are about to happen?" [8]And he replied, "Make sure that you are not led astray. For many will come in my name, saying, 'I am he!' and, 'The time is near!' Do not follow them.

[9]When you hear of wars and political upheavals, do not be terrified, for these things must take place first, however the end will not come immediately."

[10]Then he said to them, "Nation will rise against nation, and kingdom against kingdom. [11]There will be massive earthquakes, and famines and pestilences in various places, and there will be terrors and great signs in the sky. [12]But before all this happens, they will grab you and persecute you, delivering you up to the synagogues and prisons, and you will be brought in front of kings and governors for the sake of my name, [13]as your opportunity to testify. [14]So, settle your hearts now on not preparing in advance how to answer, [15]for I will give you the words, and the wisdom that none of your adversaries will be able to withstand or contradict. [16]You will be betrayed even by parents and brothers and relatives and friends, and they will put some of you to death. [17]You will be hated by all for my name's sake. [18]But not a hair of your head will perish. [19]You will win your souls by your endurance.

[20]"When you see Jerusalem surrounded by armies, you will know that its destruction is at hand. [21]Then let those who are in Judea flee to the mountains, and let those who are inside the city escape, and do not allow those who are out in the country to enter it, [22]for these are days of vengeance, to fulfill all that is written. [23]What woe for pregnant women and those who are nursing infants in those days! For there will be great distress on the earth and wrath against this people. [24]They

will fall by the edge of the sword and be taken away captive among all nations, and the Gentiles will trample Jerusalem underfoot, until the age of the Gentiles has been completed.

The Coming of the Son of Man

[25]"There will be portents in the sun and moon and stars, while on the earth the nations will be in distress, bewildered by the roaring of the sea and the waves. [26]People will faint with fear and with foreboding of what is coming on the world, for the powers of the heavens will be shaken. [27]Then they will see the Son of Man coming in a cloud with power and great glory. [28]Now when these things begin to take place, straighten up and raise your heads, because your redemption is drawing near."

The Lesson of the Fig Tree

[29]And he told them a parable: "Look at the fig tree—actually, all the trees. [30]As soon as the leaves come out, you can look for yourselves to know that the summer is already near. [31]So also, when you see these things taking place, you will know that the kingdom of God is near. [32]Truly, I say to you, this generation will not pass away until all has taken place. [33]Heaven and earth will pass away, but my words will not pass away.

Watch Yourselves

[34]"But take care that your hearts not become weighed down with dissipation and drunkenness and the anxieties of this life, such that that Day sneaks up on you suddenly like a trap. [35]For it will come on all who dwell on the face of the whole earth. [36]But be vigilant at all times, praying that you may have strength to escape all these things that are going to take place, and to stand before the Son of Man."

[37]He was teaching in the temple by day, but by night he went out and lodged on the mount called Olivet. [38]And all the people rose early in the morning to go listen to him in the temple.

Chapter 22

The Plot to Kill Jesus

[1]Now the Feast of Unleavened Bread, which is called the Passover, drew near, [2]and the chief priests and the scribes were searching for a way to have [Jesus] put to death because they feared the people. [3]Then Satan entered into Judas called Iscariot, who was numbered among the Twelve. [4]He went away and conferred with

the chief priests and officers about how he might betray him to them. ⁵They were delighted and made an agreement to pay him money. ⁶So he consented and began looking for an opportunity to betray him to them in the absence of the crowds.

The Passover with the Disciples

⁷Then came the day of Unleavened Bread, the day when the Passover lamb had to be sacrificed. ⁸So Jesus sent Peter and John, saying, "Go and prepare the Passover for us, that we may eat it." ⁹They asked him, "Where do you want us to prepare it?" ¹⁰"Listen," he replied, "when you have entered the city, a man carrying a jar of water will meet you. Follow him into the house that he enters ¹¹and tell the owner of the house, 'The Teacher asks of you, where is the guest room, where I may eat the Passover with my disciples?' ¹²He will show you a large furnished upper room; prepare it there." ¹³So, they went and found things just as he had told them, and they prepared the Passover meal.

The Lord's Supper

¹⁴When the hour came, he took his place at the table, and the apostles were with him. ¹⁵And, he said to them, "I have greatly longed to eat this Passover with you before I suffer. ¹⁶For I tell you I will not eat it again until it is fulfilled in the kingdom of God." ¹⁷And he took a cup, and when he had given thanks he said, "Take this, and portion it out among yourselves. ¹⁸For I tell you that from now on I will not drink of the fruit of the vine until the kingdom of God comes." ¹⁹Then he took bread, and when he had given thanks, he broke it and gave it to them, saying, "This is my body, which is given for you. Do this in remembrance of me." ²⁰And likewise he took the cup after they had eaten, saying, "This cup that is poured out for you is the new covenant in my blood. ²¹But take notice–the hand of the one who is to betray me is on the table with me. ²²For as it has been determined, so goes the Son of Man, but woe to that man who betrays him!" ²³Then they began to question among themselves as to which one of them it could be who was going to do this.

Who Is the Greatest?

²⁴A dispute also arose among them, as to which of them was to be regarded as the greatest. ²⁵So he said to them, "The kings of the Gentiles lord their power over them, and those in authority over them are called benefactors. ²⁶But not so with you. Rather, let the greatest among you become as the youngest, and the leader a servant. ²⁷For who is the greater—one who is seated at the table or the one who serves? Is it not the one who is seated at the table? But I am among you as the one who serves.

28"You are the ones who have stayed with me in my trials, 29and I confer a kingdom to you, as my Father conferred to me, 30that you may eat and drink at my table in my kingdom and sit on thrones judging the twelve tribes of Israel.

Jesus Foretells Peter's Denial

31"Simon, Simon, listen, Satan has been granted his demand to sift you like wheat, 32but I have prayed for you that your faith may not fail. And when you have returned again, strengthen your brothers." 33He replied, "Lord, I am ready to go with you both to prison and to death." 34But Jesus answered, "I tell you, Peter, the cock will not crow today until you have denied that you know me three times."

Scripture Must Be Fulfilled in Jesus

35He said to them, "When I sent you out with no moneybag or knapsack or sandals, did you lack anything?" They said, "Nothing." 36He said to them, "But now let the one who has a moneybag take it, and likewise a knapsack. And let the one who has no sword sell his cloak and buy one. 37For I tell you that this scripture must be fulfilled in me: 'And he was counted among the criminals.' For what is written about me has its fulfillment." 38And they replied, "Look, Lord, here are two swords." And he told them, "That is enough."

Jesus Prays on the Mount of Olives

39He came out and went, as was his habit, to the Mount of Olives, and the disciples followed him. 40When he reached the place, he said to them, "Pray that you may not fall into temptation." 41He withdrew about a stone's throw away from them, and knelt down and prayed, 42saying, "Father, if you are willing, remove this cup from me. Nevertheless, not my will, but yours, be done." 43An angel appeared to him from heaven, strengthening him. 44And being in an agony he prayed more earnestly, and his sweat became like great drops of blood falling down to the ground. 45When he stood up from praying, he came to the disciples and found them sleeping, worn out with grief, 46and he said to them, "Why are you sleeping? Get up and pray that you may not fall into temptation."

Betrayal and Arrest of Jesus

47While he was still speaking, there came a crowd, with the man called Judas, one of the Twelve, leading them. He approached Jesus to kiss him, 48but Jesus said to him, "Judas, would you betray the Son of Man with a kiss?" 49When those who were around him saw what would follow, they asked, "Lord, should we strike with the sword?" 50Then one of them struck the servant of the high priest, cutting off his right ear. [51]But Jesus said, "No more of this!" and touching his ear, he healed him. [52]Then Jesus said to the chief priests and officers of the temple and elders, who had come out to seize him, "Have you come out with swords and clubs as if I were a robber? [53]When I was with you day after day in the temple, you did not lay hands on me. But then, this is your moment: the power of darkness!"

Peter Denies Jesus

[54]Then they seized him and led him away, bringing him into the high priest's house, and Peter was following at a distance, [55]and when they had kindled a fire in the middle of the courtyard and were sitting down together, Peter sat down among them. [56]Then a servant girl, seeing him as he sat in the light and studying him closely, said, "This man was with him, too." [57]But he denied it, saying, "Woman, I do *not* know him." [58]A little later someone else saw him and said, "You are one of them, also." But Peter said, "Man, I am not." [59]Then about an hour later still another one insisted, saying, "Surely this man was with him, too, because he is a Galilean." [60]But Peter said, "Man, I do *not* know what you are talking about." Right at that moment, while he was still speaking, the cock crowed. [61]And turning, the Lord looked at Peter, and Peter remembered the Lord's words, how he had said to him, "Before the cock crows today, you will deny me three times." [62]Then he went out and wept bitterly.

Jesus Is Mocked

[63]Now the men who were holding Jesus in custody were mocking him and beating him. [64]They also blindfolded him and kept asking him, "Prophesy! Who is it that struck you?" [65]And they hurled many other blasphemous insults at him.

Jesus Before the Council

[66]When the dawn came, the council of the elders of the people—both chief priests and scribes—assembled. And they led him away to their council, and they said, [67]"If you [truly] are the Christ, tell us so." But he said to them, "If I tell you, you will not believe, [68]and if I ask you a question, you will not answer. [69]But from now on the Son of Man shall be seated at the right hand of the power of God." [70]So they all asked, "Then, are you the Son of God?" he said to them, "You say that I am." [71]Then they said, "What further testimony do we need? We have heard it ourselves from his own lips."

Chapter 23

Jesus Before Pilate and Herod

[1]Then the whole group of them arose and took Jesus to stand before Pilate. [2]They began making accusations about him, saying, "We found this man leading our nation astray and forbidding us to pay taxes to Caesar, and saying that he himself is Christ, a king." [3]Pilate questioned him, "Are you the King of the Jews?" And he answered him, "You have said so." [4]Then Pilate said to the chief priests and the crowds, "I find no guilt in this man." [5]But they were insistent, saying, "With his teaching he stirs up the people throughout all Judea, from Galilee even to this place."

[6]When Pilate heard "Galilee", he asked whether the man was a Galilean. [7]And having learned that he fell under Herod's jurisdiction, he sent him over to Herod, who was himself in Jerusalem at that time. [8]Herod was excited when he saw Jesus, for he had long desired to see him, because he had been hearing about him, and he was hoping to witness some miraculous sign performed by him. [9]So he questioned him at some length, but he made no answer. [10]The chief priests and the scribes stood by, vehemently accusing him. [11]Along with his soldiers, Herod treated him with contempt and mocked him. Then, clothing him in an elegant robe, he sent him back to Pilate. [12]So, Herod and Pilate became friends with each other that very day, for before this they had been enemies with each other.

[13]Pilate then summoned together the chief priests and the leaders and the people [14]and said to them, "You brought me this man as one who was leading the people astray. After examining him in your presence, indeed I did not find this man guilty of any of your charges against him. [15]Neither has Herod, for he sent him back to us. Listen, nothing worthy of death has been done by him. [16]So, I will just have him flogged and release him."

Jesus is Crucified

[17]Now, he was under obligation to release one prisoner to them at the festival. [18]But they all cried out in unison, "Away with this man, and release Barabbas to us." [19](He had been thrown into prison for an insurrection started in the city and for murder.) [20]Wanting to release Jesus [instead], Pilate addressed them again, [21]but they kept on shouting, "Crucify, crucify him!" [22]A third time he said to them, "What wrongdoing, then, has *this* one committed? I have found no guilt deserving death in him. I will therefore have him flogged and release him." [23]But they were insistent, demanding with loud cries that he should be crucified, and the voices of them and of the chief priests prevailed. [24]So Pilate pronounced that

their demand should be granted. ²⁵He released the man who had been thrown into prison for insurrection and murder, the one they asked for, but he handed Jesus over to their will.

²⁶And as they led him away, they seized one Simon of Cyrene, who was coming in from the country, and laid the cross on him, and made him carry it behind Jesus. ²⁷And there followed him a great crowd of the people and of women who were wailing and lamenting for him. ²⁸But Jesus turned to them and said, "Daughters of Jerusalem, do not weep for me, but weep for yourselves and for your children. ²⁹For you see, the days are coming when they will say, 'Blessed are the barren and the wombs that never bore and the breasts that never nursed!' ³⁰Then they will start saying to the mountains, 'Fall on us,' and to the hills, 'Cover us.' ³¹For if they do these things when the wood is green, what will become of them when it is dry?"

³²Two others, who were criminals, were led away to be put to death with him. ³³When they came to the place that is called The Skull, they crucified him there with the criminals, one on his right and one on his left. ³⁴Jesus said, "Father, forgive them, for they do not know what they are doing." Meanwhile they cast lots to divide his garments. ³⁵And the people stood by watching, but the leaders derided him, saying, "He saved others; let him save himself, if he is the Christ of God, his Chosen One!" ³⁶The soldiers also mocked him, coming up and offering him sour wine ³⁷and saying, "If you are the King of the Jews, save yourself!" ³⁸Also, an inscription was placed above him, written in Greek, Latin, and Hebrew script:

THIS IS THE KING OF THE JEWS.

³⁹One of the criminals who were hanged taunted him, saying, "Aren't you the Christ? Save yourself and us!" ⁴⁰But the other rebuked him, saying, "Don't you fear God, since you are under the same [death] sentence? ⁴¹Now for us this really is justice because we are receiving the penalty for what we did. But this man has done nothing wrong." ⁴²Then he said, "Jesus, remember me when you come into your kingdom." ⁴³He replied, "Truly, I say to you: today you will be with me in Paradise."

Jesus Dies and is Buried

⁴⁴It was now about noon, and darkness came over the whole land until three in the afternoon, ⁴⁵as the light of the sun was blocked. The curtain of the temple was torn in two. ⁴⁶Then Jesus, calling out with a loud voice, said, "Father, into your hands I commit my spirit!" Having said this, he breathed his last. ⁴⁷Now when the centurion saw what had happened, he gave God glory, declaring, "Certainly this

man was innocent!" [48]When all the crowds that had assembled for this spectacle saw what had taken place, they returned home beating their breasts. [49]But all those who knew him and the women who had followed him from Galilee stood at a distance observing these things.

[50]Now then, there came a man named Joseph, from the town of Arimathea in Judea. He was a member of the council, a good and righteous man, [51]who had not consented to their decision and action, and he was watching expectantly for the kingdom of God. [52]This man went to Pilate and requested the body of Jesus. [53]Then he took it down and wrapped it in a linen shroud, and he laid him in a tomb cut into rock, where no one had ever been laid. [54]It was the day of Preparation, and the Sabbath was beginning. [55]Now the women who had come with him from Galilee followed along and saw the tomb and how his body was laid. [56]Then they returned and prepared spices and ointments. They rested on the Sabbath Day in obedience to the commandment.

Chapter 24

The Resurrection

[1]But at early dawn on the first day of the week, they returned to the tomb, taking the spices they had prepared. [2]They found the stone rolled away from the tomb, [3]but when they went in they did not find the body of the Lord Jesus. [4]It so happened that while they were perplexed about this, you see, two men in dazzling apparel suddenly appeared beside them. [5]They were frightened and bowed their faces to the ground, but the men said to them, "Why do you seek the living among the dead? [6]He is not here but has risen. Remember how, while he was still in Galilee, he told you [7]that the Son of Man must be delivered into the hands of sinful men and be crucified and rise again on the third day." [8]Then they remembered his words, [9]and once they had returned from the tomb they told all these things to the eleven and to all the rest. [10]Now it was Mary Magdalene and Joanna and Mary the mother of James and the other women with them who told these things to the apostles, [11]but these words seemed like a silly fantasy to them, and they did not believe them. [12]Still, Peter did get up and run to the tomb. Stooping and looking in, he saw the linen cloths by themselves, and he went home wondering about what had happened.

On the Road to Emmaus

[13]That very day two of them were going to a village named Emmaus, located about seven miles from Jerusalem, [14]and they were talking with each other about all these things that had just taken place. [15]And it came to pass that while they

were talking and reasoning things out together, Jesus himself came up next to them and joined them. ¹⁶But their eyes were prevented from recognizing him.

¹⁷He said to them, "What are you discussing with each other as you walk along?" They stopped still, looking downcast. ¹⁸Then one of them, named Cleopas, answered him, "Are you the only visitor to Jerusalem who does not know the things that have happened there these past few days?" ¹⁹He replied to them, "What things?" And they said to him, "Things related to Jesus of Nazareth, who was a prophet mighty in deed and word before God and all the people, ²⁰and how our chief priests and leaders delivered him up to be condemned to death and crucified him. ²¹But we had hoped that he was the one to redeem Israel. Yes, and besides all this, now it is the third day since these things occurred. ²²What's more, some of the women among us have amazed us. Early in the morning they were at the tomb. ²³And when they did not find his body, they came back saying that they had even seen a vision of angels, who said that he was alive. ²⁴Some of those who were with us went to the tomb and found it just as the women had said, but they did not see him." ²⁵Then he said to them, "O how foolish you are, and so slow of heart to believe all that the prophets have spoken! ²⁶Was it not necessary that the Christ should suffer these things and enter into his glory?" ²⁷And he began with Moses and all the Prophets, and he interpreted the things concerning himself in all the scriptures to them.

²⁸As they approached the village that they were going to, he acted as if he were going farther. ²⁹But they pressed him, saying, "Stay with us, for it is almost evening and the day is now nearly over." So, he went in to stay with them. ³⁰When he was at table with them, he took the bread and blessed and broke it and gave it to them. ³¹Then their eyes were opened, and they recognized him. Then he vanished from their sight. ³²They said to each other, "Did not our hearts burn within us while he talked to us on the road, when he was opening the scriptures to us?" ³³So they got up immediately and returned to Jerusalem. They found the eleven and those who were with them gathered together, ³⁴saying, "The Lord has risen indeed, and has appeared to Simon!" ³⁵Then they related what had happened on the road, and how they recognized him in the breaking of the bread.

Jesus Appears to his Disciples

³⁶As they were talking about these things, Jesus himself stood in their midst and said to them, "Peace to you!" ³⁷But they were startled and fearful and thought they were seeing a ghost. ³⁸He said to them, "Why are you troubled, and why are doubts growing in your hearts? ³⁹Look at my hands and my feet, that I myself am He. Touch me and see. For a ghost does not have flesh and bones as you can

see that I have." ⁴⁰And when he had said this, he showed them his hands and his feet. ⁴¹While they were still incredulous in their joy and were marveling, he asked them, "Do you have anything here to eat?" ⁴²They gave him a piece of broiled fish, ⁴³and he took it and ate it right in front of them.

⁴⁴Then he said to them, "These are my words, which I spoke to you while I was still with you, that everything written about me in the law of Moses and the Prophets and the Psalms must be fulfilled." ⁴⁵Then he opened up their minds to fully comprehend the scriptures. ⁴⁶And said to them, "Thus it is written: that the Christ must suffer and on the third day rise from the dead, ⁴⁷and that repentance and forgiveness of sins is to be proclaimed in his name to all nations, starting from Jerusalem. ⁴⁸You are witnesses of these things. ⁴⁹Take notice: I am sending the promise of my Father over you. But you are to remain in the city until you have been clothed with power from on high."

The Ascension

⁵⁰Then he led them out as far as Bethany, and lifting up his hands, he blessed them. ⁵¹And it happened that while he was blessing them, he parted from them and was carried up into heaven. ⁵²And they worshiped him and then they returned to Jerusalem jubilantly, ⁵³and then they were constantly in the temple praising and blessing God.

Chapter 1

The Word Comes into the World

[1]In the beginning the Word already existed, and the Word was in union with God, and the Word was God. [2]In the beginning he existed with God. [3]All things were made through him, and not a thing was made without him. [4]What has been made in him was life, and the life was the light of men. [5]The light shines in the darkness, and the darkness has never engulfed it.

[6]A man named John was sent from God. [7]He came as a testimony, to bear witness to the light, that all might believe through him. [8]He himself was not the light, but came to bear witness to the light, [9]the true light that enlightens every man, which was coming into the world. [10]He was in the world, and the world was made through him, and yet the world did not recognize him. [11]He came to his own people, yet his own people did not accept him. [12]However, he extended the right to become children but of God to all the people who *did* accept him and believe in his name, [13]and were [thereby] born—not from a bloodline, nor by human will, nor because of the will of a man—but of God.

[14]And the Word became human and dwelled among us, full of grace and truth. We have witnessed his glory, glory as of the only Son from the Father. [15](John bore witness to him by exclaiming, "This was the one about whom I said, 'He who comes after me is greater than I, for he existed before me.'")

[16]And out of his abundance we have all received grace after grace. [17]For the law was given through Moses, but grace and truth came through Jesus Christ. [18]No one has ever seen God. It was the only Son, who is at the Father's side, who has made him known.

The Testimony of John the Baptist

[19]Now this is the testimony of John:

When the Jews sent priests and Levites from Jerusalem to ask him, "Who are you?" [20]he confessed (he did not deny, but confessed), "I am *not* the Christ." [21]And they asked him, "Well then, are you Elijah?" he said, "I am not." "Are you the prophet?" And he answered, "No." [22]So, then they said to him, "Who are you?

Let us have an answer for those who sent us. What do you say about yourself?" [23]He said, "I am the voice of one crying in the wilderness, 'Lay out a straight avenue for the Lord,' as the prophet Isaiah said."

[24]Now having been sent from the Pharisees, [25]they asked him, "Then, if you are neither the Christ, nor Elijah, nor the prophet, why are you baptizing?" [26]John answered them, "I baptize with water, but there is someone among you whom you do not know, that is [27]the one who will come after me. I am not even worthy to untie the strap of his sandal." [28]These things happened in Bethany beyond the Jordan, where John was baptizing.

The Lamb of God

[29]The next day he saw Jesus coming toward him, and said, "Look—this is the Lamb of God, who takes away the sin of the world! [30]He who comes after me is greater than I [am], for he existed before me. [31]I myself did not know him, but I came baptizing with water for this reason: that he might be revealed to Israel." [32]And John bore witness, "I saw the Spirit descend as a dove from heaven, and it remained on him. [33]I myself did not know him; but he who sent me to baptize with water said to me, 'The one you see the Spirit descend on and remain on is the one who baptizes with the Holy Spirit.' [34]And I have seen and have borne witness that this is the Son of God."

[35]The next day John was standing with two of his disciples again. [36]And he looked at Jesus as he was walking and said, "Look—this is the Lamb of God!" [37]The two disciples heard him declare this, and they followed Jesus. [38]Jesus turned, and saw them following, and said to them, "What do you seek?" And they said to him, "Rabbi" (which means "teacher"), "where are you staying?" [39]He said to them, "Come and see." They came and saw where he was staying, and they stayed with him that day, for it was about four o'clock in the afternoon.

Calling Four of the Apostles

[40]One of the two who heard John speak, and followed him, was Andrew, Simon Peter's brother. [41]He found his own brother Simon first and said to him, "We have found the Messiah" (which means "Christ"). [42]He brought him to Jesus. Jesus looked at him, and said, "So you are Simon the son of John. You shall be called Cephas" (which means "Peter").

[43]The next day Jesus decided to go to Galilee, and he found Philip and said to him, "Follow me." [44]Now Philip was from Bethsaida, the city of Andrew and Peter. [45]Philip found Nathanael, and said to him, "We have found the One whom

Moses and also the prophets wrote about: Jesus of Nazareth, the son of Joseph." [46]Nathanael replied to him, "Can anything good come out of Nazareth?" Philip said to him, "Come and see." [47]Jesus saw Nathanael coming to him and commented about him: "Look, an Israelite indeed—there is no guile in him!" [48]Nathanael asked him, "How do you know me?" Jesus answered him, "I saw you before Philip called you, when you were under the fig tree." [49]Nathanael responded to him, "Rabbi, you are the Son of God! You are the King of Israel!" [50]Jesus answered him, "Do you believe [just] because I said to you, 'I saw you under the fig tree'? You shall see greater things than these!" [51]He also said to him, "Truly, truly, I say to you, you will see heaven opened, and the angels of God ascending and descending on the Son of Man."

Chapter 2

The Wedding at Cana in Galilee

[1]On the third day a wedding occurred at Cana in Galilee, and the mother of Jesus was there. [2]Jesus was invited to the wedding also, along with his disciples. [3]When the wine ran out, the mother of Jesus said to him, "They are out of wine." [4]And Jesus answered her, "Woman, what is that to you and me? My hour has not yet come." [5]His mother said to the servants, "Do whatever he tells you." [6]Now six stone jars were standing there, for the Jewish rites of purification, and each could hold twenty or thirty gallons. [7]Jesus said to them, "Fill the jars with water." And they filled them up to the brim. [8]He said to them, "Now draw some out and take it to the master of the banquet." So, they took it. [9]When the master of the banquet tasted the water that had become wine, and did not know where it came from (though the servants who had drawn the water knew), the master of the banquet called the bridegroom [10]and said to him, "Everybody serves the best wine first, and once the men have drunk freely, then the inferior wine. But you have kept the best wine until now." [11]Jesus did this, the first of his signs, at Cana in Galilee, thereby manifesting his glory, and his disciples believed in him.

Cleansing the Temple

[12]After this he went down to Capernaum, with his mother and his brothers and his disciples, and they stayed there for a few days. [13]The Passover of the Jews was imminent, and Jesus went up to Jerusalem. [14]In the temple he found those who were selling oxen and sheep and pigeons, and the moneychangers at their business. [15]And making a whip of cords, he drove them all, with the sheep and oxen, out of the temple, and he dumped out the coins of the moneychangers and overturned their tables. [16]And he told those who sold the pigeons, "Take these things

away; you shall not make my Father's house a house of business." [17]His disciples remembered that it was written, "Zeal for your house will consume me." [18]The Jews then said to him, "What sign can you show us for [the right] to do this?" [19]Jesus answered them, "Raze this temple, and I will raise it up again in three days." [20]Then the Jews said, "It has taken forty-six years to build this temple, and yet you would raise it up in three days?" [21]But he was referring to the temple of his body.

[22]Therefore, when he was raised from the dead, his disciples remembered that he had said this, and they believed the scripture and the word that Jesus had spoken. [23]Now when he was in Jerusalem at the Passover feast, many believed in his name when they saw the signs he was doing. [24]But Jesus did not entrust himself to them, because he knew all men, [25]and needed no one else's testimony on the nature of man, for he himself already knew what lies in a man's heart.

Chapter 3

The Need to be Born Again

[1]Now there was a man of the Pharisees, named Nicodemus, a ruler of the Jews. [2]This man came to Jesus by night and said to him, "Rabbi, we know that you are a teacher come from God, for no one can do these signs that you do, unless God is with him." [3]Jesus answered him, "Truly, truly, I say to you, unless one is born anew, he cannot see the kingdom of God." [4]Nicodemus asked him, "How can a man be born when he is old? Can he enter into his mother's womb a second time and be born?" [5]Jesus answered, "Truly, truly, I say to you, unless one is born of both water and the Spirit, he cannot enter the kingdom of God. [6]What is born of the flesh is flesh, and what is born of the Spirit is spirit. [7]Do not marvel that I told you, 'You must be born anew.' [8]The wind blows where it wills, and you hear the sound of it, but you do not know where it comes from or where it goes to. So it is with everyone who is born of the Spirit."

[9]Nicodemus asked him, "How can these things be?" [10]Jesus answered him, "Are you a teacher of Israel, and yet you fail to understand these things? [11]Truly, truly, I say to you, we speak of what we know, and bear witness to what we have seen, but you people do not accept our testimony. [12]If I have told you earthly things and you have not believed [them], how would you believe if I tell you heavenly things? [13]No one has ascended into heaven except the one who descended from heaven, the Son of Man. [14]And in the same way that Moses lifted up the serpent in the wilderness, so must the Son of Man be lifted up, [15]that whoever believes in him may have eternal life. [16]For God so loved the world that he gave his only Son, that whoever believes in him should not perish but have eternal life. [17]For God

did not send the Son into the world to condemn the world, but in order that the world might be saved through him. ¹⁸Whoever believes in him is not condemned, but whoever does not believe is condemned already because he has not believed in the name of the only Son of God. ¹⁹And this is the judgment, that the light has come into the world, and people loved darkness rather than light, because their deeds were evil. ²⁰For everyone who does wicked things hates the light, and does not come to the light, so that his deeds may not be exposed. ²¹But whoever does what is true comes to the light, that it may be clearly seen that it is in God that his deeds have been performed."

Christ Exalted by John

²²After this Jesus and his disciples went into the land of Judea, and he remained there with them and was baptizing. ²³John also was baptizing at Aenon near Salim because water was plentiful there, and people were coming and were being baptized ²⁴(for John had not been put in prison yet).

²⁵Now a discussion over purification arose among John's disciples and a Jew. ²⁶And they came to John, and said to him, "Rabbi, the one who was with you beyond the Jordan, the one you bore witness to—look, he is baptizing, and everyone is going to him." ²⁷John answered, "No one can receive anything except what is given to him from heaven. ²⁸You yourselves bear me witness that I said, 'I am not the Christ,' but I have been sent before him. ²⁹The one who holds the bride is the groom. The friend of the groom, who is standing by and hears him, rejoices greatly at the voice of the groom. Therefore, this joy of mine is now complete. ³⁰He must increase, but I must decrease."

³¹He who comes from above is above all. He who is of the earth belongs to the earth, and he talks about things of the earth. He who comes from heaven is above all. ³²He bears witness to what he has seen and heard, yet no one accepts his testimony. ³³But he who does accept his testimony certifies this: that God is true. ³⁴For the one God has sent speaks the words of God, for he gives the Spirit without limit. ³⁵The Father loves the Son and has given all things into his hand. ³⁶Whoever believes in the Son has eternal life. Whoever does not obey the Son shall not see life, but instead the wrath of God rests on him.

Chapter 4

The Samaritan Woman at the Well

¹Now when the Lord realized that the Pharisees had heard that Jesus was making and baptizing more disciples than John ²(although Jesus himself did not baptize,

only his disciples did), ³he left Judea and set out again for Galilee. ⁴Since he had to pass through Samaria, ⁵he came to a city of Samaria called Sychar, near the field that Jacob gave to his son Joseph. ⁶Jacob's well was there, and so Jesus, being weary from his journey, sat down beside the well. It was about noon.

⁷A woman of Samaria came to draw water, and Jesus said to her, "Give me a drink." ⁸(For his disciples had gone away into the city to buy food.) ⁹The Samaritan woman said to him, "How is it that you, a Jew, ask for a drink from me, a woman of Samaria?" (For Jews have no dealings with Samaritans.) ¹⁰Jesus answered her, "If you knew the gift of God, and who it is that is saying to you, 'Give me a drink,' you would have asked him, and he would have given you life-giving water." ¹¹The woman said to him, "Sir, you have nothing to draw water with, and the well is deep. Where do you get that life-giving water? ¹²Are you greater than our father Jacob, who gave us the well, and drank from it himself, along with his sons, and his livestock?" ¹³Jesus replied to her, "Everyone who drinks of this water will thirst again, ¹⁴but whoever drinks of the water that I shall give him will never thirst again. The water that I shall give him will become a spring of water in him, welling up to eternal life." ¹⁵The woman said to him, "Sir, give me this water, so that I might not get thirsty, nor have to come here to draw water."

¹⁶Jesus said to her, "Go, call your husband, and return here." ¹⁷The woman answered him, "I have no husband." Jesus said to her, "You are right in saying, 'I have no husband,' ¹⁸for you have had five husbands, and the man you have now is not your husband. You have told the truth." ¹⁹The woman said to him, "I perceive that you are a prophet, sir. ²⁰Our fathers worshiped on this mountain, but you say that in Jerusalem is the place where men ought to worship." ²¹Jesus said to her, "Woman, believe me, the hour is coming when neither on this mountain nor in Jerusalem will you worship the Father. ²²You worship what you do not know. We worship what we know, for salvation is from the Jews. ²³But the hour is coming, in fact it is now, when the true worshipers will worship the Father in spirit and truth, for the Father seeks such people to worship him. ²⁴God is spirit, and those who worship him must worship in spirit and truth."

²⁵The woman said to him, "I know that Messiah is coming (he who is called Christ). When he comes, he will proclaim all things to us." ²⁶Jesus said to her, "I who am speaking to you am He."

²⁷Just then his disciples returned. They marveled that he was talking with a woman, but none of them asked, "What do you want?" or, "Why are you talking with her?" ²⁸Then the woman left her water jar, and went away into the city, and said

to the people, [29]"Come, see a man who told me all that I ever did. Can this be the Christ?" [30]So, they left the city and were on their way to him.

[31]All the while the disciples kept urging him, saying, "Rabbi, eat." [32]But he said to them, "I have food to eat that you know nothing about." [33]So the disciples asked one another, "Has anyone brought him something to eat?" [34]Jesus said to them, "My food is to do the will of him who sent me, and to accomplish his work. [35]Do you not say, 'There are still four months remaining before the harvest comes'? I tell you, lift up your eyes, and see how the fields are already white for harvest. [36]Whoever reaps receives a reward and gathers fruit for eternal life, so that sower and reaper may rejoice together. [37]For the saying holds true in this [case], 'One sows and another reaps.' [38]I sent you to reap what you did not labor for. Others have labored, and you have profited from their labor."

Samaritans Believe

[39]Many Samaritans from that city believed in him because of the woman's testimony, "He told me all that I ever did." [40]So when the Samaritans came to him, they asked him to stay with them, so he stayed there for two days. [41]And many more believed because of his word. [42]They said to the woman, "No longer do we believe due to just what you said, for we have heard for ourselves, and we know that this man is indeed the Savior of the world."

[43]After the two days he departed for Galilee. [44](For Jesus himself testified that a prophet has no honor in his own country.) [45]So when he came to Galilee, the Galileans welcomed him, having seen all that he had done in Jerusalem at the feast, for they too had gone to the feast.

Jesus Heals the Son of an Official

[46]So he came again to Cana in Galilee, where he had turned the water into wine. And at Capernaum there was an official whose son was ill. [47]When he heard that Jesus had come from Judea to Galilee, he went and begged him to come down and heal his son, for he was about to die. [48]So it was that Jesus said to him, "Unless you see signs and wonders you will not believe." [49]The official said to him, "Sir, come down before my child dies." [50]Jesus said to him, "Go—your son will live." The man believed the word that Jesus spoke to him and went on his way. [51]As he was going down, his servants met him, telling him that his son was alive. [52]So he asked them the hour when he began to revive, and they answered, "Yesterday at one in the afternoon the fever left him." [53]The father knew that was the hour when Jesus had said to him, "Your son will live," and he himself believed, and all his household. [54]This was now the second sign that Jesus performed once he had come to Galilee from Judea.

Chapter 5

Healing the Invalid at the Pool of Bethesda

[1]After this was a feast of the Jews, so Jesus went up to Jerusalem. [2]Now in Jerusalem by the Sheep Gate there is a pool, called Bethesda in Hebrew, which has five porticoes. [3]In these lay a multitude of invalids—blind, lame, and paralyzed—waiting for the moving of the water. [4]For an angel of the Lord went down into the pool occasionally, and stirred the water, and whoever stepped in first after the stirring of the water was healed of whatever disease he had. [5]A certain man was there, who had been an invalid for thirty-eight years. [6]When Jesus saw him, knowing that he had been lying there a long time, he asked him, "Do you want to be healed?" [7]The sick man answered him, "Sir, I have no one to put me into the pool when the water is stirred up, and while I am going someone else steps down before me." [8]Jesus said to him, "Get up, pick up your pallet, and walk." [9]At once the man was healed, and he picked up his pallet and walked.

Now that day was the Sabbath. [10]So the Jews said to the man who had been healed, "It is the Sabbath, so it is not lawful for you to carry your pallet." [11]But he answered them, "The man who healed me told me, 'Pick up your pallet, and walk.'" [12]They asked him, "Who is the man who told you, 'Pick up your pallet, and walk'?" [13]Now the man who had been healed did not know who it was, for Jesus had withdrawn, there being quite a crowd in the place. [14]Afterward, Jesus found him in the temple and said to him, "See, you are well! Sin no more, so that nothing worse may happen to you." [15]The man went away and told the Jews that it was Jesus who had healed him.

Jesus Criticized for Healing on the Sabbath

[16]And this was why the Jews persecuted Jesus: because he did this on the Sabbath. [17]But Jesus addressed them, "My Father is still working, and I am working." [18]This was why the Jews sought all the more to kill him, because he not only broke the Sabbath but also called God his Father, making himself equal with God.

The Raising of the Dead

[19]Jesus said to them, "Truly, truly, I say to you, the Son can do nothing of his own accord, but only what he sees the Father doing. For whatever the Father does, the Son does likewise. [20]For the Father loves the Son and shows him all that he himself is doing. And he will show him greater works than these, that you may marvel. [21]For as the Father raises the dead and gives them life, so the Son also gives life to whom he will. [22]The Father judges no one, but has given all judgment to the

Son, [23]that all may honor the Son, even as they honor the Father. Whoever does not honor the Son does not honor the Father who sent him. [24]Truly, truly, I say to you, whoever hears my word and believes him who sent me, has eternal life. He does not come into judgment, but has passed from death to life. [25]"Truly, truly, I say to you, the hour is coming, and in fact is now here, when the dead will hear the voice of the Son of God, and those who hear will live. [26]For as the Father has life in himself, so he has granted the Son to have life in himself as well, [27]and has given him authority to execute judgment, because he is the Son of Man. [28]Do not marvel at this, for the hour is coming when all who are in the tombs will hear his voice [29]and come forth– those who have done good to the resurrection of life, and those who have done evil to the resurrection of judgment.

Witnesses of the Truth

[30]"I can do nothing on my own authority. As I hear, I judge, and my judgment is just, because I seek not my own will but the will of him who sent me. [31]Just my bearing witness to myself does not make my testimony true. [32]There is another who bears witness to me, and I know that the testimony he bears to me is true. [33]You questioned John, and he has borne witness to the truth. [34]Not that the testimony that I receive is from man, but I say this that you may be saved. [35]He was a burning and shining lamp, and for a while you were willing to rejoice in his light.

[36]But the testimony that I have is greater than that of John, for the works that the Father has granted me to accomplish, these very works that I am doing, bear witness about me that the Father has sent me. [37]And the Father who sent me has himself borne witness to me. You have never heard his voice; you have never seen his form. [38]And you do not have his word abiding in you, for you do not believe in the One whom he has sent. [39]You search the scriptures because you think that in them you have eternal life. And it is the [scriptures] that bear witness to me, [40]yet you refuse to come to me so that you may have life. [41]The approval I receive is not from mankind. [42]Instead, I know that you do not have the love of God within you. [43]I have come in my Father's name, and you do not accept me. But if another were to come in his own name, you would accept *him*. [44]How can you believe, since you accept approval from one another but do not seek the approval that comes from the only God? [45]Do not think that I shall accuse you to the Father. Moses, on whom you set your hope, is the one who accuses you. [46]If you believed Moses, you would believe me, for he wrote about me. [47]But if you do not believe his writings, how will you believe my words?"

Chapter 6

Jesus Feeds the 5,000 Miraculously

[1]After this, Jesus went to the other side of the Sea of Galilee (which is the Sea of Tiberias). [2]And a large crowd followed him because they saw the signs that he was performing on the sick. [3]Jesus went up on the mountain and sat down there with his disciples. [4]Now the Passover, the feast of the Jews, was imminent. [5]Then, lifting up his eyes and seeing that a large crowd was coming to him, Jesus said to Philip, "Where shall we buy bread, so that these people may eat?" [6]He said this to test him, for he himself knew what he intended to do. [7]Philip answered him, "Two hundred denarii would not buy enough bread for each of them to get a little."

[8]One of his disciples, Andrew, Simon Peter's brother, said to him, [9]"There is a lad here who has five barley loaves and two fish. But of what use are they for so many people?" [10]Jesus said, "Have the people sit down." Now there was a lot of grass in this place, so the men sat down, about five thousand in number. [11]Jesus then took the loaves, and once he had given thanks, he distributed them to those who were seated, and did the same with the fish, as much as they wanted. [12]And when they had eaten their fill, he told his disciples, "Gather up the leftover pieces so that nothing goes to waste." [13]So they gathered them up and filled twelve baskets with leftover pieces of the five barley loaves left by those who had eaten. [14]When the people saw the sign that he had performed, they remarked, "This is indeed the prophet who is to come into the world!" [15]Perceiving then that they were about to come and take him by force to make him king, Jesus again withdrew all alone to the mountain.

Jesus Walks on Water

[16]When evening came, his disciples went down to the sea, [17]got into a boat, and started across the sea to Capernaum. It was dark by then, but Jesus had not yet come back to them. [18]The sea was churning because a strong wind was blowing. [19]When they had rowed about three or four miles, they saw Jesus walking on the sea and approaching the boat. They were frightened, [20]but he said to them, "It is I; do not be afraid." [21]Then they were glad to take him into the boat, and immediately the boat was at the land that they were going to.

[22]On the next day the people who remained on the other side of the sea saw that there had been only one boat there, and that Jesus had not entered the boat with his disciples, but that his disciples had gone away alone. [23]Other boats from Tiberias came near the place where they ate the bread after the Lord had given thanks. [24]So when the crowd saw that Jesus was not there, nor [were] his disciples, they themselves got into the boats and went to Capernaum seeking Jesus.

150

²⁵When they found him on the other side of the sea, they asked him, "Rabbi, when did you come here?" ²⁶Jesus answered them, "Truly, truly, I say to you, you seek me, not because you saw signs, but because you ate your fill of the loaves. ²⁷Do not labor for the food that perishes, but for the food that endures to eternal life, which the Son of Man will give to you, for God the Father has set his seal on him."

The Bread of Life

²⁸Then they asked of him, "What must we do, to be doing the works of God?" ²⁹Jesus answered them, "This is the work of God: that you believe in the One whom he has sent." ³⁰So they said to him, "Then what sign do you do, that we may see and believe you? What work do you perform? ³¹Our fathers ate the manna in the wilderness. As it is written, 'He gave them bread to eat from heaven.'" ³²Jesus then replied to them, "Truly, truly, I say to you, it was not Moses who gave you the bread from heaven; my Father gives you the true bread from heaven. ³³For the bread of God is the One who comes down from heaven and gives life to the world." ³⁴They said to him, "Lord, give us this bread always." ³⁵Jesus said to them, "I am the bread of life. Whoever comes to me shall never hunger, and whoever believes in me shall never thirst. ³⁶But I told you that you have seen me and yet do not believe. ³⁷Everyone whom the Father gives me will come to me, and I will not cast out whoever does come to me. ³⁸For I have come down from heaven, not to do my own will, but the will of him who sent me. ³⁹And this is the will of him who sent me: that I should lose nothing of all that he has given me, but raise it up on the last day. ⁴⁰For this is the will of my Father: that everyone who sees the Son and believes in him should have eternal life, and I will raise him up on the last day."

⁴¹Then the Jews murmured about him because he said, "I am the bread that came down from heaven." ⁴²They said, "Isn't this Jesus, the son of Joseph, whose father and mother we know? How does he now claim, 'I have come down from heaven'?" ⁴³Jesus answered them, "Do not murmur among yourselves. ⁴⁴No one can come to me unless the Father who sent me draws him, and I will raise him up at the last day. ⁴⁵It is written in the prophets, 'And they shall all be taught by God.' Everyone who has heard and learned from the Father comes to me. ⁴⁶Not that anyone has seen the Father except he who is from God: he has seen the Father. ⁴⁷Truly, truly, I say to you, whoever believes has eternal life. ⁴⁸I am the bread of life. ⁴⁹Your fathers ate the manna in the wilderness, and they died. ⁵⁰This is the bread that comes down from heaven, that a man may eat of it and not die. ⁵¹I am the living bread that down from heaven; if anyone eats of this bread, he will live forever. And the bread that I shall give for the life of the world is my flesh."

⁵²The Jews then disputed among themselves, saying, "How can this man give us his flesh to eat?" ⁵³So Jesus said to them, "Truly, truly, I say to you, unless you eat the flesh of the Son of Man and drink his blood, you have no life in you. ⁵⁴He who eats my flesh and drinks my blood has eternal life, and I will raise him up on the last day. ⁵⁵For my flesh truly is food, and my blood truly is drink. ⁵⁶Whoever eats my flesh and drinks my blood abides in me, and I in him. ⁵⁷As the living Father sent me, and I live because of the Father, in the same way whoever eats me will live because of me. ⁵⁸This is the bread that came down from heaven, not like what the fathers ate and died. The one who eats this bread will live forever." ⁵⁹He said this in the synagogue, as he taught at Capernaum.

⁶⁰When they heard it, many of his disciples commented, "This is a difficult teaching. Who can grasp it?" ⁶¹But Jesus, knowing in himself that his disciples were murmuring over it, said to them, "Do you take offense at this? ⁶²Then what if you were to see the Son of Man ascending back to where he had been before? ⁶³It is the Spirit who gives life; the flesh is of no avail. The words that I have spoken to you are spirit and life. ⁶⁴But there are some of you who do not believe." (For from the beginning Jesus had known who did not believe, and who it was who would betray him.) ⁶⁵He also said, "This is why I told you that nobody can come to me unless such is granted to him by the Father."

⁶⁶After this, many of his disciples drew back and no longer traveled about with him. ⁶⁷Jesus asked the Twelve, "Do you want to leave as well?" ⁶⁸Simon Peter answered him, "Lord, to whom shall we go? You have the words of eternal life. ⁶⁹And we have believed and have come to know that you are the Holy One of God." ⁷⁰Jesus answered them, "Did I not choose you, the Twelve? And yet, one of you is a devil." ⁷¹(He was referring to Judas the son of Simon Iscariot, for he, one of the Twelve, was going to betray him.)

Chapter 7

The Feast of the Tabernacles

¹After all this, Jesus traveled about in Galilee. He did not want to travel about in Judea because the Jews were seeking to kill him. ²Now the Jews' Feast of Tabernacles was imminent. ³So his brothers said to him, "Leave here and go to Judea so that your disciples also may see the deeds you are doing. ⁴For no man works in secret if he seeks to be known openly. If you do these things, show yourself to the world." ⁵(For even his brothers did not believe in him.) ⁶Jesus replied to them, "My time has not come yet, but your time is always here. ⁷The world cannot hate you, but it hates me because I testify about it that its deeds are evil. ⁸Go to the feast

yourselves. I am not going up to this feast, for my time has not fully come yet." [9]And having said this, he remained in Galilee.

[10]But after his brothers had gone up to the feast, then he also went up, not publicly but in private. [11]The Jews were looking for him at the feast and asking, "Where is he?" [12]And there was much muttering about him among the people. Some were saying, "He is a good man," while others said, "No, he is leading the people astray." [13]Yet for fear of the Jews no one spoke about him openly.

[14]About the middle of the feast, Jesus went up into the temple and began to teach. [15]The Jews marveled at it, saying, "How can this one be so learned, having never studied formally?" [16]So Jesus responded, declaring to them, "My teaching is not from me, but from him who sent me. [17]If anyone's will is to do [God's] will, he shall know whether the teaching is from God or whether I am speaking on my own authority. [18]The one who speaks on his own authority seeks his own glory. But the one who seeks the glory of him who sent him is true, and in him there is no falsehood. [19]Has Moses not given you the law? Yet none of you keeps the law. Why do you seek to kill me?" [20]The people answered, "You are crazy! Who is trying to kill you?" [21]Jesus answered them, "I did one deed, and you all marvel at it. [22]Moses gave you circumcision (not that it is from Moses, but from the fathers), and you circumcise a man on the Sabbath. [23]If a man receives circumcision on the Sabbath so that the law of Moses may not be broken, are you angry with me because I made a man's whole body well on the Sabbath? [24]Do not judge by appearances, but by righteous discernment."

Where Will the Christ Come From?

[25]Some of the people of Jerusalem therefore wondered, "Isn't this the man that they are seeking to kill? [26]Yet, look, here he is speaking openly, and they aren't saying anything to him! Can it be that actually the authorities know that this is the Christ? [27]Still, we know where this man comes from, and when the Christ does appear, no one is going to know where he comes from." [28]So, as he taught in the temple, Jesus proclaimed, "You know me, and you know where I come from. But I have not come of my own accord. He who sent me is true, and you do not know him. [29]I do know him, for I come from him, and he sent me." [30]So they sought to arrest him, but no one laid hands on him because his hour had not come yet. [31]Nonetheless, many of the people believed in him and they were saying, "When the Christ does appear, will he perform more signs than this man has?"

[32]The Pharisees heard the crowd muttering about him this way, so then the chief priests and Pharisees sent officers to arrest him. [33]Then Jesus said, "I will be with

you a little longer, and then I am going to him who sent me. [34]You will seek me and you will not find me— you cannot come where I am." [35]The Jews said to one another, "Where does this man intend to go to so that we are not going to find him? Does he intend to go to the Dispersion among the Greeks and teach the Greeks? [36]What does he mean by saying, 'You will seek me, and you will not find me,' and, 'You cannot come where I am'?"

[37]Now, on the last (the greatest) day of the feast, Jesus stood up and proclaimed, "If anyone should be thirsty, let him come to me and drink.[38]As for anyone who believes in me, as the scriptures have said, out of his innermost being shall flow rivers of life-giving water." [39]Now, since Jesus was not yet glorified, the Holy Spirit had not yet been [given]; he said this referring to the Spirit who was soon be received by those who believed in him.

[40]When they heard these words, some of the people said, "This really is the prophet." [41]Others said, "This is the Christ." But some asked, "Is the Christ [supposed] to come from Galilee? [42]Does not the scripture say that the Christ is to come from the descendants of David, from Bethlehem, the village that David was from?" [43]Such was the division among the people about him. [44]Some of them wanted to arrest him, but no one laid hands on him.

[45]The officers then went back to the chief priests and Pharisees, who asked them, "Why did you not bring him?" [46]The officers answered, "Never has anyone spoken like this man!" [47]The Pharisees answered them, "Have you also been taken in by him? [48]Do any of the authorities or Pharisees believe in him? [49]But [the people in] this crowd, who do not know the law, are accursed." [50]Nicodemus, who had gone to him before, and who was one of the [Pharisees], asked them, [51]"Does our law judge a man without first giving him a hearing and learning what he does?" [52]In response, they asked, "You aren't from Galilee too, are you? Search and you will see that no prophet is to rise from Galilee." [53]Then they left, each going to his own house, [8:1]but Jesus went to the Mount of Olives.

Chapter 8

A Woman Is Caught in Adultery

[8:2]Early in the morning he came to the temple again. All the people came to him, and he sat down and taught them. [3]The scribes and the Pharisees brought a woman who had been caught in adultery, and placing her in their midst, [4]they said to him, "Teacher, this woman has been caught in the act of adultery. [5]Now in the law, Moses commanded us to stone such a woman. What do you say about her?" [6]They said this to test him so that they might have some charge to bring against him. But Jesus just bent down and wrote with his finger on the ground. ⁷Since they kept on quizzing him, he stood up and said to them, "Let the one among you who is without sin be the first to throw a stone at her." ⁸And he bent down and went back to writing on the ground. ⁹But when they heard it, they went away, one by one, beginning with the older ones, until Jesus was left alone with the woman standing before him. ¹⁰Jesus looked up and said to her, "Woman, where are they? Has no one condemned you?" ¹¹"No one, Lord," she replied. So, Jesus said, "Neither do I condemn you. Go—and sin no more."

Witness and Testimony

¹²Again Jesus spoke to them, saying, "I am the Light of the World. Whoever follows me will not walk in darkness, but will have the light of life." ¹³The Pharisees then said to him, "You are bearing witness to yourself; your testimony is not true." ¹⁴Jesus answered, "Even if I do bear witness to myself, my testimony is true, for I know where I have come from and where I am going, but you know neither where I come from nor where I am going. ¹⁵You judge according to the flesh; I judge no one. ¹⁶Yet even if I do judge, my judgment is true, for it is not I alone who judges, but I and he who sent me.

¹⁷In your Law it is written that the testimony of two men is true. ¹⁸I am the one who bears witness to myself, and the Father who sent me bears witness to me." ¹⁹Therefore they asked him, "Where is your Father?" Jesus answered, "You know neither me nor my Father; if you knew me, you would know my Father also." ²⁰He spoke these words in the Treasury Room as he was teaching in the temple. But no one arrested him because his hour had not come yet.

²¹Again he said to them, "I shall go away, and you will seek me and die in your sin. Where I am going, you cannot come." ²²Then the Jews pondered, "Will he kill himself, since he says, 'Where I am going, you cannot come'?" ²³He said to them, "You are from below, I am from above. You are of this world; I am not of this world. ²⁴I told you that you would die in your sins, for unless you believe that I am He, you will die in your sins." ²⁵They asked him, "Who are you?" Jesus said to them, "Just what I have told you from the beginning. ²⁶I have much to say about you and much to judge. Now he who sent me is true, and I declare to the world what I have heard from him." ²⁷They did not understand that he was speaking to them about the Father. ²⁸So Jesus said, "When you have lifted up the Son of Man, then you will know that I am He, and that I do nothing on my own authority but speak this way, as the Father taught me. ²⁹And he who sent me is with me. He has not left me alone, for I always do what is pleasing to him."

Who Is Your Father? God, Abraham, or the Devil?

[30]Many believed in him as he was saying such things. [31]Jesus then said to the Jews who had come to believe in him, "If you abide in my word, you are truly my disciples, [32]and you will know the truth, and the truth will set you free." [33]They answered him, "We are descendants of Abraham and have never been in bondage to anyone. How is it that you say, 'You will be set free'?" [34]Jesus answered them, "Truly, truly, I say to you, everyone who commits sin is a slave to sin. [35]The slave does not remain in the house forever. The son *does* remain forever. [36]So if the Son makes you free, you will be free indeed. [37]I know that you are descendants of Abraham, yet you seek to kill me because my word finds no place in you. [38]I speak of what I have seen with my Father, and you do what you have heard from your father."

[39]They answered him, "Abraham is our father." Jesus said to them, "If you were Abraham's children, you would be doing the things Abraham did, [40]but right now you are seeking to kill *me*, a man who has told you the truth that I heard from God, which is *not* the sort of thing Abraham did. [41]You are doing the [very] things your father did." They said to him, "*We* were not born from sexual immorality; we have one Father: God." [42]Jesus said to them, "If God were your Father, you would love me, for I proceeded and came forth from God. I came not of my own accord, but [because] he sent me. [43]Why do you fail to understand what I am saying? It is because you cannot bear to hear my word. [44]You are of your father the devil, and you want to act on your father's desires. He was a murderer from the beginning and has nothing to do with the truth, because there is no truth in him. When he lies, he speaks according to his own nature, for he is a liar and the father of lies. [45]But, because I tell the truth, you do not believe me. [46]Which of you convicts me of sin? If I tell the truth, why do you not believe me? [47]He who is of God hears the words of God; you do not hear them because you are not of God."

[48]The Jews answered him, "Are we not right in saying that you are a Samaritan and demon-possessed?" [49]Jesus answered, "I am not demon-possessed. I honor my Father, and you dishonor me. [50]Yet I do not seek my own glory. There is One who seeks it, and he will be the judge. [51]Truly, truly, I say to you, if anyone keeps my word, he will never see death." [52]The Jews said to him, "Now we know that you are possessed. Abraham died, as did the prophets; and yet you say, 'If anyone keeps my word, he will never taste death.' [53]Are you greater than our father Abraham, who died? Even the prophets died! Who do you claim to be?" [54]Jesus answered, "If I glorify myself, my glory is nothing. It is my Father, whom you claim is your God, who glorifies me. [55]Though you have not known him, I *do*

know him. If I said that I do not know him, I should be a liar like you. But I *do* know him, and I keep his word. ⁵⁶Your father Abraham rejoiced that he was to see my day. He saw it and was glad." ⁵⁷The Jews then said to him, "You are not even fifty years old yet. How did Abraham see you?" ⁵⁸Jesus said to them, "Truly, truly, I say to you, before Abraham was, I am." ⁵⁹So they took up stones to throw at him, but Jesus hid himself and left the temple.

Chapter 9

A Blind Man Receives His Sight

¹As he passed by, he saw a man [who had been] blind from his birth. ²And his disciples asked him, "Rabbi, who sinned, this man or his parents, that he was born blind?" ³Jesus answered, "It was not that this man sinned, or his parents, but that God's work might be demonstrated in him. ⁴I must do the deeds of him who sent me while it is day. The night is coming—when no one can work. ⁵While I am in the world, I am the light of the world." ⁶As he said this, he spit on the ground and made mud of the saliva and anointed the man's eyes with the mud, ⁷saying to him, "Go, wash in the pool of Siloam" (which means "sent"). So, he went and washed and came back seeing.

⁸The neighbors and those who had seen him before as a beggar pondered, "Isn't this the man who used to sit and beg?" ⁹Some said, "It is he," whereas others said, "No, but he is like him." But he kept on insisting, "I *am* the man." ¹⁰They asked him, "Then how were your eyes opened?" ¹¹He answered, "The man called Jesus made mud and anointed my eyes and said to me, 'Go to Siloam and wash'; so I went and washed and received my sight." ¹²They asked him, "Where is he?" He replied, "I don't know."

¹³They brought the man who had formerly been blind to the Pharisees. ¹⁴Now when Jesus made the mud and opened his eyes it was a Sabbath day. ¹⁵So, again the Pharisees asked him how he had received his sight. And he said to them, "He put mud on my eyes, and I washed, and I see." ¹⁶Some of the Pharisees said, "This man is *not* from God because he does not keep the Sabbath." But others said, "How could a man who is a sinner do such signs?" So stood the division among them. ¹⁷So again they asked the blind man, "What do you say about him, since he has opened your eyes?" he replied, "He is a prophet."

¹⁸The Jews did not believe that he had been blind and had received his sight, until they called the parents of the man who had received his sight, ¹⁹and asked them, "Is this your son, who you say was born blind? Then how is he able to see now?" ²⁰His parents answered, "We know that this is our son and that he was born blind.

²¹But we don't know how it is that he can see now, nor do we know who opened his eyes. Ask him—he is of age; he will speak for himself." ²²(His parents said this because they feared the Jews, for the Jews had already agreed that if anyone should confess him to be Christ, he was to be put out of the synagogue.) ²³That was why his parents said, "He is of age, ask him."

²⁴So for the second time they called the man who had been blind and said to him, "Give God the praise. We know that this man is a sinner." ²⁵He answered, "I don't know whether or not he is a sinner. One thing I do know: that although I used to be blind, now I can see." ²⁶They questioned him, "What did he do to you? How did he open your eyes?" ²⁷He answered them, "I've told you already, and you wouldn't listen. Why do you want to hear it again? Do you also want to become his disciples?" ²⁸And they reviled him, saying, "You are his disciple, but we are disciples of Moses. ²⁹We know that God has spoken to Moses, but as for this man, we don't know where he comes from." ³⁰The man answered, "Well, well—this is something amazing! You don't know where he comes from, and yet he opened my eyes. ³¹We know that God does not heed sinners, but if anyone is a worshiper of God and does his will, God listens to him. ³²Since the world began it has never been heard that anyone opened the eyes of a man born blind. ³³If this man were not from God, he could do nothing." ³⁴They answered him, "You who were born in utter sin would presume to teach *us*?" And they threw him out.

³⁵Jesus heard that they had thrown him out, and having found him he asked [him], "Do you believe in the Son of Man?" ³⁶He answered, "Well, sir—so that I may believe in him—who is He?" ³⁷Jesus replied, "You have seen him, and he is the One speaking to you." ³⁸He responded, "Lord, I believe," and he worshiped him. ³⁹Jesus said, "I have come into this world for judgment, that those who do not see may see, and that those who do see may become blind." ⁴⁰Some of the Pharisees near him heard this, so they asked him, "Are we blind also?" ⁴¹Jesus answered them, "If you were blind, you would have no guilt. But since you say, 'We see,' your guilt remains.

Chapter 10

The Good Shepherd

¹"Truly, truly, I tell you: the one who does not enter the sheepfold by the door but instead climbs in by another way—that one is a thief and a robber. ²But the one who enters by the door is the shepherd of the sheep. ³The gatekeeper does open to him. The sheep hear his voice, and he calls his own sheep by name and leads them out. ⁴When he has brought out all his own, he goes before them, and the

sheep follow him because they know his voice. ⁵They will not follow a stranger—rather, they will flee from him, for they do not know the voice of strangers." ⁶Jesus used this way of explaining something with them, but they did not understand what he was saying to them.

⁷So again Jesus said to them, "Truly, truly, I say to you, I am the door of the sheep. ⁸All who came before me are thieves and robbers, but the sheep did not heed them. ⁹I am the door; if anyone enters by me, he will be saved, and will go in and out and find pasture. ¹⁰The thief comes only to steal, kill, and destroy; I have come that they may have life and have it abundantly. ¹¹I am the good shepherd; the good shepherd lays down his life for the sheep. ¹²The one who is a hired hand and *not* a shepherd, who does not own the sheep, sees the wolf coming and leaves the sheep and flees. Then the wolf snatches them and scatters them. ¹³He flees because he is a hired hand and cares nothing for the sheep. ¹⁴I am the good shepherd; I know my own and my own know me—¹⁵just as the Father knows me and I know the Father—and I lay down my life for the sheep. ¹⁶And I have other sheep that are not of this fold. I must bring them also, and they will heed my voice, making one flock, one shepherd. ¹⁷For this reason the Father loves me, because I lay down my life, that I may take it up again. ¹⁸No one takes it from me, but I lay it down of my own accord. I have power to lay it down, and I have power to take it up again. I have received this charge from my Father."

¹⁹Again there was a division among the Jews because of these words. ²⁰Many of them said, "He is demon-possessed, and he is crazy. Why listen to him?" ²¹Others stated, "These are not the sayings of one who is possessed. Can a demon open the eyes of the blind?"

I and the Father are One

²²It was the Feast of the Dedication at Jerusalem. ²³It was winter, and Jesus was walking in the temple, in the portico of Solomon. ²⁴So the Jews gathered around him and said to him, "How long will you keep us in suspense? If you are the Christ, tell us plainly." ²⁵Jesus answered them, "I told you, and you do not believe. These works that I do in my Father's name, they bear witness to me. ²⁶But you do not believe, because you are not from among my sheep. ²⁷My sheep hear my voice, and I know them, and they follow me. ²⁸And I give them eternal life, and they shall never perish, and no one shall snatch them out of my hand. ²⁹My Father, who has given them to me, is greater than all, and no one is able to snatch them out of the Father's hand. ³⁰I and the Father are one."

³¹Again the Jews picked up stones to stone him. ³²Jesus answered them, "I have shown you many good deeds from the Father. Which one of them are you stoning me for?" ³³The Jews answered him, "It's not for a good deed that we stone you, but for blasphemy, because you, being a man, make yourself out to be God." ³⁴Jesus answered them, "Is it not written in your law, 'I said, you are gods'? ³⁵If he called the ones that the word of God came to 'gods' (and scripture cannot be broken), ³⁶are you accusing the One whom the Father consecrated and sent into the world of blaspheming because I said, 'I am the Son of God'? ³⁷If I am not doing the deeds of my Father, then do not believe me. ³⁸But if I *am* doing them, even though you do not believe me, believe the deeds, that you may know and understand that the Father is in me, and I am in the Father."

³⁹Again they tried to arrest him, but he escaped from their hands. ⁴⁰He went away again across the Jordan to the place where John had first baptized, and he stayed there. ⁴¹Many people came to him and they said, "John performed no signs, but everything that John said about this man was true." ⁴²And many there believed in him.

Chapter 11

Jesus Raises Lazarus from the Dead

¹Now a certain man, Lazarus, was ill. He was from Bethany, the village of Mary and her sister Martha. ²Mary was the one who anointed the Lord with ointment and wiped his feet with her hair, and it was her brother Lazarus who was ill. ³So the sisters sent word to him, saying, "Lord, the one whom you love is ill." ⁴But when Jesus heard it he said, "This illness does not lead to death. It is for the glory of God, so that the Son of God may be glorified by means of it."

⁵Now Jesus loved Martha and her sister and Lazarus. ⁶So when he heard that Lazarus was ill, he stayed just two days longer in the place where he was, ⁷and then after that he said to the disciples, "Let's go into Judea again." ⁸The disciples said to him, "Rabbi, just now the Jews were trying to stone you, and yet you would return there?" ⁹Jesus answered, "Are there not twelve hours in the day? If anyone walks in the daytime, he does not stumble, because he sees the light of this world. ¹⁰But if anyone walks in the nighttime, he stumbles, because the light is not in him." ¹¹He spoke in that way, and then he said to them, "Our friend Lazarus has fallen asleep, but I am going [there] to awaken him." ¹²The disciples said to him, "Lord, if he's sleeping deeply, he will get well." ¹³Now Jesus had spoken about his death, but they thought that he meant resting up by sleeping. ¹⁴So, then Jesus told them plainly, "Lazarus is dead. ¹⁵Now for your sake I am glad that I was not there, so that you may believe. Now let's go to him." ¹⁶Thomas,

called the Twin, said to his fellow disciples, "We should also go, so that we may die with him."

¹⁷Now when Jesus came, he found out that Lazarus had already been in the tomb for four days. ¹⁸Bethany was near Jerusalem, about two miles away, ¹⁹and many of the Jews had come to Martha and Mary to console them concerning their brother. ²⁰When Martha heard that Jesus was coming, she went to meet him, while Mary was sitting in the house. ²¹Martha said to Jesus, "Lord, if only you had been here, my brother would not have died. ²²But even still I know that God will give to you whatever you ask from him." ²³Jesus said to her, "Your brother will rise again." ²⁴Martha said to him, "I know that he will rise again in the resurrection at the last day." ²⁵Jesus said to her, "I am the resurrection and the life. Whoever believes in me will live, even if he dies, ²⁶and whoever lives and believes in me shall never die. Do you believe this?" ²⁷She said to him, "Yes, Lord. I believe that you are the Christ, the Son of God, who has come into the world."

²⁸Having said this, she went and called her sister Mary, saying quietly, "The Teacher is here and is calling for you." ²⁹And when she heard it, she got up quickly and ran to him. ³⁰Now Jesus had not yet come to the village but was still in the place where Martha had met him. ³¹When the Jews, who were with her in the house consoling her, saw Mary get up quickly and head out, they followed her, supposing that she was going to the tomb to weep there. ³²Then Mary, when she came to where Jesus was and saw him, fell at his feet, saying to him, "Lord, if you had been here, my brother would not have died." ³³When Jesus saw her weeping, and the Jews who came with her weeping as well, he felt an angry indignation in his spirit, and being deeply troubled, ³⁴He asked, "Where have you laid him?" They replied to him, "Lord, come and see." ³⁵Jesus wept. ³⁶So the Jews said, "Look how [much] he loved him!" ³⁷But some of them asked, "Couldn't the one who opened the eyes of the blind man have kept this man from dying also?"

³⁸Then Jesus, deeply moved once more, came to the tomb. It was a cave, and a stone lay against it. ³⁹Jesus said, "Move the stone away." Martha, the sister of the dead man, said to him, "Lord, there will be a stench by this time, for he has been dead four days." ⁴⁰Jesus said to her, "Did I not tell you that you would see the glory of God if you would believe?" ⁴¹So they moved away the stone. And Jesus lifted up his eyes and said, "Father, I thank you that you have heard me. ⁴²I know that you always hear me, but I have said this for the benefit of the people standing nearby, that they may believe that you did send me." ⁴³When he had said this, he called out in a loud voice, "Lazarus, come out." ⁴⁴The dead man came out, his hands and feet bound with strips of linen, and his face wrapped with a cloth. Jesus said to them, "Unbind him, and let him go."

Jesus' Death First Prophesied

[45]Therefore, many of the Jews, who had come with Mary and had seen what he did, believed in him. [46]But some of them went to the Pharisees to report to them what Jesus had done. [47]So the chief priests and the Pharisees gathered the council, and said, "What are we going to do? For this man performs many signs. [48]If we let him go on like this, everyone will believe in him, and the Romans will come and destroy our holy place and even our nation." [49]But one of them, Caiaphas, who was high priest that year, said to them, "You do not understand at all. [50]Nor do you realize that it is better for you that one man should die for the people, rather than having the whole nation perish." [51]He did not say this of his own accord, but being high priest that year he was uttering a prophesy: that Jesus was about to die for the whole nation, [52]and not only for the nation, but also to unify the children of God who are scattered abroad.

[53]So from that day on they plotted how to put him to death. [54]So, Jesus no longer moved about among the Jews openly, but went from there to the country near the wilderness, to a town called Ephraim, and he stayed with the disciples there. [55]Now the Passover of the Jews was imminent, so before the Passover, many people went up from the country to Jerusalem to purify themselves. [56]They were searching for Jesus and saying to one another as they stood in the temple, "What do you think? That he will not come to the feast?" [57]Now the chief priests and the Pharisees had given orders that anyone who knew where he was should let them know, so that they could arrest him.

Chapter 12

Mary Anoints Jesus

[1]Six days before the Passover, Jesus came to Bethany, where Lazarus (whom Jesus had raised from the dead) was. [2]There they made him a supper; Martha served, and Lazarus was one of those at table with him. [3]Mary took a pound of costly ointment of pure spikenard and anointed the feet of Jesus and wiped his feet with her hair; and the house was filled with the fragrance of the ointment. [4]But Judas Iscariot, one of his disciples (the one who was to betray him), asked, [5]"Why was this ointment not sold for three hundred denarii and given to the poor?" [6](He did not say this because he cared about the poor, but because he was a thief, and since he kept the money box he used to help himself to what was put into it.) [7]Jesus said, "Leave her alone and let her keep it for the day of my burial. [8]You always have the poor with you, but you do not always have me."

⁹When the great crowd of the Jews learned that he was there, they came, not only on account of Jesus but also to see Lazarus, whom he had raised from the dead. ¹⁰So the chief priests planned to put Lazarus to death also, ¹¹because many of the Jews were going off to believe in Jesus on account of him.

Jesus Enters in Triumph

¹²The next day a great crowd who had come to the feast heard that Jesus was coming to Jerusalem. ¹³So they took branches of palm trees and went out to meet him, crying, "Hosanna! Blessed is he who comes in the name of the Lord. Bless the King of Israel!" ¹⁴And Jesus found a young donkey and sat on it, just as it had been written:

> ¹⁵"Do not be afraid, daughter of Zion.
> Look—your king approaches,
> seated on the colt of a donkey!"

¹⁶At first, his disciples did not understand these things, but once Jesus was glorified, then they remembered that these things that had been written about him had been done to him. ¹⁷The crowd that had been with him when he called Lazarus out of the tomb and raised him from the dead kept giving testimony. ¹⁸So because they had heard that he had done this sign, crowds went to meet him. ¹⁹The Pharisees then said to one another, "You see that you can do nothing: look, the world is following him."

²⁰Now among those who went up to worship at the feast were some Greeks. ²¹So these people went to Philip, who was from Bethsaida in Galilee, and said to him, "Sir, we wish to see Jesus." ²²Philip went and told Andrew, who then went with Philip, and they told Jesus. ²³Jesus answered them, "The hour has come for the Son of Man to be glorified. ²⁴Truly, truly, I say to you, unless a grain of wheat falls into the earth and dies, it remains alone. But if it dies, it bears much fruit. ²⁵Anyone who loves his life loses it, and anyone who hates his life in this world will keep it for eternal life. ²⁶If anyone serves me, he must follow me, and where I am, there my servant shall be also. If anyone serves me, the Father will honor him.

²⁷"Now my soul is troubled. And what shall I say? 'Father, save me from this hour'? No, I have come to this hour for this purpose. ²⁸Father, glorify your name." Then a voice came from heaven, "I have glorified it, and I will glorify it again." ²⁹The people standing nearby heard it and said that it had thundered. Others said, "An angel has spoken to him." ³⁰Jesus answered, "This voice has come for your sake, not for mine. ³¹Now is the judgment of this world, now the ruler of this world will be cast out. ³²When I am lifted up from the earth, I will draw all

mankind to myself." [33]He said this to indicate the type of death he was about to die. [34]The crowd answered him, "From the law we have heard that the Christ remains forever. How can you say that the Son of Man must be lifted up? Who is this Son of Man?" [35]Jesus said to them, "The light is with you for a little longer. Walk while you have the light, so that the darkness may not overtake you. The one who walks in the darkness does not know where he is going. [36]While you have the light, believe in the light, that you may become sons of light."

Belief and Unbelief

When Jesus had said this, he departed and hid himself from them. [37]Though he had done so many signs before them, they still did not believe in him, [38]so that the word spoken by the prophet Isaiah might be fulfilled:

> "Lord, who has believed the report from us,
> and to whom has the arm of the Lord been revealed?"

[39]Therefore they could not believe, for in addition Isaiah said:

> [40]"He has blinded their eyes and hardened their hearts, so that they
> will not be able to perceive with their eyes, and hear with their ears, and
> understand with their heart, and repent so that I might heal them."

[41]Isaiah said this because he saw his glory and spoke about him. [42]Nevertheless even many of the authorities believed in him, but for fear of the Pharisees they did not confess it, so that they would not be put out of the synagogue, [43]for they loved the praise of men more than the praise of God.

[44]And Jesus cried out and said, "Whoever believes in me, believes not in me but in him who sent me. [45]And anyone who sees me sees him who sent me. [46]I have come as light into the world, that whoever believes in me may not remain in darkness. [47]If anyone hears my sayings and does not keep them, I do not judge him. For I did not come to judge the world but to save the world. [48]Anyone who rejects me and does not receive my sayings has a judge. The word that I have spoken will be his judge on the last day. [49]For I have not spoken on my own authority. The Father who sent me has himself given me a commandment of what to say and what to speak. [50]And I know that his commandment is eternal life. Therefore, I speak as the Father has instructed me."

Chapter 13

The Last Supper

[1]Now before the feast of the Passover, when Jesus knew that his hour to depart out of this world to the Father had come, having loved his own who were in the world, he loved them to the end. [2]Now the devil had already put it into the heart of Judas Iscariot, Simon's son, to betray Jesus. But [3]Jesus knew that the Father had given all things into his hands, and that he had come from God and was returning to God.

[4]So, after supper, he rose from the table, laid aside his garments, and took up a towel and girded himself with it. [5]Then he poured water into a basin and began to wash the disciples' feet and to wipe them with the towel that girded him. [6]He came to Simon Peter, and Peter said to him, "Lord, you—washing my feet?" [7]Jesus answered him, "You do not realize what I am doing now, but afterward you will understand." [8]Peter protested to him, "You are never going to wash *my* feet." Jesus answered him, "If I do not wash you, you have no part in me." [9]Simon Peter said to him, "Lord, [then] not my feet only, but also my hands and my head!" [10]Jesus said to him, "He who has bathed does not need to wash—rather, he is clean all over, except for his feet. You are clean as well—though not every one of you [is]." [11](For he knew who was to betray him. That was why he said, "Not every one of you is clean.")

[12]Once he had washed their feet, and put his outer garments back on, and resumed his place, he said to them, "Do you realize what I have done for you? [13]You call me Teacher and Lord; and you are right, for so I am. [14]If I then, your Lord and Teacher, have washed your feet, you should wash one another's feet also. [15]For I have given you an example, that you should also do as I have done for you. [16]Truly, truly, I say to you, a servant is not greater than his master. Nor is the one who is sent greater than the one who sent him. [17]Knowing these things, you are blessed if you do them. [18]I am not speaking of you all. I know whom I have chosen. The scripture will be fulfilled: 'He who ate my bread has lifted his heel against me.' [19]I tell you this now, before it takes place, so that when it does take place you may believe that I am He. [20]Truly, truly, I say to you, whoever receives anyone whom I send receives me—and he who receives me receives him who sent me."

[21]When Jesus had said these things, he was troubled in spirit, and declared, "Truly, truly, I say to you, one of you will betray me." [22]The disciples looked at one another, not sure whom he meant. [23]One of his disciples, whom Jesus loved, was reclining at table right next to Jesus. [24]So Simon Peter beckoned to him and said,

"Tell us who it is that he is talking about." ²⁵So that disciple, leaning back against Jesus, asked him, "Lord, who is it?" ²⁶Jesus answered, "It is the one that I am about to give this morsel to, once I have dipped it." So when he had dipped the morsel, he gave it to Judas, the son of Simon Iscariot. ²⁷After he had taken the morsel, Satan entered into him. Jesus said to him, "What you are going to do, do quickly." ²⁸Now no one at the table knew why he said this to him. ²⁹Because Judas kept the money bag, some thought that Jesus was telling him, "Buy what we need for the feast"; or, that he should give something to the poor. ³⁰So, immediately after receiving the morsel, he went out. It was nighttime.

³¹Once he had gone out, Jesus said, "Now the Son of Man is glorified, and God is glorified in him. ³²If God is glorified in him, God will also glorify him in himself, and glorify him at once. ³³Little children, I am with you for only a little while more. You will seek me, and as I said to the Jews I also say to you now: 'Where I am going you cannot come.' ³⁴A new commandment I give to you: that you love one another. Just as I have loved you, you as well are to love one another. ³⁵By this everyone will know that you are my disciples, if you have love for one another." ³⁶Simon Peter said to him, "Lord, where are you going?" Jesus answered, "Where I am going you cannot follow me now; but you shall follow afterward." ³⁷Peter said to him, "Lord, why can I not follow you now? I will lay down my life for you." ³⁸Jesus answered, "Will you lay down your life for me? Truly, truly, I say to you, the cock will not crow until you have denied me three times.

Chapter 14

I Am the Way and the Truth and the Life

¹"Let not your hearts be troubled: you believe in God. Believe also in me. ²In my Father's house are many rooms. If it were not so, would I have told you that I go to prepare a place for you? ³And when I go and prepare a place for you, I will come again and will take you to myself, so that you may also be where I am. ⁴And you know the way to where I am going." ⁵Thomas said to him, "Lord, we do not even know where you are going. How can we know the way there?" ⁶Jesus said to him, "I am the way and the truth and the life. No one comes to the Father but by me. ⁷If you had known me, you would have known my Father also. From now on you do know him and have seen him."

⁸Philip said to him, "Lord, show us the Father, and we shall be satisfied." ⁹Jesus said to him, "Have I been with you so long, and yet you do not know me, Philip? He who has seen me has seen the Father. How can you say, 'Show us the Father'? ¹⁰Do you not believe that I am in the Father and the Father in me? I do not speak

the words that I say to you on my own authority. But the Father who dwells in me does his deeds. [11]Believe me that I am in the Father and the Father is in me, or else believe me by virtue of the deeds themselves. [12]Truly, truly, I say to you, he who believes in me will also do the things that I do. And he will do greater things than these because I go to the Father. [13]Whatever you ask in my name, I will do it, that the Father may be glorified in the Son. [14]If you ask anything in my name, I will do it.

The Holy Spirit is Promised

[15]"If you love me, you will keep my commandments. [16]And I will pray [to] the Father, and he will give you another Counselor, to be with you forever, [17]which is the Spirit of truth, whom the world cannot receive, because it neither sees him nor knows him. You know him, for he dwells with you, and will be in you.

[18]"I will not leave you as orphans; I will come to you. [19]In just a little while, the world will see me no more, but you will see me. Because I live, you will live also. [20]In that day you will know that I am in my Father, and you in me, and I in you. [21]Whoever has my commandments and keeps them is the one who loves me. And whoever loves me will be loved by my Father, and I will love him and manifest myself to him." [22]Judas (not Iscariot) said to him, "Lord, how is it that you will manifest yourself to us but not to the world?" [23]Jesus answered him, "If anyone loves me, he will keep my word, and my Father will love him, and we will come to him and make our home with him. [24]He who does not love me does not keep my words. And the word that you hear is not mine but the Father's. And he sent me.

[25]"I have spoken these things to you while I am still with you. [26]But the Counselor, the Holy Spirit, whom the Father will send in my name, will teach you all things and bring all that I have said to you to your remembrance. [27]I am leaving peace with you; I am giving my peace to you. I am giving this to you not as the world does. Do not let your hearts be troubled, neither let them be afraid. [28]You heard me say to you, 'I am going away, and I will come to you.' If you loved me, you would have rejoiced, because I am going to the Father—for the Father is greater than I [am]. [29]And now I have told you before it happens, so that when it does happen you may believe. [30]I will not be talking with you much longer, for the ruler of this world is coming. He has no power over me. [31]But I do as the Father has commanded me, so that the world may know that I love the Father. Now get up, and we must leave here.

Chapter 15

The Vine and the Branches

[1]"I am the true vine, and my Father is the vinedresser. [2]He removes every branch of mine that does not bear fruit, and he prunes every one that does bear fruit, that it may produce more fruit. [3]You are already made clean by the word that I have spoken to you. [4]Abide in me, and I [will abide] in you. As the branch cannot bear fruit by itself, unless it abides in the vine, neither can you, unless you abide in me. [5]I am the vine, you are the branches. Anyone who abides in me, and I in him, bears much fruit, for apart from me you can do nothing. [6]If anyone does not abide in me, as a branch he is thrown away and withers. Then the branches are gathered, thrown into the fire, and burned. [7]If you abide in me, and my words abide in you, ask whatever you want, and it shall be done for you. [8]My Father is glorified by this: that you bear much fruit, and so prove to be my disciples. [9]As the Father has loved me, so have I loved you; abide in my love. [10]If you keep my commandments, you will abide in my love, just as I have kept my Father's commandments and abide in his love. [11]I have spoken these things to you so that my joy may be in you, and your joy may be full.

[12]"This is my commandment: Love one another as I have loved you. [13]No man has a love greater than this: that he lay down his life for his friends. [14]You are my friends if you do what I command you. [15]No longer do I call you servants, for the servant does not know what his master is doing. Rather, I have called you friends, for I have made known to you all that I have heard from my Father. [16]You did not choose me, but I chose you and appointed you that you should go and bear fruit and that your fruit should abide, so that the Father may give to you whatever you ask him in my name. [17]I command these things to you so that you will love one another.

The World Will Hate You

[18]"If the world hates you, be aware that it has hated me before it hated you. [19]If you were of the world, the world would love you as its own. However, because you are not of the world, but rather I chose you out of the world, therefore the world hates you. [20]Remember the word that I said to you, 'A servant is not greater than his master.' If they persecuted me, they will persecute you. If they kept my word, they will keep yours also. [21]But they will do all this to you on account of my name because they do not know him who sent me. [22]If I had not come and spoken to them, they would not have been guilty of sin. But now they have no excuse for their sin. [23]Whoever hates me hates my Father also. [24]If I had not done the things

that no one else had ever done among them, they would not have been guilty of sin. But now they have seen and hated both me and my Father. ²⁵It is to fulfill the word that is written in their law, 'They hated me for no reason.'

²⁶But when the Counselor comes, whom I shall send to you from the Father, [and] who is the Spirit of truth who proceeds from the Father, he will bear witness to me. ²⁷And you also are witnesses because you have been with me from the beginning.

Chapter 16

¹"I have warned you about all this to keep you from falling away. ²They will shove you out of the synagogues. Indeed, the time is coming when whoever kills you will think he is offering service to God. ³And they will do this because they have not known the Father nor me. ⁴Now I have told you these things so that when their time comes you may remember that I told them to you.

The Work of the Holy Spirit

"I have not been telling you these things right from the start because I have been with you. ⁵But now I am going to him who sent me. Yet, none of you are asking me, 'Where are you going?' ⁶But because I have said these things to you, sorrow has filled your hearts. ⁷Nevertheless I tell you the truth: it is to your advantage that I go away, for if I do not go away, the Counselor will not come to you. But if I do go, I will send him to you. ⁸And when he comes, he will convince the world concerning sin and righteousness and judgment:

⁹concerning sin because they do not believe in me;

¹⁰concerning righteousness because I go to the Father, and you will see me no more;

¹¹concerning judgment because the ruler of this world is judged.

¹²"I still have many things to say to you, but you cannot handle them now. ¹³When the Spirit of truth comes, he will guide you into all the truth, for he will not speak on his own authority, but whatever he hears he will speak, and he will declare to you the things that are to come. ¹⁴He will glorify me, for he will take what is mine and declare it to you. ¹⁵All that the Father has is mine. Therefore, I said that he will take what is mine and declare it to you.

¹⁶"In a little while you will see me no more. Then after another little while, you will see me once more." ¹⁷Some of his disciples said to one another, "What is this that he is telling us, 'In a little while you will see me no more; then after another little while, you will see me once more.'; and, 'because I go to the Father'?" ¹⁸They said, "What does he mean by 'a little while'? We do not know what he means." ¹⁹Jesus

knew that they wanted to ask him, so he said to them, "Is this what you are asking each other: what I meant by saying, 'In a little while you will see me no more; then after another little while, you will see me once more'? [20]Truly, truly, I say to you, you will weep and lament, but the world will rejoice. You will be sorrowful, but your sorrow will turn into joy. [21]When a woman is in childbirth she has sorrow because her hour has come. But when she has delivered the baby, she no longer remembers the anguish, due to the joy that a child has been born into the world. [22]So you have sorrow now, but I will see you again and your hearts will rejoice, and no one will take your joy away from you. [23]In that day you will ask nothing of me. Truly, truly, I say to you, if you ask anything of the Father in my name, he will give it to you. [24]Up until now you have asked nothing in my name. Ask, and you will receive, that your joy may be full.

[25]"I have said this to you in figures of speech. The hour is coming when I shall no longer speak to you in figures of speech but tell you plainly about the Father. [26]In that day you will ask in my name, and I am not telling you that I shall ask the Father on your behalf. [27]For the Father himself loves you because you have loved me and have believed that I came from the Father. [28]I came from the Father and have come into the world. Now I am leaving the world and going to the Father."

[29]His disciples said, "Ah, now you are speaking plainly, not speaking figuratively! [30]Now we know that you know all things and need no one to question you. By this we believe that you came from God." [31]Jesus answered them, "Now do you believe? [32]Look, the hour is coming—indeed it has come—when you will be scattered, every man to his home, and you will leave me alone. Yet I am not alone, for the Father is with me. [33]I have said this to you, that in me you may have peace. In the world you have tribulation, but take courage: I have overcome the world."

Chapter 17

Jesus Prays the Prayer of a High Priest

[1]Once Jesus had spoken these words, he lifted up his eyes to heaven and said, "Father, the hour has come. Glorify your Son so that the Son may glorify you, [2]since you have given him authority over all flesh, to give eternal life to everyone whom you have given him. [3]And this is eternal life: that they know you, the only true God, and Jesus Christ, whom you have sent. [4]I glorified you on earth, having accomplished the work that you gave me to do. [5]And now, Father, glorify me in your own presence with the glory that I had with you before the world was made.

⁶"I have made your name known to the people whom you gave me out of the world. They were yours, and you gave them to me, and they have kept your word. ⁷Now they know that everything that you have given me is from you. ⁸For I have given them the words that you gave me, and they have received them and realized that I truly came from you, and they have believed that you did send me. ⁹I am praying for them; I am not praying for the world but for those whom you have given me, for they are yours. ¹⁰All mine are yours, and yours are mine, and I am glorified in them. ¹¹And now I am no longer in the world, but they are in the world, and I am coming to you. Holy Father, keep them in your name, which you have given me, that they may be one, even as we are one. ¹²While I was with them, I kept those whom you have given me in your name. I have guarded them, and none of them is lost except the son of damnation, that the scripture might be fulfilled. ¹³But now I am coming to you. And these things I speak in the world, that they may have my joy fulfilled in themselves. ¹⁴I have given them your word, and the world has hated them because they are not of the world, even as I am not of the world. ¹⁵I am not praying that you should take them out of the world, but that you should keep them from the evil one. ¹⁶They are not of the world, even as I am not of the world. ¹⁷Set them apart for holy things in the truth; your word is truth. ¹⁸As you sent me into the world, so I have sent them into the world. ¹⁹And I set myself apart for holy things for their sake so that they as well may be truly set apart for holy things.

²⁰"I am praying not only for these people, but also for those who will believe in me through their word, ²¹that they may all be one even as you, Father, are in me, and I in you, that they also may be in us, so that the world may believe that you have sent me. ²²I have given the glory that you have given me to them so that they may be one even as we are one, ²³I in them and you in me, that they may become perfectly one, so that the world may know that you have sent me and have loved them even as you have loved me. ²⁴Father, I desire that they also, whom you have given me, may be with me where I am, to gaze on my glory that you have given me in your love for me before the foundation of the world. ²⁵O righteous Father, the world has not known you, but I have known you, and these [men] know that you have sent me. ²⁶I made your name known to them, and I will keep making it known, so that the love you have loved me with may be in them, and I in them."

Chapter 18

Judas Betrays Jesus

¹When Jesus had spoken these words, he went forth with his disciples across the Kidron ravine, to where there was a garden, which he and his disciples entered. ²Now

Judas, who betrayed him, also knew the place, for Jesus often withdrew there with his disciples. ³Then Judas, having rounded up a band of soldiers and some officers from the chief priests and the Pharisees, went there with lanterns and torches and weapons. ⁴Then Jesus, knowing all that was to befall him, came forward and asked them, "Who are you looking for?" ⁵They answered him, "Jesus of Nazareth." Jesus replied to them, "I am [He]." Judas, who betrayed him, was standing with them. ⁶When he said to them, "I am [He]," they drew back and fell to the ground. ⁷Again he asked them, "Whom are you looking for?" And they said, "Jesus of Nazareth." ⁸Jesus answered, "I told you that I am he. So, if I am the one you are looking for, let these men go." ⁹This was to fulfill the word that he had spoken, "I have not lost one off those whom you gave me." ¹⁰Then Simon Peter drew a sword that he had and struck the high priest's servant [with it], cutting off his right ear. (The servant's name was Malchus.) ¹¹Jesus said to Peter, "Put your sword into its sheath. Shall I not drink of the cup that the Father has given me?"

Jesus Set Before Annas while Peter Denies Him

¹²So the band of soldiers and their captain and the officers of the Jews seized Jesus and bound him. ¹³First they led him to Annas, because he was the father-in-law of Caiaphas, who was high priest that year. ¹⁴(Caiaphas was the one who had advised the Jews that it was expedient that one man should die for the people.)

¹⁵Simon Peter followed Jesus, and so did another disciple. Now this disciple was known to the high priest, so he entered the court of the high priest along with Jesus, ¹⁶while Peter stood outside at the door. So the other disciple, the one known to the high priest, went out and spoke to the doorkeeper girl and brought Peter in. ¹⁷This maid who kept the door asked Peter, "Aren't you one of this man's disciples also?" He said, "I am not." ¹⁸Now because it was cold, the servants and officers had made a charcoal fire, and they were standing and warming themselves. Peter was also with them, standing and warming himself.

¹⁹The high priest then questioned Jesus about his disciples and his teaching. ²⁰Jesus answered him, "I have spoken openly to the world; I have always taught in synagogues and in the temple, where all Jews come together; I have said nothing secretly. ²¹Why do you ask me? Ask those who have heard me what I said to them; they know what I said." ²²When he had said this, one of the officers standing by struck Jesus with his hand, saying, "Is that how you answer the high priest?" ²³Jesus answered him, "If I have spoken wrongly, explain the error. But if I have spoken correctly, why are you striking me?" ²⁴Annas then sent him bound to Caiaphas the high priest.

Peter Denies Jesus Again

[25]Now as Simon Peter was standing and warming himself, someone asked him, "Aren't you one of his disciples, also?" He denied it, saying, "I am not." [26]One of the servants of the high priest, a kinsman of the man whose ear Peter had cut off, asked, "Didn't I see you in the garden with him?" [27]Peter again denied it, and at once the cock crowed.

Jesus Before Pilate

[28]Then they led Jesus from the house of Caiaphas to the governor's headquarters. It was early morning. They themselves did not enter the headquarters, so that they might not be defiled, but would be able to eat the Passover. [29]So Pilate went out to them and asked, "What accusation do you bring against this man?" [30]They answered him, "If this man were not doing evil, we would not have handed him over." [31]Pilate said to them, "Take him yourselves and judge him by your own law." The Jews said to him, "It is not lawful for us to put anyone to death." [32]This was to fulfill the word that Jesus had spoken to show by what death he was to die.

[33]Pilate entered the headquarters again and called Jesus and questioned him, "Are you the King of the Jews?" [34]Jesus answered, "Are you saying this of your own accord, or did others say it to you about me?" [35]Pilate answered, "Am I a Jew? Your own nation and the chief priests have handed you over to me. What have you done?" [36]Jesus answered, "My kingdom is not of this world. If my kingdom were of this world, my servants would fight, that I might not be handed over to the Jews. But, at this time, my kingdom is not from here." [37]Pilate said to him, "So you are a king?" Jesus answered, "You state that I am a king. I was born for this purpose, and I have come into the world for this: to bear witness to the truth. Everyone who is of the truth hears my voice." [38]Pilate asked him, "What is truth?"

After he had said this, he went back outside to the Jews and told them, "I find no guilt in him. [39]But a custom of yours is that at the Passover I should release one man for you. Will you have me release the King of the Jews for you?" [40]Again they exclaimed, "Not this man, but Barabbas!" (Now Barabbas was a robber.)

Chapter 19

Jesus is Crucified

[1]Then Pilate took Jesus and had him flogged. [2]And the soldiers wove a crown of thorns, and put it on his head, and arrayed him in a purple robe. [3]They kept taunting him, saying, "Hail, King of the Jews!" and slapping him with their hands. [4]Then Pilate went out again, and said to them, "See, I am bringing him out to

you, that you may know that I find no guilt in him." [5]So Jesus came out, wearing the crown of thorns and the purple robe. Pilate said to them, "Here is the man!" [6]When the chief priests and the officers saw him, they cried out, "Crucify him, crucify him!" Pilate said to them, "Take him away yourselves and you crucify him, for I find no guilt in him." [7]The Jews answered him, "We have a law, and by that law he ought to die, because he has made himself out to be the Son of God." [8]On hearing these words, Pilate was even more fearful. [9]He entered the headquarters again and asked Jesus, "Where are you from?" But Jesus gave him no response. [10]Pilate therefore said to him, "You will not speak to me? Do you not realize that I have the authority to release you or to crucify you?" [11]Jesus answered him, "You would have no authority over me unless it had been given to you from above. Therefore, the one who delivered me to you bears the greater sin."

[12]After this, Pilate tried to release him, but the Jews cried out, "If you release this man, you are not Caesar's friend. Everyone who makes himself a king opposes Caesar." [13]When Pilate heard these words, he brought Jesus out and sat down on the judgment seat at a place called The Stone Pavement (which in Hebrew is "Gabbatha"). [14]Now it was about noon on the day of Preparation of the Passover. He said to the Jews, "Here is your King!" [15]They cried out, "Away with him, away with him, crucify him!" Pilate said to them, "Should I crucify your King?" The chief priests answered, "We have no king but Caesar." [16]Then he handed him over to them to be crucified.

[17]So they took Jesus, and he went out, bearing his own cross, to the place called the place of a skull, (which in Hebrew is "Golgotha"). [18]They crucified him there, and two others with him, one on either side, with Jesus between them. [19]Pilate also wrote down a title and had it put on a placard on the cross; it read:

JESUS OF NAZARETH, THE KING OF THE JEWS.

[20]Many of the Jews read this title, for the place where Jesus was crucified was near the city, and it was written in Hebrew, in Latin, and in Greek. [21]The chief priests of the Jews then said to Pilate, "Don't write, *The King of the Jews*, but rather, *This man said, 'I am King of the Jews'.*" [22]Pilate answered, "What I have written, I have written."

[23]Once the soldiers had crucified Jesus they took his garments, dividing them into four parts, one for each soldier. But as for his tunic, it was seamless, woven in one piece from top to bottom. [24]So they said to one another, "Let's not tear it, instead [let's] cast lots for it to see whose it shall be." This was to fulfill the scripture, "They divided up my garments among them, and cast lots for my clothing." [25]So the soldiers did this. But standing by the cross of Jesus were his mother, and his mother's

sister, Mary (the wife of Clopas), and Mary Magdalene. ²⁶When Jesus saw his mother and the disciple whom he loved standing nearby, he said to his mother, "Woman, here is your son!" ²⁷Then he said to the disciple, "Here is your mother!" And from that moment on, the disciple took her into his own home.

²⁸After this, Jesus was aware that all was now finished and said (to fulfill the scripture), "I thirst." ²⁹A jar full of sour wine stood there. So, they put a sponge full of the sour wine on a hyssop branch and held it up to his mouth. ³⁰When Jesus had received the sour wine, he said, "It has been finished"; and he bowed his head and gave up his spirit.

³¹Now it was the Day of Preparation for a Sabbath that was a high holy day. So, in order to prevent the bodies from remaining on the cross on the Sabbath, the Jews requested of Pilate that their legs might be broken, and that they might be taken away. ³²So the soldiers came and broke the legs of the first one and of the other one who had been crucified with him. ³³But when they came to Jesus and saw that he was already dead, they did not break his legs. ³⁴But one of the soldiers pierced his side with a spear, and blood and fluid gushed out. ³⁵The one who saw it has borne witness—his testimony is true—and he knows that he tells the truth so that you also may believe. ³⁶For these things took place that the scripture might be fulfilled, "Not one bone of his shall be broken." ³⁷And again another scripture says, "They will look at the One whom they have pierced."

Jesus' Body is Buried

³⁸After this, Joseph of Arimathea, who was a disciple of Jesus (but secretly so, out of fear of the Jews), asked Pilate if he could take away the body of Jesus, and Pilate gave him permission. So, he came and took away his body. ³⁹Nicodemus, who earlier had come to him at night, also came, bringing a mixture of myrrh and aloes, about a hundred pounds in weight. ⁴⁰They took the body of Jesus, and bound it in linen cloths with the spices, as is the burial custom of the Jews. ⁴¹Now in the place where he was crucified there was a garden, and in the garden a new tomb where no one had ever been laid. ⁴²So because of the Jewish day of Preparation, they laid Jesus there, since the tomb was close by.

Chapter 20

The Empty Tomb

¹Now early on the first day of the week while it was still dark, Mary Magdalene came to the tomb and saw that the stone had been taken away from the tomb. ²So she ran and went to Simon Peter and the other disciple, the one whom Jesus

loved, and said to them, "They have taken the Lord out of the tomb, and we do not know where they have laid him." [3]Peter then came out with the other disciple, and they went toward the tomb. [4]They both ran, but the other disciple outran Peter and reached the tomb first. [5]Stooping to look in, he saw the linen cloths lying there, but he did not go in. [6]Then Simon Peter came, following him, and entered the tomb. He saw the linen cloths lying there, [7]and the face cloth, which had been on his head, not lying with the linen cloths but rolled up in a place by itself. [8]Then the other disciple, who reached the tomb first, also went in, and he saw and believed. [9]For as yet they did not comprehend the scripture, that he must rise from the dead. [10]Then the disciples returned to their homes.

He is Risen Indeed

[11]But Mary stood weeping outside the tomb, and as she wept, she stooped to look into the tomb. [12]And she saw two angels in white, seated where the body of Jesus had lain, one at the head and one at the feet. [13]They said to her, "Woman, why are you weeping?" She answered them, "Because they have taken away my Lord, and I do not know where they have laid him." [14]Having said this, she turned around and saw Jesus standing [there], but she did not know that it was Jesus. [15]Jesus said to her, "Woman, why are you weeping? Whom are you looking for?" Supposing him to be the gardener, she said to him, "Sir, if you have carried him away, tell me where you have laid him, and I will take him away." [16]Jesus said to her, "Mary." She turned and said to him in Hebrew, "Rabboni!" (which means "teacher"). [17]Jesus said to her, "Do not hold on to me, for I have not yet ascended to the Father, but go to my brothers and tell them I am ascending to my Father and your Father, to my God and your God." [18]Mary Magdalene went and announced to the disciples, "I have seen the Lord." And she told them that he had said these things to her.

Jesus Appears to the Disciples

[19]Then during the evening of that day, the first day of the week, the disciples were [together] with the doors locked shut, out of fear of the Jews. Jesus appeared and stood among them and said to them, "Peace be with you." [20]When he had said this, he showed them his hands and his side. When the disciples saw the Lord, they were filled with gladness. [21]Jesus said to them again, "Peace be with you. Just as the Father has sent me, so am I sending you." [22]And once he had said this, he breathed on them, and said to them, "Receive the Holy Spirit. [23]If you forgive the sins of anyone, they are forgiven. If you withhold forgiveness from anyone, they stand unforgiven."

[24]Now Thomas, one of the Twelve, called "the Twin," was not with them when

Jesus came. [25]So the other disciples told him, "We have seen the Lord." But he said to them, "Unless I see the print of the nails in his hands and place my finger in the mark of the nails, and place my hand in his side, I will not believe."

[26]Eight days later, his disciples were again in the house, and Thomas was with them. The doors were locked shut, but Jesus came and stood among them, and said, "Peace be with you." [27]Then he said to Thomas, "Put your finger here and see my hands, and put out your hand and place it in my side. Stop being faithless and believe." [28]Thomas responded to him, "My Lord and my God!" [29]Jesus said to him, "Have you believed because you have seen me? Blessed are those who have not seen but still believe."

[30]Now Jesus did many other signs in the presence of the disciples, which are not written in this book. [31]But these things are written down so that you may believe that Jesus is the Christ, the Son of God, and that by believing you may have life in his name.

Chapter 21

Jesus Provides Fish for the Fishermen

[1]After this, Jesus revealed himself again to the disciples by the Sea of Tiberias, and he revealed himself in this way: [2]Simon Peter, Thomas (called the Twin), Nathanael of Cana in Galilee, the sons of Zebedee, and two others of his disciples were together. [3]Simon Peter said to them, "I am going fishing." They said to him, "We will go with you." They went out and got into the boat, but they caught nothing all night long. [4]Then, as the day was dawning, Jesus stood on the beach, yet the disciples did not realize that it was Jesus. [5]Jesus called to them, "Children, you do not have any fish, do you?" "No," they answered him. [6]He told them, "Cast the net on the right side of the boat, and you will find some." Once they had cast it in, they were unable to haul it in, due to the abundance of fish. [7]That disciple whom Jesus loved said to Peter, "It is the Lord!" When Simon Peter heard that it was the Lord, he put on his outer garment, for he was stripped for work, and threw himself into the sea.

[8]The other disciples followed in the boat, dragging the net full of fish, for they were not far away from the shore, only about 100 yards away. [9]When they got onto land, they saw a lit charcoal fire with fish on it and bread. [10]Jesus said to them, "Bring some of the fish that you have just caught." [11]So, Simon Peter got into the boat, and he dragged the net to the shore, full of large fish—153 of them—and though there were so many, the net did not get torn. [12]Jesus said to them, "Come and have breakfast." Now none of the disciples dared ask him, "Who are you?"

They knew that it was the Lord. [13]Jesus came and took the bread and gave it to them and did the same with the fish. [14]This was now the third time after he was raised from the dead that Jesus showed himself to the disciples.

Peter, Do You Love Me?

[15]When they had finished breakfast, Jesus said to Simon Peter, "Simon, son of John, do you unconditionally love me more than these?" he answered him, "Yes, Lord, you know that I love you." he said to him, "Feed my lambs." [16]A second time he said to him, "Simon, son of John, do you love me unconditionally?" he answered him, "Yes, Lord, you know that I love you." he said to him, "Tend my sheep." [17]He said to him the third time, "Simon, son of John, do you love me?" Peter was grieved because he asked him the third time, "Do you love me?" And he responded to him, "Lord, you know everything; you know that I love you." Jesus said to him, "Feed my sheep. [18]Truly, truly, I say to you, when you were young, you dressed yourself and walked wherever you wanted. But when you are old, you will stretch out your hands, and another will dress you and carry you where you do not want to go." [19](He said this to show by what death he was to glorify God.) Having said this, he said to him, "Follow me."

Jesus and the Beloved Apostle

[20]Peter turned and saw following them the disciple whom Jesus loved, who had reclined right next to him at the last supper and had asked, "Lord, who is it that is going to betray you?" [21]When Peter saw Jesus, he asked of him, "Lord, what about this man?" [22]Jesus replied to him, "If it is my will that he remain until I return, what is that to you? You follow me!" [23]The saying spread abroad among the brothers that this disciple was not going to die. Jesus did not tell him that he was not going to die, but rather [He said]: "If it is my will that he should remain until I return, what is that to you?"

[24]This is the disciple who is bearing witness to these things, and who has written these things, and we know that his testimony is true. [25]Now Jesus did many other things also, and if every one of them were to be written, I suppose that the world itself could not contain the books that would be written.

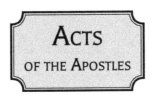

ACTS
OF THE APOSTLES

Chapter 1

The Holy Spirit is Promised

¹In the first book, O Theophilus, I have dealt with all that Jesus did and taught ²until the day when he was taken up [to Heaven], having given orders through the Holy Spirit to the apostles whom he had chosen. ³After his suffering, he showed himself alive, appearing to them in many convincing ways during a period of forty days, and speaking about the kingdom of God.

⁴Now, while he was dining with them, he commanded them not to depart from Jerusalem, but to wait for the Father's promise, which, he said, "you heard from me, ⁵for John baptized with water, but after a few days you will be baptized with the Holy Spirit."

The Ascension into Heaven

⁶So once they had gathered, they asked him, "Lord, are you going to restore the kingdom to Israel now?" ⁷He answered them, "By his own authority, the Father has fixed times and seasons; it is not for you to know them. ⁸But you will receive power when the Holy Spirit has come over you, and you will be my witnesses in Jerusalem and in all Judea and Samaria and to the end of the earth." ⁹And when he had said these things, he was lifted up as they were looking on, and a cloud took him out of their sight. ¹⁰And while they were gazing into heaven as he went—listen to this—two men [dressed] in white robes stood [there] next to them, ¹¹and said, "Men of Galilee, why are you standing [here] looking into heaven? This Jesus, who was taken up from you into heaven, will return just as you saw him go into heaven."

Matthias Chosen to Replace Judas

¹²Then they returned to Jerusalem from the hill called the Mount of Olives, which is near Jerusalem, about a half-mile away. ¹³When they got there, Peter and John and James and Andrew, Philip and Thomas, Bartholomew and Matthew, James the son of Alphaeus and Simon the Zealot and Judas the son of James went up to the upper room [at the place] where they were staying. ¹⁴Being of the same mind,

all these [men] devoted themselves to prayer, along with the women and Mary the mother of Jesus, and his brothers.

¹⁵Now in those days, Peter stood up one day when he was in a crowd of about 120 of the brothers and said,

> ¹⁶"Brothers, long ago the Holy Spirit spoke the scripture through the mouth of David concerning Judas, who led men to arrest Jesus, and this had to be fulfilled. ¹⁷For he was numbered among us and shared in his portion of this ministry. ¹⁸(Now this man bought a field with the reward of his wickedness. Falling headlong, he burst open in the middle and all his intestines gushed out. ¹⁹When all the inhabitants of Jerusalem learned of this, the field was called Akeldama in their language, that is, Field of Blood.) ²⁰For it is written in the Book of Psalms, *'Let his property fall to desolate ruin, and let there be no one to live in it'*; and *'Let another assume his leadership role.'* ²¹So, out of the group of men who have accompanied us during all the time that the Lord Jesus came and went among us—²²beginning from the baptism of John until the day when he was taken up from us—one must become a witness to his resurrection with us."

²³And they put forward two men, Joseph (who was called both Barsabbas and Justus), and Matthias. ²⁴And they prayed, saying, "Lord, you know the hearts of all men. Indicate which one of these two you have chosen ²⁵to take the place in this ministry and apostleship that Judas abandoned to go to his [rightful] place." ²⁶Then they cast lots for them, and the lot fell to Matthias, so he was enrolled with the eleven apostles.

Chapter 2

The Holy Spirit Comes Over the Disciples

¹When the day of Pentecost arrived, they were all meeting together in one place. ²And suddenly a sound came from heaven like the rush of a mighty wind, and it filled the whole house where they were sitting. ³Then tongues like flames of fire appeared to them, apportioned to each [person present], and hovered over each one of them. ⁴They were all filled with the Holy Spirit and began to speak in other languages, as the Spirit gave them words to say.

⁵Now Jews, devout men from every nation under heaven, were living there in Jerusalem. ⁶When this sound happened, the crowd came together, and they were bewildered, because each one heard them speaking in his own language. ⁷And they were amazed and astounded, exclaiming, "Aren't all these people who are speaking Galileans? ⁸So, how is it that we, each one of us, can hear [them] in his own native language? ⁹[As] Parthians and Medes and Elamites and residents of

180

Mesopotamia, Judea and Cappadocia, Pontus and Asia, [10]Phrygia and Pamphylia, Egypt and the parts of Libya belonging to Cyrene, and visitors from Rome, both Jews and proselytes, [11]Cretans and Arabians, we hear them recounting the mighty works of God in our own tongues!" [12]And all were amazed and perplexed, asking "What could this be?" [13]However, mocking [them], others commented, "They are filled with new wine."

Peter Preaches at Pentecost

[14]Then Peter stood up with the eleven others, raised his voice, and addressed them:

"Men of Judea and all you who live in Jerusalem, may you understand this, and listen to my words. [15]For these people are *not* drunk, as you suppose, since it is only nine o'clock in the morning. [16]On the contrary, this is what was spoken by the prophet Joel: [17]'And in the final era, God declares, it shall come to pass that I will pour out my Spirit upon all people, and your sons and your daughters shall prophesy, and your young men shall see visions, and your old men shall dream dreams. [18]In those days I will pour out my Spirit even on my male servants and my female servants, and they will prophesy. [19]And I will display wonders in the heavens above and signs on the earth below: blood, and fire, and smoke vapor. [20]The sun will be turned into darkness and the moon into blood, before the day of the Lord comes—the great and magnificent day. [21]And it shall come to pass that everyone who calls on the name of the Lord shall be saved.'

[22]"Men of Israel, hear these words:

[This] Jesus of Nazareth: God proved to you who he was with awesome deeds and signs and wonders that God performed through him in your midst, as you yourselves know.

[23]"This Jesus: In accordance with the pre-defined plan and God's foreknowledge, *you* handed him over to be crucified and killed by the hands of lawless men. [24]But God raised him up, having released him from the pain of death, because it was not possible for [death] to hold him. [25]David says this about him: 'I always saw the Lord before me, for he is at my right hand so that I will not be shaken. [26]Therefore my heart was glad, and my tongue rejoiced—even my body will rest with hope. [27]For you will not leave my soul in Hell, nor let your Holy One undergo decay. [28]You have explained the ways of life to me. You will fill me with gladness in your presence.' [29]Brothers, I can tell you confidently that the patriarch David both died and was buried, and his tomb is

181

with us to this day. [30]He was a prophet and knew that God had sworn an oath to him that he would put one of his descendants on his throne. [31]He was foreseeing and speaking of the resurrection of the Christ, in that he was not left in Hell, nor did his body undergo decay.

[32]"This Jesus: God raised him [from the dead], and of *that* we all are witnesses. [33]Being therefore exalted at the right hand of God, and having received from the Father the promise of the Holy Spirit, he has poured out what you are seeing and hearing. [34]For *David* did not ascend into the heavens, but he himself says, 'The Lord said to my Lord, Sit at my right hand, [35]until I make your enemies a footstool for your feet.' [36]Let all the house of Israel therefore know for certain that God has made him both Lord and Christ—

This Jesus—whom *you* crucified."

[37]Now upon hearing this, they were cut to the heart and begged Peter and the rest of the apostles, "Brothers, what should we do?" [38]And Peter said to them, "Repent and be baptized, every one of you, in the name of Jesus Christ for the forgiveness of your sins, and you shall receive the gift of the Holy Spirit. [39]For the promise is to you and to your children and to all who are far away, everyone whom the Lord our God calls to himself." [40]And he testified with many other words and encouraged them, saying, "Save yourselves from this crooked generation." [41]So those who received his word were baptized, and about three thousand souls were added that day.

Believers Fellowship

[42]And they devoted themselves to the apostles' teaching and fellowship, to the breaking of bread and the prayers. [43]Awe fell upon every soul, and many wonders and signs were done through the apostles. [44]And all the believers were together and owned everything in common. [45]They sold their possessions and goods and distributed them to all, as anyone had need [of them]. [46]And every day they attended temple together and broke bread in their homes, eating with glad and generous hearts, [47]praising God, and enjoying favor with all the people. And day by day, the Lord added those who were being saved to their number.

Chapter 3

A Lame Beggar is Healed

[1]One day Peter and John went up into the temple at the hour of prayer, 3 o'clock in the afternoon. [2]And a man [who had been] lame from birth was being carried in. Each day he was laid at that Temple gate, called Beautiful, so that he could

182

beg for handouts from people entering the temple. ³Seeing Peter and John about to go into the temple, he asked [them] for a handout. ⁴Peter looked right at him, as did John, and said, "Look at us." ⁵So he fixed his attention on them, expecting to receive something from them. ⁶But Peter said, "I have neither silver nor gold, but what I *do* have is what I will give you: in the name of Jesus Christ of Nazareth, stand up and walk!" ⁷And he took him by the right hand and raised him up, and immediately his feet and ankles became strong enough [to be used]. ⁸And leaping up, he stood and walked and entered the temple with them, walking and leaping and praising God. ⁹Then all the people saw him walking and praising God, ¹⁰and recognized him as the one who sat begging for handouts at the Beautiful Gate of the temple. They were filled with wonder and amazement at what had become of him.

Peter Preaches in the Portico

¹¹While he was clinging to Peter and John, all the people, totally astonished, ran together to them in Solomon's Portico. ¹²Now when Peter saw this, he addressed the people,

"Men of Israel, why are you wondering about this, or why are you staring at us, as though it was through our own power or piety that we have made him able to walk? ¹³The God of Abraham and of Isaac and of Jacob, the God of our fathers, glorified his servant Jesus, whom you handed over and rejected in the presence of Pilate, when he had decided to release him. ¹⁴Instead, you rejected the Holy and Righteous One, and asked for a murderer to be granted to you. ¹⁵So you killed the Author of life, but God raised him from the dead. We are witnesses to this. ¹⁶And by faith in his name, his name has healed this man whom you see and know. And in the presence of all of you, the faith that is through Jesus has given the man this perfect health.

¹⁷"And now, brothers, I know that you acted in ignorance, as your rulers did also. ¹⁸But in this way God fulfilled what he foretold through the mouths of all the prophets: that his Christ would have to suffer. ¹⁹So now, repent, and turn aside so that your sins may be blotted out, so that times of refreshing may come from the presence of the Lord, ²⁰and so that he may send the Christ appointed for you, Jesus. ²¹Heaven must hold him until the time when everything is restored, as God spoke through his holy prophets long ago. ²²Moses said: 'The Lord God will raise up a prophet for you from your brothers as he did me. You must listen earnestly to him, to all that he tells you. ²³And it will be that every soul that does not listen to that prophet shall be destroyed from the people.'

²⁴And all the prophets who have spoken, from Samuel on down through those who followed, also foretold these days. ²⁵You are the descendants of the prophets and heirs of the covenant that God gave to your fathers, saying to Abraham, 'And all the families of the earth will be blessed through your Descendant.' ²⁶Having raised up his servant, God sent him to you first, to bless you in turning each one of you from your wickedness."

Chapter 4

Peter and John Appear Before the Council

¹And while they were speaking to the people, the priests and the captain of the temple and the Sadducees came on them, ²greatly vexed that they were teaching the people and proclaiming resurrection from the dead in Jesus. ³So they arrested them and, since it was already evening, put them in custody until the next morning. ⁴But many of those who heard the word believed, and the number of the men grew to about five thousand.

⁵And so it happened that the next day their rulers and elders and scribes were gathered together in Jerusalem, ⁶with Annas the high priest and Caiaphas and John and Alexander, and all who were of the high priest's family. ⁷Once they had set them in their midst, they inquired, "By what power or by what name did you do this?" ⁸Then Peter, filled with the Holy Spirit, replied to them:

> "Rulers of the people and elders, ⁹if we are being examined today concerning a good deed done to a cripple, and how this man has been healed, ¹⁰be it known to you all, and to all the people of Israel, that this man is standing before you healed by the name of Jesus Christ of Nazareth, whom you crucified, and whom God raised from the dead. ¹¹This is the stone that was rejected by you builders, but which has become the cornerstone. ¹²And in no one else is there salvation, for under heaven there is no other name appointed to mankind by which we must be saved."

¹³Now they were astonished when they saw the boldness of Peter and John, and perceived that they were uneducated, common men, though they did note the fact that they had been with Jesus. ¹⁴Still, seeing the man that had been healed standing beside them, they had no rebuttal. ¹⁵Then, once they had commanded them to go aside out of the council, they conferred with one another, ¹⁶saying, "What are we to do with these men? Why, it's obvious to everybody who lives in Jerusalem that a noteworthy sign has been performed through them, which we cannot deny. ¹⁷But, so that it does not spread any further among the people, let's caution them to not speak to anyone in this name anymore." ¹⁸So they called them back

in and ordered them not to speak or teach at all in the name of Jesus. [19]But Peter and John answered them, "You yourselves must judge whether it is right in the sight of God to listen to you rather than to God, [20]for we cannot keep from talking about what we have seen and heard." [21]And once they had threatened [Peter and John] even more, they let them go on account of the people, finding no way to punish them, since everyone was praising God for what had happened. [22]After all, the man that this sign of healing was performed on was more than forty years old.

Believers Need Boldness

[23]Once they were released, they went to their friends and reported what the chief priests and the elders had said to them. [24]And when [their friends] heard it, they lifted their voices together to God and said,

"Sovereign Lord, you who created heaven and the earth and the sea, and everything in them, [25]said by the Holy Spirit, through the mouth of our father David, your servant: 'Why do the Gentiles furiously rage, and the peoples plot in vain? [26]The kings of the earth ready themselves, and the rulers gather themselves together, against the Lord and against his Anointed.' [27]For truly, in this city were gathered—together with the Gentiles and the peoples of Israel against your holy servant Jesus—both Herod and Pontius Pilate, who were anointed by you [28]to do whatever your hand and your plan had predetermined to take place. [29]And now, Lord, look at their threats, and enable your servants to speak your word with great boldness, [30]while you extend your healing hand, and signs and wonders are performed through the name of your holy servant Jesus."

[31]And when they had prayed, the place where they were gathered together was shaken, and they were all filled with the Holy Spirit and kept speaking the word of God with boldness.

Sharing All Things in Common

[32]Now the company of those who believed were of one heart and mind, and no one claimed any of his belongings as his own, but instead they held everything in common. [33]And the apostles were giving their testimony to the resurrection of the Lord Jesus with great power, and profound grace was on all of them. [34]No one among them was needy, for whoever owned lands or houses sold them and brought the proceeds of what was sold [35]and laid it at the apostles' feet, and it was distributed to each as anyone was in need. [36]So it was that Joseph, a Levite and a native of Cyprus, (whom the apostles called Barnabas, which means Son of encouragement) [37]sold a field that he owned and brought the money and placed it at the feet of the apostles.

Chapter 5

Ananias and Sapphira Hold Back

[1]However, a man named Ananias and his wife Sapphira sold a piece of property, [2]and with his wife's knowledge he held back some of the proceeds for himself and brought only a portion of it and placed it at the feet of the apostles. [3]Peter asked, "Ananias, why has Satan filled your heart to lie to the Holy Spirit and to hold back part of the proceeds of the land for yourself? [4]While still unsold, didn't it remain your own? And after it was sold, wasn't it at your disposal? Why have you contrived this deed in your heart? You have not lied to men but to God." [5]When Ananias heard these words, he fell down and seized up dead. Then great fear fell on everyone who heard about it. [6]The young men got up and wrapped him up and carried him out and buried him.

[7]Now it happened that about three hours later his wife came in, not knowing what had just taken place. [8]And Peter said to her, "Tell me whether you sold the land for such-and-such a price." And she said, "Yes, that was the price." [9]So Peter said to her, "How could both of you have agreed together to put the Spirit of the Lord to a test? Look—there at the door are the feet of the men who have buried your husband, and they will carry you out." [10]Immediately she fell down at his feet and seized up dead. When the young men entered, they found her dead, and they carried her out and buried her beside her husband. [11]Then a profound fear fell on the whole church and on everyone who heard about these events.

Signs and Wonders Performed

[12]Now at the hands of the apostles many signs and wonders were being performed among the people. They continued to gather in Solomon's Portico. [13]None of the rest dared to join them, although the people did hold them in high regard. [14]And more and more, believers were added to the Lord—great numbers of both men and women— [15]such that the sick were even carried into the streets and laid on beds and pallets so that as Peter passed by at least his shadow might fall on some of them. [16]People from the towns around Jerusalem also thronged in, bringing the sick and those troubled by evil spirits, and all of them were healed.

Apostles Arrested and Then Freed

[17]But the high priest took a stand, along with all who were with him, (that is, the party of the Sadducees), and being filled with jealousy, [18]they arrested the apostles and put them in the public jail. [19]But at nighttime an angel of the Lord opened the doors of the jail and brought them out and said, [20]"Go and stand in the temple and explain all about this [new] life to the people." [21]And having heard this, at daybreak they entered the temple and started teaching.

Now the high priest came, along with those who attended him, and he called together the council and all the senate of Israel and sent to the jail to have the [apostles] brought [to him]. [22]But when the officers got to the jail, they could not find them there, so they returned and reported, [23]"We found the jail locked securely and the sentries standing at the doors, but we found no one inside when we opened it up." [24]Now when the captain of the temple and the chief priests heard this report, they were quite perplexed about it, wondering what this would come to. [25]Then someone came and told them, "Those men that you put in jail are standing in the temple teaching the people." [26]So then the captain, along with the officers, went and seized them, but without violence, for they were afraid of being stoned by the crowd.

[27]Now when they had brought them [there], they set them before the council. And the high priest questioned them, [28]saying, "We gave you strict orders not to teach in this name, and look—you have filled Jerusalem with your teaching and you're intending to lay the guilt of this man's death on us." [29]But Peter and the apostles answered,

"We must obey God rather than men. [30]The God of our forefathers resurrected Jesus, whom you killed by hanging him on [the wood of] a tree. [31]God exalted him at his right hand as Prince and Savior, to grant Israel [the opportunity for] repentance and forgiveness of sins. [32]We and the Holy Spirit, whom God has given to those who obey him, are witnesses to these things."

[33]When they heard this they were enraged and wanted to kill them. [34]But a Pharisee named Gamaliel, [who was] a teacher of the law and held in honor by all the people, stood up in the council and ordered that the men be put outside for a while. [35]And he addressed them:

"Men of Israel, be careful about how you handle these men, [36]because a while back Theudas arose, claiming to be someone [special], and a number of men, about four hundred, joined him. But he was killed and all who followed him were dispersed and [it all] came to nothing. [37]After him Judas the Galilean arose, [back] in the days of the census, and convinced some of the people to follow him. He also perished, and all who followed him were scattered. [38]So in the present case I warn you: keep away from these men and leave them alone. For if this scheme—this movement—is of man, it will be overthrown. [39]But if it is of God, you will not be able to stop them. It might turn out that you are opposing God!"

[40]So they took his advice, and when they had called in the apostles, they beat them, ordered them not to speak in the name of Jesus, and released them. [41]Then the [apostles] left the presence of the council, rejoicing that they were counted

187

worthy to suffer dishonor for the name [of Christ]. [42]And every day, both in the temple and at home, they did not stop teaching and preaching Jesus as the Christ.

Chapter 6

First Seven Deacons Appointed

[1]Now in these days when the number of disciples was increasing, the Greek-speaking Jews started murmuring against the native Jews because their own widows were being neglected in the daily [food] distribution. [2]So, the Twelve summoned the body of the disciples and said, "It is not right that we should reduce our time preaching the word of God in order to wait tables. [3]Therefore, brothers, choose from among yourselves seven men of good repute, full of the Spirit and of wisdom, whom we may appoint to this duty. [4]But we will devote ourselves to prayer and to the ministry of the word." [5]And this statement pleased the whole crowd, and they chose Stephen, a man full of faith and of the Holy Spirit, and Philip, and Prochorus, and Nicanor, and Timon, and Parmenas, and Nicolaus, a proselyte of Antioch. [6]They set these men before the apostles, and they prayed and laid their hands on them.

[7]So the word of God increased, and the number of the disciples multiplied greatly in Jerusalem, and a great many of the priests even came to faith.

Stephen Dragged Before the Council

[8]Now Stephen, full of grace and power, did great wonders and signs among the people. [9]Then some of those who belonged to the synagogue of the Freedmen (as it was called), and of the Cyrenians, and of the Alexandrians, and of those from Cilicia and Asia, started a dispute with Stephen. [10]But they could not resist the wisdom and the Spirit that he spoke with. [11]So they secretly instigated some people to say, "We have heard him blaspheme Moses and God." [12]And they stirred up the people and the elders and the scribes, and they ran up and grabbed him and dragged him before the council. [13]They set up false witnesses who claimed, "This man never stops speaking words against this holy place and the law, [14]for we have heard him say that this Jesus of Nazareth will destroy this place and alter the customs handed down to us from Moses." [15]Everyone sitting in the council looked intently at him and noticed that his face resembled the face of an angel.

Chapter 7

Stephen's Speech on Jewish History

¹So the high priest asked him, "Are these things so?" ²And Stephen replied:

"Brothers and fathers, listen. The God of glory appeared to our father Abraham, when he was in Mesopotamia, before he lived in Haran, ³and said to him, 'Leave your land and your kinsmen and go into the land that I will show you.' ⁴Then he departed from the land of the Chaldeans and lived in Haran. And after his father died, God moved him from there into this land where you are now living. ⁵Yet he gave him no property in it, not even a foot's length, but promised to give it to him and to his descendants after him, as a permanent possession, even though he did not have a child. ⁶And God indicated that his descendants would sojourn in a land belonging to another people who would enslave them and oppress them for four hundred years. ⁷'But I will judge the nation that holds them in bondage,' said God, 'and after that they shall escape and [come to] worship me in this place.' ⁸And he gave him the covenant of circumcision. And so, Abraham became the father of Isaac, and circumcised him on the eighth day; and Isaac became the father of Jacob, and Jacob of the twelve patriarchs.

⁹"And the patriarchs envied Joseph and sold him into Egypt. But God was with him, ¹⁰and rescued him out of all his afflictions, giving him favor and wisdom before Pharaoh, king of Egypt, who made him governor over both Egypt and all his household. ¹¹Now there came a famine with great misery throughout all Egypt and Canaan, and our forefathers could find no food. ¹²But when Jacob heard that there was grain in Egypt, he sent out our forefathers on a first visit. ¹³Then on the second visit Joseph made himself known to his brothers, and Joseph's family was introduced to Pharaoh. ¹⁴Then Joseph sent and summoned his father Jacob and all his family, seventy-five persons in all. ¹⁵Jacob went down into Egypt and died [there]—he himself and our forefathers—¹⁶and [their bodies] were carried back to Shechem and laid in the tomb that Abraham had bought for a sum of silver from the sons of Hamor in Shechem.

¹⁷"But as the time of the promise that God had made to Abraham approached, the number of our people in Egypt increased greatly ¹⁸until another king, who had not known Joseph, came to power in Egypt. ¹⁹He dealt with our people in a scheming way to force our forefathers to leave their infants vulnerable to being killed. ²⁰Moses was born at this time, and in God's sight he was beautiful. He was brought up for three months in his father's house. ²¹And when he was no longer hidden, Pharaoh's daughter adopted him and brought him up as her own son. ²²Moses was educated in all the wisdom of the Egyptians, and he was mighty in both speech and action.

²³"When he was forty years old, he longed in his heart to visit his brothers, the sons of Israel. ²⁴And seeing one of them being mistreated, he defended the oppressed man and avenged him by striking down the Egyptian. ²⁵He assumed that his brothers understood that through him God was extending deliverance to them, but they did not understand. ²⁶On the following day he appeared to them as they were quarreling and wanted to reconcile them, saying, 'Men, you are brothers. Why are you mistreating one another?' ²⁷But the man who was mistreating his neighbor shoved him aside, saying, 'Who made you a ruler and a judge over us? ²⁸Do you intend to kill me as you killed the Egyptian yesterday?' ²⁹At this reply Moses fled, and became an exile in the land of Midian, where he fathered two sons.

³⁰"Now when forty years had passed, an angel appeared to him in the wilderness of Mount Sinai, in a flame of a burning bush. ³¹When Moses saw it he wondered at the sight; and as he drew near to look, the voice of the Lord came, ³²'I am the God of your fathers, the God of Abraham and of Isaac and of Jacob.' And Moses trembled and did not dare to look. ³³And the Lord said to him, 'Take the shoes off your feet, for the place where you are standing is holy ground. ³⁴You see, indeed I have seen the affliction of my people who are in Egypt and have heard their groaning, and so I have come down to deliver them. Come now, I will send you to Egypt.'

³⁵"God sent this Moses (whom they had rejected by saying, 'Who made you a ruler and a judge?') as both ruler and deliverer by the hand of the angel that appeared to him in the bush. ³⁶This man led them out and performed wonders and signs in Egypt and at the Red Sea, and for forty years in the wilderness. ³⁷This is the Moses who said to the Israelites, 'God will raise up a prophet like me for you from your brothers.' ³⁸This is the one who was in the assembly in the wilderness, and with the angel who spoke to him at Mount Sinai, and with our fathers. He received the living word to give to us. ³⁹Our fathers refused to obey him but pushed him aside instead. In their hearts they yearned for [the ways of] Egypt, ⁴⁰saying to Aaron, 'Fashion us [some] gods who can lead us. As for this Moses who led us out from the land of Egypt, we don't even know what has become of him.' ⁴¹And in those days they created a calf and offered a sacrifice to that idol, rejoicing in the works of their hands. ⁴²But God turned aside and gave them over to worshiping the stars of heaven, as it is written in the book of the prophets: 'Was it to me that you offered slaughtered beasts and sacrifices, during those forty years in the wilderness, O house of Israel? ⁴³You carried the tent of Moloch, and the star of your god Rephan—the images that you made to worship. So, I shall send you into exile farther than Babylon.'

⁴⁴"Our forefathers had the tent of witness in the wilderness, which was just like Moses had been directed to make it, according to the pattern that he had seen. ⁴⁵Our forefathers in turn brought it in with Joshua when they took the land from the Gentile nations that God drove out before our forefathers. And there it was until the days of David, ⁴⁶who found favor in the sight of God and asked for permission to find a dwelling place for the God of Jacob. ⁴⁷But it was Solomon who built a house for him. ⁴⁸Yet the Most High does not dwell in houses made with hands. As the prophet says, ⁴⁹'Heaven is my throne, and earth my footstool. What house will you build for me, says the Lord, or what is the place of my rest? ⁵⁰Was it not my hand that made all these things?'

⁵¹"You stiff-necked people—pagan hearted and deaf—you always resist the Holy Spirit. As your fathers once did, so you are doing. ⁵²Which one of the prophets did your forefathers *not* persecute? They killed those who foretold the coming of the Righteous One, whom you have now betrayed and murdered. ⁵³You even received the law brought by the angels and yet did not obey it."

Stephen is Martyred

⁵⁴Now when they heard these things they were infuriated, and they gnashed their teeth against him. ⁵⁵But Stephen, full of the Holy Spirit, gazed into heaven and saw the glory of God, and Jesus standing at the right hand of God. ⁵⁶And he said, "Look—I [can] see the heavens opened up and the Son of Man standing at the right hand of God." ⁵⁷But they began yelling, and they covered their ears with their hands and rushed together on top of him. ⁵⁸Then they threw him out of the city and began stoning him. The witnesses laid down their garments at the feet of a young man named Saul. ⁵⁹And as they were stoning him, Stephen called out, saying, "Lord Jesus, receive my spirit." ⁶⁰And falling on his knees, he cried out loudly, "Lord, do not hold this sin against them." And having said this, he fell into the sleep of death, and Saul heartily approved of his being killed.

Chapter 8

Saul Persecutes the Church

^{1b}And on that day a great persecution against the church in Jerusalem started, and, other than the apostles, [believers] were all scattered throughout the region of Judea and Samaria. ²Devout men buried Stephen and lamented over him greatly. ³But Saul was ravaging the church. He entered house after house and dragged off men and women and had them sent to prison.

⁴Now those who were scattered went about sharing the good news. ⁵Philip went down to a city in Samaria and proclaimed Christ to them. ⁶And in great unity the crowds heeded what Philip said when they heard him and saw the signs that he performed, ⁷because evil spirits came out of many people who were possessed, each crying out with a loud voice. In addition, many others who were paralyzed or lame were healed. ⁸So in that city there was much joy.

Simon the Magician Comes to Faith

⁹But in that city there was a man named Simon who had once practiced magic and amazed the nation of Samaria, claiming that he himself was somebody great. ¹⁰Everybody, from the least to the greatest, focused their attention on him, saying, "He surely is what is known as the Great Power of God." ¹¹So, they continued paying attention to him because he had amazed them with his magical power for such a long time. ¹²But then, as those people came to believe the good news about the kingdom of God and the name of Jesus Christ, as preached by Philip, both men and women started getting baptized. ¹³Even Simon himself believed, and after being baptized he stayed on with Philip, being awestruck at seeing signs and great miracles being performed.

¹⁴Now when the apostles at Jerusalem heard that Samaria had accepted the word of God, they sent Peter and John to them. ¹⁵They came down and prayed for them that they might receive the Holy Spirit, ¹⁶for as yet he had not yet fallen on any of them, since they had been baptized just in the name of the Lord Jesus. ¹⁷Then they laid their hands on them and they received the Holy Spirit. ¹⁸Now when Simon saw that the Spirit was imparted through the laying on of the hands of the apostles, he offered them money, ¹⁹saying, "Give this power to me, too, so that anyone that I lay my hands on may receive the Holy Spirit." ²⁰But Peter said to him, "May your silver perish with you, because you thought you could secure the gift of God with money! ²¹You do not have part or parcel in this work, because your heart is not right with God. ²²So now, repent of this wickedness of yours, and pray to the Lord that, if possible, you will be forgiven for this intent of your heart. ²³For I perceive that you are [trapped] in the gall of bitterness and in bondage to sinfulness." ²⁴And Simon answered, "Pray to the Lord for me, that nothing of what you have said may happen to me."

²⁵Once they had given testimonies and had spoken the word of the Lord, they journeyed back to Jerusalem, preaching the gospel in many Samaritan towns.

Philip Meets an Ethiopian Eunuch

[26]Now an angel of the Lord said to Philip, "Get up and go south to the road that goes down from Jerusalem to Gaza." This is a desert road. [27]And he got up and went. Now, you see, there was an Ethiopian eunuch, the high official of Candace, the queen of the Ethiopians, who was in charge of all her treasure. He had come to Jerusalem to worship, [28]and was on his way home, seated in his chariot, reading the prophet Isaiah. [29]And the Spirit said to Philip, "Go up and join this chariot." [30]So Philip ran to him, and hearing him reading Isaiah the prophet, he asked, "Can you understand what you are reading?" [31]He replied, "How can I, unless someone explains to me what it means?" And he invited Philip to come up and join him. [32]Now the passage of the scripture that he was reading was this:

"He was led like a sheep to the slaughter.
Just as a lamb is silent before its shearer,
 he does not open his mouth.
[33]He was denied justice in his humiliation.
Who can describe his generation?
 For his life is taken away from the earth."

[34]Then the eunuch said to Philip, "So I ask you, whom is the prophet saying this about? himself or someone else?" [35]Then Philip began to speak, and starting with this scripture he told him the good news of Jesus. [36]And as they went along the road they came to some water, and the eunuch said, "Look, here is water! What is to prevent my being baptized?" [37]And Philip responded, "If you believe with all your heart, you may." And he replied, "I believe that Jesus Christ is the son of God." [38]And he commanded the chariot to stop, and Philip and the eunuch both went down into the water, and he baptized him. [39]And when they came up out of the water, the Spirit of the Lord whisked Philip away, and the eunuch saw no more of him, but he did go on his way rejoicing. [40]As for Philip, he found himself at Azotus, and as he went along he preached the gospel to all the towns until he came to Caesarea.

Chapter 9

Saul Meets the Lord on Road to Damascus

[1]But, still breathing out murderous threats against the Lord's disciples, Saul went to the high priest [2]and asked him for letters to the synagogues at Damascus, so that if he found anyone belonging to The Way—men or women—he would be able to bring them back to Jerusalem in chains. [3]Now as he was on his way, he was approaching Damascus when suddenly a light from heaven flashed around

him. ⁴As he fell to the ground, he heard a voice saying to him, "Saul, Saul, why are you persecuting me?" ⁵And he asked, "Who are you, Lord?" And he replied, "I am Jesus, whom you are persecuting. ⁶But get up and enter the city, and you will be told what you are to do." ⁷The men who were traveling with him stood speechless—though hearing the voice, they could see no one. ⁸Saul got up from the ground, but when he opened his eyes, he could not see anything. So, they led him by the hand and brought him into Damascus. ⁹And for three days he remained without eyesight, and he had nothing to eat or drink.

¹⁰Now there was a disciple at Damascus named Ananias. The Lord called to him in a vision, "Ananias." And he said, "Here I am, Lord." ¹¹And the Lord said to him, "Get up and go to the street called Straight, and at the house of Judas, inquire about a man of Tarsus named Saul, because—listen—he is praying, ¹²and in a vision he has seen a man named Ananias come in and lay his hands on him so that he might regain his eyesight." ¹³But Ananias answered, "Lord, I have heard about this man from many people and about how much harm he has done to your saints in Jerusalem. ¹⁴And here he has authority from the chief priests to put all who call on your name in chains." ¹⁵But the Lord said to him, "Go, for he is an instrument of mine, chosen to carry my name before the Gentiles, and kings, and the sons of Israel. ¹⁶For I will show him how much he must suffer for my name's sake." ¹⁷So Ananias left, and he entered that house. And laying his hands on him, he said, "Brother Saul, the Lord Jesus who appeared to you on the road that you came on has sent me so that you may regain your eyesight and be filled with the Holy Spirit." ¹⁸And immediately something like scales fell from his eyes and he regained his eyesight. Then he got up and was baptized, ¹⁹had something to eat, and regained his strength.

²⁰He spent several days with the disciples at Damascus. Very soon afterward he began proclaiming Jesus in the synagogues, declaring, "He *is* the Son of God." ²¹And all who heard him were amazed and asked, "Isn't this the man who harangued everyone in Jerusalem who called on this name? And hasn't he come here for the [express] purpose of hauling [believers] before the chief priests bound in chains?" ²²But Saul became more forceful and confounded the Jews who lived in Damascus by proving that Jesus *was* the Christ.

²³After many days had passed, the Jews started plotting to kill him, ²⁴but Saul learned about their plot. They were watching the [city] gates day and night in order to kill him. ²⁵But by night his followers took him, put him through a hole in the city wall, and lowered him in a basket.

Saul Goes to Jerusalem

²⁶Now when he had arrived in Jerusalem, he attempted to join the disciples, but they were all afraid of him, not believing that he [really] *was* a disciple. ²⁷However, Barnabas took him and brought him to the apostles, and he declared to them how on the road had seen the Lord, who spoke to him, and how he had preached boldly in the name of Jesus in Damascus. ²⁸So he associated with them in Jerusalem, ²⁹boldly preaching in the name of the Lord. He was speaking and disputing against the Greek-speaking Jews, but they wanted to kill him. ³⁰And when the brothers found out about that, they brought him down to Caesarea, and sent him off to Tarsus.

³¹Now the church throughout all of Judea and Galilee and Samaria was experiencing peace and was being strengthened as it was walking in the fear of the Lord and in the comfort of the Holy Spirit. So it multiplied.

Aeneas is Healed

³²Now as Peter was going around here and there among them all, he also went down to the saints who lived in Lydda. ³³There he found a man named Aeneas, who was paralyzed and had been bedridden for eight years. ³⁴And Peter said to him, "Aeneas, Jesus Christ heals you: get up and make your bed." And he immediately got up. ³⁵All the inhabitants of Lydda and Sharon saw him, and they turned to the Lord.

Dorcas Raised from the Dead

³⁶Now at Joppa there was a disciple named Tabitha, (which in Greek is "Dorcas"). She was full of good deeds and acts of charity. ³⁷It so happened that in those days she fell sick and died. Having washed her [body], they laid her in an upper room.

³⁸Since Lydda was near Joppa, the disciples, hearing that Peter was there, sent two men to him begging him, "Please come to us without delay." ³⁹So Peter got up and went with them. And when he had come, they took him to the upper room. All the widows stood beside him weeping and showing tunics and other garments that Dorcas had made while she was still with them. ⁴⁰But Peter had all the people go outside and knelt down and prayed. Then turning to the body, he said, "Tabitha, get up." And she opened her eyes, and when she saw Peter she sat up. ⁴¹And he gave her his hand and lifted her up. Then calling the saints and the widows, he presented her to them alive. ⁴²And the news of this spread throughout all Joppa, and many believed in the Lord. ⁴³And he stayed in Joppa for many days with one Simon, a tanner.

Chapter 10

Cornelius Has a Vision

[1]Now, in Caesarea there was a man named Cornelius. He was a centurion of what was known as the Italian Cohort, [2]and he was a devoutly religious man who, along with all his household, feared God. He gave a good deal of money to the support of the poor and prayed to God continually. [3]About three o'clock in the afternoon he had a vision and clearly saw an angel of God coming in and saying to him, "Cornelius." [4]He stared at him in terror and replied, "What is it, Lord?" And he said to him, "Your prayers and your gifts to the poor have risen up as an offering before God. [5]Now send men to Joppa to bring back one Simon who is called Peter. [6]He is lodging with another Simon, a tanner, whose house is by the sea." [7]After the angel who spoke to him had left, he summoned two of his servants and a God-fearing soldier from among those that served him, [8]and having conveyed everything to them, he sent them to Joppa.

Peter Sees a Sheet Descend

[9]The next day about noon, while they were on their journey and approaching the city, Peter went up on the housetop to pray. [10]And he became hungry and wanted something to eat. Now, while it was being prepared, he fell into a trance [11]and saw the sky opened, and something like a great sheet descending, being let down onto the ground by its four corners. [12]In it were all types of animals and reptiles and birds of the air. [13]And there came a voice to him, "Rise, Peter. Kill and eat." [14]But Peter said, "No, Lord, for I have never eaten anything that is common or unclean." [15]And the voice came to him again a second time, "God has made these things clean. Do not call them common." [16]This happened three times, and then the sheet was immediately taken back up into the sky.

[17]Now while Peter was still bewildered as to what the vision that he had seen might mean—listen—the men that were sent by Cornelius, having asked for [the location of] Simon's house, were standing at the gate. [18]And they called out to ask whether the Simon who was called Peter was staying there. [19]While Peter was still pondering the vision, the Spirit said to him, "Listen, three men are [here] looking for you. [20]So, get up and go downstairs, and do not hesitate about going back with them, for I have sent them." [21]And Peter went down to the men and said, "I am the one you are looking for. What is the reason for your visit?" [22]And they answered, "Cornelius, a centurion, an upright and God-fearing man, who is well spoken of by the whole Jewish nation, was directed by a holy angel to send for you to come to his house and to hear what you have to say." [23]So he invited them in as his guests.

Peter Visits Cornelius

The next day he got up and departed with them, and some of the brothers from Joppa accompanied him, ²⁴and on the following day they reached Caesarea. Cornelius was expecting them and had called together his kinsmen and close friends. ²⁵When Peter came in, Cornelius met him and fell down at his feet and worshiped him. ²⁶But Peter made him stand, saying, "Stand up; I am a man also." ²⁷And as he talked with him, he went in and found many people gathered. ²⁸So he said to them, "You yourselves know how unlawful it is for a Jew to associate with or to even visit someone of another nation. But God has shown me that I am not to call any man common or unclean. ²⁹So, I came without any objection when I was sent for. May I ask, then, why you sent for me?"

³⁰And Cornelius replied, "About this time of day, four days ago, I was praying in my house about 3 o'clock in the afternoon—and listen—a man in bright apparel was suddenly standing in front of me, ³¹saying, 'Cornelius, your prayer has been heard and your gifts to the poor have been remembered before God. ³²Therefore send [someone] to Joppa and ask for Simon who is called Peter. He is lodging in the house of Simon, a tanner, by the sea.' ³³So I immediately sent for you, and it was kind of you to come. So, now all of us are here present in the sight of God to hear all that you have been commanded [to say] by the Lord."

Peter Leads Gentiles to the Lord

³⁴Then Peter began to speak, saying:

"Truthfully, I have come to understand that God shows no partiality, ³⁵but rather, anyone, from any nation, who fears him and does what is right is acceptable to him. ³⁶He sent his message to Israel, proclaiming the good news of peace through Jesus Christ. But he is the Lord of *all* people. ³⁷You yourselves know what happened throughout all Judea, starting from Galilee with the baptism that John preached: ³⁸how God anointed Jesus of Nazareth with the Holy Spirit and with power, and how he went about doing good and healing all those who were oppressed by the devil, for God was with him.

³⁹And we are witnesses to all that he did in both the country of the Jews and Jerusalem. They put him to death by hanging him on [the wood of] a tree, ⁴⁰but God raised him on the third day and caused him to appear, ⁴¹not to all the people but to us who were chosen by God as witnesses, who ate and drank with him after he rose from the dead. ⁴²And he commanded us to preach to the people, and to give testimony that he is the one appointed by God as judge of the living and the dead. ⁴³All the prophets declare that "everyone who believes in him receives forgiveness of sins through his name."

[44]While Peter was still saying this, the Holy Spirit fell on all those who were hearing the word. [45]And the Jewish believers who had come with Peter were amazed that the gift of the Holy Spirit had even been poured out on Gentiles, [46]for they were hearing them speaking in tongues and extolling God. Then Peter exclaimed, [47]"Would anyone withhold water to baptize these people who have received the Holy Spirit just as we have?" [48]And he commanded them to be baptized in the name of Jesus Christ. Then they asked him to stay there for several days.

Chapter 11

Salvation is Also for Gentiles

[1]Now the apostles and the brothers who were in Judea heard that the Gentiles also had received the word of God. [2]So after Peter had returned to Jerusalem, the 'circumcised-only' faction criticized him, [3]saying, "You visited uncircumcised men and ate with them!" [4]So, Peter explained it all to them in order, starting at the beginning, saying: [5]"I was in the city of Joppa praying, and in a trance I saw a vision, something like a great sheet descending, being let down from the sky by its four corners, and it came down to me. [6]Looking at it closely, I observed animals and beasts of prey and reptiles and birds of the air. [7]And I heard a voice saying to me, 'Rise, Peter, kill and eat.' [8]But I said, 'No, Lord, for nothing common or unclean has ever entered my mouth.' [9]But the voice answered a second time from heaven, 'God has made these things clean: do not call them common.' [10]This happened three times, and then it all was drawn back up again into the sky.

[11]"Listen—at that very moment three men arrived at the house where we were, sent to me from Caesarea. [12]And the Spirit told me not to hesitate about going with them. These six brothers also accompanied me, and we entered the man's house. [13]And he told us how he had seen the angel standing in his house and saying, 'Send [someone] to Joppa to bring Simon called Peter. [14]He will declare to you a message by which you will be saved— you and all your household.' [15]As I started speaking, the Holy Spirit fell on them just as on us at the beginning. [16]And I remembered the Lord's words, how he said, 'John baptized with water, but you shall be baptized with the Holy Spirit.' [17]So then, if God gave the same gift to them as he gave to us when we believed in the Lord Jesus Christ, who was I to stand in God's way?" [18]When they heard this report, they fell silent. Then they glorified God, saying, "Then God has granted repentance leading life to the Gentiles also."

Disciples First Called Christians

¹⁹Now those who were scattered because of the persecution that arose over Stephen made their way as far as Phoenicia and Cyprus and Antioch, speaking the word only to Jews. ²⁰But some of them, men from Cyprus and Cyrene, did speak to the Greeks also, preaching the Lord Jesus, when they went to Antioch. ²¹And the hand of the Lord was with them, and a great number believed and turned to the Lord. ²²News of this came to the ears of the church in Jerusalem, so they sent Barnabas to Antioch. ²³When he came and saw the grace of God, he was glad, and he encouraged them all to intentionally remain whole-heartedly faithful to the Lord, ²⁴for he was a good man, full of the Holy Spirit and of faith. And a great number of people were added to the Lord. ²⁵So Barnabas went to Tarsus to look for Saul, ²⁶and having found him, he brought him to Antioch. For a whole year they continually met with the church and taught a great number of people. It was in Antioch that the disciples were first referred to as Christians.

²⁷Now in these days prophets came down from Jerusalem to Antioch. ²⁸And one of them named Agabus stood up and foretold by the Spirit that there would be a great famine over all the world, which did take place in the days of Claudius Caesar. ²⁹And each of the disciples decided to send relief, each according to his own financial ability, to their fellow-believers who lived in Judea. ³⁰And they did so, sending it to the elders by the hands of Barnabas and Saul.

Chapter 12

Apostles Persecuted

¹About that time Herod the king violently attacked some members of the church. ²He had James the brother of John killed by sword. ³And when he saw that this act pleased the Jews, he went on to arrest Peter also. This was during the days of Unleavened Bread. ⁴And when he had seized him, he put him in prison, and handed him over to four squads of soldiers to guard him, planning to bring him out to the people after the Passover.

An Angel Rescues Peter from Prison

⁵So Peter was kept in prison, but the church kept praying earnestly to God for him. ⁶Now on the very night when Herod was about to bring him out, Peter was asleep between two soldiers, bound with two chains, and in front of the door sentries were guarding the prison. ⁷And listen—an angel of the Lord appeared, and a light shone in the cell. He struck Peter on the side to awaken him, saying, "Get up quickly." And the chains fell off his hands. ⁸And the angel told him, "Dress

yourself and put on your sandals." And he did so. And he said to him, "Wrap your cloak around yourself and follow me." ⁹And he went out and followed [the angel]. He did not realize that what the angel was doing was real, but instead, he thought he was seeing a vision. ¹⁰When they had passed the first and the second guard, they came to the iron gate leading into the city. It opened to them of its own accord, and they exited and passed along a street, and right then the angel departed from him. ¹¹Then Peter came to himself and said, "Now I am certain that the Lord has really sent his angel to rescue me from the hand of Herod and from all that the Jewish people were expecting."

¹²When he realized this, he went to the house of Mary, the mother of John, who was also called Mark, where many were gathered together and were praying. ¹³And when he knocked at the door of the gateway, a servant girl named Rhoda came to answer. ¹⁴She recognized Peter's voice and was so overjoyed that she neglected to open the gate but instead ran in and reported that Peter was standing at the gate. ¹⁵They said to her, "You're crazy." But she insisted that it was so. They said, "It is his angel!" ¹⁶But Peter continued knocking, and when they opened [the gate], they saw him and were amazed. ¹⁷But signaling to them with his hand to stay silent, he described to them how the Lord had brought him out of the prison. Then he said, "Tell this to James and to the brothers." Then he left and went somewhere else.

¹⁸Now when day came, there was no small stir among the soldiers over what had become of Peter. ¹⁹And when Herod had searched for him but was unable to find him, he questioned the sentries and ordered their execution. Then [Peter] went down from Judea to Caesarea and sojourned there a while.

The Death of Herod

²⁰Now Herod held the people of Tyre and Sidon in great contempt. So, they came to him in a united body, and having found favor with Blastus, the king's chamberlain, they asked for peace, because their country depended on the king's country for food. ²¹On the appointed day, Herod dressed in his royal robes, took his seat on the throne, and made a speech to them. ²²And the people shouted, "The voice of a god, and not of man!" ²³At once an angel of the Lord struck him down, because he did not give the glory to God, and he was consumed by worms and died.

²⁴But the word of God increased and multiplied.

²⁵And Barnabas and Saul returned from Jerusalem when they had fulfilled their mission, bringing John, who was also called Mark, with them.

Chapter 13

The Church at Antioch

[1]Now in the church at Antioch there were prophets and teachers: Barnabas, Simeon (who was called Niger), Lucius of Cyrene, Manaen (a member of the court of Herod the tetrarch), and Saul. [2]Once, while they were worshiping the Lord and fasting, the Holy Spirit said, "Set aside Barnabas and Saul for me, for the work that I have called them to." [3]Then after fasting and praying, they laid their hands on them and sent them off.

[4]So, they went down to Seleucia, being sent out by the Holy Spirit, and from there they sailed to Cyprus. [5]Having arrived at Salamis, they proclaimed the word of God in the synagogues of the Jews, and they had John to assist them. [6]When they had made their way through the whole island as far as Paphos, they encountered a certain magician, a Jewish false prophet, named Barjesus. [7]He was with the proconsul, Sergius Paulus, an intelligent man, who summoned Barnabas and Saul and was seeking to hear the word of God. [8]But Elymas the magician (for that is the meaning of his name) opposed them, in his effort to turn the proconsul away from the faith. [9]But filled with the Holy Spirit, Saul (who was also being called Paul) looked intently at him [10]and said, "You son of the devil, you enemy of all righteousness, full of all deceit and villainy, will you not stop twisting the straight paths of the Lord? [11]So now, listen: the Lord has struck you with his hand, and you shall be temporarily blind and unable to see the sun." A fog and darkness fell on him at once, and he wandered around searching for people to lead him by the hand. [12]Then, when the proconsul saw what had happened, he believed, for the teaching of the Lord astounded him.

[13]Then Paul and his company set sail from Paphos and went to Perga in Pamphylia. John left them and returned to Jerusalem, [14]but they passed on from Perga and came to Antioch of Pisidia. And on the Sabbath day they went into the synagogue and were seated. [15]After the reading from the law and the prophets, the rulers of the synagogue messaged them, saying, "Brothers, if you have any word of encouragement for the people, do say it."

Paul Preaches at the Synagogue

[16]So Paul stood up, and motioning with his hand said:

"Men of Israel, and you who fear God, listen. [17]The God of this people Israel chose our fathers and made the people great during their stay in the land of Egypt, and he stretched out his arm and led them out of it. [18]Then he endured their behavior in the wilderness for about forty years. [19]And after having destroyed seven nations in the land of Canaan, he gave [our people] their land as an inheritance. ²⁰And after these things, he gave them [a series of] judges for about 450 years, up until Samuel the prophet. ²¹Then they requested a king, and God gave them Saul the son of Kish, a man of the tribe of Benjamin, for forty years.

²²"And when he had removed him, he raised up David to be their king, whom he approved of, declaring, 'In David the son of Jesse I have found a man after my own heart, who will do all of what I want.' ²³As he promised, God provided to Israel a savior, Jesus, from this man's descendants. ²⁴In anticipation of his coming, John had preached a baptism of repentance to all the people of Israel. ²⁵And as John was finishing the course set out for him, he said, 'Who do you suppose that I am? I am not He. No, but One will come after me, and I am not even worthy to untie the sandals of his feet.'

²⁶"Brothers, sons of the family of Abraham, and those among you who do fear God, the message of this salvation has been sent to *us*. ²⁷Because the inhabitants of Jerusalem and their rulers did not recognize him nor understand the messages of the prophets, which are read aloud every Sabbath, they fulfilled them by condemning him. ²⁸Even though they could not charge him with something deserving death, they still asked Pilate to have him executed. ²⁹And when they had fulfilled all the written predictions about him, they took him down from the tree, and laid him in a tomb. ³⁰But God raised him from the dead. ³¹For many days he kept appearing to those who had accompanied him from Galilee to Jerusalem, who are now his witnesses to the people. ³²And we bring you the good news that by raising Jesus [from the dead], God has fulfilled ³³what he had promised to the fathers to us their children. As it is also written in the second psalm, 'You are my Son, on this day I have begotten you.'

³⁴"And he has spoken this about the fact that he raised him from the dead, never to return to decay: 'I will give you the holy and sure blessings of David.' ³⁵Therefore he also says in another psalm, 'You will not let your Holy One experience decay.' ³⁶For David, after he had served the purposes of God in his own generation, fell into the sleep of death, and was laid with his fathers, and experienced decay. ³⁷But the One whom God raised up experienced no decay. ³⁸Therefore, brothers, let it be known to you that forgiveness of sins through this man is being proclaimed to you, ³⁹and by him everyone who believes is freed from everything that by the law Moses he could not be freed. ⁴⁰Therefore, be careful that what was said in the prophets does not come to pass: ⁴¹'Look, you scoffers, and be astonished, and perish, for I am doing a work in your days, a work you will never believe, even if someone should explain it to you.'"

⁴²As they were leaving, the people begged to have these things explained to them [again] the next Sabbath. ⁴³And once the meeting at the synagogue had broken up, many Jews and devout converts to Judaism followed Paul and Barnabas, who talked with them, urging them to continue in the grace of God.

⁴⁴On the next Sabbath, nearly the whole community was gathered to hear the word of God. ⁴⁵But the Jews noticed the crowds, which filled them with jealousy, so they started contradicting what Paul was saying and reviling him. ⁴⁶So, Paul and Barnabas, speaking with great boldness, said, "It was necessary that the word of God should be spoken to *you* first. But, since you reject it and deem yourselves unworthy of eternal life, then listen—we are turning to the Gentiles. ⁴⁷For the Lord has commanded us to do so, saying, 'I have set you to be a light for the Gentiles, that you may bring salvation to the uttermost parts of the earth.'"

⁴⁸And when the Gentiles heard this, they were glad and glorified the word of God. And all of them who had been appointed to eternal life did believe. ⁴⁹And the word of the Lord spread throughout all the region. ⁵⁰But the Jews incited the devout women of high standing and the leading men of the city to stir up persecution against Paul and Barnabas and drove them out of their district. ⁵¹But they shook the dust off their feet against them and went on to Iconium.

⁵²Still and all, the disciples were filled with joy and with the Holy Spirit.

Chapter 14

Belief and Persecution in Iconium

¹Now it came to pass that in Iconium they both went into the Jewish synagogue and spoke in such a way that a great number of both Jews and Greeks believed. ²But the Jews who did not believe stirred up the Gentiles and poisoned their minds against the brothers. ³So they stayed there for a long time, boldly speaking on behalf of the Lord, who gave a testimony to this news of his grace by granting signs and wonders that were done by their hands. ⁴But the people of the city were split—some stood with the Jews, and some with the apostles. ⁵When both some Gentiles and some Jews, along with their rulers, made a plan to abuse them and stone them, ⁶they learned of it and fled to Lystra and Derbe, cities of Lycaonia, and to the surrounding countryside, ⁷and they kept on preaching the gospel there.

Paul and Barnabus Mistaken for gods

⁸Now in Lystra was a man who could not use his feet, being a cripple from birth who had never walked. He was sitting ⁹there listening to Paul speaking. And studying him closely, Paul perceived that he had faith to be made well, ¹⁰and

said in a loud voice, "Stand upright on your feet." And he sprang up and started walking. [11]And when the crowds saw what Paul had done, they shouted in Lycaonian, "The gods have come down to us in human form!" [12]They called Barnabas 'Zeus,' and they called Paul 'Hermes,' because he was the main speaker. [13]And the priest of Zeus, whose temple lay at the entrance to the city, brought oxen and garlands to the gates, intending to offer a sacrifice with the people. [14]But when the apostles Barnabas and Paul heard about this, they tore their garments and rushed out among the crowd, exclaiming, [15]"Men, why are you doing this? We are men, too, of the same human nature as you. We bring you good news, that you should turn from these vain things to a living God who made the heavens and the earth and the sea and all that is in them. [16]In previous generations he permitted all the nations to walk in their own ways. [17]Still and all, he has given evidence of himself, for he did good things like giving you rains from heaven and fruitful seasons to satisfy your hearts with food and gladness." [18]By making these statements, they just barely restrained the people from offering a sacrifice to them.

Paul a Victim of Stoning

[19]But some Jews arrived there from Antioch and Iconium, and having won over the minds of the people, they stoned Paul and dragged him out of the city, believing him to be dead. [20]But the disciples gathered around him, and then he got up and went back into the city. On the next day he continued on to Derbe with Barnabas. [21]When they had preached the gospel to that city and had made many disciples, they returned to Lystra and to Iconium and to Antioch, [22]strengthening the souls of the disciples, encouraging them to persevere in the faith, and saying that to enter the kingdom of God we must go through many tribulations. [23]And when they had appointed elders for them in every church, they committed them to the Lord in whom they had believed, with prayer and fasting.

[24]Then they passed through Pisidia and reached Pamphylia. [25]And when they had spoken the word in Perga, they went down to Attalia. [26]From there they sailed to Antioch, where they had been commended to the grace of God for the work that they had now completed. [27]And when they arrived, they gathered the church together and reported all that God had done through them, and how he had opened a door of faith to the Gentiles. [28]And they stayed there with the disciples for a long time.

Chapter 15

The Council of Jerusalem

[1]But some men came down from Judea and began instructing the brothers, "Unless you have yourselves circumcised according to the custom of Moses, you cannot be saved." [2]And after Paul and Barnabas had a great argument and debate with them, Paul and Barnabas and some of the others were appointed to go up to Jerusalem to [confer with] the apostles and the elders about this question. [3]So, having been sent on their way by the church, they passed through both Phoenicia and Samaria, reporting the conversion of the Gentiles, which brought great joy to all the fellow believers. [4]When they came to Jerusalem, the church and the apostles and the elders welcomed them, and they described all that God had done through them. [5]But some believers who belonged to the party of the Pharisees stood up, and stated, "It *is* necessary to circumcise the [Gentiles], and to command them to keep the law of Moses."

[6]The apostles and the elders convened to consider this matter. [7]After a lengthy debate, Peter stood up and said to them:

"Brothers, you know that early on, God decided that among us it would be by my lips that the Gentiles would hear the word of the gospel and believe. [8]And knowing their hearts, God gave evidence of this to them, by giving them the Holy Spirit just as [He had done] to us, [9]and he made no distinction between us and them, having made their hearts clean through faith. [10]Now therefore why do you provoke God by putting a yoke, which neither our fathers nor we have been able to bear, on the neck of the disciples? [11]On the contrary, we believe that we will be saved in the same way they will also—through the grace of the Lord Jesus."

[12]At that the whole assembly fell silent, and then they listened to Barnabas and Paul relating what signs and wonders God had done among the Gentiles through them. [13]After they finished speaking, James replied:

"Brothers, listen to me. [14]Simeon has related how God first visited the Gentiles, to gather a people for his name from among them. [15]Even the words of the prophets agree with this, as it is written, [16]'After this I will return, and I will rebuild the fallen House of David. I will rebuild its ruins, and I will restore it, [17]so that the rest of mankind may seek the Lord, even all the Gentiles who are called by my name, [18]says the Lord, who has made known these things from ages past.'

[19]"Therefore my opinion is that we should not make it unduly hard for the

Gentile ones who turn to God. [20]Nonetheless, we should write to them to abstain from the things tainted by idolatry, and from sexual immorality, and from what has been strangled, and from blood. [21]For from earliest generations in every city Moses' teachings have been proclaimed, for he is read in the synagogues on every Sabbath."

The Council Addresses Gentile Believers

[22]Then it seemed good to the apostles and the elders, along with the whole church, to delegate men from among them to send to Antioch with Paul and Barnabas. They sent Judas (called Barsabbas), and Silas, prominent men among the brothers, [23]with the following letter:

[From]: the brothers, both the apostles and the elders,

To: the believers, who are from the Gentiles, in Antioch and Syria and Cilicia.

Greetings.

[24]We have heard that some men have gone out from among us and have told you, without our instructions, that you must be circumcised and keep the law, which unsettled your minds. [25]So, it seemed good to us, being unanimous about the matter, to delegate men to send to you with our beloved Barnabas and Paul, [26]men who have risked their lives for the sake of our Lord Jesus Christ. [27]Therefore, we have sent Judas and Silas, who themselves will tell you the same things verbally.

[28]For it seemed good to the Holy Spirit and to us to not lay a burden beyond these necessary things on you: [29]that you abstain from what has been sacrificed to idols, and from blood, and from what was strangled, and from sexual immorality. In keeping yourselves away from these things, you will do well.

Farewell.

[30]So having been sent off, they went down to Antioch, and having gathered the congregation together, they delivered the letter. [31]And when they had read it, [the congregation] rejoiced because of its encouragement. [32]And Judas and Silas, who were themselves prophets, encouraged and strengthened the brothers with many words. [33]And after they had spent some time there, the brothers sent them off in peace back to those who had sent them, [34]though it seemed good to Silas that he should remain there. [35]But Paul and Barnabas remained in Antioch, teaching and preaching the word of the Lord, with many others also.

Paul and Barnabus Separate

[36]Some days later Paul said to Barnabas, "We should start heading back and visit

the brothers in every city where we proclaimed the word of the Lord to see how they are faring." ³⁷Now Barnabas wanted to take John (called Mark) with them. ³⁸But Paul preferred not to take along someone who had withdrawn from them in Pamphylia and had not gone with them to the work. ³⁹As it happened, they disagreed sharply, which caused them to go their separate ways. Barnabas took Mark with him and sailed away to Cyprus, ⁴⁰but Paul chose Silas and left, as the brothers commended him to the grace of the Lord, ⁴¹and he went through Syria and Cilicia, strengthening the churches.

Chapter 16

Timothy Joins Paul and Silas

¹And he also went to Derbe and then to Lystra, where there was a disciple named Timothy, who was the son of a believing Jewish woman, but whose father was a Greek. ²The believers in Lystra and Iconium spoke very highly of him. ³Paul wanted Timothy to accompany him, so he took him and circumcised him on account of the Jews who were in those areas, since they all knew that his father was a Greek. ⁴As they passed through the cities, they delivered the decisions made by the apostles and elders who were in Jerusalem, for the [churches] to abide by. ⁵So the churches were strengthened in the faith, and each day they increased in numbers.

A Call to Macedonia

⁶And they went through the region of Phrygia and Galatia, having been forbidden by the Holy Spirit to speak the word in Asia. ⁷And when they had come up to Mysia, they tried to go into Bithynia, but the Spirit of Jesus did not allow them to. ⁸So, bypassing Mysia, they went down to Troas. ⁹Then a vision came to Paul in the night: a man of Macedonia was standing there pleading with him, saying, "Come over to Macedonia and help us." ¹⁰Once he had seen the vision, we immediately began planning to go on into Macedonia, concluding that God had called us to preach the gospel to [the Macedonians].

Lydia Believes

¹¹So, setting sail from Troas, we set a direct course to Samothrace, and to Neapolis on the following day, ¹²and from there to Philippi, which is the principal city of the district of Macedonia, and a Roman colony. We sojourned in this city a number of days. ¹³On the Sabbath day we went outside the gate to the riverside, where we imagined there might be a place to pray, and we sat down and started talking near the women who had congregated there. ¹⁴One [of them] who heard us was

a woman named Lydia, a seller of purple goods, from the city of Thyatira. She was a worshiper of God, and the Lord opened her heart such that she responded to what Paul was saying. [15]And once she and the members of her household had been baptized, she kept pressing us, saying, "If you consider me to be faithful to the Lord, come and stay at my house." And she insisted we do so.

Paul and Silas Imprisoned

[16]And it so happened that as we were going to the place of prayer, we met up with a slave girl who had a spirit of fortune-telling and brought in a lot of revenue for her owners by telling fortunes. [17]She followed Paul and us, shouting, "These men are servants of the Most High God, who are proclaiming the way of salvation to you." [18]And she kept doing this for many days. At length, Paul was annoyed, and [finally] turned around and addressed the spirit: "In the name of Jesus Christ, I order you to come out of her." And it came out that very moment.

[19]But when her owners realized that their means of future profit was gone, they seized Paul and Silas and dragged them into the marketplace in front of the local officials. [20]And when they had brought them to the magistrates they said, "These men are Jews, and they are upsetting our city. [21]They advocate customs that cannot be lawfully accepted or practiced by us Romans." [22]The crowd joined in attacking them, and the magistrates had them stripped and ordered them to be flogged. [23]And once they had flogged them many times, they threw them into prison, ordering the jailer to guard them securely. [24]Having received this order, he put them into the inner prison and fastened their feet in the stocks.

A Philippian Jailer Converts

[25]Now about midnight, Paul and Silas were praying and singing hymns to God, and the [other] prisoners were listening to them. [26]Suddenly there was a great earthquake, so that the foundations of the prison were shaken, and suddenly all the doors flew open and everyone's chains were unfastened. [27]When the jailer woke up and saw that the prison doors were open, he drew his sword and was about to kill himself, assuming that the prisoners had escaped. [28]But Paul called out in a loud voice, "Don't harm yourself: we are all [still] here." [29]The [jailor] requested some lights and rushed in, and trembling with fear, he fell down in front of Paul and Silas. [30][Then] he brought them out and asked, "Sirs, what do I have to do to be saved?" [31]And they replied, "Believe in the Lord Jesus, and you will be saved, you and your household." [32]And they spoke the word of the Lord to him and to everyone in his house. [33]Next, at that hour of the night, he took them and washed their wounds. And he and all his family were baptized at once. [34]Then he brought them up into his house and set food before them. And with all his household, he rejoiced that he had put his faith in God.

[35]But when morning had come, the magistrates sent the police, saying, "Let those men go." [36]And the jailer reported the message to Paul, saying, "The magistrates have sent word to let you go. So, come out now and go in peace." [37]But Paul said to them, "They have publicly beaten us—unconvicted men who are Roman citizens—and have thrown us into prison. So now are they throwing us out secretly? No! Let them come themselves and take us out." [38]The police reported this response to the magistrates, and when they heard that they were Roman citizens, they were alarmed. [39]So they came and apologized to them, and they took them out and asked them to leave the city. [40]So they left the prison and paid a visit to Lydia. And as they visited the believers [there], they encouraged them and then departed.

Chapter 17

Paul and Silas Visit Thessalonica

[1]Now having passed through Amphipolis and Apollonia, they came to Thessalonica, where there was a synagogue of the Jews. [2]Paul went into it, and, on three Sabbath days, he debated with them from the scriptures, according to his custom. [3]He explained and proved that it was necessary for the Christ to suffer and to rise from the dead, stating, "This Jesus, whom I proclaim to you, *is* the Christ." [4]So, some of them were persuaded, and joined Paul and Silas, as did a great many of the devout Greeks and quite a few of the leading women. [5]But the Jews became jealous, and by employing some evil men from the common rabble, they formed a mob, set the city in an uproar, and attacked the house of Jason, intending to try to bring them out to the people. [6]But not being able to find them, they dragged Jason and some of the fellow believers before the city authorities, shouting, "These men who have been turning the world upside down have also come here! [7]And Jason has taken them into his home! Even more, they are all doing things that are against the decrees of Caesar, saying that there is another king, Jesus." [8]Then the people and the city authorities were all upset when they heard this. [9]And only after Jason and the rest of them had put up bond money were they released.

Paul and Silas Visit Berea

[10]The other believers quickly sent Paul and Silas away to Berea at nighttime, and once they got there they went into the Jewish synagogue. [11]Now these Jews were nobler than those in Thessalonica, for they received the word with all eagerness, and every day they examined the scriptures to see if these things were [really] true. [12]So, many of them believed, along with a quite a few Greek women of high standing, as well as [some] men. [13]But when the Jews of Thessalonica learned that Paul was proclaiming the word of God at Berea also, they came there too, stirring

up and inciting the crowds. [14]So, right away the fellow believers sent Paul off on his way to the sea, but Silas and Timothy remained there. [15]The men who were escorting Paul brought him as far as Athens, and then they headed back with a command for Silas and Timothy to come to Paul as soon as possible.

[16]Now while Paul was in Athens waiting for them, he noticed that the city was filled with idols, which grieved the spirit within him greatly. [17]So he debated with the Jews and the devout people in the synagogue, and in the market place every day with those who happened to be there. [18]Some of the Epicurean and Stoic philosophers had conversations with him, too, but some wondered, "What might this chattering fool be trying to say?" Now because he was preaching about Jesus and the resurrection, others said, "He seems to be a preacher of foreign deities." [19]So they took him and escorted him to the Areopagus, saying, "This new teaching that you are presenting—may we know what it is? [20]For, you are bringing up some things that are strange to our ears. So, we want to know what these things mean." [21]Now, all the Athenians and the foreigners who lived there spent their time in nothing but talking about or listening to novel things.

Paul Preaches at the Areopagus

[22]So Paul, standing in the middle of the Areopagus, said:

> "Men of Athens, I perceive that in every way you are very religious. [23]For as I passed through [the city], observing the objects of your worship, I even en-countered an altar with this inscription, **To the unknown god**. So, I will tell you about this one that you worship as unknown: [24]The God who made the world and everything in it, being Lord of heaven and earth, does not live in shrines made by human hands, [25]nor do human hands meet his needs, as if he were ever in need of something, since he himself gives life and breath and every-thing [else] to everyone. [26]And he created every nation of mankind that lives on all the face of the earth from just one man, having laid out their time-spans and the boundaries of their habitations, [27]so that they would seek God, hoping that they would grope for him and find him. Actually, he is not far from each one of us, [28]for 'In him we live and move and exist'. As even some of your poets have put it, 'For indeed we are his children.' [29]Since then we are the children of God, we should not imagine that the Deity is like a gold, or silver, or stone representation designed by man's imagination. [30]God used to overlook this ignorance in the past, but now he commands everyone everywhere to repent, [31]because he has fixed a day when he will judge the world in righteousness through a man whom he has appointed, and he has assured everyone about this by raising him from the dead."

[32]Now some of them mocked when they heard about the resurrection of the dead, but others stated, "We are going to listen to you about this again." [33]So Paul went out from among them. [34]But some men, including Dionysius the Areopagite, joined him and did believe, as did a woman named Damaris, and some others with them.

Chapter 18

Paul Visits Corinth

[1]After this he left Athens and went to Corinth. [2]And he found a Jew by the name of Aquila, a native of Pontus, recently arrived from Italy with his wife Priscilla, because Claudius had ordered all the Jews to leave Rome, and Paul visited them. [3]They were tentmakers by trade, so because Paul was of the same trade, he stayed and worked with them. [4]Each Sabbath he debated in the synagogue, and he was trying to win over Jews and Greeks.

[5]When Silas and Timothy arrived from Macedonia, Paul was occupied with [preaching] the word, testifying to the Jews that the Christ was Jesus. [6]And when they opposed and insulted him, he shook the dust off his garments and said to them, "May your blood be on your own heads! I am innocent. From now on I shall go to the Gentiles." [7]And having departed, he went to the house of a man named Titius Justus, a worshiper of God, whose house was next door to the synagogue. [8]Crispus, the head of the synagogue, came to belief in the Lord, along with all of his household. Also, many of the Corinthians that heard Paul came to believe and were baptized. [9]One night, the Lord said to Paul in a vision, "Do not be afraid, but rather keep speaking and do not be silent. [10]For I am with you, and no one shall assault you and injure you, for many people in this city belong to me." [11]So, he remained a year and six months, teaching the word of God among them.

[12]But when Gallio was proconsul of Achaia, the Jews unified themselves to come against Paul, and they brought him before the tribunal, [13]saying, "This one is persuading men to worship God in a way that contradicts the law." [14]But just as Paul was about to open his mouth, Gallio said to the Jews, "Listen, Jews, if this were a matter of a misdemeanor or a wicked crime, I would have cause to address your complaint. [15]But since it is quibbling over words and names and your own law, see to it yourselves. I refuse to be a judge of these matters." [16]And he drove them out of the court. [17]Then all of them grabbed Sosthenes, the head of the synagogue, and beat him in front of the judge's platform, but Gallio paid no attention to that.

Paul Returns to Antioch

[18]After this, Paul remained many days longer and then took leave of the brothers and sailed for Syria, and with him [were] Priscilla and Aquila. At Cenchreae he had his hair cut because he had taken a vow. [19]When they had come to Ephesus, he left them there, but he himself went into the synagogue and debated with the Jews. [20]Then, they asked him to stay longer, but he declined. [21]Nonetheless, as he took leave of them, he said, "I must keep the upcoming feast in Jerusalem, but I shall return to you if God wills," and he set sail from Ephesus.

[22]Once he had landed at Caesarea, he went up and greeted the church, and then went down to Antioch. [23]After spending some time there, he set out, going from place to place through the region of Galatia and Phrygia, strengthening all the disciples.

Apollos Speaks at Ephesus

[24]Now then, a Jew by the name of Apollos, a native of Alexandria, arrived in Ephesus. He was an eloquent man, well grounded in the scriptures. [25]He had been instructed in the way of the Lord. With an enthusiastic spirit he spoke and taught the things concerning Jesus diligently, though he had only experienced the baptism from John. [26]Now, once he started speaking boldly in the synagogue, and when Priscilla and Aquila heard him, they took him aside and explained God's ways to him in even greater detail. [27]And when he wished to cross over to Achaia, the brothers encouraged him and wrote to the disciples to receive him. When he arrived, he greatly helped those who had believed through grace, [28]for in public he refuted the Jews powerfully, using the scriptures to show that the Christ was [indeed] Jesus.

Chapter 19

Paul Visits Ephesus

[1]While Apollos was at Corinth, Paul traveled through the hill country and came to Ephesus and found some disciples there. [2]He asked them, "Did you receive the Holy Spirit when you believed?" And they responded, "No, we have never even heard that the Holy Spirit exists." [3]So he asked, "What then were you baptized into?" They replied, "Into John's baptism." [4]And Paul said, "John baptized with the baptism of repentance, telling the people to believe in the one who was about to appear after him, that is, Jesus." [5]On hearing this, they were baptized into the name of the Lord Jesus. [6]Once Paul had laid his hands on them, the Holy Spirit came on them, and then they were speaking in tongues and prophesying. [7]In all, there were about twelve men.

[8] [Paul] then went into the synagogue, and he spoke boldly there for three months, debating and persuading them about the kingdom of God. [9] But some were stubborn and did not believe, maligning The Way before the congregation. So, he withdrew from them, taking the disciples with him, and debated every day from eleven o'clock in the morning till four o'clock in the afternoon in the hall of Tyrannus. [10] This continued for two years, so that all the residents of Asia, both Jews and Greeks, heard the word of the Lord,.

Seven Sons of Sceva

[11] And by the hands of Paul God worked extraordinary miracles—[12] such that even handkerchiefs or aprons that had touched his skin were brought away to sick people, and their diseases were cured, and the evil spirits came out of them. [13] Then some of the itinerant Jewish exorcists started invoking the name of the Lord Jesus over those who had evil spirits, saying, "I rebuke you by the Jesus whom Paul preaches." [14] Now, once seven sons of a Jewish high priest by the name of Sceva were doing this. [15] But the evil spirit answered them, "I know Jesus, and I recognize Paul, but who are you?" [16] And the man that had the evil spirit in him jumped on them, got the best of them, and overpowered them, so that they fled from that house wounded and without their clothes. [17] All the residents of Ephesus, Jews and Greeks alike, learned of this [incident], and fear fell on them all. Then the name of the Lord Jesus was held in great honor. [18] In addition, many of those who were now believers came, confessing and revealing what they had been doing. [19] And a number of those who had once practiced magic arts assembled their books and burned them in public. When they counted up the value of them, they figured that it came to fifty thousand pieces of silver. [20] Thus the word of the Lord kept on growing and triumphing mightily.

A Riot in Ephesus

[21] Now after these [events], being guided by the Spirit, Paul determined that he would pass through Macedonia and Achaia and go to Jerusalem, saying, "After I have been there, I must see Rome as well." [22] And having sent two of his helpers, Timothy and Erastus, into Macedonia, he himself remained in Asia for a period of time.

[23] About that time there arose a large disturbance concerning The Way. [24] For a silversmith named Demetrius, who fashioned silver shrines of Artemis, brought a good deal of business to the craftsmen. [25] He gathered these men together, with the workmen of related trades, and said, "Men, you realize that we make our living from this business. [26] And you see and hear that not only at Ephesus but also

throughout almost all of Asia this Paul has turned away a considerable group of people, persuading them that gods made with [human] hands are not gods. [27]And there is danger not only that this trade of ours may fall out of favor but also that the temple of the great goddess Artemis may lose its standing, and that even she, who is worshipped by Asia and the [rest of] the world, might become dethroned from her majestic glory."

[28]When they heard this they were filled with rage, and started chanting, "Great is Artemis of the Ephesians!" [29]So the city was thrown into confusion, and people rushed together into the theater, dragging with them Gaius and Aristarchus, Macedonians who were Paul's traveling companions. [30]Paul wanted to go into the crowd, but the disciples would not allow him. [31]Even some of the rulers of Asia, who were friends of his, sent [a message] to him, begging him not to even venture into the theater. [32]Now some of them were shouting out one thing, and some another because the mob was in confusion and most of them did not even know why they had assembled. [33]Some of the crowd pushed Alexander, whom the Jews had put forward, to the forefront. So, Alexander motioned with his hand, intending to explain things to the people. [34]But once they recognized that he was a Jew, they all chanted in unison, "Great is Artemis of the Ephesians!" for about two hours.

[35]Finally, when the town clerk had quieted the crowd, he said, "Men of Ephesus, what man is there who does not know that the city of the Ephesians is keeper of the temple of the great Artemis, and of her sacred icon from the heavens? [36]Since these things cannot be denied, you should quiet down and not do anything rash. [37]For you have brought these men here who neither break religious laws nor speak evil of our goddess. [38]If therefore Demetrius and the craftsmen with him have a complaint against anyone, the courts are open, and there are judges. Let them bring charges against one another. [39]But if you are looking for anything further, it shall be settled in a legal meeting. [40]For we are in danger of being charged with rioting today, for we can give no cause to justify this commotion." [41]And having said this, he dismissed the assembly.

Chapter 20

Paul Travels to Macedonia and Greece

[1]After the uproar died down, Paul sent for the disciples and having encouraged them, he bid them farewell and left for Macedonia. [2]Once he had gone through these parts and had given them a good deal of encouragement, he went to Greece. [3]He spent three months there, and when the Jews formed a plot against him as he was about to set sail for Syria, he decided to return through Macedonia.

[4]Accompanying him were Sopater of Berea, the son of Pyrrhus; Aristarchus and Secundus from Thessalonica; Gaius of Derbe; and Timothy, and Tychicus, and Trophimus from Asia. [5]These men continued on and were waiting for us at Troas, [6]but after the Feast of Unleavened Bread, we sailed away from Philippi and in five days we came to them in Troas, where we stayed for seven days.

Eutychus is Raised from the Dead

[7]On the first day of the week, when we were gathered together to break bread, Paul talked with them, planning to leave the next morning, but he kept on speaking until midnight. [8]Now, in the room upstairs where we were gathered were many lamps. [9]As Paul kept on talking longer, a young man named Eutychus was sitting in the window, falling into a deep sleep. Being overcome by sleep, he fell down from the third story and was picked up dead. [10]But Paul went down and bent over him, and picking him up said, "Do not be alarmed, for his life is in him." [11]And when Paul had gone back up and had broken bread and eaten, he conversed with them a long while, until daybreak, and thus he departed. [12]And they took the lad away alive and were comforted greatly.

[13]But going ahead to the ship, we set sail for Assos, intending to take Paul aboard there, for he had arranged it that way, intending himself to travel by land. [14]And when he met us at Assos, we took him on board and came to Mitylene. [15]And sailing from there, the following day we came up opposite Chios; the next day we touched land at Samos; and the day after that we came to Miletus. [16]For Paul had decided to sail past Ephesus, so that he would not have to spend time in Asia, because he was hurrying to be in Jerusalem, if possible, on the day of Pentecost.

Paul Meets with the Elders from Ephesus

[17]Then from Miletus he sent a message to Ephesus, summoning the elders of the church. [18]And when they had come to him, he said to them:

"You yourselves know how I lived among you all the time from the first day that I set foot in Asia, [19]serving the Lord with all humility and with tears and with trials that happened to me through the plots of the Jews, [20]how I never shrank from declaring to you anything that was profitable, and teaching you in public and from house to house, [21]testifying both to Jews and to Greeks of repentance to God and of faith in our Lord Jesus Christ. [22]And now, listen, I am going to Jerusalem, compelled in the Spirit, not knowing what will become of me there, [23]except that in every city the Holy Spirit testifies to me, saying that prison chains and troubles await me. [24]But I do not count my life as valuable, nor as precious to me—just so long as I can finish the course [set out for] me, and [accomplish] the ministry that I received from the Lord Jesus: to give testimony to the gospel of the grace of God. ²⁵And now, listen, I have gone around preaching the kingdom among you, but I know that none of you will ever see my face again. ²⁶Therefore today I declare to you that I am innocent of the blood of you all, ²⁷because I did not shrink back from declaring God's entire plan to you.

²⁸"Give careful attention to yourselves and to the whole flock where the Holy Spirit has made you overseers to care for the Lord's church, which he purchased with his own blood. ²⁹For of this I am sure: that once I am gone fierce wolves will invade you, showing no mercy to the flock. ³⁰And even from among you yourselves will arise some men who will twist things when they speak, so as to lure away disciples after themselves. ³¹Therefore stay alert, bearing in mind that I never stopped warning everyone tearfully, night and day for three years.

³²And now I entrust you to God and to the word of his grace, which is able to build you up and to give you the inheritance shared by all those who are sanctified. ³³I have never had a longing desire to own anyone's silver or gold or clothing. ³⁴You yourselves know that these hands [of mine] ministered to my own needs, and to my companions. ³⁵I have shown you in all things that by working in this way one must help the weak, remembering the words of the Lord Jesus, how he said, 'To give is more blessed than to receive.'"

³⁶And when he had spoken these things, he knelt down and prayed with all of them. ³⁷And they all wept and embraced Paul and kissed him. ³⁸Most of all, they were grieving over what he had just said: that they would never see his face again. Then they went with him to the ship.

Chapter 21

Paul Returns to Jerusalem

¹And when we had torn ourselves away from them and set sail, we followed a straight course to Cos, and the next day to Rhodes, and from there to Patara. ²And having found a ship that was crossing to Phoenicia, we boarded and set sail. ³Having come in sight of Cyprus, we sailed to Syria, leaving Cyprus on the left, and landed at Tyre, because the ship was to unload its cargo there. ⁴Next, we sought out the disciples and stayed there for seven days. By the Spirit's [leading] they told Paul not to go on to Jerusalem. ⁵And when our days there came to an end, we left and continued our trip. All of them, along with [their] wives and children, went with us till we were outside the city, and kneeling down on the beach we prayed and said goodbye to one another. ⁶Then we boarded the ship, and they

returned home. ⁷When we had finished the voyage from Tyre, we arrived at Ptolemais. We greeted the brothers and stayed with them for one day.

⁸The next morning we departed and went to Caesarea. We entered the house of Philip the evangelist and stayed with him. He was one of the seven, ⁹and he had four unmarried daughters who spoke prophecies. ¹⁰While we were staying [there] for some days, a prophet named Agabus came down from Judea. ¹¹When visiting us, he took Paul's belt and tied up his own feet and hands, and said, "So says the Holy Spirit, 'The Jews at Jerusalem will bind the man who owns this belt in this way and deliver him into the hands of the Gentiles.'" ¹²When we heard this, we and the other people there begged Paul not to go up to Jerusalem. ¹³Then Paul replied, "What are you doing—crying and breaking my heart? For I am ready not only to be imprisoned but even to die in Jerusalem for the name of the Lord Jesus." ¹⁴And since he would not be dissuaded, we acquiesced and stated, "May the Lord's will be done."

¹⁵After these days we readied ourselves and traveled up to Jerusalem. ¹⁶Some of the disciples from Caesarea accompanied us, taking us to [the home of] Mnason of Cyprus, an early disciple, where we could spend the night.

Paul Visits James

¹⁷When we arrived in Jerusalem the fellow believers welcomed us gladly. ¹⁸On the following day we and Paul went to visit to James, and all the elders were present. ¹⁹After greeting them, one by one [Paul] related the things that God had done through his ministry among the Gentiles. ²⁰On hearing these things, they gave God the glory. However, they said to him, "Brother, you are aware how many thousands of Jewish believers there are, and they are all zealous for the law. ²¹Well, they have been told about how you instruct all the Jews [living] among the Gentiles to forsake Moses, telling them not to circumcise their sons or adhere to our customs. ²²What then should be done? Surely they will hear that you have come. ²³So, do what we tell you. We have four men who have taken a vow. ²⁴Take these men and purify yourself along with them and pay their expenses, so that they may shave their heads. That way everyone will know that there's nothing in what they have been told about you, but rather that you yourself do live in observance of the law. ²⁵But as for the Gentiles who now believe, we have sent a letter with our decision that they should abstain from food that has been sacrificed to idols, and from blood, and from the meat of strangled [animals], and from sexual immorality." ²⁶Then Paul took the men, and the next day he purified himself along with them, and he went into the temple to set the date when he would bring an offering for each one of them and so mark the completion of the time of purification.

Paul is Arrested

[27]When the seven days were almost completed, the Jews from Asia noticed [Paul] in the temple, so they stirred up the whole crowd and grabbed him, [28]shouting out, "Men of Israel, help! This is the man who is indoctrinating everybody everywhere contrary to the nation, and the law, and this [holy] place. And now he has even brought Greeks into the temple, and he has defiled this holy place." [29](Previously they had seen Trophimus the Ephesian with him in the city, and they assumed that Paul had brought him into the temple.) [30]Then the whole city was aroused, and the people began rushing together. They grabbed Paul and dragged him out of the temple, and the gates were shut immediately. [31]And as they were trying to kill him, it was reported to the commander of the [Roman] cohort that all Jerusalem was in an uproar. [32]Immediately he took soldiers and centurions and rushed down to them. Now when they saw the commander and the soldiers, they ceased beating Paul. [33]Then the commander came up and arrested him and ordered him to be bound with two chains. Paul inquired who he was and what he had done. [34]Now, some people in the crowd were shouting one thing, some another. So since he could not ascertain the facts due to the uproar, he ordered [Paul] to be brought into the barracks. [35]When he reached the steps, the crowd was so violent that the soldiers had to carry him. [36]The mob was following along behind, shouting, "Away with him!"

Paul Addresses the People

[37]As Paul was about to be brought into the barracks, he asked the commander, "May I say something to you?" And he replied, "[Oh], you can speak Greek? [38]Well, then, aren't you the Egyptian who in recent times stirred up a revolt and led the four thousand members of "The Assassins" out into the wilderness?" [39]Paul replied, "I am a Jew from Tarsus in Cilicia, a citizen of a noteworthy city. I beg you, let me speak to the people." [40]And when [the commander] had given him permission, Paul, stood on the steps and motioned with his hand to the people. When all had quieted down, he spoke to them in the Hebrew language, saying: [22:1] "Brothers and fathers, listen to the defense that I am making before you now."

Chapter 22

[2]And when they heard that he addressed them in the Hebrew language, they were even quieter. And he said:

> [3]"I am a Jew, born at Tarsus in Cilicia, but brought up in this city under the teaching of Gamaliel, educated according to the strict manner of the law of our fathers, being as zealous for God as you all are today. [4]I persecuted [mem-

bers of] The Way to the death, continually tying up and delivering both men and women to prison, [5]as the high priest and the whole council of elders will attest to. From the [elders] I received letters to our fellow Jews in Damascus, so I journeyed there to take those also who were there and bring them in chains to Jerusalem to be punished.

[6]"Now it happened that as I was traveling and drawing near Damascus, about noon a great light from heaven suddenly shone around me. [7]And I fell to the ground and heard a voice saying to me, 'Saul, Saul, why are you persecuting me?' [8]And I answered, 'Who are you, Lord?' And he said to me, 'I am Jesus of Nazareth whom you are persecuting.' [9]Now those who were with me did see the light but could not understand what the voice was saying to me. [10]And I said, 'What should I do, Lord?' And the Lord said to me, 'Get up and go into Damascus, and there you will be told all that is appointed for you to do.' [11]Since I could not see because of the brightness of that light, I was led by the hand by those who were with me and went into Damascus.

[12]"Now there was a man named Ananias who feared God according to the law and was well spoken of by all the Jews who lived there. [13]He came to me, and standing next to me, he said, 'Brother Saul, receive your sight.' At that very moment I received my sight and saw him. [14]And he said, 'The God of our fathers appointed you to know his will, to see the Righteous One and to hear a voice from his mouth. [15]For you will be a witness for him of what you have seen and heard to all men. [16]And now what are you waiting for? Get up and be baptized, and wash away your sins, calling on his name.'

[17]"When I had returned to Jerusalem and was praying in the temple, I fell into a trance [18]and saw him saying to me, 'Hurry up and get out of Jerusalem quickly, because they will not accept your testimony about me.' [19]And I said, 'Lord, they themselves know that in one synagogue after another I have imprisoned and beat those who believed in you. [20]And even when the blood of your witness Stephen was being shed, I was standing by and approving, guarding the clothes of those who were killing him.' [21]And he said to me, 'Leave, because I will send you far away to the Gentiles.'"

Paul and the Roman Tribune

[22]Up to this point they listened to him, but then they lifted up their voices and shouted, "Away with such a fellow from the earth! He is not fit to live!" [23]And as they cried out and waved their garments and threw dust into the air, [24]the tribune commanded him to be brought into the barracks and ordered him to be examined by flogging to find out why they had been shouting against him this way.

[25]But when they had tied him up with the straps, Paul asked the centurion who was standing by, "Is it lawful for you to flog a man who is a Roman citizen, and as yet not convicted?" [26]When the centurion heard that, he went to the tribune and said to him, "What are you about to do? For this man is a Roman citizen." [27]So the tribune came and said to him, "Tell me, are you a Roman citizen?" And he replied, "Yes." [28]The tribune answered, "I bought this citizenship for a large sum." Paul stated, "But I was born a citizen." [29]So those who were about to examine him instantly drew back from him. The tribune was afraid, too, for he [then] realized that Paul was a Roman citizen and that he had put him in chains.

Paul Goes Before the Council

[30]But the next day, desiring to know the real reason why the Jews accused him, he unbound him, and commanded the chief priests and all the council to meet, and he brought Paul down and set him before them.

Chapter 23

[1]Looking intently at the council, Paul said,

"Brothers, I have spent my life before God in all good conscience up to this day." [2]Consequently, the high priest Ananias ordered the men standing next to him to strike him on the mouth. [3]Then Paul said to him, "God shall strike you, you whitewashed wall! Do you sit in judgment of me according to the law, and yet you order me to be struck, contrary to the law?" [4]The men standing nearby asked, "Do you mean to insult God's high priest?" [5]Paul replied, "I did not know, brothers, that he was the high priest, for it is written, 'You shall not speak evil of a ruler of your people.'"

[6]But once Paul perceived that one section was a group of Sadducees and the other Pharisees, he cried out in the council, "Brothers, I am a Pharisee, a son of Pharisees. I am on trial concerning the hope of the resurrection of the dead." [7]And when he had said this, an angry shouting match broke out between the Pharisees and the Sadducees. Then the assembly was divided, [8]because the Sadducees assert that there is no [such thing as] a resurrection, an angel, or a spirit, but the Pharisees acknowledge [the existence of] all of them. [9]Then a great clamor arose, and some of the scribes of the Pharisees' party stood up and contended, "We find no wrongdoing in this man. What if a spirit or an angel spoke to him?" [10]And when the argument became violent, the commander, afraid that they would tear Paul to pieces, commanded the soldiers to go down and take him by force from their midst and bring him into the barracks. [11]The following night the Lord stood by him and said, "Take courage, for as you have testified about me in Jerusalem, so you must also bear witness in Rome."

Jews Plot to Kill Paul

[12]When morning came, the Jews made a plot and bound themselves by an oath to neither eat nor drink until they had killed Paul. [13]More than forty of them formed this conspiracy. [14]And then they went to the chief priests and elders, and said, "We have strictly bound ourselves by an oath to taste no food until we have killed Paul. [15]You therefore, along with the council, give notice now to the commander to bring him down to you, as though you were going to determine his case more exactly. And we will be ready to kill him before he gets here."

[16]Now the son of Paul's sister heard of their ambush [plan], so he went and entered the barracks and informed Paul. [17]So, Paul called one of the centurions and said, "Take this young man to the tribune, for he has something to tell him." [18]So [the centurion] took him and brought him to the tribune and said, "The prisoner Paul summoned me and asked me to bring this young man to you, since he has something to tell you." [19]The tribune took him by the hand, turned aside, and asked him privately, "What is it that you have to tell me?" [20]So he told him, "The Jews have conspired to ask you to bring Paul down to the council tomorrow, as if they were going to inquire something about him in more detail. [21]But do not be fooled by them, because more than forty of their men will be lying in ambush for him, having bound themselves by an oath to neither eat nor drink until they have killed him. They are ready even now, waiting for word from you." [22]So the tribune dismissed the young man, commanding him, "Do not tell anyone that you have informed me of these plans."

Paul is Sent to Felix

[23]Then he called two of the centurions and said, "At nine o'clock tonight prepare two hundred soldiers with seventy horsemen and two hundred spearmen to go as far as Caesarea, [24]and also provide mounts for Paul to ride. Bring him safely to Felix the governor." [25]And he wrote a letter in these terms:

[26]*[From]: Claudius Lysias*

To: his Excellency the governor Felix

Greetings.

[27]*This man was seized by the Jews, and was about to be killed by them, when I came on them with soldiers and rescued him, having learned that he was a Roman citizen. [28]I brought him down to their council, wanting to know the charge on which they accused him. [29]I discovered that he had been accused over issues pertaining to their [religious] law, but not charged with anything deserving death or*

imprisonment. ³⁰And when it was disclosed to me that there was a plot [to murder] the man, I immediately sent [him] to you, ordering that his accusers state before you what they have against him.

³¹So, according to their instructions, the soldiers took Paul and brought him to Antipatris by night. ³²They returned to the barracks on the next day, leaving the horsemen to go on with him. ³³When they came to Caesarea and delivered the letter to the governor, they also presented Paul before him. ³⁴On reading the letter, he asked him which province he belonged to. When he learned that he was from Cilicia ³⁵he said, "I will grant a hearing for you when your accusers have arrived." And he ordered that he be guarded in Herod's headquarters.

Chapter 24

Paul Stands Before Felix

¹Five days later Ananias the high priest came down with some elders and an expert in the law named Tertullus, and they presented their case against Paul before the governor. ²When Tertullus was called on, he began the accusation against him, saying:

"Since it is through you that we enjoy such great peace, most excellent Felix, and since by your provision, reforms have benefitted this nation, ³we acknowledge this in every way and everywhere with much gratitude. ⁴So, not to weary you any further, I beg that in your kindness you would listen to us briefly. ⁵For we have found this man a real troublemaker, an agitator among all the Jews throughout the world, and a ringleader of that Nazarene sect. ⁶He even tried to desecrate the temple, but we seized him, and we would have judged him according to our law. ⁷But the chief captain Lysias came and grabbed him out of our hands with great violence, commanding his accusers to come before you. ⁸By examining him yourself you will be able to learn from him about everything that we are accusing him of."

⁹The Jews also joined in the charge, confirming that all this was so.

¹⁰And when the governor had motioned to him to speak, Paul made his reply: "Realizing that you have been judge over this nation for many years, I am delighted to make my defense. ¹¹As you may ascertain, not more than twelve days ago I went up to Jerusalem to worship. ¹²They did not find me arguing with anyone or stirring up a crowd, either in the temple or in the synagogues, or in the city. ¹³Neither can they prove to you the charges they are now bringing up against me. ¹⁴But I do admit this to you: that according to The Way, which they call a sect, I worship the God of our fathers, believing everything within the Law and written

222

in the Prophets, [15]holding the same hope in God that these men themselves accept, that there will be a resurrection of both the righteous and the wicked. [16]So I always make the effort to keep a clear conscience toward God and other people. [17]Now after a lapse of some years I returned here to my nation to bring alms and make offerings. [18]As I was doing this, they found me in the temple, ceremonially clean, and without any mobs or disturbances. Now if some Jews from Asia have anything against me, [19]they ought to be here before you to make an accusation. [20]Or else, let these men themselves state what wrongdoing they found when I stood before the council, [21]other than one thing that I cried out while standing among them, 'I am on trial before you today concerning the resurrection of the dead.'"

Paul Held in Custody

[22]But Felix, who had quite an accurate understanding of The Way, put them off, saying, "I will decide your case when Lysias the tribune comes down." [23]Then he gave orders to the centurion that Paul should be kept in custody but should have some liberty, and that none of his friends should be forbidden to attend to his needs.

[24]A few days later Felix came with his wife Drusilla, who was a Jewess, and he summoned Paul and listened to him concerning faith in Christ Jesus. [25]And as he presented logical arguments concerning justice, and self-control, and the coming judgment, Felix was alarmed and exclaimed, "Go away for right now. When I have an opportunity, I will summon you." [26]At that moment he was in hopes that Paul would give him [bribe] money.

He did summon him often and conversed with him. [27]When two years had gone by, Porcius Festus took the place of Felix. But, since he wanted to do the Jews a favor, Felix left Paul in prison.

Chapter 25

Paul Appeals to Caesar

[1]Now Festus, three days after having come to power in the province, went up from Caesarea to Jerusalem. [2]And the chief priests and the Jewish leaders presented a case against Paul to him, urging him [3]to grant them a favor and have him sent to Jerusalem. (They were planning an ambush to kill him on the way.) [4]Festus replied that Paul was being kept at Caesarea, and that he himself intended to go there soon. [5]"So," he said, "have the men of authority among you come down with me, and if there is anything wrong concerning the man, let them make ac-

cusations against him."

⁶When he had stayed among them not more than eight or ten days, he went down to Caesarea. The next day he took his seat on the tribunal and ordered Paul to be brought. ⁷And when he had come, the Jews who had gone down from Jerusalem stood around him, bringing many serious charges against him, which they were unable to substantiate. ⁸Paul responded in his defense, "I have not committed any offense against either the law of the Jews or the temple, or against Caesar." ⁹But Festus, wishing to do the Jews a favor, asked Paul, "Do you want to go up to Jerusalem, and be tried on these charges there before me?" ¹⁰Then Paul replied, "I am standing before Caesar's court, where I should be tried. I have done no wrong to the Jews, as you know very well. ¹¹So then, if I were a wrongdoer and had committed anything that I would deserve to die for, I would not seek to escape death. But if there is no truth in their charges against me, no one can deliver me over to the [Jews]. I appeal to Caesar." ¹²Then, once Festus had conferred with his council, he answered, "You have appealed to Caesar, and to Caesar you shall go."

Paul Goes Before Agrippa

¹³Now after some days had passed, the king Agrippa and Bernice arrived in Caesarea to welcome Festus. ¹⁴And once they had been there many days, Festus laid the case about Paul before the king, saying, "There is a man [here] left a prisoner by Felix. ¹⁵And when I was in Jerusalem, the chief priests and the elders of the Jews presented their case against him, demanding him to be sentenced. ¹⁶I answered them that it was not the custom of the Romans to deliver a man over to death before the accused met the accusers face to face and had the chance to make his defense concerning the charge laid against him. ¹⁷So, when they came together here, I did not delay, but on the next day took my seat on the tribunal and ordered the man to be brought in. ¹⁸When the accusers stood up, they brought no charge in his case of the kind of wrongdoings that I had imagined. ¹⁹Instead, their dispute with him lay in certain points of their own "spirit-worship" and about a certain Jesus, who was dead, but whom Paul declared to be alive. ²⁰Being at a loss as to how to investigate these questions, I asked whether he wished to go to Jerusalem and be tried there regarding them. ²¹But when Paul had appealed to be kept in custody for the decision of the emperor, I commanded him to be held until I could send him to Caesar." ²²And Agrippa said to Festus, "I should like to hear the man myself." "Tomorrow," he said, "you shall hear him."

²³So the next morning Agrippa and Bernice arrived with ceremonious pomp, and they entered the audience hall with the military tribunes and the prominent men of the city. Then Paul was brought in by the command of Festus. ²⁴And Festus

said, "King Agrippa and all who are present with us, you see this man about whom the whole Jewish community petitioned me, both at Jerusalem and here, clamoring that he should live no longer. ²⁵But I found that he had done nothing deserving death. And since he himself appealed to the emperor, I decided to send him. ²⁶But I have nothing conclusive about him to write to my lord. Therefore, I have brought him before you, and, especially before you, King Agrippa, so that, having examined him, I would have something to write. ²⁷For it seems unreasonable to me, when sending a prisoner, not to document the charges against him."

Chapter 26

Paul Defends himself to Agrippa

¹So Agrippa said to Paul, "You have permission to speak for yourself." Then Paul stretched out his hand and made his defense:

²"I think myself fortunate that it is before you, King Agrippa, that I am to make my defense today against all the accusations of the Jews, ³because you are especially familiar with all customs and controversies of the Jews. Therefore, I beg you to listen to me patiently.

⁴"All the Jews are aware of how I have lived my life, right from my younger days, among my own people and in Jerusalem. ⁵They have known for a long time, if they are willing to testify, that I have lived as a Pharisee, the strictest party of our religion. ⁶And now I stand here on trial due to my hope in the promise made by God to our fathers. ⁷Our twelve tribes hope to attain it, as they worship earnestly day and night. And for this hope I am accused by Jews, O king! ⁸Why do any of you think it incredible that God raises the dead? ⁹I myself was once convinced that I ought to do many things in opposing the name of Jesus of Nazareth. ¹⁰And I did so in Jerusalem: I not only shut up many of the saints in prison, by getting authority from the chief priests, but also cast my vote against them when they were put to death. ¹¹And I punished them often in all the synagogues and tried to make them blaspheme. And in raging fury against them, I hunted them down, even to distant cities.

Paul Relates his Conversion Experience

¹²"So, in carrying this out, I was journeying to Damascus with the authority and commission of the chief priests. ¹³On the way, O king, about noon I saw a light from heaven, brighter than the sun, shining around me and my traveling companions. ¹⁴And when we had all fallen to the ground, I heard a voice saying to me in the Hebrew language, 'Saul, Saul, why do you persecute me? You make it hard

for yourself by kicking against the goads.' [15]And I said, 'Who are you, Lord?' And the Lord said, 'I am Jesus whom you are persecuting. [16]But get up and stand on your feet. For I have appeared to you for this purpose: to appoint you as a servant and a witness to the things you have seen already seen me do as well as to the things you have yet to see me do. [17]I will rescue you from the people and from the Gentiles. I am sending you to them [18]to open their eyes, so that they might turn from darkness to light and from the devil's power to God, so that they may receive forgiveness of sins and a place among those who are sanctified by faith in me.'

[19]"Therefore, O King Agrippa, I did not disobey the heavenly vision, [20]but rather I declared first to those at Damascus, then at Jerusalem and throughout all the country of Judea, and also to the Gentiles, that they should repent and turn to God, performing deeds in keeping with their repentance. [21]This was why the Jews seized me in the temple and tried to kill me. [22]To this day I have had the help that comes from God, and so I stand here testifying both to small and great, saying nothing but what the prophets and Moses said would come to pass: [23]that the Christ must suffer, and that, by being the first one to ever rise from the dead, he would proclaim light both to the people and to the Gentiles."

[24]And as he made his defense in this way, Festus said with a loud voice, "Paul, you are insane; your great learning is driving you mad." [25]But Paul said, "I am not insane, most excellent Festus, but I am speaking the sober truth. [26]For the king knows about these things, and I speak freely to him. For I am persuaded that none of these things has escaped his notice, for this was not done in a corner. [27]King Agrippa, do you believe the prophets? I know that you believe [them]." [28]Agrippa replied to Paul, "You imagine that you'll turn me into a Christian in just a short while!" [29]And Paul said, "Whether short or long, I would to God that not only you but also all who hear me this day might become such as I am—except for these chains."

[30]Then the king got up, as did the governor and Bernice and those who were sitting with them. [31]Once they had withdrawn, they said to one another, "This man is doing nothing to deserve death or imprisonment." [32]And Agrippa said to Festus, "This man could have been set free if he had not appealed to Caesar."

Chapter 27

Paul Sets Sail for Rome

[1]And when it was decided that we should sail for Italy, they delivered Paul and some other prisoners to a centurion of the Augustan regiment, named Julius. [2]After going on board a ship from Adramyttium, which was about to sail to the

ports along the coast of Asia, we put to sea, accompanied by Aristarchus, a Macedonian from Thessalonica. ³The next day we landed at Sidon at which point Julius treated Paul kindly, and allowed him to go to his friends and be cared for. ⁴And putting to sea from there we sailed under the shelter of Cyprus, because the winds were against us. ⁵And when we had sailed across the open sea off the coast of Cilicia and Pamphylia, we came to Myra in Lycia. ⁶There the centurion found an Alexandrian ship sailing for Italy and put us on board. ⁷We sailed slowly for a number of days, and arrived with difficulty off Cnidus, and since the wind did not allow us to go farther, we sailed under the shelter of Crete off Salmone. ⁸Coasting along it with difficulty, we came to a place called Fair Havens, near which was the city of Lasea.

⁹Since a lot of time had been lost, and because the Day of Fasting had already passed, the voyage was already dangerous. So, Paul advised them, ¹⁰saying, "Sirs, I perceive that the voyage will be with injury and much loss, not only of the cargo and the ship, but also of our lives." ¹¹But the centurion paid more attention to the captain and to the owner of the ship than to what Paul said. ¹²And because the harbor was not suitable to spend the winter in, the majority decided to put out to sea from there, on the chance that somehow they could reach Phoenix, a harbor of Crete that faces both northeast and southeast, and spend the winter there.

Storm and Shipwreck

¹³And when the south wind blew gently, supposing that they had achieved their purpose, they weighed anchor and sailed along Crete, close to shore. ¹⁴But soon a tempestuous wind, called a northeaster, struck down from the land. ¹⁵Once the ship was caught and could not face the wind, we gave way to it and were driven along. ¹⁶And running under the shelter of a small island called Cauda, we managed to secure the boat with [some] difficulty. ¹⁷After hoisting it up, they used supports to undergird the ship. Then, fearing that they should run aground on the sandbars of Syrtis, they lowered the gear, and so were driven along. ¹⁸Since we were violently storm-tossed, the next day they began to jettison the cargo. ¹⁹On the third day they threw the ship's tackle overboard. ²⁰And when neither sun nor stars appeared for many a day, and no small tempest lay on us, all hope of our being saved was at last abandoned.

²¹As they had been long without food, Paul then stood up among them and said, "Men, you should have listened to me, and should not have set sail from Crete and incurred this injury and loss. ²²Yet now I urge you to take heart for there will be no loss of life among you, but only of the ship. ²³For this very night an angel of the God that I belong to and worship stood beside me, ²⁴and he said, 'Do not

227

be afraid, Paul. You must stand before Caesar. Now look, God has given you everyone who is sailing with you.' ²⁵So take heart, men, for I have faith in God that it will be exactly as I have been told. ²⁶But we will have to run aground on some island."

²⁷When the fourteenth night had come, as we were drifting across the Adriatic Sea, about midnight the sailors suspected that they were nearing land. ²⁸So they took a sounding and found twenty fathoms. A little farther on they sounded again and found fifteen fathoms. ²⁹Then fearing that we might run up onto rocks, they let down four anchors from the stern, and prayed for day to come. ³⁰And as the sailors were seeking to escape from the ship, and had lowered the boat into the sea under the pretense of laying out anchors from the bow, ³¹Paul told the centurion and the soldiers, "Unless these men stay in the ship, you cannot be saved." ³²Then the soldiers cut away the ropes of the boat, and let it go.

³³As day was about to dawn, Paul urged them all to take some food, saying, "To-day is the fourteenth day that you have continued in suspense and without food, having taken nothing. ³⁴Therefore I urge you to take some food. It will give you strength, since not a hair is to perish from the head of any of you." ³⁵And when he had said this, he took bread, and giving thanks to God in the presence of all he broke it and began to eat. ³⁶Then they all were encouraged and ate some food themselves. ³⁷(In all we were 276 persons in the ship.) ³⁸And once they had eaten enough, they lightened the ship by dumping the wheat into the sea.

³⁹When morning came, they could not recognize the land, but they noticed a bay with a beach, on which they planned to bring the ship ashore, if possible. ⁴⁰So they cast off the anchors and left them in the sea, at the same time loosening the ropes that tied the rudders. Then, hoisting the foresail to the wind, they headed for the beach. ⁴¹But striking a reef they ran the vessel aground. The bow stuck and remained immovable, and the stern was broken up by the surf. ⁴²The soldiers' plan was to kill the prisoners, so that they could not escape by swimming away. ⁴³But the centurion, wishing to save Paul, kept them from carrying out their plan. He ordered those who could swim to jump overboard first and make for the land, ⁴⁴and the rest [to float] on planks or pieces of the ship. And so it was that all made it safely to land.

Chapter 28

On the Island of Malta

¹Once we had made it safely through [the ordeal], we then learned that the island was called Malta. ²Now the natives showed us unusual kindness in welcoming us

all by kindling a fire, because it was cold and had begun to rain. ³Paul gathered a bundle of sticks and when he put them on the fire, a viper came out because of the heat and latched onto his hand. ⁴When the natives saw the creature hanging from his hand, they said to one another, "No doubt this man is a murderer. Although he has escaped from the sea, justice has not allowed him to live." ⁵However, [Paul] shook off the creature into the fire and suffered no harm. ⁶They waited, expecting him to swell up or suddenly fall down dead. But when they had waited a long time and saw no misfortune come to him, they changed their minds and said that he was a god.

⁷Now in the area around that place were lands belonging to the chief man of the island, named Publius, who received us and entertained us hospitably for three days. ⁸It happened that Publius's father was lying sick with fever and dysentery. So, Paul visited him and prayed, and putting his hands on him he healed him. ⁹And once this had happened, the rest of the people on the island who had diseases also came and were cured. ¹⁰They also honored us with many gifts, and as we were making preparations to set sail, they put whatever we needed on board.

Paul Arrives in Rome

¹¹After three months we set sail in a ship that had wintered on the island, a ship of Alexandria, with the Twin Gods as figurehead. ¹²Putting in at Syracuse, we stayed there for three days. ¹³And from there we made a circuit and arrived at Rhegium. And after one day a south wind sprang up, and on the second day we came to Puteoli. ¹⁴There we found fellow believers who urged us to stay with them for seven days. And so we came to Rome ¹⁵and when the fellow believers heard of us, they came as far as the Forum of Appius and Three Taverns to meet us. On seeing them, Paul thanked God and took courage. ¹⁶And when we came into Rome, Paul was allowed to stay by himself with the soldier guarding him.

Paul in Rome

¹⁷After three days he called the local leaders of the Jews together. And once they were gathered, he said to them, "Brothers, though I had done nothing against the people or the customs of our fathers, I was delivered as a prisoner from Jerusalem into the hands of the Romans. ¹⁸Having examined me, they wished to set me free, because there was no reason for me to [receive] the death penalty. ¹⁹But when the Jews objected, I was compelled to appeal to Caesar, though I had no cause to accuse my nation. ²⁰Therefore, for this reason I have asked to see you and speak to you, since I am bound with this chain because of the hope of Israel." ²¹And they said to him, "We have received no notices from Judea about you, and none of the

fellow believers coming here have reported or spoken any evil about you. ²²But we would like to hear from you what you think, for we know that everywhere people are speaking out against this sect."

²³Once they had appointed a day for him, they started coming to him at his lodging in great numbers. And he explained the matter to them from morning till evening, testifying to the kingdom of God to convince them about Jesus both from the law of Moses and from the Prophets. ²⁴And some were convinced by what he said, while others did not believe. ²⁵So, as they disagreed among themselves, they departed, after Paul had made one statement:

"The Holy Spirit was right in saying to your fathers through Isaiah the prophet: ²⁶'Go to this people and say, "You will indeed hear but never understand, and you will indeed see but never perceive." ²⁷For the heart of this people has grown dull, and with their ears they can barely hear. And they have closed their eyes, so that they will not be able to perceive with their eyes, and hear with their ears, and understand with their heart, and turn for me to heal them.' ²⁸Let it be known to you then that this salvation of God has been sent to the Gentiles—and they will listen."

²⁹After he said this, the Jews left, arguing vigorously among themselves.

³⁰And he lived there for two entire years in his own rented place and welcomed everyone who visited him, ³¹preaching the kingdom of God and teaching about the Lord Jesus Christ with all boldness and without hindrance.

Chapter 1

¹[From]: Paul, a servant of Christ Jesus, called to be an apostle, set apart for the [work of the] gospel of God, ²which he promised beforehand through his prophets in the Holy Scriptures. ³This is the gospel concerning his Son, Jesus Christ our Lord, who was descended from David in terms of his human nature, ⁴and empowered as the Son of God by the Spirit of holiness through his resurrection from the dead. ⁵Through him we have received grace and apostleship to bring about the obedience of faith for the sake of his name among all the nations, ⁶including you yourselves who are called to belong to Jesus Christ.

⁷To: All God's beloved in Rome, who are called to be saints:

Grace to you and peace from God our Father and the Lord Jesus Christ.

Paul Longs to See the Believers in Rome

⁸First, I thank my God through Jesus Christ for all of you, because your faith is being proclaimed in the whole world. ⁹For God, whom I serve heartily in the gospel of his Son, is my witness that I continually mention you in my prayers, ¹⁰always asking that at long length somehow by God's will, a way may be made for me to come to you. ¹¹For I long to see you so that I may convey to you some spiritual gift to strengthen you. ¹²That is, that we may be mutually encouraged by each other's faith, both yours and mine. ¹³I want you to know, brothers, that I have often intended to come to you (but up till now have been prevented), in order that I may reap some harvest among you as well as among the rest of the Gentiles. ¹⁴I have a duty both to Greeks and to heathen nations, both to the learned and to the uneducated. ¹⁵Thus, as much as I am able to, I am eagerly willing to preach the gospel to you who are in Rome also.

¹⁶For I am not ashamed of the gospel of Christ because it is the power from God to save everyone who believes, first to the Jew and also to the Greek. ¹⁷For the righteousness of God is revealed in it, [coming] from faith, resulting in faith. As it is written, "The righteous ones shall live by faith."

God's Wrath Against Evildoers

[18]However, the wrath of God is being revealed from heaven against every [form of] ungodliness and wickedness of men who suppress the truth by their wicked deeds. [19]For what can be known about God is obvious to their minds because God has made it clear to them. [20]Ever since the creation of the world his invisible nature, namely, his eternal power and deity, has been clearly perceived in the things that he has made, so they are without excuse. [21]But even though they knew God, they did not honor him as God or give thanks to him, but rather in their worldview they imagined futile things and their foolish minds grew dark. [22]Claiming to be wise, they became fools, [23]and exchanged the glory of the immortal God for idols made in the image of mortal man, or birds, or animals, or reptiles.

[24]As a result, God gave them over to immorality through the lusts of their hearts, and to the degrading of their bodies among themselves, [25]because they exchanged the truth about God for a lie and worshiped and served the creature rather than the Creator, who is blessed forever! Amen.

[26]For this reason God abandoned them to reprehensible passions. Their women exchanged natural sexual relations for unnatural. [27]And in similar fashion, the men turned away from natural sexual relations with women and were consumed with passion for one another: men shamelessly committing acts with other men, and thereby receiving in their own persons the due penalty for their perversity.

[28]And since they did not see fit to acknowledge God, God gave them over to having a filthy mind and to improper conduct. [29]They were filled with all manner of wickedness, evil, covetousness, and malice. Being full of envy, murder, strife, deceit, and slander, they are gossips, [30]backbiters, and haters of God, insolent, haughty, and boastful inventors of evil. They are disobedient to [their] parents, [31]foolish, faithless, heartless, and ruthless. [32]Though they are aware of God's judgment that those who do such things deserve to die, not only do they do them, but they also give approval to those who practice them.

Chapter 2

Man is Without Excuse

[1]Therefore, O man, all who judge—you have no excuse when you judge another because you condemn yourself in passing judgment on another, because you, the judge, are doing the very same things. [2]Now we know that judgment of God truly is on those who do such things. [3]So do you suppose, O man, that when you judge those who do such things and yet do them yourself, you will escape the judgment of God? [4]Or do you presume that he is lavish with his kindness and forbearance

and patience, not realizing that God's kindness is for leading you to repentance? [5]But by your hard and unrepentant heart you are storing up wrath for yourself on the day of wrath when God's righteous judgment will be unleashed.

[6]He will apportion to each person by virtue of his deeds: [7]He will give eternal life to those who seek for glory and honor and immortality by patience in well-doing. [8]But there will be wrath and fury for those who are divisive and do not obey the truth but obey wickedness. [9]There will be tribulation and distress for every person who practices evil—first the Jew and also the Greek—[10]but glory and honor and peace for every person who does good—first the Jew and also the Greek—[11]for God shows no partiality.

The Law and God's Judgment

[12]Everyone who has sinned without the law will also perish without the law, and everyone who has sinned under the law will be judged by the law. [13]For it is not the hearers of the law who are righteous before God, but the doers of the law who will be justified. [14]When Gentiles, who do not have the law, do by nature what the law requires, they are a law to themselves, even though they do not have the law. [15]They show that what the law requires is written on their hearts, since their conscience also bears witness and their conflicting thoughts [will] accuse or perhaps excuse them [16]on that day when, according to my gospel, God judges the secrets of men by Christ Jesus.

[17]But if you call yourself a Jew, and rely on the law, and boast of your relation to God, [18]and know his will and discern what is excellent because you are instructed in the law, [19]and if you are a guide to the blind, a light to those who are in darkness, [20]a corrector of the foolish, a teacher of children, having the embodiment of knowledge and truth in the law, [21]then:

You who teach others, will you not teach yourself?
You preach against stealing, do you steal?
[22]You who say that one must not commit adultery, do you commit adultery?
You who despise idols, do you rob [their] temples?
[23]You who boast in the law, do you dishonor God by breaking the law?

[24]For, as it is written, "Because of you the name of God has been maligned among the Gentiles."

[25]For circumcision indeed is of value if you obey the law. But if you break the law, your circumcision ends up as uncircumcision. [26]So, if a man who is uncircumcised keeps the precepts of the law, will not his uncircumcision be regarded as circumcision? [27]Then those who are physically uncircumcised but keep the law

233

will condemn you who have the written code and circumcision but break the law. [28]For the one who is only a Jew outwardly is not a real Jew, nor is true circumcision something external and physical. [29]Rather the [real] Jew is one inwardly, and circumcision is of the heart—spiritual and not literal. his affirmation comes not from men but from God.

Chapter 3

God is Righteous

[1]Then what advantage does the Jew have? Or what is the value of circumcision? [2]Great, in every way: first of all, the Jews have been entrusted with God's word. [3]What if some were unfaithful? Could their faithlessness cancel out the faithfulness of God? [4]Certainly not! God remains true to his word, even if everyone is a liar. As the scripture says, "May you be vindicated by what you say, and prevail when you are judged." [5]But if our wickedness serves to define the justice of God, what shall we say? That God is unjust to inflict punishment on us? (I am wording it as a common man.) [6]Certainly not! For then how could God judge the world? [7]But if through my falsehood God's truthfulness abounds to his glory, why do I still deserve to be condemned as a sinner? [8]And why not do evil so that good may come [from it]? —as some people slanderously charge us with saying. The condemnation of them is just.

Scriptures Declare Man's Sin Nature

[9]What then? Are we Jews any better off? No, not at all: for I have already declared that all men, both Jews and Greeks [alike], are subject to sin. [10]As it is written:

> "None is righteous, no, not one.
> [11]No one understands; no one is searching for God.
> [12]All have turned aside, together they have gone wrong.
> No one does good, not even one."
> [13]"Their throats are an open tomb; they use their tongues to deceive."
> "The venom of asps lies under their lips."
> [14]"Their mouths are full of curses and bitterness."
> [15]"Their feet are swift to shed blood.
> [16]Destruction and misery fill their paths, [17]and they do not know the way of peace."
> [18]"No fear of God lies in front of their eyes."

[19]Now we know that whatever is stated in the law addresses those who are under the law, so that every mouth may fall silent, and the whole world may be held ac-

countable to God. ²⁰For no human being will end up justified in his sight by works of the law, since through the law comes knowledge of sin.

Righteousness Comes Through Faith

²¹But now, apart from the law, the righteousness coming from God has been brought to light, even though the law and the prophets bear witness to it: ²²the righteousness of God through faith in Jesus Christ for all who believe. For there is no distinction, ²³since all have sinned and do not measure up to the glory of God. ²⁴They are justified by his grace as a free gift, through the redemption that is in Christ Jesus, ²⁵whom God put forth as an atoning sacrifice by his blood, to be received by faith. This was to demonstrate God's righteousness, because in his divine forbearance he had passed over sins in the past. ²⁶It was to prove at the present time that he himself is righteous and that he justifies the one who has faith in Jesus. ²⁷Then what becomes of our boasting? It is ruled out. On what bais? By virtue of deeds? No, by virtue of faith. ²⁸For we conclude that a person is justified by faith apart from works of law. ²⁹Or is God the God of Jews only? Is he not also the God of Gentiles? Yes, of Gentiles also, ³⁰seeing that there is one God who will justify the circumcised on the basis of their faith and the uncircumcised through their faith [as well]. ³¹Do we then cancel out the law by this faith? Certainly not! On the contrary, we are confirming the law.

Chapter 4

Abraham Justified by Faith

¹What then shall we say about Abraham, our forefather by natural descent? ²For if Abraham was justified by works, he has cause to boast, but not before God. ³For what does the scripture say? "Abraham put his faith in God, and it was accounted to him as righteousness." ⁴Now wages are not accounted to the one who works as a gift, but as a debt. ⁵But to one who does not work but trusts him who justifies the ungodly, his faith is counted as righteousness. ⁶So also David pronounces a blessing on the man to whom God reckons righteousness apart from works: ⁷"Blessed are those whose wrongdoings are forgiven, and whose sins are covered. ⁸Blessed is the man against whose sin the Lord does not take into account."

⁹Is this blessing [pronounced] only on the circumcised, or also on the uncircumcised? We say that faith was accounted to Abraham as righteousness. ¹⁰In which way was it accounted to him? Was he as yet uncircumcised, or was he circumcised? It was not after, but before he was circumcised. ¹¹He received circumcision as a sign or seal of the righteousness that he had by faith while he was still uncircumcised. The purpose was to make him the father of all who believe without

being circumcised and thus have righteousness accounted to them, [12]and likewise the father of the circumcised who are not merely circumcised but who also walk in the example of the faith set by our as yet uncircumcised father Abraham.

God's Promise to Abraham

[13]The promise to Abraham and his descendants, that they should inherit the world, did not come through the law but through the righteousness of faith. [14]For if those of the law are to be the heirs, then faith is nullified, and the promise is void [15]because the law brings punishment. After all, where there is no law there is no transgression.

[16]That is why it depends on faith, in order that the promise may rest on grace and be guaranteed to all his descendants, not only to those of the law, but also to the one who shares the faith of Abraham, who is the father of us all. [17]As the scripture says, "I have made you the father of many nations" in the presence of the God in whom he believed, who makes the dead alive [again] and calls into being those things that do not yet exist as if they did. [18]Abraham believed, hope against hope, that he should become the father of many nations, just as he had been told, "…so shall your descendants be." [19]He did not weaken in faith when he considered his own body, which had grown impotent because he was about a hundred years old, or when he considered the infertility of Sarah's womb. [20]No distrust made him waver concerning the promise of God, but he grew strong in his faith as he gave glory to God, [21]fully convinced that he was able to do what he had promised. [22]That is why his faith was "accounted to him as righteousness." [23]But the words, "it was accounted to him," were written not only for his sake, [24]but also for ours. It will be accounted to us who believe in the One that raised from the dead Jesus our Lord, [25]who was put to death for our trespasses and raised again for our justification.

Chapter 5

Justified by Faith

[1]Therefore, being justified by faith, we have peace with God through our Lord Jesus Christ. [2]Through him we have obtained access to this grace that we stand in, and we rejoice in the hope of [partaking in] God's glory. [3]More than that, we rejoice in our sufferings, knowing that suffering produces endurance, [4]and endurance produces character, and character produces hope. [5]Now that hope does not disappoint us, because God's love has been poured into our hearts through the Holy Spirit, who has been given to us.

[6]For while we were still helpless, at the appointed time Christ died for the ungodly. [7]Now, a man will hardly die on behalf of a righteous man—though perhaps a man might even dare to die for a good man. [8]But God shows his love for us in that while we were yet sinners Christ died for us. [9]Therefore, since we are now justified by his blood, even more so shall he save us from the wrath of God. [10]For if while we were enemies we were reconciled to God by the death of his Son, even more so shall we be saved by his life, now that we stand reconciled. [11]And not only that, but we also rejoice in God through our Lord Jesus Christ, through whom we now have received reconciliation.

Adam Brought Death into the World

[12]Therefore, since sin came into the world through one man and death through sin, so death spread to all men because all men sinned. [13]Sin indeed was in the world before the law was given, but without the law sin is not counted. [14]However death did reign from Adam to Moses, even over those whose sins were not like the transgression of Adam, who was a type of the one who was to come.

[15]On the contrary, the free gift is not like the offence. For if through one man's offence many have died, even more so the grace of God and the free gift in the grace of that one man, Jesus Christ, have abounded for many. [16]And the free gift is not like the effect of that one man's sin. For the judgment following one offence brought condemnation, but the free gift due to many offences brought justification. [17]If, because of one man's offences, death reigned through that one man, even more so those who receive the abundance of grace and the free gift of righteousness will reign in life through the one man, Jesus Christ.

[18]Consequently, as one man's offence brought about condemnation for all men, so one man's act of righteousness brought about acquittal and life for all men. [19]For just as many were made sinners by one man's disobedience, so many will be made righteous by the one man's obedience. [20]Then the law entered in, which increased the offence. But where sin increased, grace abounded all the more, [21]so that, as sin reigned in death, grace might also reign through righteousness ushering in eternal life through Jesus Christ our Lord.

Chapter 6

Being Dead to Sin

[1]Then what should we conclude? Are we to continue in sin that grace may abound? [2]Certainly not! We died to sin. How could we still live in it? [3]Do you not realize that all of us who have been baptized into Christ Jesus were baptized into his death? [4]Therefore, by baptism we were buried with him into death, so that just as Christ was

raised from the dead by the glory of the Father, we also might walk in newness of life.

⁵For if we have been grafted into him in a death like his, we shall certainly be united with him in a resurrection like his [as well]. ⁶We know that our old self was crucified with him so that the sinful body might be destroyed, and we might no longer be enslaved to sin. ⁷For the one who has died is freed from sin. ⁸Now if we have died with Christ, we believe that we shall also live with him. ⁹For we know that Christ, being raised from the dead, will never die again. Death no longer has dominion over him. ¹⁰The death he died, he died to sin, once for all, but the life he lives, he lives to God. ¹¹So you also must consider yourselves to be dead to sin and alive to God in Christ Jesus.

¹²Therefore, do not let sin reign in your mortal bodies, so that you obey its lustful desires. ¹³Do not yield parts of your bodies to sin to be used for acts of wickedness, but rather yield yourselves to God as people [raised] from death to life and yield the parts of your body to God to be used for acts of righteousness. ¹⁴For sin is not meant to have power over you, since you are not under law but under grace.

Enslaved to Righteousness

¹⁵So then what? Should we sin because we are no longer under law but under grace? Certainly not! ¹⁶Do you not know that if you yield yourselves to anyone as obedient slaves, you are slaves of the one whom you obey, either of sin, which leads to death, or of obedience, which leads to righteousness? ¹⁷But thanks be to God, that you who were once slaves of sin have become obedient from the heart to the standard of teaching under which you were placed. ¹⁸So, you have become slaves of righteousness, having been set free from sin. ¹⁹(I am speaking in these terms to be understood by common men.) For just as you once yielded the parts of your body to impurity and to wickedness after wickedness, so now yield your members to righteousness [that leads] into sanctification.

²⁰When you were slaves of sin, you were free to ignore righteousness. ²¹But then what return did you get from the things that you are now ashamed of? The final result of those things is death. ²²But now that you have been set free from sin and have become slaves of God, the return you receive is sanctification and its result: eternal life. ²³For the eventual payout from sin is death, but the free gift from God is eternal life in Christ Jesus our Lord.

Chapter 7

Released from the Law

[1]Now, do you not know, brothers and sisters—for I am speaking to those who know the law—that the law has authority over a person only as long as he is alive? [2]So it is that a married woman is bound by law to her husband as long as he lives. But if her husband dies, she is discharged from the law regarding the husband. [3]Accordingly, she will be called an adulteress if she lives with another man while her husband is [still] alive. But if her husband dies, she is free from that law, and if she marries another man, she is not an adulteress.

[4]In the same way, my brothers and sisters, through the body of Christ you have died to the law, so that you may belong to another: to him who has been raised from the dead in order that we may bear fruit for God. [5]While we were living in the flesh, our sinful passions, aroused by the law, were at work in the parts of our bodies to bear fruit for death. [6]But now we are released from the law, having died to what held us captive, so that [now] we serve, not under the old written code, but in the new life of the Spirit.

[7]What then shall we say? That the law is sin? Certainly not! Yet, if it had not been for the law, I would not have known sin. I would not have known what it is to covet if the law had not said, "You shall not covet." [8]But sin, seizing an opportunity in the commandment, brought about all kinds of covetousness in me, because apart from the law sin lies dead. [9]I was once alive apart from the law, but when the commandment came, sin came back to life and I died. [10]The very commandment that promised life proved [to be] death to me. [11]For sin, seizing an opportunity in the commandment, deceived me and through it, it killed me. [12]So the law is holy, and the commandment is holy and just and good.

[13]Then, did what is good bring death to me? Certainly not! It was sin, bringing about death in me through what is good, in order that sin might be shown to be sin, and through the commandment might become immensely sinful. [14]We know that the law is spiritual, but I am of the flesh, sold under sin. [15]I do not understand my own actions. For I do not do what I want to, but I do the very thing I hate. [16]Now if I do what I do not want to, I agree that the law is good. [17]So then it is no longer I who do it, but sin that resides within me. [18]For I know that nothing good resides within me, that is, in my flesh. For I desire to do what is right, but I cannot carry it out. [19]For I do not do the good I want [to do], but rather the evil I do not want [to do] is what I do. [20]Now if I do what I do not want [to do], it is no longer I doing it, but sin that resides within me.

²¹So I have noticed the rule that when I want to do what's right, evil lurks nearby. ²²For in my inmost self I do delight in the law of God, ²³yet I see in the parts of my body another law at war with the law of my mind and making me captive to the law of sin that resides in the parts of my body. ²⁴A wretched man am I! Who will deliver me from this body of death? ²⁵Thanks be to God through Jesus Christ our Lord! So then, inside myself I serve the law of *God* with my mind, but I serve the law of *sin* with my flesh.

Chapter 8

Set Free by the Spirit of Life

¹Therefore there is now no condemnation for those who are in Christ Jesus. ²For the law of the spirit of life has set us free in Christ Jesus from the law of sin and death. ³For by sending his own Son in the likeness of sinful flesh on account of sin, God has done what the law, debilitated by the flesh, was unable to achieve. Thus, in the flesh he condemned sin, ⁴in order that the just requirement of the law might be fulfilled in us, who walk not according to the flesh but according to the Spirit. ⁵For those who live according to the flesh fix their minds on the things of the flesh, but those who live according to the Spirit fix their minds on the things of the Spirit. ⁶For fixing the mind on the flesh is death, whereas fixing the mind on the Spirit is life and peace. ⁷For the mind that is fixed on the flesh is hostile to God. It does not submit to God's Law—indeed it cannot. ⁸Thus, those who are in the flesh cannot please God.

⁹However, if the Spirit of God truly dwells in you, you are not in the flesh; you are in the Spirit. Anyone who does not have the Spirit of Christ does not belong to him. ¹⁰With Christ in you, your spirits are alive because of righteousness, even though your bodies are dead on account of sin. ¹¹If the Spirit of him who raised Jesus from the dead dwells in you, he who raised Christ Jesus from the dead will also give your mortal bodies life through his Spirit, which dwells in you.

The Spirit of Adoption

¹²So then, brothers, we are not debtors to the flesh, living according to the flesh. ¹³For if you live according to the flesh you will die, but you will live if you put to death the deeds of the body by the Spirit. ¹⁴For all who are led by the Spirit of God are sons of God. ¹⁵For you did not receive the spirit of slavery to fall back into fear. Rather, you have received the spirit of adoption as sons, by whom we cry, "Abba! Father!", ¹⁶The Spirit himself bears witness with our spirit that we are children of God. ¹⁷And if [we are] children, then heirs—heirs of God and fellow heirs with Christ, provided we suffer with him in order that we may also be glorified with him.

240

Creation Groans, Waiting for Future Glory

[18]For I consider the sufferings of this present time to be not worth comparing with the glory that is to be revealed to us. [19]For yearning eagerly, the creation awaits the revealing of the sons of God. [20]The creation was subjected to futility, not of its own will but by the will of him who subjected it in the assured hope [21]that the creation itself will be set free from its bondage to decay and obtain the glorious freedom of the children of God. [22]We know that the whole creation has been groaning together in the pains of childbirth up until now. [23]And not only the creation, but we ourselves, who have the firstfruits of the Spirit, groan inwardly as we wait eagerly to be adopted as sons, the redemption of our bodies. [24]For in this hope we were saved. Now hope for what is seen is not hope. For who hopes for what he sees? [25]But as we hope for what we do not see [yet], we wait for it with patience.

[26]Likewise the Spirit helps us in our weakness. For we do not know how to pray as we should, but the Spirit himself intercedes for us with groanings too deep for words. [27]And he who searches hearts knows what the mind of the Spirit is because the Spirit intercedes for the saints according to the will of God. [28]For we know that for those who love God all things work together for good, for those who are called according to his purpose. [29]For he also predestined those whom he foreknew to be conformed to the image of his Son, in order that he might be the first-born among many brothers. [30]And he also called those whom he predestined, and he also justified those whom he called, and he also will glorify those whom he justified.

Who Can Be Against Us?

[31]What then shall we say to this? If God [be] for us, who [can be] against us? [32]He did not spare his own Son, but gave him up for us all: will he not also graciously give us all things with him? [33]Who shall bring any charge against God's elect? It is God who justifies. [34]Who is to condemn? Christ Jesus, who died, but more importantly, who was raised from the dead, and is at the right hand of God, indeed intercedes for us. [35]Who shall separate us from the love of Christ? Shall tribulation, or distress, or persecution, or famine, or nakedness, or peril, or sword? [36]As the scripture says, "For your sake we are being killed all the day long. We are regarded as sheep to be slaughtered." [37]No, in all these things we are more than conquerors through him who loved us. [38]For I am convinced that neither death, nor life, nor angels, nor rulers, nor present things, nor future things, nor powers, [39]nor height, nor depth, nor anything else in all creation, will be able to separate us from the love of God in Christ Jesus our Lord.

Chapter 9

God's Sovereign Right to Choose

[1]I am speaking the truth in Christ—I am not lying. My conscience bears me witness in the Holy Spirit [2]that I have great sorrow and unceasing anguish in my heart. [3]For I could wish that I myself were accursed and cut off from Christ for the sake of my brothers, my kinsmen by race. [4]They are Israelites, and the adoption as sons, the glory, the covenants, the giving of the law, the worship, and the promises are theirs. [5]The patriarchs are theirs, even the Christ is of their race. May God, who is over all, be blessed forever. Amen.

[6]Now it is not as though the word of God had failed. For not all who are descended from Israel belong to Israel, [7]and not all are children of Abraham because they are his descendants, but rather "Through Isaac shall your descendants be named." [8]This means that it is not the children of the flesh who are the children of God, but rather the children of the promise are counted as descendants. [9]For this is what the promise said, "I will return about this time [next year] and Sarah shall have a son." [10]And not only so, but also when Rebecca had conceived children by one man, our forefather Isaac, [11]though they were not yet born and had done nothing either good or bad, in order that God's purpose of election might keep working, not because of deeds but because of his calling, [12]she was told, "The elder will serve the younger." [13]As the scripture says, "Jacob I loved, but Esau I hated."

[14]What shall we say then? Is there injustice on God's part? Certainly not! [15]For he says to Moses, "I will have mercy on whom I have mercy, and I will have compassion on whom I have compassion." [16]So it does not depend on man's will or striving, but on God's mercy. [17]For the scripture says to Pharaoh, "I have raised you up for the very purpose of showing my power in you, so that my name may be proclaimed in all the earth." [18]So then he has mercy on whomever he wills, and he hardens the heart of whomever he wills.

[19]You will say to me then, "Why does he still find fault? For who can resist his will?" [20]But who are you, a man, to answer back to God? Shall the thing that is molded say to its molder, "Why have you made me like this?" [21]Has the potter no right over the clay—to make create one vessel for honor and another for dishonor out of the same lump? [22]What if God, desiring to show his wrath and to make known his power, has endured the vessels of wrath prepared for destruction with much patience, [23]in order to make known the riches of his glory for the vessels of mercy, which he has prepared for glory beforehand, [24]even us whom he has called, not only from the Jews but also from the Gentiles? [25]As he also says in Hosea, "Those who were not my people I will call 'my people,' and her who was

not beloved I will call 'my beloved.'" [26]"And in the very place where it was said to them, 'You are not my people,' there they will be called 'sons of the living God.'"

[27]And Isaiah cries out concerning Israel: "Though the number of the sons of Israel be as the sand of the sea, only a remnant of them will be saved, [28]for the Lord will execute his sentence on the earth forcefully and swiftly." [29]And as Isaiah predicted, "If the Lord of hosts had not left children for us, we would have fared like Sodom and become like Gomorrah." [30]What shall we say, then? That Gentiles who did not pursue righteousness have attained it—that is, righteousness through faith—[31]but that Israel, who pursued the righteousness, which is based on Law, did not succeed in fulfilling that Law? [32]Why? Because they did not pursue it through faith, but as if it were based on deeds. They have stumbled over the stumbling stone. [33]As the scripture says, "Look: In Zion I am laying a stumbling stone, a rock to trip over—and whoever believes in him will not be put to shame."

Chapter 10

[1]Brothers, my heart's desire and [my] prayer to God for them is that they may be saved. [2]I declare about them that they have a zeal for God, but it is not based on knowledge. [3]For, being ignorant of the righteousness that comes from God, and seeking to establish their own, they did not submit to God's righteousness. [4]For Christ is the final consummation of the law, that everyone who believes may be made righteous.

Salvation Bestowed

[5]Moses writes that the man who practices the righteousness which is based on the law shall live by it. [6]But the righteousness based on faith says, "Do not say in your heart, 'Who will ascend into heaven?' (that is, to bring Christ down) [7]or 'Who will descend into the abyss?' (that is, to bring Christ up from the dead)." [8]But what does it say? The word is near you, on your lips and in your heart (that is, the word of faith that we preach), [9]because, if you confess with your lips that Jesus is Lord and believe in your heart that God raised him from the dead, you will be saved. [10]For with his heart someone believes and is justified, and with the mouth someone confesses and is saved. [11]The scripture says, "Everyone who believes in him will not be put to shame." [12]For there is no distinction between Jew and Greek. The same Lord is Lord of all and bestows his riches on all who call on him. [13]For, "everyone who calls on the name of the Lord will be saved."

[14]But how are men to call on him having not believed in him? And how are they to believe in him having not heard about him? And how are they to hear without a preacher? [15]And how can men preach unless they are sent? As the scripture

says, "How beautiful are the feet of those who preach good news!" [16]But not all of them have obeyed the gospel. For Isaiah says, "Lord, who has believed what he has heard from us?" [17]So faith comes by hearing, and hearing [comes] through the word of Christ.

[18]But I ask, have they not heard? Indeed, they have, for "Their message has gone out to all the earth, and their words to the ends of the world." [19]Still, I ask, did Israel not understand? First Moses says, "I will make you protective of those who are not a nation. Using a foolish nation, I will make you angry." [20]Then Isaiah is so bold as to say, "I have been found by those who were not seeking me. I have shown myself to those who were not asking for me." [21]But concerning Israel he says, "All day long I have spread out my hands to a disobedient and rebellious people."

Chapter 11

A Believing Remnant in Israel

[1]I ask, then, has God rejected his people? Certainly not! I myself am an Israelite, descended from Abraham, from the tribe of Benjamin. [2]God has not rejected his people whom he foreknew. Do you not know what the scripture says about Elijah—how he pleads with God against Israel? [3]"Lord, they have killed your prophets, they have demolished your altars, and I alone am left, and they seek my life." [4]But what does he say in response to him? "I have preserved for myself seven thousand men who have not bowed the knee to Baal." [5]So too at the present time there is a remnant, chosen by grace. [6]But if it is by grace, it is no longer on the basis of works; otherwise grace would no longer be grace.

[7]So now what? Israel failed to obtain what it was seeking. The elect obtained it, but the rest were hardened, [8]as it is written, "God gave them a spirit of stupor, eyes that would not see and ears that would not hear, down to this very day." [9]And David says, "Let their dinner table become a snare and a trap, a pitfall and a retribution for them. [10]Let their eyes be darkened so that they cannot see and bend their backs forever."

Gentiles Grafted In

[11]So I ask, did they stumble so that they might fall? Certainly not! Instead, through their error salvation has come to the Gentiles, so as to provoke Israel to jealousy. [12]Now if their error means riches for the world, and if their failure means riches for the Gentiles, how much more complete would be their inclusion!

[13]Now I am speaking to you Gentiles. Inasmuch then as I am an apostle to the Gentiles, I make a great deal of my ministry [14]in order to make my fellow Jews jealous, and thus save some of them. [15]For if their rejection means the reconciliation of the world, what will their acceptance mean but life from the dead? [16]If the firstfruits of the dough is holy, so [is] the whole lump—and if the root is holy, so [are] the branches.

[17]But since some of the branches were broken off, and you, a wild olive shoot, were grafted in their place to share the richness of the olive tree, [18]you must not lord it over the branches. If you do boast, remember it is not you that support the root, but the root that supports you. [19]You will say, "Branches were broken off so that I might be grafted in." [20]That is true. They were broken off because of their unbelief, but you stand fast only through faith. So, do not become proud but stand in awe. [21]For if God did not spare the natural branches, neither will he spare you. [22]Note then the kindness and the severity of God: severity toward those who have fallen, but God's kindness toward you, provided you continue in his kindness; otherwise you too will be cut off. [23]And even the others, if they do not persist in their unbelief, will be grafted in, for God has the power to graft them in again. [24]For if you have been cut from what is by nature a wild olive tree, and grafted, contrary to nature, into a cultivated olive tree, how much more will these natural branches be grafted back into their own olive tree.

The Mysterious Salvation of Israel

[25]So that you do not esteem yourselves too knowledgeable, brothers, I want you to understand this mystery: a partial hardening has come on Israel, until the complete number of Gentiles has come in. [26]And in this way all Israel will be saved. As the scripture says, "The Deliverer will come from Zion; he will banish ungodliness from Jacob. [27]And this will be my covenant with them when I take away their sins." [28]Regarding the gospel, they are enemies of God for your sake. But regarding election they are beloved for the sake of their forefathers. [29]For the gifts and the calling of God are irrevocable. [30]Just as you were once disobedient to God, but now have received mercy because of their disobedience, [31]so they have now been disobedient in order that by the mercy shown to you they also may receive mercy. [32]For God has given over everyone to disobedience, that he may have mercy on them all.

[33]*Oh, the depth of the riches and wisdom and knowledge of God!*
How unsearchable are his judgments and how inscrutable his ways!
[34]*"For who has known the mind of the Lord, or who has been his advisor?"*
[35]*"Or who has first given [God] something for which he must be paid back?"*
[36]*For from him and through him and to him are all things.*
To him be glory forever. Amen.

Chapter 12

Using Our Different Gifts

¹Therefore, brothers, I appeal to you by the mercies of God, to present your bodies as a living sacrifice, your reasoned worship being holy and acceptable to God. ²Do not let yourselves be molded by [the spirit of] this age, but rather be transformed by the renewal of your mind, so that you may grasp what is the will of God, what is good and acceptable and perfect.

³For by the grace given to me I tell everyone among you not to think of himself more highly than he ought to think, but to think with sober judgment, each according to the measure of faith that God has apportioned him. ⁴For we have many parts in one body, and the parts do not all have the same function. ⁵Likewise, though many, we are one body in Christ, and individually parts of each other. ⁶[Let's use] the gifts we have that differ according to the grace given to us:

- if prophecy, in proportion to our faith;
- ⁷if service, in our serving;
- he who teaches, in his teaching;
- ⁸he who encourages, in his encouraging;
- he who contributes, in his generous giving;
- he who gives aid, with zeal;
- he who does acts of mercy, with cheerfulness.

Commands for Christian Behavior

- ⁹Let love be genuine,
- Despise what is evil, cling to what is good.
- ¹⁰Love one another with brotherly affection,
- Outdo one another in showing honor.
- ¹¹Do not slacken off in zeal, be fervent in Spirit,
- Serve the Lord.
- ¹²Rejoice in your hope,
- Be patient in tribulation,
- Stay constant in prayer.
- ¹³Contribute to the needs of the saints,
- Practice hospitality.
- ¹⁴Bless those who persecute you, bless and do not curse them.
- ¹⁵Rejoice with those who rejoice, weep with those who weep. ¹
- ¹⁶Live in harmony with one another.
- Do not be haughty, but associate with the lowly; never be conceited.

> [17]Repay no one evil for evil, but dwell on what is noble in the sight of all.

> [18]Whenever possible, to the degree that it depends on you, live peaceably with all.

> [19]Beloved, never avenge yourselves, but leave it to the wrath of God; for it is written, "Vengeance is mine, I will repay, says the Lord." [20]Instead, "if your enemy is hungry, feed him; if he is thirsty, give him drink, for by doing so you will heap burning coals on his head." [21]Do not be overcome by evil, but rather overcome evil with good.

Chapter 13

Submit to Authorities

[1]Let every person be subject to the governing authorities. For there is no authority except from God, and those that exist have been instituted by God. [2]Therefore whoever resists the authorities resists what God has appointed, and those who do resist will incur judgment. [3]For rulers are not a terror to good conduct, but to bad. Do you desire to have no fear of the one who is in authority? [Then] do what is good, and you will receive his approval, [4]for he is God's servant for your benefit. But if you do wrong, be afraid, for he does not carry a sword for no reason. He is the servant of God, an avenger who executes his wrath on the wrongdoer. [5]Therefore one must act in submission, not only to avoid God's wrath, but also for the sake of conscience. [6]You also pay taxes for the same reason, because the authorities are ministers of God, attending to this very thing. [7]Pay all of them their dues: taxes to whom taxes are due, revenue to whom revenue is due, respect to whom respect is due, honor to whom honor is due.

Love is the Fulfillment of the law

[8]Owe no one anything, except to love one another, for the one who loves his neighbor has fulfilled the law. [9]The commandments, "You shall not commit adultery, You shall not kill, You shall not steal, You shall not covet," and any other commandment, are summed up in this sentence, "You shall love your neighbor as yourself." [10]Love does no wrong to a neighbor; therefore love is the fulfilling of the law.

[11]Besides this, you recognize this moment in time: the appointed time for you to awaken from sleep has come. For salvation is nearer to us now than when we first believed. [12]The night is far gone, the day is at hand. So then, let's cast off the deeds of darkness and put on the armor of light. [13]Let's conduct ourselves becomingly as in the daytime, not in reveling and drunkenness, not in sexual immorality and sensuality, not in quarreling and jealousy. [14]Instead, put on the Lord Jesus Christ and make no provision for gratifying the desires of the flesh.

Chapter 14

Not Judging One Another

[1]Welcome anyone who is weak in faith, but not to dispute opinions. [2]One believes he may eat anything, while the weak one eats only vegetables. [3]Do not allow the one who does eat [certain foods] to despise the one who abstains, and do not allow the one who abstains to pass judgment on the one who does eat [certain foods], for God has accepted him. [4]Who are you to judge the servant of another? [It's] up to his own master whether he stands or falls. But he will be upheld for the Master is able to make him stand.

[5]One person esteems one day as more significant than another, while another one esteems all days alike. Let everyone be fully convinced in his own mind. [6]The one who does observe the day observes it in honor of the Lord. Also, the one who eats [something], eats in honor of the Lord, since he gives thanks to God, whereas the one who abstains [from something], abstains in honor of the Lord and gives thanks to God. [7]None of us lives to himself, and none of us dies to himself. [8]For if we live, we live to the Lord, and if we die, we die to the Lord. So then, whether we live or whether we die, we belong to the Lord [9]because to this end Christ died and came back to life, so that he might be Lord of both the dead and the living.

[10]Why do you criticize your brother? Or you, why do you look down on your brother? For we shall all stand before the judgment seat of God. [11]For the scripture says, "As I live, says the Lord, to me every knee shall bow, and every tongue shall give praise to God." [12]So each of us shall give an account of himself to God.

Do not Make Someone Else Stumble

[13]So then let's not criticize one another any longer, but rather decide never to put a stumbling block or hindrance in the way of a brother. [14]I know and am persuaded in the Lord Jesus that nothing is unclean in itself, though it *is* unclean for anyone who considers it unclean. [15]If your brother is being injured by what you eat, you are no longer walking in love. Do not let what you eat cause the ruin of someone Christ died for. [16]So do not let your good be spoken of as evil. [17]For the kingdom of God is not food and drink but righteousness and peace and joy in the Holy Spirit. [18]Anyone who serves Christ in this way is acceptable to God and approved by men. [19]So then, let's pursue whatever brings about peace and mutual development.

[20]Do not destroy the work of God for the sake of food. Everything is indeed clean, but it is wrong for anyone to make others stumble by what he eats. [21]It is good to not eat meat or drink wine or do anything that makes your brother stumble.

²²Keep the [practice of] your faith between yourself and God. Blessed is the one who has no reason to judge himself for what he approves. ²³But the one who has doubts is condemned, if he does eat [something], because he is not acting from faith. For whatever does not proceed from faith is sin.

Chapter 15

Bear with Weaker Members

¹We who are strong have an obligation to bear with the failings of the weak and to not just please ourselves. ²Each of us should please his neighbor for his good, to build him up. ³For Christ did not please himself, but as the scripture says, "The accusations of those who accused you fell on me." ⁴For whatever was written in former days was written for our instruction, that through endurance and the encouragement of the scriptures we might have hope. ⁵May the God of endurance and encouragement grant that you are so like-minded, one with one another, in accord with Christ Jesus, ⁶that together you may glorify the God and Father of our Lord Jesus Christ with one voice. ⁷So then, for the glory of God—welcome one another as Christ has welcomed you.

Christ is the Hope of All

⁸For I tell you that Christ became a servant to the [nation of the] circumcised to show God's truthfulness, in order to confirm the promises given to the patriarchs, ⁹and in order that the Gentiles might glorify God for his mercy. As the scripture says, "Therefore I will praise you among the Gentiles and sing to your name." ¹⁰Again it is said, "Rejoice, O Gentiles, with his people"; ¹¹and again, "Praise the Lord, all Gentiles, and let all the peoples praise him." ¹²Furthermore Isaiah says, "The root of Jesse shall come, the One who rises to rule the Gentiles, and the Gentiles shall [place their] hope in him." ¹³May the God of hope fill you with all joy and peace in believing, so that by the power of the Holy Spirit you may abound in hope.

Paul's Ministry to Gentiles

¹⁴I myself am satisfied about you, my brothers, that you yourselves are full of goodness, filled with all knowledge, and able to instruct one another. ¹⁵But I have written to you on some points very boldly by way of reminder, because of the grace given to me by God ¹⁶to be a minister of Christ Jesus to the Gentiles in the priestly service of the gospel of God, so that the offering of the Gentiles may be acceptable, sanctified by the Holy Spirit. ¹⁷In Christ Jesus, then, I have reason to be proud of my work for God. ¹⁸For I will not venture to speak of anything except

what Christ has accomplished through me to win obedience from the Gentiles, by word and deed, [19]by the power of signs and wonders, by the power of the Holy Spirit, so that from Jerusalem and all the way around to Illyricum I have fully preached the gospel of Christ, [20]thus making it my ambition to preach the gospel, not where Christ has already been named, so that I do not build on another man's foundation, [21]but as the scripture says, "They who have never been told of him shall see, and they who have never heard of him shall understand."

Paul Hopes to Visit Rome

[22]This is the reason why so often I have been hindered from coming to you. [23]But now, since I no longer have any openings for work in these regions, and since for many years I have longed to come to you, [24]I hope to see you in passing as I go to Spain, and that you will help expedite my journey there, once I have enjoyed your company for a little while. [25]However, at the moment I am going to Jerusalem bringing aid for the saints. [26]For Macedonia and Achaia have been pleased to make some contribution for the poor among the saints at Jerusalem. [27]They were pleased to do it, and indeed they are indebted to them, for if the Gentiles have come to share in their spiritual blessings, they also ought to be of service to them in material blessings. [28]When therefore I have completed this [journey], and have delivered to them what has been raised, I shall go on by way of you to Spain. [29]I know that when I do come to you, I will come in the fullness of the blessing of Christ.

[30]By our Lord Jesus Christ and by the love of the Spirit I urge you, brothers, to strive along with me in your prayers to God concerning me, [31]such that I may be rescued from the unbelievers in Judea, and that my mission to Jerusalem would be acceptable to the saints, [32]so that by the will of God I may come to you with joy and be refreshed being with you. [33]Now then, may the God of peace be with all of you. Amen.

Chapter 16

Personal Greetings

[1]To you I am entrusting our sister Phoebe, who is a deaconess of the church at Cenchreae. [2]Please receive her in the Lord as you would a saint and help her in whatever way she may need you to do, because she has been a supporter of many people, myself included.

[3]Greet Prisca and Aquila, my fellow workers in Christ Jesus, [4]who risked their necks for my life; not only I but also all the churches of the Gentiles send thanks to them. [5]Also greet the church in their house. Greet my beloved Epaenetus, who was the first one in Asia led to Christ. [6]Greet Mary, who has worked hard among you.

[7]Greet Andronicus and Junias, my kinsmen and my fellow prisoners. They are well known among the apostles, and they were in Christ before me. [8]Greet Ampliatus, my beloved in the Lord. [9]Greet Urbanus, our fellow worker in Christ, and my beloved Stachys. [10]Greet Apelles, who is approved in Christ. Greet those who belong to [the family of] Aristobulus. [11]Greet my kinsman Herodion. Greet those in the Lord who belong to the family of Narcissus. [12]Greet those workers in the Lord, Tryphaena and Tryphosa. Greet the beloved Persis, who has worked hard in the Lord. [13]Greet Rufus, chosen in the Lord, also his mother and mine. [14]Greet Asyncritus, Phlegon, Hermes, Patrobas, Hermas, and the brothers who are with them. [15]Greet Philologus, Julia, Nereus and his sister, and Olympas, and all the saints who are with them. [16]Greet one another with a holy kiss. All the churches of Christ send their greetings to you.

A Warning About Church Members

[17]I urge you, brothers, to be on the lookout for those who create disputes and obstacles contrary to the doctrine that you have been taught and to avoid them. [18]For such people are not serving our Lord Christ, but their own appetites. And by eloquent and flattering words they deceive the hearts of the simple-minded. [19]For while your obedience is known to all, so that I rejoice over you, I want you to discern what is good and guileless from what is evil. [20]Then the God of peace will soon crush Satan under your feet. May the grace of our Lord Jesus Christ be with you.

Final Greetings

[21]Timothy, my fellow worker, sends his greetings to you, as do Lucius and Jason and Sosipater, my kinsmen. [22]I, Tertius, who physically wrote down this letter, greet you in the Lord. [23]Gaius, who is host to me and to the whole church, sends his greetings to you. Erastus, the city treasurer, and our brother Quartus send their greetings to you. [24]The grace of Lord Jesus Christ be with you all. Amen.

Benediction

[25]*Now to him who is able to strengthen you*
according to the gospel and the preaching of Jesus Christ from me,
according to the revelation of the mystery that was kept secret for long
periods of time, [26]*but has now been disclosed, and has been made known*
to all nations through the prophetic writings,
according to the command of the eternal God, to bring about the obedience of faith
[27]*–to the only wise God–*
be glory for evermore through Jesus Christ! Amen.

I CORINTHIANS

Chapter 1

¹[From]: Paul, called to be an apostle of Christ Jesus by the will of God, and from Sosthenes, our brother,

²To: God's church located in Corinth, to those who have been sanctified in Christ Jesus, called to be saints, along with all people in all places who call upon the name of our Lord Jesus Christ, who is both their Lord and ours:

³Grace be to you, and peace from God our Father and from the Lord Jesus Christ.

Giving Thanks

⁴I am always thanking my God for you, on account of God's grace given to you in Christ Jesus, ⁵that in him you were made rich in every way—in all speech, and in all knowledge—

⁶as the testimony about Christ was confirmed in your midst, ⁷such that [now] you do not lack any spiritual gift as you are awaiting the revelation of our Lord Jesus Christ. ⁸He will also sustain you to the end, to be blameless on the day of our Lord Jesus Christ. ⁹God is faithful: you were called by him into the fellowship of his Son, Jesus Christ our Lord.

Divisions in the Church

¹⁰Brothers, by the name of our Lord Jesus Christ, I urge you all to agree with one another so that there may be no divisions among you, but rather that you may be harmonious in your understandings and judgments [of things]. ¹¹For those of [the household of] Chloe have informed me about the quarreling among you, my brothers. ¹²Now what I am saying is this: Each of you is claiming, "I am with Paul," or "I am with Apollos," or I am with Cephas," or "I am with Christ." ¹³Has Christ been divided? Was Paul crucified for you? Or were you baptized in the name of Paul? ¹⁴I thank God that I did not baptize any of you except Crispus and Gaius, ¹⁵so that no one might say that I was baptizing in my own name. ¹⁶(I did baptize some of the household of Stephanus, too. But besides them, I do not know if I baptized any others.) ¹⁷For Christ did not send me to baptize but to preach the gospel –and not in lofty terms—so that the cross of Christ would not be emptied of its power.

The Wisdom of God

[18]For the message of the Cross is foolishness to those who are perishing, but to those of us who are saved, it is the power of God. [19]For, it has been written, "I will destroy the wisdom of the wise men, and I will thwart the knowledge of the scholars." [20]Where, then, is the wise man? Where, then, is the scholar? Where, then, is the skilled debater of this age? Has God not turned the wisdom of this world into foolishness? [21]For since by God's design the world could not understand God by wisdom, it pleased God to save believers through the "folly" of our preached messages. [22]For Jews insist on signs, and Greeks seek wisdom, [23]but we preach Christ crucified—a stumbling block to the Jews, and foolishness to the Greeks—[24]but to those who are called, whether Jew or Greek, Christ is the power of God and the wisdom of God. [25]For the foolishness of God is wiser than men, and the weakness of God is stronger than men.

[26]For, brothers, look at your calling: not many of you were wise (according to the world), not many powerful, not many of noble birth. [27]But, God chose the foolish things of this world to shame the wise, and God chose the weak things of this world to shame the strong. [28]God also chose the lowly and despised things of this world, and things considered to be nothing, in order to overthrow the great things of this world, [29]so that no mere human might have reason to boast in God's presence. [30]Thanks to him, you are now in Christ Jesus, who has become wisdom from God, righteousness, sanctification, and redemption, for our sake, [31]so that as it is written: "If anyone does boast, let him boast in the Lord."

Chapter 2

Paul Proclaims Christ Crucified

[1]Now brothers, when I came to you, I did not come to proclaim the testimony of God to you using lofty terms or philosophy, [2]because I had decided that while in your midst I would concentrate on nothing except Christ and him crucified. [3]I was with you in weakness, fear, and much trembling, [4]and my messages and my sermons were not in clever words of wisdom, but in the demonstration of the power of the Holy Spirit, [5]so that your faith would rest not in man's wisdom but in God's power.

Wisdom Comes from the Spirit

[6]Yet, what we say is wisdom to those who are spiritually mature, though it is not of this age, nor of the rulers of this world, who will eventually come to nothing. [7]But we speak about the wisdom of God, secret and mysterious, which God de-

creed for our glory before time [began]. [8]None of the rulers of this current age understood this because they would not have crucified the Lord of glory if they had known it. [9]But as it was written:

> "What no eye has seen,
> and what no ear has heard,
> and what has never occurred to the mind of man—
> [this is] what God has prepared for those who love him."

[10]But God has revealed them to us by his Spirit, for the Spirit searches out all things, even the depths of God. [11]For who knows what lies in [the heart of] a man, but the man himself? Likewise, no one knows the things of God except the Spirit of God. [12]Now we have not received the spirit of the world, but the Holy Spirit, which is from God, so that we might understand those things that God freely gives to us. [13]So, then, we do not speak in words of human wisdom, but by what the Holy Spirit teaches, explaining spiritual things to those who are spiritual.

The Natural Person's Thinking

[14]But the natural person does not understand spiritual things, for they are foolishness to him, and he cannot understand them because they are discerned spiritually. [15]But the spiritual person can discern all things, though no one understands [him]. [16]For who has ever understood the mind of the Lord that he should instruct Him? But we have the mind of Christ.

Chapter 3

Still Acting Carnally

[1]And, brothers, I was not able to speak to you as I would to people of the Spirit, but rather as I would to people of the flesh, even as infants in Christ. [2]I had to give you milk to drink, not solid food, because you were not able to handle it. And you still are not able to do so, [3]because you are still of the flesh. For since there is still envy and strife among you, are you not still acting according to your fleshly nature and behaving in a merely human way? [4]For when one says, "I am with Paul," or "I am with Apollos," are you not acting according to the flesh? [5]After all, who is Paul? And who is Apollos? Simply servants through whom you came to faith, each doing what God gave him to do. [6]I planted, Apollos watered, but it was God who gave the growth. [7]So, the one who matters is neither the one who plants nor the one who waters, but God who gives the growth. [8]Now then, the one who plants and the one who waters are equivalent: each one shall receive his payment according to his own labor. [9]For we are God's co-laborers; you are God's work in progress—that is, what God is building.

¹⁰According to the grace of God that has been given to me, I have laid the foundation like a skilled architect. Now someone else is building on it. But let each one who does be careful how he builds. ¹¹For no one is able to lay a foundation other than the one already laid, which is Jesus Christ. ¹²So, some will build on this foundation using gold, silver, and precious stones; others, only wood, grass and straw. ¹³On the day of the Lord each kind of work will be made known, for it is revealed by fire, and the fire will prove its true nature. ¹⁴If what anyone has built remains, he shall receive a reward. ¹⁵But if anyone's work is burned up, he will suffer loss, though he himself shall be saved, having been purified in the fire.

The Temple of the Holy Spirit

¹⁶Do you not know that you are the temple of God, and that the Holy Spirit dwells within you? ¹⁷If any man destroys the temple of God, God shall destroy him, for the temple of God is holy, and you are that temple. ¹⁸Let no one deceive himself: if anyone among you thinks himself to be wise in this world, let him become foolish, so that he may become wise. ¹⁹For the wisdom of this world is foolishness to God. As it is written: "He traps the wise in their craftiness," ²⁰and, "The Lord understands the plans of the wise, how futile they are." ²¹No one, then, should boast in [the deeds of] men.

> For actually, all things are yours:
> ²²whether Paul, Apollos, or Cephas;
> the world, life, and death;
> things present and things to come.
> These belong to you–
> ²³and you belong to Christ,
> and Christ to God.

Chapter 4

Apostolic Ministry

¹This is how one should regard us: as servants of Christ and stewards of the mysteries of God. ²In addition, stewards are required to be found trustworthy. ³Now for me it is trivial that I should be judged by you or by any human court. Actually, I do not even judge myself. ⁴I myself am not aware of any [charge], but that does not acquit me: it is the Lord who judges me. ⁵Therefore do not pronounce judgment prematurely, before the Lord comes, for he will bring to light the things now hidden in darkness and will reveal the purposes of the heart. Then every man will receive his commendation from God.

⁶For your sake, brothers, I have applied all this to myself and Apollos so that through us you may learn to not go beyond what is written, so that none of you may be puffed up in favor of one against another. ⁷Who made you special? What do you possess that you did not receive? If you received it, then why do you boast as if it were not merely a gift?

⁸You have plenty already! You have become rich already! You, not we, have become kings! Oh, that you were already reigning so that we might rule together with you! ⁹For, I figure that God has us apostles on display at the end of the line, the ones sentenced to death, because we have been made a spectacle to the world—both to angels and to men. ¹⁰For Christ's sake, we are fools, whereas in Christ you are wise. We are weak, but you are strong. You are held in high regard, but we in contempt. ¹¹For the moment, we hunger and thirst. We are poorly dressed and strongly opposed and homeless. ¹²And we toil, doing manual labor. When denounced, we bless; when persecuted, we endure; ¹³when slandered, we beg [to be understood]. We have become, and remain, like the scum of the earth, the rejects of everything.

Imitate Paul

¹⁴I am not writing these things to make you feel ashamed, but to warn you as my beloved children. ¹⁵For even if you were to have 10,000 guides in Christ, you do not have many fathers, for I became your father in Christ Jesus through the gospel. ¹⁶So then, I urge you to be imitators of me. ¹⁷This is why I am sending you Timothy, my beloved and faithful child in the Lord, who will remind you of my ways in Christ, as I teach them in every church everywhere. ¹⁸Some are acting arrogantly, as if I were never going to return. ¹⁹But I will come to you soon, if the Lord wills, and I will discover not what these arrogant ones can say, but what power they have. ²⁰For the kingdom of God does not consist in talk but in power. ²¹Which do you prefer? Shall I come to you with a rod of discipline or with love in a spirit of gentleness?

Chapter 5

Immorality in the Church

¹Sexual immorality among you has actually been reported—and of that kind that is uncommon even among pagans, such as a man having sexual relations with his father's wife. ²And yet you are proud of it! Should you not be mourning instead? The man who has done this should be driven out of your midst.

³For though I am physically absent, yet I am there in spirit. And I have already condemned the man who has done such a thing, as if I were present. ⁴Once you have assembled in the name of the Lord Jesus, and I am spiritually present, with the power of our Lord Jesus, ⁵this one is to be delivered over to Satan for the destruction of the flesh, so that on the day of the Lord Jesus his spirit may be saved.

⁶[Neither] is it a good thing that you are boasting. Do you not realize that a little yeast leavens the whole lump [of dough]? ⁷Purge the old yeast so that you may become a whole new lump [of dough], since you actually are unleavened. For Christ, our Passover lamb, has been sacrificed. ⁸So then, let's celebrate the festival, not with the old yeast, the yeast of malice and evil, but with the unleavened [bread] of sincerity and truth.

⁹In my [other] letter I told you not to associate with sexually immoral people, ¹⁰not meaning [to isolate yourselves] from the sexually immoral or greedy people, the swindlers, and the idol worshippers, since that would require you to leave this world. ¹¹But rather, I wrote to you not to associate with anyone who bears the name of brother if he is guilty of immorality or greed, or is an idolater, reviler, drunkard, or swindler—not even to have a meal with such a person. ¹²For it is not for me to judge outsiders. Are you not to judge those inside the church? ¹³God will judge the outsiders. "Drive out the wicked person from among you."

Chapter 6

Wrong to Sue Another Believer

¹When one of you has a dispute with another, how dare he take it to a court of law, before the unrighteous rather than before the saints? ²Do you not realize that the saints will judge the world? And if the world is to be judged by you, are you incompetent to decide small matters? ³Do you not realize that we are to judge angels? Then, how much more, the affairs of this life! ⁴If then you have cases from daily life, why do you lay them before those who are not respected within the church? ⁵I mention this to your shame. Could there be no man among you wise enough to settle disputes between brothers? ⁶Instead brother goes to court against brother, and that before unbelievers? ⁷To have lawsuits between one another at all is a defeat for you. Why not just suffer the wrong instead? Why not just be defrauded instead? ⁸But you yourselves wrong and defraud [others]—even your own brothers.

What is and is not Permissable

⁹Or is it that you do not know that the unrighteous will not inherit the kingdom of God? Do not be deceived; neither the sexually immoral, nor idolaters, nor adulterers, nor partners in homosexual acts, ¹⁰nor thieves, nor the greedy, nor drunkards, nor revilers, nor swindlers will inherit the kingdom of God. ¹¹And some of you were once like that. But you were washed. But you were sanctified. But you were justified in the name of the Lord Jesus Christ and in the Spirit of our God.

¹²"All things are permissible for me," but not all things are beneficial. "All things are permissible for me," but I resist being enslaved by anything. ¹³"Food is meant for the stomach and the stomach for food"—but God will do away with both of them. The body is not meant for sexual immorality, but for the Lord, and the Lord for the body. ¹⁴And God raised the Lord and will also raise us up by his power. ¹⁵Do you not know that your bodies are members of Christ? Shall I therefore take the members of Christ and make them members of a prostitute? May it never be! ¹⁶Do you not know that the man who joins himself to a prostitute becomes one body with her? For, as it is written, "The two shall become one flesh." ¹⁷But anyone who is united to the Lord becomes one spirit with him. ¹⁸Run from sexual immorality. Every other sin that a man commits is outside the body, but the sexually immoral man sins against his own body. ¹⁹Do you not know that your body is a temple of the Holy Spirit [dwelling] within you, whom you have [received] from God? You are not your own, since ²⁰you were bought with a price. So, glorify God in your body.

Chapter 7

Instructions on Marriage and Divorce

¹Now concerning the matters that you wrote about: "It is good for a man not to have sexual relations with a woman." ²Well, [to avoid] sexual immorality, each man should have his own wife and each woman her own husband. ³The husband should grant the intimate relations due to his wife, and likewise the wife to her husband. ⁴For the wife does not rule over her own body, but the husband does. Likewise, the husband does not rule over his own body, but the wife does. ⁵Do not deprive one another except perhaps if you agree to for a limited time so that you may devote yourselves to fasting and prayer. But then come together again, so that Satan does not tempt you because you lack self-control.

⁶I say this by way of concession, not as a command. ⁷I wish that all men were as I myself am. But each person has his own gift from God, one of one kind and one of another. ⁸So, I say to the unmarried and the widows that remaining single as I

do is a good thing. [9]But they should marry if they cannot control themselves. For it is better to marry than to be aflame with passion.

[10]Then to the married, not I but the Lord gives this command: that the wife should not separate from her husband [11](but if she does, she should remain single or else reconcile with her husband)—and that the husband should not divorce his wife.

[12]To the rest, not the Lord but I say that if any believer has a wife who is an unbeliever, and she consents to live with him, he should not divorce her. [13]If any woman has a husband who is an unbeliever, and he consents to live with her, she should not divorce him. [14]For the unbelieving husband is consecrated by his wife, and the unbelieving wife is consecrated by her husband. Otherwise, your children would be stained, but as it is they are holy. [15]But if the unbelieving partner desires to separate, let it be so. The believing spouses are not duty-bound in such cases. Now, God has called us to peace. [16]Wife, how do you know whether you will save your husband? Husband, how do you know whether you will save your wife?

[17]Everyone should lead the life that the Lord has assigned to him, and in which God has called him. This is my ruling in all the churches. [18]Was a man already circumcised at the time of his call? He should not seek to remove the sign of his circumcision. Was any man uncircumcised at the time of his call? Let him not seek circumcision. [19]For it is neither circumcision nor lack of circumcision that matters but rather keeping the commandments of God. [20]Each one should remain in the situation he was in when he was called. [21]Were you a slave when you were called? Let it be. But if you can gain your freedom, take the opportunity to do so. [22]For anyone who was called in the Lord as a slave is a free man in the Lord. Likewise, anyone who was free when called has become a slave of Christ. [23]You were bought with a price; do not become slaves of men. [24]So, brothers, let person remain in whatever state he was called, with God.

Better to Live Unmarried

[25]Now concerning [the matter of] the unmarried: I have no command of the Lord, but I give my opinion as one who by the Lord's mercy is trustworthy. [26]I think that in view of the impending distress it is good for a person to remain as he is. [27]Are you bound to a wife? Do not seek to be free. Are you free from a wife? Do not seek marriage. [28]But if you marry, you are not sinning, and if a girl marries, she is not sinning. Yet those who do [marry] will have worldly troubles, and I would want to spare you that. [29]Brothers, I mean this: that our allotted time is running out quickly. From now on, let those who have wives live as though they had none, [30]and those who mourn as though they were not mourning, and those

who rejoice as though they were not rejoicing, and those who buy as though they had no goods, ³¹and those who do business with the world as though they did no business with it. For the current form of this world is passing away.

³²I want you to be free from anxieties. The unmarried man is anxious about the affairs of the Lord and how to please the Lord. ³³But the married man is anxious about worldly affairs and how to please his wife, ³⁴and so his interests are divided. In addition, the woman who is not married or engaged is anxious about the affairs of the Lord and how to be holy in both body and spirit. But the married woman is anxious about the things of this world and how to please her husband. ³⁵I say this for your own benefit, not to set restrictions on you, but to promote what is proper and to secure your undivided devotion to the Lord.

³⁶Now, if any man thinks that he is not behaving properly toward his fiancée, because his passions are strong, then let him do as he desires if it must be: let them marry—it is not a sin. ³⁷But any man who is firmly established in his heart, and is not feeling such a strong need, and has his passion under control, and has determined this in his heart, will do well to leave her in an unmarried state. ³⁸Thus any man who marries his fiancée does well, and the man who does not marry will do even better. ³⁹A wife is bound to her husband as long as he lives. But, if the husband dies, she is free to marry whomever she wants to, only in the Lord. ⁴⁰Now in my thinking she will be happier if she remains single, and I think that [in this] I also have the Spirit of God.

Chapter 8

Instructions About Food Offered to Idols

¹Now concerning food offered to idols: we know that all of us possess knowledge. This "knowledge" puffs up whereas love builds up. ²Even if someone imagines that he [fully] understands something, he still does not understand [it] as he should understand [it]. ³However if someone loves God, he is known by him. ⁴Therefore, as to the eating of food offered to idols, we know that an idol is not [really anything] in this world, and that there is no other God but the one. ⁵For although in heaven or on earth there may be so-called gods—since there are many "gods" and many "lords"—⁶nonetheless for us there is [only] one God, the Father, the basis of everything and our very being, and one Lord, Jesus Christ, through whom we and everything else [have our existence].

⁷On the other hand, not everyone has this knowledge. Some people, being accustomed to idols, eat food that has been offered to an idol, and so being weak, their conscience is defiled. ⁸Food itself, though, does not commend us to God. We are

no worse off if we do not eat [some foods], and no better off if we do eat them.
⁹But be careful that this liberty of yours does not somehow become a stumbling block to the weak. ¹⁰For if anyone sees you, a man of knowledge, [sitting] at table in an idol's temple, might he not feel emboldened to eat food offered to idols, if his conscience is weakened? ¹¹And so this weak man gets destroyed on account of your knowledge—the brother for whom Christ died. ¹²Thus, in sinning against your brothers and wounding their conscience when it is weak, you sin against Christ. ¹³Therefore, if food causes my brother to stumble, then at no time will I eat meat, so that I do not cause my brother to stumble.

Chapter 9

Freedom in Christ

¹Am I not free? Am I not an apostle? Have I not seen Jesus our Lord? Are you not my handicraft in the Lord? ²Even if I am not an apostle to others, surely I am to you, for you are the seal of my apostleship in the Lord.

³To those who would criticize me, this is my defense: ⁴Do we not have the right to our food and drink? ⁵Do we not have the right to be accompanied by a wife who is a fellow believer, as the other apostles and the brothers of the Lord and Cephas? ⁶Or is it only Barnabas and I who have no right to not work for a living? ⁷Who serves in the military at his own expense? Who plants a vineyard without eating any of its fruit? Who tends a flock without getting some of the milk?

Pastors Worthy of Pay

⁸Do I say these things by man's authority? Does the law not say the same thing? ⁹For in the law of Moses it is written, "You shall not muzzle an ox when it is treading out the grain." Is it the oxen that God is concerned about? ¹⁰Does he not speak entirely for our sake? It was written for our sake, because the plowman should plow in hope and the thresher thresh in hope of a share in the crop. ¹¹If we have sown spiritual good among you, is it too much to ask that we reap some material goods from you? ¹²If others share this rightful claim on you, do we not [share it] even more? Nevertheless, we have not exercised this right. We would endure anything rather than put an obstacle in the way of the gospel of Christ. ¹³Do you not know that those who work in the temple service get their food from the temple, and those who serve at the altar share in the sacrificial offerings? ¹⁴In the same way, the Lord commanded that those who proclaim the gospel should get their living by the gospel.

¹⁵But I have not exercised any of these rights, nor am I writing this to have it done for me. For my dying would be better than having someone nullify my reason for boasting. ¹⁶For my preaching the gospel is not boasting for me, because I am burdened with that need, and so if I do not preach the gospel, woe is me! ¹⁷For if I am doing this willingly, I have a reward; but if unwillingly, I am entrusted with a commission. ¹⁸Then what is my reward? That I may make the gospel free of charge in my preaching, not making full use of my rights in the gospel.

All Things to All People

¹⁹For though I am free from all, I have made a servant of myself to all, that I might win more of them. ²⁰To the Jews I became as a Jew, in order to win Jews; to those under the law I became as one under the law—though not being under the law myself—that I might win those under the law. ²¹To those outside the law I became as one outside the law—not being without law toward God but under the law of Christ—so that I might win those outside the law. ²²To the weak I became weak, that I might win the weak. I have become all things to all people, that I might by all means save some. ²³I do it all for the sake of the gospel so that I may share in its blessings with them.

²⁴Do you not realize that in a race all the runners compete, but only one receives the prize? So run that you may obtain it. ²⁵All athletes exercise self-control in all things. They do it to receive a perishable wreath, but we an imperishable one. ²⁶So, I do not run without purpose, nor do I fight by just beating the air. ²⁷Rather, I discipline my body and force it into submission, so that, having preached to others, I myself do not get disqualified.

Chapter 10

Fleeing Temptation

¹Brothers, I do not want you to be unaware of the fact that our fathers were all under the cloud, and all passed through the sea, ²so in the cloud and in the sea all were baptized into Moses. ³And all ate the same spiritual food ⁴and all drank of the same spiritual beverage. For they drank from the spiritual Rock that followed them, and the Rock was Christ. ⁵Nonetheless, most of them were not pleasing to God, since their bodies were strewn in the desert.

⁶Now these things took place as warnings for us to not desire evil as they did. ⁷Do not be idolaters as some of them were. As it is written, "The people sat down to eat and drink and got up to dance." ⁸We must not indulge in sexual immorality. Some of them did do that and 23,000 of them fell [dead] in a single day! ⁹We must

not put Christ to the test, as some of them did and were destroyed by serpents; [10]nor grumble, as some of them did and were destroyed by the Destroyer. [11]Now these things happened to them as examples, but they were written down to instruct those of us who are alive now that the final age has come. [12]Therefore let anyone who thinks that he stands be careful so that he does not fall. [13]No temptation has overtaken you that is not common to man. God is faithful, and he will not let you be tempted beyond your strength, but with the temptation will also provide the way of escape, that you may be able to endure it.

[14]Therefore, my beloved ones, flee from idolatry. [15]I am speaking to intelligent people; judge for yourselves what I am saying. [16]As for the cup of blessing that we bless: is not that a participation in the blood of Christ? As for the bread that we break: is not that a participation in the body of Christ? [17]Because just one bread exists, we who are many are one body since we all partake of that one bread. [18]Consider the nation of Israel: are not those who eat the sacrifices partners in the altar? [19]What do I imply then? That food offered to idols matters, or that an idol matters? [20]No, I imply that pagans offer what they sacrifice to demons and not to God. I do not want you to be partners with demons. [21]You cannot drink both the cup of the Lord and the cup of demons. You cannot partake of both the table of the Lord and the table of demons. [22]Should we provoke the Lord to jealousy? Are we stronger than he is?

Do All Things to the Glory of God

[23]"All things are permissible," but not all things are productive.

"All things are permissible," but not all things are constructive.

[24]Let no one seek his own good, but rather the good of his neighbor. [25]For the sake of your conscience, eat whatever is sold in the meat market without questioning it. [26]For "the earth is the Lord's, and everything in it." [27]If an unbeliever invites you over, and you are of a mind to go, for the sake of your conscience, eat whatever is set before you without asking any questions. [28](But if someone tells you, "This [food] has been offered in sacrifice," then out of consideration for the man who informed you, and for the sake of conscience—[29]I mean his conscience, not yours—do not eat it.) For, why should the conscience of someone else determine my liberty? [30]If I partake with thankfulness, why am I denounced because of what I am thankful for? [31]So, whether you eat or drink, or whatever you do, do all to the glory of God. [32]Give no offense to Jews or to Greeks or to the church of God, [33]just as I try to please everybody in everything I do, not seeking my own advantage, but the advantage of many others, so that they may be saved. [11:1]Be imitators of me, as I am [an imitator] of Christ.

263

Chapter 11, cont.

Head Coverings in Church Services

[2] Now I do praise you because you remember me in everything and maintain the traditions even as I have delivered them to you. [3]But I want you to understand that the head of every man is Christ, the head of a woman is her husband, and the head of Christ is God. [4]Any man who prays or prophesies with his head covered dishonors his head, [5]but any woman who prays or prophesies with her head unveiled dishonors her head; it is the same as if her head were shaven. [6]For if a woman will not veil herself, then she should cut off her hair; but if it is disgraceful for a woman to be shorn or shaven, let her wear a veil. [7]For a man should not cover his head, since he is the image and glory of God, but woman is the glory of man. [8](For man was not made from woman, but woman from man. [9]Neither was man created for woman's sake, but woman for man's sake.) [10]Therefore a wife should wear a symbol of authority on her head, because of the angels. [11](Nevertheless, in the Lord woman is not independent of man nor man of woman. [12]For as woman was made from man, so man is now born of woman. [Ultimately], all things are from God.) [13]Judge for yourselves; is it proper for a woman to pray to God with her head uncovered? [14]Does not nature itself teach you that for a man to wear long hair is disgraceful to him, [15]but if a woman has long hair, it is her glory? For her hair is given to her for a covering. [16]If anyone is inclined to contend this, we recognize no such custom, nor do the churches of God.

Instructions About Communion

[17]But in the following instructions I do *not* praise you, because when you come together it is not going better, but worse. [18]In the first place, I hear that when you assemble as a church, there are divisions among you. To some degree, I would believe so [19]because factions are bound to arise among you, to make it apparent which ones among you are genuine.

[20]Now, when you meet together, are you not eating the Lord's supper? [21][When you are] eating, each person is going ahead with his own meal, while someone goes hungry and someone else gets drunk. [22]What! Do you not have houses to eat and drink in? Or do you have such little regard for the church of God as to humiliate people who have nothing [to eat]? What should I say to you? Should I praise you about this? No, I will not.

[23]For I received from the Lord what I also passed on to you: On the night when he was betrayed, the Lord Jesus took bread, [24]and when he had given thanks, he broke it, and said, "This is my body, which is broken for you. Do this in remem-

brance of me." ²⁵In the same way, after supper [He] also [took] the cup, saying, "This cup is the new covenant in my blood. Do this, as often as you drink it, in remembrance of me." ²⁶For as often as you eat this bread and drink the cup, you proclaim the Lord's death until he comes.

²⁷Therefore, whoever eats the bread or drinks the cup of the Lord in an unworthy manner will be guilty, as to the body and blood of the Lord. ²⁸Let a man examine himself, and so eat of the bread and drink of the cup. ²⁹For anyone who eats and drinks without accurately comprehending [the nature of] 'the body' eats and drinks judgment on himself. ³⁰That is why many of you are weak and sick, and some have died. ³¹But if we judged ourselves truly, we would not be judged. ³²But when we are judged by the Lord, we are disciplined so that we will not get condemned along with the world.

³³So then, my brothers, when you come together to eat, wait for one another. ³⁴If anyone is hungry, let him eat at home, so that when you do come together it [does not lead to] judgment. I will give directions about the other matters when I come.

Chapter 12

Spiritual Gifts

¹Now, brothers, I do not want you to be uninformed concerning spiritual gifts, ²You know that when you were pagans, you were led astray, however you led, to mute idols. ³Therefore I want you to understand that no one speaking by the Spirit of God ever says "Jesus be cursed!", and no one is able to declare "Jesus is Lord" except by the Holy Spirit.

⁴Now there are varieties of gifts, but [they are of] the same Spirit; ⁵and there are varieties of service, but [of] the same Lord. ⁶And there are varieties of activities, but it is the same God who empowers all of them in everyone. ⁷The manifestation of the Spirit is given to each person for the common good. ⁸Through the Spirit the utterance of wisdom is given to one person, and to another person the utterance of knowledge according to the same Spirit, ⁹to another one faith by the same Spirit, to another one gifts of healing by the one Spirit, ¹⁰to another one the working of miracles, to another one prophecy, to another one the ability to discern between spirits, to another one various kinds of tongues, to another one the interpretation of tongues. ¹¹All these [gifts] are empowered by one and the same Spirit, who apportions [them] to each person individually as he wills.

Each Member of the Body Has Value

¹²For just as the body is one and has many members, and all the members of the body, though many, are one body, so it is with Christ. ¹³For by one Spirit we all were baptized into one body—Jews or Greeks, slaves or free—and all are to drink from one Spirit. ¹⁴For the body does not consist of one member but of many. ¹⁵If the foot should say, "Because I am not a hand, I do not belong to the body," that would not make it any less a part of the body. ¹⁶And if the ear should say, "Because I am not an eye, I do not belong to the body," that would not make it any less a part of the body. ¹⁷If the whole body were an eye, where would the sense of hearing be? If the whole body were an ear, where would the sense of smell be? ¹⁸But as it is, God has arranged the organs in the body, each one of them, as he chose. ¹⁹If all of it were a single organ, where would the body be? ²⁰As it is, there are many parts, yet one body.

²¹The eye cannot say to the hand, "I have no need of you," nor again the head to the feet, "I have no need of you." ²²On the contrary, the parts of the body that seem to be weaker are indispensable. ²³And we invest those parts of the body that we deem less honorable with the greater honor, and our unpresentable parts are treated with greater modesty, ²⁴which our more presentable parts do not require. But God has so composed the body, giving the greater honor to the part that was lacking, ²⁵so that there may be no discord in the body, but that the members may have the same care for one another. ²⁶If one member suffers, all of them suffer together. If one member is honored, all of them rejoice together.

Gifted People Appointed in the Church Body

²⁷Now, you are the body of Christ and individually members of it. ²⁸And God has appointed in the church:

> ➤ first apostles, second prophets, third teachers,
> ➤ then gifts: miracles, healing, helping, administrating, and various kinds of tongues.

²⁹Are all apostles? Are all prophets? Are all teachers? Do all work miracles? ³⁰Do all possess gifts of healing? Do all speak with tongues? Do all interpret? ³¹But earnestly desire the higher gifts.

Chapter 13

The importance of Love

And I will show you an even more excellent way. ¹³:¹If I speak in the tongues of men and of angels, but have not love, I am a noisy gong or a clanging cymbal.

²And if I have prophetic powers and understand all mysteries and [possess] all knowledge, and if I have complete faith—so as to remove mountains—but do not have love, I am nothing. ³If I give away all I have, and if I hand over my body to be burned, but do not have love, I gain nothing.

Love Is

> ⁴Love is patient and kind;
> love is not envious or boastful;
> ⁵it is not arrogant or rude.
> Love does not insist on its own way;
> it is not irritable or resentful;
> ⁶it does not rejoice at wrongdoing but rejoices in the truth.
> ⁷Love bears all things, believes all things, hopes all things, and endures all things.
> ⁸Love never ends.

As for prophecies, they will pass away; as for tongues, they will cease; as for knowledge, it will pass away. ⁹For our knowledge is partial, and our prophecy is partial. ¹⁰But when the perfect comes, the imperfect will pass away. ¹¹When I was a child, I spoke like a child, I thought like a child, I reasoned like a child. When I became a man, I gave up [my] childish ways. ¹²For, currently we see in a mirror dimly, but in the future, face to face. Currently, I know partially, but in the future, I shall understand fully—even as I have been fully understood.

¹³So, faith, hope, and love abide: these three. But the greatest of these is love.

Chapter 14

Tongues and Prophecy

¹Pursue love, and earnestly desire the spiritual gifts, especially that you may prophesy. ²For one who speaks in a tongue speaks not to men but to God because no one understands him, though he utters mysteries in the Spirit. ³On the other hand, the one who prophesies speaks to men to build up, encourage, and console them. ⁴Anyone who speaks in a tongue builds up himself, but anyone who prophesies builds up the church. ⁵Now I would like for all of you to speak in tongues, but even more for you to prophesy. Anyone who prophesies is greater than the one who speaks in tongues, unless someone interprets [what is said], so that the church may be strengthened.

⁶Now, brothers, if I come to you speaking in tongues, how shall I benefit you unless I should speak out some revelation or knowledge or prophecy or teaching to

you? ⁷If an inanimate instrument, such as a flute or a harp, does not play distinct notes, how does anyone know what [tune] is being played? ⁸Or if a bugle does not play a distinct sound, who will get ready for battle? ⁹So it is with you: if you say something in a foreign tongue that is unintelligible, how will anyone know what is being said? You might just as well be speaking into the air. ¹⁰Doubtless, there are many different languages in the world, and not one of them is without meaning. ¹¹But if I do not know the meaning of the language, I will be a foreigner to the speaker and the speaker a foreigner to me. ¹²So it is with you: inasmuch as you are eager [to experience] the Spirit, strive to excel in building up the church.

¹³Therefore, anyone who speaks in tongues should pray for the ability to interpret. ¹⁴For if I pray in tongues, my spirit prays but my mind produces nothing helpful. ¹⁵Well, what then? I will pray with the spirit, and I will pray with the mind also. I will sing with the spirit, and I will sing with the mind also. ¹⁶Otherwise, if you say a blessing only in the Spirit, how can an uninitiated outsider say the "Amen" to your thanksgiving when he cannot understand what you are saying? ¹⁷For you may give thanks well enough, but the other man is not built up. ¹⁸I thank God that I speak in tongues more than all of you. ¹⁹Nevertheless, in a church [setting] I would rather speak five words with my mind in order to teach others, than ten thousand words in a [foreign] tongue.

²⁰Brothers, do not be childish in your understanding. In evil things be babies, but in your thinking be mature. ²¹In the law it is written, "By men of foreign languages and by the lips of foreigners will I speak to this people, and even then they will not listen to me, says the Lord." ²²Thus, tongues are a sign not for believers but for unbelievers, while prophecy is [a sign] not for unbelievers but for believers. ²³If, therefore, the whole church assembles, and all speak in tongues, and outsiders or unbelievers enter, will they not say that you have lost your minds? ²⁴But if everyone prophesies, and an unbeliever or outsider comes in, he is convicted by everyone, he is called to account by everyone, ²⁵the secrets of his heart are disclosed, and then, falling on his face, he will worship God and declare that God is really among you.

²⁶What then, brothers? When you come together, each one has a hymn, a lesson, a revelation, a tongue, or an interpretation. Let all things be done for the purpose of building up [the church]. ²⁷If anyone speaks in a tongue, let there be only two or at most three—and each in turn—and let one interpret. ²⁸But if there is no one to interpret, let each of them keep silent in church and speak to himself and to God. ²⁹So, let two or three prophets speak, and let the others carefully consider it. ³⁰If a revelation is made to another sitting by, let the first be silent. ³¹For all of you can prophesy one at a time, so that everyone may learn and be encouraged. ³²And the spirits of prophets are subject to prophets. ³³For God is not a God of confusion but of peace.

Women Keeping Silent in Church

As in all the churches of the saints, ³⁴the women should keep silent in the church-es. For they are not permitted to speak, but should be subordinate, as even the law says. ³⁵If there is anything they desire to know, let them ask their husbands at home. For it is shameful for a woman to speak in church. ³⁶What! Did the word of God originate with you, or are you the only ones it has reached? ³⁷If anyone thinks that he is a prophet, or spiritual, he should acknowledge that what I am writing to you is a command of the Lord. ³⁸If anyone does not recognize this, he is not recognized. ³⁹So, my brothers, earnestly desire to prophesy, and do not forbid speaking in tongues. ⁴⁰But all things should be done decently and in order.

Chapter 15

Paul has Preached the Gospel

¹Now, brothers, I would remind you of the gospel I preached to you, which you received, in which you stand, ²by which you are saved, if you grip tightly the message I preached to you–unless, [that is], you believed [it only] in a casual way.

³For I communicated to you the most important things I also received: that Christ died for our sins in accordance with the scriptures, ⁴that he was buried, that he was raised on the third day in accordance with the scriptures, ⁵and that he appeared to Cephas, then to the Twelve. ⁶Then he appeared to more than five hundred brothers at one time, most of whom are still alive, though some have gone to their rest. ⁷Then he appeared to James, then to all the apostles. ⁸Last of all he also appeared to me—as if I had been born at the wrong time. ⁹For I am the least of the apostles, unworthy to even be called an apostle, because I persecuted the church of God. ¹⁰But by the grace of God I am what I am, and his grace toward me was not in vain. On the contrary, I worked harder than any of them, though it was not I, but the grace of God that is with me. ¹¹So then whether it was I or they, so we preached and so you believed.

Resurrection of the Dead

¹²If we preach that Christ rose from the dead, how can some of you say that there is no resurrection of the dead? ¹³Now if there is no resurrection of the dead, then Christ has not been raised. ¹⁴If Christ has not been raised, then our preaching is in vain and your faith is in vain. ¹⁵We are even found to be misrepresenting God, because we have testified that God has raised Christ, whom he did *not* raise if it is true that the dead are not raised. ¹⁶For if the dead are not raised, then Christ has not been raised. ¹⁷If Christ has not been raised, then your faith is futile. and you

are still in your sins. [18]Then too, those who have gone to their rest in Christ have perished. [19]If we have placed our hope in Christ just for this present life only, then of all people, we are the most to be pitied.

[20]But in fact Christ *has* been raised from the dead, the firstfruits of those who have gone to their rest. [21]For since death came through a man, through a man has also come the resurrection of the dead. [22]For as in Adam everyone dies, so also in Christ shall everyone be brought to life. [23]But each one [will do so] in his own category: Christ the firstfruits, then at his coming those who belong to Christ. [24]Then comes the end, when he delivers the kingdom to God the Father after abolishing every government and every authority and power. [25]For he must reign until he has put all his enemies under his feet. [26]The last enemy to be abolished is death. [27]"For God has put everything in subjection under his feet." But when it says, "Everything has been put in subjection under him," it is clear that the One who put everything under him is excluded. [28]When everything has been subjected to him, then the Son himself will also be subjected to him who put everything under him, so that God may be everything to everyone.

[29]Otherwise, why are thos who are concerned about the dead being baptized? If there is no resurrection of the dead, why would people be baptized? [30]Why are we in peril every hour? [31]Brothers—as surely as I rejoice in you in Christ Jesus our Lord—I am dying every day! [32]What would I gain if I fought with beasts at Ephesus, like other men? If the dead are not raised, then "Let us eat and drink, for tomorrow we die." [33]Do not be deceived: "Bad company ruins good morals." [34]Wake up to what is right, and do not go on sinning, for some have no knowledge of God. I say this to your shame.

Our Heavenly Bodies

[35]But someone will ask, "How are the dead raised? What bodily form do they come in?" [36]You foolish person! What you sow does not come to life unless it dies. [37]And what you sow is not the body that it will become, but a bare kernel, perhaps of wheat or of some other grain. [38]But God gives it a body as he has chosen, and to each kind of seed its own body. [39]For not all flesh is alike, but there is one kind for men, another for animals, another for birds, and another for fish. [40]There are celestial bodies and there are terrestrial bodies; but the glory of the celestial is one, and the glory of the terrestrial is another. [41]There is one glory of the sun, and another glory of the moon, and another glory of the stars, for one star differs from another star in glory.

⁴²So is it with the resurrection of the dead:

> ➤ What is sown is perishable, what is raised is imperishable.
> ➤ ⁴³It is sown in dishonor, it is raised in glory.
> ➤ It is sown in weakness, it is raised in power.
> ➤ ⁴⁴It is sown a physical body, it is raised a spiritual body.
> ➤ If there is a physical body, there is also a spiritual body.

⁴⁵Thus it is written, "The first man Adam became a living being." The last Adam became a life-giving spirit. ⁴⁶But it is not the spiritual that is first, but the physical and then the spiritual. ⁴⁷The first man was from the earth, a man of dust. The second man is from heaven. ⁴⁸As the man of dust was, so are those who are of the dust. And as the man of heaven is, so are those who are of heaven. ⁴⁹Just as we have borne the image of the man of dust, we shall also bear the image of the man of heaven.

"O Death, Where is Your Victory?"

⁵⁰I tell you this, brothers: flesh and blood cannot inherit the kingdom of God, nor does the perishable inherit the imperishable. ⁵¹Listen! I tell you a mystery. We shall not all sleep, but we shall all be changed, ⁵²in a moment, in the twinkling of an eye, at the last trumpet. For the trumpet will sound, and the dead will be raised imperishable, and we shall be changed. ⁵³For this, perishable nature must put on the imperishable, and this mortal nature must put on immortality. ⁵⁴When the perishable puts on the imperishable, and the mortal puts on immortality, then the saying that is written shall come to pass: "Death is swallowed up in victory." ⁵⁵"O death, where is your victory? O death, where is your sting?" ⁵⁶The sting of death is sin, and the power of sin is the law. ⁵⁷But thanks be to God, who gives us the victory through our Lord Jesus Christ.

⁵⁸Therefore, my beloved brothers, stand firm—immovable—always abounding in the work of the Lord, keeping in mind that your labor in the Lord is not in vain.

Chapter 16

Instructions About Offerings

¹Now concerning the contribution for the saints: you are also to do it as I directed the churches of Galatia. ²On the first day of every week, each of you is to put something aside and store it up, as he may prosper, so that contributions do not need to be made when I come. ³And when I arrive, I will send the men that you approve, with credentials, to carry your gift to Jerusalem. ⁴If it seems advisable that I should go also, I will accompany them.

Plans for Travel

[5]I will visit you after passing through Macedonia, for I intend to pass through Macedonia. [6]And perhaps I will stay with you or even spend the winter, so that you may expedite my journey, wherever I go [7]because this time I do not want to see you just in passing. I hope to spend some time with you if the Lord permits. [8]But I will stay in Ephesus until Pentecost, [9]for a door has opened wide for me to do some effective work [there], but [with] many adversaries.

[10]When Timothy comes, see that you allay his fears among you, for he is doing the work of the Lord as I am. [11]So let no one despise him. Support him on his way in peace, so that he may return to me, for I am expecting him with the brothers.

Final Instructions

[12]As for our brother Apollos, I strongly urged him to visit you with the other brothers, but he was unwilling to come now. He will come when he has opportunity.

[13]Be watchful, stand firm in your faith, behave like men, be strong. [14]All you do should be done in love.

[15]Now, brothers, you know that the [members of the] household of Stephanas were the first ones in Achaia led to Christ, and they have devoted themselves to the service of the saints. [16]I urge you to be subject to such men and to every fellow worker and laborer. [17]I rejoice at the coming of Stephanas and Fortunatus and Achaicus, because they have made up for your absence, [18]for they refreshed my spirit as well as yours. Acknowledge such men.

Greetings and Benediction

[19]The churches of Asia send greetings. Aquila and Prisca, together with the church in their house, send you hearty greetings in the Lord. [20]All the brothers send greetings. Greet one another with a holy kiss. [21]I, Paul, write this greeting with my own hand. [22]If anyone has no love for the Lord, let him be accursed.

May our Lord come! [23]The grace of the Lord Jesus be with you. [24]May my love be with you all in Christ Jesus. Amen.

2 CORINTHIANS

Chapter 1

[From]: Paul, an apostle of Christ Jesus by the will of God, and Timothy our brother.

To: God's church in Corinth, along with all the saints who are in the whole area of Achaia:

²Grace to you and peace from God our Father and the Lord Jesus Christ.

God Comforts Us in Affliction

³Blessed be the God and Father of our Lord Jesus Christ, the Father of mercies and God of all comfort. ⁴He comforts us in all our affliction, so that we may be able to comfort those who are in any affliction with the comfort by which God comforts us. ⁵For as we share abundantly in Christ's *sufferings*, in the same way through Christ we do share abundantly in *comfort* as well. ⁶If we are afflicted, it is for your comfort and salvation. And if we are comforted, it is for your comfort, which you experience when you patiently endure the same sufferings that we suffer. ⁷Our hope for you is unshaken, for we know that as you share in our sufferings, [you will share] in our comfort as well.

⁸Now we do not want you to be ignorant, brothers, of the affliction we experienced in Asia, because being so utterly overwhelmed beyond our capability, we despaired of life itself. ⁹Why, we felt that we had received the sentence of death in order to make us rely not on ourselves but on God who raises the dead. ¹⁰He rescued us from so deadly a peril, and he will [still] rescue us. We have set our hope on him that he will rescue us again. ¹¹Please support us in prayer so that on our behalf many people will give thanks for the blessing granted to us, in answer to the prayers of many people.

Paul Changes his Plans

¹²For our boast is this: our conscience gives testimony that we have behaved in the world (and even more so toward you) with simplicity and godly sincerity, not by earthly wisdom but by the grace of God. ¹³For we are not writing to you anything other than what you can read and understand. I hope you will understand fully, ¹⁴as you have understood in part, that on the day of the Lord Jesus you will boast about us as we will about *you*.

[15]Because I was sure of this, I wanted to come to you first, so that you might experience grace a second time. [16]I wanted to visit you on my way to Macedonia, and to come back to you from Macedonia and have you send me on my way to Judea. [17]In planning to do that was I waffling indecisively? Do I make my plans based on human frailty, apt to answer both "Yes, yes" and "No, no"? [18]Rather, since God is faithful, our word to you has *not* been "Yes and no." [19]While among you, Silvanus, Timothy, and I preached the Son of God, Jesus Christ, who was not "Yes and no." Instead, it is always Yes in him [20]because all the promises of God become Yes in him, which is why through him we say Amen to God, for his glory.

[21]So, it is God who establishes us with you in Christ and has commissioned us. [22]He has set his seal on us and has given us his Spirit in our hearts as a deposit of guarantee.

[23]Now I invoke God to bear witness about me—I refrained from returning to Corinth to spare you. [24]It is not that we are minimizing your faith, but rather, because you do stand firm in your faith, we are working with you for your joy.

Chapter 2

[1]I made up my mind not to make another grievous visit to you. [2]For if I should cause you grief, who would be there to make me glad but the one whom I have grieved? [3]Now, I wrote such things so that when I came I might not suffer grief from the very people who should have made me rejoice, for I felt sure that for all of you, my joy would be your joy. [4]For I wrote to you out of much affliction and anguish of heart and with many tears, not to cause you grief, but to let you know the abundant love that I have for you.

Show Forgiveness

[5]Now if anyone has caused grief, he has caused it not to me, but in some way—not to put this too harshly—to all of you. [6]For having such a person be punished by most of you will suffice. [7]So instead, now you should turn around and forgive and comfort him, or he may be overwhelmed by excessive sorrow. [8]So I beg you to reaffirm your love for him. [9]For this is why I wrote: to test you and know whether you are obedient in everything. [10]Anyone whom you forgive, I also forgive. What I have forgiven—if I have forgiven anything—has been for your sake in the presence of Christ, [11]to keep Satan from gaining the advantage over us, for we are not ignorant of his schemes.

The Open Door in Troas

¹²When I arrived in Troas to preach the gospel of Christ, a door [of opportunity] was opened up for me in the Lord. ¹³Still, my mind could not rest because I did not find my brother Titus there. So, I took leave of them and proceeded to Macedonia.

Being the Aroma of Christ

¹⁴But thanks be to God, who in Christ always leads us in triumph, using us to spread the fragrance of the knowledge of him everywhere. ¹⁵For we are the aroma of Christ to God among those who are being saved and among those who are perishing: ¹⁶to one a fragrance from death to death, to the other a fragrance from life to life. Who is qualified for these things? ¹⁷For we are not men who tamper with the Word of God for financial gain as many others are, but rather, in Christ we speak sincerely, as [sent] from God, in the sight of God.

Chapter 3

A Letter of Recommendation

¹Are we beginning to commend ourselves again? Or, as some do, do we need letters of recommendation to you, or from you? ²You yourselves are our letter of recommendation, written on your hearts, to be known and read by everyone. ³And you continually show that you are a letter from Christ delivered by us, written not with ink but with the Spirit of the living God, not on tablets of stone but on tablets of human hearts.

⁴Now, we have such a confidence through Christ before God. ⁵It is not that we are competent in ourselves so as to claim anything as having come from us. Our competence is from God, ⁶who has made us competent to be ministers of a new covenant, not from a written code but of the Spirit. For the written code kills, but the Spirit gives life.

Religious versus Spiritual Service

⁷Now if the deadly religious service, carved in letters on stone, came with such splendor that the Israelites could not look at Moses' face because of its brightness, fading as this was, ⁸will not the spiritual service have greater splendor? ⁹For if there was splendor in the service [leading to] condemnation, the service [leading to] righteousness must far exceed it in splendor. ¹⁰Indeed, in this case, what once had splendor has come to have no splendor at all, because of the splendor that surpasses it. ¹¹For if what was fading away came with splendor, what is permanent must have much more splendor.

¹²Since we have such a hope, we speak boldly, ¹³unlike Moses, who used to put a veil over his face so that the Israelites could not see the result of what was fading away. ¹⁴However, their minds were hardened, for to this day, when they read the old covenant, that same veil remains unlifted, because it is only taken away through Christ. ¹⁵Indeed, to this day, whenever Moses' [writing] is read, a veil lies over their minds. ¹⁶On the contrary, when someone turns to the Lord, the veil is removed. ¹⁷Now the Lord is the Spirit, and freedom [lies] where the Spirit of the Lord is. ¹⁸And with unveiled faces, gazing on the glory of the Lord, all of us are being changed into his likeness from one degree of glory to another, for this comes from the Lord, the Spirit.

Chapter 4

The Light of the Gospel

¹Therefore, having this ministry by [God's] mercy, we do not lose heart. ²We have renounced dishonest, underhanded ways. We refuse to do things out of craftiness or to tamper with God's word. But rather, by the open statement of the truth, we would commend ourselves to every man's conscience in the sight of God. ³And even if our gospel is veiled, it is veiled only to those who are perishing. ⁴In their case, the god of this world has blinded the minds of the unbelievers to keep them from seeing the light of the gospel of the glory of Christ, who is the image of God. ⁵For we are not proclaiming ourselves, but Jesus Christ as Lord, with us being your servants for the sake of Jesus. ⁶For it is God, who said, "Let light shine out of darkness," who has shone in our hearts to give the light of the knowledge of God's glory in the face of Jesus Christ.

This Treasure in Jars of Clay

⁷But we have this treasure in jars of clay so that the extraordinary power is of God and not from us. ⁸We are afflicted in every way, but not crushed; perplexed, but not driven to despair; ⁹persecuted, but not forsaken; struck down, but not destroyed; ¹⁰always carrying around the death of Jesus physically, so that in our bodies the life of Jesus may also be demonstrated. ¹¹For while we are alive we are constantly being given up to death for the sake of Jesus, so that the life of Jesus may be demonstrated in our mortal flesh. ¹²So it is death that is at work in us, but life in you.

¹³It has been written, "I believed, and so I spoke." Since we have that same spirit of faith, we also believe, and so we speak, ¹⁴knowing that he who raised the Lord Jesus will raise us also with Jesus and bring us with you into his presence. ¹⁵For it is all for your sake so that as grace extends to more and more people it may bring

about more thanksgiving, to the glory of God. [16]So, we do not lose heart. Though our outer self is deteriorating, still our inner self is being renewed day by day. [17]For this light momentary affliction is preparing a weight of glory for us—extraordinary and eternal—[18]as we look not to the things that are seen but to the things that are unseen. For the things that *are* seen are transient, but the things that are *not* seen are eternal.

Chapter 5

Earthly and Heavenly Dwellings

[1]For we know that if the earthly tent we live in is destroyed, we have a building from God— an eternal house not made by human hands—in the heavens. [2]For indeed we are groaning in this one, longing to put on our heavenly dwelling, [3]so that by putting it on we will not be found unclothed. [4]For while we are still in this tent, we are groaning under the burden, not wishing to become unclothed, but rather to be further clothed, so that what is mortal may be swallowed up by life. [5]He who has prepared us for this very thing [is] God, who has given us the Spirit as a guarantee.

[6]So we are always cheerfully confident. We know that while we are at home in the body we are away from the Lord, [7]for we walk by faith, not by sight. [8]So, we are cheerfully confident, and we would rather be out of these bodies and at home with the Lord. [9]So whether we are at home or away, we intentionally seek to please him. [10]For we will all have to appear before the judgment seat of Christ, so that each one may receive what is due, according to what he has done in the body, whether good or evil.

[11]Therefore, knowing the fear of the Lord, we persuade people. But we are completely known by God, and I hope that we are known fully in your consciences as well. [12]We are not commending ourselves to you again but we are giving you reason to affirm us, so that you can respond to those who esteem themselves highly, based on appearance rather than on the heart. [13]For if we are beside ourselves, it is for God. If we are in our right mind, it is for you. [14]For the love of Christ motivates us because we are convinced of this: that One has died for all, therefore all have died. [15]And he died for all, that those who live might live no longer for themselves but for him who died and was raised for their sake.

[16]From now on, therefore, we regard no one from a human point of view. Even though we once regarded Christ from a human point of view, we no longer regard him that way. [17]Therefore, if anyone is in Christ, he is a new creation; the old has passed away, note this well: the new has come. [18]This all originated from

God, who reconciled us to himself through Christ and granted the ministry of reconciliation to us. [19]That is, in Christ, God was reconciling the world to himself, not counting their trespasses against them, and entrusting to us the message of reconciliation. [20]So we are ambassadors for Christ: God making his appeal through us. We implore you on behalf of Christ: be reconciled to God. [21]For our sake he made him who knew no sin to be sin, so that in him we might become the righteousness of God.

Chapter 6

Paul Lists his Afflictions

[1]Working together with God, then, we appeal to you to not receive his grace in a pointless manner. [2]For he says, "At just the right favorable moment I listened to you and helped you on the day of salvation." Look, *now* is that favorable time: take note that now is the day of salvation. [3]In no way are we putting an obstacle in anyone's way, so that no one may find fault with our ministry.

[4]Instead, as servants of God we commend ourselves in every way:

by great endurance in afflictions, hardships, calamities, [5]beatings, imprisonments,
    riots, labors, sleepless nights, and hunger;
    [6]by purity, knowledge, forbearance, and kindness;
    by the Holy Spirit, genuine love, [7]truthful speech, and the power of God;
    with the weapons of righteousness for both the right hand and the left;
    [8]in both honor and dishonor,
    in both bad and good reputation.

We are treated:

    as impostors, and yet are true,
    [9]as unknown, and yet well-known,
    as dying, and yet alive—as you will notice—
    as punished, and yet not killed,
    [10]as sorrowful, yet always rejoicing,
    as poor, yet enriching many others,
    as having nothing, and yet possessing everything.

[11]We have spoken openly to you, Corinthians; our heart is wide open. [12]You are not constricted by us, but you are constricted in your own affections. [13]I am speaking as to [spiritual] children: in return, open your hearts wide also.

Unequally Yoked with Unbelievers

[14]Do not be unequally yoked with unbelievers. For what partnership do righteousness and lawlessness have? Or what fellowship does light share with darkness? [15]How would Christ agree with Belial? Or what does a believer have in common with an unbeliever? [16]What agreement does the temple of God have with idols? For we are the temple of the living God. As God said,

> "I will dwell among them and walk among them,
> and I will be their God, and they shall be my people.
> [17]Therefore come out from them
> and be separate from them, says the Lord,
> and do not touch anything unclean.
> Then I will welcome you,
> [18]and I will be a father to you,
> and you shall be my sons and daughters,
> says the Lord Almighty."

[7:1]Beloved, since we have these promises, in the fear of God, let us purge ourselves from everything that defiles body and spirit so as to make holiness complete.

Chapter 7, cont.

Paul Rejoices in his Work in the Church

[2]Open your hearts to us. We have not wronged anyone, we have not corrupted anyone, we have not taken advantage of anyone. [3]I do not say this to condemn you, for I said before that you are in our hearts, to die together and to live together. [4]I have great confidence in you; I have great pride in you; I am filled with comfort. Even in all our affliction, I am overflowing with joy.

[5]For even when we came into Macedonia our bodies had no rest, but we were afflicted at every turn—fighting without and fearing within. [6]But God, who comforts the downcast, comforted us by the coming of Titus, [7]and not only by his coming but also by the comfort with which he was comforted in you, as he told us of your longing, your mourning, and your zeal for me, so that I rejoiced even more. [8]For even if I made you sorry with my letter, I do not regret it (though I did regret it), for I see that that letter grieved you, though only for a while. [9]As it is, I am glad, not because you were grieved, but because you were grieved into repenting. For you felt a godly grief, so that through us you did not suffer loss.

[10]For godly grief produces a repentance that leads to salvation and brings no regret, but worldly grief produces death. [11]For see what earnestness this godly

grief has produced in you, what eagerness to clear yourselves, what disgust with wrongdoing, what alarm, what longing, what zeal, what punishment [of wrongs]! At every point you have proven yourselves guiltless in the matter. [12]So although I wrote to you, it was not on account of the one who did the wrong, nor on account of the one who suffered the wrong, but in order that your zeal for us might be revealed to you in the sight of God. [13]We take comfort in that.

And besides our own comfort we rejoiced still more at Titus's joy, because his mind has been set at ease by you all. [14]For if I have expressed to him some pride in you, I was not put to shame. But just as everything we said to you was true, so our boasting before Titus has proved true. [15]And his heart goes out all the more to you, as he remembers how obedient you all are, and the fear and trembling that you received him with. [16]I rejoice because I have complete confidence in you.

Chapter 8

Give Generously

[1]We want you to know, brothers, about the grace of God that has been shown in the churches of Macedonia, [2]for in a severe test of affliction, their abundance of joy and their extreme poverty have overflowed in a wealth of generosity on their part. [3]For they gave according to their means (as I can testify), and even beyond their means, of their own free will, [4]begging us earnestly for the favor of taking part in the relief of the saints. [5]In addition, [this was] not as we expected, but they first gave themselves to the Lord and to us by the will of God. [6]Accordingly, we have urged Titus that as he had already made a beginning, he should also complete among you this act of grace. [7]Now as you excel in everything—in faith, in speech, in knowledge, in all earnestness, and in your love for us—see that you excel in this act of grace also.

[8]I say this not as a command, but to prove by the earnestness of others that your love also is genuine. [9]For you know the grace of our Lord Jesus Christ: that though he was rich, yet for your sake he became poor, so that by his poverty you might become rich. [10]And in this matter I give my advice: it is best for you now to complete what you began a year ago not only to do but to desire, [11]so that your readiness in desiring it may be matched by your completing it out of what you have. [12]For if the readiness is there, it is acceptable according to what a man has, not according to what he does not have. [13]I do not mean that others should be at ease while you are burdened, [14]but that as a matter of equality your abundance at the present time should supply their want, so that their abundance might one day supply your

needs, so that there might be equality. ¹⁵As the scripture says, "The one who gathered a lot had nothing left over, and the one who gathered little was not in need."

A Commendation of Titus

¹⁶But thanks be to God who puts the same earnest care for you into the heart of Titus. ¹⁷For he not only accepted our appeal, but being very earnest himself, he is going to you of his own accord. ¹⁸With him we are sending the brother who is famous among all the churches for his preaching of the gospel. ¹⁹And not only that, but he has also been appointed by the churches to travel with us in this work of grace as we are doing ministry for the glory of the Lord and to show our good will. ²⁰We are proceeding this way so that no one would find fault with us over this generous gift that we are administering. ²¹For we are aiming at what is honorable not only in the Lord's sight but also in the sight of men.

²²With them we are also sending our brother whom we have often tested and found earnest in many matters, but who is now more earnest than ever because of his great confidence in you. ²³As for Titus, he is my partner and fellow worker in your service. Being like brothers to us, they are messengers of the churches, the glory of Christ. ²⁴So in the presence of these churches, provide proof of your love and the grounds for our boasting about you to them.

Chapter 9

An Offering for Believers in Jerusalem

¹Now it is superfluous for me to write to you about the offering for the saints, ²for I know you are ready [to make one], and I have proudly talked about you to the people of Macedonia, telling them that Achaia has been ready since last year. Your fervor has inspired most of them. ³But I am sending the brothers so that our boasting about you may not prove vain in this case. This way you will be ready, as I said you would be, ⁴so that if some Macedonians do come with me and find that you are not ready, we will not be embarrassed—to say nothing of you—for being so confident. ⁵So, I thought it necessary to urge the brothers to go on to you ahead of me and make arrangements for this gift you have promised in advance, so that it may be ready as a gift given willingly, expecting nothing in return.

God Supplies the Needs of a Cheerful Giver

⁶The point is this: the one who sows sparingly will also reap sparingly, and the one who sows a goodly amount will also reap a goodly amount. ⁷Each one must do as he has made up his mind to do, not reluctantly or under compulsion, for

God loves a cheerful giver. [8]And God is able to provide you with every blessing in abundance, so that you may always have enough of everything and may provide in abundance for every good work. [9]As the scripture says, "He has distributed freely. He has given to the poor. His rsteadfast love endures forever."

[10]He who supplies seed to the sower and bread for food will supply and multiply your resources and increase the harvest of your righteousness. [11]You will be enriched in every way in order to be generous in every way, which through us will produce thanksgiving to God. [12]For the ministry of this service not only supplies the wants of the saints but also overflows in many thanksgivings to God. [13]By the approval of this ministry, you will glorify God by your obedience in acknowledging the gospel of Christ, and by the generosity of your contribution for them and for all others. [14]They do care about you and pray for you, because of the surpassing grace of God in you. [15]Thanks be to God for his inexpressible gift!

Chapter 10

Paul Defends himself

[1]Now I myself, Paul, plead with you, by the meekness and gentleness of Christ (I who am humble when face to face with you, but bold to you when I am away!) [2]That is, I beg of you that when I am present I may not have to act with such confident boldness as I assume I will have to use against some people who suspect us of living by worldly standards. [3]For though we dwell in human bodies, our battle is not an earthly one, [4]for the weapons of our warfare are not of this world but have divine power to tear down fortresses. [5]We are tearing down speculative arguments and everything that pridefully raises itself against the knowledge of God, so that every thought is held captive in obedience to Christ. [6]We stand ready to punish every disobedience, once your obedience is complete.

[7]Are you just looking at what lies in front of you? If anyone is confident that he belongs to Christ, may he remind himself that just as he belongs to Christ, so do we. [8]For even if I do stress our authority a little too much, the Lord gave it for building you up and not for destroying you; I shall not be put to shame. [9]I would not want to appear to be frightening you with my letters. [10]For they say, "His letters are heavy-handed and powerful, but his physical presence is frail, and his speech unimpressive." [11]Let such people understand that what we say by letter when absent, we do when present. [12]Not that we dare to classify or compare ourselves with some of those who commend themselves. But when they measure themselves by one another, and compare themselves with one another, they lack discernment.

[13]Now, we are not boasting outside our limits, but only within the sphere of influence God had assigned to us in order to reach you. [14]For this is not an overextension of ourselves, as though we did not reach you: we were the first ones to come all the way to you with the gospel of Christ. [15]We are not boasting about other people's labors, outside our limit. Rather, our hope is that as your faith increases, our sphere of influence among you may be greatly enlarged, [16]so that we may preach the gospel in lands beyond you, without boasting of work already done in another person's sphere of influence. [17]"Let the one who boasts, boast of the Lord." [18]For it is not the man who commends himself who is accepted, but the man whom the Lord commends.

Chapter 11

Beware of False Gospels

[1]I wish you would bear with me in a little foolishness. Please bear with me! [2]I feel a divine jealousy for you, for I betrothed you to one husband to present you as a pure virgin bride to Christ. [3]But I am afraid that as Eve was deceived by the serpent's trickery, your thoughts will be led astray from a sincere and pure devotion to Christ. [4]For if someone comes and preaches another Jesus than the one we preached, or if you receive a different spirit from the one you received, or if you accept a different gospel from the one you accepted, you tolerate it readily enough. [5]I think that I am not in the least inferior to these superlative apostles. [6]Even if I am unskilled in speaking, I am not so in knowledge. In every way we have made this plain to you in all ways.

[7]Did I commit a sin in humbling myself so that you might be exalted because I preached God's gospel to you without charge? [8]I robbed other churches by accepting support from them in order to be of service you. [9]And when I was with you and was in want, I did not burden anyone, for my needs were supplied by the brothers who came from Macedonia. So I refrained and will refrain from burdening you in any way. [10]As the truth of Christ is in me, this boasting of mine shall not be silenced in the regions of Achaia. [11]And why? Because I do not love you? God knows [I do]!

[12]And what I do I will continue to do, in order to undermine the claims of those who would like to claim that in the mission they boast about, they work just as we do. [13]For such men are false apostles, deceitful workmen, disguising themselves as apostles of Christ. [14]And no wonder, for even Satan can change himself into the form of an angel of light. [15]So it is not strange that his servants also disguise themselves as servants of righteousness. Their end will be in accordance with their

deeds. [16]Again I say: let no one think me foolish. But even if you do, accept me as a fool, so that I too may boast a little. [17](What I am saying I say in this boastful confidence, not with the Lord's authority but as a fool. [18]Since many people boast of worldly things, I will boast, too.) [19]For you gladly tolerate fools, being wise yourselves! [20]For you tolerate someone enslaving you, or preying upon you, or taking advantage of you, or putting on airs, or striking you in the face. [21]I must say, to my shame, we were too weak for that!

Paul Lists his Afflictions Again

But whatever anyone would dare to boast about—I am speaking facetiously—I would dare to boast about, also. [22]Are they Hebrews? So am I. Are they Israelites? So am I. Are they descendants of Abraham? So am I. [23]Are they servants of Christ? (I am talking like a madman) I am a better one:

> ➤ with far greater labors,
> ➤ with far more imprisonments,
> ➤ with countless beatings, and often near death.
> ➤ [24]Five times the Jews have given me the forty lashes less one,
> ➤ [25]three times I have been beaten with rods,
> ➤ once I was stoned.
> ➤ I have been shipwrecked three times, adrift at sea for a night and a day,
> ➤ [26]And on frequent journeys I have been:
> ➤ in danger from rivers and from robbers,
> ➤ in danger from my own people and from Gentiles,
> ➤ in danger in the city, in the wilderness, and at sea,
> ➤ in danger from false brothers,
> ➤ [27]in toil and hardship through many a sleepless night,
> ➤ in hunger and thirst often without food,
> ➤ in cold and exposure.

[28]And, apart from other things, there is the daily pressure on me of my anxiety for all the churches. [29]If someone else is powerless, aren't I also? If someone gets offended, don't I also burn with indignation? [30]If I must boast, I will boast of the things that show my weakness. [31]The God and Father of the Lord Jesus, who is blessed forever, knows that I am not lying. [32]At Damascus, the governor under King Aretas was guarding the city of Damascus in order to capture me, [33]but I was let down in a basket through a window in the wall and escaped his hands.

284

Chapter 12

On Boasting and Having a Thorn in the Flesh

[1]My need of boasting, though, profits me nothing, so I will continue on to visions and revelations of the Lord. [2]I know a man in Christ who was caught up to the third heaven fourteen years ago—whether in the body or out of the body I do not know; God knows. [3]And I know that this man was caught up into paradise—whether in the body or out of the body I do not know, God knows—[4]and he heard things not allowed to be told, which man may not utter. [5]I will boast on behalf of this man, but on my own behalf I will not boast, except of my weaknesses. [6]Though if I were to boast, I would not be a fool, for I would be speaking the truth. But I refrain from that, so that no one would think more of me than what he sees in me or hears from me. [7]And to keep me from being conceited due to the awesomeness of the revelations, a thorn in the flesh was given to me—a messenger from Satan—to harass me, and to keep me from being conceited. [8]I pleaded with the Lord three times that it would leave me. [9]But he replied to me, "My grace is sufficient for you, for my power is made perfect in weakness." So, I will boast of my weaknesses all the more gladly, so that the power of Christ may rest on me. [10]Then, for the sake of Christ, I remain content with weaknesses, insults, hardships, persecutions, and calamities. For when I am weak, then I am strong.

[11]I have made a fool of myself, [but] you forced me to do it, for I should have been commended by you. For I was not at all inferior to these superlative apostles, even though I am nothing. [12]The signs of a true apostle were performed among you in all patience, with signs and wonders and mighty works. [13]For in what [way] were you any less favored than the rest of the churches, except that I myself was not a burden to you? Forgive me this wrong!

Paul's Concern for the Church in Corinth

[14]Now here it is the third time I am ready to come to you. And I refuse to be a burden, for I am not after your possessions but you, because children should not have to save up for their parents, but parents for their children. [15]I will most gladly spend and be spent for your souls. If I love you more, am I to be loved less? [16]But seeing as I myself wasn't a burden to you, you say I was crafty and got the better of you through deceit. [17]Did I take advantage of you through any of those that I sent to you? [18]I urged Titus to go and sent the brother with him. Did Titus take advantage of you? Did we not behave in the same spirit and take the same steps?

[19]Have you been thinking all along that we have been defending ourselves before you? Beloved ones, we have been speaking in Christ in the sight of God, and all

for building you up. [20]For I fear that perhaps I may come and find you not as I wish, and that you may find me not as you wish, that perhaps there may be quarreling, jealousy, anger, selfishness, slander, gossip, conceit, and disorder. [21]I fear that when I return among you, my God may humble me, and I may have to mourn over many of those who had sinned in the past and have not repented of the impurity, sexual immorality, and licentiousness that they have practiced.

Chapter 13

Instructions in Advance of Paul's Next Visit

[1]This is the third time I am coming to you. All charges must be supported by the evidence of two or three witnesses. [2]I warned those who sinned before and all the others, and while absent, I am warning them now, as I did when present on my second visit, that if I come again I will not spare them– [3]since you desire proof that Christ is speaking in me. He is not weak in dealing with you but is mighty among you. [4]For in weakness he was crucified but by the power of God he is alive. For we are weak in him, but we shall live with him by the power of God in dealing with you. [5]Examine yourselves, to see whether you are holding to your faith. Test yourselves, or do you not yourselves realize that Jesus Christ is in you? (unless indeed you fail to meet the test!) [6]I hope you will discover that we have not failed the test. [7]But we pray to God that you may not do wrong—not that we may appear to have met the test—but that you may do what is right, though we may seem to have failed. [8]For we cannot do anything against the truth, but only for the truth. [9]For we are glad when we are weak, and you are strong, and what we are praying for is your restoration. [10]That is why I write this while I am away from you, so that when I come [back], I might not have to be severe in my use of the authority that the Lord has given me for building up and not for tearing down.

Final Greetings

[11]Finally, brothers and sisters, farewell. Seek restoration, comfort one another, agree with one another, be at peace, and the God of love and peace will be with you. [12]Greet one another with a holy kiss. [13]All the saints [send their] greetings to you. [14]May the grace of the Lord Jesus Christ and the love of God and the fellowship of the Holy Spirit be with all of you.

Chapter 1

¹[From]: Paul, being an apostle—not from men, nor by man's [authority] but through Jesus Christ and God the Father, who raised him from the dead– ²and [from] all the brothers who are with me,

To: the churches of Galatia:

³Grace to you and peace from God our Father and the Lord Jesus Christ, ⁴who gave himself for our sins to deliver us from the present evil age, according to the will of our God and Father, ⁵to whom be the glory forever and ever. Amen.

One True Gospel from God

⁶I am astonished that you are so quickly deserting him who called you in the grace of Christ [to seek] a different gospel, ⁷not that there is another gospel. But, some people are disturbing you and want to distort the gospel of Christ. ⁸But if we, or an angel from heaven, should preach to you a gospel contrary to the one we preached to you, let him be accursed. ⁹As we have said before, so I now say again: if anyone is preaching to you a gospel contrary to the one that you received, let him be accursed. ¹⁰Am I now seeking the approval of men, or of God? Or am I trying to please men? If I were still trying to please men, I would not be a servant of Christ. ¹¹For I would have you know, brothers, that the gospel that I preached is not man's gospel. ¹²For I did not receive it from man, nor was I taught it, but it came through a revelation of Jesus Christ.

Paul's Past Life

¹³For you have heard of my former life in Judaism, and how horribly I persecuted the church of God and tried to destroy it. ¹⁴And I was advancing in Judaism beyond many of my peers among my people, since I was so extremely zealous for the traditions of my fathers. ¹⁵But when he who had set me apart before I was born, and had called me through his grace, ¹⁶was pleased to reveal his Son to me, in order that I might preach him among the Gentiles, I did not immediately confer with anyone, ¹⁷nor did I go up to Jerusalem to those who had become apostles before me. Instead I went away into Arabia and then returned again to Damascus.

¹⁸Then after three years I went up to Jerusalem to visit Cephas and stayed with him for fifteen days. ¹⁹But I saw none of the other apostles except James, the Lord's brother. ²⁰(In what I am writing to you—listen—before God, I am not lying) ²¹Then I went into the regions of Syria and Cilicia. ²²And I was still not known by sight to Christ's churches in Judea. ²³They only heard it said, "The one who used to persecute us is now preaching the faith he once tried to destroy." ²⁴And they glorified God because of me.

Chapter 2

Paul's Acceptance into the Church

¹Then after fourteen years I went with Barnabus up to Jerusalem again, taking Titus along as well. ²I went up on account of a revelation and laid before them (but privately before those deemed influential) the gospel that I preach among the Gentiles, to verify that I was not going forward, nor had I raced on ahead, in vain. ³Now Titus, a Greek, was with me but was not forced to be circumcised. ⁴Yet because of [this], false brothers (who slipped in to spy out our freedom that we have in Christ Jesus) were secretly brought in to enslave us. ⁵We did not yield in submission to them for even a moment, so that the truth of the gospel might be preserved for you. ⁶Now it makes no difference to me who they were—God shows no partiality—but from those who were deemed influential (those whom I say were deemed influential) nothing was added to my [words]. ⁷But on the contrary, they saw that I had been entrusted with the gospel to the uncircumcised, just as Peter had been entrusted with the gospel to the circumcised ⁸(for he who worked through Peter for the mission to the circumcised worked through me also for the Gentiles). ⁹And when they perceived the grace that was given to me, James and Cephas and John, who were considered pillars, gave to me and Barnabas the right hand of fellowship, [deciding] that we should go to the Gentiles and they [should go] to the circumcised, ¹⁰except that they wanted us to be mindful of the poor—exactly what I was eager to do.

Paul Rebukes Peter

¹¹But when Cephas came to Antioch, I opposed him to his face because he stood condemned. ¹²For before certain men came from James, he had been eating with the Gentiles. But when they came, he drew back and separated himself, fearing the circumcision sect. ¹³And the rest of the Jews behaved hypocritically along with him, so that even Barnabas was led astray by their hypocrisy. ¹⁴But when I saw that they were not acting in step with the truth of the gospel, I said to Cephas in the presence of all of them, "If you, though a Jew, live like a Gentile and not like a Jew, how can you force the Gentiles to live like Jews?"

Justification by Faith, not Works

[15]By birth, we ourselves are Jews and not Gentile sinners. [16]Yet we know that a person is not justified by works of the law but through faith in Jesus Christ, so we also have believed in Christ Jesus, in order to be justified by faith in Christ, and not by works of the law, because no person will be justified by works of the law. [17]But if, in our endeavor to be justified in Christ, we ourselves were found to be sinners, is Christ then a minister of sin? May it never be so! [18]For if I rebuild what I tore down, then I prove myself to be a transgressor. [19]For through the law I died to the law that I might live to God. [20]I have been crucified with Christ. It is no longer I who live, but Christ who lives in me. The life I now live in the flesh I live by faith in the Son of God, who loved me and gave himself for me. [21]I do not nullify the grace of God, for if justification were through the law, then Christ died for no reason.

Chapter 3

[1]O foolish Galatians! Who has bewitched you? Jesus Christ was publicly portrayed as crucified before your very eyes. [2]Let me just ask you this: Did you receive the Spirit by works of the law, or by hearing with faith? [3]Are you so foolish? Having started out with the Spirit, will you reach maturity by the flesh? [4]Did you experience so many things in vain, if indeed it was in vain? [5]Does he who supplies the Spirit to you and works miracles among you do so by works of the law, or by hearing with faith, [6]just as Abraham "believed God, and it was reckoned to him as righteousness"?

[7]So realize that it is men of faith who are the sons of Abraham. [8]And the scripture, foreseeing that God would justify the Gentiles by faith, preached the good news to Abraham beforehand when it said, "In you all the nations shall be blessed." [9]So then, those who are men of faith are blessed along with Abraham, the faithful one.

Live by Faith

[10]For all who depend on works of the law are under a curse, for it is written, "Cursed be everyone who does not abide by all the things written in the Book of the law, and do them." [11]Now it is evident that no one is justified before God by the law, for "The righteous shall live by faith." [12]But the law does not rest on faith, for "The one who does them shall live by them." [13]Christ redeemed us from the curse of the law, having become a curse on our behalf–for it is written, "Cursed is everyone hanged on a tree"—[14]so that in Christ Jesus the blessing of Abraham might come to the Gentiles, so that, though faith, we might receive the Spirit that was promised.

¹⁵Brothers, humanly speaking, even with a man-made covenant, no one annuls or adds to it once it has been ratified. ¹⁶Now the promises were made to Abraham and to his offspring. It does not say, "And to *offsprings*," referring to many—but referring to one—"And to your *offspring*," who is Christ. ¹⁷This is what I mean: the law, which came 430 years afterward, does not nullify a covenant previously ratified by God, so as to make the promise void. ¹⁸For if the inheritance comes by the law, it is no longer based on a promise. Rather, God gave it to Abraham by a promise.

¹⁹Why then the law? It was added on because of transgressions, until that off-spring should come to those whom promise had been made to. Further, it was set up by an intermediary through angels. ²⁰Now, [having] an intermediary involves more than one [party], but God is one.

²¹Is the law then against the promises of God? Absolutely not! For if a life-giving law could have been given, then righteousness would indeed come by the law. ²²On the contrary, the scripture locked up everything under sin, so that the promise, by faith in Jesus Christ, might be given to those who believe.

²³Now before faith came, we were held captive under the law, kept under restraint until faith should be revealed. ²⁴So then, the law acted as our guardian until Christ came, that we might be justified by faith. ²⁵But with faith having come, we are no longer under a guardian, ²⁶for you are all children of God through faith in Christ Jesus. ²⁷For each of you who were baptized into Christ has put on Christ. ²⁸There is neither Jew nor Greek, there is neither slave nor free, there is neither male nor female: for you are all one in Christ Jesus. ²⁹And if you are of Christ, then you are Abraham's offspring: heirs according to promise.

Chapter 4

From Slaves to Heirs

¹I mean that the heir, as long as he is a child, is no different from a slave, even though he is the Lord of all [the estate]. ²But he is under guardians and trustees until the date appointed by the father. ³So it is with us: when we were children, we were slaves to the elementary principles of the world. ⁴But when the time was fully ripe, God sent forth his Son, born of woman, born under the law, ⁵to redeem those who were under the law, so that we might receive adoption as sons. ⁶And because you are sons, God has sent the Spirit of his Son into your hearts, crying, "Abba! Father!" ⁷So no longer are you a slave, but a son—and if a son, then an heir, through God.

⁸Formerly, when you did not know God, you served beings that are not gods by nature. ⁹But now that you have come to know God, or rather to be known by God, how can you turn back again to the weak and shabby elementary principles [of the world], to which you are wanting to be enslaved again? ¹⁰You have special observances for [some] days, and months, and occasions, and years! ¹¹I fear that I may have labored over you in vain.

Paul Begs the Brethren

¹²Brothers, I beg you to become as I am, for I also have become like you. You did me no wrong. ¹³You know that a sickness of the body caused me to preach the gospel to you the first time, ¹⁴and even though my physical [condition] was hard for you to endure, you did not despise me or throw me out, but received me as an angel of God, [even] as Christ Jesus. ¹⁵What has become of that blessing of yours? For I declare that, if possible, you would have gouged out your own eyes and given them to me. ¹⁶Then, have I become your enemy by telling you the truth? ¹⁷They make much of you, but not for a good purpose. They want to shut you out, so that you may make much of them. ¹⁸It is always good to be made much of for a good purpose, and not only when I am present with you. ¹⁹My little children, I am again in the anguish of childbirth with you until Christ is formed in you! ²⁰I long to be present with you now and to change my tone, for I am perplexed about you.

Two Women and Two Covenants

²¹Tell me, you who desire to be under the law, are you not paying attention to the law? ²²For it is written that Abraham had two sons, one by a slave woman and one by a free woman. ²³Now, the son of the slave was born according to the flesh, whereas the son of the free woman was born through promise. ²⁴Now this is an allegory: these women are two covenants. One is from Mount Sinai, bearing children for slavery; she is Hagar. ²⁵Now Hagar is Mount Sinai in Arabia and corresponds to the present Jerusalem, for she is in slavery with her children. ²⁶But the Jerusalem above is free: she is our mother. ²⁷For it is written, "Rejoice, O barren one who does not bear. Break forth and shout, you who are not in labor! For the children of the desolate one number more than the children of the one who has a husband." ²⁸Now you, brothers, like Isaac, are children of promise. ²⁹But just as before when the one born according to the flesh persecuted the one born according to the Spirit, so it is again now. ³⁰But what does the scripture say? "Drive out the slave woman and her son, for the son of the slave woman shall not inherit along with the son of the free woman." ³¹So, brothers, we are not children of the *slave* woman but of the *free* woman.

Chapter 5

Maintain Your Freedom

[1]For [the sake of] freedom Christ has set us free. Therefore, stand firm, and do not submit to a yoke of slavery again. [2]Listen! I, Paul, tell you that if you acquiesce to [the need for] circumcision, Christ will be of no advantage to you. [3]To every man who thus accepts circumcision I testify again that he is obligated to keep the whole law. [4]You have severed yourselves from Christ, you who would be justified by the law. You have fallen away from grace. [5]For by faith, through the Spirit we eagerly await the hope of righteousness. [6]For in Christ Jesus what matters is neither circumcision nor uncircumcision, but rather faith working through love.

[7]You were running the race well. Who has abruptly blocked you from obeying the truth? [8]This persuasion is not from the one who calls you. [9]A little leaven leavens the whole lump [of dough]. [10]I am confident in the Lord that you will have no other view [of this] than mine. And the one who is troubling you, whoever he is, will bear his penalty. [11]But if I, brothers, am still preaching circumcision, why am I still being persecuted? In that case the stumbling block of the cross has been removed. [12]I wish that those who unsettle you would [go the next step and just] castrate themselves! [13]For you were called to freedom, brothers. Only do not use your freedom as an opportunity for the flesh, but through love serve each other. [14]For the whole law is fulfilled in one saying, "You shall love your neighbor as yourself." [15]But if you keep on biting and devouring each other be careful that you are not consumed by one another.

Desires and Deeds of the Flesh

[16]So I say, walk by the Spirit, and you will not gratify the desires of the flesh. [17]For the desires of the flesh are against the Spirit, and the desires of the Spirit are against the flesh, for these oppose each other, which prevents you from doing what you want to do. [18]But if you are led by the Spirit you are not under the law. [19]Now the deeds of the flesh are obvious: fornication, impurity, sensuality, [20]idolatry, sorcery, hatred, strife, jealousy, raging, selfish rivalries, dissensions, divisiveness, [21]envy, murder, drunkenness, orgies, and other such things. I warn you, as I warned you before, that people who do such things will *not* inherit the kingdom of God.

Fruit of the Spirit

[22]But the fruit of the Spirit is love, joy, peace, patience, kindness, goodness, faithfulness, [23]gentleness, [and] self-control. No law stands opposed to such things.

²⁴And those who belong to Christ Jesus have crucified the flesh with its passions and lusts.

²⁵If we live by the Spirit, let us also march forward in line with the Spirit. ²⁶Let us not become conceited, provoking one another and envying one another.

Chapter 6

Restore the Fallen in Humility

¹Brothers, if a man has been snared by any transgression, you who are spiritual should restore him in a spirit of gentleness. Watch yourself so that you are not tempted as well. ²Bear one another's burdens; in doing so you fulfill the law of Christ. ³For if anyone thinks he is something, whereas [actually] he is nothing, he deceives himself. ⁴But let each one test his own work, and then his reason to boast will lie in himself alone and not in his neighbor. ⁵For each person will have to bear his own load.

Sow in the Spirit

⁶The one who is taught the Word must share all good things with the teacher. ⁷Do not be deceived: God is not mocked, for whatever a man sows, that will he reap also. ⁸For the one who sows to his own flesh will reap corruption from the flesh, whereas the one who sows to the Spirit will reap eternal life from the Spirit. ⁹And let us not grow weary in well-doing, for in due season we shall reap if we do not lose heart. ¹⁰So then, let us do good to everyone whenever we have the chance—especially to those who are of the household of faith.

Closing and Benediction

¹¹Notice what large letters I have used in writing to you with my own hand.

¹²It is those who want to make a good outward impression that would compel you to be circumcised, and only in order that they may not be persecuted for the cross of Christ. ¹³For even those who agree to circumcision do not keep the law themselves, but they desire to have you circumcised so that they may boast about your deeds in the flesh. ¹⁴But far be it from me to boast except in the cross of our Lord Jesus Christ, by which the world has been crucified to me, and I to the world. ¹⁵For what matters is neither circumcision nor uncircumcision, but a new creation.

¹⁶Peace and mercy be on all who walk by this principle, and on the Israel of God.

¹⁷From now on let no one give me grief, for my body has been branded with the marks of Jesus. ¹⁸May the grace of our Lord Jesus Christ be with your spirit, brothers. Amen.

EPHESIANS

Chapter 1

¹[From]: Paul, an apostle of Christ Jesus by the will of God,

To: the saints who are in Ephesus and are faithful in Christ Jesus:

²Grace to you and peace from God our Father and the Lord Jesus Christ.

Spiritual Blessings

³Blessed be God, the Father of our Lord Jesus Christ, who in Christ has blessed us with every spiritual blessing in the heavenly realms, ⁴since even before the foundation of the world he chose us in him, that we should be holy and blameless before him. ⁵In love he predestined us to be adopted as his sons through Jesus Christ, according to the purpose of his will, ⁶to the praise of his glorious grace, which in the Beloved he freely bestowed on us. ⁷We have redemption in him through his blood, the forgiveness of our sins, according to the riches of his grace, ⁸which he lavished on us. With completely wise perception, ⁹according to his intentions, he revealed the mystery of his will to us, which he demonstrated in Christ, ¹⁰as a plan to be put into action when the time was ripe, in order to bring together in him all things—things in heaven and things on earth.

¹¹According to the purpose of the One who works out all things according to the counsel of his will, we have an inheritance in him that we were predestined for: ¹²that we who first hoped in Christ are to live for the praise of his glory. ¹³Having heard the word of truth, the gospel of your salvation, and having believed in him, you were also sealed in him with the promised Holy Spirit, ¹⁴who is the down payment guarantee of our inheritance until we acquire possession of it, to the praise of his glory.

Prayer for Spiritual Wisdom

¹⁵For this reason, because I have heard of your faith in the Lord Jesus and your love toward all the saints, ¹⁶I do not stop giving thanks for you, remembering you in my prayers, ¹⁷that the God of our Lord Jesus Christ, the Father of glory, may give you a spirit of wisdom and of revelation in the knowledge of him. ¹⁸Having the eyes of your hearts enlightened, may you understand

what is the hope that he has called you to,

what are the riches of his glorious inheritance in the saints, [19]and what is the immeasurable greatness of his power in us believers,

according to the working of his tremendous power [20]that he accomplished in Christ when he raised him from the dead and seated him at his right hand in the heavenly realms, [21]far above all rule and authority and power and dominion, and above every name that is named, not only in this age but also in the one that is to come. [22]He has also put all things under his feet and presented him, the ruler over all things, to the church, [23]which is his body, the fullness of him who fills all things in all ways.

Chapter 2

Saved by Grace Through Faith

[1]Now, at one time you were dead due to the trespasses and sins [2]that you used to live in, going along with the course of this world, following the prince of the power of the air, the spirit that is now at work in the sons of disobedience. [3]All of us used to live among them in the passions of our flesh, fulfilling the desires of body and mind, and so by nature we were children of wrath, like the rest [of mankind]. [4]But God, who is rich in mercy, out of the great love that he loved us with, [5]even when we were dead due to our trespasses, made us alive in union with Christ. By grace you have been saved. [6]And he raised us up with him, and in Christ Jesus he seated us in the heavenly realms with him, [7]so that in the ages to come he might kindly display the immeasurable riches of his grace toward us in Christ Jesus. [8]For by grace you have been saved through faith. And this is not of your own action; it is a gift from God, [9]not based on deeds, thus no one can boast. [10]For we are his workmanship, created in Christ Jesus for good deeds, which God had ordained previously, so that we would walk in them.

Oneness in Christ

[11]Therefore, remember that at one time you Gentiles by birth—referred to as "the uncircumcision" by those who call themselves "the circumcised", which is done to the body by human hands—[12]remember that at that time you were separated from Christ, left outside the house of Israel, and foreigners to the covenants of promise, having no hope, and without God in this world. [13]But now in Christ Jesus you who once were far off have been brought near though Christ's [shed] blood. [14]For he himself is our peace; he has made both of us one and in his flesh has broken down the dividing wall of hostility, [15]by abolishing in his flesh the legal system of decreed commandments, so that in himself he might create one new man in place of the two, so making peace, [16]and that he might reconcile us both to

God in one body through the cross, having thereby wiped out the hostility. [17]And he came and preached peace to you who were far off and peace to those who were near, [18]for through him both of us have access to the Father in one Spirit. [19]So then you are no longer strangers and sojourners, but you are fellow citizens with the saints as well as members of the household of God, [20]built on the foundation of the apostles and prophets, with Christ Jesus himself as the cornerstone, [21]in whom the whole structure being joined together grows into a holy temple in the Lord. [22]In him you are also being built together into a dwelling place of God in the Spirit.

Chapter 3

Revelation of the Mystery

[1]For this reason I, Paul, [am] a prisoner for Christ Jesus for the sake of you Gentiles, [2]if indeed you have heard about the commission of God's grace that was given to me for you, [3]and how the mystery was made known to me through [divine] revelation, which I have briefly written about. [4]Reading this, you are able to perceive my insight into the mystery of Christ, [5]which was not made known to the sons of men in other generations as the Spirit has now revealed it to his holy apostles and prophets; [6]that is, how through the gospel the Gentiles have become fellow heirs, members of the same body, and partakers of the promise in Christ Jesus.

[7]According to the gift of God's grace that was given to me by the working of his power, I was made a minister of this gospel. [8]Though I be the very least of all the saints, this grace was given to me, to bring the good news of the infinite treasure of Christ to the Gentiles, [9]and to enlighten everyone about the plan of the mystery, which had been kept hidden for ages by God (who created everything), [10]so that the church might now make known the multifaceted wisdom of God to the rulers and authorities in the heavenly realms. [11]This was [done] for the eternal purpose that he has now brought to pass in Christ Jesus our Lord. [12]Through our faith in him, we have the boldness and confidence to approach him. [13]So, I beg you not to be disheartened over what I am suffering for you, which is your glory.

Prayer for Strength

[14]For this reason I kneel before the Father, [15]from whom every family lineage in heaven and on earth derives its name, [16]that according to the riches of his glory he may grant you to be strengthened in the inner man with power through his Spirit, [17]and that Christ may dwell in your hearts through faith, so that then you, along with the saints, being rooted and grounded in love, [18]may have the power to

fully grasp its breadth and length and height and depth, [19]and knowing the love of Christ, which surpasses knowledge, that you may be completely filled with all the fullness of God.

> [20]*Now to him who is able*
> *to do far more abundantly than all that we ask or think,*
> *according to the power at work within us–*
> [21]*to him be glory in the church and in Christ Jesus*
> *throughout all generations, forever and ever.*
> *Amen.*

Chapter 4

Spiritual Living

[1]Therefore I, a prisoner for the Lord, beg you to lead a life worthy of the calling you have been called to, [2]with all humility and gentleness, with patience, bearing with one another in love, [3]being eager to maintain the unity of the Spirit in the bond of peace. [4]There is one body and one Spirit, just as you were called to the one hope that belongs to your call, [5]one Lord, one faith, one baptism, [6]one God and Father of us all, who is over all and through all and in all. [7]But grace was given to each of us according to the measure of Christ's gift. [8]Therefore it is said, "When he ascended on high he led a host of captives, and he gave gifts to [his] people." [9](In saying, "He ascended," what does it mean but that he had also descended into the lower parts of the earth? [10]He who descended is he who also ascended far above all the heavens, that he might complete everything.)

[11]Now, he gave some to be apostles, some to be prophets, some to be evangelists, and some pastors and teachers [12]for equipping the saints for the work of ministry for building up the body of Christ, [13]until we all attain to the unity of the faith and of the knowledge of the Son of God, to mature manhood, to the measure of the stature of the completeness of Christ, [14]so that we may no longer be children, wildly tossed and blown around by every wind of doctrine, by the cunning of men, by their craftiness in deceitful schemes. [15]Rather, speaking the truth in love, we are to grow up in every way into him who is the head, [that is,] into Christ. [16]He causes the whole body to grow and build itself up in love when each part, joined and fitted together by every joint that it is supplied with, is working properly.

[17]Now I state this and declare in the Lord: you must no longer live like the Gentiles, in the futility of their minds. [18]In their understanding they are darkened, alienated from the life of God because of the ignorance that lies in them, due to their hardness of heart. [19]They have become callous and have given themselves up

to sensuality, eagerly desiring to practice every kind of impurity. [20]But that is not the way you learned [the ways of] Christ, [21]assuming that you have heard about him and were taught in him, since truth is in Jesus. [22]Take off your old nature, which belongs to your former lifestyle and is corrupt due to its deceitful desires, [23]and be renewed in the spirit of your minds. [24]Put on the new nature, created after the likeness of God in true righteousness and holiness.

Kind and Truthful Speech

[25]Therefore, having set aside falseness, let everyone speak the truth with his neighbor, for we are members one of another. [26]Be angry, but do not sin. Do not let the sun go down on your anger [27]and give no opportunity to the devil. [28]The thief should no longer steal, but rather he should labor, doing honest work with his own hands, so that he may be able to share with someone in need. [29]Do not allow corrupt speech to come out of your mouths, but only such speech that is good for building up, as is fitting to the moment, that it may bring grace to those are listening.

[30]And do not grieve the Holy Spirit of God, who has sealed you for the day of redemption. [31]Let all bitterness and wrath and anger and clamor and slander be put away from you, along with all malice. [32]Be kind to one another, tenderhearted, forgiving one another, as God forgave you in Christ.

Chapter 5

[1]Therefore be imitators of God, as beloved children, [2]and live a life of love, as Christ loved us and gave himself up for us, a fragrant offering and sacrifice to God.

Walk in the Light

[3]But as is proper among saints, sexual immorality and all forms of impurity or covetousness should not even be mentioned in relation to you. [4]Let there be no filthiness, nor silly talk, nor coarse jesting, which are not fitting, but instead let there be thanksgiving. [5]For you can be certain of this: that everyone who is sexually immoral, or is greedy (that is, who idolizes things), has no inheritance in the kingdom of Christ and of God. [6]Let no one deceive you with empty talk, for because of these things, the wrath of God is coming on the sons of disobedience. [7]Therefore do not enter into partnerships with them, [8]for once you were darkness, but now in the Lord you are light. So, walk as children of light— [9]for light produces all that is good and right and true—[10]discerning what pleases the Lord. [11]Take no part in the futile deeds of darkness, but instead expose them. [12]For even speaking of the things that are done in secret is shameful. [13]But when anything is

exposed by the light it becomes visible, for anything that becomes visible is light. [14]Therefore it is said, "Awake, O sleeper, and arise from the dead, and Christ shall shine on you."

[15]Carefully examine then how you walk, not as unwise men but as wise, [16]making the best use of your time, because the days are [filled with] evil. [17]Therefore do not be foolish but rather figure out what the Lord's will is. [18]And do not get drunk with wine—which is debauchery—but instead be continually filled with the Spirit, [19]addressing one another in psalms and hymns and spiritual songs, singing and making melody to the Lord with all your heart, [20]always giving thanks to God the Father for everything, in the name of our Lord Jesus Christ, [21][and] submitting to one another out of reverence for Christ.

Submission and Love in Marriage

[22]Wives, submit to your husbands, as you would to the Lord, [23]for the husband is the head of the wife as Christ is the head of the church, his body; and he himself is its Savior. [24]So then, as the church submits to Christ, in the same way wives also should submit in everything to their husbands.

[25]Husbands, love your wives, just as Christ also loved the church and gave himself up for her, [26]so that he might her make her holy, having cleansed her by the washing of water with the word. [27]He did so that he might present the church to himself in splendor, without spot or wrinkle or any such thing, that she might be holy and without blemish. [28]Likewise husbands must love their wives as their own bodies. The man who loves his wife loves himself, [29]because a man does not despise his own flesh, but nourishes and cherishes it, as Christ does the church, [30]because we are members of his body. [31]"For this reason a man shall leave his father and mother and be fitted together to his wife, and the two shall become one flesh." [32]This mystery is a profound one, and I am implying a reference to Christ and the church. [33]Nevertheless, each one of you should love his wife as himself, and the wife should respect her husband.

Chapter 6

Submission and Love in Parenting

[1]Children, obey your parents in the Lord, for this is right. [2]"Honor your father and mother" is the first commandment with an added promise: [3]"that things may go well with you and that you may live long on the earth." [4]Fathers, do not provoke your children to anger, but bring them up in the discipline and instruction of the Lord.

Submission and Love in Work

[5]Slaves, be obedient to your human masters, with fear and trembling, with a sincere heart, as you would to Christ, [6]not in the way of eye-service, as people-pleasers, but as servants of Christ, doing the will of God from the heart, [7]rendering service with a good will as to the Lord and not to men, [8]knowing that whatever good someone (slave or free) does, he will receive the same from the Lord. [9]Masters, do the same for them and refrain from making threats, knowing that he who is both their Master and yours is in heaven, and no partiality exists with him.

Put on the Whole Armor

[10]Finally, be strong in the Lord and in the power of his might. [11]Put on the whole armor of God, so that you may be able to stand against the devil's schemes. [12]For we do not wrestle against flesh and blood, but against the rulers, against the authorities, against the worldly forces ruling over this present darkness, against the spiritual forces of wickedness in the heavenly realms. [13]Therefore, make use of the whole armor of God, so that you may be able to withstand in bad times, and to stand firm, having completed everything. [14]Therefore, stand, having put on the belt of truth, and the breastplate of righteousness, [15]and having prepared yourselves with the gospel of peace as shoes for your feet. [16]In all situations, take the shield of faith, with which you can extinguish all the flaming darts of the evil one, [17]and take the helmet of salvation, and the sword of the Spirit, which is the word of God.

[18]Pray in the Spirit at all times, with prayers and requests to God for help. For that [goal], keep alert with all perseverance, making requests to God on behalf of all the saints, [19]and also for me, that the right words may be given to me when I open my mouth to boldly proclaim the mystery of the gospel, [20]for which I am an ambassador in chains, so that I may declare it boldly, as I ought to speak.

Final Messages

[21]Now, Tychicus, the beloved brother and faithful minister in the Lord, will tell you everything so that you also may know how I am and what I am doing. [22]I have sent him to you for this very purpose, so that you may know how we are, and that he may encourage your hearts.

Benediction

[23]Peace be to the brothers, and love with faith, from God the Father and the Lord Jesus Christ. [24]Grace be with all who love our Lord Jesus Christ with an undying love.

300

PHILIPPIANS

Chapter 1

[From]: Paul and Timothy, servants of Christ Jesus,

To: All the saints in Christ Jesus who are in Philippi, along with the overseers and deacons:

[2]Grace to you and peace from God our Father and from the Lord Jesus Christ.

Thanksgiving and Prayer

[3]I thank my God every time I think of you, [4]and always—every time I pray for you all—offer prayers with joy [5]because of your partnership in the work of the gospel from the beginning until now. [6]And I remain convinced of this same thing: that he who has begun a good work in you will see it through to completion until the day of Christ Jesus. [7]Just as it is right for me to think of you all in this way, because I have you in my heart, so too you are fellow partakers in grace with me, both while I am in bonds, and while I am in the defense and confirmation of the gospel. [8]For as God is my witness, how greatly I long for you all, in the compassion of Christ Jesus. [9]And this I pray: that your love may abound more and more, in knowledge and in all judgment [10]so that you may knowingly choose what is excellent, and so that you will be found pure and blameless on the day of Christ, [11]being filled with the fruits of righteousness, which are from Jesus Christ to the glory and praise of God.

[12]But, brothers, I want you to know that the things that happened to me have turned out to be for the groundbreaking furtherance of the gospel, [13]so that it may become known in all the palace guard and everywhere else that I am in bonds [for the sake] of Christ, [14]and that most of the brothers in the Lord, gaining confidence by understanding why I am imprisoned, may preach the Word more fearlessly.

[15]Some indeed are proclaiming Christ out of envy and a striving for self-promotion, but some others are [doing so] from good will. [16][That first group] preaches Christ out of contention, not out of sincerity, thinking that they will add affliction to my bondage. [17]But, the others preach out of love, knowing that my purpose is the defense of the gospel. [18]What of it? Regardless, Christ is preached in every way, whether in pretense or in truth, and I do rejoice in that. And I will keep rejoicing, [19]because for me, I know that through your prayers and the provision of the spirit of Jesus Christ this shall result in deliverance.

²⁰It is my earnest desire and eager expectation that I shall be ashamed in nothing, but rather that in all boldness, now and always, Christ shall be magnified in my body, whether it be by life or by death. ²¹For to me, to go on living is Christ, and to die is gain. ²²But if I go on living in the flesh this means fruitful labor on my part, and I cannot say which I would choose. ²³For I am pressed hard between the two: having the desire to depart, and to be with Christ is far, far better, ²⁴but for your sake, it is more important for me to remain in the flesh. ²⁵And being convinced of this, I know that I am to stay—and keep on staying—with you all, for the sake of your progress and joy in the faith, ²⁶so that through my being with you again your rejoicing in Christ Jesus for me may abound even more. ²⁷Only, conduct yourselves in a manner worthy of the gospel of Christ, so that, whether having come to see you or being away, I might hear of how you are doing: that you are standing firm in one spirit, and with one mind are striving together for the faith of the gospel. ²⁸Now, not being terrified by your opponents in anything will show them that they shall be destroyed, but that you shall be saved. And this [is] from God, ²⁹because you have been given the privilege to not only believe on Christ, but also to suffer for his sake, ³⁰as you have seen me doing, and now hear that I am still doing.

Chapter 2

Christ's Humility

¹So then, if there be any encouragement in Christ, if any loving comfort, if any fellowship of the Spirit, if any heart-felt compassion, ²then complete my joy– that you might be like-minded, having the same love, being of one accord and one mind. ³Let nothing be done out of contention or vainglory, but in humility let each man esteem others above himself. ⁴Let each man consider not only his own affairs, but also the affairs of others.

> ⁵*For let this mindset be in you,*
> *which also was in Christ Jesus,*
> ⁶*who, being in the form and nature of God,*
> *did not consider being equal with God something to cling to,*
> ⁷*but rather emptied himself,*
> *having taken on the form of a slave,*
> *and was born in the likeness of men.*
> ⁸*And having been found in the figure of a man,*
> *He humbled himself, having become obedient to death–*
> *even death on a cross.*
> ⁹*For this reason, God also highly exalted him*

and granted him a name that is above all names,
[10]that at the name of Jesus every knee should bow,
in heaven, and on earth, and under the earth,
[11]and every tongue confess that Jesus Christ is Lord,
to the glory of God the Father.

[12]For this reason, my beloved, as you have always obeyed in my presence, do so even much more now in my absence: work out your own salvation with fear and trembling, [13]for God is working in you, that you would both desire and do what pleases him.

Be a Light in the World

[14]Do everything without grumbling or arguing, [15]so that you may become blameless and pure, children of God, faultless in the midst of a crooked and perverse generation, among whom you appear as lights in the world, [16]as you hold on to the word of life, so that I may rejoice in the day of Christ that I did not run or labor in vain. [17]But even if I am to be poured out like a drink offering in sacrificial service of your faith, then I celebrate and rejoice with you all. [18]In the same way, you are to celebrate and rejoice with me.

Fellow Workers: Timothy and Epaphroditus

[19]But I trust in the Lord Jesus that soon I will be able to send Timothy to you so that I may rest assured once I know how things are going for you. [20]For I have no one else who is likeminded and genuinely cares about what state you are in [21]because they all are concerned about their own affairs, and not the things of Jesus Christ. [22]But you know how [Timothy] proved himself—how he, like son with a father, has toiled with me for the sake of the gospel. [23]Therefore I hope to send him as soon as I see how things turn out for me. [24]But, I am persuaded in the Lord that I myself shall come soon, also.

[25]But I deemed it necessary to send you Epaphroditus, *my* brother, and fellow-worker, and fellow soldier, but *your* messenger, and the one who ministered to my needs. [26]For he longed to see you all and was very heavy-hearted because you heard that he was sick. [27]For indeed he was sick, deathly sick, but God had mercy on him– and not only on him but on me, too, so that I would not endure sorrow after sorrow. [28]Therefore I all the more diligently did send him so that by seeing him again you might rejoice, which would also make me less sorrowful. [29]Therefore receive him in the Lord with all joy, and hold such a man in honor, [30]for he disregarded his own safety and risked death for the sake of the work of Christ in order to meet those needs of mine that you could not meet.

Chapter 3

Righteousness Comes Through Faith

[1]Finally, my brothers, rejoice in the Lord. I do not mind writing the same things to you again, and it is for your safety.

[2]Beware of evildoers—those dogs—and of the mutilation of the body. [3]For we who worship God in spirit, and rejoice in Christ, and do not trust in the flesh, are the [true] circumcision—

[4]though I could trust in the flesh, and I have more reason to do so than any other man: [5]circumcised on the eighth day, of the nation of Israel, of the tribe of Benjamin, a Hebrew of Hebrews; concerning the law, a Pharisee; [6]concerning zeal, a persecutor of the church; as to the righteousness that is in the law, having become blameless. [7]But whatever things that I had counted as profitable, I have come to count as loss on account of Christ, [8]and I consider all things to be loss in exchange for the far greater gain of knowing Jesus Christ my Lord, for whom I suffered the loss of all things, and consider them to be vile excrement, so that I might gain Christ, [9]and be found in him, not having my own righteousness that is of the law, but that which is of faith in Christ, the righteousness that is of God by faith, [10]in order to know him and the power of his resurrection, and the fellowship of his sufferings, being conformed to his death, [11]so that somehow I might attain the resurrection from the dead.

Pressing On Toward the Goal

[12]Not that I have already obtained this, or have already been perfected, but I keep pressing on so that I might take hold of it as Christ Jesus has also taken hold of me. [13]Brothers, I do not figure that I have attained this. But [this] one thing [I do]: not being constrained by what lies in the past, and straining forward to what is to come, [14]I press on toward the finish line for the prize of the high calling of God in Christ Jesus. [15]Therefore, we who are mature should have this kind of mindset, and if you think otherwise, God will reveal it to you. [16]Nevertheless, let us stay in step with what we have learned, and be like-minded.

[17]Brothers, imitate me in unison, and study those who walk in such a way, so that in us you may have a model. [18]For I have often told you, and now do so again in tears, about many who conduct themselves as enemies of the cross of Christ. [19]Their end is destruction, their god is their appetite, their glory is their shame, and they set their hearts on earthly things. [20]For our citizenship lies in heaven, from which we are also awaiting a savior, the Lord Jesus Christ [21]who will transform our weak earthly body, so that it may be made like his glorious body,

through the power by which he is able to subdue all things to himself. ^{4:1}Therefore, my brothers whom I dearly love and long for—my joy and my crown—stand fast in the Lord in such a way, beloved ones.

Chapter 4

Encouragement Towards Godliness

²I beg Euodia and I beg Syntyche to be of the same mind in the Lord. ³And, true partner, I also beg you to assist these women who labored on behalf of the gospel with me, and also with Clement, and the rest of my fellow workers whose names are in the Book of Life. ⁴Rejoice in the Lord always; again, I say rejoice. ⁵Let your fairness be known to everyone. The Lord is near. ⁶Do not be anxious about anything, but in everything by prayer and petition, make your requests known to God with thanksgiving. ⁷And the peace of God, which surpasses all understanding, shall guard your hearts and thoughts in Christ Jesus.

⁸Finally, brothers, whatever is true, whatever is honorable, whatever is just, whatever is pure, whatever is lovely, whatever is of good report—should there be anything virtuous or anything praiseworthy–focus your minds on these things. ⁹Also keep practicing the things that you learned and received and heard and saw in me, and the God of peace shall be with you.

¹⁰But, I rejoiced in the Lord greatly that at last now you have started thinking about me again. Though you had thought of me, you did not have the chance to show it. ¹¹Not that I am speaking out of great need, for I have learned the secret of being content in whatever circumstances I am in. ¹²And I know how to be brought low, and to how to live in plenty. In everything and in all ways I have learned both to be full and to be hungry, both to abound and to be in need. ¹³I am able to do all things through Christ who empowers me.

God Provides

¹⁴Nevertheless, you did well, taking part in my tribulation. ¹⁵Now you Philippians also know that when I came out of Macedonia, at the beginning of the spread of the gospel, no church except you shared the receiving and giving with me. ¹⁶For time and time again you even sent me things to meet my needs while I was in Thessalonica. ¹⁷Not that I am doing this to get a gift, but rather I am working so that gains will be credited to your account. ¹⁸Nonetheless, I have everything that I need, and more. I am full, having received from Epaphroditus those things from you–a sweet-smelling sacrifice, acceptable and pleasing to God. ¹⁹With his riches in glory in Christ Jesus, my God will meet all your needs. ²⁰So, glory be to God and our Father forever and ever, Amen.

Final Greetings.

[21]Greet every saint in Christ Jesus. The brothers who are with me send their greetings to you. [22]All the saints, especially the ones from Caesar's household, [also] send their greetings to you.

Benediction

[23]May the grace of the Lord Jesus Christ be with your spirit.

COLOSSIANS

Chapter 1

¹[From]: Paul, an apostle of Christ Jesus by the will of God,

and [from] Timothy our brother,

²To: The holy and faithful brothers in Colossae:

Grace and peace be to you from God our father.

Prayer for the Colossian Saints

³We always give thanks to God the Father of our Lord Jesus Christ whenever we pray for you, ⁴because we have heard of your faith in Christ Jesus and of the love that you show to all the saints, ⁵the faith and love [that spring] from the assured hope of what is stored up for you in heaven. You heard about this hope in the truthful message, the gospel ⁶that has come to you. All over the world this gospel is bearing fruit and growing, just as it has been doing among you since the day when you heard it and comprehended the grace of God truthfully. ⁷You learned it from Epaphras, our beloved fellow servant, who is a faithful minister of Christ for your sake, and ⁸he has told us about your love in the Spirit.

⁹Therefore, since the day when we heard of it we have not stopped praying for you, asking that you might be filled with the knowledge of his will in all spiritual wisdom and understanding, ¹⁰so as to conduct yourselves in a manner worthy of the Lord:

- ➤ being fully pleasing to him,
- ➤ bearing fruit in every good deed,
- ➤ growing in the knowledge of God,
- ➤ ¹¹being strengthened with all power according to his glorious might [so that you will have] complete endurance and joyful patience,
- ➤ ¹²and giving thanks to the Father.

He has made you fit to share in the inheritance of the saints in [the realm of] light, and ¹³has delivered you from the realm of darkness and has transferred you into the kingdom of his beloved Son, ¹⁴ in whom we have redemption [in his blood], that is, the forgiveness of sins.

Christ's Preeminence

[15]He is the image of the invisible God, the firstborn of all creation. [16]For all things were created through him, both in heaven and on earth, both the visible and the invisible— whether thrones or governments, or rulers or authorities—all things have been created by him and for him. [17]Indeed he has existed before everything else, and in him all things hold together. [18]And he is the head of the body, the church. He is the beginning, the firstborn from among the dead, so that in all things he might be preeminent. [19]For God was pleased to have his full nature dwell in him, [20]and to reconcile all things, both on earth and in heaven, to himself through him, having made peace by the blood of his cross. [21]In the past you were once alienated, even hostile [toward God] in your minds, by virtue of your wicked deeds. [22]But now he has reconciled you by the death of his fleshly body in order to present you holy in his sight, blameless and free from accusation, [23]if indeed you do continue in your faith, established and steadfast, not drifting away from the hope offered in the gospel that you have heard. [This gospel] was proclaimed to everyone under heaven, and I, Paul, have become a minister of it.

Paul's Concern for the Church

[24]Now on your behalf, I rejoice in sufferings, and I take on in my own body what suffering still remains in regard to Christ's afflictions for the sake of his body, meaning the church. [25]I have become its minister through the commission that God gave me to show you, in its fulness, the word of God—[26]the mystery that has been kept hidden for ages and generations, but now is revealed to the saints. [27]God has chosen to make known among the Gentiles the glorious riches of this mystery, which is Christ in you, the hope of glory. [28]We proclaim him, warning and teaching everyone with all wisdom, so that we may present everyone mature in Christ. [29]I labor for this goal, striving with all the energy that he so powerfully works within me.

Chapter 2

[1]For I want you to know how greatly I strive for you, and for those at Laodicea, and for all who have not seen me face to face, [2]that their hearts may be encouraged being knit together in love, so [they may have] all the riches of assured understanding and the knowledge of God's mystery, which is Christ, [3]in whom are hidden all the treasures of wisdom and knowledge. [4]I say this so that no one may delude you with clever arguments.

[5]For though I am absent in body, yet I am with you in spirit, rejoicing to see your orderliness and the steadfastness of your faith in Christ. [6]Therefore, as you

received Christ Jesus the Lord, so live in him, [7]rooted and built up in him and established in the faith, just as you have been taught, overflowing with thankfulness.

[8]Make sure that no one ensnares you through philosophy and vain deceit, according to men's traditions, or according to the elementary principles of the universe, rather than according to Christ. [9]For the whole fullness of deity dwells in bodily form in him, [10]and you have been made complete in him. He is the head of all rule and authority. [11]You were also circumcised in him with a circumcision not done with hands but by laying aside the fleshly body through the circumcision [that comes] from Christ. [12]You were buried with him in baptism, in which you were also raised with him through faith in the powerful acts of God, who raised him from the dead. [13]And he made you, who were dead in your trespasses and the uncircumcision of your flesh, alive together with him. Having forgiven us all our trespasses, [14]he canceled the record of debt, along with its legal demands, which stood against us, and laid it aside, nailing it to the cross. [15]He disarmed the rulers and authorities, and made a public spectacle of them, triumphing over them in him.

Let No One Judge You

[16]Therefore, let no one pass judgment on you in matters of food and drink, or regarding a holiday, or a new moon event, or a Sabbath. [17]These are only a shadow of what is to come, but the substantial [reality lies in] Christ. [18]Let no one judge you unworthy by requiring self-abasement and the worship of angels. Such a one claiming to have had visions is conceited without reason due to [having] a sensuous mind. [19]He is not connected to [Christ], the Head, from whom the whole body, nourished and joined together through its joints and ligaments, grows as God causes it to grow.

[20]If with Christ you died to the world's value system, why are still living in a worldly way? Why, according to human ideas and teachings, do you submit to regulations such as: [21]"Do not handle, Do not taste, Do not touch."? [22]They refer to things that all perish as they are used. [23]Indeed, these things—self-abasement and severity to the body—seem like wisdom in promoting self-made religions but they are ineffectual in [truly controlling] the cravings of the flesh.

Chapter 3

Putting on the New Man

[1]So then, since you have been raised with Christ, seek the things that are above, where Christ is, seated at the right hand of God. [2]Keep focusing your minds on

things that are above, not on things that are on earth. ³For you have died, and now your life lies hidden with Christ in God. ⁴When Christ, who is your life, appears, then you also will appear with him in glory. ⁵Therefore, put to death the earthly part of you: sexual immorality, impurity, passion, evil desire, and covetousness, which amounts to idolatry. ⁶The wrath of God is coming because of these things. ⁷You once walked in these ways when you were living in them. ⁸But now you must eliminate all these: anger, wrath, malice, slander, and speaking obscenities. ⁹Do not lie to each other, seeing that you have put off the old nature with its practices ¹⁰and have put on the new nature, which is being renewed in knowledge in the likeness of its creator. ¹¹Here there is no longer Greek and Jew, circumcised and uncircumcised, barbarian and Scythian, slave and free man—rather Christ is all, and is in all.

¹²So then, as God's chosen ones who are holy and beloved, put on hearts [full] of compassion, kindness, humility, meekness, and patience. ¹³Bear with one another and, if one has a complaint against another, forgive each other. As the Lord has forgiven you, so must you do as well. ¹⁴And above all these things, put on love, which binds together everything in perfect harmony. ¹⁵And let the peace of Christ rule in your hearts, into which you were truly called in one body. And be thankful. ¹⁶Let the word of Christ dwell richly in you, instructing and advising one another wisely, and singing psalms and hymns and spiritual songs to God with thankfulness in your hearts. ¹⁷And whatever you do, in word or deed, do everything in the name of the Lord Jesus, giving thanks to God the Father through him.

Christian Family Living

¹⁸Wives, submit to your husbands, as is fitting in the Lord. ¹⁹Husbands, love your wives, and do not treat them harshly. ²⁰Children, obey your parents in everything, for this pleases the Lord. ²¹Fathers, do not provoke your children, so that they will not become discouraged. ²²Slaves, in everything obey those who are your earthly masters, not with eye-service to please people, but with sincerity of heart, fearing the Lord. ²³Whatever your task, work heartily, as serving the Lord and not men, ²⁴knowing that you will receive the inheritance from the Lord as your reward. You are serving the Lord Christ. ²⁵For the wrongdoer will be paid back for the wrong he has done, and no partiality exists. ⁴·¹Masters, treat your slaves justly and fairly, keeping in mind that in heaven you also have a Master.

Chapter 4

Further Commandments

4:2As you pray continually, stay vigilant, and thankful. 3And meanwhile pray for us also, that God may open up a door for the word, for us to declare the mystery of Christ, because of which I am in prison. 4Pray that I may make it clear, as I should speak. 5Interact with those outside [the faith] wisely, making the best use of the opportunity. 6Let your speech always be gracious, seasoned with salt, so that you may know how you should respond to each person.

Final Greetings

7Tychicus will tell you all things concerning me. He is a beloved brother and faithful minister and fellow servant in the Lord. 8I have sent him to you for this very purpose, that you may know things about us and that he may encourage your hearts. 9And Onesimus, the faithful and beloved brother, who is one of you, [is] with him. They will tell you about everything that has happened here.

10Aristarchus my fellow prisoner greets you, along with Mark the cousin of Barnabas (You have received instructions about him; do welcome him if he comes to you), 11and Jesus who is called Justus. Of those who work along with me for the kingdom of God, these are the only men from the Circumcision [Sect], and they have been a comfort to me. 12Epaphras, who is one of you, a servant of Christ Jesus, greets you, always contending earnestly in his prayers for your sake, that you may stand mature and in total assurance in all the will of God. 13For I can attest that he has worked hard for you and for those in Laodicea and in Hierapolis. 14The beloved physician Luke and Demas greet you. 15Give my greetings to the brothers at Laodicea, and to Nympha and the congregation in her house. 16And when this letter has been read among you, have it read also in the church of the Laodiceans, and see that you also read the letter from Laodicea. 17And tell Archippus, "See to it that you fulfill the ministry that you have received in the Lord."

Closing

18I, Paul, write this greeting with my own hand. Be mindful of my chains. Grace be with you.

I THESSALONIANS

Chapter 1

[From]: Paul and Silvanus and Timothy,

To: The church of the Thessalonians in God the Father and the Lord Jesus Christ:

Grace to you and peace.

The Faith of the Brothers

[2]We always give thanks to God for all of you, mentioning you in our prayers constantly, [3]as we are remembering before our God and Father your work of faith and your labor of love and your steadfastness of hope in our Lord Jesus Christ. [4]We know that you, brothers beloved by God, have been chosen by God, [5]because our gospel came to you not only in word, but also in power and in the Holy Spirit and with deep conviction. You know how we proved ourselves for your sake. [6]You became imitators of us and of the Lord because you welcomed the word, in spite of a great deal of suffering, with joy from the Holy Spirit, [7]so that you became an example to all the believers in Macedonia and Achaia. [8]For not only have you sounded forth the word of the Lord in Macedonia and Achaia, but also your faith has spread everywhere, so that we have no need to comment. [9]For [people] are reporting how you received us, and how you turned away from idols toward God, to serve the living and true God, [10]and to await his Son from heaven, whom he raised from the dead—Jesus, who rescues us from the coming wrath.

Chapter 2

Paul Explains his Ministry

[1]For, brothers, you yourselves know that our visit to you was not in vain. [2]On the contrary, though having previously suffered and been mistreated in Phillipi (as you know), nonetheless because of our God we had the boldness to speak the gospel of God to you in the midst of much opposition. [3]For this appeal from us does not come from error, nor from impure motives, nor from deceitfulness, [4]but since we were approved by God to be entrusted with the gospel, we speak this way, not to please man, but to please God, who examines our heart motives. [5]For we did not come with flattering words, nor as a disguise for reed—God is witness of this—[6]nor seeking praise from people, neither from you nor from others, though

as apostles of Christ we could have made demands. [7]We treated you gently like a nursing mother caring for her children. [8]So, being greatly fond of you, we were pleased to share with you not only the gospel of God but also our very own selves, because you had become so precious to us.

[9]For, brothers, you remember our labor and toil: we worked night and day so as not to be a financial burden to any of you while we were proclaiming the gospel of God to you. [10]You are witnesses, and God is as well, to how our conduct toward you believers was holy and righteous and blameless. [11]For you know how, like a father with his own children, [12]we advised and encouraged you and commanded you to walk in a manner worthy of God who calls you into his own kingdom and glory.

[13]In addition, we continually thank God that when you received the word of God that you heard from us, you embraced it not as the word of men, but what it truly is: the word of God, which is at work in you believers. [14]For you, brothers, have started to mimic the churches of God in Christ Jesus that are in Judea, in that you have suffered the same treatment from your own countrymen as they have from the Jews [15]who killed both the Lord Jesus and the prophets. They drove us out, and they displease God, and form a blockade against all mankind [16]by hindering us from informing the Gentiles so that they might be saved. Thus, they are always full of their own sins. Yet God's wrath has fallen on them for all time!

[17]Now then, brothers, ever since we were torn away from you (for a short while, in person but not in heart) we have been trying even harder to see you face to face. [18]We wanted to come to you–I, Paul, especially, repeatedly wanted to come but Satan prevented us. [19]For, what is our hope or joy or crown of boasting before our Lord Jesus at his coming? Is it not you? [20]You are our pride and joy!

Chapter 3

[1]So when we could not stand it any longer, we were content to be left behind alone at Athens [2]and we sent Timothy, our brother, minister of God, and fellow worker in the gospel of Christ, to establish and encourage you concerning your faith, [3]so that no one would be set back by these afflictions. You yourselves know that we are appointed to this work. [4]For truly when we were there with you, we predicted to you then that we would suffer affliction; and so it has happened, as you know. [5]Therefore, when I could no long endure not knowing, I made an inquiry about your faithfulness, hoping that the tempter had not tempted you, making our labor in vain.

Timothy's Report

[6]Well, now Timothy has come from you to us and has brought us a good report about your faithfulness and love, and how you always remember us fondly, and how you are longing to see us, as we are also longing to see you. [7]Therefore, brothers, in all our troubles and sufferings, your faithfulness has been a great comfort to us, [8]because now we feel alive [again, knowing] you stand firmly in the Lord. [9]For, what thanks can we give to God again for you, for all the joy with which we rejoice over you before our God? [10]Night and day we are praying in earnest that we might see your faces again and be able to complement what is lacking in your faith.

[11]Now may our God and Father himself, and our Lord Jesus Christ direct our return to you. [12]And may the Lord increase and multiply your love for one another, and toward all people, even as we love you. [13]By this he will strengthen your hearts and make you blameless and holy before our God and Father, when our Lord Jesus comes with all his saints.

Chapter 4

Please God in Your Lives

[1]Finally, then, brothers, we ask you—we even strongly urge you in the Lord Jesus—to keep on living in a way that pleases God as we taught you, and as you are doing now, so that you might abound even more. [2]For you know what training we gave you by the authority of the Lord Jesus, [3]because this is God's will:

> ➢ that you should be made holy;
> ➢ that you keep yourselves free from sexual immorality;
> ➢ [4]that each of you should control his body in a holy and honorable way, [5]not in passionate lust like the heathen who do not know God;
> ➢ [6]and that no one should wrong his brother or take advantage of him.

The Lord is the avenger concerning all these things, as we have already told you and warned you. [7]For God did not call us to be unclean, but to be made holy. [8]So, anyone who rejects this instruction does not reject man, but God, who gives you his Holy Spirit.

[9]Now nobody needs to write to you concerning brotherly love, for you yourselves have been taught by God to love one another. [10]And indeed, you do show love toward all the brothers in Macedonia. Still, brothers, we urge you to do so more and more. [11]Make it your goal to lead quiet lives, to mind your own business, and to work with your hands, just as we told you, [12]so that you conduct yourselves properly in the presence of outsiders, and so that you will not need things from anyone.

The Second Coming of Christ

¹³Now, brothers, we do not want you to stay uninformed as to [the fate of] those who have fallen asleep [in death], so that you will not have to grieve as others who have no hope do. ¹⁴For since we do believe that Jesus died and rose again, and that through Jesus, God will bring those who have fallen asleep in him, ¹⁵then, according to the word of the Lord, we tell you that we who are still alive and remain until the coming of the Lord will not precede those who have fallen asleep [in death]. ¹⁶For the Lord himself will descend from heaven with a commanding shout, with the voice of an archangel, and with the trumpet call of God, and the dead in Christ shall rise first. ¹⁷Then, we who are still alive and are left will be caught up with them in the clouds to meet the Lord in the air. And so, we will be with the Lord forever. ¹⁸So, encourage each other with these words.

Chapter 5

The Day of the Lord

¹Now then, brothers, concerning the times and seasons, you have no need of being written to ²because you yourselves know full well that the day of the Lord shall come like a thief in the night. ³While people will be declaring peace and safety, destruction shall come on them suddenly, like labor pains on a pregnant woman, and they will not escape. ⁴But, you, brothers, are not in the dark such that this day should overtake you like a thief, ⁵because you are sons of the light and sons of the day. We do not belong to the darkness or the night. ⁶So then, we should not sleep as others do, but we should keep watch and be sober. ⁷For those who sleep by night sleep, and those who get drunk at night get drunk. ⁸We, however, who are of the day, should be sober, having put on the breastplate of faith and love, and the hope of salvation for a helmet, ⁹because God has not appointed us for wrath, but for obtaining salvation through our Lord Jesus Christ ¹⁰who died for us, so that whether we are awake or asleep, we may one day live with him. ¹¹So, encourage one another and build up one another as you are already doing.

Instructions for Holy Living

¹²Therefore, brothers, we urge you to respect those who are working among you, and have authority over you in the Lord and advise you, ¹³and to lovingly hold them in high esteem on account of their work, and to be at peace among yourselves. ¹⁴Now, brothers, we ask you to:

➢ warn those who are disorderly,
➢ comfort the fainthearted,

- ➤ support the weak,
- ➤ and be patient with everyone.
- ➤ [15]See that no one returns evil for evil, but always pursue what is good both toward one another and toward all.
- ➤ [16]Rejoice always.
- ➤ [17]Pray continually.
- ➤ [18]Give thanks in every situation, for this is God's will for you in Christ Jesus.
- ➤ [19]Do not quench the Spirit.
- ➤ [20]Do not despise prophecies.
- ➤ [21]Test all things and hold on to what is good.
- ➤ [22]Stay away from anything that even appears evil.

Benediction and Closing

[23]Now may the God of peace make you completely holy, and may your whole spirit and soul and body be preserved blameless at the coming of our Lord Jesus Christ. [24]The One who called you will succeed in doing this, because he is faithful. [25]Brothers, pray for us. [26]Greet all the brothers with a holy kiss. [27]I charge you, by the authority of the Lord, to read this letter to all the holy brothers. [28]May the grace of our Lord Jesus Christ be with you all.

2 THESSALONIANS

Chapter 1

[From]: Paul, Silvanus, and Timothy,

To: The church of the Thessalonians in God our Father and the Lord Jesus Christ:

²Grace to you and peace from God the Father and the Lord Jesus Christ.

Thanksgiving

³We are obligated to always give thanks to God for you, brothers, as is fitting, because your faith is growing greatly, and the love that each of you has for one another is increasing. ⁴Therefore, in God's churches we ourselves are boasting about you because of the steadfastness of your faith throughout all your persecutions and in the tribulations you are enduring.

Judgment Day

⁵This is evidence of the righteous judgment of God: that you may be deemed worthy of the kingdom of God that you are suffering for, ⁶since God does consider it just to repay those who trouble you with affliction, ⁷and to give relief to you who are afflicted, as well as to us, when the Lord Jesus is revealed from heaven with his mighty angels in flaming fire. ⁸He will be inflicting vengeance on those who do not know God and on those who do not obey the gospel of our Lord Jesus. ⁹They shall suffer the punishment of eternal destruction, [removed] from the presence of the Lord and from the glory of his might, ¹⁰when he comes on that day to be glorified in his saints, and to be marveled at among all who have believed, because our testimony to you was believed. ¹¹We are always praying for you to this end: that our God may make you worthy of his calling and bring to fruition every plan for goodness and work of faith by [his] power, ¹²so that the name of our Lord Jesus may be glorified in you, as well as you in him, according to the grace of our God and the Lord Jesus Christ.

Chapter 2

The Coming of the Man of Lawlessness

[1]Now as for the coming of our Lord Jesus Christ and our being gathered up to him, we beg you, brothers [2]not to be shaken and alarmed hastily, because of something spiritual, or someone's words, or a letter purporting to be from us claiming that the day of the Lord has come. [3]Let no one deceive you in any way; for [that day] shall not come until after the [great] rebellion comes, and the man of lawlessness is revealed. [Being] the son of utter doom, [4]he antagonistically exalts himself above every so-called god or object of worship– and then seats himself in the temple of God, proclaiming himself to be God. [5]Do you not remember that I told you these things when I was still with you? [6]And, you know something is restraining him now so that he may be revealed in his time. [7]For the mystery of lawlessness is already at work. He alone who is restraining it now will keep doing so until he is removed. [8]And then the lawless one will be revealed, and the Lord Jesus will slay him with the breath of his mouth and annihilate him by the very act of his coming. [9]The coming of the lawless one will be through the activity of Satan, by means of great power, false signs and wonders, [10]and total, wicked deception for those who are to perish, because of their refusal to embrace the truth and be saved by it. [11]Therefore God will send a strong delusion on them such that they will believe what is false, [12]so that all who did not believe the truth, but took pleasure in sinfulness, may be condemned.

Standing Firm

[13]But we are obligated to always give thanks to God for you, [our] brothers beloved by the Lord, because from the beginning God chose you to be saved, through sanctification by the Spirit and belief in the truth. [14]He called you to this through our gospel, so that you may obtain the glory of our Lord Jesus Christ. [15]So then, brothers, stand firm and hold to the traditions that we taught you, either by our spoken words or by our letter.

> [16]*Now may our Lord Jesus Christ himself,*
> *and God our Father,*
> *who loved us and gave us eternal comfort and good hope through grace,*
> [17]*comfort your hearts and build you up in every good deed and word.*

Chapter 3

Remain in Prayer

[1]Finally, brothers, pray on our behalf that the word of the Lord may speed ahead triumphantly and bring glory, as it happened among you, [2]and that we may be rescued from wicked and evil men, for not all have faith. [3]But the Lord is faithful; he will build you up and guard you from evil. [4]And we have confidence in the Lord about you, that you are doing and will keep doing what we are commanding. [5]May the Lord direct your hearts to God's love and to Christ's enduring nature.

Do not be Idle

[6]Now, in the name of our Lord Jesus Christ we command you, brothers, to you keep away from any brother who is living in idleness and not in line with the tradition that you received from us. [7]For you yourselves know how you should imitate us: with you, we were not idle. [8]Nor did we eat anyone's bread as a gift—rather, we worked night and day with toil and labor so that we would not be a burden to any of you. [9]It was not because we do not have that right, but [instead, it was] to give you, in ourselves, an example to imitate. [10]For even when we were with you, we gave you this command: If anyone is unwilling to work, let him not eat. [11]For we hear that some of you are living in idleness—mere busybodies instead of being busy at work. [12]Now, in the Lord Jesus Christ we appeal to such people, and advise them strongly to do their work quietly to earn their own bread to eat. [13]But, as for you, brothers, do not grow weary in doing good. [14]If anyone refuses to obey what we say in this letter, take note of that person, and have nothing to do with him, so that he may be ashamed. [15]Do not view him as an enemy, but do warn him as a brother.

Benediction

[16]Now may the Lord of peace himself give you peace at all times in all ways. The Lord be with you all. [17]I, Paul, write this greeting with my own hand. This is my special mark in all [my] letters; it is how I write. [18]May the grace of our Lord Jesus Christ be with all of you.

I TIMOTHY

Chapter 1

¹[From]: Paul, an apostle of Christ Jesus by command of God our Savior and of Christ Jesus our hope,

²To: Timothy, my true child in the faith:

Grace, mercy, and peace from God the Father and Christ Jesus our Lord.

Warnings About False Teachings

³As I urged you when I was going to Macedonia, remain at Ephesus so that you may command certain persons not to teach different doctrines, ⁴nor to devote themselves to myths and endless genealogies that promote speculations rather than an orderly life. ⁵Instead, the goal of our commands is a love that flows from a pure heart, a good conscience, and a sincere faith. ⁶By straying away from these, certain persons have wandered away into futile discussions, ⁷wanting to be teachers of the law, without understanding either what they are saying or the things that they are making claims about.

⁸Now we know that the law is good, if anyone uses it judiciously, ⁹[with the] understanding that the law is not established for the sake of the just but for the lawless and disobedient, for the ungodly and sinners, for the unholy and profane, for those who beat their fathers and mothers, for murderers, ¹⁰immoral persons, men who practice homosexuality, slave-traders, liars, perjurers, and others who do what is contrary to sound doctrine. ¹¹[This is] in accordance with the glorious gospel of the blessed God that I have been entrusted with.

¹²I thank Christ Jesus our Lord, who has empowered me, because he deemed me faithful and appointed me to his service, ¹³even though previously I had blasphemed and persecuted and insulted him. But I received mercy because I had acted ignorantly in unbelief, ¹⁴and the grace of our Lord overflowed for me with the faith and love that are in Christ Jesus. ¹⁵This saying is trustworthy and deserves full acceptance: Christ Jesus came into the world to save sinners. Now, I am the foremost of sinners, ¹⁶but I received mercy for this reason, that in me, as the foremost, Jesus Christ might display his perfect patience as an example to those who were to put their faith in him for eternal life.

17 To the King of ages, immortal, invisible–the only God–
   be honor and glory forever and ever.   Amen.

Hold on

18 I entrust this commission to you, Timothy, my child, in accordance with the earlier prophesies made about you, that you may fight the battle for what is the good through them, 19 holding [onto] faith and a good conscience. Certain people have made a shipwreck of their faith by rejecting this, 20 among them Hymenaeus and Alexander, whom I have turned over to Satan that they may learn not to blaspheme.

Chapter 2

On Prayer

1 First of all, then, I urge that prayers, prayer requests, intercessions, and the giving of thanks be made for everyone, 2 for kings and all who are in high positions, that we may lead a peaceful and quiet life, godly and dignified in every way. 3 This is good and pleasing in the sight of God our Savior, 4 who wants all to be saved and to come to the knowledge of the truth. 5 For there is one God, and there is one mediator between God and men, the man Christ Jesus, 6 who gave himself as a ransom for all, a testimony given at the appointed time. 7 I was appointed a preacher and apostle for this reason (I am telling the truth, I am not lying), a teacher of the Gentiles in faith and truth.

Instructions for Men and Women

8 In every place, then, I want men to be lifting holy hands to pray, without any anger or arguing. 9 Also, women should adorn themselves modestly and sensibly in seemly apparel, not with braided hair or gold or pearls or expensive clothing 10 but with what is fitting to women who profess godliness: good deeds. 11 A woman is to learn in silence with all submissiveness. 12 I do not permit a woman to teach men, or to have authority over them; she is to remain quiet. 13 For Adam was formed first, then Eve. 14 And Adam was not deceived, but the woman was deceived and became a transgressor. 15 Still, [women] will be saved through childbearing, if they continue in faith and love and holiness, with modesty.

Chapter 3

Qualifications for Overseers

1 This saying is trustworthy: If a man aspires to the office of overseer, he desires a noble task. 2 Now then, an overseer must be above reproach, a man who has one wife, and be:

- sober-minded
- self-controlled
- respectable
- hospitable
- able to teach
- [3]not addicted to alcohol
- not violent but gentle
- not quarrelsome
- and not avaricious.
- [4]He must manage his own household well, keeping his children submissive in a dignified way, [5]for if a man does not know how to manage his own household, how would he be able to care for God's church?
- [6]He must not be a new believer, or he may become conceited and fall into the condemnation of the devil.
- [7]Moreover, he must be held in high opinion by outsiders, so that he may not fall into disgrace, the snare of the devil.

Qualifications for Deacons and Their Wives

[8]Deacons likewise must be:

- dignified
- not double-tongued
- not addicted to alcohol
- and not greedy for material gain
- [9]holding onto the mystery of the faith with a clear conscience.
- [10]Also, let them be tested first; then once proved blameless let them serve as deacons.

[11]Likewise, their wives must be:

- dignified
- not slanderous, but sober-minded
- faithful in everything.

[12]A deacon is to be a man with one wife, and the deacons must manage their children and their households well. [13]For those who serve well as deacons gain a good standing for themselves and also great confidence in the faith that is in Christ Jesus.

The Mystery of the Christian Faith

[14]I hope to come to you soon, but I am writing these instructions to you so that [15]in case I am delayed, you may know how someone should behave in the house-

hold of God, which as the church of the living God is the pillar and upholder of truth. [16]We confess that the mystery of our religion is great. He was:

manifested in human form,
justified by the Spirit,
seen by angels,
proclaimed among the nations,
believed on in the world, and
taken up in glory.

Chapter 4

[1]Now the Spirit expressly says that in the latter times some will depart from the faith by devoting themselves to deceitful spirits and doctrines of demons, [2]through the false teachings made up by liars with seared consciences. [3]They forbid marriage and demand abstinence from foods that God created to be received with thanksgiving by those who believe and know the truth. [4]For everything created by God is good, and nothing is to be rejected if it is received with thanksgiving, [5]for then it becomes sanctified by the word of God and prayer. [6]If you convey these instructions to the brothers, you will be a good minister of Christ Jesus, one who has been trained by the words of the faith and the good doctrine that you have followed. [7]Have nothing to do with irreverent and silly myths. Instead, train yourself for godliness. [8]While physical training is of some value, godliness is of value in every way since it holds promise for [both] the present life as well as for the one to come. [9]This saying is trustworthy and deserves to be fully accepted. [10]For this purpose we labor and strive because we have set our hope on the living God, who is the Savior of all people, in particular of believers.

Teach and Preach

[11]Command and teach these things. [12]Let no one hold you in contempt on account of your youth, but set an example for the believers in speech and conduct, in love, in faith, and in purity. [13]Until I come, devote time to the public reading of scripture, to giving encouraging messages, and teaching. [14]Do not neglect your gift, which was given to you by prophecy when the council of elders laid their hands on you. [15]Practice these [duties], immerse yourself in them so that all may see your progress. [16]Guard yourself and your teaching carefully. Persist in this, for by doing so you will save both yourself and those who heed your words.

Chapter 5

How to Treat Others

[1]Do not rebuke an older man, instead advise him as you would a father. Treat younger men like brothers, [2]older women like mothers, younger women like sisters, in a totally pure way.

How to Treat Widows and Families

[3]Honor widows who truly are [needy] widows. [4]If a widow has children or grandchildren, let them first learn their godly duty to their own family by taking care of their parents, for this is acceptable in the sight of God. [5]She who is really a widow, and is left all alone, has set her hope on God and continues in prayer requests and [other] prayers night and day; [6]whereas she who is self-indulgent is dead even while she is alive. [7]Also command these things, so that they may be without reproach. [8]But if anyone does not provide for his relatives, and especially for his own household, he has denied the faith and is worse than an unbeliever.

[9]Let a widow be enrolled if she is at least sixty years of age, having been the wife of one husband. [10]In addition, she must have a reputation for good deeds, as one who has raised children, shown hospitality, washed the feet of the saints, cared for the afflicted, and devoted herself to doing good in every way. [11]But refuse to enroll younger widows, for when their passions pull them away from Christ they want to marry, [12]and so incur condemnation for having abandoned their former faith. [13]Besides that, they learn to be idlers, flitting about from house to house, and not only idlers but gossips and busybodies, saying what they should not. [14]So I would have younger widows remarry, bear children, manage their households, and give the enemy no occasion to revile us. [15]For some have already strayed, following Satan. [16]If any believing woman has relatives who are widows, she should give them assistance, so that the church is not so burdened and can assist those who are truly widows.

How to Treat Elders

[17]Let the elders who rule well be considered worthy of double honor, especially those who labor in preaching and teaching. [18]For the scripture says, "You shall not muzzle an ox when it is treading out the grain," and, "The laborer deserves his wages." [19]Never admit any charge against an elder except on the evidence of two or three witnesses. [20]As for those who persist in sin, rebuke them in the presence of all, so that the rest may stand in fear. [21]I command you, in the presence of God and of Christ Jesus and of the chosen angels, to keep these rules without showing favoritism, doing nothing out of partiality.

Other Instructions

[22]Do not be hasty in the laying on of hands. Do not participate in another man's sins; keep yourself pure. [23]No longer drink only water but take a little wine for the sake of your stomach and your frequent illnesses. [24]Some men's sins are conspicuous; they presage a coming judgment. But the sins of others come to light later on. [25]In the same way good deeds are also conspicuous, and even when they are not, they cannot remain hidden.

Chapter 6

Slaves with Believing Masters

[1]Let all who are under the yoke of slavery regard their masters as worthy of all honor, so that the name of God and the teaching may not be defamed. [2]Those who have believing masters must not be disrespectful on the grounds that they are brothers; rather they must serve all the better since those who benefit by their service are believers and beloved.

Teach and urge these duties:

Lead a Godly Life

[3]If anyone teaches otherwise and does not agree with the sound words of our Lord Jesus Christ and the teaching that is in accordance with godliness, [4]he is puffed up with conceit and understands nothing. He has an unhealthy craving for controversy and for disputes about words, which produce envy, dissension, slander, evil suspicions, [5]and wrangling among people who are depraved in mind and deprived of the truth, imagining that godliness is a means of gain. [6]Now then, in godliness with contentment there *is* great gain, [7]for we brought nothing into this world, and we cannot take anything out of this world. [8]Still, if we have food and clothing, we shall be content with these things. [9]However, those who want to be rich fall into temptation, into a snare, into many needless and harmful desires that plunge people into ruin and destruction. [10]For a root of all sorts of evil is the love of money, and by yearning after it some have wandered away from the faith and pierced their own souls with many sorrows.

Fight the Good Fight

[11]But as for you, man of God, flee from all this. Pursue righteousness, godliness, faith, love, steadfastness, and gentleness. [12]Fight the good fight of the faith. Take hold of the eternal life that you were called to when you made the good confession in the presence of many witnesses. [13]In the presence of God who gives life to all

things, and of Christ Jesus who made the good confession in his testimony before Pontius Pilate, I charge you [14]to keep the commandment unstained and free from reproach until the appearing of our Lord Jesus Christ. [15]And it will be revealed at the proper time by the blessed and only Sovereign, the King of kings and Lord of lords, [16]who alone has immortality and dwells in unapproachable light, whom no man has ever seen or can see. To him be honor and eternal dominion. Amen.

Instructions for the Rich

[17]As for the rich in this present age, command them not to be haughty, nor to set their hopes on the uncertainty of riches, but on God who richly provides us with everything to enjoy. [18]They are to do good, to be rich in good deeds, ready to share generously. [19]In doing so they are laying up treasure for themselves—a good foundation for the future so that they may take hold of what life truly consists of.

Closing

[20]O Timothy, guard what has been entrusted to you. Avoid irreverent chatter and the contradictions in what bears the false name of "knowledge", [21]for by professing it some have strayed away from the faith.

Grace be with you.

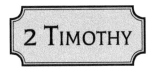

2 TIMOTHY

Chapter 1

¹[From]: Paul, an apostle of Christ Jesus by the will of God according to the promise of the life that is in Christ Jesus,

²To: Timothy, my beloved child.

Grace, mercy, and peace from God the Father and Christ Jesus our Lord.

Serve Without Being Ashamed

³I thank God—whom I serve as my ancestors did—with a clear consciensce, when night and day I remember you constantly in my prayers. ⁴Remembering your tears, I long to see you, that I may be filled with joy. ⁵I am reminded of your sincere faith, a faith that first dwelled in your grandmother Lois and your mother Eunice and now, I am sure, dwells also in you. ⁶For this reason I remind you to rekindle the gift of God, which is [now] within you due to the laying on of my hands. ⁷For God did not give us a spirit of cowardice, but rather one of power and love and self-control.

⁸Do not be ashamed therefore of the testimony about our Lord, nor of me his prisoner, but share in suffering for the gospel in the power of God ⁹who saved us and called us with a holy calling, not by virtue of our own deeds but by virtue of his own purpose and the grace that he gave us in Christ Jesus ages ago. ¹⁰This grace has now been made manifest through the appearing of our Savior Christ Jesus, who abolished death and brought to light [both] life and immortality through the gospel. ¹¹I was appointed a preacher and apostle and teacher for this gospel, ¹²which is why I suffer these things. But I am not ashamed because I know whom I have believed in, and I am convinced that he is able to protect the trust that is being held for me until that Day. ¹³Follow the pattern of sound words that you have heard from me, in the faith and love that are in Christ Jesus. ¹⁴Guard the good deposit entrusted to you by the Holy Spirit who dwells within us.

¹⁵You are aware that all who are in Asia turned away from me, among whom are Phygelus and Hermogenes. ¹⁶May the Lord grant mercy to the household of Onesiphorus, for he often renewed my spirit, and he was not ashamed of my chains. ¹⁷Rather, when he arrived in Rome, he searched for me earnestly and

found me—[18]may the Lord grant him to find mercy from the Lord on that Day—and well you know how much he ministered [to me] in Ephesus.

Chapter 2

Serve as a Good Soldier

[1]You then, my child, strengthen yourself in the grace that is in Christ Jesus, [2]and entrust what you have heard from me before many witnesses to faithful men, who will be worthily qualified to teach others as well. [3]Take your share in suffering as a good soldier of Christ Jesus. [4]No active duty soldier lets himself get entangled in civilian pursuits, since his aim is to dutifully obey the one who enlisted him. [5]Also, an athlete is not crowned unless he competes according to the rules. [6]The hard-working farmer should take the first share of the crops. [7]Keep thinking over what I say, for the Lord will grant you understanding in everything.

[8]Remember Jesus Christ, risen from the dead, descended from David, as preached in my gospel, [9]for which I am suffering and wearing fetters like a criminal. But the word of God is not fettered. [10]Therefore I endure everything for the sake of the chosen ones, that they also may obtain salvation in Christ Jesus with eternal glory. [11]This is a trustworthy saying, for:

> *If we have died with him, we will also live with him.*
> [12]*If we endure, we will also reign with him.*
> *If we deny him, he will also deny us.*
> [13]*If we are faithless, he remains faithful–for he cannot deny himself.*

Workers that God Approves

[14]Keep on reminding them of this and charge them before the Lord to avoid disputing about words, which does no good, but only ruins the hearers. [15]Do your best to present yourself to God as someone tested and approved, a worker unashamed, accurately analyzing and handling the Word of Truth. [16]Avoid irreverent chatter, for it will lead people into more and more ungodliness, [17]and their talk will spread like gangrene. [Among such people] are Hymenaeus and Philetus, [18]who have veered from the truth by holding that the resurrection is already past. They are upsetting the faith of some. [19]But God's firm foundation stands, bearing this seal: "The Lord knows those who are his," and, "Let everyone who names the name of the Lord walk away from wickedness."

[20]In a great house there are vessels not only of gold and silver but also of wood and earthenware: some for noble use, and some for ordinary use. [21]If anyone cleanses himself from what is dirty, then he will be a vessel for noble use, consecrated, and useful to the master of the house, fit for every good work.

²²So flee from youthful passions and aim at righteousness, faith, love, and peace, along with those who call on the Lord from a pure heart. ²³Have nothing to do with stupid, senseless controversies; you know that they breed quarrels. ²⁴And the Lord's servant must not be quarrelsome, but kind to everyone, good at teaching, [and] forbearing, ²⁵correcting his opponents with gentleness. God may perhaps grant that [the opponents] will repent and come to know the truth, ²⁶and they may escape from the snare of the devil, after having been captured by him to do his will.

Chapter 3

Godlessness in the Last Era

¹But understand this: in the final era difficult times will come. ²For people will be lovers of self, lovers of money–proud, arrogant, abusive, disobedient to their parents, ungrateful, unholy, ³heartless, unappeasable, slanderous, unruly, brutal, despising what is good, ⁴treacherous, reckless, swollen with conceit–lovers of pleasure rather than lovers of God. ⁵[They] will have the appearance of godliness but deny its power. Avoid such people. ⁶For among them are those who work their way into households and captivate weak-willed women who are weighed down by their sinful actions and swayed by their passions, ⁷and who, [though] always learning, can never become able to grasp the truth. ⁸Just as Jannes and Jambres opposed Moses, so these men—men of corrupt mind and counterfeit faith—also oppose the truth. ⁹But, they will not get very far, for their folly will be plain to all, as was the folly of those two men.

¹⁰Now you have observed my teaching, my lifestyle, my purpose in life, my faith, my patience, my love, my steadfastness, ¹¹my persecutions, my sufferings, what happened to me in Antioch, in Iconium, and in Lystra, and what persecutions I endured. Yet the Lord rescued me from them all. ¹²Indeed, all who desire to live a godly life in Christ Jesus will be persecuted, ¹³while evil people and impostors will proceed from bad to worse, deceiving and being deceived. ¹⁴But as for you, continue in what you have learned and have firmly believed, knowing whom you learned it from, ¹⁵and how from childhood you have been acquainted with the sacred writings that can instruct you for salvation through faith in Christ Jesus. ¹⁶All scripture is breathed out by God and is profitable for teaching, for refuting error, for correcting, and for training in righteousness, ¹⁷so that the man of God may be competent, fully equipped for every good deed.

Chapter 4

Keep Preaching Sound Doctrine

[1]I solemnly charge you in the presence of God and of Christ Jesus, who is to judge the living and the dead, and by his appearing, and by his kingdom: [2]preach the word, be eagerly prepared at times both opportune and inopportune. Persuade, rebuke, and encourage, with unfailing patience and teaching. [3]For the time is coming when people will not endure sound teaching, but having itching ears, they will surround themselves with teachers that suit their own tastes [4]and will turn away from listening to the truth and wander off into myths. [5]As for you, always be steadfastly alert, endure suffering, do the work of an evangelist, fulfill your ministry.

[6]For I am already being expended as a sacrifice; the time of my departure has come. [7]I have fought the good fight, I have finished the race, I have kept the faith. [8]From here on, there is laid up for me the crown of righteousness, which the Lord, the righteous judge, will award to me on that Day, and not only to me but also to all who have loved his appearing.

Final Instructions and Greetings

[9]Do your best to come to me soon. [10]For Demas, enthralled with this present world, has deserted me and gone to Thessalonica. Crescens has gone to Galatia, Titus to Dalmatia. [11]Only Luke is with me. Take Mark and bring him with you because he is very useful to me in ministry. [12]I have sent Tychicus to Ephesus. [13]When you come, bring the cloak that I left with Carpus at Troas, the books as well, and above all the parchments.

[14]Alexander the coppersmith did me great harm; the Lord will repay him for his deeds. [15]Beware of him yourself, for he strongly opposed our message. [16]At my first defense no one came to stand with me; all deserted me. May it not be charged against them! [17]But the Lord stood by me and strengthened me, so that the message might be fully proclaimed through me, and all the Gentiles might hear it. Thus, even I was rescued from the lion's mouth. [18]The Lord will deliver me from every evil deed and deliver me into his heavenly kingdom. To him be the glory forever and ever. Amen.

[19]Greet Prisca and Aquila, and the household of Onesiphorus. [20]Erastus remained at Corinth; I left Trophimus ill at Miletus. [21]Do your best to come before winter. Eubulus sends greetings to you, as do Pudens and Linus and Claudia and all the brothers. [22]May the Lord be with your spirit. Grace be with you.

TITUS

Chapter 1

[From]: Paul, a servant of God and an apostle of Jesus Christ for the promotion of the faith of God's elect and their knowledge of the truth in accordance with godliness, [2]in hope of eternal life that God, who never lies, promised before the dawn of time [3]and at the proper time made known in his word through the preaching that I have been entrusted with by the command of God our Savior.

[4]To: Titus, my true child in a common faith.

Grace and peace from God the Father and Christ Jesus our Savior.

Qualifications of Elders

[5]For this purpose I left you in Crete: that you might organize the remaining work, and that in every town, as I directed, you might appoint men as elders, [6][choosing] only those who are:

- ➤ blameless,
- ➤ the husband of one wife,
- ➤ [parents of] believeing children
- ➤ and are not accused of indecent behavior or rebellion.
- ➤ [7]For an overseer, as God's steward, must be blameless.
- ➤ He must not be arrogant or quick-tempered or given to drunkenness or violent or greedy for material gain.
- ➤ [8]But, he must be hospitable, devoted to what is good, self-controlled, upright, holy, and disciplined.
- ➤ [9]He must hold firm to the trustworthy word as taught, so that he may be able to instruct in sound doctrine and to rebuke those who contradict it, as well.

Dealing with the Insubordinate

[10]For there are many unruly men, empty talkers and deceivers, especially those from the circumcision sect. [11]They must be silenced, since they are upsetting entire households by teaching what they have no right to teach for their own unethical profit. [12]One of them, a Cretan himself and prophet of their own, said, "Cretans are always liars, evil beasts, lazy gluttons." [13]This testimony is true, so rebuke them sharply, that they may be sound in the faith, [14]instead of paying attention

to Jewish myths or to commands of men who reject the truth. [15]To the pure all things are pure, but nothing is pure to the corrupt and unbelieving. Their very minds and consciences are corrupted. [16]They profess to know God, but they deny him by their deeds. They are detestable, disobedient, and unfit for any noble task.

Chapter 2

Teach Sound Doctrine

[1]But as for you, teach what is in line with sound doctrine. [2]Older men are to be temperate, serious, self-controlled, and sound in faith, love, and steadfastness. [3]Likewise, older women are to behave reverently, and not to accuse people falsely or be addicted to alcohol. They are to teach what is good, [4]and thereby train the young women to love their husbands and children, [5]to be sensible, chaste, domestic, kind, and submissive to their husbands, that the word of God may not be discredited. [6]Likewise, urge the younger men to control themselves. [7]In all respects show yourself to be a model of good deeds, show integrity and dignity in your teaching. [8]Speak in a [doctrinally] sound way that cannot be criticized, so that an opponent may be put to shame, having nothing bad to say about us. [9]Servants are to be submissive to their masters, satisfying their demands in every respect. They are not to be argumentative, [10]nor to pilfer, but to show themselves completely trustworthy, so that in every way they may add a beautiful [testimony] to the doctrine of God our Savior.

[11]For the grace of God has appeared, a salvation [offered] to all men, [12]which teaches us to renounce ungodliness and worldly passions, and to live self-controlled, upright, and godly lives in this world, [13]waiting for our blessed hope: the appearing of the glory of our great God and Savior Jesus Christ. [14]He gave himself for us to redeem us from all lawlessness and to purify for himself a people of his own who are eager to do good things.

Chapter 3

Be Ready to Do Good Deeds

[2:15]Declare these things: encourage and reprove with all authority. Let no one hold you in contempt. [3:1]Remind people to be submissive to rulers and authorities, to be obedient, to be ready to do whatever is good, [2]to slander no one, to avoid arguing, to be gentle, and to show complete courtesy to everyone. [3]For we ourselves used to be foolish, disobedient, led astray, enslaved to various passions and pleasures. We once passed our days in malice and envy, hated by others and hating one another. [4]But when the goodness and loving kindness of God our Savior appeared, [5]He saved us, not because of the righteous things we had done, but by virtue of his own mercy, by the washing of regeneration and renewal of the Holy Spirit, [6]whom he poured out on us richly through Jesus Christ our Savior, [7]so that being justified by that grace we might become heirs in the assured hope of eternal life. [8]This saying is trustworthy. I want you to insist on these things, so that those who have believed in God may take care to devote themselves to doing good deeds; such things are excellent and profitable for people [to do]. [9]On the other hand, avoid foolish controversies, [obsession with] genealogies, dissensions, and quarrels over the law, for they profit nothing and are futile. [10]As for someone who is divisive, after sternly warning him once or twice, have nothing more to do with him, [11]knowing that such a person is warped and sinful, being self-condemned.

Final Instructions and Greetings

[12]When I send Artemas or Tychicus to you, do try to come to me in Nicopolis, for I have decided to pass the winter there. [13]Do try to speed Zenas the lawyer and Apollos on their way. See that they are not lacking anything. [14]Also, see that our people learn to devote themselves to good deeds, so as to help out in cases of urgent need, and not to be unfruitful. [15]Everyone with me sends greetings to you. Greet those who love us in the faith.

Grace be with you all.

PHILEMON

Chapter 1

¹[From]: Paul, a prisoner for Christ Jesus,
and Timothy our brother,

To: Philemon our beloved fellow worker,
²and Apphia our sister and Archippus our fellow soldier, and your house church.

³Grace to you and peace from God our Father and the Lord Jesus Christ.

⁴I always thank my God whenever I remember you in my prayers, ⁵as I hear of the faith that you have toward the Lord Jesus and your love for all the saints. ⁶By living out your faith together, may you profoundly realize all the benefits that are ours in Christ. ⁷For I have derived much joy and comfort from your love, brother, because through you the hearts of the saints have been refreshed.

⁸Therefore, though in Christ I am bold enough to command you to do what is required, ⁹yet out of love I would rather make an appeal to you. This is the Paul—who is an old man and at present also a prisoner on account of Christ Jesus –¹⁰who appeals to you for my child, Onesimus, whose [spiritual] father I have become during my imprisonment. ¹¹ (Formerly he was useless to you, but now he is indeed useful to both you and me.) ¹²I am sending him back to you, sending my very heart. ¹³I would have been glad to keep him with me, so that in place of you he might take care of me during my imprisonment for the sake of the gospel. ¹⁴But, I preferred to do nothing without your consent in order that your kindness might not be done by compulsion but of your own free will. ¹⁵Perhaps he was taken from you for a short while so that you might have him back forever, ¹⁶no longer as a slave but more than a slave, as a brother, especially beloved to me but how much more to you, both in person and in the Lord.

¹⁷So if you consider me a partner, welcome him as you would welcome me. ¹⁸If he has wronged you in any way, or owes you anything, charge it to me. ¹⁹I, Paul, write this with my own hand, I will repay it—not to mention that you are indebted to me for your very life. ²⁰Yes, brother, I am seeking some blessing from you in the Lord. Refresh my heart in Christ. ²¹Confident of your obedience, I have written to you, knowing that you will do even more than what I am asking. ²²And another thing—please prepare a guest room for me, for I am hoping that as a result of your prayers I will be given back to you.

²³Epaphras, my fellow prisoner in Christ Jesus, sends greetings to you, ²⁴as do Mark, Aristarchus, Demas, and Luke, my fellow workers.

²⁵May the grace of the Lord Jesus Christ be with your spirit.

HEBREWS

Chapter 1

God's Son is Supreme

[1]In days of old, God used to speak to our forefathers by the prophets at various times and in many ways. [2]But in this final era he has spoken to us by his Son, whom he appointed the heir of everything, and through whom he created the world. [3]As the radiance of [God's] glory—the precise imprint of his nature—[the Son] upholds the universe by the word of his power.

Once he had achieved purification for sins, he sat down at the right hand of the Majesty on high, [4]having become superior to angels to the same degree that the name he has inherited is more excellent than theirs.

[5]For to what angel did God ever say, "You are my Son; today I have begotten you"? Or even, "I will be a father to him, and he shall be a son to me"? [6]Furthermore, when he brought the firstborn into the world, he declared, "Let all God's angels worship him." [7]Of the angels he says, "He makes his angels winds, and his servants flames of fire." [8]But of the Son he says:

"Your throne, O God, is forever and ever;
the scepter of righteousness is the scepter of your kingdom.
[9]You have loved righteousness and hated wickedness.
 Therefore, God, your God, has anointed you
with the oil of gladness surpassing that of your companions."

[10]And,

"In the beginning it was you, Lord,
who laid the foundation of the earth,
and the heavens are the work of your hands.
[11]They will perish, but you remain;
they will all wear out like a garment.
[12]You will roll them up like a robe,
and they will be changed.
 But you are the same,
and your years will never come to an end."

[13]But to what angel has he ever said, "Sit at my right hand until I make your enemies a footstool for your feet"? [14]Are not [angels] all ministering spirits sent out to serve for the sake of those who are to inherit salvation?

Chapter 2

Warnings Concerning Neglecting Salvation

[1]Therefore we must pay much closer attention to what we have heard, so that we do not meander away. [2]For since the message declared by angels indeed proved valid, and every transgression or disobedience receives a just penalty, [3]then how shall we escape if we neglect so great a salvation? First the Lord declared it, and then those who heard it attested it to us [4]while God was also bearing witness to it through signs and wonders and various miracles and by gifts of the Holy Spirit, given out as he willed.

The Only True Source of Salvation

[5]For he has not subjected the world to come, which we are talking about, to angels. [6]Now, somewhere someone gave testimony about it, saying:

> "What is man that you are mindful of him,
> or the Son of Man, that you care for him?
> [7]You did make him lower than the angels for a little while.
> You have crowned him with glory and honor,
> [8]putting everything in subjection under his feet."

Now in putting everything in subjection to him, he left nothing that was *not* in subjection to him. Currently, we do not see everything as being in subjection to him yet. [9]But we do see him, Jesus, who was made lower than the angels for a little while, crowned with glory and honor because of the suffering of death, so that by the grace of God he might taste death for everyone.

[10]For it was fitting that he, for whom and by whom all things exist, should make the originator of their salvation perfect through suffering in bringing many sons to glory. [11]For he who sanctifies and those who are sanctified are all in union, which is why he is not ashamed to call them brothers, [12]saying, "I will proclaim your name to my brothers, in the midst of the congregation I will sing your praises." [13]And again, "I will put my trust in him." And again, "Here am I, along with the children God has given me."

[14]Therefore, since all these children are flesh and blood, he himself also took on the same nature, that through death he might destroy the one who has the power of death, that is, the devil, [15]and deliver all those who were subject to lifelong slav-

337

ery through the fear of death. [16]For surely he did not take on himself the needs of angels, but rather he took on himself the needs of the descendants of Abraham. [17]Therefore it was necessary that he be made like his brothers in every way, so that he could become a merciful and faithful high priest in the things of God, to make a sacrifice of atonement for the sins of the people. [18]For he is capable of helping those who are being tempted because he himself suffered when he was tempted.

Chapter 3

Moses and Jesus Compared

[1]Therefore, holy brothers, who share in a heavenly call, consider Jesus, the envoy and high priest of our confession, [2]who was faithful to the One who appointed him, just as Moses also acted faithfully in all [God's] house. [3]For Jesus is deemed worthy of more glory than Moses to the same degree that the builder of a house has more honor than the house itself. [4](For every house is built by someone, but God is the builder of all things.) [5]Now Moses was faithful in all God's house as a servant, being a witness to the things that were to be spoken later. [6]Now, as a son Christ is faithful over God's house. And we are his house if we firmly hold on to our confidence, asserting our hope right to the end.

Entering his Rest

[7]Therefore, as the Holy Spirit says,

> "Today, if you hear his voice,
> [8]do not harden your hearts as in the rebellion,
> on the day of testing in the wilderness,
> [9]where your fathers put me to the test
> and saw my works for forty years.
> [10]Therefore I was provoked with that generation and said,
> 'They always go astray in their hearts;
> they have not known my ways.'
> [11]As I swore in my wrath,
> 'They shall not enter my rest.'"

[12]Brothers, watch out, so that in not one of you is there a wicked, unbelieving heart that falls away from the living God. [13]But encourage one another every day—as long as it is called "today"—so that none of you may end up hardened by the deceitfulness of sin. [14]For if indeed we firmly hold on to our original confidence right to the end, we will have come to share in Christ. [15]As it is said, "Today, if you hear his voice, do not harden your hearts as in the rebellion." [16]After

all, who were the ones who heard and yet rebelled? Was it not all those who left Egypt, [led] by Moses? [17]And who was he provoked with for forty years? Was it not those who sinned, whose bodies fell in the wilderness? [18]And who did he vow would not enter into his rest, but those who were disobedient? [19]So we see that they were unable to enter because of unbelief.

Chapter 4

[1]Therefore, while the promise of entering his rest still remains, we should be in fear, so that none of you appear to have failed to [enter it]. [2]For the good news has come to us just as it has to unbelievers, though the message they heard did not benefit them because those who heard it did not combine it with faith. [3]But we believers *do* enter into that rest that he spoke about in "As I swore in my wrath, 'They shall not enter my rest.'"

Nonetheless, his works have been finished from [the time of] the foundation of the world. [4]For somewhere he has spoken of the seventh day like this: "And God rested from all his works on the seventh day." [5]And in this place again he said, "They shall not enter my rest." [6]Therefore, since it remains that some will enter it, and since those who had formerly received the good news failed to enter because of disobedience, [7]again he sets a certain day, "today," saying through David a long time later, as quoted before, "Today, if you hear his voice, do not harden your hearts."

[8]For if Joshua had given them rest, he would not have spoken of another day after that. [9]So then, for the people of God there does remain a Sabbath rest, [10]for whoever has entered into God's rest has also rested from his labors as God did from his. [11]Therefore we should make every effort to enter into that rest, so that no one may fall due to the same type of disobedience.

[12]For the word of God is living and active, sharper than any two-edged sword, piercing to the division of soul and spirit, of joints and marrow, and discerning the thoughts and intentions of the heart. [13]And no creature is hidden from his sight, but all are unclothed and exposed to the eyes of the One whom we must give an account to.

Our Great High Priest

[14]Since then we have a great high priest
who has passed through the heavens,
Jesus, the Son of God,
let us hold firmly to our confession.
[15]For we do not have a high priest

who is unable to sympathize with our weaknesses,
but one who has been tempted as we are in every respect,
yet without sin.
[16]Let us then with confidence approach the throne of grace,
so that we may receive mercy
and find grace to help in times of need.

Chapter 5

[1]For every high priest chosen from among men is ordained in the things of God for duty so that he may offer up gifts and sacrifices for sins on behalf of the people. [2]He can sympathize compassionately with the ignorant and wayward since he himself is limited by human weakness. [3]Because of this, he is obligated to offer sacrifice for his own sins as well, as he does for the people. [4]And no one may assume this honor for himself, but rather he, like Aaron, must also be called by God. [5]So likewise Christ did not exalt himself to be made a high priest, but instead he was appointed by the One who declared to him, "You are my Son, today I have begotten you". [6]As he also says elsewhere, "You are a priest forever, after the order of Melchizedek."

[7]In the days when [Jesus] was in human flesh, he offered up prayers and prayer requests, with loud cries and tears to the One who was able to save him from death, and he was heard on account of his reverence. [8]Even though he was a Son, he learned obedience by what he suffered. [9]And being made perfect, he became the source of eternal salvation to all who obey him, [10]being designated by God a high priest after the order of Melchizedek.

Moving on to Maturity

[11]We have much to say about this, which is hard to explain, since you have grown lazy about learning. [12]For though you ought to be teachers by now, you need someone to teach you the elementary principles of God's word again. It has come to the point where you are in need of milk, not solid food, [13]for everyone who lives on milk stays unskilled in the word of righteousness, since he remains a child. [14]But solid food is for the mature, for those who have had their abilities of discernment trained by exercise in order to be able to distinguish good from evil.

Chapter 6

[1]Therefore, leaving behind the elementary doctrine of Christ, let us press on to maturity, not laying again a foundation of repentance from dead works, faith toward God, [2]instruction about ceremonial cleansings, the laying on of hands, the resurrection of the dead, and eternal judgment. [3]And we will do this if God

allows. [4]Now then, as for those who have once been enlightened, who have tasted the heavenly gift, and have partaken of the Holy Spirit, [5]and have tasted the goodness of the word of God and the powers of the coming age: [6]if they then commit apostasy, it is impossible to restore [them] again to repentance since to their own peril they are crucifying the Son of God yet again and holding him up to contempt. [7]For land that has absorbed the rain that often lands on it, and then brings forth plants useful to those that it was cultivated for, receives a blessing from God. [8]But if it produces thorns and thistles, it is worthless and ready to be cursed: its destiny is to be burned.

[9]Even though we are speaking in this manner, nonetheless in your case, beloved, we are assured of better things that indicate salvation. [10]For God is not so unjust that he would overlook your work and the love that you have shown for his name's sake in serving the saints, and that you are still serving. [11]And we want each one of you to show the same diligence, in order to realize the full assurance of hope right to the end, [12]so that you do not grow lazy, but instead imitate those who inherit the promises through faith and patience.

God Makes a Promise

[13]For when God made a promise to Abraham, since he had no one greater to swear by, he swore by himself, [14]saying, "Surely I will bless you and exponentially multiply you." [15]And so, Abraham, having waited patiently, *did* obtain that promise. [16]Men do swear by something greater than themselves, and an oath can finally settle all disputes. [17]So, when God desired to show the unalterable nature of his purpose more convincingly to the heirs of the promise, he confirmed it with an oath, [18]so that through two unalterable things, in which it is impossible for God to lie, we who have fled for refuge might have strong encouragement to keep a tight hold on the hope offered. [19]We hold this as a certain and steadfast anchor of the soul—a hope that enters into the inner sanctum behind the veil, [20]where for our sake a forerunner, Jesus, has gone, having become a high priest after the order of Melchizedek forever.

Chapter 7

Melchizedek and Priesthood

[1]This Melchizedek, king of Salem, priest of the Most High God, encountered Abraham as he was returning from slaying the kings and blessed him, [2]and Abraham tithed one tenth of everything to him. By the translation of his name, first he is the king of righteousness, and then he is also the king of Salem, that is, the king of peace. [3]Being fatherless, motherless, and without any ancestors, he has neither

341

beginning of days nor end of life, but resembling the Son of God, he continues a priest forever.

⁴Now, notice how great was this one whom Abraham the patriarch gave a tenth of the spoils to. ⁵And those descendants of Levi who are received into the priesthood have a commandment according to the law to receive tithes from the people, that is, from their brothers, though these people are also the offspring of Abraham. ⁶But this man who did not share in their ancestry received tithes from Abraham and blessed the one who had the promises. ⁷Without any dispute, the inferior one is blessed by the superior one. ⁸In one case tithes are received by mortal men, but in another case by one who is declared to be alive. ⁹It might even be said that Levi himself, who received tithes, paid tithes through Abraham, ¹⁰for he was still in the loins of his forefather when Melchizedek encountered him.

¹¹Now if perfection could have been [reached] through the Levitical priesthood (for the people received the law on the basis of it), why the need for another priest to arise after the order of Melchizedek, instead of one named after the order of Aaron? ¹²After all, a change in the priesthood would necessitate a change in the law as well. ¹³The one being discussed here belonged to another tribe, from which no man has ever officiated at the altar. ¹⁴For it is obvious that our Lord was descended from Judah, and as for *that* tribe, Moses said nothing about priests.

¹⁵This becomes even more apparent when another priest arises in the likeness of Melchizedek, ¹⁶who has become a priest, not by means of a legal requirement concerning one's physical lineage but by the power of a life that cannot be destroyed. ¹⁷For it has been testified about him: "You are a priest forever, after the order of Melchizedek."

¹⁸For even though a previous mandate is done away with because of its weakness and ineffectiveness ¹⁹(for the law made nothing perfect), still, a better hope is introduced, through which we approach God.

²⁰And it was not without an oath. ²¹Those who formerly became priests did so without an oath, but this one with an oath: "The Lord has sworn and will not change his mind, 'You are a priest forever.'" ²²This [oath] makes Jesus the guarantor of a better covenant.

²³The former priests were many in number because death prevented each one from staying in office. ²⁴But he maintains his priesthood permanently because he continues forever. ²⁵Consequently, he is completely able to save those who approach God through him, since he lives forever to intercede on their behalf.

²⁶For it was indeed fitting that we should have such a high priest—holy, blameless, unstained, separated from sinners, and exalted above the heavens. ²⁷He has no need, like those high priests, to offer sacrifices daily, first for his own sins and then for those of the people, because when he offered up himself he did this once for all. ²⁸Whereas the law appointed men, having an imperfect nature, as high priests, then after the law the word of the oath appointed a Son made perfect forever.

Chapter 8

The High Priest of a New Covenant

¹Now the important thing that we are saying is: we *do* have such a high priest, one who is seated at the right hand of the throne of the Majesty in heaven, ²a minister in the Holy Places and the true tabernacle that the Lord, not man, erected. ³For every high priest is appointed to offer gifts and sacrifices. So, it is necessary for this priest to actually have something to offer. ⁴Now if he were on earth, he would not be a priest at all, since there are priests who offer gifts according to the law. ⁵They do their service in a representative copy and shadow of the heavenly things, for when Moses was about to erect the tabernacle, he was instructed by God, saying, "Now then, see to it that you construct everything according to the pattern that was shown to you on the mountain." ⁶But as it is, [Christ] has obtained a ministry that is far superior to the old one to the same degree that the covenant he mediates is far better, since it is enacted on far better promises. ⁷For if that first [covenant] had been without fault, there would have been no cause to seek a second one.

⁸For he finds fault with them as he says:

> "The days will come, the Lord declares,
>   when I will establish a new covenant with the house of Israel
>   and with the house of Judah,
> ⁹unlike the covenant that I made with their fathers
>   on the day when I took them by the hand
>   to lead them out of the land of Egypt.
> For they abandoned my covenant,
>   and so I showed no concern for them, says the Lord.
> ¹⁰This is the covenant that I will make
>   with the house of Israel
>   after those days, says the Lord:
> I will put my laws into their minds and write them on their hearts,
>   and I will be their God, and they shall be my people.

¹¹And each one of them
> shall not need to teach his neighbor or his brother,
> saying, 'Know the Lord,'
> for they all shall know me,
> from the least of them to the greatest.
> ¹²For I will be merciful in regard to their wrongdoings,
> and I will remember their sins no more."

¹³In declaring a "new" [covenant], he renders the first one obsolete. And what is becoming old and worn out is now ready to disappear.

Chapter 9

Earthly Sanctuary

¹Now even the first [covenant] contained regulations for worship and an earthly sanctuary. ²For a tabernacle was prepared, the outer one, in which were the lampstand and the table and the bread of the Presence; it is called the Holy Places. ³Behind the second veil stood a tent called the Holy of Holies, ⁴having the golden altar of incense and the ark of the covenant covered with gold on all sides, which contained a golden urn holding the manna, and Aaron's rod that budded, and the tablets of the covenant. ⁵Above it were the cherubim of glory overshadowing the mercy seat. We cannot speak of these things in detail now.

⁶With these preparations having been made in this way, the priests periodically go into the outer tent, performing their ritual duties. ⁷But only the high priest goes into the second one, and he just once a year, and not without taking the blood that he offers for himself and for the unintended wrongdoings of the people. ⁸By this the Holy Spirit indicates that the way into the sanctuary is not yet opened as long as the outer tent is still standing ⁹(which symbolizes the present age). According to this arrangement, gifts and sacrifices are offered that cannot possibly clear the worshiper's conscience perfectly, ¹⁰but instead they deal only with food and drink and various ceremonial cleansings—regulations for the body imposed until the time of reformation.

The Blood of Christ Redeems

¹¹But when Christ, the high priest of the good things to come, appeared, then through the greater and more perfect tent not made with hands (that is, not of this creation), ¹²he entered into the Holy Place once for all, not by the blood of goats and calves but by his own blood, securing an eternal redemption. ¹³For sprinkling the blood of goats and bulls, and the ashes of a burned heifer onto a ritually un-

clean person sanctifies him to purify the body. ¹⁴How much more, then, will the blood of Christ, who offered himself to God without blemish through the eternal Spirit, purify your conscience from deeds leading to death in order to serve the living God.

¹⁵Therefore he is the mediator of a new covenant, such that those who are called may receive the promised eternal inheritance, since a death has brought about a redemption from [what were] transgressions under the first covenant. ¹⁶For where a [last] will is involved, the death of the testator must be established. ¹⁷For a will goes into effect only at the time of death since it is not in force as long as the testator remains alive. ¹⁸Thus even the first covenant was not ratified without blood. ¹⁹For when Moses had declared every commandment of the law to all the people, he took the blood of calves and goats, with water and scarlet wool and hyssop, and sprinkled both the book itself and all the people, ²⁰saying, "This is the blood of the covenant that God commanded of you." ²¹And in the same way he sprinkled both the tent and all the vessels used in worship with the blood. ²²Indeed, under the law almost everything is purified with blood, and without the shedding of blood there is no forgiveness of sins.

²³Thus it was necessary for the representative copies of the heavenly things to be purified with these rites, but for the heavenly things themselves [to be purified] with sacrifices superior to these. ²⁴For Christ has entered, not into holy places made by human hands—copies representing the true things—but even into heaven itself, to appear in the presence of God now on our behalf, ²⁵not to keep offering himself repeatedly, as the high priest does when he enters the holy places once each year with the blood of another. ²⁶For then he would have had to suffer repeatedly since the foundation of the world. Instead of that, he has appeared in this final age to abolish sin once and for all by the sacrifice of himself. ²⁷And just as it is appointed for men to die once, and after that comes judgment, ²⁸so Christ, having been offered up once to take on the sins of many, will appear a second time, with sin gone, to save those eagerly awaiting him.

Chapter 10

Sufficiency of Christ's Sacrifice

¹For since the law contains merely a shadow of the good things to come, rather than the true form of these realities, it can never, by means of the same sacrifices that are continually offered year after year, perfect those who come to it. ²Otherwise, would not the [sacrifices] have ceased being offered? If the worshipers had been cleansed once, would they no longer have any consciousness of sin? ³But

345

year after year a reminder of sin lies in these sacrifices, [4]for it is impossible for the blood of bulls and goats to take away sins.

[5]Consequently, when [Christ] came into the world, he said,

"You have not desired sacrifices and offerings,
   instead you have prepared a body for me.
[6]You have taken no pleasure
   in burnt offerings and sin offerings.
[7]Then I said, 'See, I have come to do your will, O God,'
   as it is written of me in the scroll of the book."

[8]Up above when he said, "You have neither desired nor taken pleasure in sacrifices and offerings and burnt offerings and sin offerings" (these are offered according to the law), [9]he then added, "See, I have come to do your will." He abolishes the first in order to establish the second. [10]And we have been sanctified by that will, through the offering of the body of Jesus Christ once for all.

[11]And every priest stands daily at his service, repeatedly offering the same sacrifices, which can never take away sins. [12]But when [Christ] had offered a single sacrifice for sins for all time, he sat down at the right hand of God, [13]then to wait until his enemies are made a footstool for his feet. [14]For by a single offering he has made those who are being sanctified perfect for all time.

[15]And the Holy Spirit also bears witness to us. For after saying,

[16]"This is the covenant that I will make with them
   after those days, says the Lord:
I will put my laws on their hearts,
   and write them on their minds,"

[17]then he adds,

"I will remember their sins and their lawlessness no more."

[18]Where forgiveness of these exists, there is no longer any offering for sin.

Confident by Faith

[19]Therefore, brothers, since we have confidence to enter the Holy Places by the blood of Jesus, [20]by the new and living way that he opened for us through the veil, that is, through his flesh, [21]and since we have a great priest [presiding] over the house of God, [22]let us draw near with a true heart in full assurance of faith, with our hearts sprinkled clean from an evil conscience and our bodies washed with pure water. [23]We should grip the confession of our hope tightly, not wavering, for he who promised is faithful. [24]And we should ponder how we can inspire one

another to love and good deeds, [25]not neglecting meeting together, as is the habit of some, but rather encouraging one another, and all the more so, as you see the Day drawing near.

[26]For if we go on sinning deliberately after receiving the knowledge of the truth, there no longer remains a sacrifice for sins, [27]but the dreadful prospect of judgment, and a fiery fury that will consume the adversaries. [28]Anyone who has dismissed the law of Moses dies without mercy at the testimony of two or three witnesses. [29]How much worse punishment do you think will be deserved by the man who has trampled the Son of God underfoot, and profaned the blood of the covenant by which he was sanctified, and outraged the Spirit of grace? [30]For we know him who said, "Vengeance is mine, I will repay." And again, "The Lord will judge his people." [31]It is a terrifying thing to fall into the hands of the living God.

[32]But recall the days in the past when, having been enlightened, you endured a difficult struggle with sufferings, [33]sometimes being publicly exposed to insults and affliction, and sometimes being friends with people being treated in that way. [34]For you had compassion on the prisoners, and you accepted the seizing of your property with joy, since you knew that you yourselves had a better and more enduring possession. [35]Therefore, do not throw away your confidence, which has great reward. [36]For you have need of endurance, so that having done the will of God you will receive what is promised. [37]"For,

> "Just a little while more,
>   and then the coming one shall come
>   and shall not tarry.
> [38]But my righteous one shall live by faith,
>   and if he shrinks back,
>   my soul has no pleasure in him."

[39]But we are not among those who shrink back and get destroyed, but among the ones who keep believing until the saving of the soul.

Chapter 11

Faith Defined

[1]Now faith is the assurance of things hoped for, the conviction of things not seen. [2]For people from long ago won approval by their faith. [3]By faith we understand that God created the universe by his word. Therefore, what can be seen was not made out of visible things.

The Hall of Faith

Abel

[4]By faith Abel offered a more acceptable sacrifice to God than Cain did, through which he won approval as righteous, and God certified that by accepting his gifts. Through his [faith] he still speaks, even though he is dead.

Enoch

[5]By faith Enoch was taken up so that he should not see death, and was found no more, because God had taken him. Now before he was taken, he was commended for having pleased God. [6]Now without faith it is impossible to please him, for whoever would approach God must do so believing that he exists and that he rewards those who seek him.

Noah

[7]By faith Noah, being warned by God about events still unseen, took heed and constructed an ark to save his household. By this [action] he condemned the world and became an heir of the righteousness that comes by faith.

Abraham and Sarah

[8]By faith Abraham obeyed when he was called to depart for a place that he was to receive as an inheritance, and he did depart, not knowing where he was to go. [9]By faith he camped out in the land of promise, as in a foreign land, living in tents with Isaac and Jacob, who, along with him were heirs of the same promise. [10]For he was looking forward to the city with solid foundations, designed and built by God. [11]By faith Sarah herself received the ability to conceive a child, even though she was well past the age, since she considered the one who had promised it to be faithful. [12]Therefore from one man, who was as good as dead, were born descendants as many as the stars of heaven or the innumerable grains of sand at the seashore.

Sojourners of the Promise

[13]All these people died in faith, not having received what was promised, but having seen it and greeted it from afar, and having acknowledged that they were strangers and exiles on the earth. [14]For people who speak as they did make it obvious that they are looking for a homeland. [15]Had they been yearning for the land that they had left behind, they would have had the chance to return. [16]But then—they desired a better country, that is, a heavenly one. Therefore, God has no shame in being called their God because he has prepared a city for them.

Abraham and Isaac

¹⁷By faith Abraham offered up Isaac when he was tested, and having received the promises, he was getting ready to offer up his only son, ¹⁸of whom it had been said, "Through Isaac shall your descendants be named." ¹⁹He considered that God was even able to raise him from the dead—from which he did receive him back, in a manner of speaking. ²⁰By faith Isaac blessed Jacob and Esau concerning things to come.

Jacob

²¹By faith Jacob, when he was dying, bowed in worship over the head of his staff and blessed each of Joseph's sons.

Joseph

²²By faith Joseph, at the end [of his life], predicted the exodus of the Israelites and told what to do with his bones.

Moses

²³By faith the infant Moses was hidden by his parents for three months, because they saw him as a beautiful child, and they were not afraid of the edict of the king. ²⁴By faith Moses, when he was grown up, refused to be called the son of Pharaoh's daughter, ²⁵choosing instead to suffer mistreatment along with the people of God rather than to enjoy the fleeting pleasures of sin. ²⁶He considered the abuse he suffered for Christ greater wealth than the treasures of Egypt, for he was looking to the reward. ²⁷By faith he left Egypt, not fearing the king's anger, because he persevered as if he was able to see him who is invisible. ²⁸By faith he kept the Passover and sprinkled the blood, so that the Destroyer of the first-born might not touch [the firstborn of Israel].

The Israelites

²⁹By faith the people crossed the Red Sea as if on dry land, whereas the Egyptians, attempting to do the same, were drowned. ³⁰By faith the walls of Jericho, having been encircled for seven days, collapsed. ³¹By faith Rahab the harlot did not perish with the unbelievers, because she had welcomed the spy scouts hospitably.

Conquerors

³²And what more shall I say? I lack the time to tell of Gideon, Barak, Samson, Jephthah—or of David and Samuel and the prophets—³³who through faith conquered kingdoms, enforced justice, obtained promises, closed the mouths of lions, ³⁴quenched powerful fire, escaped the edge of the sword, faced temptations, were strengthened

out of weakness, became mighty in war, and chased away foreign armies. [35]Women received back their dead by resurrection. Some were tortured, refusing to accept release, that they might rise again to a better life. [36]Others suffered mocking and scourging, and even chains and imprisonment. [37]They were stoned, they were sawn in two, they were killed with the sword. They wandered around in the skins of sheep and goats, destitute, afflicted, tormented—[38]the world was not worthy of them—wandering over deserts and mountains, and in dens and caves in the ground.

[39]And all these people, though well-attested by their faith, did not receive what was promised, [40]since God had preplanned something better for our sake, such that without us their [faith] would not be made perfectly complete.

Chapter 12

Author and Perfecter of Our Faith

[1]Therefore, since so great a cloud of witnesses surrounds us, let us also shove off every burden and clinging sin that entangles [us], and let us run the race laid out before us with perseverance, [2]focusing our eyes on Jesus, the author and perfecter of our faith, who endured the cross for the joy that was laid out before him, despising the shame, and is seated at the right hand of the throne of God.

Press On

[3]So that you do not grow weary or fainthearted, keep thinking about him who endured such great hostility against himself from sinful man. [4]In your own struggle against sin, you have not yet had to resist to the point of bloodshed. [5]And have you forgotten the encouraging message that addresses you as sons?

> "My son, do not regard the discipline of the Lord lightly,
> nor lose heart when he reproves you.
> [6]For the Lord disciplines the one that he loves
> and chastises every son that he receives."

[7]You must endure for the sake of discipline. God is treating you as sons—for what son is not disciplined by his father? [8]If you go without discipline, which everyone participates in, then you are illegitimate children and not sons. [9]In addition, we have had human fathers who disciplined us, and we did respect them. Should we not submit even more to the Father of spirits—and live? [10]For [our human fathers] disciplined us for a short time as they saw fit, but [God] disciplines us for our benefit so that we may share his holiness. [11]Of course, all discipline seems painful rather than pleasant at the moment—but later it yields the peaceful fruit of righteousness to those who have been trained by it.

[12]Therefore hold up your sagging hands and strengthen your feeble knees, [13]and make straight paths for your feet, so that instead of your aching body slipping out of joint, it gets cured. [14]Strive for peace with everybody, and for holiness because no one will see the Lord without it. [15]Diligently make sure that no one fails to obtain the grace of God, that no "root of bitterness" springs up, causing trouble, and contaminating many people. [16]And [make sure] that no one is sexually immoral, or godless like Esau, who sold his birthright for just one meal. [17]Now you know that afterward, when he wanted to inherit the blessing, he was rejected, for he found no chance for a change of heart, though he tearfully pursued one.

An Unshakable Kingdom

[18]For you have not come to some mountain that could be touched, or a blazing fire, or darkness and gloom, or a tempest, [19]or the sound of a trumpet, or a voice whose words made those who heard it beg that no more words would be spoken to them. [20]For they could not endure the stated order, "If a beast even touches the mountain, it must be killed by stoning." [21]Indeed, that sight was so terrifying that Moses said, "Even I tremble with fear." [22]But instead, you have come to Mount Zion, and to the city of the living God, the heavenly Jerusalem, and to myriads of angels at a celebration, [23]and to the congregation of the first-born whose names are written in heaven, and to God, who is judge of everything, and to the spirits of perfected righteous ones, [24]and to Jesus, the mediator of a new covenant, and to the sprinkled blood that conveys the message better than the [blood] of Abel.

[25]See that you do not refuse him who is speaking. For if they did not escape when they refused the one who warned them on earth, much less shall we escape if we reject him who is warning from heaven. [26]In days of old, his voice shook the earth. But now he has promised, "Yet once more will I shake not only the earth, but also the heavens." [27]This phrase, "Yet once more," indicates the elimination of things that are shaken, that is, the created things, so that all that remains is the things that cannot be shaken. [28]Therefore we should be grateful for receiving an unshakable kingdom, and in that way let us offer acceptable worship to God—with reverence and awe—[29]for our God is a consuming fire.

Chapter 13

Commands for Living a Godly Life

- ➤ [1]Continue to love one another as brothers.
- ➤ [2]Do not neglect showing hospitality to strangers, for in doing so, some have unknowingly entertained angels.
- ➤ [3]Remember those who are in prison, as if you were in prison with them, as

351

well as those who are being mistreated since you also belong to the body.

> ⁴May marriage be held in honor among all and may the marriage bed be undefiled, for God will judge the sexually immoral and adulterous.

> ⁵Keep your way of life free from the love of money and be content with what you possess. For he has said, "I will never leave you nor forsake you." ⁶So we can confidently say, "The Lord is on my side, I will not be afraid. What can man do to me?"

> ⁷Remember your leaders, who have spoken the word of God to you. Contemplate the outcome of how they spent their lives and imitate their faith.

> ⁸Jesus Christ is the same yesterday and today and forever.

> ⁹Do not be led astray by a variety of strange teachings.

> It is good that the heart be strengthened by grace, rather than by foods, which have not benefitted the people who pursue them.

Sacrifice of Praise

¹⁰We have an altar where the ministers of the tabernacle have no right to eat. ¹¹For the bodies of those animals whose blood is taken into the sanctuary by the high priest as a sin-offering are burned outside the camp. ¹²Likewise Jesus also suffered outside the gate in order to make the people holy through his own blood. ¹³So we ought to go out and join him outside the camp and bear the abuse he endured. ¹⁴For we have no permanent city here, but we look for the city that is to come. ¹⁵May we then continually offer up through him a sacrifice of praise to God, that is, the fruit of lips that confess his name. ¹⁶Do not neglect doing good and sharing what you own, for such sacrifices are pleasing to God.

¹⁷Obey your leaders and submit to them, for they are keeping watch over your souls, as men who will have to give an account. Let them do this joyfully, and not as a burden, for that would not benefit you.

¹⁸Pray for us, for we are sure that we have a clear conscience, desiring to act honorably in all things. ¹⁹I beg you to do this especially so that I may be brought back to you even sooner.

Benediction

²⁰Now may the God of peace who brought our Lord Jesus, the great shepherd of the sheep, back from the dead, by the blood of the eternal covenant, ²¹equip you with every good thing so that you may do his will, working in you what is pleasing in his sight, through Jesus Christ, to whom be glory throughout all the ages. Amen.

Final Greetings

[22]Brothers, I beg you to attend to [my] words of encouragement, for I have written a brief message to you. [23]Be aware that our brother Timothy has been released. If he comes soon, I shall see you along with him. [24]Greet all your leaders and all the saints [for us]. The ones from Italy send you greetings. [25]Grace be with all of you. Amen.

JAMES

Chapter 1

¹[From]: James, a servant of God and of the Lord Jesus Christ,

To: The twelve tribes that are scattered abroad

Greetings.

The Testing of Your Faith

²Consider it all joy, my brothers, when you find yourselves in various trials, ³knowing that the testing of your faith produces endurance. ⁴So allow endurance to complete its work in you, so that you will be made perfect and complete, lacking in nothing. ⁵But if anyone lacks wisdom, let him request it from God who gives freely to all without finding fault, and it shall be given to him. ⁶But let him ask in faith, doubting nothing, for the one who doubts is like a wave of the sea being tossed about and driven by the wind. ⁷For that person cannot presume that he shall receive anything from the Lord; ⁸he is a double-minded man, unstable in all his ways.

⁹Rather, let the brother of little means rejoice in being exalted ¹⁰and let the rich one rejoice in being humbled, for he shall pass away like the flower of the grass. ¹¹For the sun rises with a scorching heat and dries up the grass, and its flower falls off, and its lovely appearance perishes. In the same way, the man of wealth will also wither away in the midst of his business.

¹²Blessed is the man who endures tribulation, because having been tried he shall receive the crown of life that the Lord promised to those who love him. ¹³No one who is being tempted ought to say, "I am being tempted by God," for God is not tempted by evil things, and he himself tempts no one. ¹⁴But each man is tempted when he is lured by his own evil desire and enticed. ¹⁵Then when evil desire has conceived, it gives birth to sin, and when it is fully matured, sin produces death.

The Father of Lights

¹⁶Do not be deceived, my beloved brothers: ¹⁷every good and perfect gift is from above, coming down from the Father of lights, in whom there is neither variation nor changing shadow. ¹⁸By his own will he conceived us with the word of truth so that we would be a sort of firstfruits of his creatures.

Slow to Speak

[19]Therefore, my beloved brothers, let every man be quick to hear, but slow to speak, and slow to get angry. [20]For man's anger does not accomplish God's righteous purposes. [21]So set aside all filthiness and overwhelming wickedness. In meekness accept the Word that has been implanted into you, which is able to save your souls.

Doers of the Word

[22]But you should be doers of the word, not deceiving yourselves by being only hearers of it. [23]For if any man is a hearer of the word, and not also a doer, he is like a man who sees his own face in a mirror, [24]and then having looked at himself, forgets what he looks like once he walks away. [25]But the one who looks into the perfect law of freedom, and abides in it, is not just someone who hears and forgets but a doer who takes action. This one shall be blessed in what he does.

[26]If anyone among you should deem himself religious, but does not control his tongue and thereby deceives himself, this man's religion is useless. [27]Before God the Father, this is pure and undefiled religion: to go take care of widows and orphans in their times of distress, and to keep oneself untainted by the world.

Chapter 2

Treating Others with Integrity

[1]My brothers, in practicing the faith of our Lord Jesus Christ, the Lord of glory, do not show partiality. [2]For if a man with a gold ring, dressed in splendid apparel, should come into your church, and a poor man in ragged clothes should come in also, [3]and if you should notice the well-dressed one and say to him, "Sit here in this nice chair," and you say to the poor one, "You sit over there or sit down on the floor," [4]then are you not also guilty of showing partiality, and of judging people with evil motives in [your] mind? [5]Listen, my beloved brothers, has not God chosen the poor people of this world to be rich in faith, and to be heirs of the kingdom that he has promised to those who love him? [6]Yet you still dishonor the poor. Is it not the rich people who oppress you, and drag you into courts of law? [7]And do they not blaspheme that worthy name that you are known by? [8]Indeed you do well if you keep the royal law according to the scripture, "You shall love your neighbor as yourself."

[9]But if you do discriminate, you commit a sin, being convicted by the law as a transgressor. [10]For whoever keeps the whole law but breaks it in one small way shall be guilty of all of it. [11]For he who said, "You shall not commit adultery," also

said, "You shall not murder." So, even if you do not commit adultery, yet you murder, you are still a lawbreaker, nonetheless. [12]So, speak and act as people who shall be judged by the law of liberty. [13]For the one who has not shown mercy will receive judgment without mercy: mercy triumphs over judgment.

Faith Produces Good Deeds

[14]My brothers, what does it profit a man to say that he has faith, and yet does not act on it? Can that faith save him? [15]If a brother or sister is without clothing, destitute, and hungry, [16]and if one of you should say to him, "Go in peace, be warm, and well-fed," but then you do not meet his physical needs, what good is that? [17]Likewise, faith by itself, without deeds, is dead. [18]So, if a man should say, "One person has faith, and another has deeds," then I would respond, "You show me a faith that is without deeds, and I will show you my faith *by* my deeds."

[19]So you believe there is one God; you do well. But even the demons believe that— and tremble! [20]Fool, do you need to be shown that faith without deeds is useless? [21]Was not our father Abraham justified by deeds when he offered his son Isaac on the altar? [22]Do you see that his faith worked in tandem with his actions? His faith was completed through his actions. [23]And so the scripture that says, "Abraham believed God, and it was counted to him as righteousness," was fulfilled, and he was called a friend of God. [24]You can see then how a man is justified by deeds, and not through faith alone. [25]In the same way, was not Rahab the prostitute also justified by deeds when she received the messengers and sent them out a different way? [26]For, just as a body without the spirit is dead, so also faith without deeds is dead.

Chapter 3

Who Can Tame the Tongue?

[1]My brothers, not many of you should become teachers, knowing that they are judged more strictly. [2]For all of us often make mistakes. In fact, if someone does not *ever* say the wrong thing, he is a perfect man, able to keep his entire body under control. [3]Look, we put a bit in a horse's mouth so that it will obey us, and thereby we turn its whole body. [4]Also notice ships, though they are so large, and driven by strong winds, yet they are steered by a very small rudder, in whatever direction a pilot wants to steer it.

[5]So, the tongue is a small body part also, and yet it boasts of great things. How great a forest can be set on fire by such a tiny spark! [6]And the tongue is a fire, a world of evildoing. The tongue, placed in our bodies in such a way that it can defile the whole body, sets the entire course of our existence on fire and is itself set

on fire by hell. [7]For every kind of beast and bird, of reptile and sea creature, can be tamed and has been tamed by mankind, [8]but nobody can tame the tongue. It is a restless evil, full of deadly poison. [9]With it we bless the Lord and Father, and with it we curse others, who are made in the likeness of God. [10]Both blessing and cursing come from the same mouth. My brothers, it should not be like this. [11]Does a spring pour forth both fresh water and saltwater from the same opening? [12]My brothers, can a fig tree yield olives? Or can a grapevine produce figs? Nor can a salt lake yield fresh water.

Heavenly Wisdom

[13]Who among you is wise and understanding? Let him show his good deeds by his good conduct, through the meekness of wisdom. [14]But if you have bitter jealousy and selfish ambition in your hearts, do not boast and lie against the truth. [15]This is not the wisdom that comes down from above, but is earthly, unspiritual, and demonic. [16]For where jealousy and selfish ambition exist, there will be disorder and every vile practice. [17]But the wisdom from above is first pure, then peaceable, gentle, reasonable, full of mercy and good fruits, impartial and sincere. [18]Thus those who make peace sow a harvest of righteousness.

Chapter 4

Avoid Worldliness

[1]What is causing quarrels and causing fights among you? Is it not your passionate desires that are at conflict with each other within you? [2]You desire but do not possess [something], so you commit murder. You covet but cannot obtain [something], so you fight and quarrel. You do not have because you do not ask. [3]When you *do* ask, yet do not receive, it is because you ask with the wrong [motive] of spending to fulfill your own desires. [4]Unfaithful people! Do you not realize that friendship with the world is hostility with God? Therefore, whoever wishes to be a friend of the world makes himself an enemy of God. [5]Or do you suppose it is in vain that the scripture says, "Wanting to guard [his own], he woos back the spirit he has created to dwell within us"? [6]But he gives more grace. Therefore, it says, "God opposes the proud, but gives grace to the humble." [7]Submit yourselves therefore to God. Resist the devil and he will flee from you. [8]Draw near to God and he will draw near to you. Cleanse your hands, you sinners, and purify your hearts, you double-minded people. [9]Be wretched and mourn and weep. Let your laughter be turned to mourning and your joy to gloom. [10]Humble yourselves before the Lord and he will exalt you.

[11]Do not speak evil against one another, brothers. The one who speaks evil against a brother or judges his brother, speaks evil against the law and judges the law. But if you judge the law, you are not a doer of the law but a judge. [12]There is one lawgiver and judge, the one who is able to save and to destroy. But who are you that you judge your neighbor?

The Lord Holds Tomorrow

[13]Come now, you who say, "Today or tomorrow we will go into such and such a town and spend a year there and do business and make a profit." [14]Yet you know nothing about tomorrow. What is your life? For you are a mist that appears for a short time and then vanishes. [15]Instead you ought to say, "If the Lord wills, we shall live and we shall do such and such." [16]As it is, you boast in your arrogance; all such boasting is evil. [17]It is sin for someone to know what is right to do and fail to do it.

Chapter 5

Warnings to the Rich

[1]Come now, you rich, weep and howl over the miseries that are coming on you. [2]Your riches have rotted and your garments are moth-eaten. [3]Your gold and silver have corroded, and their corrosion will be evidence against you and will eat your flesh like fire. You have laid up treasure for the last days. [4]Look, the wages of the laborers who mowed your fields, which you kept back by fraud, cry out. And the cries of the harvesters have reached the ears of the Lord of hosts. [5]You have lived in luxury on the earth and have indulged yourselves. You have overfed your hearts at the time of slaughter. [6]You have condemned and have murdered the righteous man, [though] he does not resist you.

Bear Suffering with Patience

[7]Therefore, brothers, be patient until the coming of the Lord. Notice how the farmer waits for the precious fruit of the earth, being patient with it until it receives the early and the late rains. [8]You also, be patient. Strengthen your hearts, for the coming of the Lord is at hand. [9]Brothers, do not grumble against one another, so that you may not be judged. Look, the Judge is standing at the door. [10]Brothers, take for an example of suffering and patience the prophets who spoke in the name of the Lord. [11]Now, we consider blessed those who remained steadfast. You have heard of the steadfastness of Job, and you have seen the purpose of the Lord, and how compassionate and merciful the Lord is.

[12]But above all, my brothers, do not swear, either by heaven or by earth or with any other oath, but let your yes be yes and your no be no, so that you may not fall under condemnation.

Faithful Prayers

[13]Is anyone among you suffering? Let him pray. Is anyone cheerful? Let him sing praise. [14]Is anyone among you sick? Let him call for the elders of the church, and let them pray over him, anointing him with oil in the name of the Lord. [15]The faithful prayer will save the sick person, and the Lord will raise him up. Also, if he has committed sins, he will be forgiven. [16]Therefore confess your sins to one another, and pray for one another, that you may be healed. The earnest prayer of a righteous man releases great, effective power. [17]Elijah was a man of the same nature as ours, and he prayed fervently that it might not rain, and for three years and six months it did not rain on the earth. [18]Then he prayed again, and the heavens gave forth rain, and the earth brought forth its fruit.

Restoration of a Believer

[19]My brothers, if anyone among you wanders from the truth and someone brings him back, [20]let him know that someone who brings back a sinner from the error of his way will rescue [the sinner's] soul from death and will overlay a multitude of sins.

Chapter 1

¹[From]: Peter, an apostle of Jesus Christ,

To: the chosen ones, exiled and scattered throughout Pontus, Galatia, Cappa-docia, Asia, and Bithynia, ²according to the foreknowledge of God the Father, in the sanctification of the Spirit, with obedience to Jesus Christ and his sprin-kled sacrificial blood.

May grace and peace be multiplied to you.

Imperishable Inheritance

³Blessed be the God and Father of our Lord Jesus Christ! Through his great mer-cy we have been born again to a living hope through the resurrection of Jesus Christ from the dead, ⁴to an imperishable, undefiled, and unfading inheritance, preserved in heaven for you. ⁵By God's power you are guarded through faith for a salvation set to be revealed in the last time. ⁶You rejoice in this, even though you may have to suffer various trials for a little while now, ⁷so that the genuineness of your faith—which is more precious than gold which, even though it is perishabl,e is tested by fire—may become praise and glory and honor at the revelation of Je-sus Christ. ⁸Though you have not seen him, yet you do love him. Even though you do not see him now, you believe in him and rejoice with inexpressible and glorious joy. ⁹As the result of your faith you obtain the salvation of your souls.

Ransomed from Futility

¹⁰Now, as to this salvation, the prophets who prophesied of the grace that was to be yours carefully searched and inquired, ¹¹seeking to know what person or time the Spirit of Christ within them was indicating when he predicted the sufferings of Christ and the glories to follow. ¹²It was revealed to them that they were serving not themselves but you, in the things that have now been announced to you by those who proclaimed the good news to you through the Holy Spirit sent from heaven. Angels long to look into these things. ¹³Accordingly, you must prepare your minds for battle. Be serious and set your hope fully on the grace that will be delivered to you at the revelation of Jesus Christ. ¹⁴As obedient children, do not be shaped by the passions you had in your previous ignorance, ¹⁵but as he who called you is holy, be holy yourselves in all your conduct. ¹⁶After all, it is written,

"You shall be holy, for I am holy." ¹⁷And if you call on the Father who judges each one impartially according to his deeds, conduct yourselves with reverence throughout your sojourn in exile. ¹⁸You know that you were ransomed from the futile ways passed down to you from your forefathers, not with perishable things such as silver or gold, ¹⁹but with the precious blood of Christ, which is like that of a lamb without blemish or spot. ²⁰He was foreknown before the foundation of the world, but he was made manifest in the last era for your sake. ²¹Through him you have confidence in God, who raised him from the dead and gave him glory, so that your faith and hope are in God.

Purify Souls and Eliminate Evil

²²By your obedience to the truth, out of a sincere love of the brothers, you have purified your souls, so love one another earnestly from the heart. ²³You have been born again, not of perishable but of imperishable seed, through the living and abiding word of God. ²⁴For:

> "All humanity is like grass,
> and all its glory like the flower of grass.
> The grass withers, and the flower falls—
> ²⁵but the word of the Lord abides forever."

This word is the good news that was proclaimed to you.

Chapter 2

¹So eliminate all malice and all guile and hypocrisy and envy and all slander. ²Desire the pure spiritual milk, like newborn babies, so that you may grow up to salvation by it, ³since indeed you have tasted the Lord's kindness. ⁴By coming to him—the living stone rejected by men but chosen and precious to God—⁵you yourselves are being built into a spiritual house like living stones, [becoming] a holy priesthood to offer spiritual sacrifices that through Jesus Christ are acceptable to God. ⁶For scripture contains this: "Take note: in Zion I am laying a stone, a cornerstone chosen and precious, and he who believes in him will not be put to shame." ⁷So you who believe regard him as precious, but for those who do not believe: "The very stone that the builders rejected has become the chief cornerstone," ⁸and "A stumbling block, a rock that will trip them up." They stumble because they disobey the word, as they were destined to do.

A Royal Priesthood

⁹But you are a chosen race, a royal priesthood, a holy nation, God's own people, that you may proclaim the wonderful deeds of him who called you out of darkness

into his wonderful light. [10]In the past, you were not a people, but now you are God's people. In the past you had not received mercy, but now you have received mercy.

[11]I urge you, beloved ones—sojourners and pilgrims—to abstain from fleshly passions that wage war against the soul. [12]Among the Gentiles, keep conducting yourselves honorably, so that if they should speak against you as evildoers, they may notice your good deeds and glorify God on the day of visitation.

Honor Authorities

[13]For the Lord's sake, submit to every human institution, whether it be to the emperor as supreme, [14]or to governors as sent by him to punish those who do evil and to praise those who do right. [15]For it is God's will that you should silence the ignorance of foolish people by doing what is right. [16]Live as free people, yet without using your freedom as a cover-up for evil, but rather living as God's servants. [17]Honor everyone, love the brotherhood. Fear God, honor the emperor.

[18]Servants, be submissive to your masters with all respect, not only to the kind and gentle ones but also to the unjust ones. [19]For this is gracious: when someone being mindful of God endures sorrows while suffering unjustly. [20]For what credit lies in your patient endurance of being beaten for having done something wrong? But this is gracious in God's eyes: if you patiently endure suffering for having done what is right. [21]For you have been called to this because Christ also suffered for you, leaving you an example, that you should follow in his footsteps. [22]He committed no sin; no guile was found on his lips. [23]When he was being reviled, he did not revile in return. When he suffered, he did not threaten, but rather he kept on entrusting himself to him who judges justly. [24]He himself bore our sins in his body on the [wood] of a tree, that we might die to sin and live to righteousness. By his wounds you have been healed. [25]For you were straying like sheep but have now returned to the shepherd and overseer of your souls.

Chapter 3

Submission and Honor in Marriage

[1]Likewise, [you] wives, be submissive to your husbands, so that some of them, even though they do not obey the word, may be won without a word by the conduct of their wives, [2]as they observe your reverent and pure-hearted conduct. [3]Do not have your adorning be on the outside, with the braiding of hair, wearing of gold, and dressing in fine clothing. [4]Instead, let [your adorning] be the hidden person of the heart with the imperishable jewel of a gentle and quiet spirit, which is very precious in God's sight. [5]Long ago the holy women who placed their hope

in God used to adorn themselves in this way, and were submissive to their husbands, [6]such as Sarah being obedient to Abraham by calling him lord. And you are now her children if you do right and let nothing frighten you.

[7]Likewise, [you] husbands, live with your wives in a considerate way, bestowing honor on the woman as the weaker vessel, since you are joint heirs of the grace of life, so that your prayers may not be hindered.

Righteous Suffering

[8]Finally, all of you, have unity of spirit, sympathy, love of the brothers, a tender heart, and a humble mind. [9]Do not return evil for evil or reviling for reviling. But on the contrary, bless, for you have been called to this to obtain a blessing. [10]For

> "Whoever desires to love life and see good days,
> let him keep his tongue from evil and his lips from speaking lies.
> [11]Let him turn away from evil to do what is right.
> Let him seek peace and pursue it.
> [12]For the eyes of the Lord are on the righteous,
> and his ears are open to their prayer.
> But the face of the Lord is against those who do evil."

[13]Now who would harm you if you are zealous for what is good? [14]But even if you do suffer this, you will be blessed. Do not be afraid of that, nor be troubled, [15]but keep Christ the Lord holy in your hearts. Always be prepared to make a defense to anyone who requires you to account for the assured hope that is in you; yet do so with gentleness and respect. [16]Keep your conscience clear so that, when you are slandered, those who revile your good behavior in Christ may be put to shame. [17]For it is better to suffer for doing right, if God should will it to be, than for doing wrong.

[18]For Christ also suffered death for sins once for all—the righteous for the unrighteous—that he might bring us to God, being put to death in the flesh but made alive in the Spirit, [19]in which he went and preached to the spirits in prison, [20]who formerly had not obeyed, when God's patience waited in the days of Noah, during the building of the ark, in which a few—that is, eight persons—were saved through water. [21]Corresponding to this is baptism, which now saves you, not as a removal of dirt from the body but as an appeal to God for a clear conscience, through the resurrection of Jesus Christ, [22]who has gone into heaven and is at the right hand of God with the angels, with authorities and powers subjected to him.

Chapter 4

Avoid Your Sinful Ways of the Past

[1]Therefore, since Christ suffered in the flesh, equip yourselves with the same mindset. For the one who has suffered physically is no longer totally given over to sin, [2]so as to live out the rest of his earthly lifetime no longer just for the sake of human passions, but for the will of God. [3]Let the time that is past suffice for doing what the Gentiles like to do: living in sensuality, passions, drunkenness, orgies, drinking parties, and lawless idolatry. [4]Regarding this, they are surprised that you do not run off to join them in the same immoral lifestyle, so, and they malign you. [5]But, they will give an account to him who is prepared to judge the living and the dead. [6]For this is why the gospel was preached even to the dead, so that though they were judged in the flesh as human beings, they might live in the spirit as God does.

[7]The end of all things is imminent. Therefore, be self-controlled and sober-minded for the sake of your prayers. [8]Above all, keep loving one another earnestly, since love overlays a multitude of sins. [9]Practice hospitality to one another without grumbling. [10]Each one of you should be using the gift he has been given in service to others, as good stewards of the variety of God's grace: [11]the one who speaks should be speaking the very words of God; the one who serves should serve by the strength that God supplies, so that God may be glorified in all things through Jesus Christ.

Glory and dominion belong to him forever and ever. Amen.

The Fiery Trial

[12]Beloved ones, when the fiery trial comes on you to test you, do not be surprised as though something unusual were happening to you. [13]But rejoice as you share in Christ's sufferings, so that you may also rejoice and be glad when his glory is revealed. [14]When you are insulted for the name of Christ, you are blessed, since the spirit of glory and of God rests on you. [15]But let none of you suffer as a murderer, or a thief, or an evildoer, or a meddler. [16]Yet if anyone suffers for being as a Christian, let him not be ashamed, but let him glorify God in that name. [17]For the time has come for judgment to begin with the household of God. And if it begins with us, what will be the destiny of those who do not obey the gospel of God? [18]And "If the righteous person is scarcely saved, what will happen to the ungodly and the sinner?" [19]Therefore let those who suffer according to God's will entrust their souls to a faithful Creator as they are doing good.

Chapter 5

[1]So as a fellow elder and a witness of the sufferings of Christ as well as a partaker in the glory that is to be revealed, I encourage the elders among you [2]to tend the flock of God, overseeing them not under compulsion; but willingly, not for shameful material gain but with eagerness; [3]not by dominating those in your charge but by being examples to the flock. [4]And when the chief Shepherd appears you will obtain the unfading crown of glory.

[5]Likewise you younger ones are to be subject to the elders. Clothe yourselves, all of you, with humility toward one another, for "God opposes the proud, but gives grace to the humble." [6]So, humble yourselves under the mighty hand of God, so that he may exalt you in due time, [7]casting all your anxieties on him because he takes care of you. [8]Be sober-minded and be vigilant. Your adversary the devil prowls around like a roaring lion, looking for someone to devour. [9]Resist him, firm in your faith, knowing that your brotherhood throughout the world is experiencing the same types of suffering.

> [10]*And after you have suffered a little while,*
> *the God of all grace,*
> *who has called you to his eternal glory in Christ,*
> *will himself restore, confirm, strengthen, and establish you.*
> [11]*To him be the dominion forever and ever. Amen.*

Final Instructions and Closing

[12]I have written briefly to you with [the help of] Silvanus, whom I regard as a faithful brother, encouraging and declaring that this is the true grace of God; stand fast in it. [13]Your sister church [here] in [this] Babylon, sends you greetings, as does my son Mark. [14]Greet one another with the kiss of love. Peace to all of you who are in Christ.

2 Peter

Chapter 1

¹[From]: Simon Peter, a servant and apostle of Jesus Christ,

To: those who have obtained a faith equally as precious as ours through the righteousness of our God and Savior Jesus Christ.

Spiritual Maturity

²May grace and peace be multiplied to you in the knowledge of God and of Jesus our Lord. ³His divine power has granted all things pertaining to life and godliness to us, through the knowledge of him who called us to his own glory and excellence. ⁴Through this he has granted his precious and awesome promises to us, in order that through them you may escape from the corruption that is in the world because of sinful desire and become partakers of the divine nature. ⁵For this very reason, put forth the effort to supplement your faith with virtue, and virtue with knowledge, ⁶and knowledge with self-control, and self-control with steadfastness, and steadfastness with godliness, ⁷and godliness with brotherly affection, and brotherly affection with love. ⁸For if these things are in you and are increasing, they will keep you from being ineffective or unfruitful in the knowledge of our Lord Jesus Christ. ⁹For whoever lacks these qualities is so short-sighted as to be blind and has forgotten that he was cleansed from his former sins. ¹⁰Therefore, brothers, be all the more diligent to confirm your calling and election, for if you practice this you will never fall. ¹¹For in doing so an entrance into the eternal kingdom of our Lord and Savior Jesus Christ will be richly provided for you.

¹²Therefore I intend to remind you of these things at all times, though you know them and are established in the truth that you have. ¹³As long as I am in this body, I think it right to stir you up by way of reminder, ¹⁴since I know that the time for me to depart my physical body will be soon, as our Lord Jesus Christ showed me. ¹⁵And I will see to it that after my departure you will always be able to recall these things.

¹⁶For we did not follow cleverly devised myths when we made known the power and coming of our Lord Jesus Christ to you. On the contrary, we were eyewitnesses of his majesty. ¹⁷He received honor and glory from God the Father and the Majestic Glory brought the voice to him: "This is my beloved Son, with whom I am well pleased." ¹⁸We ourselves heard this voice brought from heaven, for we

were with him on the holy mountain. ¹⁹And we have an even surer thing: the prophetic word– and you will do well to pay attention to it as to a lamp shining in a dark place, until the day dawns and the morning star rises in your hearts. ²⁰First of all you must understand this: spiritual prophecy arises out of one's own interpretation, ²¹because no prophecy ever came by the will of man, but men spoke from God being moved by the Holy Spirit.

Chapter 2

False Prophets Will Come

¹But false prophets have also come among our people, just as false teachers will come among you. They will sneak in destructive heresies, even denying the Master who redeemed them, and thus bring swift destruction on themselves. ²And many others will go along with their open immorality, and because of them the way of truth will be blasphemed. ³In their greed they will exploit you with false words, but their longstanding condemnation has not been idle, and their destruction has not lain dormant.

⁴For:

—If God did not spare the angels that sinned but cast them into hell and condemned them to be kept in gloomy pits until the judgment;

—⁵If he did not spare the ancient world, but preserved Noah, a herald of righteousness, as one of eight people, when he brought a flood on the world of the ungodly;

—⁶If by turning the cities of Sodom and Gomorrah to ashes he condemned them to extinction and made them an example to those who were going to be ungodly; ⁷and,

—If he rescued righteous Lot, greatly distressed by the sensual conduct of the wicked ⁸(for as that righteous man lived among them, he was tormented in his righteous soul day after day with their wicked deeds),

⁹Then:

the Lord knows how to rescue the godly from adversity, and he knows how to keep the unrighteous under punishment until the day of judgment, ¹⁰especially those who indulge in the lust of defiling passion and who despise authority.

The Ways of the Wicked and Their Final End

Bold and arrogant, they do not tremble as they blaspheme the glorious ones. ¹¹Whereas angels, though greater in might and power, do not pronounce a blasphemous judgment against them before the Lord. ¹²But these people—who are like animals who cannot reason—creatures of instinct born to be caught and killed—are blaspheming about matters that they are ignorant of. They will perish along with the [angels] in the same destruction, ¹³suffering affliction as the payoff for their wrong-doing. They take pleasure in reveling in the daytime. They are blots and blemishes, reveling in their deceptions, even as they are dining with you. ¹⁴They have eyes full of adultery; their lust for sinfulness cannot be satisfied; they entice unstable souls; they have hearts trained in greed. Accursed children! ¹⁵Forsaking the right way they have gone astray. They have followed the way of Balaam, the son of Beor, who loved to profit from wrongdoing. ¹⁶He was rebuked for his own transgression when a speechless donkey spoke with human voice and restrained the prophet's madness.

¹⁷These people are springs without water and vaporous clouds driven by a storm, and the gloom of utter darkness has been reserved for them! ¹⁸For, uttering loud, foolish boasts, they entice men who have barely escaped from those who live in error with sensual passions of the flesh. ¹⁹They promise them freedom, but they themselves are slaves of corruption. For whatever overcomes a man enslaves him. ²⁰For if, after they have escaped the defilements of the world through the knowledge of our Lord and Savior Jesus Christ, they are again entangled in them and overpowered, the last state has become worse for them than the first. ²¹For it would have been better for them never to have known the way of righteousness than having known it to turn back from the holy commandment delivered to them. ²²That truthful proverb has come on them: "The dog returns to his own vomit, and the sow is washed only to wallow in the mire."

Chapter 3

The Coming of the Day of the Lord

¹My beloved ones, this is now the second letter that I am writing to you. In both I [seek to] awaken your sincere mind by way of this reminder: ²You should remember the predictions of the holy prophets and the commandment of the Lord and Savior [sent] through your apostles. ³First [of all], you must realize this: that scoffers will come in the final era with scoffing, following their own sinful desires ⁴and saying, "Where is the promise of his coming? For [ever since] the fathers fell asleep, all things have continued as they were from the beginning of creation." ⁵They deliberately ignore this fact: that by the word of God the heavens existed long ago, and the earth was formed out of water and by means of water. ⁶And by that means the world that existed then was flooded with water and destroyed. ⁷But by the same word the heavens and earth that now exist are being stored up for fire, being kept until the Day of Judgment and destruction of the ungodly.

[8]But, beloved, do not overlook this one fact: that with the Lord one day is as a thousand years, and a thousand years as one day. [9]The Lord is not slow [in fulfilling] *his* promise as some would measure slowness. Rather, he is patient with you, not wanting that anyone should perish, but rather that all should come to repentance. [10]But the day of the Lord will come like a thief: the heavens will pass away with a roar, and the elements of the universe will be burned up and dissolved, and the earth and what man built on it will be burned up. [11]Since all these things are to be dissolved in this way, what sort of persons should you be in lives of holiness and godliness, [12]waiting for and hastening the coming of the day of God, because of which the heavens will be set ablaze and dissolved, and the elements will melt as they burn! [13]But according to his promise we are waiting for the New Heavens and a New Earth where righteousness dwells.

[14]Therefore, beloved, since you are waiting for these things, be diligent to have [the Lord] find you without spot or blemish, and at peace. [15]And regard our Lord's patience as a [chance for] salvation. Our beloved brother Paul also wrote to you in the same way, by the wisdom given to him, [16]speaking of this as he does in all his letters. Some things in them are hard to understand, which ignorant and unstable people twist as they do with other scriptures to their own destruction. [17]Therefore, you, beloved, knowing this beforehand, take care not to be carried away by the error of lawless men and lose your own strong foothold. [18]But grow in the grace and knowledge of our Lord and Savior Jesus Christ. To him be the glory both now and to the day of eternity. Amen.

I JOHN

Chapter 1

¹The One who was from the beginning,
whom we have heard,
whom we have seen with our eyes,
whom we have looked on
and touched with our hands:

We proclaim him to you concerning the Word of life. ²The life was made manifest, and we have seen it and do testify to the eternal life that was with the Father and was made manifest to us. ³We also proclaim to you what we have seen and heard so that you may have fellowship with us—and indeed our fellowship is with the Father and with his Son Jesus Christ. ⁴And we are writing these things so that your joy may be complete.

Walking in the Light

⁵This is the message that we have heard from him and proclaim to you: that God is light and in him there is no darkness at all. ⁶If we claim we have fellowship with him while we walk in darkness, we lie and do not practice the truth. ⁷But if we walk in the light, as he is in the light, we have fellowship with one another, and the blood of Jesus his Son cleanses us from all sin. ⁸If we claim we have no sin, we deceive ourselves, and the truth is not in us. ⁹If we confess our sins, he is faithful and just to forgive our sins and to cleanse us from all unrighteousness. ¹⁰If we claim we have not sinned, we make him a liar, and his word is not in us.

Chapter 2

Jesus Advocates for Us

¹My little children, I am writing this to you so that you may not sin. But if anyone *does* sin, we have an advocate with the Father, Jesus Christ the righteous, ²and he is the sacrifice of atonement for our sins, and not only for ours but also for the sins of the whole world. ³Now this is how we are certain that we have come to know him: if we keep his commandments. ⁴Anyone who says "I know him" but disobeys his commandments is a liar, and the truth is not in him. ⁵But love for God truly is made perfect in anyone who keeps his word. By this we may be sure

that we are in him: 6anyone who claims that he abides in him ought to walk the same way he walked.

My Reasons for Writing

7Beloved, to you I am writing no new commandment, but an old commandment that you had from the beginning. The old commandment is the word that you have heard. 8Yet to you I am writing a new commandment, which is true in him and in you, because the darkness is passing away, and the true light is already shining. 9Anyone who claims to be in the light and yet hates his brother is still in the darkness. 10Anyone who loves his brother abides in the light, and in it lies no cause for stumbling. 11But anyone who hates his brother is in the darkness and walks in the darkness, and does not know where he is going, because the darkness has blinded his eyes.

12I am writing to you, little children, because your sins are forgiven for [the sake of] his name.

13I am writing to you, fathers, because you know him [who has been] from the beginning.

I am writing to you, young men, because you have overcome the evil one.

I write to you, children, because you know the Father.

14I write to you, fathers, because you know him [who has been] from the beginning.

I write to you, young men, because you are strong, and the word of God abides in you, and you have overcome the evil one.

Do Not Love the Things of This World

15Do not love the world or the things in the world. If anyone loves the world, love for the Father is not in him. 16For all that is in the world—the lust of the flesh and the desires of the eyes and the pride of life's [goods]—is not of the Father but is of the world. 17The [things of this] world pass away, [as does] the lust for them. But anyone who does the will of God abides forever.

Antichrist in the World

18Children, it is the last hour! You have heard that antichrist is coming, and many antichrists have already come. Therefore, we know that it is the last hour. 19They parted ways with us. But then, they were not [really part] of us. For if they had *really* been [part] of us, they would have continued with us. Instead, they parted ways, so that it might be obvious that they all are not [part] of us. ²⁰But you have been anointed by the Holy One, so you understand all things. ²¹I write to you, not because you do not know the truth, but because you know it, and know that no lie is of the truth. ²²Who is the liar but someone who denies that Jesus is the Christ? This is the antichrist: anyone who denies the Father and the Son. ²³No one who denies the Son has the Father. Anyone who confesses the Son has the Father also. ²⁴Let what you heard from the beginning abide in you. If what you heard from the beginning abides in you, then you will abide in the Son and in the Father. ²⁵And this is what he has promised us: eternal life.

²⁶I write these things to you about those who would deceive you. ²⁷But the anointing that you received from him abides in you, and you have no need for anyone to teach you. Rather, abide in him as his anointing teaches you about everything, and is true, and is not a lie, just as it has instructed you.

Be Children of God

²⁸And now, little children, abide in him, so that when he appears, we may have confidence and not shy away from him in shame at his coming. ²⁹If you know that he is righteous, you may be assured that everyone who practices what is right has been born of him. ³:¹See what love the Father has given us: that we should be called children of God, and so we are. The world does not know us because it did not know him. ³:²Beloved, now we are God's children. What we shall be has not yet come to pass, but we know that when he appears, we shall be like him, for we shall see him as he is. ³:³And everyone who hopes in him purifies himself as he is pure.

Chapter 3, cont.

³:⁴Everyone who commits sins practices lawlessness because sin is lawlessness. ⁵You know that he was made manifest to take away sins, and in him there is no sin. ⁶No one who abides in him keeps on sinning; anyone who *does* keep on sinning has neither seen nor known him. ⁷Little children, let no one deceive you. Anyone who does right is righteous, as he is righteous. ⁸Anyone who makes a practice of sinning is of the devil, for the devil has been sinning from the beginning. The reason the Son of God appeared was to destroy the works of the devil. ⁹No one who is born of God makes a practice of sinning, for God's seed resides in him, and he cannot keep on sinning because he is born of God. ¹⁰It is evident by this who the children of God are, and who the children of the devil are: anyone who does not practice righteousness and does not love his brother is not of God.

Love One Another

[11]For this is the message that you have heard from the beginning: that we should love one another, [12]unlike Cain who was of the evil one and murdered his brother. And why did he murder him? Because his own deeds were evil, whereas his brother's were righteous. [13]Brothers, do not be surprised that the world hates you. [14]Because we *do* love the brothers, we know that we have passed out of death into life. Anyone who does not love remains in death. [15]Anyone who hates his brother is a murderer, and you know that no murderer has eternal life abiding in him.

[16]We fully realize what love is by this: he laid down his life for us. And we ought to lay down our lives for the brothers. [17]But if anyone owns worldly goods and sees his brother in need, yet closes his heart against him, how does God's love abide in him? [18]Little children, let us love not in word or speech, but rather in deed and in truth.

[19]We will know that we are of the truth by this and reassure our hearts before him. [20]For whenever our heart condemns us, God is greater than our heart, and he knows everything. [21]Beloved, if our heart does not condemn us, we have confidence before God. [22]And we receive from him whatever we ask because we keep his commandments and do what pleases him. [23]And this is his commandment: that we should believe in the name of his Son Jesus Christ and love one another, just as he has commanded us. [24]Anyone who is keeping his commandments is abiding in God, and he is in him; by this we know that he abides in us through the Spirit that he has given us.

Chapter 4

Test Every Spirit

[1]Beloved, do not believe every spirit, but test the spirits as to whether they are from God, for many false prophets have gone out into the world. [2]This is how you know the Spirit of God: every spirit that confesses that Jesus Christ has come in the flesh is from God, [3]and every spirit that does not confess Jesus is *not* from God. This is the [spirit of] the antichrist, which you heard was coming, and now is already in the world. [4]Little children, you are from God, and have overcome them, for the One who is in you is greater than the one who is in the world. [5]They are from the world, therefore what they say is from the world, and the world listens to them. [6]We are from God. Anyone who knows God listens to us, and anyone who is *not* from God does not listen to us. By this we know the spirit of truth and the spirit of error.

God is Love

[7]Beloved, let us love one another, for love is of God, and anyone who loves has been born of God and knows God. [8]Anyone who does not love does *not* know God, for God is love. [9]The love of God was made manifest among us in this: that God sent his only Son into the world, so that we might live through him. [10]In this is love, not that we loved God but that he loved us and sent his Son to be the sacrifice of atonement for our sins. [11]Beloved, if God loved us in this way, we also ought to love one another. [12]No one has ever seen God. If we love one another, God abides in us and his love is made perfect in us. [13]By this we know that we abide in him and he in us, because he has given of his own Spirit to us.

[14]And we have seen and do testify that the Father has sent his Son as the Savior of the world. [15]God abides in anyone who confesses that Jesus is the Son of God, and he abides in God. [16]So we have come to know and to trust in the love God has for us. God is love, and anyone who abides in love abides in God, and God abides in him. [17]In this, love is made perfect with us, so that we may have confidence for the day of judgment, because as he is so are we in this world.

[18]There is no fear in love, but perfect love casts out fear. For fear has to do with punishment, and anyone who fears has not been made perfect in love. [19]We love because he first loved us. [20]If anyone claims, "I love God," yet hates his brother, he is a liar. For anyone who does not love his brother, whom he has seen, cannot love God, whom he has not seen. [21]And we have this commandment from him: that anyone who loves God must love his brother as well.

Chapter 5

Overcome the World

[1]Everyone who believes that Jesus is the Christ is a child of God, and everyone who loves the Father loves his offspring. [2]By this we know that we love the children of God: when we love God and obey his commandments. [3]For this is the love of God: that we keep his commandments. And his commandments are not burdensome. [4]For anyone who has been born of God overcomes the world; and this is the victory that overcomes the world: our faith. [5]Who is the one who overcomes the world? Only the one who believes that Jesus is the Son of God.

Three Witnesses

[6]This is the One who came by water and blood: Jesus Christ—not only by the water, but by the water and by the blood. And the Spirit is the witness because the Spirit is the truth. [7]There are three witnesses: [8]the Spirit, the water, and the

blood; and these three are in agreement. [9]If we receive the testimony of men, the testimony of God is greater, for this is the testimony of God that he has borne about his Son. [10]Anyone who believes in the Son of God has the testimony in himself. Anyone who does not believe God has made him a liar, because he has not believed in the testimony that God has borne about his Son. [11]And this is the testimony: that God gave us eternal life, and this life is in his Son. [12]Anyone who has the Son has life; anyone who does not have the Son of God does not have life.

Praying About Sins

[13]I write these things to you who believe in the name of the Son of God so that you may know that you have eternal life. [14]And this is the confidence we have in him: that if we ask anything according to his will, he hears us. [15]And if we know that he hears us in whatever we ask, we know that we have obtained what we requested of him. [16]If anyone sees his brother committing a sin that does not bring death, he should make a request, and God will grant life for those whose sin does not bring death. There is sin that does bring death; I am not saying that someone is to pray about that [kind]. [17]All wrongdoing is sin, but there is sin that is not mortal. [18]We know that everyone who is born of God does not keep on sinning, but the One born of God guards him, and the evil one does not touch him. [19]We know that we are of God, and the whole world remains in wickedness. [20]And we know that the Son of God has come and has given us understanding, so that we may know him who is true. And we are in him who is true, in his Son Jesus Christ. This is the true God and eternal life.

And in closing—

[21]Little children, guard yourselves from idols.

2 JOHN

[1]From]: the elder

To: the chosen lady and her children, who are loved not only by me but also by all who have known the truth, [2]because of the truth that lives in us and shall be with us forever.

[3]May grace, mercy, and peace be with you from God the Father and from the Lord Jesus Christ, the son of the Father, in truth and love.

Love One Another

[4]I rejoiced greatly on finding out that some of your children are walking in the truth, according to the commandments we received from the Father. [5]And now I ask you, lady, not as if I were writing a new commandment to you, but rather this being one that we have had right from the beginning, that we love one another. [6]And this is what love is: that we should walk according to the commandments. This is the commandment, being the same one that you have heard right from the beginning, so that you would walk in it.

Deception and Truth

[7]Many deceivers have entered into this world–those who do not confess that Jesus Christ came in the flesh–such is the deceiver and the antichrist. [8]Guard yourselves, so that you do not lose what we have worked for, but that we might receive a full reward. [9]Anyone who violates, and does not stay within, Christ's teaching does not have God. Anyone who does stay within the teaching has both the Father and the Son. [10]If anyone comes to you not bearing this teaching, do not welcome him into your house, and do not wish him well, [11]for anyone who wishes him well takes part in his evildoings. [12]Though I have many things to write to you, I would prefer not to with pen and paper. Rather, I am in hopes of coming to you, and speaking face to face, so that our joy may be full.

[13]The children of your chosen sister send you their greetings.

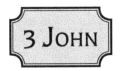

3 John

¹From: the elder–

To: the cherished Gaius, whom I truly love.

Walk in the Faith

²My cherished friend, I wish above all else that you may prosper and be in good health, just as you are prospering spiritually. ³For I rejoiced greatly when the brothers came and testified of the truth that is in you, just as you are walking in the truth. ⁴No greater joy do I experience than hearing that my children are walking in the truth.

⁵My cherished friend, whatever you do both for the brothers and for strangers ⁶who have borne witness to the church of your godly love is a faithful thing. You will do well to help them on their spiritual journey in a godly way. ⁷For they went out for his name's sake, taking along nothing from the Gentiles. ⁸So, we ought to be supportive of such people, so that we may be fellow workers for the truth.

Diotrephes Causing Trouble

⁹Now then, I wrote to the church about this, but Diotrephes, who loves being first in all things, does not accept us. ¹⁰Because of this, if I come, I will remember the things that he does, speaking nonsense about us with malicious words. And furthermore, not content with this, he does not accept the brothers, and forbids those who would come from coming, and instead throws them out of the church.

¹¹My cherished friend, do not imitate what is evil, but rather what is good. The one who does good is of God, but the one who does evil has *not* seen God.

In closing

¹²Everyone speaks well of Demetrius, and so the truth stands, and we also speak well of him, and you know that our word is true. ¹³I had many things to write about, but I prefer to not write of them to you with pen and ink. ¹⁴Rather, I hope to see you soon and we shall be able to speak face-to-face. ¹⁵Peace be with you. Our friends send their greetings. Greet our friends by name.

JUDE

[1][From]: Jude, a servant of Jesus Christ, and the brother of James,

To: those who have been called and sanctified by God the Father, and preserved in Jesus Christ.

[2]May mercy and peace and love be given to you in abundance.

Destruction of Unbelievers

[3]Beloved, though I was striving diligently to write to you about the salvation that we share in common, it became necessary for me to write to you and encourage you to contend earnestly for the faith that was delivered to the saints. [4]For certain ungodly men, who were ordained long ago to this condemnation, have snuck in, distorting the grace of our God to excuse immorality, and denying the only Lord God and our Lord Jesus Christ. [5]So I should like to remind you of this—though you used to be aware of it—that the Lord, having saved the people out of the land of Egypt, destroyed the unbelievers afterward.

[6]He has kept the angels who overstepped their authority—and left their assigned dwelling place—in everlasting chains in the gloomy darkness below, awaiting the great Day of judgment. [7]In the same way, Sodom and Gomorrah, and the cities around them, having given themselves over to fornication and pursued unnatural sexuality, are put forth as an example, suffering the penalty of eternal fire. [8]Furthermore, these fantasizers defile the flesh, dismiss authority, and malign heavenly glory.

[9]Yet, Michael the Archangel, while contending with the Devil, disputed about the body of Moses. He did not dare to bring a railing accusation against him, but rather said, "May the Lord rebuke you." [10]But these people speak evil of things that they do not understand, and, using what they do not know through basic human nature, they corrupt themselves like wild animals. [11]Woe to them! Because having gone the way of Cain, seeking after profit, they rushed into the error of Balaam and perished in Korah's rebellion.

[12]These [men] are moldy spots at your love feasts, eating along with you without a qualm–shepherds who only feed themselves. They are rainless clouds, blown along by the wind, trees uprooted at harvest time having borne no fruit–twice dead. [13]They are wild ocean waves, foaming up their shame, wandering stars for whom an eternity of gloomy darkness has been reserved.

[14]Even Enoch, the seventh generation from Adam, prophesied about these men saying: "See, the Lord is coming with thousands and thousands of his holy ones[15] to judge all men and to condemn the wicked for all their ungodly deeds and ways, and for the harsh things that these sinners said against him." [16]These men are the grumblers and murderers who follow their own evil desires. They speak arrogantly and flatter others for their own advantage.

Be Wise and Faithful

[17]But, you, beloved, be mindful of the words that have been spoken by the apostles of our Lord Jesus Christ, [18]because they told you that in the last times there would come mockers who follow their own ungodly desires. [19]These are divisive, worldly people who lack the Spirit.

[20]But, you, beloved, build yourselves up in the most holy faith, praying in the Holy Spirit. [21]Keep yourselves in the love of God, waiting with expectation for the mercy of our Lord Jesus Christ [leading] to eternal life.

[22]Be merciful towards those who waver spiritually. [23]Snatch them from the fire and save them, and in fear be merciful towards them, hating even the clothing tainted by corrupted flesh.

Benediction

[24]Now to him who is able to keep you from falling, and to present you blameless before his glorious presence with great joy– [25]to the only wise God our savior be glory and majesty, power and dominion through Jesus Christ our Lord, before all the ages, now, and forevermore! Amen.

Chapter 1

Preface

¹The revelation from Jesus Christ, which God gave him to show to his servants what must soon take place. He made this known by sending his angel to his servant John, ²who bore witness to the word of God and to the testimony of Jesus Christ, to all that he saw. ³Blessed is anyone who reads aloud the words of the prophecy, and blessed are those who listen, and who heed what is written in it, for the time is at hand.

Greeting

⁴[From] John to the seven churches that are in Asia: Grace to you and peace from the One who is and who was and who is to come, and from the seven spirits who stand in front of his throne, ⁵and from Jesus Christ the faithful witness, the first-born among the dead, and the ruler over the kings of the earth.

To him who loves us and has freed us from our sins by his blood ⁶and made us a kingdom, priests to his God and Father, to him be glory and dominion forever and ever. Amen. ⁷Behold, he is coming with the clouds, and every eye will see him, everyone who pierced him, and all tribes of the earth will wail on account of him. May it be so. Amen.

⁸"I am the Alpha and the Omega," says the Lord God, "who is and who was and who is to come, the Almighty."

John Has a Vision

⁹I John, your brother and partner in the tribulation and kingdom and patient endurance that are in Jesus, was on the island called Patmos on account of the word of God and [my] testimony about Jesus. ¹⁰I was in the Spirit on the Lord's Day when from behind me I heard a loud voice like a trumpet ¹¹saying, "Write what you see in a book and send it to the seven churches, to Ephesus and to Smyrna and to Pergamum and to Thyatira and to Sardis and to Philadelphia and to Laodicea."

¹²Then I turned to see the voice that was speaking to me, and having turned around around I saw seven golden lampstands, ¹³and in the midst of the lampstands One like a son of man,

clothed with a long robe and with a golden sash around his chest.

[14]The hairs on his head were white like white wool—like snow.

His eyes resembled a flame of fire.

[15]His feet resembled burnished bronze, refined as in a furnace.

And his voice resembled the roar of many waters.

[16]In his right hand he held seven stars.

From his mouth a sharp two-edged sword came forth,

and his face was like the sun shining mightily.

[17]When I saw him, I fell at his feet as though dead. But he placed his right hand on me, saying, "Fear not, I am the first and the last, [18]and the living One. I died, but look—I am alive for evermore, and I possess the keys of Death and Hades. [19]Now write what you see—things that are and things that are to happen after this. [20][Regarding] the mystery of the seven stars you saw in my right hand, and the seven golden lampstands: the seven stars are the angels of the seven churches, and the seven lampstands are the seven churches.

Chapter 2

To the Church in Ephesus

[1]"To the angel of the church in Ephesus write: 'The words of the one who holds the seven stars in his right hand, who walks among the seven golden lampstands.

[2]"I know your deeds, your toil and your patient endurance, and how you cannot tolerate evil people, but have tested those who call themselves apostles and are not, and found them to be false. [3]I know you are enduring patiently and bearing up for my name's sake, and you have not grown weary. [4]But I hold this against you: that you have left behind the love you had at first. [5]Think back to the place where you have fallen from, repent and do the things you did at first. If not, I will come to you and remove your lampstand from its place, unless you repent. [6]Yet you do have this: you hate the activities of the Nicolaitans, which I also hate. [7]Let anyone who has an ear hear what the Spirit says to the churches: I will grant [the privilege] to eat of the tree of life, which is in the paradise of God, to anyone who wins the victory.'

To the Church in Smyrna

[8]"And to the angel of the church in Smyrna write: 'The words of the first and the last, who died and came to life.

[9]"I know your tribulation and your poverty (actually you are rich) and the verbal abuse of those who claim to be Jews but are not—they are a synagogue of Satan.

[10]Do not be afraid of what you are about to suffer. Look, the devil is about to throw some of you into prison—to test you—and for ten days you will have tribulation. Be faithful until death, and I will award you the crown of life. [11]Let anyone who has an ear hear what the Spirit says to the churches: The one who wins the victory will not be hurt by the second death.'

To the Church in Pergamum

[12]"And to the angel of the church in Pergamum write: 'The words of the one who has the sharp two-edged sword.

[13]"'I know that you live where Satan is on the throne. Still, you cling to my name and you did not betray my faith in me even in the days when my faithful witness, Antipas was killed in your midst—where Satan lives. [14]But I hold a few things against you: you have some people there who follow the teaching of Balaam, who taught Balak to put a stumbling block before the sons of Israel, namely, to eat food sacrificed to idols and practice sexual immorality. [15]So you also have some people who follow the teaching of the Nicolaitans. [16]So repent. But if not, I will come to you soon and war against them with the sword of my mouth. [17]Let anyone who has an ear hear what the Spirit says to the churches: To the one who wins the victory I will give some of the hidden manna, and I will give him a white stone, with a new name written on the stone, which no one knows except the one who receives it.'

To the Church in Thyatira

[18]"And to the angel of the church in Thyatira write: 'The words of the Son of God, who has eyes like a flame of fire, and whose feet are like burnished bronze.

[19]"'I know your deeds, your love and faith and service and patient endurance, and that your latter works exceed the first. [20]But I have this against you, that you tolerate the woman Jezebel, who calls herself a prophetess and is teaching and beguiling my servants to practice sexual immorality and to eat food sacrificed to idols. [21]I gave her time to repent, but she refuses to repent of her sexual immorality. [22]Look, I will throw her onto a sickbed, and I will throw those who commit adultery with her into great tribulation, unless they repent of her actions. [23]Even more—I will strike her children dead. Then all the churches shall know that I am he who searches mind and heart, and I will repay each of you according to what you have done.

[24]But to the rest of you in Thyatira, who do not hold this teaching, who have not learned what some call the deep things of Satan, I tell you that I do not lay any

other burden on you. ²⁵Just hold on tightly to what you have, until I come. ²⁶I will give authority over the nations to anyone who wins the victory and keeps my works until the end. ²⁷That person shall rule them with a rod of iron, as when clay pots are broken in pieces, even as I myself have received authority from my Father. ²⁸And I will give him the morning star. ²⁹Let anyone who has an ear hear what the Spirit says to the churches.'

Chapter 3

To the Church in Sardis

¹"And to the angel of the church in Sardis write: 'The words of the One who holds the seven spirits of God and the seven stars.

"'I know your deeds: you have the reputation of being alive, but you are dead. ²Awaken and strengthen those parts that remain, which are about to perish, for I have not found your deeds complete in the sight of my God. ³Recall, then, what you received and heard—hold onto that, and repent. If you will not stay awake, I will come like a thief, and you will not know at what hour I will come back to you. ⁴Yet you do still have a few names in Sardis—people who have not soiled their garments—who will walk with me [dressed] in white, for they are worthy. ⁵The one who wins the victory shall be dressed in such a way—in white garments—and I will not blot his name out of the Book of Life. I will confess his name before my Father and before his angel. ⁶Let anyone who has an ear hear what the Spirit says to the churches.'

To the Church in Philadelphia

⁷"And to the angel of the church in Philadelphia write: 'The words of the holy one, the true one, who has the key of David, who opens what no one shall shut, who shuts what no one shall open.

⁸"'I know your deeds. Look—I have put an open door in front of you, which no one is able to shut. I know that you have but little power, and yet you have kept my word and have not denied my name. ⁹Some people of the synagogue of Satan claim to be Jews, though they are not, and are lying. Look—I will make them come and bow down before your feet and learn that I have loved you. ¹⁰Because you have kept my word of patient endurance, I will keep you from the hour of trial that is coming on the whole world, to try those who dwell on the earth. ¹¹I am coming soon; cling tightly to what you have, so that no one may seize your crown. ¹²I will make the one who wins the victory a pillar in the temple of my God. He shall never leave it, and on him I will write the name of my God, and the name of the city of my God, the new Jerusalem which comes down from my God out

of heaven, and my own new name. [13]Let anyone who has an ear hear what the Spirit says to the churches.'

To the Church in Laodicea

[14]"And to the angel of the church in Laodicea write: 'The words of the Amen, the faithful and true witness, the beginning of God's creation.

[15]"I know your deeds: you are neither cold nor hot. O that you were either cold or hot! [16]So, because you are lukewarm, and neither cold nor hot, I will spew you out of my mouth. [17]For you say, I am rich, I have prospered, and I need nothing, not perceiving that you are wretched, pitiable, poor, blind, and naked. [18]Therefore I advise you to buy gold refined by fire from me to make you rich, and white garments to clothe you and hide the shame of your nakedness, and salve to anoint your eyes and let you see. [19]I correct and discipline the people I love, so be zealous and repent. [20]Take notice of this—I stand at the door and knock: if anyone hears my voice and opens the door, I will come in to him and eat with him, and he with me. [21]I will grant [the privilege] to sit with me on my throne to anyone who wins the victory, as I myself won the victory and sat down with my Father on his throne. [22]Let anyone who has an ear hear what the Spirit says to the churches.'"

Chapter 4

The Throne in Heaven Described

[1]After this I looked, and there was a door in heaven standing open! And the first voice, which I had heard speaking to me like a trumpet, said, "Come up here, and I will show you what must take place after this." [2]Immediately I was in the Spirit, and a throne stood there in heaven, with someone seated on the throne! [3]Now, the One who sat there had the appearance of jasper and carnelian, and around the throne was a rainbow that looked like an emerald. [4]Surrounding the throne were twenty-four thrones, and seated on the thrones were twenty-four elders, dressed in white garments, with golden crowns on their heads. [5]From the throne came forth flashes of lightning, and voices and peals of thunder, and before the throne were burning seven torches of fire, which are the seven spirits of God. [6]In front of the throne was something like a sea of glass, like crystal.

And around the throne, in the middle of each side of the throne, covered with eyes both in front and behind, were four living creatures: [7]the first living creature like a lion, the second living creature like an ox, the third living creature with the face of a man, and the fourth living creature like a flying eagle. [8]And the four living creatures, each of them with six wings, were covered with eyes all round and within, and day and night they never stop singing, "Holy, holy, holy, is the Lord God Almighty, who always was and is now and ever shall be!" [9]And whenever the living creatures gave glory and honor and thanks to the One seated on the throne, who lives forever and ever, [10]the twenty-four elders fell down before the One seated on the throne and worshiped the One who lives forever and ever. They cast their crowns before the throne, singing, [11]"Worthy are you, our Lord and God, to receive glory and honor and power, because you created all things, and by your will they existed and were created."

Chapter 5

The Lamb is Worthy to Open the Scroll

[1]In the right hand of the One who was seated on the throne I saw a scroll with writing on the inside and on the back, sealed up with seven seals. [2]Then I saw a powerful angel [who asked], projecting with a loud voice, "Who is worthy to open the scroll and break its seals?" [3]Now, no one in heaven or on earth or under the earth was able to open the scroll or to look into it, [4]and I wept greatly because no one was found worthy to open the scroll or to look into it. [5]Then one of the elders said to me, "Weep no more: you see, the Lion of the tribe of Judah, the Root of David, has won the victory in order to open the scroll and its seven seals."

[6]And between the throne and the four living creatures and among the elders, I saw a Lamb standing, as though it had been slain, with seven horns and with seven eyes, which are the seven spirits of God sent out into all the earth. [7]He went and took the scroll from the right hand of the One who was seated on the throne. [8]And when he had taken the scroll, the four living creatures and the twenty-four elders fell down before the Lamb, each holding a harp, and golden bowls full of incense, which are the prayers of the saints. [9]Then they sang a new song, saying, "Worthy are you to take the scroll and to open its seals, for you were slain and by your blood you ransomed men for God from every tribe and tongue and people and nation. [10]And you have made them a kingdom and priests to our God, and they shall reign on the earth."

[11]Then I looked, and I heard around the throne and the living creatures and the elders the voice of many angels, numbering myriads of myriads and thousands of thousands, [12]saying with a loud voice, "Worthy is the Lamb who was slain, to receive power and wealth and wisdom and might and honor and glory and blessing!" [13]And I heard every creature in heaven and on earth and under the earth and in the sea, and everything in them, saying, "To the One who sits on the throne and to the Lamb be blessing and honor and glory and power forever and ever!" [14]And the four living creatures said, "Amen!" and the elders fell down and worshiped.

Chapter 6

The Seven Seals Are Opened

[1]Then I watched as the Lamb broke open one of the seven seals, and I heard one of the four living creatures exclaim with a voice like thunder, "Come!" [2]And I looked and there was a white horse, and its rider had a bow. He was given a crown, and he took off as a conqueror going out to conquer.

[3]When he broke open the second seal, I heard the second living creature exclaim, "Come!" [4]And out came another horse [that was] fiery red whose rider was permitted to remove peace from the earth, so that men would slaughter one another, and he was given a large sword.

[5]When he broke open the third seal, I heard the third living creature exclaim, "Come!" And I looked and there was a black horse, and its rider had a set of scales in his hand. [6]I heard a voice that seemed to come from the midst of the four living creatures saying, "A quart of wheat for a denarius, and three quarts of barley for a denarius; but do not damage the oil and wine!"

[7]When he broke open the fourth seal, I heard the voice of the fourth living creature exclaim, "Come!" [8]And I saw a pale-green horse, and its rider's name was Death, and Hades followed him. They were given power over a quarter of the earth, to kill with sword and with famine and with pestilence and by wild beasts of the earth.

[9]When he broke open the fifth seal, under the altar I saw the souls of those who had been slain for [being faithful] to the word of God and for the testimony they had borne. [10]They cried out with a loud voice, "O Sovereign Lord, holy and true, how much longer before you judge those who live on the earth and avenge our blood?" [11]Then they were each given a white robe and told to wait quietly a little longer, until the number of their fellow servants and their brothers, who were to be killed as they themselves had been, was complete.

[12]When he broke open the sixth seal, I looked, and there was a great earthquake, and the sun became black as sackcloth. The full moon became like blood, [13]and the stars of the sky fell to the earth like a fig tree dropping its winter fruit when shaken by a gale-force wind. [14]The sky vanished like a scroll being rolled up, and every mountain and island was shaken out of its place. [15]Then the kings of the earth and the great men and the generals and the rich and the strong, and everyone, slave and free, hid in the caves and among the rocks of the mountains, [16]calling to the mountains and rocks, "Fall on us and hide us from the face of the One who is seated on the throne, and from the wrath of the Lamb, [17]for the great day of their wrath has come, and who can withstand it?"

Chapter 7

144,000 Witnesses Sealed

[1]After this I saw four angels standing at the four corners of the earth, holding back the four winds of the earth, so that no wind would blow on the earth or on the sea or against any tree. [2]Then I saw another angel ascending from the rising of the sun, with the seal of the living God, and he called with a loud voice to the four angels who had been given power to harm earth and sea, [3]saying, "Do not harm the earth or the sea or the trees, until we have sealed the servants of our God on their foreheads." [4]And then I heard the number of the sealed, 144,000, sealed from all the tribes of the sons of Israel:

> [5]12,000 were sealed out of the tribe of Judah,
> 12,000 out of the tribe of Reuben,
> 12,000 out of the tribe of Gad,
> [6]12,000 out of the tribe of Asher,
> 12,000 out of the tribe of Naphtali,
> 12,000 out of the tribe of Manasseh,
> [7]12,000 out of the tribe of Simeon,
> 12,000 out of the tribe of Levi,
> 12,000 out of the tribe of Issachar,
> [8]12,000 out of the tribe of Zebulun,
> 12,000 out of the tribe of Joseph, and
> 12,000 were sealed out of the tribe of Benjamin.

[9]After this I looked, and there was a great multitude that no one could number, from every nation, from all tribes and peoples and tongues, standing before the throne and before the Lamb, clothed in white robes, with palm branches in their hands, [10]and crying out with a loud voice, "Salvation belongs to our God who sits on the throne, and to the Lamb!" [11]And all the angels stood around the throne and the elders and the four living creatures. And they fell on their faces before the throne and worshiped God, [12]saying, "Amen! Blessing and glory and wisdom and thanksgiving and honor and power and might be to our God forever and ever! Amen."

[13]Then one of the elders addressed me, asking, "Who are these, clothed in white robes, and where have they come from?" [14]I answered him, "Sir, you know." And he said to me, "These are the ones who have come out of the great tribulation. They have washed their robes and made them white in the blood of the Lamb. [15]For this reason they are before the throne of God and serve him day and night within his temple; and he who sits on the throne will shelter them with his

presence. [16]They will never be hungry or thirsty again. Neither the sun nor any scorching heat will ever strike them again. [17]For the Lamb in the midst of the throne will be their shepherd, and he will guide them to springs of life-giving water. And God will wipe away every tear from their eyes."

Chapter 8

The First Four Trumpets

[1]When the Lamb broke open the seventh seal, heaven fell silent for about half an hour. [2]Then I saw the seven angels who stand before God, and seven trumpets were given to them. [3]And another angel came and stood at the altar with a golden censer, and he was given a great deal of incense to offer up with the prayers of all the saints on the golden altar before the throne. [4]Then the smoke of the incense, with the prayers of the saints, rose from the hand of the angel before God. [5]Then the angel took the censer and filled it with fire from the altar and threw it on the earth, and there were thunderclaps, rumbling sounds, flashes of lightning, and an earthquake.

Hail and Fire

[6]Now the seven angels who had the seven trumpets got ready to blow them. [7]The first angel blew his trumpet, and hail and fire, mixed with blood, followed, and fell on the earth. So a third of the earth was burned up, and a third of the trees were burned up, and all the green grass was burned up.

One-Third Destroyed

[8]The second angel blew his trumpet, and something like a great mountain, burning with fire, was thrown into the sea. [9]And a third of the sea became blood, a third of the living creatures in the sea died, and a third of the ships were destroyed.

Wormwood Falls from Heaven

[10]The third angel blew his trumpet, and a great star fell from heaven, blazing like a torch, and it fell on a third of the rivers and on the springs of water. [11]The name of the star is Wormwood. A third of the waters became wormwood, and many people died of the water, because it had been made bitter.

One-Third Darkened

[12]The fourth angel blew his trumpet, and a third of the sun was struck, and a third of the moon, and a third of the stars, so that a third of their light was darkened. Thus, it was dark for a third of the day, and likewise a third of the night. [13]Then I looked, and I heard an eagle crying with a loud voice, as it flew in midair, "Woe,

woe, woe to those who live on the earth, because of the blasts of the other trumpets that the three angels are about to blow!"

Chapter 9

Tormenting Locusts

[1]And the fifth angel blew his trumpet, and I saw a star fallen from heaven to earth, and he was given the key to the shaft of the bottomless pit. [2]He opened the shaft of the bottomless pit, and from the shaft rose smoke like the smoke of a great furnace, and the sun and the air were darkened with the smoke from the shaft. [3]Then from the smoke came locusts on the earth, and they were given power like the power of scorpions of the earth. [4]They were told not to harm the grass of the earth nor any green growth or any tree, but only those people who do not have the seal of God on their foreheads. [5]They were allowed to torment them for five months, but not to kill them, and their torture was like the torture of a scorpion stinging someone. [6]And in those days men will seek death and will not find it. They will long to die, though death will evade them.

[7]In appearance the locusts resembled horses arrayed for battle:

➢ on their heads were what looked like golden crowns,
➢ their faces were like human faces,
➢ [8]their hair like women's hair,
➢ and their teeth like lions' teeth.
➢ [9]They had scales like iron breastplates,
➢ and the noise of their wings was like the noise of many chariots with horses rushing into battle. [10]They had tails that sting like scorpions, and in their tails they had the power to injure people for five months.
➢ [11]They had the angel of the bottomless pit as king over them. In Hebrew, his name is Abaddon, and in Greek he is called Apollyon.

[12]The first woe has passed. But take note—two woes are still to come.

Two-hundred-million-man Army

[13]Then the sixth angel blew his trumpet, and I heard a voice from the four horns of the golden altar before God, [14]saying to the sixth angel who had the trumpet, "Release the four angels who are bound at the great river Euphrates." [15]So the four angels were released to kill a third of mankind. They had been held ready for this very hour, day, month, and year. [16]The number of the cavalry troops was 200 million; I heard their number. [17]And this was how I saw the horses in my vision: the riders wore breastplates the color of fire and of sapphire and of sulfur, and the heads of the horses were like lions' heads, and fire and smoke and sulfur

poured forth from their mouths. ¹⁸A third of mankind was killed by these three plagues, that is, by the fire and smoke and sulfur pouring from their mouths. ¹⁹For the power of the horses is in their mouths and in their tails. Their tails are like serpents with heads, and they inflict wounds with them.

No Repentance

²⁰The rest of mankind, who were not killed by these plagues, did not repent of their deeds, nor give up worshiping demons and idols of gold and silver and bronze and stone and wood, which cannot either see or hear or walk. ²¹Nor did they repent of their murders or their sorceries or their sexual immorality or their thievery.

Chapter 10

Eating the Scroll

¹Then I saw another mighty angel coming down from heaven, wrapped in a cloud, with a rainbow over his head, and his face was like the sun, and his legs like pillars of fire. ²He had a little scroll open in his hand. He set his right foot on the sea, and his left foot on the land, ³and called out with a loud voice, like a lion roaring. When he called out, the seven thunders spoke. ⁴And when the seven thunders had spoken, I was about to write [it down], but I heard a voice from heaven telling [me], "Seal up what the seven thunders have told, and do not write it down." ⁵And the angel that I saw standing on sea and land lifted up his right hand to heaven. ⁶And he swore by the One who lives forever and ever, who created heaven and what is in it, the earth and what is in it, and the sea and what is in it, that there should be no more delay, ⁷but that in the days of the trumpet call to be sounded by the seventh angel, the mystery of God should be fulfilled, as he announced to his servants the prophets.

⁸Then the voice that I had heard from heaven spoke to me again, saying, "Go, take the scroll that is open in the hand of the angel who is standing on the sea and on the land." ⁹So I went to the angel and told him to give me the little scroll. And he said to me, "Take it and eat. It will be bitter to your stomach, though sweet as honey in your mouth." ¹⁰And I took the little scroll from the hand of the angel and ate it. It was sweet as honey in my mouth, but when I had eaten it, it made my stomach bitter. ¹¹Then I was told, "You must prophesy again in the presence of many peoples and nations and languages and kings."

Chapter 11

The Seven-Year Tribulation Begins

[1]Then I was given a measuring rod like a staff, and I was told: "Rise up and measure the temple of God and the altar and those who worship there, [2]but do not measure the court outside the temple. Leave that out, for it is given over to the nations, and they will trample over the holy city for 42 months. [3]And I will grant my two witnesses authority to prophesy clothed in sackcloth for 1,260 days."

[4]These are the two olive trees and the two lampstands that stand before the Lord of the earth. [5]And if anyone wants to harm them, fire will pour out from their mouths and consume their foes. So, if anyone should want to harm them, that is how he is doomed to be killed. [6]They have authority to close up the sky and keep rain from falling during the days of their prophesying. And they have authority over the waters to turn them into blood, and to strike the earth with every plague, as often as they desire. [7]And when they have finished their testimony, the beast that ascends from the bottomless pit will war against them and conquer them and kill them. [8]And their dead bodies will lie in the street of the great city where also their Lord was crucified, which is called 'Sodom' and 'Egypt' in spiritual terms. [9]For three and a half days men from the peoples and tribes and languages and nations will gaze at their dead bodies and refuse to let them be put into graves. [10]And those who dwell on the earth will rejoice over them and celebrate and exchange gifts, because these two prophets had been a torment to those who live on the earth.

[11]But after the three and a half days, a breath of life from God entered them, and they stood up on their feet, and great fear fell on those who saw them. [12]Then they heard a loud voice from heaven saying to them, "Come up here!" And as their enemies watched them, they ascended to heaven in a cloud. [13]And a great earthquake happened at that hour, and a tenth of the city collapsed. Seven thousand people were killed in the earthquake, and the rest were terrified and gave glory to the God of heaven.

[14]The second woe has passed; look, the third woe is soon to come.

The Seventh Trumpet

[15]Then the seventh angel blew his trumpet, and there were loud voices in heaven, saying, "The kingdom of the world has become the kingdom of our Lord and of his Christ, and he shall reign forever and ever." [16]And the twenty-four elders who sit on their thrones before God fell on their faces and worshiped God, [17]declaring, "We give thanks to you, Lord God Almighty, who is and who was, that you have

391

assumed your great power and begun to reign. [18]The nations raged, but your wrath came, and the time for the dead to be judged, and to reward your servants, the prophets and saints, and those, both small and great, who fear your name, and to destroy those who are destroying the earth."

[19]Then God's temple in heaven was opened, and the ark of his covenant was seen within his temple. And [then] there were flashes of lightning, rumbling sounds, thunderclaps, an earthquake, and large hail.

Chapter 12

The Woman and the Dragon

[1]Then a great sign appeared in heaven: a woman clothed with the sun, with the moon under her feet, and on her head a crown of twelve stars. [2]She was pregnant and she cried out in birth pangs, and the agony of childbirth. [3]And another sign appeared in heaven: look—a great red dragon, with seven heads and ten horns, and seven diadems on his heads. [4]His tail swept down a third of the stars of heaven and threw them to the earth. And the dragon stood in front of the woman who was about to bear a child, so that when she bore her child, he might devour it. [5]She gave birth to a son, one who is to rule all the nations with an iron rod, but her child was snatched away up to God and to his throne. [6]And the woman fled into the wilderness, where she has a place prepared by God, where she is to be nourished for 1,260 days.

[7]Now war arose in heaven: Michael and his angels fighting against the dragon. And the dragon and his angels fought, [8]but they were overpowered so no longer was any place found for them in heaven. [9]And the great dragon was thrown down; that ancient serpent who is called the devil and Satan, the deceiver of the whole world, was thrown down to the earth, and his angels were thrown down with him. [10]And I heard a loud voice in heaven, saying, "Now salvation and power and the kingdom of our God and the authority of his Christ have come, for the accuser of our brothers, who accuses them day and night before our God, has been thrown down. [11]And they have conquered him by the blood of the Lamb and by the word of their testimony, for they did not cling to their lives, being willing to die. [12]So then, rejoice, O heavens and you who live in them! But woe to you, O earth and sea, for the devil has come down to you in great wrath, because he knows that his [remaining] time is brief!"

[13]And when the dragon saw that he had been hurled down to the earth, he pursued the woman who had given birth to the male child. [14]But the woman had been given the two wings of the great eagle so that she could fly from the serpent

into the wilderness, to the place where she is to be provided for, for a [year's] time, plus two [more years'] time, plus half a [year's] time. ¹⁵The serpent poured water like a river out of his mouth after the woman, to carry her off in a flood. ¹⁶But the earth came to the aid of the woman, and it opened its mouth and swallowed the river that the dragon had poured from his mouth. ¹⁷Then the dragon grew furious with the woman and went off to make war on the rest of her offspring—those who keep the commandments of God and bear testimony to Jesus. He stood on the sand by the sea.

Chapter 13

A First Beast with Ten Horns and Seven Heads

¹And I saw, rising out of the sea, a beast that had ten horns and seven heads, with ten crowns on its horns and blasphemous names on its heads. ²And the beast that I saw was like a leopard; its feet were like a bear's, and its mouth was like a lion's mouth. And the dragon gave his power and his throne and great authority to it. ³One of its heads seemed to have a mortal wound, but its mortal wound was healed, and the whole earth followed the beast with wonder. ⁴They worshiped the dragon because he had given his authority to the beast, and they worshiped the beast, saying, "Who can compare with the beast, and who can fight against it?"

⁵And [the beast] was given a mouth uttering boastful and blasphemous words, and it was allowed to exercise authority for 42 months. ⁶When [the beast] spoke, it was to utter blasphemies against God, blaspheming his name and his dwelling, that is, those who dwell in heaven. ⁷Also, it was allowed to make war on the saints and to conquer them. And it was given authority over every tribe and people and language and nation. ⁸Everyone who lives on the earth will worship it—that is, everyone whose name has not been written before the foundation of the world in the Book of Life of the Lamb who was slain. ⁹Let anyone who has an ear listen: ¹⁰If anyone is to be taken captive, to captivity he goes. If anyone slays with the sword, with the sword he must be slain. Here is [a need for] the endurance and faith of the saints.

A Second Beast with Two Horns

¹¹Then I saw, rising out of the earth, another beast, and this one had two horns like a lamb and spoke like a dragon. ¹²It exercises all authority on behalf of the first beast and makes the earth and its inhabitants worship the first beast, whose mortal wound was healed. ¹³It works great signs, even making fire come down from heaven to earth in the sight of men. ¹⁴So it deceives the inhabitants of the earth by the signs that it is allowed to perform in the presence of the beast, forc-

ing them to make an image for the beast that was wounded by the sword and yet lived. ¹⁵And it is allowed to bring the image of the beast to life so that the image of the beast could even speak, and to have those who would not worship the image of the beast be killed. ¹⁶It also forces everyone—both small and great, both rich and poor, both free and slave—to be marked on the right hand or the forehead, ¹⁷so that no one can buy or sell unless he has the mark, that is, the name of the beast or the number of its name. ¹⁸Here wisdom is needed: let the man who has understanding figure out the number of the beast, for it is the number of a man, and his number is 666.

Chapter 14

The 144,000 on Mount Zion

¹Then I looked, and listen—on Mount Zion stood the Lamb, and with him the 144,000 people who had his name and his Father's name written on their foreheads. ²And I heard a voice from heaven like the sound of many waters and like the sound of loud thunder. The voice I heard was like the sound of harpists playing on their harps, ³and who sing a new song before the throne and before the four living creatures and before the elders. No one could learn that song except the 144,000 people who had been redeemed from the earth. ⁴These are the ones who have not defiled themselves with women, for they are chaste and follow the Lamb wherever he goes. They have been redeemed from mankind as firstfruits for God and the Lamb, ⁵and no lies were found in their mouths, for they are spotless.

⁶Then I saw another angel flying in midair, with an eternal gospel to proclaim to the inhabitants of earth, to every nation and tribe and language and people. ⁷And he declared with a loud voice, "Fear God and give him glory, for the hour of his judgment has come. Worship the One who made heaven and earth, and the sea and the springs of water." ⁸Another angel, a second, followed, declaring, "Fallen, fallen is Babylon the great, who made all nations drink the wine of the wrath of her sexual immorality."

The Mark of the Beast

⁹And another angel, a third, followed them, saying with a loud voice, "If anyone worships the beast and its image, and receives a mark on his forehead or on his hand, ¹⁰he also shall drink the wine of God's wrath, poured unmixed into the cup of his anger, and he shall be tormented with fire and sulfur in the presence of the holy angels and in the presence of the Lamb. ¹¹And the smoke of their torment goes up forever and ever. And [so] these worshipers of the beast and its image, and whoever receives the mark of its name have no rest, day or night."

¹²Here then, is the [need for] patient endurance on the part of the saints, those who keep the commandments of God and their faith in Jesus.

¹³And I heard a voice from heaven saying, "Write this: Blessed are the dead who die in the Lord from this point forward." "Blessed indeed," says the Spirit, "that they may rest from their labors, for their deeds do follow after them!"

The Reapers and their Sickles

¹⁴Then I looked, and look—a white cloud, and seated on the cloud one like a son of man, with a golden crown on his head, and a sharp sickle in his hand. ¹⁵And another angel came out of the temple, calling with a loud voice to him who sat on the cloud, "Put in your sickle, and reap, for the hour to reap has come, for the harvest of the earth is fully ripe." ¹⁶So he who sat on the cloud swung his sickle on the earth, and the earth was reaped.

¹⁷And another angel came out of the temple in heaven, and he too had a sharp sickle. ¹⁸Then another angel came out from the altar, the angel who has power over fire, and he called with a loud voice to him who had the sharp sickle, "Put in your sickle, and gather the clusters of the vine of the earth, for its grapes are ripe." ¹⁹So the angel swung his sickle on the earth and gathered the grape harvest of the earth and threw it into the great wine press of the wrath of God. ²⁰And outside the city the wine press was trodden, and blood flowed from the wine press, as high as a horse's bridle, for 185 miles.

Chapter 15

Seven Plagues

¹Then I saw another great and wonderful sign in heaven: seven angels with seven plagues, which are the last, for with them the wrath of God is ended.

²And I saw what appeared to be a sea of glass mingled with fire, and those who had conquered the beast and its image and the number of its name, standing beside the sea of glass with harps of God in their hands. ³And they sing the song of Moses, the servant of God, and the song of the Lamb, saying, "Great and wonderful are your deeds, O Lord God the Almighty! Just and true are your ways, O King of the ages! ⁴Who shall not fear and glorify your name, O Lord? For you alone are holy. All nations shall come and worship you, for your judgments have been revealed."

⁵After this I looked, and the temple of the tabernacle of witness in heaven was opened, ⁶and out of the temple came the seven angels with the seven plagues, robed in pure bright linen, with golden sashes around their chests. ⁷And one of the four living creatures gave the seven angels seven golden bowls full of the wrath of the eternal God. ⁸Then the temple was filled with smoke from the glory of God and from his power, and no one could enter the temple until the seven plagues of the seven angels were ended.

Chapter 16

Seven Bowls of Wrath

¹Then I heard a loud voice from the temple telling the seven angels, "Go and pour out the seven bowls of God's wrath onto the earth."

²So the first angel went and poured his bowl onto the earth, and vile, horrible sores came on the people who bore the mark of the beast and worshiped its image.

³The second angel poured his bowl into the sea, and it became like the blood of a corpse, and every living thing that was in the sea died.

⁴The third angel poured his bowl into the rivers and the springs of water, and they turned to blood. ⁵And I heard the angel of water say, "You are just in these your judgments, you who are now and always was, O Holy One. ⁶For people have shed the blood of saints and prophets, and you have given them blood to drink. It is their just reward!" ⁷And I heard the altar cry, "Yes, Lord God the Almighty, true and just are your judgments!"

⁸The fourth angel poured his bowl on the sun, and it was allowed to scorch people with fire. ⁹People were scorched by the fierce heat, and they cursed the name of God who had power over these plagues, and yet they did not repent and give him glory.

¹⁰The fifth angel poured his bowl on the throne of the beast, and its kingdom was plunged into darkness. People gnawed their tongues in anguish ¹¹and cursed the God of heaven for their pain and sores, and [still] did not repent of their deeds.

¹²The sixth angel poured his bowl on the great river Euphrates, and its water was dried up, to prepare the way for the kings from the East. ¹³And I saw three vile spirits like frogs coming out from the mouth of the dragon and from the mouth of the beast and from the mouth of the false prophet. ¹⁴For they are spirits of demons that perform signs, and they are going abroad to the kings of the whole world to assemble them for battle on the great day of God the Almighty. ¹⁵("Look, I am coming like a thief! Blessed is he who stays awake, keeping his clothes ready so

that he does not go around naked and be seen exposed!") ¹⁶And they assembled them at the place that is called Armageddon in Hebrew.

¹⁷The seventh angel poured his bowl into the air, and a loud voice came out of the temple, from the throne, saying, "It is done!" ¹⁸And there were flashes of lightning, rumbling sounds, thunderclaps, and a powerful earthquake, the likes of which had never been seen for as long as people had lived on the earth. ¹⁹The great city was split into three parts, and the cities of the nations fell. As God remembered Babylon the great, he forced her to drink down the wine of the fury of his wrath. ²⁰And every island fled away, and no mountains were to be found. ²¹And great hailstones, each a hundred pounds in weight, dropped out of the sky onto people until they cursed God for the plague of the hail because that plague was so severe.

Chapter 17

Babylon the Great Harlot

¹Then one of the seven angels who held the seven bowls came and said to me, "Come, I will show you the judgment of the great harlot who is seated on many waters. ²The kings of the earth have lived in sexual sin with her, and the inhabitants of the earth have gotten drunk with the wine of her sexual vice." ³And he carried me away in the Spirit into a wilderness, and I saw a woman sitting on a scarlet beast that was full of blasphemous names, and it had seven heads and ten horns. ⁴The woman was arrayed in purple and scarlet, and adorned with gold and jewels and pearls, holding in her hand a golden cup full of abominations and the impurities of her sexual sin. ⁵And on her forehead was written a name of hidden meaning: "Babylon the great, mother of harlots and of earth's abominations." ⁶And I saw the woman, drunk with the blood of the saints and the blood of the martyrs of Jesus.

When I saw her, I wondered [about her] in great amazement. ⁷But the angel said to me, "What are you wondering about? I will explain to you the mystery of the woman, and of the beast with seven heads and ten horns that carries her. ⁸The beast that you saw existed once, and now does not, but it will ascend from the bottomless pit and go to its utter destruction. The inhabitants of the earth whose names have not been written in the Book of Life from the foundation of the world will be amazed to see the beast, because it existed once, and now does not, and is yet to come. ⁹This is for a mind with wisdom: the seven heads are seven mountains on which the woman is seated. ¹⁰They are also seven kings: five of them have fallen, one exists, the other has not yet come. And when he comes, he must remain only a little while. ¹¹As for the beast that once was and does not exist now:

it is an eighth, but it belongs to the seven, and it is headed for utter destruction. [12]And the ten horns that you saw are ten kings who have not yet received royal power, but they are to receive authority as kings for one hour, together with the beast. [13]These are of one mind and give over their power and authority to the beast. [14]They will make war on the Lamb, but the Lamb will conquer them, for he is Lord of lords and King of kings, and those with him are called and chosen and faithful."

[15]He also said to me, "The waters that you saw, where the harlot is seated, are peoples and multitudes and nations and languages. [16]Now as for the ten horns that you saw, they and the beast will hate the harlot. They will devastate her and strip her naked and devour her flesh and burn her up with fire, [17]for God has put it into their hearts to carry out his purpose by being of one mind and giving over their royal power to the beast, until the words of God are fulfilled. [18]The woman that you saw is the great city that has dominion over the kings of the earth."

Chapter 18

Fallen is Babylon

[1]After this I saw another angel, one that had great authority, coming down from heaven, and his splendor illuminated the earth. [2]And he called out with a mighty voice, "Fallen, fallen is Babylon the great! It has become a hall of demons, a dungeon of every foul spirit, a perch for every foul and detestable bird, and a haunt for every unclean and detestable beast. [3]For all nations have drunk the wine of her sexual immorality, and the kings of the earth have lived in sexual sin with her. Even the merchants of the earth have grown rich with the wealth of her luxury."
[4]Then I heard another voice from heaven saying, "Come out of her, my people, so that you do not take part in her sins or share in her plagues. [5]For her sins are heaped high as heaven, and God has remembered her crimes. [6]Do to her as she herself has done to others and repay her double for her deeds. Mix a double dose for her in the cup she mixed. [7]In the same way that she glorified herself and lived in luxury, give her a similar portion of torment and mourning. Since in her heart she says, 'I sit like a queen, I am not a widow. I shall never [have to] face mourning.' [8]So shall her plagues come in a single day—death and mourning and famine—and she will be burned up with fire, for mighty is the Lord God who judges her."

[9]And the kings of the earth, who lived in sexual sin and luxury with her, will weep and wail over her when they see the smoke from her burning. [10]They will stand far off, in fear of her torment, and say, "Alas! alas! you great city, you mighty city, Babylon! In one hour your judgment has come."

¹¹And the merchants of the earth weep and mourn for her, since no one buys their cargoes anymore, ¹²cargoes of gold, silver, jewels and pearls, fine linen, purple cloth, silk and scarlet cloth, all kinds of scented wood, ivory goods, all kinds of things made of expensive wood, bronze, iron and marble; ¹³cinnamon, spice, incense, myrrh, frankincense, wine, oil, fine flour and wheat; cattle and sheep, horses and chariots, and slaves, that is, human souls. ¹⁴"The fruit your soul longed for has gone from you, and your delicacies and your splendor are taken from you, never to be found again!" ¹⁵The merchants of these wares, who gained wealth from her, will stand far off, in fear of her torment, weeping and mourning aloud, ¹⁶"Oh! What a horror for the great city that was clothed in fine linen, in purple and scarlet, adorned with gold, with jewels, and with pearls! ¹⁷In one hour all this wealth has been laid waste."

And all the shipmasters, seafaring men, sailors and all whose trade is on the sea, stood far off ¹⁸and cried out as they saw the smoke from her burning, "What city could compare with that great city?" ¹⁹And they threw dust on their heads, as they wept and mourned, crying out, "Oh! What a horror for the great city where all those that had ships at sea grew rich by her wealth! In one hour she has been laid waste. ²⁰Rejoice over her, O heaven, O saints and apostles and prophets, for God has pronounced judgment against her on your behalf!"

²¹Then a mighty angel took up a stone like a great millstone and threw it into the sea, saying, "So will Babylon the great city be violently thrown down, and will be found no more. ²²And the sound of harpists and minstrels, of flute players and trumpeters, will not be heard in you anymore. And craftsmen of all crafts will not be found in you anymore. And the sound of the mill will not be heard in you anymore. ²³And the light of a lamp will not shine in you anymore. And the voice of a bridegroom and a bride will not be heard in you anymore. Your merchants were the great men of the earth, and all the nations were deceived by your sorcery. ²⁴And the blood of prophets and of saints, and of all who have been slain on earth was found in her."

Chapter 19

Justice and Retribution

¹After this I heard what seemed to be the loud voice of a great multitude in heaven, crying, "Hallelujah! Salvation and glory and power belong to our God, ²for his judgments are true and just. He has judged the great harlot who corrupted the earth with her sexual immorality, and he has avenged the blood of his servants on her."

³Once more they cried, "Hallelujah! The smoke from her goes up forever and ever." ⁴And the twenty-four elders and the four living creatures fell down and worshiped God who is seated on the throne, saying, "Amen. Hallelujah!" ⁵And from the throne came a voice crying, "Praise our God, all you his servants, you who fear him, small and great."

The Marriage Supper of the Lamb

⁶Then I heard what seemed to be the voice of a great multitude, like the sound of many waters and like the sound of mighty thunder peals, crying, "Hallelujah! For the Lord our God the Almighty reigns. ⁷Let us rejoice and be glad and give him the glory, for the marriage of the Lamb has come, and his Bride has made herself ready. ⁸She has been permitted to be clothed with dazzling, pure fine linen." For the fine linen is the righteous deeds of the saints.

⁹And the angel said to me, "Write this: Blessed are those who are invited to the marriage supper of the Lamb." And he said to me, "These are true words of God." ¹⁰Then I fell down at his feet to worship him, but he said to me, "You must not do that! I am a fellow servant with you and your brothers who hold the testimony of Jesus. Worship God." For the testimony of Jesus is the spirit of prophecy.

The Rider on a White Horse

¹¹Then I saw heaven opened, and there was a white horse! He who sat on it is called Faithful and True, and in righteousness he judges and makes war. ¹²His eyes are like a flame of fire, and on his head are many diadems. And he has a name inscribed that no one else knows. ¹³He is clad in a robe dipped in blood, and the name by which he is called is The Word of God. ¹⁴And the armies of heaven, arrayed in fine linen, white and pure, followed him on white horses. ¹⁵From his mouth comes forth a sharp sword to strike down the nations with, and he will rule them with a rod of iron. He will tread the wine press of the fury of the wrath of God the Almighty. ¹⁶On his robe and on his thigh he has a name inscribed: King of kings and Lord of lords.

¹⁷Then I saw an angel standing in the sun, and with a loud voice he called to all the birds that fly in midair, "Come, gather for the great supper of God, ¹⁸to eat the flesh of kings, the flesh of captains, the flesh of mighty men, the flesh of horses and their riders, and the flesh of all men, both free and slave, both small and great." ¹⁹And I saw the beast and the kings of the earth with their armies gathered to make war against the one who sits on the horse and against his army. ²⁰And the beast was captured, and with it the false prophet who in its presence had worked the signs by which he deceived those who had received the mark of the beast and

those who worshiped its image. These two were thrown alive into the Lake of Fire that burns with sulfur. ²¹And the rest were slain by the sword of the one who sits on the horse—the sword that comes from his mouth. And all the birds gorged themselves on their bodies.

Chapter 20

The Devil is Defeated

¹Then I saw an angel coming down from heaven, holding the key to the bottomless pit and a great chain in his hand. ²And he seized the dragon, that ancient serpent, who is the devil and Satan, and bound him for a thousand years, ³and threw him into the pit, and shut it and sealed it over him, so that he should deceive the nations no more, until the thousand years were ended. After that he must be let loose for a little while.

⁴Then I saw thrones, and seated on them were the ones who the right to judge was granted to. I also saw the souls of those who had been beheaded for their testimony to Jesus and for the word of God, and who had not worshiped the beast or its image and had not received its mark on their foreheads or their hands. They came to life and reigned with Christ for a thousand years. ⁵The rest of the dead did not come to life until the thousand years had ended. This is the first resurrection. ⁶Blessed and holy is anyone who shares in the first resurrection! The second death has no power over them, but they will be priests of God and of Christ, and they will reign with him for a thousand years.

⁷And when the thousand years are over, Satan will be let loose from his prison ⁸and will come out to deceive the nations that are at the four corners of the earth, [that is], Gog and Magog, to gather them for battle. Their number is like the sand of the sea, ⁹and they marched up over the broad expanse of the earth and surrounded the camp of the saints and the beloved city. But fire came down from heaven and consumed them, ¹⁰and the devil who had deceived them was thrown into the Lake of Fire and sulfur where the beast and the false prophet were, and they will be tormented day and night forever and ever.

Judgment at the Great White Throne

¹¹Then I saw a great white throne and the One who sat on it. Earth and sky fled away from his presence, and no place was found for them. ¹²And I saw the dead, great and small, standing before the throne, and the books were opened. Also, another book, which is the Book of Life, was opened. And the dead were judged by what was written in the books, [that is], by their deeds. ¹³And the sea gave up

the dead in it. Death and Hades gave up the dead in them. And all were judged by their deeds. [14]Then Death and Hades were thrown into the Lake of Fire. This is the second death, the Lake of Fire. [15]Now if anyone's name was not found written in the Book of Life, he was thrown into the Lake of Fire.

Chapter 21

New Heaven and New Earth

[1]Then I saw a new heaven and a new earth, for the first heaven and the first earth had passed away, and the sea was no more. [2]And I saw the holy city, new Jerusalem, coming down out of heaven from God, prepared as a bride adorned for her husband. [3]And I heard a loud voice from the throne saying, "Look: the dwelling place of God is with mankind. He will dwell with them, and they shall be his people, and God himself will be with them as their God. [4]He will wipe away every tear from their eyes, and death shall be no more, neither shall there be mourning nor crying nor pain anymore, for the former things have passed away."

[5]And the One who was seated on the throne declared, "Look: I am making all things new." He also said, "Write this, for these words are trustworthy and true." [6]And he said to me, "It is done! I am the Alpha and the Omega, the beginning and the end. To the thirsty I will give freely from the fountain of the water of life. [7]Anyone who conquers shall inherit this, and I will be his God and he shall be my son. [8]But as for the cowardly, the faithless, and the detestable people, as for the murderers, the sexually immoral, the sorcerers, the idolaters, and all the liars, their lot shall be in the lake that burns with fire and sulfur, which is the second death."

The New Jerusalem

[9]Then came one of the seven angels who had the seven bowls full of the seven last plagues, and spoke to me, saying, "Come, I will show you the Bride, the wife of the Lamb." [10]And in the Spirit he carried me away to a great, high mountain, and showed me the holy city Jerusalem coming down out of heaven from God, [11]having the glory of God, its radiance like a very rare jewel, like a jasper, clear as crystal. [12]It had a great, high wall, with twelve gates, and at the gates twelve angels, and on the gates the names of the twelve tribes of the sons of Israel were inscribed: [13]on the east three gates, on the north three gates, on the south three gates, and on the west three gates. [14]And the wall of the city had twelve foundations, and on them were the twelve names of the twelve apostles of the Lamb.

¹⁵Now the one who spoke with me had a golden measuring rod to measure the city and its gates and walls. ¹⁶The city lies foursquare, its length the same as its width. With his rod he measured the city to be 185 miles, equal in length, width and height. ¹⁷He also measured its wall as 216 feet by a man's or an angel's measurement. ¹⁸The wall was built of jasper, while the city was pure gold, clear as glass. ¹⁹The foundations of the wall of the city were each adorned with a jewel: the first was jasper, the second sapphire, the third agate, the fourth emerald, ²⁰the fifth onyx, the sixth carnelian, the seventh chrysolite, the eighth beryl, the ninth topaz, the tenth chrysoprase, the eleventh jacinth, the twelfth amethyst. ²¹And the twelve gates were twelve pearls each of the gates being made of a single pearl, and the street of the city was pure gold, transparent as glass.

²²And I saw no temple in the city, for its temple is the Lord God the Almighty and the Lamb. ²³And the city has no need of sun or moon to shine on it, for the glory of God is its light, and its lamp is the Lamb. ²⁴The nations shall walk by its light, and the kings of the earth shall bring their glory into it. ²⁵Its gates shall never be shut by day, and there shall be no night there. ²⁶Into it they shall bring the glory and the honor of the nations. ²⁷But nothing unclean shall enter it, nor shall anyone who practices abomination or falsehood, but only those who have been are recorded in the Lamb's Book of Life.

Chapter 22

The River of the Water of Life

¹Then he showed me the river of the water of life, bright as crystal, flowing from the throne of God and of the Lamb ²through the middle of the street of the city. Also, on either side of the river, was the tree of life with its twelve kinds of fruit, yielding its fruit each month, and the leaves of the tree were for the healing of the nations. ³No longer will any accursed things be there, but the throne of God and of the Lamb shall be in [the city], and his servants shall worship him. ⁴They shall see his face, and his name shall be on their foreheads. ⁵And night will be no more: they will need light from neither lamp nor sun, for the Lord God will be their light, and they shall reign forever and ever.

Jesus is Coming

⁶And he said to me, "These words are trustworthy and true. And the Lord, the God of the spirits of the prophets, has sent his angel to show his servants what must soon take place. ⁷And note this—I am coming soon." Blessed is the person who keeps the words of the prophecy of this book.

[8]I, John, am the one who heard and saw these things. And when I heard and saw them, I fell down to worship at the feet of the angel who showed them to me. [9]But he said to me, "You must not do that! I am a fellow servant with you and your brothers the prophets, and with those who keep the words of this book. Worship *God*."

[10]And he said to me, "Do not seal up the words of the prophecy of this book, for the time is at hand. [11]Let the evildoer still do evil, and the filthy still be filthy, and the righteous still do right, and the holy still be holy."

[12]"Look, I am coming soon, bringing my recompense, to repay everyone for what he has done. [13]I am the Alpha and the Omega, the first and the last, the beginning and the end."

[14]Blessed are the ones who wash their robes, that they may have the right to the tree of life and that they may enter the city by the gates. [15]Outside are the dogs and the sorcerers and the sexually immoral and the murderers and the idolaters, and everyone who loves and practices falsehood.

[16]"I Jesus have sent my angel to you with this testimony for the churches. I am the root and the offspring of David, the bright morning star."

[17]The Spirit and the Bride say, "Come." And let him who hears say, "Come." And let whoever is thirsty come. Let whoever desires the water of life take it for free.

Closing with Warnings

[18]I warn everyone who hears the words of the prophecy of this book: if anyone adds to them, God will add to him the plagues described in this book, [19]and if anyone takes away from the words of the book of this prophecy, God will take away his share in the tree of life and in the holy city, which are described in this book.

[20]The one who testifies to these things says, "Surely I am coming soon." Amen. Come, Lord Jesus! [21]May the grace of the Lord Jesus be with all the saints. Amen.

HELPFUL INDEX to the NEW TESTAMENT:

a guide to locating names, places, topics, and passages

beast with 10 horns   *Rev. 13*

Beatitudes   *Mat. 5:1-11; Lk. 6:20-23*

believers

—restore the fallen   *Gal. 6:1-5*

—unequally yoked   *2 Cor. 6:14*

Bethlehem, Jesus' birth   *Mat. 2:1-6; Lk. 2:1-20*

blasphemy against Holy Spirit   *Mat. 12:31-32;*
                    Mk. 3:22-30

Book of Life   *Phil.4:3; Rev.3:5,13:8,17:8,20:12-*
           15,21:27

born again

—need to be   *Jn. 3:1-17*

—you have been   *1 Pet. 1:3-5*

bowls, seven   *Rev. 16*

Caiaphas   *Matt. 26:3,57-68; Lk. 3:2, 11:45-57;*
          18:12-32; Acts 4:5-6

centurion, faithful Roman   *Mat. 8:5-13; Lk. 7:1-10*

children   *Eph. 6:1-4; Col. 3:20-21*

children of God   *1 Jn. 3:1-7*

Christian behavior   *Rom. 12:9-21; 1 Thes. 4:1-12 &*
           5:12-22

Christians (first use of the term)   *Acts 11:19-26*

church,

—division in the   *1 Cor. 1:10-17*

—officers   *Eph. 4:11-15*

churches, seven   *Rev. 2-3*

comfort in affliction   *2 Cor. 1:1-11*

commandment, greatest   *Mat. 22:34-38*

communion   *1 Cor. 11:17-33*

conquerors, more than   *Rom. 8:31-39*

controversy, avoid   *Titus 3:9-11*

Council of Jerusalem   *Acts 15:1-35*

covenant   *Luke 22:20-23; Heb. 8:1-10:39*

creation groans   *Rom. 8:18-30*

crown of righteousness   *2 Tim. 4:8*

crown of thorns   *Mat. 27:28-29; Mk.15:16-17;*
           Jn.19:1-2

courteous, be   *Titus 3:1-2*

deacons

—first ones chosen   *Acts 7:1-7*

—qualifications   *1 Tim. 3:8-13*

death, the sting of   *1 Cor. 15:50-58*

deeds vs. faith   *Jam. 2:14-26*

demons

—believe and tremble   *Jam. 2:19*

—cast into hogs   *Mat. 8:28-34*

devil

—bound for 1,000 years   *Rev. 20-1-10*

—roaring around like a lion   *1 Pet.5:8-9*

disciples, make   *Mat. 28:16-20*

divorce   *Mat. 5:31-32, Mat. 19:1-12; Mk. 10:1-9;*
         Lk.16:18; 1 Cor. 7:1-40

doctrine, sound   *Titus 2:1-10*

doers of the word   *Jam. 1:22-25*

double-minded man   *Jam. 1:6-8*

doubting   *Jam. 1:6-8*

dragon, and the woman   *Rev. 12*

dust, shake off feet   *Mat. 10:14; Acts 18:6*

Egypt

—Israelites left   *Heb. 3:15-19*

—Joseph's flight to   *Mat. 2:13-23*

elders

—24 around the throne   *Rev. 4:4-11; 11:16*

—double honor   *1 Tim. 5:17-18*

—qualifications of   *1 Tim. 3:1-7 & 5:17-21; Titus*
1:5-9

—rebuking   *1 Tim. 5:1-2*

—shepherding   *1 Pet. 5:1-5*

Elijah   *Jam. 5:16-18*

Elizabeth   *Lk. 1:5-25 & 39-66*

end of the world   *2 Pet. 3:1-13*

end times prophecies   *Mat. 24:1-44; Mk. 13:1-37;*
                Lk. 21:5-36; 1 Thes. 4:12-5:10;
                2 Thes. 1:5-2:12; 2 Tim. 3:1-9

enemies, loving your   *Mat. 5:43-48; Lk. 6:27-36*

Enoch   *Jude 14-16; Heb. 11:5-6*

envy   *Mk. 7:21-23; Rom. 1:29-31; 1 Cor. 3:3;*
       Gal. 5:19-21; Titus 3:4; 1 Pet. 2:1

New Heavens, New Earth, New Jerusalem   *Rev. 21:1-7*

Nicodemus   *Jn. 3:1-21*

Noah   *Heb. 11:7; 1 Pet. 3:20*

oaths, swearing   *Mat. 5:33-37; Jam. 5:12*

offerings   *1 Cor. 16:1-3*

orphans   *Jam. 1:26-27*

Parables of Jesus

—banquet guests   *Lk. 14:12-24*

—fig tree   *Lk. 13:6-9*

—good Samaritan   *Lk. 10:25-37*

—lamp under basket   *Mk.4:21-25; Lk. 8:16-18*

—Lazarus and the rich man   *Lk. 16:19-31*

—lost coin   *Lk. 15:8-10*

—lost sheep   *Lk. 15:3-7*

—marriage feast   *Mat. 22:1-14*

—minas, ten   *Lk. 19:11-27*

—mustard seed   *Mat. 13:31-32; Mk.4-30-32; Lk. 13:18-21*

—prodigal son   *Lk. 15:11-32*

—shrewd manager   *Lk. 16:1-13*

—sower of the seeds   *Mat. 13:1-23; Mk. 4:1-20; Lk. 8:4-15*

—talents   *Mat. 25:14-30*

—tenants, wicked   *Mat. 21:33-41; Lk. 20:9-18*

—unforgiving servant   *Mat. 18:23-34*

—vineyard workers   *Mat. 20:1-16; Mk. 12:1-12*

—virgins, wise and foolish   *Mat. 25:1-13*

—wedding feast   *Lk. 14:7-11*

—weeds   *Mat. 13:24-30,36-43*

—widow, persistent   *Lk. 17:1-8*

parenting   *Eph. 6:1-4; Col. 3:20-21*

partiality   *Jam. 2:1-13*

passions   *Jam. 4:1-12; 1 Pet. 2:11-12 & 4:2-6*

pastors—worthy of pay   *1 Cor. 9:8-18*

patience   *Jam. 5:7-11*

Paul, the Apostle (first known as Saul)

—afflictions   *2 Cor. 6:1-10, 2 Cor. 11:21-32*

—Agrippa, testimony to   *Acts 25:13-26:32*

—Areopagus preaching   **Acts 17:16-33**

—Corinth visit   *Acts 18:1-16*

—conversion on road to Damascus   *Acts 9:1-23*

—Felix, testimony to   *Acts 23:23-24:27*

—Festus, testimony to   *Acts 25:1-12*

—imitate   *1 Cor 4:14-21; 1 Cor 10:23-11:1; 1 Thes. 1:6-7*

—James, visit with   *Acts 21:17-26*

—Jerusalem, in   *Acts 21:1ff*

—Malta, stranded on   *Acts 28:1-10*

—mistaken for a Greek god   *Acts 14: 8-18*

—persecutes the church   *Acts 8:1-4*

—Philippi, jailed in   *Acts 16:16-40*

—Rome, journey to   *Acts 27*

—Rome, in   *Acts 28:11-30*

—stoned   *Acts 14:19-23*

—thorn in the flesh   *2 Cor. 12:7-10*

—visions   *2 Cor. 12:1-6*

peace

—fruit of the Spirit   *Gal. 5:22-23*

—not, but a sword   *Mat. 10:34*

—of Christ   *Rom. 3:15*

pearls, casting   *Mat. 7:6*

Pentecost   *Acts 2*

Pergamum, church at   *Rev.2:12-17*

perseverance   *Phil. 3:1-11; Heb. 12:3-17*

Peter

—denies Jesus   *Mat. 26:30-35 & 69-75; Mk. 14:66-72; Lk. 22:31-35 & 54-62; Jn. 13:36-38, Jn. 18:26-27*

—healing miraculously   *Acts 5:12-16*

—imprisoned and rescued   *Acts 12:1-19*

—preaches at Pentecost   *Acts 2:14-41*

—preaches in the temple portico   *Acts 3:11-26*

—vision of the sheet of animals   *Acts 10:1-48*

Pharisees: woe to you,   *Mat. 22:13-36; Lk. 11:37-54*

Philadelphia, church at   *Rev.3:7-13*

Philip and Ethiopian eunuch   *Acts 8:26-40*

412

PSALTER

PSALM 1

[1]Blessed is the man who does not conduct himself according to the advice of the ungodly, nor associate with sinners, nor sit in the company of scoffers.
[2]Rather, his delight is in the law of the LORD, and he meditates on his law day and night.

[3]And he will be like a tree, planted by the rivers of water, that produces its fruit in season, and whose leaf does not wither. He will prosper in whatever he undertakes.
[4]The ungodly are not like that; rather, they are like chaff blown away by the wind.

[5]Therefore at the time of judgment the ungodly will not be able to stand, nor will sinners be able to stand in the assembly of the righteous.
[6]For the LORD takes note of the ways of the righteous, but the ways of the ungodly will come to an end.

PSALM 2

[1]Why do the nations rage, and the peoples plot action in vain?
[2]The kings of the earth rise to prepare themselves, and the rulers gather to confer against the LORD and against his anointed, saying,
[3]"Let us break their bonds into pieces and throw their ropes off us."

[4]He who sits in the heavens laughs; the LORD holds them in derision.
[5]Then he speaks to them in his wrath and terrifies them in his furious displeasure, saying:
[6]"Nonetheless, I have set my king on my holy hill of Zion."

[7]I will declare the decree that the LORD has said to me:

> "You are my Son; today I have begotten you. [8]Ask of me, and I shall give you the nations for your inheritance, and the ends of the earth for your possession. [9]You will break them with an iron rod; you will smash them into pieces like a clay pot."

[10]Now therefore, be wise, O you kings. Be warned, O judges of the earth.
[11]Serve the Lord with fear and rejoice with trembling.
[12]Kiss the Son so that he might not become angry, and then when his wrath is stirred up in a flash you perish along the way. Blessed are all those who place their trust in him.

PSALM 3

[A Psalm of David when he fled from his son Absalom.]

[1]LORD, how greatly the number of my enemies has increased! Many of them are rising up against me.

²Many of them are talking about my life, claiming "There is no help for him in God."

³But you, O Lord, are a shield for me, my glory, the one who lifts up my head.
⁴I cried out loud to the Lord, and he answered me from his holy hill.
⁵I laid myself down and slept; then I woke up again because the Lord had sustained me.
⁶I will not be afraid of ten thousand opponents who surround me.
⁷Arise, O Lord. Save me, O my God!
Strike all my enemies on the cheek, breaking the teeth of the ungodly.

⁸Salvation belongs to the Lord. May your blessing rest on your people.

PSALM 4

[To the choirmaster: With stringed instruments, a Psalm of David.]

¹Hear me when I call, O God of my righteousness. You have encouraged me in my time of distress. Have mercy on me and hear my prayer!

²O you sons of men, how long will my honor be turned into shame? How long will you love empty words and pursue lies? Selah
³But know that the Lord has set apart the godly man for himself, so the Lord will hear me when I call to him.

⁴When you are angered, do not sin. Consider things in your own heart while on your couch and remain silent. Selah
⁵Offer the right sacrifices and place your trust in the Lord.

⁶Many ask, "Who will show us something good?" Lord, lift up the light of your face on us.
⁷You have put joy in my heart, even more than in the time when the harvest of grain and wine was plentiful.

⁸I will lay myself down in peace and sleep, for only you, Lord, can make me dwell in safety.

PSALM 5

[To the choirmaster. For the flutes. A Psalm of David.]

¹Listen to my words, O Lord—consider my groaning.
²Give your attention to the voice of my cry, my King and my God, for it is to you that I pray.
³You hear my voice in the morning, O Lord.
Each morning I direct my prayer to you as I look upward.

⁴For you are not a God who takes pleasure in wickedness, and evil cannot exist with you.
⁵Boastful fools shall not stand in your sight.
You hate all evildoers.
⁶You wipe out those who speak lies.
The LORD despises bloodthirsty and deceitful men.
⁷But as for me, I come into your house though the abundance of your enduring love, and I worship you in your holy temple in reverence.
⁸O LORD, lead me in your righteous ways with regard to my enemies, making your way plain before my eyes.

⁹For truthfulness is not found in their mouth.
Their innermost part is destruction.
Their throat is an open grave.
They flatter with their tongue.
¹⁰Destroy them, O God—let them fall because of their own schemes.
Cast them out because of the abundance of their sins, for they have rebelled against you.

¹¹But may all those who do place their trust in you rejoice. May they always shout for joy as you protect them. May those who love your name also be jubilant in you, ¹²for you, O LORD, bless the righteous; you surround them like a shield of protection.

PSALM 6

[To the choirmaster: with stringed instruments, according to The Sheminith. A Psalm of David.]

¹O LORD, do not rebuke me in your anger, nor discipline me in your wrath.
²Show mercy to me, O LORD, for I am languishing.
O LORD, heal me for my bones are aching.
³My soul is also in deep distress—but you, O LORD, how long?
⁴Turn, O LORD, and preserve my life. Deliver me for the sake of your enduring love.
⁵For in death there is no one to remember you. Who could praise you from the grave?

⁶I am weary from my groaning. All night long my crying floods my bed with tears. I soak my couch with my tears.
⁷My eye is wasting away on account of my grief, and it is wearing out because of all my enemies.

⁸Get away from me, all you evildoers, for the LORD does hear the sound of my weeping.
⁹The LORD has listened to my prayerful requests. The LORD accepts my prayer.
¹⁰All my enemies will come to shame and be troubled greatly; they will retreat and suddenly be humiliated.

PSALM 7

[A Shiggaion of David that he sang to the Lord concerning the words of Cush, a Benjamite.]

¹O Lord my God, I take my refuge in you.
 Save me from all those who pursue me with evil intent and deliver me ²so that one of them does not rip my soul apart like a lion, tearing it to shreds, with no one to rescue me.

³O Lord my God,
  if I have done this—
  if there be guilt on my hands—
  ⁴if I have returned evil to my ally—
  if I have plundered my enemy without just cause—

⁵Then let the enemy chase me down and overtake me.
Indeed, let him trample me down to the ground and leave my honor in the dust. Selah

⁶Arise, O Lord, in your anger!
Take a stand against the raging of my enemies!
Arouse yourself on my account to bring the justice you have appointed.
⁷May the assembly of the peoples gather around you as you are enthroned above them on high.

⁸Let the Lord judge the peoples. Vindicate me, O Lord, according to my righteous life and according to the integrity within me.
⁹Oh, may the evil ways of the wicked ones come to an end, and may you establish the righteous ones, for the righteous God tests the hearts and minds.
¹⁰My shield of defense lies with God, who saves the upright in heart.
¹¹God is a righteous judge and a God who is indignant every day.

¹²If someone refuses to repent, God will sharpen His sword. He has bent and readied his bow, ¹³preparing deadly weapons for him and his flaming arrows against those who pursue evil.
¹⁴Take note that the wicked one plots evil things, thinking up plans of destruction and hatching lies.
¹⁵He digs out a hole but then falls into the pit he made.
¹⁶His plans for destruction return to his own head, and his violence lands back on his own scalp.

¹⁷I will praise the Lord on account of his justice and sing praise to the name of the sovereign Lord.

PSALM 8

[To the choirmaster. A Psalm of David.]

¹O LORD, our Lord,
how majestic is your name in all the earth!
You have set your glory above the heavens.
²Because of your enemies, you have established strength out of the mouth of
babes and infants, to still the enemy and the avenger.

³When I consider your heavens—the work of your fingers—
the moon and the stars, which you have put in place,
⁴what is man that you are mindful of him,
and the son of man that you care for him?
⁵Yet you have made him a little lower than the angels
and crowned him with glory and honor.
⁶You have given him dominion over the works of your hands;
you have put everything under his feet,
⁷all sheep and oxen,
and even the beasts of the field,
⁸the birds of the air, and the fish of the sea,
and whatever travels the currents in the seas.

⁹O LORD, our Lord,
how majestic is your name in all the earth!

PSALM 9

[To the choirmaster: in Muthlabben. A Psalm of David.]

¹I will praise you, O LORD, with my whole heart.
I will declare all your wonderful deeds.
²I will be glad and rejoice in you.
I will sing praise to your name, O Most High.

³My enemies retreat, stumbling and falling dead before your presence.
⁴For you have upheld my just cause.
You sat on the throne judging in righteousness.

⁵You have rebuked the nations.
You have destroyed the wicked, wiping out their names forever and ever.
⁶The enemy was destroyed, left in perpetual ruins.
You have laid waste to their cities.
The memory of them has perished with them.

⁷But the LORD sits on his throne forever.
He has established his throne for justice.

⁸And he judges the world with righteousness.
He judges the people with uprightness.

⁹The LORD is a stronghold of refuge for the oppressed—a stronghold of refuge in times of trouble.
¹⁰And they who know your name place their trust in you, for you,
O LORD, have not abandoned those who seek you.

¹¹Sing praises to the LORD, who dwells in Zion!
Declare his deeds among the people.

¹²As he avenges blood, he is mindful of them.
He does not forget the cry of the afflicted.

¹³Have mercy on me, O LORD!
Take notice of the affliction that I receive from those who hate me,
It is you who lifts me up from the gates of death
¹⁴so that I may recount all your praises.
May I rejoice in your salvation in the gates of the daughter of Zion!

¹⁵The nations have sunk down into the pit that they dug.
Their own foot is now snared in the net that they themselves had laid.
¹⁶The LORD has made himself known by the judgments he executes.
The wicked are snared in the work of their own hands. Selah
¹⁷The wicked will end up in Sheol—all the nations that deny God.
¹⁸For the needy shall not be forgotten for all time.
The hope of the poor shall not perish forever.

¹⁹Arise, O LORD!
Do not let man prevail.
Let the nations stand in judgment before you.
²⁰Strike terror into them, O LORD.
Make the nations realize that they are only men. Selah

PSALM 10

[To the choirmaster. A Psalm of David.]

¹O LORD, why do you stand far off?
Why do you hide yourself in times of trouble?

²The wicked one arrogantly chases down the poor, letting them be captured in the schemes that he has devised.
³The wicked one brags about his heart's desires, praising the greedy but cursing the LORD.
⁴With a prideful face, the wicked one does not seek after God.
He thinks "There is no God."

422

⁵His ways are always prosperous,
[whereas] your judgments are high and lofty—far above his vision.
  As for all his enemies, he sneers at them.
⁶He says in his heart, "I will not be shaken, nor will I ever see adversity."
⁷His mouth is full of cursing and deceit and extortion.
  Under his tongue lie destruction and wickedness.
⁸He sits in the villages ready to ambush.
  He murders the innocent in hidden places, secretly setting his eye against the helpless.
⁹He lurks in ambush like a lion in his thicket.
  He lurks, ready to ambush the poor.
  Then he snatches the poor when he draws them into his net.
¹⁰The helpless ones fall prey to him because of the wicked one's strength.
¹¹He says in his heart, "God has forgotten; he looked the other way. He will never notice this."

¹²Arise, O LORD; O God, lift up your hand.
  Do not forget the afflicted.
¹³Why does the wicked one renounce God, saying in his heart, "You do not require anything"?
¹⁴But you *do* see this, for you observe destruction and spitefulness so that you may deal with it.
  The poor commit themselves to you to avenge them.
    You are the helper of the fatherless.
¹⁵Break the arm of the wicked one and the evildoer.
  Deal with all his wickedness until you find no more of it.

¹⁶The LORD is King forever and ever.
  The nations perish from his land.
¹⁷LORD, you have heard the desire of the lowly.
  You will strengthen their heart.
  You will lend them your ear ¹⁸to bring justice to the fatherless and the oppressed, so that the worldly man may oppress no more.

PSALM 11

[To the choirmaster. A Psalm of David.]

¹It is in the LORD that I take refuge.
Why then would you say to my soul
  "Flee like a bird to your mountain.
  ²For, look—the wicked bend their bow.
    They have readied their arrow on the string to shoot from the shadows
        at the upright.
  ³If the foundations are destroyed, what can the righteous do?"

⁴The LORD is in his holy temple—the LORD's throne—which is in heaven.

His eyes observe—his eyelids examine— the children of men.

⁵The LORD examines the righteous, but his soul hates the wicked and those who love violence.

⁶He rains down coals on the wicked—fire and sulfur—and a scorching wind.

Such shall be the portion of their cup.

⁷For the LORD, who is righteous, delights in justice.

The upright will see his face.

PSALM 12

[To the choirmaster: according to The Sheminith, A Psalm of David.]

¹LORD, send help because the godly man is gone, for the faithful have vanished from among the children of men.

²Everyone speaks lies to his neighbors, speaking with flattering lips and a duplicitous heart.

³May the LORD cut off all the flattering lips and the tongues that arrogantly boast—⁴"With our tongues we will prevail. Our lips belong to us. Who is lord over us?"

⁵Because the poor are oppressed, because the needy are groaning, I will rise up now," says the LORD. "I will move them to the safety that they are desiring."

⁶The words of the LORD are pure words, like silver refined in an earthen furnace, purified seven times.

⁷You will protect them, O LORD, you will preserve them from this generation forever.

⁸The wicked prowl on every side as the children of man exalt what is vile.

PSALM 13

[To the choirmaster: A Psalm of David.]

¹How long will you forget me, O LORD? Forever?

How long will you hide your face from me?

²How long must my soul wrangle, and my heart be in sorrow each day?

How long will my enemy be exalted over me?

³Consider and hear me, O LORD my God.

Give light to my eyes

so that I do not sleep the sleep of death,

⁴so that my enemy cannot say he has prevailed over me,

so that those who trouble me cannot rejoice because I am undone.

⁵Still, I have placed my trust in your enduring love.

My heart shall rejoice in your salvation.
⁶I will sing to the LORD because he has dealt generously with me.

PSALM 14

[To the choirmaster: Of David.]

¹The fool says in his heart, "There is no God."
Such people are corrupt and do abominable things.
There is no one who does good.

²The LORD looks down from heaven on the children of men to see if there are
any who *do* understand and seek God.
³They are all gone astray; all of them are corrupted.
There is no one who does good—no, not one.
⁴Do all the evildoers have no knowledge—those who devour my people as if they
were bread and do not call on the LORD?
⁵There they remain, terrified because God resides with the generation of the righteous.

⁶You have dismissed the intentions of the poor man, but the LORD is still his refuge.
⁷O that the salvation of Israel would come from Zion!
When the LORD restores his people, may Jacob rejoice and Israel be glad.

PSALM 15

[A Psalm of David.]

¹LORD, who shall dwell in your tabernacle?
Who shall live on your holy hill?
²The one who walks blamelessly and does righteous things and speaks truth in
his heart.
³He does not slander with his tongue,
and does no evil to his neighbor,
and speaks no evil of his friends.
⁴In his eyes, he holds a vile person in contempt,
but he honors those who fear the LORD.
He swears promises at his own risk and holds steady to them.
⁵He does not charge interest when he lends money, nor does he take a bribe to
condemn the innocent. The one who does these things will never be undone.

PSALM 16

[A Miktam of David.]

¹Preserve me, O God, for it is in you that I take refuge.
²I say to the LORD, "You are my Lord—apart from you I have nothing good."

³As for the saints that are on earth, they are excellent, and I take delight in them.

⁴The sorrows of those who go chasing after another god shall multiply.
 I will not pour out their drink offerings of blood nor will their names be on my lips.
⁵The LORD is my chosen portion and my cup.
 You determine my lot in life.
⁶The lines have fallen in pleasant places for me.
 Surely I have a bountiful heritage.

⁷I will bless the LORD, who gives me advice.
 In the night hours my own heart also instructs me.
⁸I have always set the LORD before me.
 Because he is at my right hand, I will not be shaken.
⁹Therefore my heart is glad, and my soul rejoices.
 My body also dwells secure.
¹⁰For you will not abandon my soul in Sheol or allow your Holy One to see corruption.

¹¹You show me the path of life.
 In your presence is complete rejoicing.
 Pleasures lie at your right hand forevermore.

PSALM 17

[A Prayer of David.]

¹Listen to this just cause, O LORD.
 Attend to my cry!
 Lend an ear to my prayer from lips that do not deceive.

²Let my vindication come from your presence.
 Let your eyes observe what is right.
³You have tested my heart.
 You have visited me in the night.
 You have put me to the test, but you will find nothing.
 I have intentionally decided to keep my mouth from transgressing.
⁴As for the deeds of men, I have kept myself away from the ways of the violent ones in keeping with the word of your lips.
⁵I have held my steps within your paths so that my feet would not slip.
⁶I call on you, for you will hear me, O God.
 Lend me your ear and hear my words.
⁷Show your wondrous enduring love to those who place their trust in you to save them from their adversaries at your right hand.

⁸Keep me as the apple of your eye.

Hide me in the shadow of your wings ⁹from the wicked ones who oppress me—
my deadly enemies who surround me.

¹⁰They secure themselves within their own abundance.
  They speak in proud arrogance.
¹¹Now they have surrounded our steps, having set their sights on throwing us
down to the ground, ¹²like a lion greedy for his prey—like a young lion lurking in
ambush.

¹³Arise, O LORD! Block him and throw him down.
  Deliver my soul
  from the wicked by your sword—
¹⁴from men, O LORD, by your hand—
  from worldly men whose portion lies in this life.
  You fill their womb with hidden treasure. They are satisfied with children
  and bequeath their abundance to their infants.
¹⁵As for me, I shall see your face in righteousness.
  When I awaken, I shall be satisfied with the sight of you.

PSALM 18

[To the choirmaster. A Psalm of David, the servant of the LORD, who addressed the words of this
song to the LORD on the day when the LORD delivered him from the hand of all his enemies,
and from the hand of Saul.]

¹He said,
"I love you, O LORD, my strength.
²The LORD is my rock and my fortress and my deliverer,
my God, my rock, in whom I take refuge,
my shield, the horn of my salvation, and my high tower."

³I call on the LORD—who is worthy to be praised—and so I am saved from my
enemies.
⁴The sorrows of death surrounded me;
the torrents of destruction terrified me.
⁵The cords of Sheol wrapped around me;
the snares of death stood before me.
⁶In my distress I called on the LORD;
crying out to my God.
From his temple he heard my voice,
and my cry to him reached his ears.

⁷Then the earth shook and rocked;
even the foundations of the mountains trembled and quaked,
because he was angry.
⁸Smoke rose from his nostrils,

and a devouring fire from his mouth, which kindled coals.
⁹He rolled back the heavens as well and came down,
with dense darkness under his feet.
¹⁰He rode on a cherub and flew—
indeed, he came swiftly on the wings of the wind.
¹¹He clothed himself with darkness as his canopy around him—
thick clouds that were dark with moisture.
¹²Out of the brightness before him hailstones and coals of fire
broke through his clouds.

¹³The LORD also thundered in the heavens,
and the Most High spoke aloud with hailstones and coals of fire.
¹⁴And he sent out his arrows and scattered them.
He flashed forth lightning bolts and routed them.
¹⁵Then the channels in the sea became visible,
and the foundations of the world were laid open
at your rebuke, O LORD,
at the blast of breath from your nostrils.

¹⁶He reached down from on high, laying hold of me,
and pulled me up out of deep waters.
¹⁷He rescued me from my strong enemy
and from those who hated me,
for they were too strong for me.
¹⁸They confronted me in the day of my calamity,
but the LORD supported me.
¹⁹He carried me out into a broad expanse.
  He rescued me because he took delight in me.

²⁰The LORD dealt with me by virtue of my righteous ways—
he rewarded me according to the cleanness of my hands.
²¹For I have kept the ways of the LORD
and have not forsaken my God in wickedness.
²²For all his rules remained in front of me,
and I did not push his statutes away from myself.
²³I was before him without blame,
and I kept myself from my guilt.
²⁴So the LORD has rewarded me according to my righteousness,
according to the cleanness of my hands in his sight.

²⁵To those who are merciful, you show yourself merciful.
  To those who are blameless, you show yourself blameless.
²⁶To those who have been purified, you show yourself pure.
  To those who are underhanded, you show yourself shrewd.

²⁷For you save a humble people,
but you bring down those with haughty eyes.
²⁸For you are the one who lights my lamp.
The LORD my God lights up my darkness.
²⁹For by you I can run against a troop,
and by my God I can jump over a wall.

³⁰As for God—his way is perfect.
The word of the LORD proves true;
he is a shield for all those who take refuge in him.
³¹For who is God besides the LORD?
And who is the rock, except our God?

³²God is the one who equipped me with strength
and made my way blameless.
³³He made my feet like the feet of a deer
and set me secure on the heights.
³⁴He trains my hands for war,
so that my arms can bend a bow of bronze.
³⁵You have given me the shield of your salvation,
and your right hand supports me,
and by your gentleness you have made me great.
³⁶You widened my path under me,
so that my feet did not slip.

³⁷I pursued my enemies and overtook them,
and did not turn back till they were consumed.
³⁸I broke them so that they were not able to get up;
they fell under my feet.

³⁹For you equipped me with strength for the battle;
you forced those who rose against me to fall under me.
⁴⁰You made my enemies turn their backs to me,
so that I could destroy those who hated me.

⁴¹They cried for help, but there was no one to save them.
Though they cried out to the LORD, he did not answer them.
⁴²I beat them fine-- like dust caught up by the wind;
I dumped them out like mire from the streets.

⁴³You delivered me from contentions with the people;
you made me the head of the nations;
people whom I had not known served me.
⁴⁴As soon as they heard of me they obeyed me.
  Foreigners cringed before me.

⁴⁵The foreigners lost heart.
They came out of their fortresses trembling.

⁴⁶The LORD lives, and blessed be my rock,
and let the God of my salvation be exalted.
⁴⁷God avenged me and subdued peoples under me,
⁴⁸rescuing me from my enemies.
Yes, you exalted me above those who rose against me.
You rescued me from the man of violence.

⁴⁹O LORD, I will give thanks to you for this among the nations,
and I will sing praises to your name.
⁵⁰He brings great deliverance to his king and shows enduring love to David, his
anointed one, and his offspring forever.

PSALM 19

[To the choirmaster: A Prayer of David.]

¹The heavens declare the glory of God,
and the skies proclaim his handiwork,
²day after day conveying it,
and night after night revealing knowledge,
³without speech or words,
with no voice to be heard.
⁴Yet their message goes out through all the earth,
and their words to the end of the world.

In them he has built a tabernacle for the sun,
⁵which is like a bridegroom coming out of his chamber,
and like a strong man, it runs its course joyfully.
⁶Its rising is from one end of the heavens, with its circuit to the other end, and
nothing is hidden from its heat.

⁷The law of the LORD is faultless, revitalizing the soul.
The testimony of the LORD is certain, making the simple one wise.
⁸The precepts of the LORD are right, rejoicing the heart.
The commandment of the LORD is pure, enlightening the eyes.
⁹The fear of the LORD is clean, enduring forever.
The judgments of the LORD are true and completely righteous.
¹⁰They are more worthy of one's desire than gold—yes, than much fine gold—
and sweeter than honey and the honeycomb.
¹¹In addition, your servant is guarded by them, and there is great reward in keep-
ing them.

¹²Who can discern his own errors?

Wash me clean from unseen faults.

¹³Hold back your servant from presumptuous sins also.

Do not let them have victory over me, so that I will then be blameless and innocent of great transgression.

¹⁴Let the words of my mouth and the meditation of my heart be acceptable in your sight, O Lord, my rock and my redeemer.

PSALM 20

[To the choirmaster: a Psalm of David.]

¹May the Lord answer you in the day of trouble.

May the name of the God of Jacob keep you safe.

²May he send help from the sanctuary to you and may he send support from Zion.

³May he remember all your offerings and regard your burnt sacrifices favorably. Selah

⁴May he grant your heart's desire and fulfill all your plans.

⁵May we rejoice in your salvation and hang up our banners in the name of our God.

May the Lord fulfill all your requests.

⁶Now I know that the Lord saves his anointed.

He will answer him from his holy heaven with the saving strength of his right hand.

⁷Some place their trust in chariots, and some in horses—but we place our trust in the name of the Lord our God.

⁸They are struck down and fallen but we rise and stand upright.

⁹O Lord, save the king and answer us when we call!

PSALM 21

[Praise for Deliverance. To the choirmaster: a Psalm of David.]

¹O Lord, the king takes joy in your strength, and how greatly he rejoices in your salvation!

²You have given him the desire of his heart and have not withheld the request of his lips. Selah

³For you come before him with the good blessings.

You place a crown of pure gold on his head.

⁴He requested life of you, and you gave it to him—days extending forever and ever.

⁵Through your salvation his glory is great, for you have bestowed splendor and majesty on him.

⁶You have made him most blessed forever.

By the presence of your face, you have made him jubilant.

⁷For the king has placed his trust in the Lord, and on account of the steadfastness of the most High he will not be shaken.

⁸Your hand will find out all your enemies.

 Your right hand will find out the ones who despise you.

⁹You shall turn them into a blazing oven in the time of your revenge.

 The LORD will swallow them up in His wrath, and fire will devour them.

¹⁰You shall wipe out their descendants from the earth, and their offspring from among the children of mankind.

¹¹For they plotted evil against you.

 Even though they devised mischievous deeds, they were unable to carry them out.

¹²Therefore you will drive them away when you aim the arrows that you have set on your bows at their faces.

¹³Be exalted, O LORD, in your own strength.

 And so we will sing and praise your power.

PSALM 22

[To the choirmaster: to the tune of *The Doe of the Dawn*. A Psalm of David.]

¹My God, my God, why have you forsaken me? The words of my groaning lie far away from my deliverance.

²O my God, I cry out in the daytime, but you do not respond, in the nighttime as well, but I am not comforted.

³But you are holy, O you who inhabits the praises of Israel.

⁴Our fathers trusted in you. They trusted, and you delivered them.

⁵They cried to you and were delivered. They trusted in you and were not disappointed.

⁶But I am a worm, not a man—held as an object of contempt, despised by the people.

⁷All those looking at me ridicule me. They make faces and wag their heads, taunting, ⁸"He committed himself to the LORD—let *Him* save him. Since he delights in the LORD, let *Him* rescue him."

⁹But you are the One who took me from the womb.

 You made me trust in you while I was still at my mother's breasts.

¹⁰My life was laid on you since my birth.

 You have been my God since I was in my mother's womb.

¹¹Be not far from me, for trouble is nearby, and there is no other to help.

¹²Many bulls have surrounded me—strong bulls of Bashan have surrounded me.

¹³They gaped at me with open mouths, like a hungry, roaring lion.

¹⁴I am poured out like water, and all my bones are out of joint. My heart is like wax, melted inside my abdomen.

¹⁵My strength is wasted away like a broken piece of a clay pot, and my tongue clings to my jaws. You set me down in the dust of death.

¹⁶For dogs have surrounded me.

A wicked mob has closed me in and pierced my hands and my feet.
¹⁷I can count all my bones. They gape and gloat over me.
¹⁸They divide up my garments among themselves and cast lots for my cloak.

¹⁹But be not far from me, O LORD. O my strength, hurry to help me.
²⁰Deliver my soul from the sword and my precious soul from the power of the dog.
²¹Save me from the mouth of the lion; snatch me from the horns of the wild oxen.

²²I will declare your name to my brothers.
  I will praise you in the midst of the congregation.
²³You who fear the LORD, praise him.
  All you descendants of Jacob, glorify him.
  Revere him, all you descendants of Israel.
²⁴For the LORD has not despised or shunned the affliction of the afflicted one—
neither has he hidden his face from him; but when he cried to him, he listened.

²⁵You will praise me in the great assembly, and I will perform my vows before
those who fear him.
²⁶The meek shall eat and be satisfied. Those who seek the LORD shall praise him.
May your heart live forever!

²⁷All the ends of the earth shall remember and turn to the LORD, and all the clans
of the nations shall worship before you.
²⁸For the kingdom belongs to the LORD, and he rules over the nations.
²⁹All the prosperous ones of the earth eat and worship. All those who go down to
the dust shall bow before him—even the one who could not survive.

³⁰Descendants shall serve him and tell of the LORD to the next generation,
³¹proclaiming his deliverance—that he has brought it about—to a people yet to be born.

PSALM 23

¹The LORD is my shepherd; I shall lack for nothing.
²He settles me down in green pastures; he leads me beside restful waters.
³He restores my soul; he leads me in the paths of righteousness for the sake of
his name.

⁴Indeed, even when I walk through the valley of the shadow of death, I will fear
no evil, for you are with me; your rod and your staff comfort me.
⁵You prepare a table before me in the presence of my enemies.
  You anoint my head with oil.
  My cup overflows.

⁶Certainly goodness and mercy will follow me all the days of my life,
and I shall dwell in the house of the LORD forever.

PSALM 24

[A Psalm of David.]

¹The earth and everything in it belongs to the LORD—yes the entire world and all who inhabit it.
²For he has founded it on the seas and established it on the waters.

³Who shall ascend to the hill of the LORD?
 Or who shall stand in his holy place?
⁴He whose hands are undefiled, and whose heart is pure—who has not exalted himself in vain nor made claims deceitfully.
⁵He shall receive the blessing from the LORD and righteousness from the God of his salvation.
⁶This is the generation of those who seek him—who seek your face, O Jacob. Selah

⁷Lift up your heads, O you gates.
 And be lifted up, you everlasting doors.
 And the King of glory shall enter.
⁸Who is this King of glory?
    The LORD strong and mighty, the LORD mighty in battle.
⁹Lift up your heads, O you gates.
 Even you everlasting doors, be lifted up.
 And the King of glory shall enter.
¹⁰Who is this King of glory?
    The LORD of hosts—he is the King of glory. Selah

PSALM 25

[An acrostic of the Hebrew alphabet.]

¹Aloft to you, O LORD, do I lift my soul.

²But, O my God, I trust in you. May I not be ashamed, may my enemies not triumph over me.

³Grant that no one who waits for you is ashamed, but instead that it is those who commit treason who come to shame.

⁴Do show me your ways, O LORD; teach me your paths.

⁵Even lead me in your truth and instruct me, for you are the God of my salvation. I wait for you all day long.

⁶We beg you, O LORD, to remember your tender mercies and your enduring love, for they have existed from olden times.

⁷Zealously I beg you, O LORD, not to remember the sins of my youth, nor my transgressions. According to your mercy remember me for the sake of your goodness, O LORD.

⁸How good and upright is the LORD; therefore he instructs sinners in his ways.

⁹The LORD guides the meek in righteousness, and he instructs the meek about his ways.

¹⁰Yes, all the paths of the LORD are mercy and truth to those who keep his covenant and his testimonies.

¹¹King and LORD, for the sake of your name, forgive me of my wickedness, for it is great.

¹²Lo, who is the man who fears the LORD, who instructs him the way to choose?

¹³Mercifully his soul will live at ease, and his descendants will inherit the earth.

¹⁴Now the secret of the LORD is with those who fear him, and he will reveal his covenant to them.

¹⁵So, my eyes are always set toward the LORD, for he pulls my feet out of the net.

¹⁶Turn to me and have mercy on me for I am lonely and afflicted.

¹⁷Painful troubles of my heart have grown large. Oh, rescue me from my sorrows!

¹⁸Come and take note of my affliction and my pain and forgive all my sins.

¹⁹Quickly consider my enemies for they are many, and they hate me with cruel hatred.

²⁰Remember to preserve my soul and deliver me. Because I find my refuge in you, let me not be ashamed.

²¹So, let integrity and uprightness preserve me because I wait for you.

²²Then, O God, rescue Israel out of all his troubles.

PSALM 26

[Of David.]

¹Vindicate me, O LORD, for I have walked in integrity.
 I also have not wavered in my trust the LORD.
²Examine me, O LORD, and test me. Try my mind and my heart.
³For your enduring love is ever before my eyes, and I have walked in your truth.

⁴I do not pass my time with deceitful liars, nor do I associate with evil men.
⁵I have contempt for assemblies of evildoers and will not associate with the wicked.

⁶I wash my hands in innocence as I walk around your altar, O LORD, ⁷to announce my thankfulness and proclaim all your wonderful deeds.
⁸LORD, I love the dwelling of your house and the place where your glory resides.
⁹Do not let my soul be gathered up with sinners, nor my life with bloodthirsty men ¹⁰whose hands hold evil things, and whose right hands are filled with bribes.

¹¹But as for me, I shall walk in integrity.
   Redeem me and show mercy to me.
¹²My feet stand solidly on the ground.
   I will bless the LORD in the large assemblies.

PSALM 27

[A Psalm of David.]

¹The LORD is my light and my salvation—whom should I fear?
   The LORD is the fortress of my life—whom should I be afraid of?

²When the wicked—my enemies and my foes—attack me to consume my flesh, they are the ones who stumble and fall.
³Even if an army should encamp against me, my heart shall not fear.
   Though a war should arise against me, yet will I remain confident.
⁴I have desired one thing of the LORD, which I will pursue: that I may dwell in the house of the LORD all the days of my life, to look on the beauty of the LORD, and to study in his temple.
⁵For in the time of trouble he will hide me in his shelter, 'neath the cover of his tent will he hide me. He will place me high up on a rock.
⁶And now my head will be lifted up above my enemies surrounding me. Therefore I will offer sacrifices of joy in his tent.
I will sing—indeed—I will sing praises to the LORD.

⁷Hear, O LORD, when I cry out loud.
   Take mercy on me and answer me.
⁸You have said, "Seek my face."
   My heart replies to you, "It is your face, LORD, that I shall seek."
⁹Do not hide your face from me. Do not send your servant away in anger.
   O you who have been my help, do not leave me nor forsake me, O God of my salvation.
¹⁰If my father and my mother forsake me, then the LORD will take me in.
¹¹Teach me your way, O LORD, and lead me on a level path on account of my enemies.
¹²Do not hand me over to the plans of my enemies, for liars have risen up against me, making cruel threats.
¹³How could I not believe that I will see the goodness of the LORD in the land of the living?

¹⁴Wait for the LORD.
 Take heart and he will strengthen your resolve.
 Wait for the LORD!

PSALM 28

[A Psalm of David.]

¹I will cry out to you, O LORD, my rock.
 Do not be deaf to me and do not stay silent to me, so that I do not become like those who descend into the pit.
²Hear the voice of my pleas for mercy when I cry out to you—when I raise my hands toward the source of your holy voice.
³Do not drag me away along with the wicked and the evildoers who speak kindly to their neighbors, though evil lies in their hearts.

⁴Reward them according to their deeds, and according to the wickedness of their efforts.
 Reward them in light of the work of their hands. Give them what they deserve
⁵Because they have no regard for the works of the LORD nor the workings of his hands, he will demolish them and build them up no more.

⁶Blessed be the LORD because he has heard the voice of my pleas for mercy.
⁷The LORD is my strength and my shield.
  My heart trusts in him, and I receive help.
  So my heart rejoices greatly, and I will praise him with my song.

⁸The LORD is their strength—the saving strength of his anointed.
⁹Save your people and bless your heritage.
 Provide for them and support them forever.

PSALM 29

[A Psalm of David.]

¹Ascribe to the LORD, O sons of heaven, ascribe to the LORD glory and strength.
²Ascribe to the LORD the glory due to his name.
 Worship the LORD dressed in holiness.

³The voice of the LORD is over the waters.
 The God of glory thunders—the LORD—over many waters.
⁴The voice of the LORD is powerful;
 the voice of the LORD is majestic.
⁵The voice of the LORD breaks the cedars;
 the LORD shatters the cedars of Lebanon.
⁶He makes Lebanon skip like a calf,
 and Sirion like a young wild ox.

⁷The voice of the LORD flashes out lightning.
⁸The voice of the LORD shakes the wilderness.
The LORD shakes the wilderness of Kadesh.
⁹The voice of the LORD makes the deer give birth and strips the forests bare.
And in his temple everything shouts, "Glory!"

¹⁰The LORD is enthroned over the waters.
The LORD sits enthroned as king forever.
¹¹May the LORD strengthen his people!
May the LORD bless his people with peace!

PSALM 30

[A Psalm of David: a song at the dedication of the temple.]

¹I will extol you, O LORD, for you have raised me up and not allowed my enemies
to gloat over me.
²O LORD my God, I cried out to you, and you have healed me.
³O LORD, you have brought my soul up from the grave.
You have restored my life, so that I would not have to go down to the pit.

⁴Sing to the LORD, O you, his saints.
Give thanks as you remember his holiness.
⁵For his anger lasts only a moment; in his favor is life.
Weeping may endure all night but rejoicing comes in the morning.

⁶And in my prosperity I said, "I shall never be shaken."
⁷LORD, by your favor you have caused my mountain to stand strong.
When you hid your face, I was troubled.
⁸I cry to you, O LORD, and I plead for mercy to the LORD.
⁹What profit is there in the blood [of my death], if I go down to the pit?
Will the dust praise you? Will it declare your faithfulness?
¹⁰Hear, O LORD, and have mercy on me.
LORD, come to my aid.

¹¹You have turned my mourning into dancing.
You have taken off my sackcloth and wrapped me in gladness ¹²so that
my glory would be to sing praise to you and not be silent.
¹³O LORD my God, I will give thanks to you forever!

PSALM 31

[To the choirmaster: a Psalm of David.]

¹O LORD, it is in you that I place my trust.
Let me never be ashamed.
In your righteousness, deliver me!

²Lend me your ear; deliver me speedily.
Be my rock of refuge—a strong fortress to save me!
³For you are my rock and my fortress.
 You lead me and guide me for your name's sake.
⁴You remove me from the net that was laid for me, for you are my refuge.
⁵I commit my spirit into your hands.
 You have redeemed me, O Lord God of truth.

⁶I reject those who adore false idols; instead, I trust in the Lord.
⁷I will be glad and rejoice in your enduring love because you have taken notice of my affliction.
You have recognized the distress of my soul.
⁸Instead of delivering me over into the hands of my enemy, you have set my feet down safely in a large open space.

⁹Have mercy on me, O Lord, for I am in distress.
 My eye is worn out from grief—my soul and my body as well.
¹⁰For my life is spent with sorrow, and my years with sighing.
 My strength fails me because of my guilt, and my bones waste away.

¹¹I was disgraced among all my enemies and despised by my neighbors—even my friends are loath to visit me; when they see me out in public they run the other way.
¹²I am ignored as if I were dead—like a broken pot.
¹³For I have heard that many slander me.
 I am surrounded by terrors on every side.
 Men conspire against me, devising schemes to take my life.

¹⁴Nonetheless, I place my trust in you, O Lord, saying, "You are my God."
¹⁵My times are in your hand; deliver me from the hands of my enemies and from those who persecute me!
¹⁶Make your face shine on your servant.
 Save me on account of your enduring love.
¹⁷Let me not be ashamed, O Lord, for I have called on you.
  Let the wicked be put to shame.
  Let them be silent in the grave.
¹⁸Let the lying lips be silenced—the lips that speak insolently against the righteous ones with pride and contempt.

¹⁹How great is your goodness, which you have stored up for those who revere you.
You lavish it on those who have done for those who trust in you, in view of the children of mankind!
²⁰You hide them from the plots of men under the cover of your presence.
 In a secret shelter, you preserve them from the strife of [accusing] tongues.
²¹Blessed be the Lord, for when I was in a besieged city, he demonstrated his marvelous kindness to me.

²²Then when I was anxious, I said, "I am cut off from your sight." Nonetheless, you heard the voice of my pleas for mercy when I cried out to you for help.

²³O love the LORD, all you his saints!
The LORD preserves the faithful, but he repays the one who behaves proudly with great punishment.
²⁴Be of good courage, and he will strengthen your heart, all you who put your hope in the LORD.

PSALM 32

[A Psalm of David.]

¹Blessed is the one whose transgression is forgiven, whose sin is covered.
²Blessed is the man for whom the LORD has recorded no wrongdoing, and whose spirit is without guile.

³When I remained silent, my bones wasted away through my groaning all the day long.
⁴For day and night your hand was heavy on me, and my vigor was dried up as it is in the dry heat of summer. Selah
⁵I acknowledged my sin to you, and I have not concealed my wrongdoing.
I said, "I will confess my transgressions to the LORD," and you forgave the evil of my sin. Selah
⁶Therefore let everyone who is godly pray to you in a time when you may be found.
Surely in the rush of great waters they shall not reach him.
⁷You are my hiding place.
You keep me safe from trouble.
You surround me with shouts of deliverance. Selah

⁸I will instruct you and teach you in the way that you should go. I will guide you, keeping my eye on you.
⁹Do not be like a horse or a mule, which have no understanding and must be directed with bit and bridle or else it will not stay near you.

¹⁰The sorrows of the wicked are many, but merciful love surrounds the one who trusts in the LORD.
¹¹Be glad in the LORD and rejoice, O righteous ones.
And shout for joy, all you who are upright in heart!

PSALM 33

¹Rejoice in the LORD, O you righteous ones, for praise is fitting for the upright.
²Praise the LORD with the lyre; make music to him with the ten-stringed harp.
³Sing a new song to him, playing skillfully with a great shout.

440

⁴For the word of the LORD is right, and all his works are done faithfully.
⁵He loves righteousness and justice.
The earth is full of the enduring love of the LORD.

⁶By the word of the LORD the heavens were created, and all their starry host by the breath of his mouth.
⁷He gathers up the waters of the sea together into a heap, putting the deep into storehouses.
⁸Let all the earth fear the LORD!
Let all the inhabitants of the world regard him with awe.
⁹For he spoke, and it came into being.
    He commanded, and it stood firm.

¹⁰The LORD brings the schemes of the nations to nothing, frustrating the plans of the people.
¹¹The counsel of the LORD stands forever—the thoughts of his heart to all generations.
¹²Blessed is the nation whose God is the LORD, and the people whom he has chosen for his heritage!

¹³The LORD looks down from heaven regarding all the sons of men.
¹⁴From where he sits on his throne he looks down on all the inhabitants of the earth.
¹⁵He fashions the hearts of all of them and observes all they do.
¹⁶No king is saved by the greatness of his army, nor is a mighty warrior delivered by his great strength.
¹⁷A war horse is inadequate for salvation, nor can he rescue by his might.

¹⁸Take note—the eye of the LORD is on those who fear him, on those who hope in his enduring love ¹⁹to deliver their soul from death, and to keep them alive in famine.

²⁰Our soul waits for the LORD; he is our help and our shield.
²¹For our heart is made glad in him because we have trusted in his holy name.
²²Let your enduring love be on us, O LORD, as we place our hope in you.

PSALM 34

[An acrostic poem of the Hebrew alphabet.]

¹At all times I will bless the LORD; his praise shall continually be on my lips.

²Boasting in the LORD is what my soul shall do. The humble shall hear about it and rejoice.

³Greatly magnify the LORD with me, and let us exalt his name together.

⁴Desperately I sought the LORD, and he *did* hear me and deliver me from all I feared.

⁵Earnestly they looked toward him, and they beamed. Their faces will show no shame.

⁶When this poor man cried, the LORD *did* hear him and rescued him from all his troubles.

⁷Zealously the angel of the LORD encircles those who fear him, and he delivers them.

⁸Here—taste and see that the LORD is good; blessed is the man who trusts in him.

⁹Then fear the LORD, you his saints, for those who fear him shall lack for nothing.

¹⁰Young lions are lacking and suffering hunger, but those who seek the LORD shall lack for nothing.

¹¹Keep coming, you children, to listen to me; I will teach you the fear of the Lord.

¹²Listen—who is it that desires life and loves many days, so that he may see good?

¹³May you keep your tongue from evil, and your lips from telling lies.

¹⁴Neglect doing evil and instead do good; seek peace and pursue it.

¹⁵Surely the eyes of the Lord are on the righteous, and his ears harken to their cry.

¹⁶The LORD sets his face against evildoers to blot out the memory of them from the earth.

¹⁷Painfully the righteous cry, and the LORD hears and rescues them from all their troubles.

¹⁸Certainly the Lord is near those who are of a broken heart and saves those with a contrite spirit.

¹⁹Quite numerous are the afflictions of the righteous man, but the Lord delivers him out of them all.

²⁰Retaining all his bones, not one of them is broken.

²¹Suffering will slay the wicked; those who hate the righteous will be laid waste.

²²The LORD redeems the soul of his servants, and none of them who trust in him will be destroyed.

PSALM 35

[A Psalm of David.]

¹O LORD, contend with those who strive against me.
Fight against those who fight against me.

²Take up shield and armor and rise up to help me.
³Wield the spear and javelin to bar those who pursue me.
  Reassure my soul with "I am your salvation."

⁴Let those who seek after my life be shamed and dishonored.
  Let those who plot evil against me be turned back and disappointed.
⁵Let them be like chaff before the wind as the angel of the LORD drives them away.
⁶Let their path be dark and slippery as the angel of the LORD pursues them, ⁷because without cause they hid their net to snare me, and without cause they have dug a pit for me.
⁸Let destruction overtake them by surprise—let the net they have hidden snare them and let them fall into the pit, to their own ruin.

⁹Then shall my soul rejoice in the LORD and delight in his salvation!
¹⁰All my bones shall say, "LORD, who is like you, who delivers the poor man from the one who is too strong for him—the poor and the needy from those who rob them?"

¹¹False witnesses rise up, charging things against me that I was unaware of.
¹²They repay me evil for good, depleting my very soul.
¹³However, as for me, I wore sackcloth when *they* were sick; I humbled myself by fasting; and I prayed with my head down on my chest.
¹⁴I acted as if I was grieving for my friend or my brother; I bowed down in mourning, as someone who was mourning his mother.

¹⁵On the contrary, they rejoiced and gathered themselves together—yes, the wretched people gathered themselves together against me, and without my knowledge, they did not stop speaking evil things about me behind my back.
¹⁶At feasts, these mockers tore me apart with profanities.
¹⁷O Lord, how long will you stand by watching?
  Rescue me from being destroyed by them.
  Rescue my precious life from the lions.
¹⁸I will give you thanks in the great assembly.
  I will praise you in the presence of many people.
¹⁹Do not let these, my enemies, wrongfully rejoice over my woe.
  And do not let these who hate me without just cause wink with the eye.
²⁰For they do not speak peace—rather, they devise deceitful plans against those in the land who are peaceable.
²¹Yes, they open their mouth wide against me, and claim, "Aha, aha, our eyes have seen such-and-such."

²²You have seen this, O LORD—do not keep silent.
  O LORD, do not be far from me!
²³Wake up and rouse yourself to vindicate me, my God and my Lord!
²⁴Vindicate me according to your righteousness, O LORD my God, do not let them rejoice over me!

[25]Let them not say in their hearts, "Aha—just what we wanted!" Do not let them say, "We have swallowed him up."

[26]Let those who are rejoicing at my calamity be ashamed and brought to complete failure; let those who puff up themselves against me be clothed with shame and dishonor.

[27]Let those who delight in righteousness shout for joy and be glad.

Yes, let them always say, "Great is the LORD, who takes pleasure in the prosperity of his servant!"

[28]Then my tongue shall praise you and tell about your righteousness all day long!

PSALM 36

[To the choirmaster: a Psalm of David the servant of the LORD.]

[1]The transgression of the wicked one speaks within his heart.

No fear of God in his eyes! [2]In his own eyes he fools himself that his wickedness will not be discovered and despised.

[3]The words of his mouth [speak] evildoing and deceit; he has stopped being wise and doing good.

[4]He thinks up evil plans while on his couch, committing his ways to what is of no good, and not hating evil.

[5]O LORD, your enduring love stretches to the heavens, and your faithfulness to the clouds.

[6]Your righteousness is like the great mountains.

Your judgments are deep like the oceans.

O LORD, you save both man and beast.

[7]O God, how awesome is your enduring love!

Therefore the children of mankind find refuge in the shadow of your wings.

[8]They feast on the great abundance of your house, and you have them drink from the river of your delights.

[9]For with you is the fountain of life. In your light we see light.

[10]Yes, maintain your enduring love to those who know you, and your righteousness to the upright in heart!

[11]Do not let the foot of arrogance strike me, and do not let the hand of the wicked drive me away.

[12]Those who practice wickedness lie there fallen—hurled down and unable to get up.

PSALM 37

[A Psalm of David.]

[1]Do not fret yourself on account of evildoers and do not envy those who do evil, [2]for they shall soon fade like grass and wither like green herbs.

444

³Trust in the LORD and do good as you dwell in the land, and truly you will be fed.
⁴Delight yourself in the LORD, and he will give you the desires of your heart.
⁵Commit your way to the LORD; trust in him and he will bring things to pass.
⁶He will bring forth your righteousness like the daylight, and your justice like the noonday.

⁷Rest in the LORD and wait patiently for him.
 Do not fret yourself on account of the man who prospers in his doings—on account of a man who carries out evil schemes.
⁸Refrain from anger and forsake wrath! Do not fret yourself in a way that leads to doing wrong.
⁹For evildoers shall be cut off, whereas those who wait on the LORD shall inherit the land.
¹⁰For in just a little while the wicked one will be no more—you will carefully examine his place, but he will no longer be there.
¹¹But the meek shall inherit the land and delight themselves in abundant peace.
¹²The wicked one plots against the righteous and gnashes his teeth against him,
¹³but the Lord laughs at him, for he knows that his day is coming.
¹⁴Though the wicked draw out the swords and bend their bows to bring down the poor and needy and to slay those who live uprightly, ¹⁵their swords will end up in their own hearts, and their bows will be broken.

¹⁶The small amount owned by a righteous man is better than the riches of many wicked ones.
¹⁷For the arms of the wicked shall be broken, but the LORD upholds the righteous.
¹⁸The LORD knows the days of the righteous, and that their inheritance will last forever.
¹⁹They are not put to shame in hard times, and in the days of famine they will have plenty of food.
²⁰However the wicked ones will perish, and the enemies of the LORD are like the glory of the pastures that is consumed. They vanish like smoke.

²¹The wicked borrows and then does not repay, whereas the righteous gives generously.
²²Those blessed by the LORD shall inherit the earth, whereas those cursed by him shall be cut off.
²³The steps of a man are established by the LORD, when he delights in His way.
²⁴If he should fall, he shall not be completely cast down, for the LORD holds him up with His hand.
²⁵I have been young, and now am old, yet I have not seen the righteous man forsaken, nor his children begging for bread.
²⁶He is continually lending generously, and his children are blessed.
²⁷Turn away from evil and instead do good, and in doing so you will live forever.
²⁸For the LORD loves justice and does not forsake his saints.
 They are preserved forever unlike the children of the wicked, who shall be cut off.
²⁹The righteous shall inherit the land and live in it forever.

³⁰The mouth of the righteous speaks wisdom, and his tongue speaks justice.
³¹The law of his God is in his heart, in his steps he does not slip.
³²The wicked one watches for the righteous, seeking to kill him.
³³The LORD will not abandon the righteous to the hand of the wicked one, nor allow him to be condemned when he is on trial.

³⁴Wait for the LORD and keep his way, and he will exalt you to inherit the land.
Then when the wicked are cut off, you will watch it happen.
³⁵I have seen a powerful, wicked man spreading himself like a green laurel tree
³⁶yet he died and was no more. Yes, I looked for him, but he could not be found anymore.

³⁷Mark well the godly, mature man, and observe the one who is upright, for his ways lead to peace.
³⁸However, the transgressor shall be altogether destroyed because his ways lead to being cut off.

³⁹But the salvation of the righteous comes from the LORD, who is their strength in the time of trouble.
⁴⁰The LORD helps them and delivers them.
He delivers them from the wicked and saves them because they trust in him.

PSALM 38

[A Psalm of David, for the memorial offering.]

¹O LORD, in your anger, do not rebuke me, nor discipline me in your wrath.
²For your arrows have lodged in me, and your hand is heavy on me.

³My flesh is so unhealthy because of your indignant anger.
Because of my sin, my bones are not at peace.
⁴For my wrongdoings have overwhelmed me; like a huge burden they are too heavy for me.
⁵My wounds stink and fester because of my foolishness.
⁶I am laid low, lying prostrate; all day long I go about mourning.
⁷For in my gut is a detestable aching, and my flesh is so unhealthy.
⁸I feel feeble and my health is broken; I groan due to the tumult in my heart.

⁹Lord, all my desires lie before you and my sighing is not hidden from you.
¹⁰My heart is throbbing and my strength is failing me.
As for the light of my eyes, it too has vanished.
¹¹Those who love me, and my friends, stay clear from my plague—even my family members keep clear of me.
¹²Those who seek after my life lay snares for me, and those who seek my harm plan my destruction and constantly plot treacherous things.
¹³But I, as if I were deaf, do not hear that, and as if I were dumb, say nothing.

¹⁴So, I am like a man who cannot hear, and in whose mouth are no rebukes.
¹⁵For in you, O LORD, do I place my hope; you listen, O Lord my God.
¹⁶For I said, let them not rejoice over my demise; when my foot slips, they puff up themselves against me.

¹⁷For I am ready to give up, and my sorrow lies continually before me.
¹⁸For I will declare my wrongdoing, being sorry for my sin.

¹⁹But my enemies are vigorous and strong, and those who wrongfully hate me have increased in number.
²⁰Those who return evil for good are my adversaries because I pursue what is good.

²¹Do not forsake me, O LORD.
 O my God, be not far from me.
²²Make haste to help me, O Lord my salvation.

PSALM 39

[To the choirmaster, especially to Jeduthun, a Psalm of David.]

¹I said, "I will guard my ways, so that I do not sin with my tongue.
I will muzzle my mouth while the wicked ones are in my presence."
²I remained mute. In silence I held my peace, but it was no use—my distress only worsened.
³My heart grew hot inside me, and the fire burned while I was musing.
 Then I spoke with my tongue:

⁴"O, LORD, make me realize what my end is, and what the length of my days is; show me how momentary I am.
⁵Indeed, you have made my days just a few handspans,
and my lifespan is like nothing compared to you.
Truly—at the most every man's life is but a breath. Selah
⁶Surely everyone goes around like a mere shadow.
Surely they live in turmoil for nothing, accumulating wealth without knowing who will own it someday.
⁷And now, Lord, what am I waiting for? My hope is in you.
⁸Deliver me from all my transgressions and do not let me become a laughingstock for fools.
⁹I am mute, not opening my mouth because of what you have done.
¹⁰Remove your punishments from me, for I am wasting away from the blows of your hand.
¹¹When you discipline someone by rebuking them for sinning, you consume the object of his desire like a moth. Surely everyone is a mere breath. Selah
¹²Hear my prayer, O LORD, and lend your ear to my cry. Do not remain silent at my tears, for I am a sojourner with you, merely a temporary

guest, like all my ancestors.

¹³Spare me so that I may recover my strength before I depart and am no more."

PSALM 40

[To the choirmaster: a Psalm of David.]

¹I waited patiently for the LORD, and he inclined his ear to me and heard my cry.
²He pulled me up out of a pit of destruction—out of the miry bog—and set my feet on a rock, making my steps secure.
³Now he has put a new song in my mouth—a song of praise to our God.
Let many see it and fear and trust in the LORD.

⁴Blessed is that man who places his trust in the LORD and does not seek the ways of those who are proud and chase after lies.
⁵O LORD my God, how numerous are the wonderful things that you have done, and your thoughts on our behalf. No one can compare with you!
I will proclaim and talk about them, but they are more than can be told.
⁶You have not taken delight in sacrifice and burnt offerings.
You have opened my ears; it was not burnt offerings and sin offerings that you have required.
⁷Then I said,

"Look—I have come. Things are written about me in the scroll of the book.
⁸I delight to do your will, O my God. Truly, your law is within my heart."

⁹I have preached righteousness in the great assemblies. Look—I have not refrained from speaking out, as you know, O LORD.
¹⁰I have not concealed your enduring love within my heart—rather, I have declared your faithfulness and your salvation.
I have not concealed your enduring loving and your truth from the great assemblies.
¹¹May you never withhold your tender mercies from me, O LORD.
Let your enduring love and your faithfulness continuously preserve me.
¹²For innumerable evils have enveloped me.
My own wrongdoings have seized me, so that I am not able to look up.
They outnumber the hairs of my head, so my heart fails me.

¹³May you, O LORD, be pleased to deliver me. O LORD, quickly help me.
¹⁴Let those who seek to extinguish my soul be put to shame and fail completely.
Let those would delight in harming me be driven away and brought to dishonor.
¹⁵Let those who deride me saying, "Aha, aha!" be appalled because of their own shame.

¹⁶Let all those who seek you rejoice and be glad in you.
Let the ones who love your salvation say continually, "Great is the LORD."
¹⁷But as for me, I am poor and needy…and yet the Lord is mindful of me.
You are my help and my deliverer. Do not delay, O my God.

PSALM 41

¹Blessed is the one who shows concern for the lowly.
  In a time of trouble the LORD will deliver him.
²The LORD protects him and preserves his life.
  Others in the land call him blessed.
  You will not hand him over to the schemes of his enemies.
³The LORD still sustains him on his sickbed.
  You restore him to health in times of sickness.

⁴I said, "LORD, have mercy on me and heal my being, for I have sinned against you."
⁵My enemies hatefully say this about me: "How soon will he die, and his
name perish?"
⁶And when one visits me, he makes empty statements.
  His heart devises wicked things, which he then reports abroad to others.
⁷All who hate me gather together and whisper about me.
  They imagine calamities happening to me.
⁸They say, "A deadly disease has befallen him. Now that he lies stricken, he will
never get up again."
⁹Even my close friend whom I trusted and who ate my bread has lifted
his heel against me.
¹⁰But you, O LORD, have mercy on me, and raise me up so that I may repay them.

¹¹By this I know that I am in your favor: my enemy cannot shout in triumph over me.
¹²But you uphold me on account of my integrity and will set me before your
face forever.

¹³Blessed be the LORD God of Israel from eternity past to eternity future.
  Amen and amen.

PSALM 42

[To the choirmaster: a maskil for the sons of Korah]
¹As the deer pants after streams of water, so my soul pants after you, O God.
²My soul thirsts for God, for the living God.
  When shall I come face to face with God?
³Day and night my tears have been my food. Meanwhile others continually taunt
me saying "Where is your God?"
⁴I remember these things as I pour out my soul—how I once used to go with a
crowd, leading them to the house of God, with the voice of joy and praise—
  a crowd celebrating at festival time.

⁵Why are you cast down, O my soul?
  And why are you in turmoil within me?
  Hope in God—for I shall once again praise the one who him who is my salvation.

⁶My soul is cast down within me.

So I will remember you from the land of Jordan, and of Hermon, from Mount Mizar.

⁷Deep calls to deep at the roar of your waterfalls.

All your breaking waves have crashed over me.

⁸Still, the LORD commands his enduring love by day, and by night his song is with me—a prayer to the God of my life.

⁹I will say to God, my rock, "Why have you forgotten me?

Why am I going around mourning because of oppression from the enemy?"

¹⁰My enemies taunt me like a sword in my bones. Meanwhile every day others say to me, "Where is your God?"

¹¹Why are you cast down, O my soul? And why are you in turmoil within me? Hope in God—for I shall once again praise him who is my salvation.

PSALM 43

[A Song of Ascents.]

¹Vindicate me, O God, and defend me from an ungodly nation.

Deliver me from the deceitful and unjust man.

²For you are the God of my strength.

Why do you reject me?

Why must I go around mourning because of the oppression of the enemy?

³Send out your light and your truth that they may lead me.

Let them bring me to your holy hill—to where you reside.

⁴Then will I go to the altar of God—to God, my exceeding joy.

Yes, I will praise you, O God my God—on the harp.

⁵Why are you cast down, O my soul?

And why are you in turmoil within me?

Hope in God because once again I shall praise him, the source of my health, and my God.

PSALM 44

[To the choirmaster for the sons of Korah: a Maskil.]

¹O God, we have heard with our ears—our forefathers have told us—the things that you did in their days, in the olden times.

²With your own hand, you drove out the nations and relocated them elsewhere. You afflicted the nations and removed them.

³For our forefathers did not gain possession by their own sword, neither did their own arms save them. Rather, it was achieved by your right hand, and your arm, and the light of your face, because you took delight in them.

⁴You are my King, O God. Bring about salvation for Jacob.

⁵Through you we subdue our enemies.

It is by your name that we tread down those who rise up against us.

⁶For I do not trust in my bow, nor can my sword save me.

⁷But you have rescued us from our enemies and have put those who despise us to shame.

⁸We boast in God continually and we shall keep praising your name forever.

Selah

⁹But now you have rejected and disgraced us, and you no longer accompany our armies.

¹⁰You have forced us to retreat from the enemy, allowing them to plunder.

¹¹You have made us into sheep for slaughter and have scattered us among the nations.

¹²You have sold off your people for a pittance, not getting a good price for them.

¹³You have turned us into something for our neighbors to taunt—an object of scorn and derision to those around us.

¹⁴You have made us into an example for the nations, a laughingstock among the peoples.

¹⁵My disgrace lies before me continually, and shame covers my face ¹⁶at the very sound of taunters and revilers and at the sight of enemies and avengers.

¹⁷All this has happened to us, even though we have not forgotten you, nor have we been untrue to your covenant.

¹⁸Our heart has not retreated, neither have our steps fallen away from your way,

¹⁹yet you have broken us in the place of jackals and covered us with the shadow of death.

²⁰If we had forgotten the name of our God, or reached out to a strange god,

²¹would not God find out about it? For he knows the secrets of the heart.

²²Yes, for your sake we are being killed all day long.

We are considered sheep for the slaughter.

²³Awake! Why do you sleep, O Lord?

Arise, do not reject us forever.

²⁴Why do you conceal your face, and ignore our affliction and our oppression?

²⁵For our soul is bowed down to the dust; we are crawling on our stomachs.

²⁶Arise to help us and redeem us for the sake of your enduring love.

PSALM 45

[To the choirmaster on Shoshannim, for the sons of Korah: a Maskil, a love song.]

¹My heart is inspired by something noble as I write verses about the king.

My tongue is the pen of a skilled writer.

²You are exceedingly handsome among the sons of men.

Grace is poured into your lips.

Therefore God has blessed you forever.

³Gird your sword on your thigh, O mighty one, with your splendor and majesty.

⁴In your majesty ride forth victoriously to promote truth and meekness and righteousness.

May your right hand achieve great things.
⁵Let your sharp arrows pierce the heart of the king's enemies, causing the nations to submit to you.

⁶Your throne, O God, lasts forever and ever.
The scepter of your kingdom is the scepter of justice.
⁷You love righteousness and hate wickedness.
 So God—your God—has placed you over your peers by anointing you with the oil of gladness.
⁸All your robes have the fragrance of myrrh and aloes and cassia.
 The stringed instruments from the ivory palaces have delighted you.
⁹The daughters of kings are among your women of honor.
 At your right hand stands the queen arrayed in gold from Ophir.
¹⁰Listen carefully, O daughter, and consider, and incline your ear to this: forget your own people and your father's house, for ¹¹the king greatly desires your beauty.
 Now he is your Lord, and you are to submit to him.
¹²The daughters of Tyre, the richest of the people, will seek your favor with gifts.
¹³Inside her chamber, the princess is glorious with robes interwoven with gold.
¹⁴She is led to the king in robes of many colors with her virgin companions following her.
¹⁵With joy and gladness they are brought along, entering the king's palace.

¹⁶Your sons shall now take the place of your ancestors, and you will make them princes throughout the land.
¹⁷I will perpetuate the memory of you through all generations, and so the people will praise you forever and ever.

PSALM 46

[To the choirmaster. For the sons of Korah]

¹God is our refuge and strength—a proven help in times of trouble.
²Therefore we will not fear,
    though the earth should collapse,
    though the mountains should be moved into the middle of the sea,
        ³thought its waters should roar and foam,
    though the mountains should tremble because of the swelling. Selah

⁴There is a river whose streams delight the city of God, the holy place of the tabernacles of the Most High.
⁵God is in the midst of her; she shall not be moved.
 God shall come to her aid early in the morning.
⁶The nations rage and the kingdoms shake.
 He speaks and the earth melts.
⁷The LORD of hosts is with us. The God of Jacob is our refuge. Selah

⁸Come, see what the LORD has accomplished—what desolations he has brought about on earth.
⁹All over the whole earth, he causes wars to cease.
 He breaks the bow and shatters the spear into pieces.
 He burns the chariots with fire.
¹⁰Be still and know that I am God.
 I will be exalted among the nations.
 I will be exalted on the earth.
¹¹The LORD of hosts is with us.
 The God of Jacob is our refuge. Selah

PSALM 47

[To the choirmaster: a psalm for the sons of Korah.]

¹Clap your hands, all you peoples!
 Shout to God with the voice of triumph.
²For the LORD most high is to be feared—a great King over all the earth.
³He has subdued peoples under us, and the nations under our feet.
⁴He has chosen our inheritance for us, the pride of Jacob whom he loves.
Selah

⁵God has gone up with a shout—the LORD with the sound of a trumpet.
⁶Sing praises to God, sing praises!
 Sing praises to our King, sing praises!
⁷For God is the King of all the earth: sing praise using a psalm!
⁸God reigns over the nations.
 God is seated on the throne of his holiness.
⁹The princes of the peoples gathered together, along with the people of the God of Abraham, for the shields of the earth belong to God, who is highly exalted.

PSALM 48

[A Song and Psalm for the sons of Korah.]

¹Great is the LORD, and worthy of great praise
   in the city of our God,
   on the mountain of his holiness,
—beautiful, so high and lofty, the joy of the whole earth—
   is mount Zion in the land of the north, the city of the great King!
³God has made himself known in her palaces as a place of refuge.

⁴For, indeed, the kings assembled themselves and together they came toward her.
⁵When they saw her, they marveled in astonishment and fled away.
⁶Fear and trembling seized them there—pain like that of a woman in labor.

⁷You smashed the ships of Tarshish with an east wind.

⁸As we have heard, so we have seen in the city of the L<small>ORD</small> of hosts, in the city of our God, which God will establish forever. Selah

⁹We have pondered your enduring love, O God, in the midst of your temple.

¹⁰Like your name, O God, your praise reaches to the ends of the earth.
   Your right hand is filled with righteousness.

¹¹Let Mount Zion rejoice.
   Let the daughters of Judah be glad because of your just decrees!

¹²Stroll about Zion and walk all around her, counting her towers.

¹³Take notice of her ramparts and explore her palaces so that you may tell the next generation ¹⁴that this is God—our God forever and ever.
He will guide us for all time.

PSALM 49

[To the choirmaster: a psalm for the sons of Korah.]

¹Hear this, all you peoples!
   Listen, all you inhabitants of the world—²both lowly and high, rich and
   poor, together!

³My mouth will speak wisdom, and the meditation of my heart will be understanding.

⁴I will incline my ear to a proverb.
   I will solve my riddle with a harp.

⁵Why should I fear in the days of trouble when I am surrounded by the evil of those who cheat me—⁶those who trust in their wealth and boast of the abundance of their riches?

⁷None of them can use their means to redeem another, nor to give a ransom to God for him.

⁸For the ransom of a life is very costly; it could be enough to empower someone to ⁹live on forever and not see the pit of corruption.

¹⁰For we see that wise men die, and likewise fools and stupid men also die, leaving their wealth to others.

¹¹They imagine that their line of descendants will continue forever, and that their homes will remain standing for all generations, so they name their lands after themselves.

¹²Nonetheless, even a man arrayed in honor will not remain; he is like the animals that perish.

¹³Such is the path of those who trust in their folly, yet posterity approves of their claims. Selah

¹⁴Like sheep they are destined for Sheol.
   Death will herd them, and the righteous will rule over them when a new day dawns.
   Sheol will consume their bodies, and they will no longer have great houses.

¹⁵But God will redeem my soul from the power of Sheol for he shall receive me.
Selah

¹⁶Do not be intimidated by a man who becomes rich, when the glory of his
house increases.
¹⁷For when he dies he will take nothing away—his glory will not go down along
with him.
¹⁸Though he counts himself as blessed while he is still alive—and though people will praise the one who does well for himself—¹⁹his soul shall one day go to
the generation of his forefathers, who never see light again.
²⁰A man arrayed in honor but lacking in understanding is, nonetheless, like any
animal that dies.

PSALM 50

[A Psalm of Asaph.]

¹The Almighty God, the LORD, speaks, and he calls to the earth from the
rising of the sun until its setting.
²Out of Zion, the perfection of beauty, God shines forth.
³Our God comes, not staying silent, with a devouring fire before him and a powerful tempest all around him.
⁴So that he may judge his people, he calls to the earth from heaven above:

> ⁵"Gather my faithful ones to me—those who made a covenant with me
> by sacrifice."

⁶(Even the heavens declare his righteousness, for God himself is judge.)
Selah

⁷Hear, O my people, and I will speak:

> "O Israel, I testify against you. I am God, your God.
> ⁸I do not rebuke you for your sacrifices; your burnt offerings
> are continually before me.
> ⁹I will not accept a young bull from your house, nor goats from your folds.
> ¹⁰For every beast of the forest is mine—even the cattle on a thousand hills.
> ¹¹I know all the birds of the hills, and the beasts of the field are mine as well.
> ¹²If I were hungry, I would not tell you because the world, and all that
> lies within it, is mine.
> ¹³Do I eat the flesh of bulls or drink the blood of goats?
> ¹⁴Offer to God a sacrifice of thanksgiving and perform your vows to the
> most High, ¹⁵and call on me in the day of trouble. I will deliver you, and
> you will glorify me."

[16]But God says to the wicked:

> "What right do you have to declare my statutes or to take my covenant on your lips, [17]since you hate instruction, and throw my words behind you?"
> [18]If you see a thief, you condone him, and you keep company with adulterers.
> [19]You allow your mouth to speak evil things and your tongue to deceive.
> [20]You sit around maligning your brother, slandering your own mother's son.
> [21]You have done these things, and I kept silent.
>   You thought that I was just like you, but I rebuke you and lay out these charges for you to see.
> [22]Now carefully consider this, you who forget God, so that I do not tear you in pieces, with no one to rescue you.

[23]Whoever offers thanksgiving does glorify me, and I will show the salvation of God to whoever conducts his life righteously."

PSALM 51

[To the choirmaster: A Psalm of David, when Nathan the prophet went to him, after David had sinned with Bathsheba.]

[1]Have mercy on me, O God, according to your enduring love.
  According to your abundant mercy blot out my transgressions.
[2]Wash me thoroughly from my wicked deeds and cleanse me from my sin!
[3]For I am aware of my transgressions, and my sin is always there in front of me.
[4]It is against you and you only that I have sinned and done what is evil in your sight, such that your verdict is correct and your judgment against me is just.
[5]Indeed, I was formed in a state of sinfulness, and in sin my mother conceived me.
[6]Yet you desire truthfulness in my innermost being, and there in private you teach me wisdom.
[7]Cleanse me with hyssop, and I shall be clean.
  Wash me, and I shall be whiter than snow.
[8]Let me hear joy and gladness so that the bones that you have broken may rejoice.
[9]Hide your face from my sins and blot out all my wicked deeds.
[10]Create in me a clean heart, O God, and renew a right spirit within me.
[11]Do not cast me out of your presence, and do not remove your holy spirit from me.
[12]Restore to me the joy of your salvation and uphold me with your free spirit.
[13]Then I will teach transgressors your ways, and sinners will repent and turn to you.

[14]Deliver me from the guilt of shed blood, O God—God of my salvation—
and my tongue will sing aloud of your righteousness.
[15]O Lord, open my lips, and my mouth will declare your praise.
[16]For you do not desire sacrifice—otherwise I would give it—no, you do not take

delight in a burnt offering.

[17]The sacrifices God [desires] are a broken spirit—O God, you will not reject a broken and contrite heart.

[18]In your good pleasure, do good things for Zion and fortify the walls of Jerusalem.

[19]Then you will be pleased with righteous sacrifices, with burnt offerings and whole burnt offerings. And then young bulls will be sacrificed on your altar.

PSALM 52

[To the choirmaster. A Psalm of David.]

[1]Why do you boast of evil, O mighty man?
The enduring love of God goes on forever.
[2]Your tongue speaks plots for destruction, like a sharp razor, you who practice deceitfulness.
[3]You value evil over good and lying over speaking truth. Selah
[4]You love all destructive words, you of a deceitful tongue.

[5]God will destroy you forever. He will snatch you away, plucking you from your home, and uprooting you from the land of the living. Selah
[6]The righteous ones will see [that] and fear; then they will scoff at him, saying,
[7]"Look at the man who refused to make God his refuge, but instead trusted in his own abundant wealth, fortifying himself in what would become his own destruction."

[8]However, like a green olive tree in the house of God, I place my trust in the enduring love of God forever and ever. [9]I will praise you forever because of what you have done, and I will wait for your good name in the presence of the holy people.

PSALM 53

[For the choirmaster: According to Mahalath. A maskil of David.]

[1]The fool says in his heart, 'There is no God.'
Such people are corrupt and do abominable, evil things.
There is no one who does good.
[2]God looks down from heaven on all mankind to see if there are any who do act with understanding and do seek God.
[3]Every one of them has fallen away; they have become totally corrupt.
There is no one who does good—no, not one.
[4]Do these evildoers understand nothing? They consume my people as if they were eating bread. They do not call on God.
[5]They are there in great terror, where there used to be no terror, for God has scattered the bones of those who position themselves against you. You put them to shame because God holds them in contempt.
[6]May the salvation of Israel come from Zion! When God restores the wealth of his people, may Jacob rejoice, and may Israel be glad.

PSALM 54

[To the choirmaster: with stringed instruments. A Maskil of David, when the Ziphites went and told Saul, "Is not David hiding among us?"]

[1]Save me, O God, by your name and vindicate me by your strength.
[2]Hear my prayer, O God. Listen to the words of my mouth.

[3]For strangers have risen up against me, and cruel men seek my life.
They have not placed God before themselves. Selah

[4]Take notice—God is my helper: the Lord is with those who uphold my life.
[5]He will reward my enemies with calamity.
Wipe them out in your faithfulness.

[6]I will freely make my sacrifice to you.
I will praise your name, O LORD, for it is good.
[7]For he has delivered me from every trouble—now my eye looks at my enemies in triumph.

PSALM 55

[To the choirmaster: with stringed instruments. A Maskil of David.]

[1]O God, lend an ear to my prayer and do not hide yourself from my pleas for mercy.
[2]Attend to me and hear me, for I am distraught as I complain and moan.
I am groaning [3]because of the noise of the enemy, because of the oppression of the wicked who burden me with troubles and wrathfully despise me.

[4]My heart is full of anguish within me, and the terrors of death have fallen on me.
[5]Fearfulness and trembling have come on me, and horror overwhelms me.
[6]And I say, "Oh, if only I had wings like a dove! I would fly away and rest peacefully."
[7]Indeed—I would wander far away and stay in the wilderness. Selah
[8]I would flee away to find shelter from this fierce wind and storm.
[9]O Lord, bring them to ruin and confuse their language, for I witness violence and strife in the city.
[10]Day and night they march around it on its walls, while trouble and evil practices lie within it.
[11]In the middle of it is decay; deceitfulness and fraud are always present in her marketplace.

[12]Now it was not an enemy that jeered at me—that I could have borne.
Neither was it someone who hates me and vaunted himself against me— then I would have hidden myself from him.
[13]But rather it was you—a man, my peer, my companion, and my friend.
[14]We had sweet fellowship together and together we entered the house of God.

¹⁵May death overtake them and may they sink into Sheol alive, for wickedness is found both in their houses and in their hearts.
¹⁶As for me, I will call on God, and the LORD shall save me.
¹⁷Evening, and morning, and at noon I complain and moan, and he hears my voice.
¹⁸He delivers my soul to safety from the battle I am waging, for many stand against me.
¹⁹God—yes, He who abides from before time—shall afflict them because they do not repent, and therefore they do not fear God.
²⁰One of them extended his hands [to attack] his allies, breaking his covenant.
²¹His words were as smooth as butter, but war was in his heart.
  Though his words were softer than butter, they were drawn swords.

²²Cast your burden on the LORD, and he will sustain you.
  He will never allow the righteous to be shaken.
²³But you, O God, will bring bloody and treacherous men down into the pit of destruction; they shall not live out even half their days.
I, however, will trust in you.

PSALM 56

[To the choirmaster: a psalm of David when the Philistines seized him in Gath.]

¹Be gracious to me, O God, for people abuse me—all day long attackers oppress me.
²All day long my enemies mistreat me, for many of them pridefully attack me.
³Whenever I am afraid, I place my trust in you.
⁴In God—whose word I praise—in God I place my trust.
  I will not fear what people can do to me.

⁵Every day they twist my words.
  All their thoughts are against me for evil.
⁶They plot together and they lurk, watching my steps, as they wait for my soul.
⁷Shall they escape punishment for their evil?
  In your anger, O God, cast down these people.
⁸You keep track of all my movements.
  Put my tears into your bottle.
  Are they not in your book?
⁹When I call to you, then my enemies will turn back to retreat.
I know this because God is for me.
  ¹⁰In God—whose word I praise—
    In the LORD—whose word I praise—
  ¹¹In God have I put my trust—I will not be afraid.
    What can man do to me?

¹²Your vows are my duty, O God. I will render praises to you.

^{13}For you have delivered my soul from death—even kept my feet from falling—that I may walk before God in the light of the living.

PSALM 57

[To the choirmaster: Do not destroy. A Miktam of David, when he fled from Saul, in the cave.]

^{1}Show your mercy to me, O God, show your mercy to me,
   for my soul takes refuges in you.
 Indeed, I will take refuge in the shadow of your wings until these destructive storms have passed.
^{2}I will cry to the sovereign God—to God who completes his purposes for me.
^{3}From heaven he will send a deliverance for me, to shame the one who tramples on me. Selah
God will send out his enduring love and his faithfulness!
^{4}My soul is in the midst of lions; I am lying among beasts of fire, the children of man, whose teeth are spears and arrows, and their tongues are sharp swords.

^{5}Be exalted, O God, above the heavens!
 May your glory be over all the earth.

^{6}They laid a snare in my path; my soul was bowed down. They dug a pit in the path ahead of me, but they themselves have fallen into the middle of it.
Selah
^{7}My heart remains steadfast—O God—my heart remains steadfast.
 I will sing and give praise.
^{8}Awaken, my heart and soul!
 Awaken, O harp and lyre!
 I will awaken at dawn!
^{9}I will praise you, O Lord, among the people.
 I will sing to you among the nations.
^{10}For your enduring love is great to the heavens, and your faithfulness to the clouds.

^{11}Be exalted, O God, above the heavens!
 May your glory be over all the earth.

PSALM 58

[To the choirmaster: Do not destroy. A Miktam of David.]

^{1}O, you mighty overlords—do you really declare what is right?
 Do you judge the children of man uprightly?
^{2}Actually, you devise wrongdoing in your hearts.
 You hand out violence in the world.

³From the womb, the wicked are estranged.
 They go astray as soon as they are born, spreading falsehood.
⁴Their venom resembles the venom of a serpent,
 like the deaf adder that plugs its ears,
⁵so as to not hear the voice of charmers, ignoring the cunning enchanter.

⁶Break the teeth in their mouths, O God.
 Rip out the fangs of the young lions, O LORD.
⁷May they disappear like streams of water running off.
 When he takes aim with his arrows, let them be cut down.
⁸May all of them be like snails dissolving into slime,
 passing away like a stillborn child who never sees the sun.
⁹Faster than pots heat up over burning brambles,
 May they be swept away—both young and old.

¹⁰The righteous man will rejoice when he sees this act of vengeance.
 He will wash his feet in the blood of the wicked.
¹¹So that mankind will say,
  "Truly there is a reward for the righteous.
  Truly there is a God who judges the world."

PSALM 59

[To the choirmaster: Do Not Destroy. A Miktam of David, when Saul sent men to watch his house in order to kill him.]

¹O my God, deliver me from my enemies.
 Defend me from those who rise up against me.
²Rescue me from evildoers and save me from bloodthirsty men.
³See—they are lying in wait for my life.
Fierce men are stirring up trouble against me, but not on account of my transgression, nor because of my sin, O LORD.
⁴They are running to get ready—through no fault of my own.
  Wake up and help me, and look!
⁵So, O LORD God of hosts, the God of Israel, rouse yourself to bring punishment on all the nations.
Do not spare any of these wicked evildoers. Selah

⁶Each evening they return, like barking dogs prowling around the city.
⁷There they are—bellowing with their mouths, with swords in their lips, imagining, "Now who is going to hear us?"

⁸But you, O LORD—you laugh at them.
 You hold all the nations in derision.
⁹I shall keep watch, waiting for you, my strength—because you, O God, are
my fortress.

¹⁰In his enduring love, my God will go before me.
  God will allow me to look on my enemies in triumph.
¹¹Do not kill them, or else my people will forget.
  By your power, bowl them over and bring them down, O Lord our shield.
¹²On account of the sin of their mouths and the words of their lips, let them be ensnared by their own pride—even on account of the curses and lies that they speak.
¹³Consume them in wrath; consume them till they are no more.
  Make them realize that God rules over Jacob to the ends of the earth. Selah

¹⁴So, may they return one evening, barking like dogs and prowling around the city.
¹⁵[But this time] let them be wandering around looking for food and growling when they do not get their fill.

¹⁶I, however, will sing of your power.
Yes, in the morning I will sing aloud of your enduring love.
For you have been my fortress and my refuge in the day of distress.
¹⁷O my strength, I will sing praise to you.
  For you, O God, are my fortress—the one who shows me enduring love.

PSALM 60

[To the choirmaster: according to Shushan Eduth. A Miktam of David; for instruction; when he strove with Aram-naharaim and with Aram-zobah, and when Joab, on his return, struck down 12,000 men of Edom in the Valley of Salt.]

¹O God, you have cast us aside and left us defenseless.
You have been angry with us. Oh, turn your face toward us again.
²You have caused the earth to quake, splitting it open.
 Mend the fracture for it is still quaking.
³You have shown your people hard times.
 You made us drink a wine that made us stagger.
⁴You have given a banner to those who fear you—a display to rally those led by truth. Selah
⁵Send a rescue with your right hand and hear us so that your beloved may be delivered.

⁶God has spoken in his holiness:

> "With rejoicing I will divide up Shechem,
> and portion out the Valley of Succoth.
> ⁷Gilead is mine, and Manasseh is mine;
> Ephraim is my helmet; Judah is my scepter.
> ⁸Moab is my washbasin; I throw out my shoe on Edom.
> I shout in triumph over Philistia."

⁹Who will bring me into the fortified city? Who will lead me into Edom?
¹⁰O God, have you not rejected us?

462

O God, will you not go forth with our armies?

^{11}Grant us help against the enemy, for man's assistance is in vain.

^{12}With God we shall do valiantly, for He is the one who will tread down our enemies.

PSALM 61

[To the choirmaster. With stringed instruments. A Psalm of David.]

^{1}Hear my cry, O God—listen to my prayer.

^{2}I call to you from the end of the earth when my heart is overwhelmed. Lead me to the rock that is higher than I am.

^{3}For you have been a refuge for me—a tower of protection from the enemy.

^{4}Let me reside in your tent forever.
 Give me refuge in the shelter of your wings. Selah

^{5}For you, O God, have heard my vows.
 You have granted to me the heritage of those who fear your name.

^{6}Let the king's life be prolonged and let his years extend to many generations.

^{7}Let him abide before God forever.
 Establish mercy and faithfulness to preserve him!

^{8}So I will always sing praise to your name as day after day I go about performing my vows.

PSALM 62

[To the choirmaster: according to Jeduthun, A Psalm of David.]

^{1}My soul waits on God alone; it is from *him* that my salvation comes.

^{2}He alone is my rock and my salvation and my fortress.
 I will not be shaken.

^{3}How long will all of you plot to waylay a man?
 You will all be pushed down like a bowing wall, or a wobbling fence.

^{4}They only plot to throw him down from his high position.
 They delight in falsehood.
 They bless with their mouths, but inwardly they curse. Selah

^{5}O my soul, wait for God alone, for my hope comes from him.

^{6}He alone is my rock and my salvation and my fortress.
 I will not be shaken.

^{7}My salvation and my glory are found in God, my mighty rock.
 My refuge is in God.

^{8}O people, place your trust in him at all times.
 Pour out your hearts before him. God is our refuge. Selah

⁹Men of low degree are but a breath, and men of high degree are a delusion.
When placed on a scale they rise—even together they are lighter than air.
¹⁰Do not place your trust in extortion, do not set vain hopes on robbery.
If wealth does increase, do not set your heart on it.
¹¹God has spoken once; I have heard this twice:

That power belongs to God,
¹²and that enduring love belongs to you, O Lord,
for you reward every man according to his deeds.

PSALM 63

[A psalm of David when he was in the wilderness of Judah.]

¹O God, you are my God.
I seek you at the dawn.
My soul thirsts for you.
My body faints for you, as in a dry and weary land that is without water.
²So I have looked for you in the sanctuary to see your power and glory.
³Because your enduring love is better than life, my lips will praise you.
⁴So as long as I am alive I will bless you, lifting up my hands in your name.
⁵My soul will be satisfied as with many rich foods,
and my mouth will praise you with joyful lips,
⁶when I remember you while in bed,
and meditate on you during the watches of the night,
⁷for you have come to my assistance.
I will sing for joy in the shadow of your wings.
⁸My soul clings to you; your right hand upholds me.

⁹But those who seek to kill me will go down into the depths of the earth.
¹⁰They will be given over to the power of the sword and be prey for foxes.
¹¹However, the king will rejoice in God.
All who swear by him will rejoice, for the mouths of liars will be silenced.

PSALM 64

[To the choirmaster. A Psalm of David.]

¹O God, hear my voice, in my plea that you preserve my life from a dreaded enemy.
²Protect me from the secret plots of the wicked, from mobs of evildoers ³who
sharpen their tongues like swords

to shoot biting words like arrows,
to take shots at the blameless from an ambush,
to shoot at him suddenly and fearlessly.
⁵They encourage each other devising evil.
They plot together in secret about laying snares, thinking, "Who is going to
see them?"

⁶They pursue injustice, which they do with a diligent search, both in their innermost thoughts and deep in the heart.

⁷But God shoots arrows at them, and suddenly they are wounded.
⁸So they are brought to ruin by their own tongues; all of those who watch them shake their heads.
⁹And then mankind shall fear.
 They will declare the works of God, pondering deeply what he has done.

¹⁰Let the righteous ones rejoice in the LORD and hide themselves in him.
 Let all the upright in heart be jubilant.

PSALM 65

[To the choirmaster. A Psalm of David. A song.]

¹O God, praise awaits you in Zion, and the vows shall be made to you.
²O you who hear prayer, all mankind shall come to you.
³When deeds of wickedness prevail against me, you make atonement for our transgressions.

⁴Blessed is the one whom you choose and draw close to yourself, to dwell in your courts!
We shall be satisfied with the goodness of your house, your holy temple.
⁵You answer us in righteousness through awesome deeds, O God of our salvation.
You are the hope of all the ends of the earth—even those from the farthest seas.
⁶Being girded with power, you established the mountains by your power, and you
⁷still the roaring of the seas, the roaring of their waves, and the tumult of the peoples.

⁸Everyone—even those who dwell in the most distant lands—stands in awe at your wonders.
You cause rejoicing as the morning comes to a close, as well as in the evening.
⁹You visit the earth to water it, greatly enriching it with the river of God, which is full of water.
You provide grain for it, for you have designed it to be so.
¹⁰You water its furrowed valleys abundantly, settling the ridges between, and softening them with showers. You bless the growth.
¹¹You crown the growing season with your abundance—even the rutted wagon tracks overflow with bounty.
¹²The pastures of the wilderness overflow, and joy resounds between the hills.
¹³The pastures are clothed with flocks—even the valleys are coated with fields of corn. They shout for joy—they even sing!

PSALM 66

[To the choirmaster: A Song or Psalm.]

[1]Let all the earth shout to God with joy!
[2]Sing out the glory of his name and give him glorious praise!
[3]Say to God, "How awesome are the things you have done!"
Because of the magnitude of your power, your enemies come to you cringing.
[4]The whole earth worships you and sings to you; they sing praises to your
name. Selah

[5]Come and look at what God has done; he is awesome in his dealings with mankind.
[6]He once turned the sea into dry land and the [Hebrews] passed through on foot.
There we rejoiced in him [7]who rules by his power forever, and whose eyes observe the nations. The rebellious must not exalt themselves. Selah

[8]O peoples, bless our God and let the sound of his praise be heard.
[9]He keeps our souls among the living and does not permit our feet to slip.
[10]For you, O God, have tested us; you have tried us in the fire like silver.
[11]You brought us into the net and laid affliction on our backs.
[12]You have allowed men to ride over our heads; we went through fire and
through water, but you brought us out into a place of abundance.

[13]I will come into your house with burnt offerings, and to you I will perform my
vows [14]that my lips have uttered, and my mouth has spoken, when I was in trouble.
[15]I will offer to you burnt sacrifices of fattened animals.
   Along with the smoke of sacrificed rams I will offer bulls and goats. Selah

[16]Come and listen, all you who fear God, and I will tell about what he has
done for my soul.
[17]I cried to him with my mouth, with high praise on my tongue.
[18]If I had been harboring wickedness in my heart, the Lord would not have paid
attention to me.
[19]But truly God did listen to me; he has attended to the words of my prayer.

[20]Blessed be God who has not turned away my prayer, nor taken his enduring
love away from me.

PSALM 67

[To the choirmaster: with stringed instruments. A Psalm.]

[1]May God take mercy on us and bless us and make his face shine on us Selah
[2]May your way may be known on the earth, and your saving power among all
the nations.

³Let the peoples praise you, O God.
  Let all the people praise you!
⁴Let the nations be glad and sing for joy,
  for you will judge the people fairly
  and guide the nations on earth. Selah
⁵Let the peoples praise you, O God.
  Let all the people praise you!

⁶The earth yields its crops, and God—our own God—blesses us.
⁷God blesses us; let all the ends of the earth fear him.

PSALM 68

[To the choirmaster: a Psalm, or Song of David.]

¹May God rise up, and his enemies be scattered.
  May those who hate him flee from his presence.
²May they be driven away like smoke being blown away.
  May the wicked perish at the presence of God like wax melting by a fire.
³However—
    the righteous shall be glad.
    They shall rejoice before God.
    They shall be jubilant with great joy!

⁴Sing to God, sing praises to his name.
  Prepare a praise to him who rides through the desert.
  His name is the LORD—rejoice before him.
⁵The father of the fatherless and an advocate for widows—such is God in his
holy dwelling place.
⁶God prepares homes for the lonely, and he elevates the prisoners into prosperity.
  However, the rebellious inhabit a dry and thirsty land.

⁷O God, when you went forth before your people—when you were marching
through the desert (Selah)—⁸the earth shook, the skies poured down rain at the
presence of God, the One of Sinai, the God of Israel.

⁹O God, you sent a plentiful rain to restore your inheritance when it was weary,
and in it ¹⁰your congregation has found a place to live.
  O God, you have provided for those in need.
¹¹The Lord gives the word; great in number are the women who broadcast the
good news.
¹²The kings of armies fled, and although the men lie among the sheepfolds, the
women who remained at home divided the spoils: ¹³the wings of a dove covered with silver, and its pinions with yellow gold.
¹⁴When the Almighty scatters kings there, let there be snow on Zalmon.

¹⁵The mountain of God is like Mount Bashan—a high mountain like Mount Bashan. ¹⁶Why do you gaze enviously, you jagged mountains? This is the mountain where God desires to dwell, where the LORD will dwell forever.
¹⁷The chariots of God number twenty thousand—thousands upon thousands— and the Lord is among them, in Sinai, in the holy place.
¹⁸You ascended on high, leading a host of captives in your train.

You received gifts among the people, even from the rebellious also, so that the LORD God might dwell there.
¹⁹Blessed be the Lord, who bears us up every day. God is our salvation. Selah
²⁰*Our* God is the God of salvation, and GOD, the Lord, is in charge of deliverance from death.
²¹But God will strike the head of his enemies, and the hairy scalp of whoever goes about guilty in his misdeeds.

²²The Lord said, "I will bring [my people] back from Bashan, I will bring them back from the depths of the sea, so²³ that you may dip your foot in the blood of your enemies, and the tongue of your dogs may take their share in the spoils of your enemies."

²⁴O God, your procession is seen—the procession of my God, my King, into the sanctuary, ²⁵with the singers first, the musicians last, and young maidens playing their tambourines between them.
²⁶Praise God in the great congregations.

Praise the LORD, all of you who have sprung from the fountain of Israel:
²⁷Benjamin, the least of all of them, in the lead,
with the princes of Judah in their company—
the princes of Zebulun,
and the princes of Naphtali.

²⁸Your God has commanded your strength.

Show forth the power that you used, O God, to accomplish things on our behalf.
²⁹Because of your temple at Jerusalem, kings will bring gifts of tribute to you.
³⁰Rebuke the animals in the reeds, the herd of bulls with the calves of the people.

Trample down those who lust after tribute and scatter the people who delight in war.
³¹Princes shall come from Egypt; Ethiopia shall soon stretch out her hands to God.

³²Sing to God, you kingdoms of the earth.

O sing praises to the Lord (Selah), ³³to him who rides in the ancient heaven above the skies. Listen—he sends out his voice, his mighty voice.
³⁴Proclaim the power that belongs to God.

His majesty covers Israel, and his power resides in the heavens.
³⁵O God, you are awesome in your holy places. The God of Israel—He is the one who gives strength and power to his people. Blessed be God!

PSALM 69

[To the choirmaster: according to Lilies. Of David.]

¹Save me, O God, for the waters have risen up to my neck.

²I sink in deep mire, where I find no foothold.
 I have come into deep waters, where the flood overwhelms me.

³I am weary of my own crying out and my throat is parched.
 My eyes are dimming as I wait for my God.

⁴Those who hate me with no just cause outnumber the hairs of my head.
 Those who seek to destroy me are my enemies for no good reason and they are
  mighty.
 Must I now restore what I did not steal?

⁵O God, you know my foolishness, and my sins are not hidden from you.

⁶O Lord GOD of hosts, do not let those who hope in you be put to shame on
account of me.
 O God of Israel, do not let those who seek you be dishonored on account of me.

⁷For I have endured reproach, and shame has covered my face for your sake.

⁸I have now become a stranger to my brothers, and an alien to my mother's children.

⁹For zeal for your house has consumed me, and the insults of those who insult you have landed on me.

¹⁰When I wept and humbled myself by fasting I became an object of scorn.

¹¹When I dressed in sackcloth I became an object of ridicule.

¹²Those who sat by the gate derided me; even drunkards sang about me.

¹³But as for me, my prayer is to you, O LORD.

 In your perfect timing, O God, hear me in the greatness of your enduring love
and answer me in the faithfulness of your salvation.

¹⁴Rescue me from sinking down into the mire.
 Let me be delivered from those who hate me, and snatched out of the deep waters.

¹⁵Do not let waters flood over me, or the deep swallow me up, or the pit engulf me.

¹⁶Listen to me, O LORD, for your enduring love is good.
 Turn to me according to the abundance of your tender mercies.

¹⁷Do not hide your face from your servant, as I am in distress.
 Please answer me quickly.

¹⁸Come close to my soul and redeem it.
 Rescue me from my adversaries!

¹⁹You have known about my ridicule, and my shame, and my dishonor.
 My adversaries are all known to you.

²⁰Ridicule has broken my heart, and I am full of despair.
  I searched for pity, but there was none to be found.
  I searched for someone to comfort me, but I found no one.

²¹They gave me poison for food, and in my thirst they gave me sour wine to drink.

²²Let their own tables become a snare before them, and their security a trap.
²³Let their eyes be darkened so that they can no longer see and let their joints shake continually.
²⁴Pour out your wrath on them, and let your fierce anger overtake them.
²⁵Let their dwelling places be desolate and let none of them dwell in their tents.
²⁶For they insult the one whom you have struck down, and they talk about the pain of those you have wounded.
²⁷Give punishment in return for their wrongdoing and let them not receive your forgiveness.
²⁸Let them be blotted out of the book of the living, and not be recorded along with the righteous.

²⁹As for me, I am poor and sorrowful. O God, let your salvation place me up on high.
³⁰I will praise the name of God with a song and will magnify him with thanksgiving.
³¹Doing so will please the LORD better than sacrificing an ox or bull with horns and hooves.
³²Seeing this, the humble shall be glad.
  You who seek God, may your hearts be revived.
³³For the LORD hears the poor and does not despise his own people who are prisoners.

³⁴Let the heaven and earth praise him—the seas and everything that moves in them.
³⁵For God will save Zion and will build the cities of Judah; those who shall dwell there will have possession of it.
³⁶The offspring of his servants shall also inherit it, and those who love his name shall dwell there.

PSALM 70

[To the choirmaster: A Psalm of David, for the memorial offering]

¹Hasten to deliver me, O God.
  Hasten to help me, O LORD.
²May those who seek my life be put to shame and dishonored.
  May those who desire to hurt me be fended off and disgraced.
³May those who say "Aha, Aha!" be pushed back because of their shame.
⁴May all those who seek you rejoice and be glad in you!
  And may those who love your salvation continually say, 'How great is God!'

⁵Yet I am poor and needy.
  Hasten to me, O God.
  You are my help and my deliverer.
  O LORD, do not delay!

PSALM 71

¹I place my trust in you, O LORD—let me never be put to shame.
²In your righteousness, deliver me and rescue me; lend me your ear and save me.
³Be a tower of refuge for me, where I may continually hide myself.
You have given the command to save me, for you are my rock and my fortress.

⁴Deliver me, O my God, out of the hand of the wicked, from the palm of the unjust and cruel man.
⁵For you are my hope, O Lord GOD.
Since my youth you have been my trust.
⁶I have depended on you since I was in the womb.
It was you who brought me out of my mother's womb; my praise of you shall flow continually.

⁷To many I am something to marvel at, but you are my strong refuge.
⁸My mouth is full of praise for you—and with honor all day long.
⁹Do not toss me aside in the time of old age; do not forsake me when my strength fails.
¹⁰For my enemies speak ill of me, and those who lay in wait for my soul gather together, to plot, ¹¹saying, "God has forsaken him. Let's pursue him and grab him because there's no one to rescue him."

¹²O God, be not far from me; O my God, please hurry to help me.
¹³May my enemies be ashamed and consumed; may those who seek to harm me be buried in scorn and disgrace.
¹⁴But I will hope continually and will still praise you more and more.
¹⁵My mouth will extol your deeds of righteousness and salvation all day long, for they are innumerable.
¹⁶I will go about my days in the strength of the Lord GOD, making mention of your righteousness—yes, and yours alone.
¹⁷O God, you have taught me from my youth, and still do I proclaim your wonderful works.
¹⁸So even when I am old and gray-headed, O God, do not forsake me, until I have proclaimed your power to the next generation—yes, your power to all who are yet to come.
¹⁹Your righteousness, O God, is as high as the heavens—you who have done great things. O God, who could compare with you?
²⁰You have brought me through troubles and calamities. You will revive me and bring me back up from the depths of the earth.
²¹You will increase my greatness and surround me with comfort.

²²I will also praise you with the harp, for your faithfulness, O my God; to you will I sing with the lyre, O Holy One of Israel.
²³My lips shall greatly rejoice when I sing to you—even my entire soul, which you

have redeemed!

²⁴My tongue will also speak about your righteousness all day long, for those who were seeking to hurt me have been humiliated and disappointed.

PSALM 72

[A Psalm for Solomon.]

¹Give your justice to the king, O God, and your righteousness to the son of the king.
²He will judge your people with righteousness, and your poor with justice.
³May the mountains bring stability for the people—and the hills—in righteousness.
⁴May he defend the poor of the community; may he rescue the children of the needy and shatter their oppressors.

⁵May they fear you as long as the sun and the moon endure—throughout all generations!
⁶May he be like rain falling on the new-mown grass, like the showers watering the earth.
⁷May the righteous ones flourish in their allotted time and see an abundance of peace so long as the moon endures.
⁸May he have dominion from sea to sea, and from the River to the ends of the earth.
⁹May the tribes in the desert bow down before him, and his enemies lick the dust.
¹⁰May the kings of Tarshish and the coastal lands bring tribute; may the kings of Sheba and Seba offer gifts.
¹¹Indeed, all the kings will fall down before him; all the nations will serve him.
¹²For he shall deliver the needy when he cries out—the poor as well—and those without help.
¹³He spares the poor and needy and saves the souls of the needy.
¹⁴He shall redeem their lives from oppression and violence, and in his eyes their blood is precious.
¹⁵May he live long, and may the gold of Sheba be given to him!
May prayer be made for him continually, and blessings invoked for him continually.

¹⁶May there be armfuls and armfuls of corn on the earth and on top of the mountains.
May its fruit be abundant as it is in Lebanon.
May city dwellers flourish like the grass of the field.
¹⁷May his name endure forever, with his fame continuing as long as the sun.
May people be blessed in him!
May all the nations call him blessed!

¹⁸Blessed be the LORD, the God of Israel—the only one who can do wondrous things!
¹⁹And may his glorious name be blessed forever.
May the whole earth be filled with his glory!
Amen and Amen!

²⁰So end the prayers of David, the son of Jesse.

PSALM 73

[A Song or Psalm of Asaph.]

¹Truly God is good to Israel—to those who are pure in heart.
²But as for me, my feet were about to stumble, and I was beginning to slip.
³For I was envious of the arrogant, as I realized the prosperity of the wicked.
⁴For they feel no pain until death; their bodies are robust and sleek.
⁵They do not live with the troubles others do, nor are they plagued like other people.
⁶So, they wear their pride like a necklace and clothe themselves with violence.
⁷Their eyes swell with luxurious abundance; their hearts overflow with folly.
⁸They scoff and speak maliciously; they haughtily boast of oppressing others.
⁹They set their mouth against the heavens while with their tongues they strut through this world.
¹⁰Therefore their followers keep returning to them to drink deeply from their wells.
¹¹And they ask, "How would God know? Does the Most High know anything?"
¹²Look—such are the ungodly, who prosper in this world, continuing to accumulate wealth.
¹³Surely I have kept my heart pure and my hands innocent in vain!
¹⁴For I have felt stricken all day long and then punished every morning.

¹⁵If I had mused, "I am going to say what is on my mind," listen—I would have harmed this generation of your children.
¹⁶But when I struggled to understand this, it was so burdensome for me ¹⁷until I went into the sanctuary of God, where I came to understand their destiny.
¹⁸Surely you have set them in slippery places to be cast down into destruction.
¹⁹How they are destroyed in a momentary flash! Then they are swept away in a torrent of terrors.
²⁰Like the remnants of a dream when one awakens, O Lord, they will be merely despicable phantoms when you rouse yourself.
²¹And so my heart was deeply grieved, and this realization pricked my conscience.
²²I had been brutishly ignorant, acting like an animal in your presence.

²³In contrast to them, I am continuously with you who upholds me by my right hand.
²⁴You guide me with your counsel, and afterward you will take me to glory.
²⁵Whom do I have in heaven other than you?
   I desire nothing else on earth other than you.
²⁶Though my flesh and my courage should fail me, you strengthen my heart; you are my portion forever.

²⁷For look—those who are far from you will perish.
   You will destroy all those who turn from you to join themselves to other gods.
²⁸It is good for me to draw near to God.
   In the Lord GOD I have put my trust, so that I may declare all his works.

PSALM 74

[A Maskil of Asaph.]

[1]O God, why have you cast us off forever?
 Why is your anger still burning against the sheep of your pasture?
[2]Remember your congregation, which you purchased long ago, and which you redeemed to be the tribe of your heritage!
 Remember Mount Zion, where you have dwelled.
[3]Make your way to the perpetual ruins where enemies have destroyed all the contents of the sanctuary.
[4]Your enemies made an uproar in the middle of your meeting place and they replaced the signs with their own.
[5]Behaving like men wildly swinging axes to cut down thick trees, [6]they swiftly broke down the carved woodwork with axes and hammers.
[7]Then they set your sanctuary on fire, defiling it and burning down the dwelling place of your name.
[8]Saying in their hearts, "Let's utterly destroy them," they burned down all the synagogues of God in the land.
[9]We no longer see our signs; there are no prophets anymore; none of us know how long this will go on.

[10]O God, how long shall the enemies go on scoffing?
 Shall the enemy go on blaspheming your name forever?
[11]Why do you hold back your hand—your right hand?
 Please take it out of your pocket and destroy them.
[12]Yet—God is my King from ancient times, working salvation in the midst of the earth.
[13]You parted the sea with your might; you smashed the heads of the sea monsters on the waters.
[14]You crushed the heads of Leviathan into pieces and gave them as food to the people living in the wilderness.
[15]You split open springs and creeks; you dried up mighty rivers.
[16]The day belongs to you, as well as the night.
You established all the lights of the heavens and the sun.
[17]You fixed all the boundaries on the earth.
 You established both summer and winter.
[18]Remember that the enemies scoff, O Lord, and the foolish people revile your name.
[19]O do not deliver the soul of your dove into the wicked crowd.
 Do not forget forever the life of your poor.
[20]Have regard for the covenant, for the dark places of the land are filled with those who live in cruelty.
[21]O do not let the downtrodden return in shame; may the poor and needy praise your name.

²²Arise, O God, defend your own cause.

Remember how the foolish man scoffs at you all day long.
²³Do not forget the clamor of your enemies— the uproar of those who rise up against you—which increases continually.

PSALM 75

[To the choirmaster. Do not destroy. A Psalm of Asaph.]

¹We give thanks to you, O God—we give thanks because your name is near. We declare your wondrous deeds.

²"At my appointed time I shall judge uprightly.
³When the earth and all its inhabitants are crumbling, it is I who steadies its pillars. Selah
⁴I said to the boastful fools, 'Do not boast,' and to the wicked, 'Do not blow your own horn. ⁵Do not display your horn of power for all to see, nor speak haughtily with a stiff, prideful neck.'"

⁶For promotion comes neither from the east, nor from the west, nor from the south.
⁷But it is God who judges, lowering one man, and elevating another.
⁸For in the hand of the LORD is a cup [of judgment], full of foaming wine, mixed with spices, which he pours out, and all the wicked of the earth must drink it down to the dregs.

⁹But I will declare this forever, singing praises to the God of Jacob.
¹⁰I will also cut off the horns of the wicked, but the horns of the righteous shall be lifted up.

PSALM 76

[To the choirmaster. With stringed instruments. A Psalm of Asaph.]

¹In Judah God is known. His name is great in Israel.
²In Salem is his tabernacle. His dwelling place is in Zion.

³There he broke the arrows of the bow, the shield, the sword, and the battle [weapons]. Selah ⁴You are more glorious and more majestic than the mountains filled with game.

⁵The stouthearted have been stripped of their possessions and are now sunk into sleep. All of the warriors cannot even use their hands.
⁶At your rebuke, O God of Jacob, both the rider and his horse lie in stunned silence.
⁷Now it is you—yes, you—who are to be feared.

Who could remain standing in your sight when your anger has been aroused?
⁸You pronounced judgment from heaven.

The earth feared and lay still ⁹when God arose to establish justice and to save all the downtrodden of the earth. Selah

¹⁰Surely your wrath against man will result in your praise, and you will restrain those who survive your wrath.
¹¹Make a vow to the LORD your God and fulfill it.

Let all those from neighboring lands bring gifts to the One who is to be feared.
¹²He breaks the spirit of princes; he is a terror to the kings of the earth.

PSALM 77

[To the choirmaster, to Jeduthun: A Psalm of Asaph.]

¹I cry aloud to God—aloud to God—and he attends to my cry.
²In the day of my trouble I seek the Lord; I stretch out my hand all night long, but my soul refuses to be comforted.
³When I remember God I moan, and my spirit faints within me. Selah
⁴You hold my eyelids wide open; I am so distressed that I cannot speak.
⁵I consider the days of old, the years long ago.

⁶I said, "Oh, that I might remember my song in the night; let me meditate in my own heart." Then my spirit searched diligently.
⁷Will the Lord spurn forever, never showing me his favor again?
⁸Is his enduring love gone completely forever?

Have his promises come to an end forevermore?
⁹Has God forgotten to be gracious?

In his anger, has he closed off his tender mercies? Selah

¹⁰Then I said, "This is my sorrow, but I must remember the years of the right hand of the most High."
¹¹I will remember the deeds of the LORD—surely I will remember your wondrous acts of long ago.
¹²I will ponder all your work and talk about what you have done.
¹³Your way, O God, is in the sanctuary.
Who is *so* great a God as our God?

¹⁴You are the God who does wonders; you have declared your strength among the people.
¹⁵You have redeemed your people—the sons of Jacob and Joseph—with your arm. Selah
¹⁶When the waters saw you, O God, when the waters saw you they were afraid—yes, even the depths trembled.
¹⁷The clouds poured out water; the skies thundered, and your arrows flashed all around.
¹⁸Your thunder crashed in the heavens, and flashes of lightning lit the world; the earth trembled and shook.
¹⁹Your way was through the sea, and your path was in the great waters—yet your footsteps still remained unseen.
²⁰By the hand of Moses and Aaron you led your people like a flock.

476

PSALM 78

[a Maskil of Asaph.]

¹O my people, listen to my discourse; lend your ears to the words from my mouth. ²I will begin speaking with a narrative, telling an old story from ancient times, ³which we have heard and known, and our forefathers have told us. ⁴We must not hide these things from their descendants, but rather we must convey them to the coming generation–the praises of the LORD, his power, and the wonderful things that he has done.

⁵For he decreed a testimony for Jacob and established a law in Israel, which he commanded our forefathers to teach to their children,⁶so that the next generation would come to know them–even the children yet to be born, who would then declare them to their children, ⁷so that they would place their trust in God and would not forget what God had done, but would keep his commandments, ⁸and might not be like their forefathers–a stubborn and rebellious generation who did not keep themselves loyal, and whose spirits were not faithful to God.

⁹The men of Ephraim, though armed carrying bows, retreated on the day of battle. ¹⁰They did not keep the covenant of God and refused to live by his law ¹¹and forgot his deeds and his wonders that he had shown them.

¹²He did marvelous things in the sight of their forefathers, in the land of Egypt, in the region of Zoan. ¹³He divided the sea and ushered them through it, and he made the waters stand up like a wall. ¹⁴In the daytime he guided them with a cloud, and in the nighttime with the light of a fire.

¹⁵In the wilderness he split the rocks and gave them an abundance of water. ¹⁶He even brought streams out of the rock and made water flow down like rivers. ¹⁷And yet they kept sinning against him by rebelling against the Most High while in the wilderness. ¹⁸And they put God to the test by demanding meat for their cravings. ¹⁹They murmured against God by asking, "Can God provide a table in the wilderness? ²⁰Yes—he did strike the rock to make the waters gush out, and the streams did flow greatly, but can he also give bread? Can he provide meat for his people?"

²¹When the LORD heard this, he was angry, which sparked a fire against Jacob, and his anger also rose up against Israel ²²because they did not believe in God and did not trust in his salvation, ²³even though he had commanded the clouds above and had opened the doors of heaven, ²⁴and had rained down manna on them to eat, and had given them bread from the skies. ²⁵People ate the food of angels, and he sent them an abundance of meat.

²⁶He made an east wind blow in the skies, and by his power he made the south wind blow. ²⁷He also showered down meat on them like dust, and as many birds as the grains of sand on the seashore. ²⁸And he let this fall in the midst of their

camp, all around their tents. ²⁹So they ate and were well filled, for he gave them the object of their desire.

³⁰Yet while they were enjoying their fill—while their meat was still in their mouths— ³¹ The wrath of God rose against them, and he killed the most robust of them, cutting down the sturdy young men of Israel. ³²For in spite of all this, they kept on sinning and still did not believe, even despite his marvelous works. ³³Therefore their days vanished in futility, and they passed their years in fear.

³⁴When he killed them, then others sought him and returned earnestly seeking after God. ³⁵Then they remembered that God was their rock, that the most high God was their redeemer. ³⁶But though they flattered him with their mouths, they were lying to him with their tongues. ³⁷For their hearts were not right with him, neither did they remain faithful to his covenant.

³⁸But being full of compassion, he forgave their iniquities and did not kill them. Indeed, many times he restrained his anger and did not arouse all his wrath. ³⁹For he remembered that they were but flesh—a wind that passes once, never to return. ⁴⁰How often they rebelled against him in the wilderness and grieved him in the desert! ⁴¹Indeed, they put God to the test repeatedly, provoking the Holy One of Israel.

⁴²They did not remember his hand of deliverance, nor the day when he redeemed them from the enemy, and ⁴³how he had displayed signs in Egypt, and his wonders in the region of Zoan:

> ⁴⁴He turned their rivers into blood so that they could not drink out of the stream.
> ⁴⁵He sent swarms of flies that devoured them, and frogs that destroyed them.
> ⁴⁶He also gave over their crops to the grasshopper, and the fruit of their labor to the locust.
> ⁴⁷He destroyed their vines with hail, and their sycamore trees with frost.
> ⁴⁸He gave over their cattle to the hail as well, and their livestock to lightning bolts.
> ⁴⁹He unleashed his anger, wrath, and indignation, and woe against them, with a host of avenging angels.
> ⁵⁰He gave vent to his anger by not sparing their souls from death, but rather he gave their lives over to the plague.
> ⁵¹Thus he struck down all the firstborn of Egypt—the eldest son in each tent of Ham.

⁵²But he led forth his own people like a flock, guiding the sheep through the wilderness. ⁵³And he led them on safely, so that they were not afraid, though the sea overwhelmed their enemies. ⁵⁴And he brought them to the border of his holy place, right to this mountain, which he had claimed with his right hand.

⁵⁵He also drove out the nations before them, and allotted lands to them as an inheritance, and settled the tribes of Israel in their tents. ⁵⁶And still they put the Most High God to the test, rebelling against him and not keeping his statutes. ⁵⁷Like their forefathers, they backslid and dealt unfaithfully, veering off to the side like a faulty bow. ⁵⁸For they angered him with their tall shrines and aroused his jealousy with their carved idols.

⁵⁹When God heard this, he burned with anger and utterly despised Israel. ⁶⁰So he abandoned the tabernacle of Shiloh—the tent he had placed among men, ⁶¹and delivered the ark of his power into captivity—his glory into the hands of his enemy. ⁶²He also gave his people over to the sword and was angry with his inheritance. ⁶³The fire consumed their young men so their maidens had no one to marry. ⁶⁴Their priests fell by the sword, but their widows did not lament.

⁶⁵Then the Lord awoke as if from sleep, like a mighty warrior would from the effect of wine. ⁶⁶And he drove back his enemies, putting them into disgrace forever.

⁶⁷He then overlooked the tent of Joseph and did not choose the tribe of Ephraim, ⁶⁸choosing instead the tribe of Judah, Mount Zion, which he loved. ⁶⁹And he built his sanctuary like high [palaces], like the earth that he has established forever. ⁷⁰He also chose David as his servant, taking him from the sheepfolds, ⁷¹from tending the pregnant ewes, and he brought him to shepherd Jacob his people, and Israel his inheritance. ⁷²So David fed them in the pureness of his heart and guided them with his skillful hands.

PSALM 79

[A Psalm of Asaph.]

¹O God, the nations have come into your inheritance.
They have defiled your holy temple and they have laid waste to Jerusalem.
²They have given the bodies of your servants as food to the birds of the air, and the flesh of your faithful ones to the beasts of the earth.
³They have poured out their blood like water all around Jerusalem, and there was no one to bury them.
⁴We have become a laughingstock to the neighboring nations—mocked and derided by those around us.
⁵How long, LORD? Will you be angry forever?
Will your jealousy burn like fire?
⁶Pour out your wrath on the nations who do not know you, and on the kingdoms that do not call on your name.
⁷For they have devoured Jacob and laid waste his home.

⁸Do not hold our evil deeds of the past against us.
Let your tender compassion come to us quickly, for we are brought very low.
⁹Help us, O God of our salvation, for the glory of your name.

479

Deliver us and purge away our sins, for the sake of your name!

¹⁰Why should the nations ask, "Where is their God?"

Let [God] be known among the nations in sight of us through the revenging of the spilled blood of your servants.

¹¹Let the groans of the prisoners come before you.

With your great power, preserve those who are doomed to die!

¹²And return back to our neighbors seven times the mocking of our neighbors, with which they have mocked you, O Lord!

¹³But we your people and the sheep of your pasture will thank you forever. We will recount your praise from each generation to the next.

PSALM 80

[To the choirmaster: according to Lilies. A Testimony. A Psalm of Asaph.]

¹Lend us your ear, O Shepherd of Israel, you who lead Joseph like a flock.
Shine forth, you who are seated on a throne above the cherubim.

²Arouse your might before Ephraim and Benjamin and Manasseh and come and save us.

³Restore us, O LORD God of hosts. Shine your face on us to save us.

⁴O LORD God of hosts, how long will your anger smolder against the prayers of your people?

⁵You have fed them with the bread of tears—even given them a full dose of tears to drink.

⁶You have made us the laughingstock of our neighbors, and our foes laugh about us.

⁷Restore us, O LORD God of hosts. Shine your face on us to save us.

⁸Once you brought a vine out of Egypt, drove the nations out, and planted it.

⁹You cleared the land for it; it has taken deep root and spread through the land to fill it.

¹⁰Its shade covered the hills, and its boughs resembled mighty cedars.

¹¹Its branches have reached the sea, and its roots as far as the River.

¹²Why then have you let its walls be broken down, so that all who pass by pick its grapes?

¹³The boar from the forest ravages it, and animals of the field devour it.

¹⁴Return, we beg you, O God of hosts—look down from heaven to see and visit this vine, ¹⁵and the vineyard that your right hand planted, and the branch that you strengthened for yourself.

¹⁶Others have burned it with fire and cut it down; may they perish at the rebuke of your countenance.

¹⁷Let your hand rest on the man of your right hand, on the son of man whom you strengthened for yourself.

¹⁸Then we shall not run away from you. Revive us, and we will call on your name.

¹⁹Restore us, O LORD God of hosts. Shine your face on us to save us.

PSALM 81

[To the choirmaster on Gittith: A Psalm of Asaph.]

¹Sing aloud to God, our strength!
 Make a joyful noise to the God of Jacob.
²Raise up a song; play the tambourine, the sweet lyre, and the harp.
³Sound the ram's horn on the day of the New Moon and the Full Moon when our festival begins.
⁴For this is a statute for Israel, an ordinance from the God of Jacob.
⁵Through Joseph he made this a decree when he went out through the land of Egypt, where I heard this in a language that I did not know:
 ⁶I removed the burden from your shoulder; your hands were freed up from the baskets. ⁷In distress you called out, and I delivered you; I answered you in the secret place of thunder; I tested you at the waters of Meribah. Selah
 ⁸Listen, O my people, as I warn you. O Israel, if you will just listen to me. ⁹You shall have no foreign god in your midst, neither shall you worship any strange god. ¹⁰I am the LORD your God, who brought you out of the land of Egypt; open your mouth wide, and I will fill it. ¹¹But my people would not attend to my voice, and Israel would not obey me. ¹²So I gave them over to the lust of their own hearts, and they behaved as they saw fit. ¹³O that my people had listened to me so that Israel had walked in my ways! ¹⁴How swiftly would I subdue their enemies and turn my hand against their adversaries! ¹⁵Then those who despise the LORD would cringe before him, and their time of condemnation would endure forever. ¹⁶However, you would be nourished with the finest wheat, and I would satisfy you with honey out of the rock."

PSALM 82

[a Psalm of Asaph.]

¹God has assumed his place among the powers that be;
 Among the gods it is he who has the power to judge.

²How long will you defend the unjust and show partiality to the wicked? Selah
³Defend the poor and fatherless.
 Bring justice to the afflicted and the needy.
⁴Rescue the poor and needy.
 Deliver them from the hand of the wicked.
⁵They lack knowledge and understanding.
 They walk around in darkness.
 All the foundations of the earth are off balance.

⁶I said, "You are gods, and all of you are children of the most High.
⁷However, you will die like all men do and fall as a prince would."

⁸Rise up, O God, to judge the earth, for all the nations are yours to inherit.

PSALM 83

[A Song or Psalm of Asaph.]

¹Do not remain silent, O God.
 Do not hold your peace or be still, O God.

²For, look—your enemies are making an uproar, and those who despise you have
reared their heads.
³They have made devious plans against your people and have consulted together against those who you cherish.
⁴They are saying, "Come, and let us wipe out this nation so that the name of
Israel may no longer be remembered," ⁵for they gather together to conspire,
 [nations] plotting together against you:
  ⁶the tents of Edom, and the Ishmaelites;
   of Moab, and the Hagarenes;
  ⁷Gebal, and Ammon, and Amalek;
   the Philistines with the inhabitants of Tyre;
  ⁸Asshur has also joined them to assist the children of Lot. Selah

⁹Deal with them as you did the Midianites and those of Sisera and of Jabin, at
the brook of Kison, who ¹⁰perished at Endor and became rubbish to be buried in
the ground.
¹¹Make their nobles like Oreb, and like Zeeb—indeed, all their princes like
Zebah, and like Zalmunna ¹²who said, "Let us take possession of the houses of
God for ourselves."

¹³O my God, make them like a whirling powder—like chaff blown by the wind.
¹⁴As the fire consumes the forest, and as the flame sets the mountains on fire,
¹⁵may you persecute them with your tempest and terrify them with your violent
storm.
¹⁶Fill their faces with shame so that they may seek your name, O LORD.
¹⁷Let them be humiliated and crushed in spirit forever.
 Indeed let them be disgraced and perish ¹⁸so that people may know that you,
whose name alone is Jehovah, are the most high over all the earth.

PSALM 84

[To the choirmaster: according to The Gittith. A Psalm of the Sons of Korah.]

¹How lovely is the place of your dwelling, O LORD of hosts!
²My soul longs—yes, it even faints—for the courts of the LORD.
 My heart—yes, even my whole being—cries out for the living God.

³Even the sparrow finds a home,
 and the swallow finds herself a nest

where she may lay her young at your altars,
  O Lord of hosts, my King and my God.
[4]Blessed are those who dwell in your house, singing your praises constantly.
Selah
[5]Blessed are the ones whose strength lies in you, in whose hearts are the highways [of Zion], and [6]who make the valley of Baca a place of springs as they pass
through it. Even the rain fills the pools!
[7]They move from strength to strength; all of them appear before God in Zion.
[8]O Lord God of hosts, hear my prayer.

  Lend me your ear, O God of Jacob. Selah
[9]O God, see our shield and look on the face of your anointed ones!
[10]For one day in your courts is better than a thousand elsewhere.
  I would rather be just a doorkeeper in the house of my God than live in the
tents of wickedness.
[11]For the Lord God is a sun and a shield.
  The Lord grants favor and honor.
  He will withhold no good thing from those who walk uprightly.
[12]O Lord of hosts, blessed is the one who places his trust in you.

PSALM 85

[To the choirmaster. A Psalm of the Sons of Korah.]

[1]Lord, you once looked with favor on your land, restoring the fortunes of Jacob.
[2]You forgave the wicked deeds of your people, covering all their sin. Selah
[3]You pulled back all your wrath, turning from your hot anger.

[4]Restore us once more, O God of our salvation, set aside your anger toward us!
[5]Will you be angry with us forever?
  Will you extend your anger to all generations?
[6]Will you not revive us again, that your people may rejoice in you?
[7]Treat us according to your enduring love, O Lord, and grant us your salvation.

[8]O, that I would hear what God the Lord says, for he speaks peace to his
people, and to his holy ones!
  But let them not return to foolish ways.
[9]Surely his salvation is close to those who fear him, that glory may dwell in our land.
[10]Enduring love and faithfulness come together.
  Righteousness and peace kiss each other.
[11]Faithfulness springs out of the ground, and righteousness shall look down from
the sky.
[12]Yes, the Lord will give what is good, and our land will yield its produce.
[13]Righteousness will go before him, making a path for his footsteps.

PSALM 86

[A Prayer of David.]

¹Lend your ear, O LORD, to hear me, for I am poor and needy.
²Preserve my life, for I am godly.

 You are my God—save your servant who trusts in you.
³Be merciful to me, O Lord, for I cry out to you all day long.
⁴Make your servant's soul glad, for it is to you, O Lord, that I lift up my soul.
⁵For you, Lord, are good, and ready to forgive, and abundant in enduring love to all those who call on you.

⁶Lend your ear, O LORD, to my prayer and listen to my pleas.
⁷I will call on you on the day of my distress, for you answer me.
⁸There is none like you, O Lord, among the gods, nor are there any works like yours.
⁹All the nations that you have made shall come and worship before you, O Lord, and shall give glory to your name.
¹⁰For you are great, and you do wondrous things.

 You alone are God.
¹¹Teach me your ways, LORD, so that I may walk in your truth.

 Make me fear your name wholeheartedly.
¹²I will praise you, O Lord my God, with all my heart, and I will glorify your name forever.
¹³For great is your enduring love toward me, and you have delivered my soul from Sheol.

¹⁴O God, arrogant men have risen up against me, and a mob of violent men seek my life, and they do not have regard for you.
¹⁵But you, O Lord, are a God who is compassionate and gracious, slow to anger, and abounding in enduring love and truth.
¹⁶Turn toward me and take mercy on me.

 Give your strength to your servant and save the son of your handmaiden.
¹⁷Show me a sign of your favor so that those who despise me may see it and be ashamed, because you, LORD, have given me help and comfort.

PSALM 87

[A Psalm or Song for the sons of Korah.]

¹The city he founded stands on the holy mountain.
²The LORD loves the gates of Zion more than all the houses of Jacob.
³Glorious things are spoken of you, O city of God. Selah
⁴I will make mention of Rahab and Babylon among those who know me. Take note, Philistia, and Tyre, with Ethiopia—this one was born there.
⁵And it shall be said of Zion, "This one and that one were born on her,"

for the Most High will himself establish her.

⁶When he registers the peoples, the LORD records which one was born there. Selah

⁷Both singers as well as musicians shall declare, "All my springs are in you."

PSALM 88

[A Song or Psalm for the sons of Korah, to the choirmaster on Mahalath Leannoth, Maskil of Heman the Ezrahite.]

¹ O LORD God of my salvation, I cry out before you day and night.

²May my prayer come before you.

Lend an ear to my cry!

³For my soul is full of troubles, and my life is approaching death.

⁴I am numbered with those who go down into the pit.

I am a man without strength, ⁵left among the dead, like slain ones lying in the grave, no longer remembered by you, and cut off from your caring hand.

⁶You have laid me in the depths of the pit, deep down in darkness.

⁷Your wrath lies heavy on me, and you have overwhelmed me with all your waves. Selah

⁸You have made my friends shun me.

You have made me repulsive to them.

I am shut in and cannot escape.

⁹Sorrow dims my eye.

LORD, I call on you daily, stretching out my hands to you.

¹⁰Do you perform wonders for the sake of the dead?

Do the dead rise up to praise you? Selah

¹¹Is your enduring love declared in the grave, or your faithfulness in Abaddon?

¹²Are your wonders known in the darkness, or your righteousness in the land of oblivion?

¹³But, O LORD, I cry to you, and my prayer comes before you in the morning.

¹⁴LORD, why do you cast away my soul, hiding your face from me?

¹⁵From my youth I have been afflicted and ready to die.

I am helpless as I endure your terrors.

¹⁶Your fierce wrath sweeps over me; your assaults bring me to ruin.

¹⁷They surround me each day like flood waters closing in on me.

¹⁸You have made my loved one and my friend shun me.

Darkness has become my companion.

PSALM 89

[A Maskil of Ethan the Ezrahite.]

¹I will sing of the enduring love of the LORD forever.

I will declare your faithfulness to all generations with my mouth.

²For I said, "Enduring love will stand forever. You establish your faithfulness in the heavens."

³You have said, "I have made a covenant with my chosen one. I have sworn to David my servant, ⁴'I will establish your line of descendants forever and hold your throne firm for all generations.'" Selah

⁵May the heavens praise your wonders, O LORD, and your faithfulness in the assembly of the holy ones.

⁶For who else up in the heavens could be compared to the LORD? What heavenly being is equal in nature with the LORD?

⁷God is greatly to be feared in the council of the holy ones, and to be held in reverence by those who surround him.

⁸O LORD God of hosts, who is as powerful as you are, O LORD, with your faithfulness all around you?

⁹You rule the raging of the sea, and when its waves surge, you still them.

¹⁰You have crushed Rahab—it lies in pieces like a corpse.
   You have scattered your enemies with your strong arm.

¹¹The heavens are yours, the earth also is yours.
   You have founded the world and all it contains.

¹²You have created both the North and the South.
   Tabor and Hermon shall rejoice in your name.

¹³You have a mighty arm.
   Your hand is strong; your right hand is raised up high.

¹⁴ Righteousness and justice form the foundation of your throne.
   Enduring love and faithfulness precede you.

¹⁵Blessed are the people who have experienced the sound of jubilation, and who walk in the light of your face, O LORD, ¹⁶rejoicing in your name all day long; they are exalted in your righteousness.

¹⁷For you are the glory of their strength; your favor exalts our horn.

¹⁸For our shield of defense lies in the LORD, the Holy One of Israel, our king.

¹⁹Long ago you spoke in a vision to your godly one and said,
   "I have helped a mighty warrior; I have exalted him, chosen from the people.
   ²⁰I have found David my servant and l have I anointed him with my holy oil.
   ²¹My hand shall be established through him, and my arm shall strengthen him as well.
   ²²The enemy shall not be able to take advantage of him; the wicked shall not be able to dominate him.
   ²³And I will crush his foes before him and strike down those who oppose him.
   ²⁴But my faithfulness and my enduring love shall rest on him, and his horn shall be exalted in my name.
   ²⁵I will set his hand on the sea as well—and his right hand on the rivers.
   ²⁶He shall exclaim to me, You are my father, my God, and the rock of my salvation.
   ²⁷I will also appoint him to be my firstborn, the highest king of the earth.
   ²⁸I will maintain my enduring love for him forever, and my covenant with him will remain intact.

²⁹I will also make his descendants last forever, and his throne will be like the days of heaven.

³⁰If his children forsake my law, not walking according to my rules—

³¹If they violate my statutes, and do not keep my commandments, ³²then I will repay their transgression with the rod of discipline, and their wickedness with a scourging.

³³However I will not completely remove my enduring love from him, nor lapse in my faithfulness.

³⁴I will not break my covenants, nor alter the promise that has gone forth from my lips.

³⁵I have made an oath by my holiness once and for all; I will not lie to David.

³⁶His lineage shall last forever, and his throne as long as the sun before me.

³⁷It shall be established forever, like the moon, for a faithful witness in the sky." Selah

³⁸But you have rejected, despised, and been angry toward your anointed one.

³⁹You have renounced the covenant with your servant.

  You have defiled his crown, leaving it in the dirt.

⁴⁰You have breached all his walls, and laid waste to his strongholds.

⁴¹All who pass by plunder him; he is a laughingstock to his neighbors.

⁴²You have lifted the right hand of his adversaries [in triumph], causing all his enemies to rejoice.

⁴³You have also turned back the edge of his sword, and in battle you have not kept him standing.

⁴⁴You have brought his glory to an end and have cast his throne down to the ground.

⁴⁵You have shortened the days of his youth; you have covered him with a shroud of shame. Selah

⁴⁶How long, Lord? Will you hide yourself forever?

  How long will your wrath burn like fire?

⁴⁷Remember how brief my time is!

  Why have you made all men in vain?

⁴⁸What living man will not see death?

  Can he rescue his soul from the hand of the grave? Selah

⁴⁹Lord, where is your enduring love from bygone days, which you faithfully vowed to David?

⁵⁰Be mindful, Lord, how your servants are being mocked, and how I endure insults from all the mighty nations in my heart.

⁵¹O Lord, your enemies mock with insults—they mock the footsteps of your anointed.

⁵²Blessed be the Lord forever!

  Amen, and Amen.

PSALM 90

[A Prayer of Moses the man of God.]

[1]Lord, you have been our dwelling place in all generations.
[2]Before the mountains were brought forth, or you had even formed the earth and the world—from eternity past to eternity future—you are God.
[3]You return man to dust and say, "Return, O children of man."

[4]For in your sight a thousand years are like yesterday when it is gone, or like a watch in the night.
[5]You whisk them away like with a flood.
They resemble a dream.
They are like grass springing up: [6]in the morning it flourishes and grows up; in the evening it is cut down and withers.

[7]For we are consumed by your anger, and by your wrath we are brought to ruin.
[8]You have placed the record of our misdeeds before you—our secret sins in the light of your face.
[9]For we spend all our days in your wrath.
Our years are used up and end with a groaning sigh.
[10]The years of our lives number seventy—perhaps with strength, eighty—yet their span is just toil and trouble.
The years are soon gone, and we fly away.
[11]Who can ponder the power of your anger and your wrath by virtue of the fear of you?
[12]So teach us to count our days such that we acquire hearts filled with wisdom.

[13]Return, O LORD!
How long? Take pity on your servants.
[14]Satisfy us in the early morning with your enduring love so that we may rejoice and be glad all our days.
[15]Grant us glad days for as many days as you have afflicted us, for as many years as we have witnessed evil.
[16]May your work be shown to your servants, and your glory to their children.
[17]And may the favor of the LORD our God be on us.
Establish the work of our hands on us—indeed, establish the work of our hands.

PSALM 91

[1]Whoever dwells in the shelter of the Most High shall abide within the shadow of the Almighty, [2]I shall address the LORD: "My refuge and my fortress, my God, in whom I trust."

[3]Surely he will rescue you from the fowler's net, and from the deadly plague.
[4]He will cover you with his feathers, and you will find refuge under his wings. His faithfulness is a shield and a rampart.

⁵You will not fear the terror that comes at night, nor the arrow that flies by day, ⁶nor the plague that lurks in the darkness, nor the destruction that desolates at noontime.

⁷Though a thousand should fall by your side—even ten thousand at your right hand—this will not come near you.
⁸You need only look with your eyes to observe what reward the wicked receive.

⁹Because you have made the LORD—my refuge and the Most High—your dwelling place, ¹⁰no evil will be allowed to happen to you, nor will any plague come near your home.
¹¹For on your behalf he will command his angels to keep guard over you in all your ways.
¹²They will hold you up in their hands, so that you do not strike your foot against a stone.
¹³You will step on the lion and the adder—you will trample the young lion and the serpent under foot.

¹⁴"Because he has placed his love in me, I will deliver him.
   I will keep him safe because he knows my name.
¹⁵When he calls to me I will answer him.
   In times of trouble I will be with him and rescue him and honor him.
¹⁶I will satisfy him with long life and show him my salvation."

PSALM 92

[A Psalm for the Sabbath Day.]

¹It is good to give thanks to the LORD—
  to sing praises to your name, O Most High,
²To declare your enduring love by morning,
  and your faithfulness by night,
³To the music of the lute and the harp, and to the melody of the lyre.
⁴For you, LORD, have delighted me with your works.
  I sing joyously because of the works of your hands.

⁵O LORD, how great are your works!
  Your thoughts are profound.
⁶An ignorant man has no knowledge of this, nor does a fool understand this:
   ⁷that the wicked spring up like grass,
    and all the workers of evil do flourish,
    but they are doomed to be destroyed forever.
⁸But you, LORD, are Most High for evermore.
⁹For, surely your enemies—O LORD—for surely your enemies shall perish.
  All the evildoers will be scattered.

¹⁰You have exalted my horn of strength like that of a wild ox.

You have poured out fresh oil on me.

¹¹My eyes have witnessed the downfall of my enemies.

My ears have heard the doom of those who attacked me.

¹²The righteous will flourish like a palm tree.

They will grow like a cedar of Lebanon.

¹³Those who are planted in the house of the LORD will flourish in the courts of our God.

¹⁴They will still bear fruit in their old age.

They will be robust and healthy, ¹⁵declaring,

"The LORD is upright.

He is my rock, and there is no wickedness in him."

PSALM 93

[A Song of Ascents.]

¹The LORD reigns.

He has robed himself with majesty; the LORD has girded himself with a belt of strength.

And the world is established and shall never be moved.

²Your throne has been established since ancient times.

You are from eternity past.

³The waters have risen, O LORD, the waters have lifted up their voice.

The waters lift up their waves.

⁴The LORD on high is mighty—mightier than the thunder of many waters—yes, than the mighty waves of the sea.

⁵Your decrees stand without question.

O LORD, holiness suits your house forever.

PSALM 94

[A Psalm for the Sabbath Day.]

¹O LORD God of vengeance!

Vengeance belongs to you, O God—show yourself.

²Raise yourself, O judge of the earth, to repay the haughty what they deserve.

³How long shall the wicked— LORD—how long shall the wicked triumph?

⁴They speak with great arrogance.

All the evildoers boast about themselves.

⁵They crush your people, O LORD, and afflict your heritage.

⁶They kill the widow and the sojourner and murder the fatherless.

⁷Yet they claim, "The LORD does not see, nor does the God of Jacob notice it."

⁸Gain understanding, you ignorant ones among the people,
  and you foolish ones—you must become wise:
   ⁹He who created the ear, can he not hear?
   He who formed the eye, can he not see?
   ¹⁰He who chastises the nations, does he not rebuke?
   He who teaches man knowledge, what does he not know?
¹¹The LORD knows that the thoughts of man are but vapor.

¹²Blessed is the man whom you discipline, O LORD, teaching him from your law
¹³so that you might grant him a reprieve from the days of trouble, until the pit is
dug for the wicked.
¹⁴For the LORD will not cast off his people, neither will he forsake his inheritance.
¹⁵But justice will return to the righteous, and all the upright in heart will follow it.

¹⁶Who will rise up against the wicked for my sake?
  Who will stand up against the evildoers for my sake?
¹⁷If the LORD had not come to my aid, my soul would have soon dwelled in silence.
¹⁸When I thought, "My foot is slipping," your enduring love, O LORD, held me up.
¹⁹When my inner cares are many, your consolations comfort my soul.
²⁰Can wicked princes be your allies?
  Those who use laws to create injustice ²¹band together against the life of the
righteous and condemn the innocent to death.
²²But the LORD is now my stronghold, and my God is the rock of my refuge.
²³And he will return their own evil to them and wipe them out because of their
own wickedness.
  Indeed, the LORD our God will destroy them.

PSALM 95

[To the choirmaster: A Psalm of Asaph.]

¹O come, let us sing to the LORD.
  Let us make a joyful noise to the rock of our salvation.
²Let us enter his presence with thanksgiving and make a joyful noise to him with
songs of praise.
³For the LORD is a great God, and a great King above all gods.
⁴In his hand are the depths of the earth, and the loftiness of the mountains is his
as well.
⁵The sea is his because he created it, and his hands formed the dry land.

⁶O come, let us worship and bow down.
  Let us kneel before the LORD our maker.
⁷For he is our God, and we are the people of his pasture, and the sheep of his
hand. Today if you hear his voice, ⁸do not harden your hearts, as you did at
Meribah, and as you did at Massah in the wilderness, ⁹when your fathers tested

me. They put me to the test, even though they had seen my work.
¹⁰For forty years I was vexed with that generation and said, "They are a people who go astray in their hearts, and they have not known my ways."
¹¹So in my anger I swore, "They shall not enter into my rest."

PSALM 96

[A Psalm for the Sabbath Day.]

¹Oh sing a new song to the LORD!
  Sing to the LORD, all the earth.
²Sing to the LORD, bless his name; tell about his salvation from day to day.
³Declare his glory among the nations, his marvelous works among all peoples.
⁴For great is the LORD and worthy of great praise.
  He is to be feared above all gods.
⁵For all the gods of the nations are but idols, whereas the LORD created the heavens.
⁶Splendour and majesty go before him; strength and beauty are in his sanctuary.

⁷Ascribe to the LORD—O clans within the peoples—ascribe glory and strength to the LORD.
⁸Ascribe to the LORD the glory that his name deserves, bringing an offering as you come into his courts.
⁹O worship the LORD in the splendor of holiness.
  Tremble before him, all the earth.

¹⁰Tell the nations that the LORD reigns.
  Indeed the world is established; it shall never be moved; he shall judge the people justly.

¹¹Let the heavens rejoice, and let the earth be glad.
  Let the sea roar, and everything in it.
¹²Let the field be joyful, and everything in it.
  Then shall all the trees of the wood rejoice ¹³before the LORD.
  For he is coming—for he is coming—to judge the earth.
  He will judge the world with righteousness, and the peoples with fairness.

PSALM 97

[A Psalm for the Sabbath Day.]

¹The LORD reigns, let the earth rejoice!
  Let the lands by the sea be glad!
²Clouds and dark fog surround him.
  Righteousness and justice form the foundation of his throne.
³Fire goes before him and burns up his adversaries all around.

4His flashes of lightning light up the world; the earth sees and trembles.
5The mountains melt like wax in the presence of the LORD, before the Lord of the whole earth.
6The heavens declare his righteousness, and all the people see his glory.
7All those who worship idols are put to shame—those who boast in powerless idols. Worship *him*, all you gods.
8Zion hears and is glad, and the daughters of Judah rejoice because of your just decrees, O LORD.

9For you, LORD, are high above all the earth. You are exalted far above all gods.
10O you who love the LORD, hate evil!
He preserves the lives of his saints. He delivers them from the hand of the wicked.
11Light bursts forth for the righteous, and gladness for the upright in heart.
12Rejoice in the LORD, O you righteous ones, and give thanks to his holy name!

PSALM 98

1Oh sing to the LORD a new song, for he has done wondrous things!
His right hand and his holy arm have achieved salvation.
2The LORD has made his salvation known.
He has demonstrated his righteousness for the nations to see.
3He has remembered his enduring love and his truth to the house of Israel.
All the ends of the earth have witnessed the salvation of our God.

4Make a joyful noise to the LORD, all the earth.
Break forth into jubilant song and sing praise.
5Sing to the LORD with the lyre—with the lyre and the voice of a psalm.
6Make a joyful noise before the king, the LORD, with trumpets and the sound of a horn.

7Let the sea roar, and all that is in it—the world, and all its inhabitants.
8Let the rivers applaud.
Let the hills sing together for joy 9before the LORD.
For he comes to judge the earth.
He will judge the world with righteousness, and the peoples with fairness.

PSALM 99

1The LORD reigns; may the people tremble!
He sits above the cherubim. May the earth be shaken.
2The LORD is great in Zion. He is exalted high over all the peoples.
3Let them praise your great and reverent name, for he is holy.
4With his strength, the King loves justice.
You establish equity, and you mete out justice and righteousness in Jacob.
5Exalt the LORD our God, and worship at his footstool, for he is holy.

6Among the priests were Moses and Aaron, and among those who call on his name was Samuel.

They called on the LORD, and he answered them.
[7]He spoke to them in the pillar of the cloud.
They kept his testimonies and the statutes that he gave them.
[8]O LORD our God, you answered them.
You were a God that forgave them, though you took revenge on their wrongdoings.
[9]Exalt the LORD our God, and worship at his holy mountain, for the LORD our God is holy.

PSALM 100

[1]Shout in grateful jubilation to the LORD, all the earth.
[2]Serve the LORD with gladness.
Enter His presence with singing.
[3]Know that the LORD, He is God!
It is He, and not we ourselves, who created us.

We are His people and the sheep of His pasture.

[4]Come through His gates with thanksgiving
and enter His courts with praise
Give thanks to Him; bless His name!
[5]For the LORD is good.
His unfailing love endures forever,
and His faithfulness to all generations.

PSALM 101

[a Psalm of David.]

[1]I shall sing of enduring love and justice; O LORD, I shall sing of it to you.
[2]I shall focus on leading a life that is blameless.
Oh, when will you visit me?
Within my own home I shall conduct myself with a heart of integrity.
[3]I shall not make any vile, filthy thing the desire of my eyes.
I despise the work of those who have fallen away, and I shall not allow it to lay hold of me.
[4]The perverse heart shall be far from me—I shall not participate in evil doings.
[5]I shall wipe out whoever slanders his neighbor in secret.
I shall not endure the one who has a haughty look and a proud heart.
[6]I shall regard the faithful of the land favorably so that they might dwell with me.
The one who lives uprightly shall minister to me.

[7]Anyone who practices deceit shall not dwell within my house.
I shall give no regard to anyone who tells lies.
[8]I shall rise early to destroy all the wicked in the land so that I may wipe out all evildoers from the city of the LORD.

PSALM 102

[A Prayer of the afflicted, when he is overwhelmed and pouring out his complaint before the LORD.]

¹Hear my prayer, O LORD, and let my cry come to you.

²Please do not hide your face from me in my time of affliction.

Lend your ear to me, and on the day when I call, answer me swiftly.

³For my days vanish quickly like smoke, and my bones are burning up like embers in a fire.

⁴My heart is so stricken and withered like grass that I even neglect eating my bread.

⁵Because of the sound of my groaning my bones cling to my flesh.

⁶I am like a wilderness owl—like an owl of the desert.

⁷I lie awake at night like a lonely sparrow on a housetop.

⁸My enemies ridicule me all day long, and those who taunt me use my name as a curse word.

⁹For I eat ashes like bread and mingle my drink with tears ¹⁰because of your indignation and your wrath.

For you have lifted me up and then thrown me down.

¹¹My days resemble a fading shadow, and I am withered like grass.

¹²But you, O LORD, are on your throne forever, and the memory of you will last to all generations.

¹³You will arise and take mercy on Zion, for the time to favor her—indeed the appointed time—has come.

¹⁴For your servants cherish its stones and the very dust of it moves their hearts.

¹⁵The nations shall come to fear the name of the LORD, and all the kings of the earth shall be in awe of your glory.

¹⁶When the LORD builds up Zion, he will appear in his glory.

¹⁷He will have regard for the prayer of the destitute and will not despise their requests.

¹⁸Let this be written down—a record for the generation yet to come—so that the people yet to be created will praise the LORD.

¹⁹For he looked down from the height of his sanctuary. From heaven the LORD took notice of the earth ²⁰to hear the groaning of the prisoner, and to set free those who were appointed to die, so that they might ²¹declare the name of the LORD in Zion, and his praise in Jerusalem ²²when the people are gathered together, along with the kingdoms, to serve the LORD.

²³In the middle of my life's journey, he has broken my strength and shortened the span of my days. ²⁴I begged, "O my God—your years last throughout all generations—please do not take me away in the middle of my days!"

²⁵Long ago you laid the foundations of the earth, and the heavens are the work of your hands.

²⁶They will perish, but you will endure. Indeed, all of them will wear out like a garment. You will change them like you change clothes, and they will pass away. ²⁷But you remain the same, and your years shall have no end.
²⁸The children of your servants shall live in safety, and their descendants shall be established before you.

PSALM 103

[of David.]

¹Bless the LORD, O my soul, may my innermost being bless his holy name.
²Bless the LORD, O my soul, and forget not all the benefits of the One
      ³who forgives all your wicked deeds,
     who heals all your diseases,
      ⁴who redeems your life from the pit,
     who crowns you with enduring love and tender mercies,
      ⁵who satisfies your mouth with what is good,
     so that your youthful strength is renewed like the eagle›s.

⁶The LORD works out righteousness and justice for all those who are oppressed.
⁷He made known his ways to Moses, his deeds to the children of Israel.
⁸The LORD is merciful and gracious, slow to anger, and abundantly merciful.
⁹He will not always chide, nor will he remain angry forever.
¹⁰He does not deal with us according to our sins, nor repay us according to our wicked deeds.
¹¹His enduring love extends toward those who fear him. His love is as high as the heavens are above the earth.
¹²He removes our transgressions from us, as far as the east is from the west.
¹³The LORD shows compassion on those who fear him, as a father is compassionate to his own children.
¹⁴For he understands what we are made of—he bears in mind that we are dust.

¹⁵As for man, his days are like grass or like a wildflower—he only flourishes so long.
¹⁶For the wind passes over it, and it is gone; and the spot where it was knows it no longer.
¹⁷But for those who fear him the enduring love of the LORD is from eternity past to eternity future. And his righteousness is
   to the children of the children—
   ¹⁸to those who keep his covenant, and
   to those who remember to carry out his commandments.
¹⁹The LORD has built his throne in the heavens, and his kingdom reigns over all.

²⁰Bless the LORD, O you his angels, mighty ones who carry out
  his commandments, obediently minding the voice of his word.
²¹Bless the LORD, all his hosts, his ministers who carry out his will.

²²Bless the LORD, all his works everywhere in his kingdom.
 Bless the LORD, O my soul.

PSALM 104
¹Bless the LORD, O my soul.

O LORD my God, you are very great! You clothe yourself in splendor and majesty, ²covering yourself with light as your clothing, stretching out the heavens like a tent.
³He lays the beams of his chambers on the waters; he uses the clouds as his chariot and rides on the wings of the wind.
⁴He turns his messengers into winds and his ministers into a flaming fire.

⁵He laid the foundations of the earth so that it cannot ever be moved.
⁶You covered it with the deep waters like a garment; the waters stood above the mountains.
⁷At your command they fled; at the sound of your thunder they took flight.
⁸The mountains rose up and the valleys sank down to the places you had appointed for them.
⁹You fixed a boundary that the deep waters may not pass, so that they may never cover the earth again.
¹⁰He created springs gushing forth in the valleys and running between hills.
¹¹They provide water for every beast of the field—even the wild donkeys quench their thirst.
¹²Alongside them the birds of the air make their homes, singing among the tree branches.
¹³You water the mountains from your abode; the earth is satisfied with the fruit of your work.
¹⁴You make grass grow for livestock, and plants for people to cultivate, that they may bring forth food out of the earth, ¹⁵and wine to gladden the heart of man, and oil to make his face shine, and bread to sustain man›s strength.
¹⁶The trees of the LORD are well watered—the cedars of Lebanon that he planted.
¹⁷There the birds make their nests; the stork makes her home in the fir trees.
¹⁸The mountains are a refuge for the wild goats and the rocks for the badgers.
¹⁹He made the moon to mark the times of the year; the sun knows its time to set.
²⁰You cause darkness, and night falls—when all the beasts of the forest creep around.
²¹The young lions roar for their prey, looking for their food from God.
²²When sun rises, they steal away to lay themselves down in their dens.
²³Then mankind does his work and his labor until the evening.
²⁴O LORD, how multi-faceted are your works!
 In wisdom you have made them all; the earth is full of your creatures.

²⁵So great and wide is the sea, teeming with innumerable creatures—living things both large and small.

²⁶There the ships travel, along with Leviathan, which you created to play in it.
²⁷All these creatures look to you to give them their food in due season.
²⁸When you give it to them, they gobble it up; when you open your hand, they are filled with good things.

²⁹When you hide your face, they are dismayed.
  When you take away their breath, they die and return to dust.
³⁰When you send forth your spirit, they are created, and you renew the land.

³¹May the glory of the LORD last forever!
  May the LORD rejoice in his works.
³²He looks on the earth, and it trembles.
  He touches the mountains, and they smoke.

³³I will sing to the LORD as long as I live.
  I will sing praise to my God while I still have my being.
³⁴May my meditation please him, for I delight in the LORD.
³⁵Let the sinners be consumed from the earth, and let the wicked be no more!
  Bless the LORD, O my soul!
  Praise ye the LORD!

PSALM 105

¹O give thanks to the LORD; call on his name.
  Make his deeds known among the people.
²Sing to him, sing praises to him.
  Speak about all his wondrous works.
³Glory in his holy name.
  Let the hearts of those who seek the LORD rejoice!
⁴Seek the LORD and his strength.
  Continually seek his face.
⁵Remember the marvelous works that he has done—his wonders, and the just decrees he has spoken.
⁶O you descendants of Abraham his servant, children of Jacob, his chosen ones!
⁷He is the LORD our God; his justice is found on all the earth.

⁸For all time he remembers his covenant—the word he commanded to a thousand generations, ⁹the covenant he made with Abraham, and his oath to Isaac,
¹⁰which he confirmed to Jacob as law, and to all Israel as an everlasting covenant,
¹¹saying, "I will give the land of Canaan to you as your portion, for your inheritance."

¹²When they were only a few men in number, and of little account, just sojourners in it, ¹³wandering from one nation to another, from one kingdom to another people, ¹⁴he allowed no man to oppress them. Indeed he rebuked kings on their behalf, ¹⁵saying, "Do not hurt my anointed, and do not harm my prophets."

¹⁶Then he brought about a famine in the land by breaking the supply of bread.
¹⁷But he had sent a man before them, Joseph, who was sold as a slave.
¹⁸They bound his feet with chains, and his neck with a collar of iron.
¹⁹The word of the LORD put him to the test until the time when His word finally came to pass.
²⁰The king sent for him to be released, and in doing so, the ruler of the people let him go free.
²¹He even appointed Joseph
>to be lord of his house,
>to manage all his estate,
>   ²²to bind his princes at his pleasure, and
>to teach wisdom to the elders.

²³Then all Israel also moved into Egypt, and [the people of] Jacob sojourned as foreigners in the land of Ham.
²⁴And the LORD made his people so fruitful that they became too numerous for their enemies.
²⁵He permitted the heart of the Egyptians to have contempt for his people and to deal shrewdly with his servants.

²⁶He sent his servant Moses, and Aaron, whom he had chosen.
²⁷They performed his signs among them, and wonders in the land of Ham.
²⁸He sent darkness and turned the land dark; and they did not rebel against his words.
²⁹He turned their waters into blood, which killed their fish.
³⁰Their land brought forth frogs in abundance, even in the rooms of their kings.
³¹He spoke, and there came swarms of flies and gnats throughout the country.
³²He gave them hail for rain, and fiery bolts of lightning in their land.
³³He struck down their vines and their fig trees and laid waste to the trees of their country.
³⁴He spoke, and the locusts came—innumerable locusts—³⁵that consumed all the plants in their land and devoured the produce of their ground.
³⁶He struck down all the firstborn in their land—the prominent men of power.

³⁷Then he brought Israel out with silver and gold; no one among their tribes faltered.
³⁸Egypt was glad when they left because a dreadful fear of Israel had fallen on them.

³⁹He spread a cloud for a covering and fire to give light in the night.
⁴⁰When the people asked, he sent them quails and satisfied them bountifully with bread from heaven.
⁴¹He split open a rock, and the waters gushed out, running in the dry place like a river.
⁴²For he remembered his holy promise, and Abraham, his servant.

⁴³And he brought forth his people with joy—his chosen ones with gladness—

⁴⁴and gave them the lands of the nations, and they inherited the fruit of the labor of the people so ⁴⁵that they might keep his statutes and obey his laws. Praise the LORD!

PSALM 106

¹Praise ye the LORD. O give thanks to the LORD, for he is good.
 For his unfailing love endures forever.
²Who is able to recount all the mighty acts of the LORD?
 Who can declare all his praise?
³Blessed are those who act justly and who act in righteousness at all times.

⁴Remember me, O LORD, when you show favor to your people; grant me your salvation
> ⁵that I may see the prosperity of your chosen ones,
> that I may rejoice in the gladness of thy nation,
> that I may glory with your inheritance.

⁶Like our forefathers,
> we have sinned,
> we have done wrong,
> we have acted wickedly.

⁷When they were in Egypt our forefathers did not comprehend your miraculous works. Rather than remembering the abundance of your mercies, they rebelled at the sea—at the Red sea.
⁸Nonetheless, he rescued them for his name's sake, that he might make his mighty power known.
⁹He rebuked the Red Sea and it dried up. Thus he led them through the depths, as if it were a dry desert.
¹⁰So he redeemed them from the hand of their foes and saved them from the power of the enemy.
¹¹And the waters covered their enemies so that not one of them was left.
¹²Then they believed his words, singing his praise.

¹³However, they soon forgot what he had done; they did not wait for his decrees.
¹⁴Instead, they acted out their wanton lust there in the wilderness and put God to the test in the desert.
¹⁵And he granted them what they lusted after, but also plagued them with a disease that wasted their flesh.
¹⁶When men in the camp envied Moses and Aaron, the holy one of the LORD,
¹⁷the earth opened and swallowed up Dathan and covered the company of Abiram.
¹⁸Also a fire started in their company, and its flames burned up the wicked.
¹⁹In Horeb they fashioned a calf and worshipped that metal image, thus ²⁰exchanging the glory of God for the image of a bovine that eats grass.

²¹They forgot God their savior, who had done great things in Egypt, ²²wondrous works in the land of Ham, and awesome things by the Red sea.
²³Therefore he decided that he would destroy them, but Moses, his chosen one, stood before him on their behalf to turn away his wrath, so that he would not destroy them.

²⁴Then they gave up the hope of reaching a pleasant land, putting no faith in his promise.
²⁵So in their tents they grumbled and did not listen to and obey the voice of the LORD.
²⁶Therefore he lifted up his hand against them, threatening to let them die in the wilderness, and ²⁷to disperse their offspring among the nations, and to scatter them in the lands.
²⁸Then they avowed themselves to worship Baal of Peor and ate the sacrifices offered to the dead.

²⁹Their actions provoked the LORD to anger, causing a plague to break out among them.
³⁰Then Phineas arose and intervened, which stopped the spread of the plague.
³¹And that act was ascribed to him as righteousness from one generation to the next forever.
³²They angered the LORD also at the waters of Meribah, so that it went badly for Moses on their account ³³because they provoked his spirit so much that rash words came from his lips.

³⁴They did not destroy the nations, as the LORD had commanded them to.
³⁵Instead they mingled themselves among the nations and learned their ways.
³⁶And they served their idols, which became a deadly trap for them.
³⁷They also sacrificed their sons and their daughters to demons, ³⁸and shed innocent blood, including the blood of their sons and of their daughters, whom they sacrificed to the idols of Canaan, so the land was polluted with blood.

³⁹Thus they made themselves unclean with these deeds, and they went about in lustful pursuit of their own desires.
⁴⁰Therefore the wrath of the LORD was kindled against his people—so much so that he despised his own heritage.
⁴¹So he handed them over into the hands of the nations, and those that hated them ruled over them.
⁴²Their enemies oppressed them, and they were brought into submission under their hand.
⁴³He delivered them many times, and yet they rebelliously went their own way, and were brought low for their wrongdoing.
⁴⁴Nonetheless, he looked on their affliction when he heard their cry, ⁴⁵and he remembered his covenant for their sake, and he relented in accordance with his enduring love.

⁴⁶He made those who held them in captivity pity them.

⁴⁷Save us, O LORD our God, and gather us from among the nations, to give thanks to your holy name, and to triumph in your praise.

⁴⁸Blessed be the LORD God of Israel from eternity past to eternity future.
Let all the people say Amen.
Praise the LORD.

PSALM 107

[A Song or Psalm of Asaph.]

¹O give thanks to the LORD, for he is good, for his enduring love shall last forever!
²Let those who are redeemed of the LORD proclaim it is so—those whom he has rescued from the hand of the enemy ³and gathered in from the lands, from the east and the west, from the north and the south.

⁴Some of them wandered in the roadless desert finding no town to live in, and ⁵hungry and thirsty, their souls fainted within them.
⁶Then in their distress they cried to the LORD, and he delivered them out of their anguish,
⁷and he led them forward in the right way directly to a town to live in.
⁸Let them praise the LORD for his enduring love and the wondrous things he does for the children of man! ⁹For he satisfies the longing soul and fills the hungry soul with good things.

¹⁰Others sat in darkness and in the shadow of death, prisoners bound by both affliction and iron chains ¹¹because they rebelled against the words of God and rebuffed the counsel of the Most High.
¹²So he broke their hearts with labor; they collapsed with no one to help.
¹³Then in their distress they cried to the LORD, and he delivered them out of their anguish.
¹⁴He brought them out of darkness and the shadow of death, and he broke apart their bonds.
¹⁵Let them praise the LORD for his enduring love, for the wondrous things he does for the children of man! ¹⁶For he smashes the doors of bronze and cuts the bars of iron apart.

¹⁷Because of their transgressions and their wrongdoings, fools were suffering afflictions.
¹⁸Being revulsed by all kinds of food, they were drawing near the gates of death.
¹⁹Then in their distress they cried to the LORD, and he delivered them out of their anguish.
²⁰He sent out his word and healed them, and he rescued them from their destruction.
²¹Let them praise the LORD for his enduring love and the wondrous things he

does for the children of man! ²²And let them offer up sacrifices of thanksgiving and declare his deeds with joyous songs.

²³Others went down to the sea in ships to do business in the deep waters. ²⁴They saw the works of the LORD and his wondrous creations in the deep. ²⁵For by his command he raised a raging wind that lifted up the ocean waves. ²⁶They soared up into the sky and then crashed down again to the depths. The [sailors'] souls melted because of their trouble. ²⁷They reeled about, staggering like drunken men and were at their wits' end. ²⁸Then in their distress they cried to the LORD, and he delivered them out of their anguish. ²⁹He calmed the raging storm, so that the waves were stilled as well. ³⁰Then they were glad because all was quiet, and thus he brought them to their desired haven. ³¹Let them praise the LORD for his enduring love and the wondrous things he does for the children of man! ³²Let them extol him also in the assembly of the people and praise him in the gathering of the elders.

³³He turns rivers into a desert, springs of water into dry ground, and ³⁴ fruitful lands into salty wastelands—because of the wickedness of the inhabitants. ³⁵He turns a desert into pools of water, and parched ground into springs of water, ³⁶letting the hungry dwell there so that they may build a city to live in ³⁷and sow the fields and plant vineyards producing much fruit. ³⁸Because of his blessing they multiply greatly, and he does not allow their herds of cattle to diminish.

³⁹Some suffer loss and are brought low through oppression, affliction, and sorrow. ⁴⁰He pours contempt on princes, making them wander in the roadless deserts. ⁴¹But he raises up the needy above affliction, giving them families like flocks. ⁴²The upright one sees this and rejoices, which silences the voice of wickedness. ⁴³Whoever is wise—

Let him observe all these things carefully.

Let him meditate on the enduring love of the LORD.

PSALM 108

[A Psalm of David.]

¹O God, my heart is unmovable.

I will sing melodies of thankfulness with all my strength.

²Awake, O harp and lyre! I awaken at the dawn.

³I will praise you, O LORD, among the people, and I will sing praises to you among the nations.

⁴For your enduring love is great above the heavens.

Your faithfulness extends to the clouds.

503

⁵Be exalted, O God, above the heavens! May your glory be over all the earth ⁶so that your beloved ones may be delivered. Bring salvation with your right hand to answer me.

⁷In his holiness, God has given a promise:
    "With rejoicing I will divide up Shechem,
      and portion out the Valley of Succoth.
   ⁸Gilead is mine.
    Manasseh is mine.
    Ephraim is my helmet.
    Judah is my scepter.
   ⁹Moab is my wash basin.
    I tread on Edom with my boot.
    I will triumph over Philistia."

¹⁰Who will bring me to the fortified city?
  Who will lead me into Edom?
¹¹O God, have you rejected us?
  O God, will you not go forward with our armies?
¹²Help us in times of danger, for man's power to save is futile.
¹³With God we shall do valiantly; he is the one who will trample our enemies.

PSALM 109

[To the choirmaster: a Psalm of David.]

¹O God of my praise, do not remain silent, ²for the wicked and the deceitful open their mouths to malign me.
They have spoken against me with lying tongues, ³and they surround me with hateful words, attacking me without just cause.
⁴In return for my love, they oppose me, but I devote myself to prayer.
⁵And they have rewarded my good with evil and returned hatred for my love.
⁶Place a wicked man over him, and let the accuser stand at his right hand.
⁷When he is judged, let him be found guilty, and let his prayer be reckoned as sin.
⁸May his days be few and may another assume his position.
⁹May his children be fatherless, and his wife a widow.
¹⁰May his children be continually wandering and begging as they scavenge for food from the ruins they live in!
¹¹May a creditor seize all his assets, and may strangers pillage the fruit of his labor!
¹²May there be no one to show kindness to him, nor anyone to assist his fatherless children!
¹³May his descendants be cut off, and his name be blotted out from the next generation!
¹⁴May the wicked deeds of his fathers be remembered by the LORD.
  May the sin of his mother not be removed!

¹⁵Let them be before the LORD continually so that he may cut off the memory of them from the earth!

¹⁶For he did not remember to show mercy, but instead pursued the poor and the brokenhearted to put them to death.

¹⁷Since he loved pronouncing curses, may his curses come back upon him. Since he found no pleasure in blessing, may it be far from him.

¹⁸He clothed himself with a garment of cursing, so now may that seep into his body like water, into his bones like oil.

¹⁹To him, may it be like a garment strapped around him, like a belt that he puts on each day.

²⁰May all these things be the recompense from the LORD to my enemies, and to all those who speak evil against my life.

²¹But, O GOD my Lord, for your name›s sake, take action on my behalf.

Because your enduring love is good, deliver me, ²²for I am poor and needy, and within me my heart is stricken.

²³I am spent—like a lengthening shadow.

I am shaken off like a locust.

²⁴My knees are weak from fasting, and my body is gaunt and emaciated.

²⁵I am a laughingstock to my foes; when they look at me, they shake their heads.

²⁶Help me, O LORD my God!

Save me according to your enduring love!

²⁷Let them know that this is [by] your hand—that you, LORD, have accomplished it.

²⁸Let them curse, but you still bless!

When they arise, let them be ashamed, but let your servant rejoice.

²⁹Let my enemies be clothed with dishonor—may they be cloaked in their own shame.

³⁰I will greatly praise the LORD with my mouth.

Indeed I will praise him in the midst of the assembly.

³¹For he stands beside the destitute one to save him from those who condemn his soul to death.

PSALM 110

¹The LORD said to my Lord, "Sit at my right hand until I make your enemies a footstool for your feet."

²The LORD sends forth your mighty scepter from Zion.

Rule in the midst of your enemies!

³Your troops will serve willingly on the day of your conflict, clothed in holiness.

Your young men will serve you like dew from the womb of the morning.

⁴The LORD has sworn and will not change his mind: "You are a priest forever, after the order of Melchizedek."

⁵The Lord at your right hand will crush kings on the day of his wrath.
⁶He will execute judgment among the nations, filling such places with dead bodies.
 He will devastate rulers all over the earth.
⁷On the way, he will drink from the brook—thereby lifting his head high
[in triumph].

PSALM 111

¹Praise the LORD!
 I will praise the LORD wholeheartedly, in the assembly of the godly—in the
congregation.
²The great works of the LORD are pursued by all who take delight in them.
³How magnificent and majestic is his work, and his righteousness shall last forever.
⁴He causes his wondrous works to be remembered.
The LORD is gracious and full of compassion.
⁵Being ever mindful of his covenant, he has provided food to those who fear him.
⁶He has shown his people the power of his works by giving them the inheritance
of the nations.
⁷Truthful and judicious are the works of his hands.
 All his precepts are trustworthy.
⁸They stand firm forever and ever, to be followed in faithfulness and righteousness.
⁹He provided redemption to his people.
 He has commanded his covenant forever.
 Holy and worthy of awe is his name.
¹⁰The fear of the LORD is the beginning of wisdom.
 All those who act on his commandments have good understanding.
¹¹May his praise last forever.

PSALM 112

[An acrostic poem of the Hebrew alphabet.]

¹Ah, Praise the LORD!

 Blessed is the man who fears the LORD, and whose

 Great delight lies in keeping his commandments.

²Descendants of this man will be mighty in the land.

 Here the generation of the godly will be blessed.

³Wealth and riches are in his house, and his godliness lasts for all time.

⁴Zeal for God brings light, dawning in the darkness.

 He is gracious, compassionate, and righteous.

⁵The good man acts generously and lends, conducting his business justly.

⁶Yes, he will not ever be shaken.

Known he will be—for all time.

⁷Lo, he does not fear bad news.

May his heart remain ever steadfast, as he trusts in the LORD.

⁸Now and always may his heart be steadfast.

See, he shall not be afraid, and so he shall look at his foes in triumph.

⁹Indeed, he has distributed freely,

Providing for the destitute.

Certainly his righteousness endures forever.

Quite exalted—with honor—shall be the horn of his power.

¹⁰Rather, the wicked sees it and gets angry.

Surely, he grinds his teeth—but he will melt away.

The desire of the wicked shall perish.

PSALM 113

[a Psalm of David.]

¹Praise the LORD!
Praise—O servants of the LORD—praise the name of the LORD.
²Blessed be the name of the LORD from this time forth and forevermore!
³From the rising of the sun
till the time of its setting
the LORD's name is to be praised.

⁴The LORD is high above all nations, and his glory above the heavens!
⁵Who is like the LORD our God, who resides on high,
⁶who looks down to see the skies and the earth?
⁷He elevates the poor from the dust, and raises the needy out of a heap of ashes,
⁸to have them sit with princes—yes, with the princes of his people.
⁹He provides a home for the barren woman whom he makes a joyful mother of children.
Praise the LORD!

PSALM 114

¹When Israel departed from Egypt—the house of Jacob leaving a people of a foreign tongue—²Judah became His sanctuary, Israel His dominion.

³The sea looked and fled; Jordan was driven back.

507

⁴The mountains skipped like rams, the small hills like lambs.
  ⁵O sea, what troubled you that made you flee?
    O Jordan, that you were driven back?
    ⁶O mountains, that you skipped like rams,
    O little hills, like lambs?

⁷O earth, tremble at the presence of the Lord—at the presence of the God of Jacob ⁸who turned rock into a pool of water, the flint into a fountain of water.

PSALM 115

¹Give glory not to us, O Lord—no, not to us—but to your name, for your enduring love, and for the sake of your truth.
²Why should the nations ask, "So, where is their God?"
³Rather, our God is in the heavens. He does as he pleases.

  ⁴Their idols are silver and gold—the work of men's hands.
  ⁵They have mouths, but they cannot speak.
  They have eyes, but they cannot see.
  ⁶They have ears, but they cannot hear.
  They have noses, but they cannot smell.
  ⁷They have hands, but they cannot use them.
  They have feet, but they cannot walk—nor do they speak with their throats.
⁸Those who create them end up just like them, and so shall everyone who puts his trust in them.

⁹O Israel, place your trust in the Lord.
        He is their help and their shield.
¹⁰O house of Aaron, place your trust in the Lord.
        He is their help and their shield.
¹¹You who fear the Lord, place your trust in the Lord.
        He is their help and their shield.

¹²The Lord has been mindful of us. He will bless us; he will bless the house of Israel; he will bless the house of Aaron.
¹³He will bless those who fear the Lord—both the insignificant and the great.
¹⁴The Lord shall grant abundance to you more and more—to you and your children.
¹⁵You are blessed of the Lord who created heaven and earth.
¹⁶The heavens—indeed the heavens—are the Lord's, but he has given the earth to the descendants of men.
¹⁷The dead do not praise the Lord, neither do any of those who descend into silence.
¹⁸But *we* shall bless the Lord from now on and for evermore. Praise the Lord!

PSALM 116

[1]I love the LORD because he has heard my voice and my cries for mercy.

[2]I shall call on him as long as I live because he inclined his ear to me.

[3]Death wrapped me in its cords; the anguish of the grave overwhelmed me, and I suffered distress and sorrow.

[4]Then I called on the name of the LORD, "O LORD, I beg you to deliver my soul!"

[5]The LORD is gracious; he is righteous; our God is merciful.

[6]The LORD preserves the humble; he saved me when I was laid low.

[7]O my soul, you may rest easily again, for the LORD has treated you generously.

[8]For you have delivered my soul from death, my eyes from tears, and my feet from stumbling.

[9]Before the LORD I will walk in the land of the living.

[10]Even when I said, "I am suffering great affliction," I still did believe.

[11]In my alarm, I declared "All people are liars."

[12]What should I give the LORD in return for all his goodness to me?

[13]I will raise the cup of salvation and I will call on the name of the LORD,

[14]I will pay tribute to the LORD in the presence of all His people.

[15]The death of his saints is precious in the sight of the LORD.

[16]I am your servant, O LORD; I am your servant, even the son of your maidservant. You have released me from bondage.

[17]I will offer the sacrifice of thanksgiving to you as I call on the name of the LORD.

[18]I will fulfill my vows to the LORD in the presence of all his people,

[19]in the courts of the house of the LORD, there in your midst, O Jerusalem. Praise the LORD!

PSALM 117

[1]Praise the LORD, all you nations, and let all the people praise him.

[2]For his enduring love toward us is great, and the truth of the LORD lasts for all time. Praise the LORD!

PSALM 118

[1]Oh give thanks to the LORD for he is good, for his unfailing love endures for all time.

[2]Let Israel declare that his unfailing love endures for all time.

[3]Let the house of Aaron declare that his unfailing love endures for all time.

[4]Let those who fear the LORD declare that his unfailing love endures for all time.

[5]In my distress I called on the LORD. He answered me and released me from bondage.

[6]The LORD is on my side; I will not be afraid.

   What can man do to me?

[7]The LORD is on my side, as one who comes to my aid.

   So, I shall look triumphantly at those who despise me.

⁸It is better to trust in the LORD than to put confidence in man.

⁹It is better to trust in the LORD than to put confidence in princes.

¹⁰All nations surrounded me. But I destroyed them in the name of the LORD.

¹¹They surrounded me! Indeed they surrounded me, but I destroyed them in the name of the LORD.

¹²They swarmed around me like bees; they were extinguished like a fire in the brambles, for I destroyed them in the name of the LORD.

¹³You [enemies] shoved me to make me fall, but the LORD helped me.

¹⁴The LORD is my strength and song, and He has become my salvation.

¹⁵The voices of rejoicing and salvation are in the tents of the righteous.
   The right hand of the LORD works valiantly.

¹⁶The right hand of the LORD is exalted.
   The right hand of the LORD works valiantly.

¹⁷I will not die—rather, I will live and proclaim the works of the LORD.

¹⁸The LORD has chastened me hard, but he has not given me over to death.

¹⁹Open the gates of righteousness to me. I will enter them, and I will praise the LORD.

²⁰This gate of the LORD is where the righteous shall enter.

²¹I will praise you, for you have heard me and have become my salvation.

²²The very stone that the builders rejected has become the capstone.

²³This was the LORD's doing, and it is marvelous in our eyes.

²⁴This is the day that the LORD has made; let us rejoice and be glad in it.

²⁵Rescue us, I beg you, O LORD!
   O LORD, I beg you, help us succeed!

²⁶Blessed is the one who comes in the name of the LORD.
   From the house of the LORD, we bless you.

²⁷The LORD is God; he has shone light on us.
Bind the sacrifice with cords, up to the horns of the altar.

²⁸You are my God, and I will thank you.
   You are my God, and I will praise you.

²⁹Oh give thanks to the LORD because he is good, because his enduring love goes on forever and ever.

PSALM 119

[An acrostic poem of the Hebrew alphabet.]

Aleph

¹A man whose way is blameless is blessed.
   He walks in the law of the LORD!

²A man who keeps His testimonies is blessed,
   He seeks Him with his whole heart,

³Also he is not erring,

but rather he is walking in His ways!

⁴Aye, you have commanded that your precepts
    be kept with great diligence.
⁵Alas—that my ways may be steadfast
    in holding to your statutes!
⁶Anon I shall not be put to shame,
    having set my sight on all your commandments.
⁷And I shall praise you with an upright heart,
    as I learn your righteous rules.
⁸As I keep your statutes,
    so that you do not entirely forsake me!

Beth

⁹But how does a young man keep his conduct pure?
    By conforming it to your word.
¹⁰Bearing my whole heart, I seek you.
    May I never stray from your commandments.
¹¹By hiding your word in my heart,
    may I never sin against you.
¹²Blessed are you, O LORD;
    teach me your rules!
¹³By my lips I am declaring
    all the just statutes from your mouth.
¹⁴Bountifully I delight in the way of your testimonies
    as much as I would in the sum of all treasure.
¹⁵Being in meditation on your precepts
    I set my sights on your ways.
¹⁶Because I take delight in your statutes,
    I will never forget your word.

Gimel

¹⁷Graciously deal with your servant,
    that my life may be preserved and I keep your word.
¹⁸Grant that when I open my eyes I may see
    wondrous things from your law.
¹⁹Globe—this globe—is my temporary home;
    do not conceal your commandments from me!
²⁰Greatly consumed with longing for your rules—
    such is my soul at all times.
²¹Grandiose, arrogant, and accursed are those you rebuke;
    they wander from your commandments.
²²Get scorn and contempt away from me,
    because I have kept your testimonies.

²³Great princes may sit scheming against me,

but your servant will still meditate on your statutes.

²⁴Gladness comes to me from your statutes—

which are indeed my counselors.

Daleth

²⁵Dust is what my soul clings to;

preserve my life according to your word!

²⁶Daily you have answered me when I told you about my ways;

teach me your statutes!

²⁷Do let me understand the way of your precepts,

and I will meditate on your works so wondrous.

²⁸Dissolute is my soul from sorrow.

Fortify me according to your word!

²⁹Do cast false ways far from me

and teach me your law with grace and mercy!

³⁰Deciding on the way of faithfulness,

I have placed your rules in front of me.

³¹Do not allow me to be shamed, O LORD;

for to your testimonies I cling.

³²Delighted, I will conduct myself in the way of your commandments

when you build up my courage!

He

³³Educate me, O LORD, in the way of your statutes;

and I will remain in it until the time of reward.

³⁴Endow me with understanding, that I may keep your law

observing it wholeheartedly.

³⁵Escort me in the path of your commandments,

for in them shall I find my delight.

³⁶Edge my heart toward your testimonies,

that I may not seek my own gain!

³⁷Encourage my eyes to avoid worthless things;

and in your ways, preserve my life.

³⁸Establish your promise to your servant,

that he would revere you.

³⁹Eliminate the reproach that I dread,

for your rules are good.

⁴⁰Even so, it is your statutes that I long for;

by your tender mercy preserve my life!

Waw

⁴¹Would that your enduring love might come to me, O LORD—

the salvation that you have promised.

⁴²When it does come, I shall have an answer for whoever taunts me,
　for in your word I have placed my trust.
⁴³Withdraw not the word of truth entirely from my mouth,
　for within your rules—therein lies my hope.
⁴⁴When shall I keep your law?
　Continually, age after age.
⁴⁵Walking in a wide place—this I shall do
　having searched out your precepts.
⁴⁶Why—before kings I will also declare your testimonies
　and shall not be ashamed,
⁴⁷Wherein I find my delight in your commandments,
　which I love.
⁴⁸Willingly I raise my hands to embrace your commandments,
　which I love, and deeply will I ponder your statutes.

Zayin

⁴⁹Zealously remember your word to your servant,
　for you have caused me to **hope** in it.
⁵⁰Zenith of comfort in my affliction;
　such is your promise that gives me life.
⁵¹Zany, arrogant men deride me greatly,
　but I do not abandon your law.
⁵²Zestfully considering your ancient rules,
　O Lord, I find comfort there.
⁵³Zapped with indignation am I,
　because wicked ones disregard your rules.
⁵⁴Zeal for your statutes has been my song
　as I sojourn in this house.
⁵⁵Zealously, O Lord, in the night I recall your name
　and hold fast to your law.
⁵⁶Zion's blessing has come to me:
　that I have held fast to your precepts.

Heth

⁵⁷Heritage of mine are you, Lord;
　I promise to keep your words.
⁵⁸How wholeheartedly I beg your favor!
　According to your promise, be gracious to me.
⁵⁹Hard-pressed, I consider my ways,
　and direct myself toward your testimonies.
⁶⁰Hastening, I do not delay
　in the keeping of your commandments.
⁶¹Hateful ones ensnare me with cords;

nonetheless I do not forget your law.

⁶²Having risen at midnight, I praise you
on account of your righteous laws.
⁶³Happily, my companions are those who revere you—
the ones who keep your precepts.
⁶⁴How full of your enduring love is this world.
O LORD, teach me your statutes!

Teth

⁶⁵Truly, O LORD, your dealings with your servant
have been beneficent, in accordance with your word.
⁶⁶Teach me prudence and wisdom,
for I believe in your commandments.
⁶⁷There was a time when I strayed, and I suffered affliction,
but now I obey your word.
⁶⁸Teach me your statutes—
you *are* good so you *do* what is good.
⁶⁹The arrogant try to smear my name with lies,
but I wholeheartedly hold to your precepts;
⁷⁰Their careless hearts are swelled with excess,
but it is in your law that I find my **delight**.
⁷¹Thus it was good for me to suffer affliction,
so that I would learn your statutes.
⁷²The law that came forth from your mouth is worth more to me
than thousands of pieces of gold and silver.

Yodh

⁷³Your hands created me and formed my design;
give me the wisdom to learn your commandments.
⁷⁴Yes, may those who revere you rejoice when they see me
for I have placed my hope in your word.
⁷⁵Your rules are righteous, O LORD, and I realize
that you have afflicted me as a discipline.
⁷⁶Your enduring love: may it be my comfort
in accordance with the promise you made to your servant.
⁷⁷Your enduring mercy: may it come to me so that I might live,
for I find my delight in your law.
⁷⁸Yet, may the arrogant ones be put to shame, for they have done me wrong
with their lies, [whereas] I will meditate on your precepts.
⁷⁹Your worshipers—let them come to me
to learn about your statutes.
⁸⁰Yes, as for your statutes, may my heart remain blameless
so that I may not be put to shame!

Kaph

⁸¹Keep longing for your salvation, oh my soul;

My **hope** is in your word.

⁸²Know that my eyes fail, looking for you to fulfill your promise;

I keep asking, "When will you comfort me?"

⁸³Knowing that I have become like a wineskin in the smoke,

even still I have not abandoned your statutes.

⁸⁴Keep enduring? How much longer must your servant endure?

When will you punish those who do me wrong?

⁸⁵Knowingly, the arrogant ones have dug pitfalls for me;

they do not conduct themselves according to your law.

⁸⁶Key are all your commandments;

they are doing me wrong with lies. Help me!

⁸⁷Killers have almost brought my time on earth to an end,

even still I have not abandoned your precepts.

⁸⁸Keeping the testimonies of your mouth is what I must do;

may your enduring love preserve my life.

Lamedh

⁸⁹LORD, O LORD, your word is eternal,

steadfastly fixed in the heavens.

⁹⁰Lasting to all generations is your faithfulness;

you have established the earth, and it stands firm.

⁹¹Laws of yours have endured to this day,

for all things are your servants.

⁹²Lo—if your laws had not been my delight,

I would have died in the time of my affliction.

⁹³Life you have preserved in me by your precepts,

Never will I forget them.

⁹⁴Lord, I am yours; save me,

for I have pursued your precepts.

⁹⁵Lying in wait to destroy me are the wicked,

however I focus my mind on your testimonies.

⁹⁶Limits to excellence have I seen,

yet your commandments are boundless.

Mem

⁹⁷Meditating on your law throughout the day am I;

Oh, how I love it.

⁹⁸May your commandments always be at work within me,

making me wiser than my adversaries.

⁹⁹Meditation, for me, is to study your testimonies such that I gain more

understanding than all my teachers.

[100]More so than the elders, I have understanding—
       for I obey your commandments.
[101]Maintaining my stance to avoid evil in every way,
       I seek to keep your word.
[102]Mindful of your rules I always remain,
       for you have instructed me in them.
[103]My mouth tastes the sweetness of honey,
      but sweeter are your words to my taste!
[104]My understanding I get through your precepts;
       and so I hold every falsehood in contempt.

Nun

[105]Nightly your word is a lamp to my feet
       and daily a light to my path.
[106]Now I have sworn and confirmed an oath
       to live by your righteous rules.
[107]Nonetheless, I am suffering severely;
       according to your word O LORD, preserve my life!
[108]Never refuse my freely given offerings of praise, O LORD,
       and teach me your rules.
[109]Noon and night I hold my life in my hand,
       but I do not neglect your law.
[110]Not led stray from your precepts I remain,
      though the wicked have set a trap for me—
[111]Nay, your testimonies are my heritage forever,
       for they are the joy of my heart.
[112]Now and always shall I incline my heart to abide by your statutes
   until the end.

Samekh

[113]Statutes of yours I love,
       though I hate those who are double-minded.
[114]Shield and hiding place are you to me;
       I put my hope in your word.
[115]So depart from me, you who practice wickedness,
       that I may keep my God's commandments.
[116]Secure me as you have promised, to preserve my life,
       and may this hope not bring me shame!
[117]Safe shall I be if you but hold me up,
       and thus will I continually hold your statutes in every way.
[118]Spurn all who go astray from your statutes,
       for their schemes come to nothingness.
[119]Sinful, wicked men of the earth you discard like dross,
       therefore I love all your statutes.

¹²⁰Shaking, my flesh trembles for fear of you,
>and I fear your just decrees.

Ayin
¹²¹I have done what is just and righteous;
>do not abandon me to those who would oppress me.
¹²²Impart to your servant a pledge of good will;
>do not let the arrogant ones oppress me.
¹²³I look longingly for your salvation
>and for your righteous promise to be fulfilled.
¹²⁴I beg you to deal with your servant according to your enduring love,
>and to teach me your statutes.
¹²⁵I am your servant; give me wisdom
>to understand your statutes!
¹²⁶It is time for you to act, O Lord,
>for your law is being broken.
¹²⁷I, therefore, love your commandments
>more than gold—even more than refined gold.
¹²⁸I strive to align myself with your precepts in all things;
>therefore, I hold every falsehood in contempt.

Pe
¹²⁹Phenomenally wonderful are your statutes;
>therefore my soul obeys them.
¹³⁰Pondering and unfolding your words gives light,
>imparting understanding to the simple.
¹³¹Panting, I open my mouth,
>because I long for your commandments.
¹³²Please turn to me and be gracious to me,
>as is your way with those who love your name.
¹³³Pattern my steps steadily after your promise,
>and allow no wickedness to overwhelm me.
¹³⁴Precepts—may I keep yours;
>redeem me from being oppressed by other men.
¹³⁵Please make your face shine on your servant,
>and teach me your statutes.
¹³⁶People are not keeping your law,
>which makes my eyes shed streams of tears.

Tsadhe
¹³⁷Completely righteous are you, O Lord,
>and right are your rules.
¹³⁸Confirmed and appointed, your testimonies stand in righteousness

and in total faithfulness.
¹³⁹Consuming me—such is my zeal,

because my enemies are neglecting your words.
¹⁴⁰Convinced that your promise has been well tried,

your servant loves it.
¹⁴¹Committed to your precepts I remain,

though I am young and despised.
¹⁴²Constantly righteous is your righteousness forever,

and your law is true.
¹⁴³Commandments of yours are my delight,

though trouble and tribulation have pursued me and found me.
¹⁴⁴Completely righteous are your testimonies forever;

give me understanding so that I may live.

Qoph

¹⁴⁵Quaking I cry in my heart, "Answer me, O LORD!"

I will obey your statutes.
¹⁴⁶ Quietly I cry to you, "Save me!"

May I keep your statutes.
¹⁴⁷Quickly I rise before dawn and cry for help;

My hope rests in your word.
¹⁴⁸Quitting sleep, my eyes are open during the watches of the night,

that I may meditate on your promise.
¹⁴⁹Quickly hear my voice according to your enduring love;

O LORD, preserve my life in accordance with your judgment.
¹⁵⁰Quite near are those who devise evil schemes;

they are far from your law.
¹⁵¹Quite nearer still are you, O LORD,

and all your commandments are true.
¹⁵²Quite long have I known this from your testimonies,

which you established to last forever.

Resh

¹⁵³Regard my affliction and deliver me,

for I have not forgotten your law.
¹⁵⁴Redeem me by pleading my cause;

preserve my life according to your promise!
¹⁵⁵Rescue lies far off from the wicked,

for they do not seek your statutes.
¹⁵⁶Resplendent is your enduring love;

in accordance with your laws, O LORD, preserve my life.
¹⁵⁷Remaining steadfast, I do not stray from your testimonies,

though many are my enemies and those who persecute me.

¹⁵⁸Repulsed by the deeds of the faithless am I,
because they do not keep your commands.
¹⁵⁹Reckon how I love your precepts!
In accordance with your enduring love, preserve my life.
¹⁶⁰Righteous rules of yours endure forever—each one!
The origin of your words is truth.

Sin / Shin

¹⁶¹Should princes trouble me unjustly,
Yet my heart will regard your word in awe.
¹⁶²So I rejoice at your word like the man
who after a battle finds great treasure.
¹⁶³Sacred law of yours I love,
but I hate and abhor falsehood.
¹⁶⁴Seven times each day I praise you
for the righteousness of your rules.
¹⁶⁵Such great peace have those who love your law;
nothing causes them to stumble!
¹⁶⁶Salvation is what I hope for, O LORD,
and I obey your commandments.
¹⁶⁷Soul—my soul—it obeys your commandments,
which I love greatly.
¹⁶⁸Still I keep your precepts and commands,
for all my ways are laid bare before you.

Taw

¹⁶⁹To you, O LORD, let my cry ever come;
give me wisdom according to your word!
¹⁷⁰Thus let my plea come before you;
rescue me according to your promise.
¹⁷¹Teach me your statutes
so that my lips may be fountains of praise.
¹⁷²Then my tongue shall sing of your word,
for all your commandments are righteous.
¹⁷³To help me, may your hand always be ready,
because I have chosen your precepts.
¹⁷⁴Trusting in your salvation, O LORD, is what I yearn for;
your law is my delight.
¹⁷⁵Therefore, preserve my soul so that I may praise you,
and let your law sustain me.
¹⁷⁶Though I have gone astray like a lost sheep, seek your servant,
for I have not forgotten your commandments.

PSALM 120

[A Song of Ascents.]

¹I cried out to the LORD in my distress, and he attended to me.
²Deliver me, O LORD, from lips that lie, from a tongue that deceives.
³O you deceitful tongue—what should be given to you, and how should you be dealt with?
⁴The sharp arrows of a warrior, with the [glowing] coals of a juniper!

⁵Woe is me, that I am on sojourn in Meshech, staying among the tents of Kedar!
⁶For too long my soul has dwelled here among those who hate peace.
⁷I want peace. But when I declare so, they want war!

PSALM 121

[A Song of Ascents.]

¹I lift up my eyes toward the mountains.
 Where does my help come from?
²My help comes from the LORD, who created heaven and earth.
³He will not allow your foot to be moved.
 He who protects you does not slumber.
⁴Take note—He who protects Israel neither slumbers nor sleeps.
⁵The LORD is your protecter. The LORD is your guard on your right hand.
⁶The sun will not beat you down by day, nor the moon by night.
⁷The LORD shall protect you from all harm, preserving your soul.
⁸The LORD shall watch over your going out and your coming in from this time forth, and forevermore.

PSALM 122

[A Song of Ascents of David.]

¹I was glad when they said to me, "Let us go into the house of the LORD!"
²Our feet are standing within your gates, O Jerusalem!
³Jerusalem—constructed as a city firmly bound together—⁴is where the tribes go up—the tribes of the LORD—as a testimony for Israel, to express their thanks to the name of the LORD.
⁵Thrones of judgment have been set up there—the thrones of the house of David.
⁶Pray for the peace of Jerusalem!
 May those who love you prosper.
⁷Peace be within your walls, prosperity within your palaces.
⁸For the sake of my brothers and companions, I will say, "Peace be within you."
⁹I will seek your good on account of the house of the LORD our God.

PSALM 123

[A Song of Ascents.]

¹I lift up my eyes to you, O you who dwell in the heavens.
²Take notice:
    as the eyes of servants look to the hand of their masters,
    and as the eyes of a maiden to the hand of her mistress,
    so our eyes wait on the LORD our God, until he has mercy on us.
³Have mercy on us, O LORD, have mercy on us, for we have had our fill of being
held in contempt.
⁴Our souls have had their fill of the scorn of those who live in leisure,
  and with the contempt of the haughty.

PSALM 124

[A Song of Ascents. Of David.]

¹"If the LORD had not been on our side"—may Israel now say—"²If the LORD had
not been on our side, when men rose up against us, ³then they would have swallowed us up alive, when they became furious with us."
⁴Then the waters would have overwhelmed us. The stream would have gushed
over us. ⁵Then the raging torrents would have swept over our soul.

⁶Blessed be the LORD, who did not allow us to become prey for their teeth!
⁷We have escaped like a bird out of the trap of the fowlers. The trap is broken
open, and we have escaped. ⁸Our help is in the name of the LORD, who made
heaven and earth.

PSALM 125

[A Song of Ascents.]

¹Those who trust in the LORD are like Mount Zion, which cannot be moved and
remains forever.
²As the mountains surround Jerusalem, so the LORD surrounds his people from
now until forever.
³For the wicked shall not be permitted to rule over the land of the righteous, so
that the righteous will not err by practicing evil.
⁴O LORD, bless those who are good and those who are upright in heart.
⁵As for those who stray away into crooked ways—the LORD shall banish them
along with those who practice wickedness.
Let there be peace on Israel!

PSALM 126

[A Song of Ascents.]

¹When the LORD restored the fortunes of Zion, we thought we were dreaming.
²Our mouths were filled with laughter, and our tongues with singing.
 Then among the nations it was said, "What awesome things the LORD has done for them."
³The LORD *has* done awesome things for us, and we are glad!
⁴Restore our fortunes again, O LORD, like the streams in the south!
⁵Those who plant in tears will harvest with shouts of joy!
⁶Those who weep as they go out to plant their seed will surely return home with shouts of joy, carrying sheaves.

PSALM 127

[A Song of Ascents of Solomon.]

¹Unless the LORD builds the house, those who build it labor in vain.
 Unless the LORD guards the city, the watchmen keep vigil in vain.
²It is vain for you to get up early and to stay up late, eating the bread of anxious toil, for it is the LORD who grants sleep to his beloved.
³Listen—children are a heritage from the LORD—the fruit of the womb is a reward.
⁴Like arrows in the hand of a mighty man—such are the children of one's youth.
⁵Blessed is the man whose his quiver is filled with them!
 He shall not be ashamed when he contends with his foes in the marketplace.

PSALM 128

[A Song of Ascents.]

¹Blessed is everyone who fears the LORD and walks in his ways.
²For you shall eat the fruit of the labor of your hands.
 You shall be happy, and things shall go well with you.
³Your wife will be like a fruitful vine on a wall in your house.
 Your children will be like olive plants around your table.
⁴Note that this is how the man who fears the LORD will be blessed.
⁵May the LORD bless you from Zion, and may you see Jerusalem prosper all the days of your life!
⁶Yes—may you live to see your grandchildren!
 Let there be peace on Israel!

PSALM 129

[A Song of Ascents.]

¹"Since my youth they have attacked me a great deal."
—let Israel now say—

²"Since my youth they have attacked me a great deal,
   yet they have never prevailed against me."
³The plowers plowed on my back, making their long furrows.
⁴The LORD *is* righteous; he has sliced the ropes of the wicked in two.
⁵Let all those who hate Zion be humiliated and forced to retreat.
⁶Let them be like the grass on the housetops that withers before it even grows;
⁷no reaper fills his hand with it, and no gatherer fills his arms with it.
⁸Nor do those who pass by say, "May the blessing of the LORD be on you. We
bless you in the name of the LORD."

PSALM 130

[A Song of Ascents.]

¹O LORD, out of the depths I cry to you!
²Lord, hear my voice! Let your ears be attentive to my cry for mercy.
³O LORD, if you should keep a record of sins—Lord—who could stand?
⁴But there is forgiveness with you—that we should fear you.
⁵I wait for the LORD; my soul waits, and I put my hope in his word.
⁶I wait for the Lord more than watchmen wait for the morning,
more than watchmen wait for the morning.
⁷O Israel, put your hope in the LORD, for with the LORD there is enduring love,
and with him is abundant redemption.
⁸He himself will redeem Israel from all his sins.

PSALM 131

[A Song of Ascents of David.]

¹LORD, my heart is not haughty,
 nor are my eyes raised up too high.
 I do not concern myself with weighty matters
 nor things too lofty for me.
²Yes, I have steadied and quieted myself,
 like a child who is weaned from its mother—
 my soul within me is like a weaned child.

³May Israel hope in the LORD from now until forever.

PSALM 132

[A Song of Ascents.]

¹O LORD, remember David in all his afflictions,
²how he swore to the LORD, making a vow to the Mighty One of Jacob:
 ³"Surely I shall not enter my house nor lie down on my bed.
  ⁴I shall not grant sleep to my eyes—nor slumber to my eyelids—

⁵until I determine a place for the LORD,
   a dwelling place for the Mighty One of Jacob."

⁶Yes, we heard about it at Ephratha.
   We discovered it in the fields of Jaar.
⁷So let us go to his dwelling place. Let us worship at his footstool.

⁸"Arise, O LORD—come into your residence—you and the ark of your power.
⁹Let your priests clothe themselves with your righteousness and let your holy
ones shout for joy."
¹⁰For the sake of your servant David, do not reject the one you have anointed.

¹¹The LORD has sworn truthfully to David and will not go back on his word:
   "I will set one of your sons on your throne.
   ¹²If your sons do keep my covenant and my rules that I will teach them, their
sons shall also sit on your throne forever."

¹³For the LORD has chosen Zion, desiring it to be his dwelling place:
   ¹⁴"May this be my residence forever.
      I will dwell here for I have desired it.
   ¹⁵I will bless her with abundant provisions.
      I will provide bread to her poor.
   ¹⁶I will also clothe her priests with salvation, and her saints shall shout
      aloud for joy.
   ¹⁷I will make the ruling power of the house of David grow there.
      I have ordained a lamp for my anointed.
   ¹⁸I will clothe his enemies with humiliation, but the crown on his head will shine."

PSALM 133

[A Psalm of Ascents. From David.]

¹See how good and how pleasant it is for brothers to live together in unity!
²It is like the precious oil on the head, running down on the beard—
on Aaron's beard, running down to the hem of his robes.
³It resembles the dew of Hermon, the dew that descends onto the mountains of
Zion! For there the LORD has commanded the blessing of life eternal.

PSALM 134

[Greetings of Night Watchers, A Song of Ascents.]

¹Bless the LORD, indeed, all you servants of the LORD, who gather at the house of
the LORD in the night.
²Raise your hands in the sanctuary and bless the LORD.
³The LORD who made heaven and earth blesses you from Zion.

PSALM 135

¹Praise the LORD! Praise the name of the LORD.
 Give praise, you servants of the LORD ²who stand in the house of the LORD—in the courts of the house of our God,
³Praise the LORD, for the LORD is good!
 Sing praises to his name, for that is pleasant.
⁴For the LORD has chosen Jacob for himself—yes, Israel for his very own possession.

⁵For I know the LORD to be great, and our Lord to be above all gods.
⁶The LORD does whatever pleases him in heaven, and on earth, in the seas, and in all the deep:
 ⁷He makes rainclouds rise at the ends of the earth.
 He sends the lightning in the rainstorm.
 He brings out the winds from his storehouses.

⁸It was he who struck down the firstborn of Egypt, both of man and beast, ⁹and displayed signs and wonders in your midst, O Egypt, against Pharaoh and all his servants, ¹⁰and struck down great nations, and killed powerful kings— ¹¹Sihon king of the Amorites, and Og king of Bashan, and all the kingdoms of Canaan—¹²and gave their land as a heritage, a heritage to Israel his people.

¹³Your name, O LORD, endures forever,
 and your deeds are known, O LORD, throughout all the ages.
¹⁴For the LORD will vindicate his people, and he will take compassion on his servants.

¹⁵The idols of the nations are made of silver and gold, the work of men's hands:
 ¹⁶They have mouths, but they cannot speak.
 They have eyes, but they cannot see.
 ¹⁷They have ears, but they cannot hear.
 Nor is there any breath in their mouths.
¹⁸Those who create them end up just like them, and so shall everyone who puts his trust in them.

¹⁹Bless the LORD, O house of Israel.
 Bless the LORD, O house of Aaron.
²⁰Bless the LORD, O house of Levi.
 You who fear the LORD, bless the LORD.
²¹Blessed be the LORD from Zion, who dwells at Jerusalem.
 Praise the LORD!

PSALM 136

¹Give thanks to the LORD, for he is good.
 –His unfailing love endures forever–

²Give thanks to the God of gods.
  –His unfailing love endures forever–

³Give thanks to the Lord of lords,
  –His unfailing love endures forever–
⁴to him, the only One who performs marvelous wonders,
  –His unfailing love endures forever–
⁵to him who used his skill to create the heavens,
  –His unfailing love endures forever–
⁶to him who spread out the lands higher than waters
  –His unfailing love endures forever–
⁷to him who fashioned great lights:
  –His unfailing love endures forever–
  ⁸the sun to rule the day,
  –His unfailing love endures forever–
  ⁹the moon and stars to rule the night,
  –His unfailing love endures forever–
¹⁰to him who struck down the firstborn of Egypt,
  –His unfailing love endures forever–
¹¹and ushered Israel out from among them,
  –His unfailing love endures forever–
¹²with a mighty hand, and with an outstretched arm,
  –His unfailing love endures forever–
¹³to him who parted the Red Sea,
  –His unfailing love endures forever–
¹⁴and enabled Israel to pass through the middle of it,
  –His unfailing love endures forever–
¹⁵but then overthrew Pharaoh and his army in the Red Sea,
  –His unfailing love endures forever–
¹⁶to him who led his people through the wilderness,
  –His unfailing love endures forever–
¹⁷to him who struck down great kings,
  –His unfailing love endures forever–
¹⁸and killed eminent kings:
  –His unfailing love endures forever–
  ¹⁹Sihon king of the Amorites,
  –His unfailing love endures forever–
  ²⁰and Og the king of Bashan,
  –His unfailing love endures forever–
²¹and gave their land for a heritage,
  –His unfailing love endures forever–
²²yes, a heritage to Israel his servant,
  –His unfailing love endures forever–
²³and who was mindful of us in our lowly estate,

–His unfailing love endures forever–
²⁴and has rescued us from our enemies,
  –His unfailing love endures forever–
²⁵and who provides food to all people.
  –His unfailing love endures forever–

²⁶Give thanks to the God of heaven.
  –His unfailing love endures forever–

PSALM 137

¹By the waters of Babylon, there we sat down; we wept indeed when we remembered Zion.
²We hung up our harps on the willows that were there.
³For there our captors requested songs from us, and our torturers demanded mirth, saying "Sing us something from the songs of Zion."
⁴How could we sing the LORD's song in a strange land?
⁵If I forget you, O Jerusalem, then let my right hand forget its skill.
⁶If I do not remember you, let my tongue stick to the roof of my mouth—
if I do not place Jerusalem above my greatest joy.

⁷Remember, O LORD, on that day in Jerusalem, the Edomites who shouted, "Demolish it, demolish it, right down to its foundation."
⁸O daughter of Babylon, who is doomed to be destroyed, blessed shall be the one who repays you for how you have treated us.
⁹Blessed shall be the one who takes your children to dash them against the rocks.

PSALM 138

[A Psalm of David.]

¹I thank you with my whole heart, O LORD; I sing your praise before the gods.
²I bow down facing your holy temple and give thanks to your name for your enduring love and for your truth, because you have exalted your name and your word above all things.
³On the same day I cried out, you answered me and strengthened my soul.
⁴All the kings of the earth shall praise you, O LORD, for they have heard the words of your mouth.
⁵Indeed they shall sing of the ways of the LORD, for the glory of the LORD is great.
⁶Though the LORD is lofty, yet he has a close regard for the lowly, but as for the haughty—he has distanced himself from them.

⁷Even if I should walk in the midst of trouble, you will preserve my life.
 You will stretch out your hand against the wrath of my enemies, and your right hand will rescue me.
⁸The LORD will fulfill all his purposes for my life.

Your unfailing love, O LORD, endures forever.
Do not forsake the works of your own hands.

PSALM 139

[To the choirmaster: a Psalm of David.]

¹O LORD, you have searched me and known me!
²You know my sitting down and my getting up; you understand my
thoughts from afar.
³You plot out my path and my lying down, and you are familiar with all my ways.
⁴For not a word, O LORD, forms on my tongue, but that you already know it
completely.
⁵You block me in, behind and before, and place your hand on me.
⁶Such a concept is too lofty for me. It is too high for me to grasp.
⁷Where could I escape your spirit? Or where could I go to, to escape your presence?
⁸If I ascend to heaven, you are there.
 If I make my bed in the grave, you are even there.
⁹If I take the wings of the morning, and dwell in the uttermost parts of the sea—
¹⁰even there your hand will guide me, and your right hand shall hold me.
¹¹If I say, "Surely the darkness shall cover me, and the light around me even seem
like night, ¹²even the darkness cannot hide from you—the night shines as bright
as the day, for darkness and light are the same to you.

¹³For you formed my innermost parts; you wove me together in my mother's womb.
¹⁴I praise you for I am fearfully and wonderfully made; your works are marvelous, which my soul knows so well.
¹⁵My frame was not hidden from you, when I was being formed in
secret, intricately woven in the depths of the earth.
¹⁶Your eyes saw my substance, as yet unformed.
 And all my days were written in your book—every one of them—when none of
them existed yet.
¹⁷How precious are your thoughts to me, O God! How vast is the sum of them!
¹⁸If I were to count them, they would be more numerous than the grains of sand.
 I wake up, and I am still with you.

¹⁹May you slay the wicked, O God; depart from me, bloodthirsty men.
²⁰They speak maliciously against you, and your enemies take your name in vain.
²¹Do I not hate those who hate you, O LORD? Do I not despise those who rise
up against you?
²²I hate them with absolute hatred; I consider them my enemies.

²³Search me, O God, to know my heart!
 Test me to know my thoughts.
²⁴ See if there is any offensive way in me and lead me in the way everlasting.

528

PSALM 140

[To the choirmaster: a Psalm of David.]

¹Deliver me, O LORD, from evil men.
 Preserve me from violent men ²who devise evil plans in their heart and constantly stir up battles.
³Their tongues become sharp like a serpent and the venom of adders lies under their lips. Selah

⁴Keep me, O LORD, keep me safe from the hands of the wicked; preserve me from violent men who have determined to trip me up.
⁵The arrogant have laid a trap for me, and with cords they have spread a net; they have set snares for me along the way. Selah

⁶I say to the LORD,
"You are my God. Listen to the cry of my pleas for mercy, O LORD!"
⁷O LORD, my Lord and the strength of my salvation, you protect my head in the day of battle.
⁸O LORD, do not grant the desires of the wicked.
 Do not support their wicked schemes, or they will be exalted. Selah

⁹As for the leader of those who surround me, let the wicked plans from their own lips overwhelm them.
¹⁰Let burning coals fall on them!
  Let them be hurled into the fire—into deep pits—never to escape.
¹¹Do not let slanderers get established in the land; let misfortune swiftly hunt down the violent men.
¹²I know that the LORD will support the afflicted and bring justice for the poor.
¹³Surely the righteous shall give thanks to your name, and the upright shall dwell in your presence.

PSALM 141

¹I cry out to you, O LORD!
 Hurry to me.
 Lend your ear to my voice when I cry out to you!
²Let my prayer rise to you like incense, and the lifting of my hands like the evening sacrifice.
³Set up a safeguard over my mouth, O LORD.
 Keep watch on the door of my lips.
⁴Do not allow my heart to be attracted to doing evil or to wasting time doing things with evildoers or partaking of their delicacies.

⁵Let a righteous man smack sense into me—that would be a kindness. And let him reprove me—that would be an excellent oil, which would benefit my head.

My prayers are still against their evil deeds.
⁶When their judges are hurled over the edge down to the rocks, then they shall heed my well-spoken words.
⁷Our bones shall be scattered at the mouth of the grave, as when someone plows up the ground.

⁸But my eyes look toward you, O GOD my Lord—in you is my refuge.
 Do not leave me destitute.
⁹Keep me from the trap laid out for me, and the snares of those who practice evil.
¹⁰May the wicked fall into their own nets while I walk by them unharmed.

PSALM 142

[A Maskil of David; A Prayer when he was in the cave.]

¹I cry to the LORD with my voice—with my voice I plead to the LORD for mercy.
²I pour out my complaint before him, laying out my trouble before him.

³When my spirit within me is overwhelmed, you know my way.
 In the path where I walk they have secretly laid a snare for me.
⁴I look to the right and see that no one takes notice of me.
 For me no refuge remains—no one cares about my soul.

⁵I cry to you, O LORD, saying, "You are my refuge—my portion in the land of the living."
⁶Attend to my cry, for I am brought down very low.
 Rescue me from those who afflict me, for they are stronger than I am.
⁷Bring my soul out of prison, that I may praise your name.
 Then the righteous ones will be all around me because you have dealt generously with me.

PSALM 143

¹Hear my prayer, O LORD; lend your ear to my pleas for mercy.
 Answer me in your faithfulness and your righteousness.
²And do not bring judgment on your servant, for no living person could be completely righteous in your sight.

³For the enemy has chased after my soul, crushing my life to the ground.
 He has forced me to sit in darkness, like those who are long dead.
⁴Therefore my spirit faints within me; inside my heart is devastated.

⁵I remember the olden days.
 I ruminate on all your works.
 I reflect on the work of your hands.
⁶I spread out my hands up to you.
 Like a parched land, my soul thirsts for you. Selah

⁷Answer me quickly, O Lᴏʀᴅ. My spirit is faltering!
 Do not hide your face from me, so that I do not end up like those who descend to the pit.
⁸In the morning let me hear about your enduring love, for I trust in you.
 Show me the way in which I should walk, for I lift up my life to you.

⁹Deliver me, O Lᴏʀᴅ, from my enemies; I have fled to you for refuge.
¹⁰Teach me to do your will; for you are my God.
 Let your good spirit lead me along the even path.

¹¹Preserve my life, O Lᴏʀᴅ, for the sake of your name.
 For the sake of your righteousness carry my soul out of adversity.
¹²In your mercy cut off my enemies and destroy all the enemies of my soul, for I am your servant.

PSALM 144

¹Blessed be the Lᴏʀᴅ, my rock—
  who trains my hands for warfare and my fingers for battle,
 ²who is my unfailing goodness and my fortress,
  who is my high tower, my deliverer, my shield and my place of refuge.
 He subdues others under me.

³O Lᴏʀᴅ, what is man, that you are mindful of him?
 Or the son of man, that you consider him?
⁴Man is like an empty breath whose days resemble a fleeting shadow.

⁵Bend your heavens, O Lᴏʀᴅ, and come down!
 Touch the mountains to make them smoke.
⁶Flash forth lightning to scatter them.
 Shoot out your arrows to rout them.
⁷Stretch out your hand from on high.
 Save me and deliver me from overwhelming waters, from the hands of the foreigner ⁸whose mouth speaks empty falsehoods and whose right hand is a right hand of deception.

⁹I will sing a new song to you, O God.
 I will play on a ten-stringed lyre for you who gives kings the victory,
¹⁰and who delivers his servant David from the destructive sword.
¹¹Save me and deliver me from the hands of the foreigner whose mouth speaks empty falsehoods and whose right hand is a right hand of deception.

¹²May our sons be like full-grown plants in their youth.
 May our daughters be like pillars—trimmed, polished, and fit for a palace.
¹³May our barns be filled with all kinds of produce.
 May our sheep bring forth thousands and tens of thousands in our fields.

¹⁴May our cattle be heavy with young, not suffering loss or mishap in bearing their young.

   May there be no cries of distress in our streets!

¹⁵Blessed are the people whose lives are such.

   Blessed are the people whose God is the LORD.

PSALM 145

[David's Psalm of praise.]

¹I will extol you, my God, O King.

 I will bless your name forever and ever.
²Every day I will bless you, praising your name forever and ever.
³Great is the LORD, and greatly to be praised.

   His greatness is unfathomable.

⁴One generation shall commend your works to another and shall declare your mighty deeds.
⁵I will meditate on the glorious splendor of your majesty and on your wondrous works.
⁶The power of your awesome deeds shall be spoken of, and I will declare your greatness.
⁷The record of your bountiful goodness shall be told, as people sing of your righteousness.

⁸The LORD is gracious and full of compassion, slow to anger and abounding in enduring love.
⁹The LORD is good to all, with his tender mercies spreading over all his creation.

¹⁰All your works shall praise you, O LORD, and all your holy ones shall bless you.
¹¹They shall speak of the glory of your kingdom and talk of your power to ¹²tell of your mighty deeds and the glorious majesty of your kingdom to mankind.
¹³Your kingdom is an everlasting kingdom, and your dominion endures throughout all generations.
¹⁴The LORD upholds all who fall and raises up all who are bowed down.
¹⁵The eyes of all look to you in expectation, and you feed them in due season.
¹⁶You open your hand, satisfying the desire of every living thing.
¹⁷The LORD is righteous in all his ways and beneficent in all that he does.
¹⁸The LORD is near all those who call on him—to all those who call on him truthfully.
¹⁹He fulfills the desire of those who fear him.

   He also hears their cries and will save them.
²⁰The LORD preserves all those who love him, but he will destroy all the wicked.

²¹My mouth will speak the praise of the LORD.

   Let all people bless his holy name forever and ever!

PSALM 146

¹Praise the LORD!
 Praise the LORD, O my soul.
²As long as I live I will praise the LORD.
 I will sing praises to my God as long as I have any being.

³Do not place your trust in princes, nor in the son of man, in whom there is no salvation.
⁴When his breath leaves him, he returns to his earth; on that very day his plans come to an end.

⁵Happy is the one who has the God of Jacob for his help, whose hope is in the LORD his God
⁶who created heaven and earth, the sea, and all that lies inside it,
 who remains faithful forever,
⁷who brings about justice for the oppressed, and
 who gives food to the hungry.
The LORD sets the captives free.

⁸The LORD opens the eyes of the blind.
The LORD raises those who are bowed down.
The LORD loves the righteous.
⁹The LORD preserves the strangers.
He upholds the fatherless and widow.
But he overturns the way of the wicked.

¹⁰The LORD shall reign forever—yes, your God, O Zion—to all generations.
Praise the LORD!

PSALM 147

¹Praise the LORD, for it is good to sing praises to our God—it is pleasant,
and praise is fitting.
²The LORD builds up Jerusalem; he gathers together the exiles of Israel.
³He heals the brokenhearted and binds up their wounds.
⁴He sets the number of the stars, giving each one its name.
⁵Great is our Lord, and great is his power. His understanding is infinite.
⁶The LORD elevates the humble but the wicked he throws down to the ground.

⁷Sing to the LORD with thanksgiving; sing praise on the harp to our God
 ⁸who covers the heavens with clouds,
 who supplies rain for the earth,
 ⁹who makes grass grow on the hills,
 who provides food for the animals—even to the young ravens that call out.
¹⁰He does not delight in the strength of a horse; he does not take pleasure in the legs of a man.

[11]Instead, the LORD takes pleasure in those who fear him—in those who place their hope in his enduring love.

[12]Praise the LORD, O Jerusalem; praise your God, O Zion.
[13]For he has reinforced the bars of your gates; he has blessed your   children within you.
[14]He makes peace in your borders and fills you with the finest wheat.
[15]He sends forth his commandment on the earth; his word runs rapidly.
[16]He distributes snow like wool; he scatters the frost like ashes.
[17]He casts forth his hail like pebbles. Who could withstand his cold?
[18]He sends out his word and melts them. He stirs up the blowing winds and makes the waters flow.
[19]He reveals his word to Jacob, declaring his statutes and his just decrees to Israel.
[20]He has not dealt with any other nation in this way, nor have they known about his law. Praise ye the LORD.

PSALM 148

[To the choirmaster: A Psalm of David.]
[1]Praise the LORD!
 Praise the LORD from the heavens.
 Praise him in the high places!
[2]Praise him, all his angels
 Praise him, all his heavenly hosts!
[3]Praise him, sun and moon!
 Praise him, all you shining stars!
[4]Praise him, highest heavens, and vapors above the heavens!

[5]Let them praise the name of the LORD, for they were created at his command.
[6]He established them forever and ever.
 He decreed it so, and it shall not pass away.

[7]Praise the LORD from the earth, you great creatures of the sea and all the deeps,
[8]fire, and hail; snow and fog; and stormy gale that fulfills his word!
[9]Mountains, and all the hills; fruit trees, and all the cedars!
[10]Beasts, and all the livestock; creeping things, and birds of flight!

[11]Kings of the earth, and all the nations; princes, and all the rulers of the earth!
[12]Both the young men and the maidens; old men, and children!

[13]Let them praise the name of the LORD, for his name alone is exalted.
 His majesty is above the earth and heaven.
[14]He has established a powerful honor for his people, praise for all his saints—for the people of Israel who are close to him.
 Praise the LORD!

PSALM 149

[To the choirmaster. A Psalm of David.]

¹Praise the LORD!
 Sing a new song of his praise in the assembly of the godly.
²May Israel rejoice in his Maker.
 May the children of Zion rejoice in their King.
³May they praise his name by dancing.
 May they sing praises to him with the tambourine and the lyre.
⁴For the LORD delights in his people.
 He crowns the humble with deliverance.
⁵May the godly rejoice in glory.
 May they sing joyfully on their beds.
⁶May their mouths be filled with great praises of God,
 but may their hands brandish two-edged swords:
        ⁷to bring about vengeance on the nations
        and punishments on the peoples,
        ⁸to tie up their kings with chains, and their nobles with iron fetters,
        ⁹to execute the written judgment on them.
All his godly ones have this honor.
Praise the LORD.

PSALM 150

[A Song of Ascents.]

¹Praise the LORD!
 Praise God in his sanctuary.
 Praise him in his mighty heavens!
²Praise him for his mighty deeds.
 Praise him because of his excellent greatness.

³Praise him with the sound of the trumpet.
 Praise him with the lute and harp!
⁴Praise him with the tambourine and dance.
 Praise him with stringed instruments and pipes.
⁵Praise him on the loud cymbals—praise him on loud, clashing cymbals!

⁶Let everything that has breath praise the LORD.
 Praise the LORD!

Printed in the USA
CPSIA information can be obtained
at www.ICGtesting.com
LVHW041958270124
768938LV00004B/12